D1212701

UNITED STATES ARMY IN WORLD WAR II

The European Theater of Operations

THE LORRAINE CAMPAIGN

Whitman Publishing Edition

Hugh M. Cole

ATLANTA, GA
2012

The Lorraine Campaign
Whitman Publishing Edition

3101 Clairmont Road • Suite G • Atlanta, GA 30329

Correspondence concerning this book may be directed to Whitman Publishing, Attn: WWII (Lorraine Campaign), at the address above.

ISBN: 0794837689
Printed in China

If you enjoy this book, you will also enjoy *World War II: Saving the Reality—A Collector's Vault* (by Kenneth W. Rendell).

Each of the following volumes about the European Theater of Operations can be read and enjoyed separately; at the same time, each takes a natural place in the framework of the whole history of the war. *Cross-Channel Attack* • *Breakout and Pursuit* • *The Lorraine Campaign* • *The Siegfried Line Campaign* • *The Ardennes: Battle of the Bulge* • *Riviera to the Rhine* • *The Last Offensive.* For a day-by-day study of all the war's ground actions, see *Chronology: 1941–1945.*

For a complete catalog of history, hobby, sports, and other books and products, visit Whitman Publishing at www.whitman.com.

. . . to Those Who Served

Foreword to the First Printing

In publishing the series, U.S. ARMY IN WORLD WAR II, the Department of the Army has three objectives. The first is to provide the Army itself with an accurate and timely account of its varied activities in mobilizing, organizing, and employing its forces for the conduct of war—an account that will be available to the service schools and to individual members of the Armed Services who wish to extend their professional reading. The second objective is to help enlarge the thoughtful citizen's concept of national security by describing the basic problems of war and the manner in which these problems were met. The third objective is to preserve for the record a well-merited tribute to the devotion and sacrifice of those who served.

The authors of the combat volumes were selected from among trained civilian historians, many of whom served as historical officers attached to the headquarters of larger units engaged in the campaigns about which the histories are written. Their material has been gathered from their own observations and research as well as from the gleanings of other trained historians who served in the wartime Army. All pertinent official records, interviews with both Allied and enemy participants in the actions, and captured enemy records were made available in the preparation of these volumes. Although no claim is made that the series constitutes a final history, the authors have weighed the evidence in accordance with the Chief of Staff's directive that Army histories must present a full and factual account, thoroughly documented and completely objective. They are under no restrictions in their work except those imposed by the requirements of national security and by the standards of historical scholarship.

The level on which the volumes are written necessarily varies. When an action is confined to a comparatively small number of units in a limited area, it has been possible to carry the narrative down to companies, platoons, and even individuals. When an action involves many large units moving rapidly over extensive areas, the small-unit level is not feasible. In the writing of combat history, as in combat itself, the solution to the problem "depends on the situation."

Hugh M. Cole, the author of this volume, obtained his Ph.D. in Military History from the University of Minnesota in 1937. He taught Military History at the University of Chicago until the spring of 1942 when he accepted a commission as an intelligence officer in the U.S. Army. A graduate in 1943 from the Command and General Staff School, Dr. Cole subsequently joined the Historical section, G–2, War Department, and in 1944 was assigned to Headquarters, Third United States Army, then in England. After serving in four campaigns with the Third Army, he became Deputy Theater Historian, European Theater of Operations. In 1946 he was reassigned to the Historical Division, WDSS, and started the research and writing that culminated in this volume.

The Department of the Army gratefully acknowledges the co-operation of the U. S. Air Force in making available such of their records and research facilities as were pertinent to the preparation of this volume.

HARRY J. MALONY
Maj. Gen., U. S. A.
Chief, Historical Division

Washington, D. C.
15 March 1949

Foreword to the Whitman Publishing Edition

In the fall of 1944, the Lorraine region in northwest France was pure "mud, blood and misery" for the soldiers of Lieutenant General George S. Patton Jr.'s U.S. Third Army. The heady days of August pursuing shattered German armies hundreds of miles across France after the Normandy breakout had in September turned into a psychologically numbing slugfest against a surprisingly revitalized enemy. The Lorraine Campaign, September 1–December 18, 1944, sandwiched between two more-dramatic, headline-grabbing operations—the exhilarating July–August war of mobility liberating France and the massive late-December surprise German Ardennes Offensive (the Battle of the Bulge)—is often unfairly overlooked by historians studying U.S. Army European Theater operations. But it was a vital, hard-fought, months-long battle of attrition that positioned Supreme Allied Commander General Dwight D. Eisenhower's armies to later crack the Siegfried Line, survive the Battle of the Bulge, cross the Rhine River barrier, and overrun Germany to the Elbe River. Operations in Lorraine proved, in effect, a necessary evil—the bloody precursor to the war's final campaigns that helped pave the way to Allied victory by battering and wearing down an outnumbered, out-gunned, out-supplied enemy.

Yet, the German army's incredible resilience and ability to create new fighting forces seemingly out of thin air—often demonstrated on the Eastern Front in the wake of Red Army offensives, but now being manifested against the western Allies—came as a shock in September 1944 to Allied soldiers and leaders alike. Moreover, the numbers of soldiers added to the German battle line was not the only reason for the enemy's revitalized defense—their ferocity was suddenly fueled by the stark knowledge that they were now defending the very borders of their German homeland against Allied invaders, not merely fighting to retain conquered territory. Although the Allied logistical bottleneck of late August–early September was a principal reason for giving the enemy some breathing space to solidify defenses, the men and machines of Patton's Third Army were by then also exhausted from the breakneck pace of the summer's pursuit—the Americans badly needed the time provided them by the logistics snarl to catch their breath, too. By mid-September, like boxers in the middle rounds of a prizefight, both sides had caught their breath and resumed their contest, which suddenly turned into a brutal slugging match.

German defenders greatly benefitted from an insidious, seemingly ever-present ally: the coldest, wettest autumn weather in Europeans' memory plagued all aspects of Lorraine Campaign combat operations. Bad weather particularly hampered the Americans' offensive operations by seriously restricting the maneuver and fire support that was absolutely essential to mount successful attacks. Pea soup–thick fog often shrouded Allied airfields, grounding vital fighter and bomber air support. Incessant rain turned Lorraine's clay-based soil into a sticky quagmire, making off-road movement by infantrymen agonizingly slow and restricting vehicles—including tracked armor and artillery—to the region's roads (one American armored division commander decried the road-bound situation as being forced to attack on "a one-tank front"). Waterlogged G.I.s became afflicted by a debilitating disease known as "trench foot"—constantly saturated footgear and socks led to painfully swollen, horribly discolored, and sometimes gangrenous feet. In November, trench foot reached epidemic proportions within Third Army: although the army's battle casualties for the September–December 1944 Lorraine Campaign totaled over 55,000, additional non-battle casualties—many due to trench foot—put *42,000 more* of Patton's officers and men out of action (some permanently when gangrenous toes or feet had to be amputated). Their German enemies, in addition to greatly benefitting from the weather's debilitating effect on American offensive operations, coped much better with the cold, wet misery than their G.I. opponents. This was partly due to those East Front veterans among the German defenders having learned valuable lessons in fighting in miserable Russian weather, but it can be more widely attributed to the result of German infantrymen's feet generally being in better conditioning due to becoming "inured to long marches on foot" necessitated by the German army's chronic lack of motor transport. The American army's surfeit of vehicles was not always entirely beneficial—feet brutally suffered when G.I.s used to riding instead of walking (and who had forgotten how to properly care for their most basic means of transportation) were forced to fall back on the foot soldier's oldest form of mobility.

The miserable Lorraine fighting not only destroyed lives, it shattered careers. The most tragic example is Major General John S. "P" Wood, the dynamic, ebullient commander of U.S. 4th Armored Division who, until falling from grace in early December 1944, was widely acclaimed as the American army in Europe's best division commander (famed British historian and influential military theorist B.H. Liddell Hart called Wood the "American Rommel"). Wood's 4th Armored Division (justifiably nicknamed "Patton's Best") had spearheaded Third Army's phenomenal pursuit across France in August; but his division's "heartbreaking actions in the autumn mud" of the Lorraine Campaign left Wood physically and psychologically "fatigued"—he could "no longer carry the strain of battle" or bear seeing his division's soldiers broken, bleeding, or, too often, dead. The sad task of relieving from command of his beloved division one of the U.S. Army's "best and brightest" fell to

Wood's closest and oldest friend—George Patton. On December 3, 1944, two weeks before the end of the Lorraine Campaign, the Third Army commander reluctantly sent his friend "P" Wood back home to finish the war training armored troops.

Dr. Hugh M. Cole (1910–2005) can rightly be acknowledged the "dean" of the Office of the Chief of Military History's efforts to write the official history of U.S. Army operations in northwest Europe. Cole supervised the efforts of the other Army civilian historians preparing the 10-volume European Theater of Operations histories and wrote two volumes himself: *The Ardennes: Battle of the Bulge* (1965) and this volume, *The Lorraine Campaign*. Published in 1950, *The Lorraine Campaign* was not only the very first book in the *U.S. Army in World War II* series, it set the standard of excellence for intellectual integrity, comprehensive thoroughness, format, and style for all volumes that followed. Cole's superb account covers the three main phases of the Lorraine Campaign: the September push to the Moselle River line and its crossing; the November stalemate at Metz and the fortress city's final capture; and the subsequent advance to the in-depth enemy defenses of the Siegfried Line (Westwall).

Cole's *The Lorraine Campaign* is a groundbreaking masterpiece of scholarship and narrative, written by a gifted historian who served as Third Army historical officer during four World War II campaigns that army fought in Europe—including Lorraine—and who in 1945 became the U.S. Army's chief European Theater historian.

Jerry D. Morelock, PhD
Colonel, U.S. Army, ret.
Editor in Chief, *Armchair General* Magazine

Jerry D. Morelock, a 1969 West Point graduate, served 36 years in uniform. He is a decorated combat veteran whose military assignments included Chief of Russia Branch on the Pentagon's Joint Chiefs of Staff and head of the history department at the Army's Command and General Staff College. After retiring from the Army, he was executive director of the Winston Churchill Memorial and Library at Westminster College, Fulton, Missouri—the site of Churchill's famous 1946 "Iron Curtain Speech"—and is adjunct professor of history and political science at Westminster College. Since 2004, he has been editor in chief of *Armchair General* magazine, the only military-history magazine selected by the *Chicago Tribune* as one of its "50 Best Magazines" in the world. Among the award-winning historian's numerous publications is his acclaimed book, *Generals of the Ardennes: American Leadership in the Battle of the Bulge.* He is married to the Russian artist Inessa Kazaryan Morelock.

The Author

Hugh M. Cole received his Ph.D. from the University of Minnesota in 1937 in the field of European military history. He taught military history at the University of Chicago until 1942, when he joined the Army as an intelligence officer. After graduating from the Command and General Staff School he was assigned to the staff of the Third Army during its operations in Europe. At the close of hostilities he became Deputy Theater Historian, European Theater of Operations. From 1946 to 1952 Dr. Cole directed the work of the European Theater Section, Office of the Chief of Military History, wrote *The Lorraine Campaign,* a volume that appeared in this series in 1950, and undertook much of the work that has culminated in this volume on the Ardennes Campaign. He joined the Operations Research Office of The Johns Hopkins University in 1952 and has continued his active interest in military history and his service to the Army both as a scholar and as colonel in the U.S. Army Reserve.

Preface

In 1946 the Historical Division of the War Department made plans for the preparation of a nine-volume series recounting the history of the European Theater of Operations. There was no precedent in the experience of the United States Army for an official narrative account of military operations on the grand scale. Careful study of the official histories produced by the European combatants after World War I showed that these histories could offer little in the way of a pattern for recording the European campaigns of 1944 and 1945. The drastic change from the trench warfare of 1914–18 to the mobile operations of 1944–45 had complicated the task of the military historian. In World War I, a tactical situation represented by three divisions rising from the trenches in simultaneous attack on a narrow front permitted a reasonable unity in treatment and allowed the historian to write at the level of the army corps. Thirty years later, that same frontage might be held by a single reinforced regiment. The fluid condition of the combat zone in World War II and the wide dispersion of troops over the battle area resulting from the impact of the tank, the plane, the machine gun, the truck, and the radio telephone inevitably induced a degree of fragmentization and an unavoidable lack of sequence in the narrative of events on the battlefields of 1944 and 1945. It was decided, therefore, that the common denominator in the present series would be the division, since the division represents the basic tactical and administrative unit of the combined arms. Although emphasis is placed on the division, organization by chapters generally will follow the story of the army corps as a means of achieving narrative and tactical unity.

The limits of the individual volumes in this series have been set according to well-defined phases of the operations in the ETO. But it has been impossible in most individual volumes to cover the entire Western Front and include all phases of the action. As a result the individual volume will deal with one or more armies in a given area at a given time and will not necessarily present the complete story of American ground operations during that phase of the war in Western Europe. The importance of logistics in the history of the

ETO has been recognized by the allocation of a separate volume to this subject. The story of command and decision at the level of SHAEF also has required treatment in a separate volume, particularly since this story reaches beyond the purely American forces on the Continent. Insofar as is practicable the history of air-ground co-operation at the tactical level has been introduced in the separate operational volumes.

The Lorraine Campaign is the first volume to be published in the projected series embracing the history of the American armies in the European Theater of Operations. This volume deals with the campaign waged by the Third Army in Lorraine during the period 1 September–18 December 1944. Since it has been impossible to organize the writing of individual volumes so that they may be published in the chronological sequence followed by military operations, the reader interested in the history of the Third Army before or after the events here set forth must wait until the appropriate volumes are completed.

The present volume is concerned with the tactical operations of the Third Army and its subordinate units. The story of command and decision in higher headquarters is told only when it has a direct bearing on the campaign in Lorraine. The logistics of this campaign likewise have been subordinated to the tactical narrative. The basic unit in the present narrative is the infantry or armored division. The story of the division has been told in terms of its regiments and battalions, but swerves on occasion to the company or the platoon, just as the operations themselves turned on the exploits of these smaller units.

Comparatively little attention can be given to the exploits of the individual soldier within the confines of a single volume such as this. Deeds of valor that were officially recognized by the award of the Medal of Honor or the Distinguished Service Cross have been cited in the text or in footnotes. Unfortunately the records of the Department of the Army do not provide a complete chronological listing of such citations for bravery. Every care has been exercised to mention all recipients, but it is possible that some have been omitted inadvertently. No attempt has been made to provide a complete order of battle or a troop list of all the numbered units that were assigned or attached to the Third Army during the Lorraine Campaign. Attention has been focused throughout the volume on the combat formations actually in the line. It is hoped, however, that the reader will gain some impression of the vital combination of arms and services which in the long run bring the infantry and the tanks to victory. At certain points in the narrative the reader will find a slowing pace and a monotony induced by the similarity of detail, inasmuch as the historian, unlike the novelist or poet, is not the master of his material. The campaign in Lorraine seldom showed the dash of the August pursuit; the advance toward the Rhine sometimes seemed unbearably slow to those who took part in it. The progression from village to village was monotonous and repetitious; and a sustained, sequential, realistic account cannot shirk the event.

Precise military terminology has been employed, except in those cases where clarity and economy of style have dictated usage of a more general nature. Thus, the Third Army operations in Lorraine are considered to be a "campaign" in the general sense of the term, despite the fact that the Department of the Army does not award a separate campaign star for these operations. The regimental combat team has not been distinguished from the conventional regimental organization, because of the difficulty in determining the precise form of the regimental command at any given time. Armored organizations present a similar problem. The Reserve Command of the armored division therefore is named as one of the combat commands. The designations reinforced (reinf) and minus (—) have been used only when needed to call attention to particularly important attachments or detachments. The conventional designations, "21st Army Group" and "12th Army Group," commonly used throughout the operations in Europe, are employed in the text; the official designations, "Northern Group of Armies" and "Central Group of Armies," introduced by SHAEF when General Eisenhower assumed direct operational control on 1 September 1944, are employed in the maps. German nomenclature has been determined arbitrarily, with an eye to limitations of space and a meaningful rather than a literal translation. The umlaut vowels in the text have been indicated by addition of the letter *e*, as in Saarbr*ue*cken. In the maps, the original umlaut designation has been retained, as in Saarbr*ü*cken. For the sake of clarity, the names of enemy military units have been italicized. Such treatment has not been accorded, however, to certain German terms, such as Luftwaffe, panzer, and Reichswehr, which have been virtually assimilated into the English language.

All clock time given is that officially designated by the Allies. Prior to 17 September, 1944, British Double Summer Time is used. After that date hours are given in British Summer Time.

The author has received much help, beginning with the accumulation of information during the Lorraine Campaign and continuing through the subsequent stages of writing and editing. He gratefully acknowledges this assistance. Col. W. A. Ganoe, Theater Historian, USFET, and Col. John M. Kemper, Chief, Historical Branch, MID G–2, were instrumental in securing the assignment of the author as an officer on the Third Army staff. The members of the 3d Information and Historical Service, both officers and enlisted men, are responsible for whatever merit this volume has as a departure from the skeletal and fragmentary form of the official journals and reports. I am especially indebted for the Combat Interviews obtained during the campaign by the following officers and men: Capt. Dello G. Dayton, Capt. Ledyard B. Clark, Capt. Harry A. Morris, 1st Lt. Theron Burts. 1st Lt. Samuel Tobin, M. Sgt. Gordon A. Harrison, and M. Sgt. Monroe Ludden. The many administrative difficulties encountered by the army historian were solved in the main by the persistent and helpful efforts of Col. S. L. A. Marshall, Deputy Theater Historian, and Col. A. F. Clark, Deputy Chief, Historical Division, War Department.

The presentation of the story on the enemy side of the hill owes much to Capt. Frank Mahin, Capt. James Scoggin, and Mr. Detmar Finke, whose tireless work in exploring the German documents and in fathoming the individual memories of the German officers who took part in the Lorraine Campaign merits especial praise. The maps in this volume represent seventeen months of research and work at the drafting board by Mr. Wsevolod Aglaimoff, Miss Ann Coward, and other members of the Cartographic Unit. Mr. Aglaimoff has always been ready to place his extensive knowledge of European terrain at the disposal of the author; no military historian could hope for a better military cartographer. Maj. Charles A. Warner, USAF, collaborated with the writer in preparing the story of air-ground co-operation. Maj. John Hatlem selected and prepared the photographs used herein. Aerial photographs were made especially for the volume by the 45th Reconnaissance Squadron, USAF. Mr. Israel Wice and his very competent assistants expended much time and effort in checking names, awards, and dates. Mr. W. Brooks Phillips and Mrs. Frances T. Fritz of the Editorial Unit provided an additional check of the many names, both of persons and of places, that appear in the text. Details on the Third Army order of battle have been taken from the valuable preliminary study, *Order of Battle: European Theater of Operations* (Paris, 1945), prepared under the direction of Capt. Robert J. Greenwald. It has been a pleasure to work with Mr. Joseph R. Friedman, Associate Editor in charge of the ETO series, whose professional knowledge and skill have greatly aided the writer. Preparation of the index was in the capable hands of Mr. David Jaffé. Mrs. Jean Embry and Mrs. R. Constance Beatty carried out the tedious business of typing and retyping the manuscript.

Brigadier H. B. Latham of the War Cabinet Historical Section, Committee for Imperial Defense, London, has kindly furnished data from Luftwaffe files in British possession. Additional information on the 2d French Armored Division has been provided through the courtesy of the Ministère de la Défense Nationale, Paris; the Service Historique de l'Armée, Etat-Major des Forces Armées (Guerre); and the Groupement blindé No. 2, St. Germain-en-Laye.

Reference in the footnotes can give only partial credit to the scores of officers and men who were called upon to furnish additional information or to unravel questions of fact. Nearly every officer who held the post of division commander or above during the campaign has read the initial manuscript of this volume. Their comments and criticisms have been invaluable, but they are in no way responsible for the statements of fact contained herein.

Washington, D. C.
1 November 1949

H. M. COLE
Colonel, ORC

Contents

Maps

Illustrations

Illustrations are from the following sources:

U.S. Army Photos, pages: 14, 19, 59, 64, 73, 74, 76, 92, 113, 133, 136, 147, 186, 188, 267, 268, 279, 291, 292, 327, 341, 343, 347, 356, 364, 378, 383, 392, 424, 439, 445, 448, 455, 474, 481, 523, 545, 585.

U.S. Air Force Photos, pages: 67, 82, 98, 101, 110, 138, 155, 173, 179, 200, 265, 277, 297, 321, 329, 334, 360, 411, 484, 494, 507, 516, 555, 562, 564, 573, 580.

Captured German Photos, page: 44.

United Features Syndicate, Inc., page: 294.

CHAPTER I

The Halt at the Meuse

At the beginning of September 1944, the American Third Army under the command of Lt. Gen. George S. Patton entered upon operations against the German forces defending the territory between the Moselle and the Sarre Rivers. These operations, which lasted well into December, were subsequently to be known, although quite unofficially, as the Lorraine Campaign. The troops under General Patton's command faced the Moselle line and the advance into Lorraine with an extraordinary spirit of optimism and a contagious feeling that the final victory of World War II was close at hand.[1] They had just completed, in their pursuit of the enemy across northern France, one of the most successful operations in modern military history—and that with comparatively slight losses. Their present mission of driving through Lorraine was to be an important part of the strategy of advance on a wide front which had been laid down by Gen. Dwight D. Eisenhower, the Supreme Allied Commander, who on 1 September assumed direct operational command of the Allied forces in northern France.

Two corps, the XII and XX, were to take a continuous part in the battles for Lorraine fought by the Third Army. Both of these corps had participated earlier in the Third Army dash across northern France. The XV Corps, originally assigned to General Patton's command, fought for some time with the American First Army, but was to rejoin the Third Army during the latter part of September to take a brief though important part in the Lorraine offensive. Some of the divisions now with the Third Army were still licking wounds suffered earlier in Normandy and in the enemy counterattack at Mortain. The 90th Infantry Division had been badly mauled during the June fighting west of the Merderet River. The 35th Infantry Division had sustained some 3,000 casualties in operations at St. Lô, Vire, and Mortain. The 4th Armored Division had lost about 400 of its trained and irreplaceable armored infantry in July while holding defensive positions. But on the whole relatively few officers and

[1] The Third Army official Diary (MS), hereafter cited as TUSA Diary, well reflects this optimism.

men of the Third Army had taken part in the bloody, tiring, and often demoralizing hedgerow battles in Normandy; for the most their portion had been speedy advance and quick successes. General Patton's victories in northern France, following those of Africa and Sicily, had not only added to his own characteristic assurance but had infected the Third Army as a whole.

A series of happenings just at the close of August had acted to heighten still further the spirits of General Patton's command and gloss over the first sobering effects of the oncoming gasoline shortage. First, the advancing army had captured the champagne caves and warehouses at Reims and Epernay. It is unnecessary to dwell on the importance of this event. Second, the Third Army had passed through the obstacle of the Argonne without a fight—in spite of the gloomy and frequently expressed forebodings of the older officers whose memories harked back to the bloody experiences of the AEF in the autumn of 1918. Finally, with hardly a blow being struck, on the last day of August Patton's tanks had seized Verdun, where scores of thousands had died in World War I.

Troop Dispositions

The last German troops west of the Seine River had been mopped up on 31 August; but in point of fact the area between the Seine and the Loire Rivers, designated in the OVERLORD plan as the "Initial Lodgment Area," had to all intents and purposes been secured as early as 25 August, ten days ahead of the OVERLORD timetable.[2] By 1 September the Allied forces were across the Seine, not having met the stubborn and time-consuming opposition that had been expected at this river, and were moving speedily northeast and east of Paris in pursuit of the fleeing German armies. (*Map I*)* Thus far the Allied losses had been moderate, when viewed in relation to the territory won and the casualties inflicted on the enemy since 6 June. The build-up of the Allied armies in Northern France had been markedly successful. On the afternoon of 31 August the rosters of Supreme Headquarters, Allied Expeditionary Forces (SHAEF), showed that a cumulative total of 2,052,297 men and 438,471 vehicles had landed in the American and British zones. Although losses and withdrawals had reduced this strength, at the moment General Eisenhower assumed direct command he had at his disposal on the Continent

* All maps numbered in Roman are placed in inverse order inside the back cover.

[2] The OVERLORD plan is discussed in Gordon A. Harrison, The Cross-Channel Attack, the first volume in the present series.

23 infantry divisions and the equivalent of 15 armored divisions. Of this total the British and Canadians had furnished 17 divisions (including 1 Polish armored division). The Americans had provided 21 divisions (including 1 French armored division).[3] Further increase in the number of Allied divisions in northern France would have to be produced by American effort. The British, whose effective manpower had been drained away in five years of war, could at most be expected to keep their existing divisions up to strength.

General Eisenhower's 38 divisions were opposed, on 1 September, by 41 German divisions—5 of which were already penned in the coastal fortresses and the Channel Islands. An additional 5 enemy divisions were on the march to reinforce the German Western Front. Below the Loire River 2 reserve divisions were withdrawing from western and southwestern France. In Holland 1½ German divisions still remained in garrison.[4] This apparent general parity between the Allied and German forces existed only on paper—and in the mind of Hitler. The ratio of combat effectives was approximately 2 to 1 in favor of the Allies. Hardly a German division was at normal strength. Most had sustained very severe losses in men and equipment. Many were badly demoralized as the result of constant defeats in the field. At no point since the Seine River crossings had any large German force been able to dig in and make a stand in the face of the persistent Allied pursuit. The Allied superiority in heavy weapons and motor transport was far greater than a comparative numerical tabulation of the opposing divisions would indicate. No complete materiel figures for this period now exist in either the Allied or captured German files, but the Allied superiority in guns was at least 2½ to 1, that in tanks approximately 20 to 1.[5]

[3] SHAEF G–3 Daily Summary 88; 12th A Gp Situation Map, 1 Sep 44; OPD Situation Map, 31 Aug 44.

[4] These strength figures include neither the German *Nineteenth Army* nor the U.S. Seventh Army, both in southern France.

[5] Estimates of Allied materiel are based on the following: 21st A Gp Basic Statistical Rpt No. 5; 21st A Gp Daily Adm Bull No. 84, 2 Sep 44; 12th A Gp Armed Sec, Allocation of Equipment, 1 Sep 44; FUSA (First U.S. Army) Am Sup Rpt, 1–31 Aug 44; ETOUSA Progress Rpts CXI, 4 Sep 44, and CXV, 2 Oct 44. Estimates of German materiel are based on MSS #D–319 (Zimmermann), D–320 (Blumentritt), and D–321 (Blumentritt). See also *Oberkommando des Heeres* (hereafter cited as *OKH*), *Stab General der Artillerie beim Chef Generalstab des Heeres, Anlagenheft Nr. 9 zum Kriegstagebuch* (hereafter cited as *KTB*) *Nr. 4/Band 2, 31. VII.–26. IX. 44, Anlage Nr. 699,* 27 Aug 44. The dislocation and disregard of administrative routine and normal reporting procedures, during the August operations, show in the records of both the pursued and the pursuer. The 12th Army Group Ordnance Section Daily Journal has numerous complaints, during August, on the incomplete and inaccurate materiel figures supplied by the Third Army. The Journal concludes: "They don't know what they do have. . . ." Materiel status reports maintained by the First Army and 21st Army Group are somewhat better, but are by no means complete.

The transcendent strength of the Allied ground forces at the beginning of September was eclipsed by the overwhelming superiority which the Allied air forces held over the Luftwaffe in western Europe. SHAEF had three tactical air forces capable of providing air cover and close tactical support for the armies advancing on the ground: IX Tactical Air Command, XIX Tactical Air Command (both under Ninth Air Force), and the 2d Tactical Air Force (British). The combined Allied air strength operating from bases in the United Kingdom and France consisted of 5,059 American bombers, 3,728 American fighter planes, 5,104 combat aircraft in the Royal Air Force, and additional hundreds of miscellaneous types for reconnaissance, liaison, and transport.[6] The German armies on the Western Front were supported by one weak tactical air force, *Third Air Force* (*Luftflotte* 3), which possessed only 573 serviceable aircraft—and these of all types. The total number of first-line planes in the entire Luftwaffe (including every type) was 6,232, of which number 4,507 were reckoned to be serviceable. These planes, however, had to be divided between the air defense of the Third Reich and the several theaters of German operations.[7] Generalfeldmarschall Walter Model, the German commander in chief in the West, and Generaloberst Otto Dessloch, commander of the *Third Air Force*, had pleaded in vain for additional air support. On 21 August they asked Hitler to send at least 700 fighter planes to France, plus the new jet fighter, the Messerschmitt 262, for which great things had been promised. Hitler, however, could not or would not release any of his fighter reserve; as for the new jet type there were only a few test models in existence.

On 31 August and 1 September Allied tanks and mechanized cavalry squadrons, operating far beyond Paris, seized crossings over the Somme, the Aisne, and the Meuse Rivers. The Allied left, formed by the two armies under the 21st Army Group (Field Marshal Sir Bernard L. Montgomery), was moving rapidly in a zone about fifty-eight miles wide. In the north the First Canadian Army (Gen. H. D. G. Crerar) swept along the Channel coast in a drive aimed at the Belgian city of Bruges. On 1 September Canadian troops re-entered Dieppe, the scene, two years before, of one of the most heroic episodes in Canadian military history. The following day, Canadian tanks crossed the Somme River. To the south the Second British Army (Lt. Gen. Sir Miles C. Demp-

[6] AAF Staff Control Aircraft Inventory, Combined Allied vs. Axis Air Strength Reports, 1 Sep 44.

[7] Figures furnished by the British Historical Section and based on Luftwaffe records. Cf. MSS #B–190 (Rendulic) and T–42 (Guderian).

sey) advanced in the direction of Brussels and Antwerp, the latter, with its deepwater port, now a main target for the Allied arms. British armor crossed the Somme River midway between Amiens and Abbeville on 1 September, striking toward Belgium with such speed as to win the plaudits of that most severe of American critics, General Patton.

The Allied center, driving northeastward in support of the 21st Army Group, was formed by the First U.S. Army (Lt. Gen. Courtney H. Hodges), which, teamed with the Third U.S. Army, comprised Lt. Gen. Omar N. Bradley's 12th Army Group. The First U.S. Army was making its advance in a zone some sixty-five miles across, with armored divisions pushed forward on the wings like prongs. On 31 August elements of Hodges' right wing were across the Aisne River and operating between St. Quentin and Rethel. The next day, however, General Hodges turned the VII Corps, which held the right-wing position, directly north, in a maneuver to trap the Germans who were retreating from the British front in the area west of Mons.

The Allied right, composed of two corps under General Patton's Third U.S. Army, was engaged in the eastward drive toward Metz and Nancy as a subsidiary to the main Allied effort being made in the northeast. The VIII Corps (Maj. Gen. Troy H. Middleton), also a part of General Patton's command, had been left in Brittany to reduce the Brest defenses and contain the other German coastal garrisons. By this time, however, the VIII Corps was so far removed from the rest of the Third Army that of necessity it had become a semi-independent force both for tactics and supply. General Patton's "eastern" front was about ninety miles in width. But in addition the Third Army held the line of the Loire River, marking the right flank of the Allied armies in northern France, which gave the Third Army front and flank a length of some 450 miles. On 31 August, Third Army tanks and cavalry crossed the Meuse River at Verdun and Commercy. By 1 September small cavalry patrols had arrived on the west bank of the Moselle River.

One hundred and seventy-five miles south of the Third Army, advance detachments of the Seventh U.S. Army were fighting in the vicinity of the great French industrial city of Lyon. (*Map Ia*) The Allied invasion of the French Mediterranean coast, begun on 15 August under the code name DRAGOON, auxiliary to the main Allied operations in northern France, had cut off the German garrisons in the port cities of Marseille and Toulon and pushed rapidly northward through the valley of the Rhone. The DRAGOON forces, under the tactical command of the commanding general of the Seventh Army,

Lt. Gen. Alexander M. Patch, consisted of the Seventh Army and French Army "B" (Gen. Jean de Lattre de Tassigny)—the latter functioning as a provisional corps.[8] Of this force the French had provided five divisions (including one armored division); an additional French infantry division was in process of landing on 1 September. The American complement numbered three infantry divisions and an airborne task force of approximately divisional strength. At the beginning of September the DRAGOON forces had the German *Nineteenth Army* on the run. The Allied plans then in force called for a continuation of the northward advance to the line Autun–Dijon–Langres. Such a drive would establish contact between the Seventh and Third Armies, thus sealing off the escape routes along which the enemy troops were fleeing from western and southern France and permitting the creation of a continuous Allied front from the Mediterranean to the English Channel.

Allied Strategy

On 29 August General Eisenhower had dispatched a letter to all his major commanders, outlining his intentions for the conduct of future operations. This letter reflected the optimism current throughout the Allied armies and the general feeling that now was the moment to deal the final and destroying blows against Hitler's forces west of the Rhine:

> The German Army in the West has suffered a signal defeat in the campaign of the Seine and the Loire at the hands of the combined Allied Forces. The enemy is being defeated in the East, in the South and in the North; he has experienced internal dissension and signs are not wanting that he is nearing collapse. . . . We, in the West, must seize this opportunity by acting swiftly and relentlessly and by accepting risks in our determination to close with the German wherever met. . . . It is my intention to complete the destruction of the enemy forces in the West, and then—to strike directly into the heart of the enemy homeland.

This letter directed the Allied commanders to undertake a general advance —an advance which in fact was already under way—but assigned the principal offensive mission to the British and American armies in the north. General Bradley, however, was ordered to build up incoming forces east of Paris, in

[8] The somewhat involved command situation represented here is explained in the *Report by the Supreme Allied Commander Mediterranean: August 1944* (Washington, D.C., 1946), pp. 28 ff. Lt. Gen. J. L. Devers would assume command in southern France on 15 September 1944. For explanation of the creation of the 6th Army Group see Maj. James D. T. Hamilton, Southern France and Alsace, a volume now under preparation in this series.

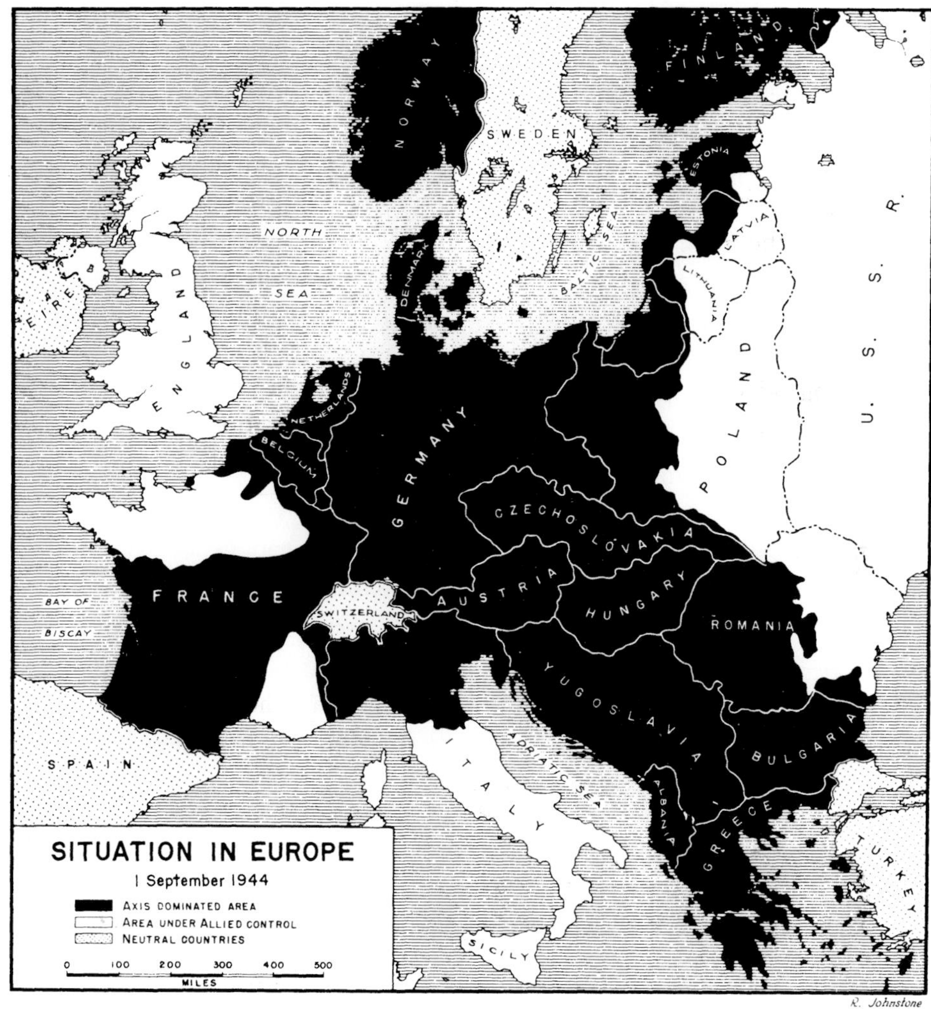

MAP NO. 1

preparation for a rapid advance toward the Sarre Valley designed to reinforce the main effort in the north and assist the Seventh Army advance "to and beyond Dijon."[9] *(Map 1)*

So rapid was the Allied advance and so complete the disintegration of the German field forces that by 1 September much of the instructional detail in the Supreme Commander's letter of 29 August was out of date. The Allied

[9] Directive, Eisenhower to Commanders, 29 Aug 44, SHAEF SGS file, Post OVERLORD Planning, 381, I.

Expeditionary Air Force (AEAF), for example, had been instructed to deny the enemy the crossings of the Somme, the Oise, and the Marne. But by 1 September the fleeing enemy already was behind these rivers. General Eisenhower's letter had directed Montgomery and Bradley to destroy the German forces still in front of the Oise and the Somme, then seize a hold across the Somme in preparation for further advances toward Antwerp and the Sarre Valley. This maneuver was close to completion on 1 September, for the enemy retained his position only on the lower Somme and the middle Oise. Under these circumstances the SHAEF operations staff advised the Supreme Commander that the directive of 29 August "should be followed without delay by additional instructions." [10]

During the preparatory period just preceding the Normandy invasion, General Eisenhower and the SHAEF planners had agreed on a strategic concept—eventually to assume the status of strategic doctrine—derived from the basic directive which the Combined Chiefs of Staff had given the Supreme Allied Commander: "to undertake operations aimed at the heart of Germany and the destruction of her armed forces." [11] The ultimate goal, obviously, was the "political heart" of Germany—Berlin. But, it was agreed, the Third Reich had an "economic heart"—the great industrial center of the Ruhr. It could be assumed that the German forces in the West would concentrate to defend the Ruhr. Therefore, an Allied advance directed toward the Ruhr, if successful, would fulfill a dual mission, crippling beyond repair the German war production, and engaging and destroying the main German armed forces on the Western Front.

Geography offered four avenues leading from northern France to the Ruhr: south of the Ardennes, by way of Metz, Saarbruecken, and Frankfurt; straight through the Ardennes, on a west-east axis; north of the Ardennes, via Maubeuge and Liége; and through the plains of Flanders. But even before the Allied invasion SHAEF planners had ruled out two of the four possible avenues to the Ruhr because of their difficult terrain—at least insofar as the direction of the main Allied effort was concerned. Two approaches to the Ruhr still seemed feasible, although not equally so: the direct route north of the Ardennes and the circuitous route along the Metz–Saarbruecken–Frankfurt axis. On 3 May the SHAEF Planning Staff had reviewed the possible

[10] *Ibid.*

[11] For this basic directive see the discussion in Forrest C. Pogue, The Supreme Command, a volume now under preparation in this series.

courses of action after the capture of a lodgment area on the Continent and recommended that the advance eastward be made on a broad front along two mutually supporting axes: the main advance to be aimed toward the northeast "with the object of striking directly at the Ruhr by the route north of the Ardennes"; the "subsidiary axis" to lie south of the Ardennes and provide a threat to Metz and the Saar.[12] General Eisenhower had concurred in this plan.

The Supreme Commander's pre-D-Day decision to direct the main Allied attack along the route which led northeast from Paris to the lower Rhine and the Ruhr, via Maubeuge and Liége, could and would be defined in modern terms: the extent of terrain suitable for airfields, the number of flying bomb sites, and the war potential of the Ruhr. Additional factors probably had weight in this great strategic decision, even if applied subconsciously, factors that appeared only indirectly in planning papers but whose importance antedated fighter planes and Bessemer furnaces. The route along which Eisenhower intended to direct the Allied main effort had been through history the most important of the invasion routes between France and Germany. This military avenue had exercised an almost obligatory attraction in wars of modern date, as in those of earlier centuries. It provided the most direct approach to the heart of Germany. It presented the best facilities for military traffic, whether tanks, trucks, or marching columns. Although canalized, this approach to Germany followed terrain well suited to maneuver and debouched onto the level expanse of the North German Plain. The western entryways to the historic highway lay adjacent to the Channel ports, through which support for the Allied armies would come. The eastern termini gave direct access to the most important strategic objectives in Germany, the Ruhr and Berlin.

The Metz–Saarbruecken–Frankfurt route also had considerable historical significance and prior military usage. It should be noticed, however, that armies had taken this road in periods when the neutrality of Belgium and the Netherlands had checked maneuver farther to the north, or in a time before

[12] SHAEF Planning Staff draft of Post NEPTUNE Courses of Action after Capture of the Lodgment Area, 3 May 44, SHAEF SGS File, Post OVERLORD Planning, 381, I. Since most of the Lorraine Campaign was fought on French territory, French spelling is used for the Sarre River throughout the text of this narrative, although German spelling is retained in references to the Saar Basin, the industrial area that lies entirely in German territory. The maps accompanying the text use the German spelling, Saar, when the river lies on the German side of the boundary, and the French spelling when it lies on the French side. Names of places along the river generally retain the spelling of the country in which they are located.

the hegemony of Prussia and the impact of the industrial revolution had shifted the strategic center of gravity to northern Germany. This eastern route offered an opening into Germany, but was less direct than the route northeast from Paris. Operations in this area would suffer from a rather rigid localization, both as to development and results. The immediate strategic objectives on the eastern axis, Rhine cities such as Mannheim and Frankfurt, no longer had any great military value. The Saar Basin, with its mines and smelters, lay on the Metz–Frankfurt axis. But the industrial capacity of the Saar, although of considerable military importance, was far less than that of the Ruhr. Once across the Rhine the eastern route was constricted by the Mittelgebirge, whose western ranges left only a narrow exit from Frankfurt. Given the conquest of the Ruhr as a necessary preliminary to the defeat of Germany, an advance on the eastern axis would have to make a wide turning movement and negotiate the unsatisfactory approach to the Ruhr along the narrow Rhine Valley. Translated in terms of those weapons of modern war in which the Allies might expect superiority, tanks and planes, the Metz–Frankfurt route and Rhine Valley approach would offer more difficult tank going and fewer airfield sites than the road via Paris, Liége, and the lower Rhine.

Behind the pre-D-Day decision for a main drive on the northeast axis and a subsidiary thrust to the east lay the desire to secure the greatest freedom of maneuver and the most advantageous application of force by widening the front of the Allied advance. This line of thought had been stated in brief but precise form in the 3 May draft of post-OVERLORD plans:

> It may be as long as eight months after D Day . . . before the allied land forces can be assured of a steadily increasing superiority in the field. . . . We must, therefore, avoid a line of advance which leads us to a head-on collision with the main German forces without opportunity for maneuvre . . . we must advance on a front sufficiently broad to threaten an advance by more than one of the "gaps" into Germany. By so doing we should be able to keep the Germans guessing as to the direction of our main thrust, cause them to extend their forces, and lay the German forces open to defeat in detail.

In the weeks that followed the invasion, strategy bowed to tactics as the Allied armies fought to break out of Normandy and to secure the lodgment area between the Seine and the Loire. The beginning of the pursuit across northern France introduced logistical complications of a complexity which had not been anticipated in the strategic planning of the pre-D-Day period. The systematic development of a supply system adequate to support the type of orthodox advance envisaged in the OVERLORD plan failed to meet the requirements of the war of movement suddenly begun in August. The strategic possibilities offered by the collapse of the German armies east of the Seine were attractive and varied, but the Supreme Allied Commander had at his disposal neither the strength nor the supplies necessary to take advantage simultaneously of all the glittering opportunities presented.

As early as 24 August General Eisenhower had written to Gen. George C. Marshall, the United States Chief of Staff, explaining the quandary in which he found himself: "For a very considerable time I was of the belief that we could carry out the operation of the northeast simultaneously with a thrust eastward, but later have concluded that due to the tremendous importance of the objectives in the northeast we must first concentrate on that movement." The objectives to which General Eisenhower referred were those which in earlier plans had long underscored the paramount importance of the northeastern approach to the Ruhr. In the first place the principal concentration of enemy forces in western Europe would be met in this area, including some divisions from the Pas-de-Calais strategic reserve which had not yet been fully committed against the Allies. Next, and highly important to the hard-pressed civilian population of London and southeastern England, was the opportunity to seize the CROSSBOW (flying bomb) sites in the Pas-de-Calais area before new and more-destructive missiles could be hurled across the Channel. In addition, a drive into western Belgium would give the Allies access to the best airfields between the Seine Basin and Germany proper, while denying these forward bases to the Luftwaffe. Finally, an advance astride the northeastern axis would bring the Allies to the deepwater port of Antwerp, which General Eisenhower and his operational and supply staffs regarded as "a permanent and adequate base," essential to further operations to and across the Rhine.[13]

Although General Eisenhower assigned priority to the northeastern operation, he was nevertheless unwilling to relinquish the idea of the subsidiary thrust to the east via Metz. On this point General Eisenhower and Field Marshal Montgomery were in fundamental disagreement. Montgomery categorized Eisenhower's strategic concept as the "broad front policy," his own as the "single concentrated thrust." The 21st Army Group commander's thesis, advanced in the last days of August and recurrent in various forms for some months afterward, held that the war could be brought to a quick conclusion by "one powerful full-blooded thrust across the Rhine and into the heart of Germany, backed by the whole of the resources of the Allied Armies. . . ."

[13] Ltr, Eisenhower to Marshall, 24 Aug 44, Gen Eisenhower's files.

Montgomery contended that a quick concentration of men and supplies on the Allied left wing and an energetic employment of the same in the 21st Army Group zone of advance would make it possible to force a breach in the German West Wall (the Siegfried Line) and "bounce" a crossing over the Rhine while the enemy was in full retreat.[14] He had insisted that one whole American army should be moved in on his right flank during the drive toward Brussels and Antwerp, but Eisenhower refused on the grounds that the enemy strength in front of the 21st Army Group did not warrant such a reinforcement. However, the Supreme Commander did agree that the objectives to be attained by an advance toward the northeast had an overriding priority; for this reason the First U.S. Army, by orders issued on 26 August, was committed to a drive close along the right boundary of the 21st Army Group.

By 1 September the marked inability of the enemy to offer any really effective resistance and the speed with which the highly mobile Allied formations were cutting in on the German escape routes led General Eisenhower to order a maneuver in which a part of the American forces would be turned to the north. In the Pas-de-Calais area west and north of the line Laon–Sedan, Allied intelligence estimated that the main German forces were grouped in a strength equivalent to the combat effectiveness of two panzer and eight to ten infantry divisions. General Eisenhower wished to engage and destroy this enemy concentration before driving on toward the Rhine and the Ruhr. Because Montgomery's divisions were insufficient for this task the Supreme Commander assigned two corps from the First U.S. Army to move north in the direction of Antwerp and Ghent, this maneuver, in conjunction with the British, being intended to trap the retreating enemy in the vicinity of Mons.

The execution of the maneuver to close the Mons pocket would shift the 12th Army Group center of gravity far from General Patton's Third Army, which at this time was deployed with its main body between the Marne and the Meuse Rivers. But General Eisenhower still was anxious to start the Third Army driving east as soon as the supply situation on the Continent would permit. On 2 September he called Bradley, Patton, Hodges, and Maj. Gen. Hoyt Vandenberg, the new commander of the Ninth Air Force, to his headquarters near Granville, outlined his plans for the proximate future, and indicated the role envisaged for the Third Army. He told his field commanders that as soon as the First Army forces had completed the move to the north

[14] Bernard L. Montgomery, *Normandy to the Baltic* (London, 1947), Ch. 11, *passim*. For a study of this basic controversy see Pogue, The Supreme Command.

both the First and Third Armies would remain "generally static" until sufficient gasoline and other supplies could be accumulated "to permit the Third Army and the V Corps of the First Army to move to the Siegfried Line [West Wall] and seize and hold that line with at least a part of each Corps."

This last outlined the general directive under which General Patton and his Third Army would begin the sixteen-week Lorraine Campaign. But at this juncture in the victorious Allied march toward Germany the eyes of the high command—and the common soldier as well—were drawn irresistibly to the Rhine River, a goal seemingly close at hand. Following Eisenhower's statement of the over-all plan, Bradley sketched in the army plans, giving General Patton a future axis of advance calculated to take the Third Army across the Rhine in the Mannheim–Frankfurt sector. General Bradley added that two more divisions, the 79th Infantry Division and the 2d French Armored Division, would be given to the Third Army, but pointed out that Patton would not need the first of these divisions (the 79th) until after the Third Army was *beyond* the West Wall and attacking toward the Rhine.[15] Such was the optimism prevalent in all echelons of the Allied armies at this stage of the war in western Europe.

In the middle of the afternoon General Patton telephoned the Third Army headquarters from the meeting of the commanders, giving orders that the army should not advance beyond the Meuse bridgehead line. Cavalry reconnaissance, he added, might continue to push to the east. These orders were promptly relayed to the commanders of the XII and XX Corps—gratuitously, it may have appeared to General Eddy and General Walker, whose forward formations already were immobilized at the borders of Lorraine by the shortage of gasoline.

Composition of the Third Army

The Third Army staff, as well as most of its combat formations, was by this time experienced and battlewise. General Patton's immediate headquarters was filled with men who had served as his staff officers in the Western Task Force and the Seventh Army during the North African and Sicilian campaigns. Many of them had come from the cavalry arm, as had Patton, and were thoroughly imbued with the cavalry traditions of speed and audacity.

[15] Memo for record, 2 Sep 44, sub: Notes on meeting of Supreme Commander with subordinate commanders, 12th A Gp files, Military Objectives, 371.3.

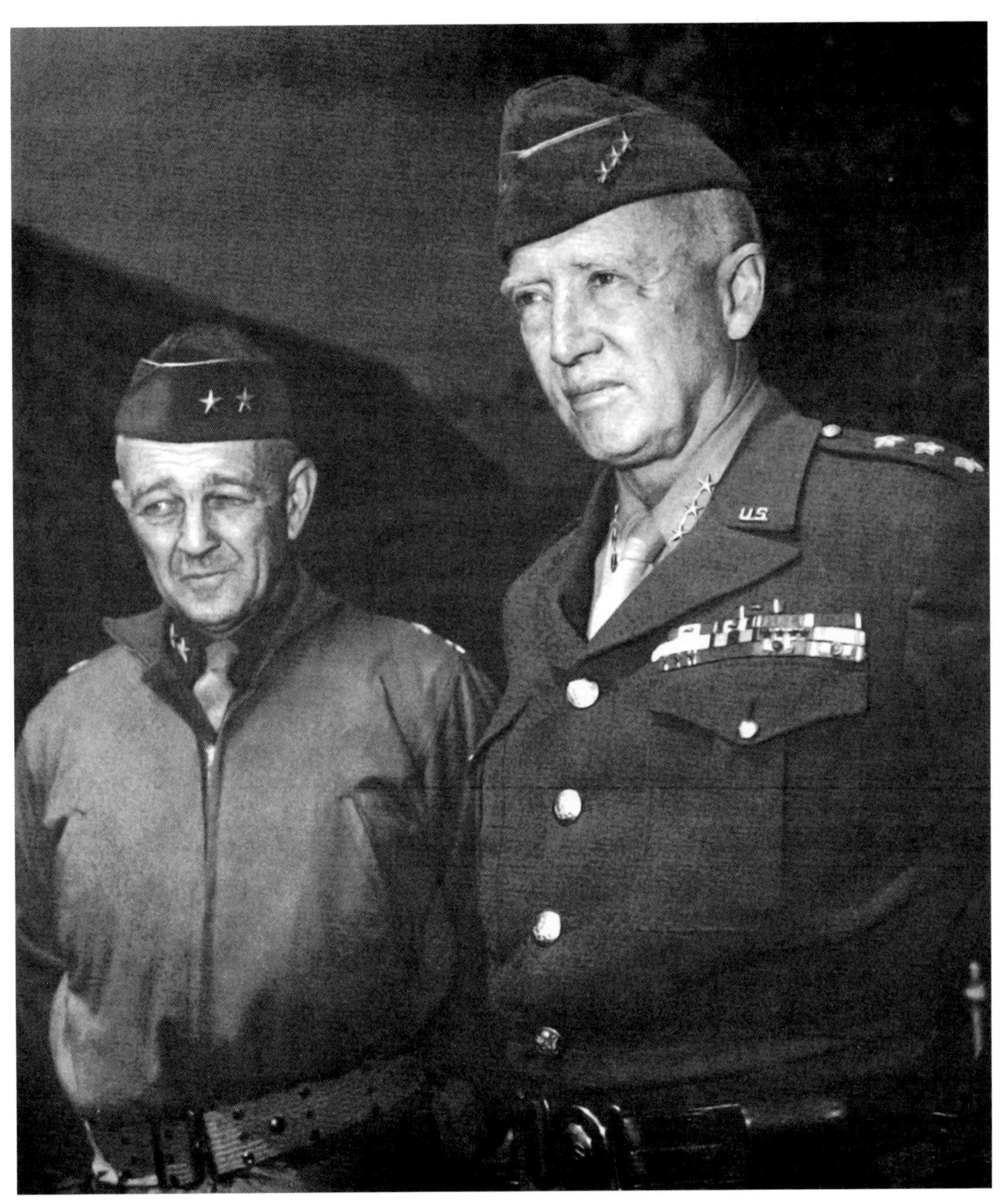

GENERAL PATTON AND HIS CHIEF OF STAFF, *Maj. Gen. Hugh J. Gaffey.*

Although the Third Army commander was by nature prone to make decisions on his own, he was equally inclined to place responsibility on his staff and subordinate commanders in matters pertaining to the implementation of his decisions. As a result the Third Army staff was a tightly knit and smoothly functioning body, although its members all were overshadowed by the personality of the army commander.

The chief of staff, Maj. Gen. Hugh J. Gaffey, was an armored expert who had served for a brief period as chief of staff of the II Corps while it was under General Patton's command in North Africa. He had subsequently commanded the 2d Armored Division in Sicily and in April 1944 had joined the Third Army in England, again as Patton's chief of staff. The deputy chief of staff, Brig. Gen. Hobart R. Gay, had been well known in the prewar Army as a horseman and cavalry instructor. Like many another cavalryman he had transferred to armor. He had been chief of staff for General Patton in both North Africa and Sicily. During the Lorraine Campaign General Gay and Col. Paul D. Harkins, who was the Third Army deputy chief of staff for Operations and had held the same post during the Sicilian campaign, were to act as Patton's closest tactical advisers.

Most of the other top-ranking members of the Third Army general staff had shared a common experience in the peacetime cavalry and armored force, in North Africa and in Sicily. Col. Oscar W. Koch, G–2, and Col. Walter J. Muller, G–4, had held these same positions on the staffs of the Western Task Force and the Seventh Army. The G–3, Col. Halley G. Maddox, a well-known army horseman, had been a member of the G–3 Section of the Western Task Force and then, in Sicily, had served as Patton's G–3. Only the G–1, Col. Frederick S. Matthews, was a newcomer to Patton's general staff. The Third Army special staff also included officers who had earlier served with General Patton in the same positions they now occupied: the Adjutant General, the Army Engineer, the Army Signal Officer, and the Army Ordnance Officer.[16]

General Patton had three army corps under his command at the opening of the Lorraine operation (VIII, XII, and XX). The VIII Corps, commanded by General Middleton, was still fighting in Brittany, far from the scene of the forthcoming campaign, and on 5 September would become a part of the new Ninth Army.

[16] These officers were Col. R. E. Cummings, Col. J. F. Conklin, Col. E. F. Hammond, and Col. T. H. Nixon. See also page 608.

The XII Corps had fought its first battle, at Orléans, under Maj. Gen. Gilbert Cook, an officer admired by both Eisenhower and Patton. General Cook's physical condition was poor when he left the United States and proved unequal to the strain imposed by a field command. On 19 August, therefore, Maj. Gen. Manton S. Eddy, who had won distinction as division commander, was named commanding general of the XII Corps. General Eddy had been a Regular Army officer since 1916, but was not a West Pointer. During World War I he saw much combat, served with a machine gun detachment, and was wounded. Eddy was well known to General Patton and the Third Army staff since he had commanded the 9th Infantry Division in North Africa and Sicily. Later, in Normandy, Eddy received the DSC for his brave and aggressive leadership of the 9th during the Cherbourg operation.

The XII Corps included the 4th Armored Division and the 80th and 35th Infantry Divisions. The 4th Armored commander, Maj. Gen. John S. Wood, was a onetime field artillery officer who had entered the young Armored Force in 1941 as an artillery commander. He was graduated from West Point in 1912 and in the course of World War I took part in the operations at Château Thierry and St. Mihiel as a division staff officer. General Wood and most of his officers had been with the 4th Armored Division, a Regular Army outfit, since the spring of 1942. During the lightning sweep into Brittany and the dash across France the 4th Armored won a considerable reputation and endeared itself to the heart of the Third Army commander. General Wood had already received the DSC on General Patton's recommendation.

Maj. Gen. Horace L. McBride, who commanded the 80th Infantry Division, was graduated from West Point in 1916 and later served as a field artillery battalion commander in the Meuse–Argonne offensive. He had joined the 80th Infantry Division, a Reserve formation, as its artillery commander. In March, 1943, McBride was promoted to command the division; he completed its training and brought it to Europe. The 80th saw its initial action in the second week of August during the battle of the Falaise pocket, but had sustained relatively few casualties. The 35th Infantry Division commander was Maj. Gen. Paul W. Baade, who had held this post since January 1943. A West Point graduate of 1911, General Baade joined the infantry, served on the Mexican border in 1914, and acted as a regimental officer in the Vosges and Verdun sectors in 1918. The 35th, a National Guard division, landed on the Continent during the second week of July. It received its baptism of fire at St. Lô and incurred severe losses there and in the Mortain counterattack.

Maj. Gen. Walton H. Walker commanded the XX Corps, which, like the XII Corps, was one of the formations originally assigned to the Third Army in the United Kingdom. General Walker was graduated from West Point in 1912. Two years later he took part in Funston's expedition to Vera Cruz. During World War I he commanded a machine gun battalion in the St. Mihiel and Meuse-Argonne offensives, where he was twice cited for gallantry in action. Although originally an infantry officer, Walker had joined the Armored Force in 1941 and there won a reputation in armored training. He was commanding general of the IV Armored Corps at the time it was redesignated as the XX Corps. At the beginning of August the XX Corps had become an operational command. Shortly after his corps entered action Walker was awarded the DSC for his part in the Seine crossings.

Like the XII Corps the XX Corps contained one armored division, the 7th, and two infantry divisions, the 5th and 90th. Maj. Gen. Lindsay McD. Silvester's 7th Armored Division, an AUS formation, first saw combat during the pursuit across France but as yet had taken part in no major fighting. Although not a graduate of West Point, General Silvester had been commissioned as a Regular Army officer in 1911. His combat record as an infantry officer in World War I was outstanding: he had fought in all of the major American engagements, been wounded, and awarded the DSC. The 5th Infantry Division, now under the command of Maj. Gen. S. LeRoy Irwin, was a Regular Army division which had been sent to outpost duty in Iceland early in the war. The first elements of this division were committed in Normandy in mid-July, but thus far losses in the 5th had been small. General Irwin, a West Point graduate in the class of 1915, already had fought the Germans at Kasserine Pass and El Guettar in North Africa as artillery commander of the 9th Infantry Division. In December 1943, he was promoted to the command of the 5th Infantry Division. It may be mentioned in passing that such a transition—from artillery commander to division commander—would be a fairly common occurrence in the European Theater of Operations.

The 90th Infantry Division, a Reserve unit, got off to an unfortunate start in Normandy[17] and by 31 August had an accumulated casualty list equal to 59 percent of its T/O strength. During August the 90th was settling into a veteran outfit under Brig. Gen. Raymond S. McLain, the division's third commander since D Day. General McLain, a National Guard officer, saw ac-

[17] The earlier history of the 90th Infantry Division is given in R. G. Ruppenthal's *Utah Beach to Cherbourg* (AMERICAN FORCES IN ACTION).

tion in World War I as a machine gun officer in the Champagne and Meuse–Argonne offensives. He next encountered the Germans in 1943 during the Sicilian campaign and there received the DSC from General Patton. Later McLain took part in the Salerno and Anzio operations in Italy. On the strength of his record in the Mediterranean, General Eisenhower brought General McLain to the European Theater of Operations as a prospective division commander. However, the 30th Infantry Division had been in need of an artillery commander and McLain served with the 30th through the Normandy campaign, leaving it at the end of July to assume command of the 90th Infantry Division.

The Third Army numbered an estimated 314,814 officers and men at the end of August, including the three divisions and supporting troops assigned to the VIII Corps in Brittany.[18] The first troop list for the Lorraine Campaign, issued on 5 September, shows five separate tank battalions assigned to the Third Army, which, added to the armored divisions, gave General Patton 669 medium tanks. Contrary to the flamboyant reports reaching the American press during this period, the Third Army could hardly be considered "top-heavy with armor"; indeed, during the month of September, the Third Army would average 150 to 200 fewer medium tanks than in the First Army. The troop assignments as of 5 September also included 8 squadrons of mechanized cavalry, 23 antiaircraft battalions, 15 tank destroyer battalions, 51 field artillery battalions, 20 engineer combat battalions, and 3 engineer general service regiments. However, the constant shifting of army and corps troops along the front would mean that on the average a lesser strength than that shown on the troop list of 5 September would participate in the Lorraine Campaign.

No appraisal of the Third Army strength at the opening of the Lorraine Campaign is complete without reference to the XIX Tactical Air Command. Although the XIX TAC did not "support" the Third Army but rather—according to regulations—"co-operated" with General Patton's troops, the tightly knit character of this air-ground team had already set a pattern for operations in the ETO. Brig. Gen. Otto P. Weyland, who had taken command of the XIX TAC early in 1944 after considerable combat experience with the 84th Fighter Wing, was held in high esteem by the Third Army commander and staff. The forward tactical headquarters of the two commands were kept close together. And at the morning briefings held in the Third Army war tent

[18] TUSA G–1 Periodic Rpt, 26 Aug–2 Sep 44.

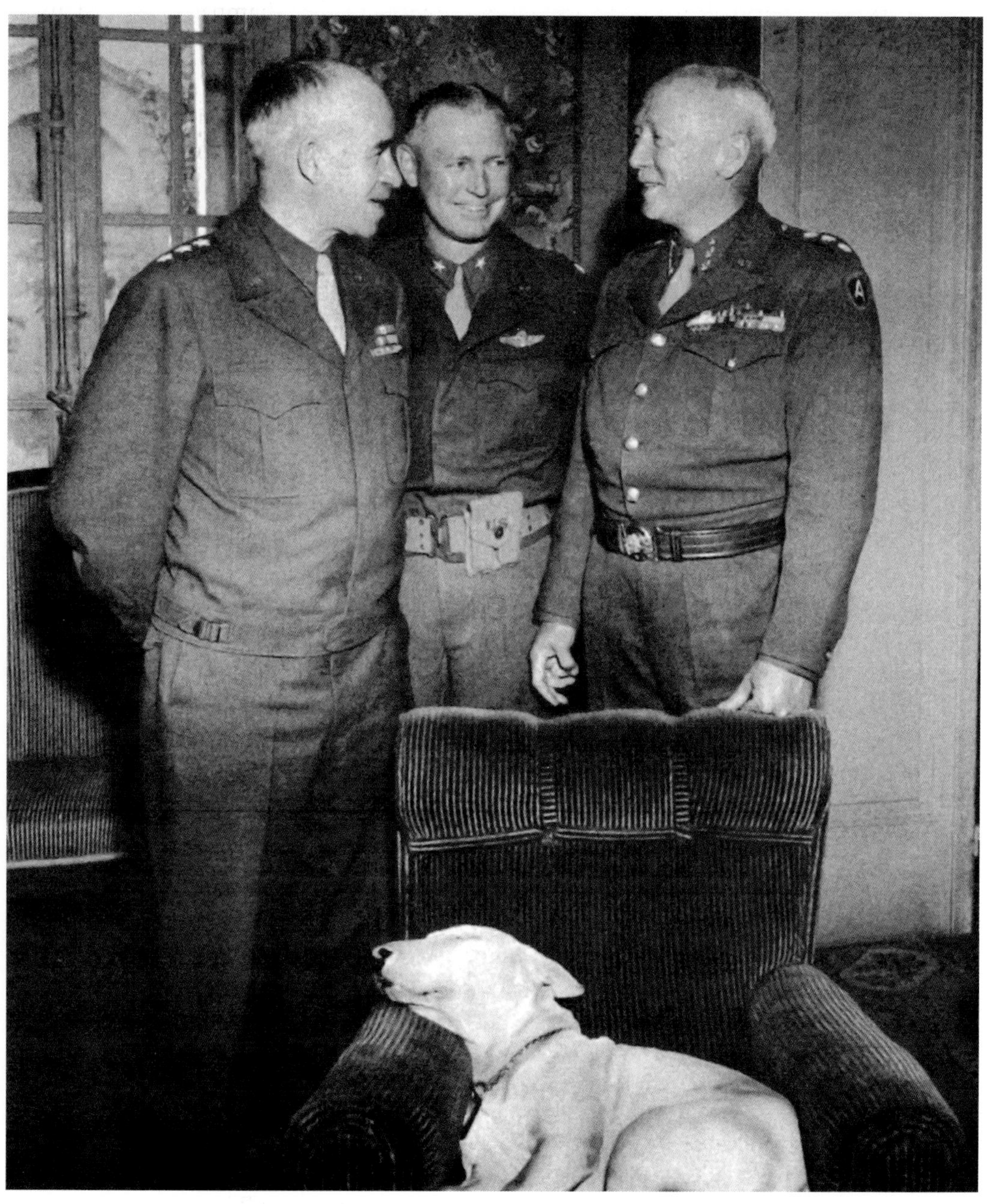

AMERICAN COMMANDERS. *Left to right: Lt. Gen. Omar N. Bradley, 12th Army Group; Brig. Gen. Otto P. Weyland, XIX Tactical Air Command; Lt. Gen. George S. Patton, Third Army. General Patton's dog, Willie, is shown in the foreground.*

General Weyland sat next to General Patton. This close co-operation assured the Third Army of very effective tactical air support, except, of course, when larger operational considerations intervened.

On 1 September the XIX TAC had in operation on the Continent two fighter wings, the 100th and 303d, comprising eight fighter-bomber groups and one photo reconnaissance group. The airfields used by General Weyland's 600 planes were distributed from the neck of the Brittany peninsula as far east as Le Mans. Since the Third Army had just overrun excellent Luftwaffe airfields in the Reims and Châlons-sur-Marne area the XIX TAC would be able, on 10 September, to move reconnaissance planes and some P-47's forward to the Marne.

During the penetration and pursuit phases of the Third Army's August drive the XIX TAC had been given three major tasks: (1) flying cover for the mechanized spearheads, together with air reconnaissance ahead of the ground advance; (2) sealing off the battlefield; (3) protecting the lengthy and exposed right flank of the Third Army. This combination of missions required a considerable dispersal of Weyland's squadrons; for example, on 1 September the XIX TAC was flying missions as far apart as Brest and Metz, while still other forays were being made 150–200 miles south of the Loire River. But although the speed and extent of the Third Army advance presented numerous problems in the matter of air-ground co-operation it also provided a wealth of targets for the American fighter-bombers. On 1 September XIX TAC was able to claim the largest bag of any single day since it had begun operations: 833 enemy motor vehicles destroyed or damaged.[19] The kill on 1 September, however, would not be soon repeated. The following day poor flying weather intervened. Then, on 3 September, General Eisenhower ordered the Ninth Air Force—with the XIX TAC—to turn its main effort against the fortified city of Brest, nearly five hundred air-line miles away from the Meuse bridgeheads occupied by the Third Army, in an attempt to open that Atlantic port.

The Pause in the Third Army Pursuit

The seizure of bridgeheads east of the Meuse River on the last day of August marked the end of the Third Army's rapid pursuit across northern France. (*Map II—inside back cover*) The brief lull which now ensued, and

[19] TUSA After Action Report (hereafter cited as AAR) II.

which would be followed by operations of a far less mobile character than those of August, must be explained in terms of logistics rather than tactics.

As early as 27 August the growing realization that the Allied armies had outrun their supplies and that there was not sufficient logistical support for a double-headed advance toward the east and northeast had forced the 12th Army Group to allocate priority in supply to the First Army, in accordance with the Supreme Commander's decision to strike toward Antwerp and the Ruhr.[20] General Bradley visited General Patton on 28 August, discussed the unfavorable supply position, and then authorized the Third Army commander to continue the advance to the Meuse River if he deemed it "advisable and feasible." Patton had not even considered a halt short of the Meuse and the following day ordered his corps commanders to continue the drive eastward, General Walker's XX Corps to establish a bridgehead over the Meuse at Verdun and General Eddy's XII Corps to cross the river in the vicinity of St. Mihiel and Commercy.

At this time the Third Army was beginning to experience the first serious effects of a logistical situation which its own dashing successes had helped create. On 28 August the Third Army G–4 reported that the amount of gasoline received was markedly short of the daily consumption. General Gay noted in the Third Army Diary "a small bit of anxiety for the time," but in general the first reaction to the gasoline shortage was irritation rather than pessimism. General Patton took his supply problem to General Bradley's headquarters the following day but was told that the Third Army could expect no appreciable amount of gasoline until 3 September. General Gay wrote: "If this is correct . . . the Third Army is halted short of its objective, the Meuse River." Actually the Third Army had enough fuel in its leading armored columns to make the last jump which would carry the advance across the Meuse. There were no signs of any enemy determination to stand and fight, and when General Eddy raised the question as to whether he could allow his tanks to become stranded east of the Meuse General Gaffey assured him that the army commander would not object.

On 31 August, Combat Command A, of the 4th Armored Division (Col. B. C. Clarke), raced across the Meuse bridges at Commercy and Pont-sur-Meuse, three miles to the north, before the German rear guard could set off

[20] The allocation of supplies in late August and early September is treated in R. G. Ruppenthal, Logistical Support of the Armies, a volume now under preparation in this series. See also 12th A Gp Rpt of Opns VI.

the demolition charges planted on the structures. In the north a task force led by Lt. Col. Edward McConnell, from CCA, 7th Armored Division (Col. Dwight A. Rosebaum), entered Verdun and seized a bridge that the demoralized Germans had left intact. By the night of 1 September the XX Corps bridgehead at Verdun and the XII Corps bridgehead at Commercy were held solidly by infantry, artillery, and armor. Other crossing sites now were in American hands; additional bridges were under construction; and the corps cavalry was pushing out from the Meuse toward the north, the east, and the south, attempting to regain contact with the fleeing enemy and scouting along the Moselle. The Third Army had achieved its objective and secured the line of the Meuse—but this was the last gasp of the month-long dash across northern France. On the morning of 2 September reports from immobile formations flooded into the army and corps headquarters. The Third Army was at a standstill.

Much ink has been spilled in varied and polemic explanations of the Third Army halt west of the Moselle River. For the historian it is sufficient to say that at this period the iron rules of logistics were in full operation and that the Third Army, making an attack subsidiary to the Allied main effort, would be the first to suffer therefrom.[21]

All through August General Patton's determination to override every obstacle and continue to advance had so inspired his army that it had violated with impunity many an accepted tactical or logistical dictum and had surpassed the most sanguine expectations of success. However, the Third Army successes in August had been matched all along the Allied front, in concrete results if not in brilliance. The total impact of these successes could not but disrupt a system of supply based on the expectation of a more gradual and evenly paced advance across France. During late June and the month of July determined German resistance had held the Allies to an exceedingly constricted area, making it impossible to carry out the scheduled and methodical forward movement of supplies, supply installations, and transportation facilities on the Continent. In August the great Allied advance had quickly regained the operational schedule which had been lost in Normandy and then had as quickly outrun it. Motorized and mechanized columns fighting a war of movement could function on a flexible tactical timetable. But the time element in the movement of low-priority service troops, cargo unloading, the creation

[21] An exhaustive study of the supply problem in this period will be found in Ruppenthal, Logistical Support.

of forward supply dumps and depots, the construction of pipe lines, the rebuilding of railroads, and the acquisition of adequate rolling stock could not be treated so cavalierly. In short, the tactical situation which had resulted from the stalemate in Normandy and the unexpected speed of the advance over the Seine and across France had created an extraordinary logistical lag.

On 31 August the Third Army was 150 air-line miles beyond the line of the Seine, which, in the OVERLORD plan, was to have been attained by the Allied armies on 3 September. According to the more tentative phase lines laid down in the POST-OVERLORD Outline Plan, the Third Army forward positions on this date were at the phase line set for 2 April 1945 (D plus 300). Obviously the phase lines set forth in the OVERLORD schedule had been tentative and hypothetical; they were probably even more so in the case of the POST-OVERLORD timetable.[22] Admittedly the papers showing these phase lines had been issued "for planning and procurement purposes only." But on this basis supply plans had been made, and improvisation in the field of logistics would prove to be far more difficult than in the sphere of tactics.

In the last days of August the Allied armies had reached the stage of "frantic supply." The bulk of all supply was still coming in over the Normandy beaches and being carried by truck directly from coastal dumps and depots to the combat zone. The beach areas were congested. An insufficient number of transport vehicles, coupled with the long haul from the beaches to the front lines, made it impossible to move supplies forward in the quantities required for the daily maintenance of the armies. The stalemate in Normany and the hand-to-mouth supply in August had prevented the stocking of supplies between the Normandy coast and the army dumps. None of the Allied armies had been able to build up large operational reserves. The railroads west of the Seine had been crippled by Allied air bombardment in the weeks before D Day and could not be rebuilt overnight. The heavy landing craft shuttling between cargo ships and the beaches were busy bringing much-needed motor trucks ashore and could not be diverted to handling locomotives and freight cars. Pipe lines and pumping stations to carry gasoline forward took long in building; meanwhile gasoline was being drained out so fast for immediate use that the sections of pipe line which were finished could not be

[22] Maps in Post NEPTUNE Planning Forecast 1, 27 May 44, SHAEF SGS File, Post OVERLORD Planning, 381, I. German surrender was assumed as of D plus 360; Reims was to be reached by D plus 180, Verdun between D plus 270 and D plus 330. These phase lines were based on the assumption that the German armies would make a stand at the Seine and Meuse Rivers.

kept full. Attempts to supplement an inadequate ground transport by the use of air transport proved markedly effective, but such attempts could be made only when the AEAF was not engaged in mounting or carrying out large-scale air operations.

The most telling shortages in this period were gasoline and transportation. As stores accumulated at the Normandy beaches and ports, the logistical problem turned on the allocation of transportation rather than on the allocation of the supply items themselves. Ammunition, which had a low priority in the unloading schedules then in force, presented no immediate supply problem, nor would it while the German armies were in retreat. Rations took a fixed but limited portion of the tonnage reaching the army dumps. During these days food would be monotonous—mostly K and C rations—but available in sufficient quantity. In the Third Army area the capture of the great Wehrmacht warehouses in and around Reims provided huge stores of beef, sauerkraut, and tinned fish, which added another kind of monotony to the army diet but freed some of the truck space hitherto given to rations.

At the end of August, Third Army trucks still were picking up their loads west of Paris, where the famous Red Ball Express had established the forward communications zone dumps, or were driving clear back to the beaches. The *average* round trip from the Third Army zone took three days. It was intended that the First and Third Armies would each have a supporting railroad. On 31 August a railway bridge was completed at Laval and rail operations were extended from Cherbourg to Chartres. But the first train movement to the Third Army zone would not commence until 6 September. The POL (petrol, oil, and lubricants) pipe line reached Alençon on 27 August, but it carried relatively small amounts of gasoline and was to have little immediate effect.[23]

Gasoline was the one item which was essential to further movement by the Third Army. The first severe impact of the supply shortage on Patton's operations had been staved off for a brief period when, on 26 and 27 August, over a thousand planes were used to fly gasoline and rations to the Third Army. On 28 August, however, gasoline deliveries were 100,000 gallons short of the daily Third Army consumption—an amount roughly equivalent to that used by one of Patton's armored divisions in a single day of cross-country fighting. On 29 August the Third Army was given priority on supply by air, and gaso-

[23] See TUSA AAR II, G–4 Sec.

line was flown to the airstrip at Bricy, near Orléans; but this delivery accounted for only about half the daily army consumption, and the over-all shortage was increased. Gasoline receipts on 30 August amounted to 31,975 gallons, approximately 368,025 gallons short of the estimated daily consumption in the Third Army. When, on 31 August, the 12th Army Group sent out an order that the Third Army would not build up more than a one-day reserve of gasoline, the Third Army G–4 was forced to reply that the army had no gasoline reserve of any kind. By 1 September gasoline was reaching the Third Army only in driblets, precluding even limited operations.[24] Fortunately, however, the enemy forces in front of the Third Army were in no position to counterattack General Patton's immobilized and widely dispersed formations; the month of September would begin with relative quiet along the western borders of Lorraine.

The Military Topography of Lorraine[25]

That part of eastern France conventionally known as Lorraine roughly corresponds to the departments of the Meuse, Meurthe-et-Moselle, Moselle, and the Vosges—although the western part of the department of the Meuse and the southern section of the department of the Vosges lie outside of Lorraine. Historically, Lorraine represents the territories belonging to the three bishoprics (Trois-Evêchés) of Metz, Toul, and Verdun in the upper basins of the Meuse and Moselle Rivers. (*Map III*) Geographically, the area of Lorraine is more difficult to define and French geographers have never agreed on a precise and commonly accepted delimitation of its natural boundaries. In general Lorraine exists as a plateau, with elevations ranging from 600 to 1,300 feet. The western boundary may be designated by the Moselle valley, although some geographers extend the western limits of the plateau to the Meuse Heights (the Côtes de Meuse). From the viewpoint of military geography Lorraine is bounded on the east by the Sarre River, on the north by Luxembourg and the western German mountains, and on the southeast by the Vosges Mountains.

[24] *Ibid.* See also Ruppenthal, Logistical Support.

[25] E. de Martonne, *Les Régions géographiques de la France* (Paris, 1921); *Lorraine Annexée*, ed. Ministère de la guerre (Paris, 1917); *OKH, Generalstab des Heeres* (hereafter cited as *OKH, Gen. St. d. H.*), *Abteilung fuer Kriegskarten und Vermessungswesen, Militaergeographische Beschreibung von Frankreich, 1940;* TUSA Target Area Analysis No. 10, 5 Sep 44; Douglas W. Johnson, *Battlefields of the World War*, Chs. IX and X, *passim; A Manual of Alsace–Lorraine*, ed. The Admiralty (London, 1920).

Insofar as military topography is concerned Lorraine through the centuries has been a route of invasion for armies moving from central to western Europe. On the western side of the Lorraine plateau, however, a succession of escarpments rises out of the plains of northern France (the so-called "Paris Basin") in a series of military barriers. These escarpments, the Argonne, the Meuse Heights, and the Moselle Plateau, all have gradual western slopes but drop abruptly on their eastern faces, presenting a difficult military approach from the east and affording the defender greater advantages if he faces to the east. But it should be noted that a hostile advance from the west across the Moselle River will have to traverse a long natural glacis and negotiate a deep river trench, beyond which lie still other heights representing the eastern continuation of the Moselle Plateau, generally somewhat lower than those on the west bank of the Moselle River but still of very considerable tactical importance.

The sector of the Moselle toward which the Third Army faced at the beginning of September was reinforced by two nodal defenses—the outposts of Lorraine—one of which might properly be said to face west, one east. In the north the river line was barricaded by the so-called Metz-Thionville *Stellung*, a position based on the fortifications around Metz and Thionville. Originally built for the defense of France, these works had passed into German hands during the period 1870–1918 and again in 1940, with the result that the most modern parts of the Metz-Thionville system of fortifications were oriented to face the west. On the eve of 1914 the Germans had constructed two new works north of Thionville at Illange and Koenigsmacker, thus extending the original Metz-Thionville *Stellung* and further strengthening the line against attack from the west.

Thirty miles south of Metz lies Nancy, the historic ruling city of Lorraine. Unlike Metz the city of Nancy has never been fortified in modern times. The French had looked upon Nancy as a "bridgehead" from which their armies could debouch to the east, and had relied upon a combination of natural barriers and strong forces in the field to give it adequate protection. On the east Nancy is covered by a bastion of scarps and buttes, erupting from the Moselle Plateau, known as the Grand Couronné. On the west the city is protected by a triangular, heavily wooded, and rugged plateau known as the Massif de Haye. Still farther to the west the Moselle River swings out to pass around Nancy in a wide loop, adding one more barrier to defend the city. At the extremity of this loop the city of Toul guards the western approach to Nancy and the Massif de Haye and, conversely, provides a bridgehead east of the Moselle. Toul itself possessed some outdated forts and was the center of a circular series of small works, such as those at Gondreville and Villey-le Sec, which had been partially modernized prior to 1940.

Between Toul and Epinal, a little over forty miles to the southeast, an opening known as the "Charmes trough" (Trouée de Charmes) offered a western entry into Lorraine and the means of flanking the Metz–Thionville *Stellung* and the Nancy–Massif de Haye position. Prior to 1914 the French frontier defense system built by Gen. Sere De Rivières had purposely left this sector undefended as an open trap for the invading German armies. French military thought therefore had accepted the necessity of a "Bataille de la Trouée de Charmes," an action that finally took place in September 1914 and resulted in defeat for the Germans. In 1940 the German *First Army* followed this same path and outflanked Nancy, this time successfully. In 1944 the Charmes Gap still afforded a convenient route bypassing Nancy. But an advance from west to east would be made more difficult by the three major "M" rivers—the Moselle, the Mortagne, and the Meurthe—which formed traverses barring the exit from the "gap."

The Moselle River in particular is a military obstacle of no mean proportion. Unlike the neighboring rivers it has a high rate of flow and a relatively steep gradient. It drains the western slopes of the Vosges and during the rainy season is torrential and flooded. West of Nancy the Moselle valley is relatively narrow, but expands as it wends northward until, between Metz and Thionville, it attains a width of between four and five miles. North of Remich the Moselle enters a narrow, tortuous gorge, finally emptying its waters into the middle Rhine near Koblenz.

East of the Moselle, as has been noted, the plateau formation continues for some distances. Metz and Nancy lie close to the wide valleys of the Nied and Seille Rivers, known as "the Lorraine plain" (La Plaine). This rich, rolling agricultural region is interlaced with small streams, dotted with occasional woods and isolated buttes, and intersected at intervals by flat-topped ridges. Here are found the characteristic Lorraine villages, small, compact, and with buildings and walls of stone.

Moving from south to north across Lorraine, the following features, important in the course of the Third Army campaign, should be noted. Bisecting the southern section of Lorraine runs the Marne-Rhin Canal—between sixteen and twenty yards in width—which originates at Vitry-le-François and ends at Strasbourg on the Rhine. West of Sarrebourg another artificial waterway, the Canal des Houillères de la Sarre, connects the Sarre River and the Marne-Rhin Canal. In this area a complex of swamps and forests forms a triangle pointing toward Dieuze, an impassable sector which canalizes large-scale troop movements through the narrow Dieuze corridor. West of Dieuze two roughly parallel ridges form another corridor, extending diagonally from Château-Salins toward the tableland at Morhange. Once past Morhange the country leading to Sarreguemines and the Sarre forms a pond-studded corridor some sixteen miles wide, perhaps the most open area east of the Moselle. Farther north the ground is much rougher and more wooded, especially as it nears the Sarre River. Still farther north the Sarre River runs into the Moselle, which here curves away to the northeast. The triangle formed by the confluence of the two rivers is in effect a kind of cul-de-sac at the northern edge of Lorraine. Since the Lorraine plateau narrows as it approaches its eastern terminus, hemmed in as it is by the middle and lower Vosges and the western German mountains, there is not enough room to accommodate a modern army in advance on a wide front. As a rule, therefore, any advance east of the Moselle will tend to move diagonally toward the northeast on a constantly narrowing front.

The main Lorraine gateway on the northeast opens at the Sarre River, with its center at Saarbruecken and the gateposts in the vicinity of Saarlautern, on the left, and Zweibruecken, on the right. Beyond this opening the Hunsrueck tableland and the Hardt mountains rise to deflect any large-scale northeastward march to the Rhine Valley onto a flat-topped, forested plateau, known as the Palatine Hills (Pfaelzer Bergland). Beyond this plateau lie the Rhine Valley and the cities of Mannheim, Darmstadt, and Frankfurt. This gateway has always been important in the military topography of Europe. In 1814 the Allies took possession of Saarlautern in order to provide an immediate entry into France in case it should become necessary to deal again with Napoleon. In 1870 the main German armies crossed the Sarre in this sector to invade France and defeat General Bazaine's army at Metz. And here, in the period before 1940, Hitler had built the strongest section of the West Wall facing the strongest part of the Maginot Line.

Two main highways pass across Lorraine. One follows the old Roman road from Metz to Saarbruecken and thence to Mannheim. The other leads from Nancy, across the Vosges to Strasbourg. In general the area east of the Moselle is covered with an adequate road net, often hard-surfaced, which spreads out from the great road centers at Metz, Nancy, and Lunéville. The main trunk railroad lines which cross Lorraine largely follow the routes of the two primary highways.[26] At the Sarre River two junction points—Saarbruecken and Sarreguemines—tie the French railroad system to the German. A third important rail center, at Sarrebourg, continues this lateral line to the south, and with the other two permits considerable movement by rail on the eastern edge of Lorraine.

The climate of Lorraine—due to play so important a role in the operations of the Third Army—tends to extremes of heat and cold, precipitation and dryness. The westerly winds do not lose their moisture until after passing over the plateaus east of the Paris Basin, with the result that two to three times as much rain falls in Lorraine as in the Champagne country just to the west. Weather records—which have been kept for a ninety-year period in Lorraine—show that in normal times the wet season begins in September and that October has the greatest amount of rainfall of any of the autumn and winter months. The average monthly precipitation in Lorraine during September, October, and November, is between 2.4 and 3.0 inches. In the autumn of 1944, however, the rain which fell on the underlying Lorraine clay was two and three times the amount usually recorded; in November 1944, 6.95 inches of rain fell during the month.[27]

The Enemy Situation on the Western Front

At the beginning of September 1944, the collective ground forces of the Third Reich numbered 327 divisions and brigades, greatly varied as to strength and capabilities. Of this total, in some respects a paper roster, 31 divisions and 13 brigades were armored. The confusion introduced in the German reporting system by the reverses suffered during August makes it difficult to determine what proportion of this strength was actively engaged on battle fronts. A careful study of the German situation maps maintained by OKH (Oberkommando des Heeres) and OKW (Oberkommando der Wehrmacht) indicates that elements of some 252 divisions and 15 to 20 brigades were deployed within the

[26] Nancy is a rail center of international importance since it is the junction point for the Calais–Basel and the Paris–Vienna–Orient lines.

[27] Wea Div Hq AAF, Weather and Climate as related to military operations in France, Sep 46; Hq Air Wea Serv, Weather conditions in the European Theater of Operations on D Day and in November, 1944, Sep 46.

combat zones of the several German theaters of operations on 1 September. In addition, the ground forces of the Wehrmacht were augmented by the presence of approximately 55 allied divisions (Finnish, Hungarian, and Bulgarian) on the Finnish front, the Eastern Front, and in the Balkans. One German division, it may be noted, was reckoned as the equivalent of two of these allied divisions.[28]

In the five years of war that had elapsed since the invasion of Poland cumulative German losses had mounted to 3,630,274 men and 114,215 officers. The Army accounted for the largest share of these losses: 3,266,686 men and 92,811 officers. These enormous casualty figures included only the dead, the missing in action, and soldiers demobilized by reason of physical disability or extreme cases of family hardship. Nonetheless the numerical strength of the German armed forces still represented a relatively high proportion of the population, although the quality had deteriorated somewhat as conscription broadened to make good the earlier losses by reaching into older and younger mobilization classes, and as training periods of necessity were shortened. The total paper strength of the Wehrmacht, at the beginning of September, was estimated to be 10,165,303.

Army and Waffen-SS	7,536,946
Navy	703,066
Luftwaffe	1,925,291

In actual fact the available fighting strength of the German ground forces was considerably below the total ration strength. This disparity had increased as the war progressed and was a continuing source of irritation to Hitler. The Field Army (*Feldheer*) now was estimated to number 3,421,000 officers and men. The Replacement Army (*Ersatzheer*), whose composition could be determined with a little more precision, totaled 2,387,973. Units of the *Waffen-SS* which were serving in the field independent of Army control had a strength reckoned as 207,276. The remaining million and a half members of the Army included miscellaneous Luftwaffe ground troops and SS personnel, police, foreign volunteers such as Italians, Indians, Frenchmen, and Spaniards, members of the services of supply, East European auxiliaries (*Hilfswillige*), and so forth. The greater part of the German Field Army was concentrated on

[28] The total roster for German divisions and brigades is taken from a tabulation in *OKH, Gen. St. d. H./Organisations Abteilung* (hereafter cited as *OKH/Org. Abt.*) *KTB*, 13 October 1944, with some revisions, such as the deletion of divisions which had headquarters but no troops. The figure given for German divisions actually engaged has been compiled from situation maps now in the possession of GMDS.

the Eastern Front. Of the 3,421,000 men on the rosters of the Field Army, 2,046,000 belonged to the East Army (*Ostheer*).

The months of June, July, and August had brought one German defeat after another on both the Eastern and Western Fronts. The resultant breakdown of communications, the loss or destruction of personnel records in hasty retreats, and the failure to retake the battlefields where the German dead and wounded lay made any strict accounting of battle losses impossible. Casualty tables dated in April 1945, but still incomplete at that time, give some idea of the losses inflicted on the Field Army in the summer disasters of 1944. In July the number of wounded who had to be hospitalized on all the German fronts was at least 195,332, the largest total of seriously wounded for any month of the war. August was marked by the greatest number of killed and missing which the collective German Field Army would endure in any month of the entire war. Incomplete returns show 60,625 officers and men officially declared dead, and 405,398 missing. The mobility of the Field Army also had been gravely impaired in August, with the loss of 254,225 horses during the great retreats in the East and the West.

The Russian offensives against *Army Group Center* and the forces in the Ukraine had accounted for the largest proportion of German ground force casualties during June, July, and August: at least 916,860 dead, wounded, and missing. On the Western Front, where substantially fewer divisions were engaged on both sides of the line, the German Field Army had lost a minimum of 293,802 dead, wounded, and missing in the battles from D Day to 1 September. To this number may be added 230,320 officers and men of the Wehrmacht (86,337 of these belonged to the Field Army) who had retired into the Western fortresses, there to be contained with relatively small effort on the part of the Allies, and eventually to surrender.

At this late date it is impossible to give more than the approximate strength of the German armies in the West on 1 September. Casualty returns were only "estimates." The changes in the Replacement Army, following the attempt on Hitler's life and the appointment of Himmler to its command, seem to have caused extensive confusion and disorder throughout the replacement system. As a result the Germans themselves could not be certain as to the exact number of replacements sent to the Western Front during this period. They later estimated the fighting strength of the ground forces in the West on 1 August 1944, as 770,000 officers and men. Tables compiled at the same time for the status on 1 September give a fighting strength of 543,000. These tables, however, do not include the division and army troops which had been sent to the Western Front during August, or the numerous separate replacement battalions. It is probable, therefore, that the 49½ German divisions and supporting troops in the West at the opening of September numbered over 700,000.[29]

The heavy losses suffered in the West and the continuing high rate of attrition on the Eastern Front forced Hitler to provide some program for bolstering up the two main fronts with new or reconstructed divisions. In early July, while the Allies still were held in check in Normandy, Hitler had ordered the formation of fifteen new divisions to strengthen the German lines in the East and stem the Soviet tide. These fresh formations were obtained by utilizing troops returning to duty from the hospitals, drastically reducing the number of ground troops assigned to the Luftwaffe, converting naval personnel to infantrymen, enrolling new classes that had come of military age, and stripping industry of able-bodied men who previously had been exempted from the operation of the conscription laws. By the beginning of September, the fifteen new divisions and three "static" divisions had been raised and dispatched to the combat zones, fifteen of the total going to the East, two to the West, and one to Norway.[30]

During the early summer of 1944, Hitler and his closest military advisers had showed more concern with the collapse of the central section of the Eastern Front and the Soviet threat to East Prussia than with the Allied drive toward the boundaries of western Germany. The number of divisions engaged on the Russian front was much greater than the number engaged in the West. The Eastern theater of operations had been draining German resources since 1941. A long-continued, virulent, and effective propaganda had made the primacy of the struggle against "Bolshevism" an article of faith with the German people and the German Army. Equally important was the reliance which

[29] The strength, loss, and replacement statistics used in this section have been taken from a variety of *KTB*'s and *Anlagen* files for 1944 and 1945. The most useful sources are *Oberkommando der Wehrmacht, Organisations Abteilung* (hereafter cited as *OKW/Org. Abt.*); *OKH/Org. Abt.*; *OKW/Allgemeines Wehrmachts Amt, "Verluste der Wehrmacht bis 1944,"* 1 Dec 44; and *OKH/Generalquartiermeister, der Heeresarzt KTB* and *Anlagen*. German losses given for this period are only approximate. The card files of the *Heeres-Personalamt* have been partially destroyed; many have been lost. However, the figures used in the text are very close to those found in MSS #T–121, T–122, *Geschichte des Oberbefehlshaber West* (Zimmermann *et al.*). See also the loss statistics Major Percy Schramm, OKW historian, obtained from the 14 March 1945 issue of the *OKW, Wehrmachtfuehrungsstab* (hereafter cited as *OKW/WFSt*) monthly publication, *Beurteilung der personellen und materiellen Ruestungslage der Wehrmacht*. MS #B–716 (Schramm).

[30] *OKH/Org. Abt. KTB* and *Anlagen* 1944; see also the respective *OKH/Org. Abt. Karteiblaetter*, 1942–45.

Hitler and the higher staff officers in OKW placed in the West Wall, regarding this fortified line as a final and impenetrable barrier to an invasion of western Germany. On the Eastern Front, however, there was no such system of fortifications—indeed Hitler had decided against any thoroughgoing program of permanent defenses[31]—and the only barrier between the Soviet armies and the Third Reich was that constituted by the German armies in the field.

Nevertheless, the rapid disintegration of the western German forces during August forced Hitler to turn his attention from the East and consider ways and means of shoring up the armies in front of the West Wall. It appears also that Hitler was already thinking in terms of some large-scale operation to regain the initiative, which had been everywhere surrendered. On 2 September Hitler gave instructions for the creation of an "operational reserve" of twenty-five new divisions, to be made available between 1 October and 1 December. Nearly all of these formations were destined for the Western Front.

The twenty-five new divisions and the eighteen raised in July and August now were designated volksgrenadier divisions, an honorific selected by Hitler to appeal to the national and military pride of the German people (*das Volk*). Reichsfuehrer-SS Heinrich Himmler and the SS were assigned the political indoctrination and training of these units, although they would not be included in the *Waffen-SS*, and Hitler personally concerned himself with attempting to secure the best arms and equipment for the new formations. Some of these divisions were assigned new members, generally in the "500" series. Many, however, would carry the numbers belonging to divisions that had been totally wrecked or destroyed, for on 10 August Hitler had forbidden the practice of erasing such divisions from the Wehrmacht rolls.

The organization and equipment of the new volksgrenadier divisions reflected the tendency, current in the German Army since 1943, to reduce the manpower in the combat division while increasing its fire power. Early in 1944 the standard infantry division had been formally reduced in strength from about 17,000 to 12,500 officers and men.[32] The volksgrenadier division represented a further reduction to a strength of some 10,000, this generally being effected by reducing the conventional three infantry regiments to two rifle battalions apiece and paring down the number of organic service troops. Although equipment varied, an attempt was made to arm two platoons in each company with the 1944 model machine pistol, add more field artillery,

[31] Hitler relaxed this order in late August 1944.

[32] See discussion in Harrison, Cross-Channel Attack.

and provide a slightly larger complement of antitank weapons and assault guns. Theoretically, fourteen assault guns, the basic accompanying weapon for the German infantry platoon in attack, were assigned to each division, but this number seldom would be available in the field. Approximately three-quarters of the divisional transportation was horse-drawn. One unit, the *Fuesilier* battalion, was equipped with bicycles.

Although a desperate shortage of heavy weapons had forced Hitler to accept a Table of Equipment for the volksgrenadier divisions much weaker in antitank guns and artillery than he desired, he sought to remedy this weakness by ordering the construction of twelve motorized artillery brigades (requiring about 1,000 guns), ten *Werfer* (rocket projector) brigades, ten tank destroyer battalions, and twelve 20-mm. machine gun battalions. These GHQ (*Heeres*) units were intended to reach combat at the same time as the last twenty-five volksgrenadier divisions; most were slated for the Western Front.

In addition, ten panzer brigades were in the process of formation or just going into action on 1 September. Their equipment varied according to the ebb and flow of German industrial production, but in general these first brigades, numbered from 101 through 110, would be built around a panzer battalion that contained some forty Panther tanks (Mark V). As early as 26 June Hitler had ruled, on the basis of the German tank losses in Normandy, that the basic tank model, the Mark IV, should be matched one for one by the heavier Panther. Since even the most sanguine heads of the various German armaments offices were as one in agreement that the Third Reich could not equal the tank production of the United States, Hitler hoped to redress the armored balance on the battlefield by giving priority to the production of tank models tactically superior to the American Sherman. During July and August, therefore, the German factories stepped up the output of the Panther and the superheavy Tiger—the latter optimistically estimated to be equal to twenty Sherman tanks. In spite of the Allied air effort against German industrial centers, tank output during these two months fell only slightly short of production schedules, with tanks actually delivered as follows:

	July	*August*[33]
Mark IV	282	279
Panther	373	358
Tiger	140	97

[33] Monthly tables appearing in *OKH, Der Generalinspekteur der Panzertruppen, Fuehrer Vortrag-Notizen*, Jul–Dec 44.

Early in August Hitler ordered that the Western Front should be given priority on the tanks coming off the assembly lines. Contrary to the advice of his armored experts he decreed that the Panthers should not be used to refit the depleted and burned-out panzer divisions already in being but should go straight from the factory to the new panzer brigades, which he envisaged as mobile reserves capable of immediate commitment.

Still other drastic steps were taken in midsummer to meet the crisis in the West. Approximately a hundred fortress infantry battalions, made up of the older military classes and heretofore used in rear areas, were hastily and scantily re-equipped and sent forward to the field armies. About four-fifths of these battalions eventually would be sent to the West; by the beginning of September many were already in the line. On 4 September OKW took note of "the threatening situation" in the West and assigned priority on all new artillery and assault guns to that theater, following this with orders for a general movement of the artillery units in the Balkans back to the Western Front.[34]

Unlike the German high command of World War I, Hitler and his household military staff were unable to utilize fully the play of internal lines by shuttling divisions back and forth between the two main German fronts. Continuous pressure in the East and the West made it impossible to strip one front in order to reinforce the other, and, equally important, the great Allied air offensive against the railroad systems of Central Europe denied any rapid and direct large-scale troop movements.

In general the carry-over from the older Eastern Front to the newly opened Western Front would be indirect in nature. The survivors of divisions destroyed by the Soviet armies in many cases would be returned to Germany, there be used as cadres in the formation of new divisions, and finally be sent to the Western Front as the veteran core of these inexperienced formations. In addition, the long campaigning in Russia had produced a number of rank-

[34] *OKW/WFSt KTB Ausarbeitung, "Der Westen"* 1. IV.–16. XII. 44 (hereafter cited as *OKW/WFSt KTB Ausarbeitung Der Westen*), 4 and 8 Sep 44. This draft War Diary (*KTB*) is based on the detailed daily working notes kept by Major Schramm in his capacity as historian at the headquarters of OKW. Until the end of 1943 the Diary was arranged purely chronologically, supplemented by information from participants in operations. After 1943 the Diary was arranged according to subject matter and fronts (*Ausarbeitungen*), for example, the Anzio Beachhead, Shifting of Divisions between Fronts, and so forth, and was supplemented by a *Merkbuch* kept by Schramm, with notes of the discussions at the situation meetings he attended and notes obtained from special interviews with the Deputy Chief of *WFSt,* General Warlimont. From 1 January 1945 the chronological order was reintroduced. In view of the subsequent destruction of the OKW records ordered by General Scherff, the copies of the *Ausarbeitungen* for 1944 and the personal commentaries preserved by Schramm represent a unique and valuable source. Also in Historical Division files as MS #B–034 (Schramm).

ing and experienced commanders who were ready for promotion to higher posts. As vacancies occurred, or were purposely created on the Western Front, many high-ranking officers would be relieved from duty in the East and promoted to still higher commands in the West, bringing with them the experience, tactics, and techniques derived from the hard months and years of battle in the Russian theater of operations. This carry-over in experience would have some important effects on the conduct of the war in the West—not all favorable to the Germans.

Hitler's intense and direct personal concern with every small detail involved in the preparation of new forces during the summer of 1944 was indicative of the degree to which the direction of the war had passed from the hands of the higher field commanders and the General Staff Corps to those of Hitler and his immediate entourage in the headquarters of OKW. The Polish campaign of 1939 had been fought by the field commanders and the General Staff planners in general accordance with the conventional German theories of command responsibility. In 1940 Hitler had intervened in the conduct of the campaign in France on two occasions, personally selecting Sedan as the point of penetration for the drive through the Maginot Line and personally halting the German armored formations from pursuing the British Expeditionary Force through the flooded areas in the Dunkerque sector.[35] Up to this point in the war the prestige of the Wehrmacht generals and the German General Staff had been sustained by quick and easy victories. The reverses suffered on the Russian front during the winter of 1941–42, however, gave Hitler the excuse for entering more and more into the picture as the supreme military leader. Through 1942 and 1943 he tried to run the war from his headquarters in East Prussia. By 1944 Hitler's personal control over military matters was so well established that a general with the prestige of Rundstedt could not move an army corps a few miles without the permission of Hitler and the OKW staff. The unsuccessful attempt on Hitler's life in July 1944 ended most of what little influence the field commanders and the General Staff had managed to retain.

Now Hitler stood alone as the supreme arbiter in all phases of the German war effort, embodying in himself the "Fuehrer Prinzip" so long the core of

[35] *Gruppe von Kleist (GKdo XXII A.K.), Ia: Anlagenheft 3 zu KTB Nr. 4*, 24–31 May 40; *Heeresgruppe A, KTB West II. Teil*, 17–25 May 40. See also interrogations of Warlimont (State Department Special Interrogation Mission, 20 Sep 45), Guderian (State Department Special Interrogation Mission, 7–8 Sep 45), and Rundstedt (CPM, MIS, 6 Sep 45).

Nazi faith. Directly below Hitler the OKW acted as his personal military staff. Generalfeldmarschall William Keitel, the head of OKW, and Generaloberst Alfred Jodl, Chief of the Armed Forces Operations Staff (*Wehrmachtfuehrungsstab*), served here as technical advisers only, seldom making any decisions on their own. But the importance of Keitel, Jodl, and the OKW staff should not be underestimated; through them Hitler received his impression of the situation in the field, and through them the field commanders had to go to reach Hitler. The complete abandonment of the prewar system of German command organization also brought still another staff under Hitler's direct domination, that of OKH, which had responsibility for the conduct of the war on the Eastern Front. All other theaters of operation were subordinate to OKW.

On the Western Front *OB WEST*[36] exercised an illusory "supreme command" in the field under OKW. The relations between OKW and *OB WEST*, in the summer of 1944, indicate the disrepute and desuetude into which all the field commands had fallen. Hitler and the OKW staff mistrusted the field commanders and sought evidence of treason in each defeat suffered at the hands of the Allies. Even successful operations, such as the *Nineteenth Army* withdrawal from southern France, more often than not would be rewarded with suspicion, calumny, and the relief of the commanders concerned. The field commanders and staffs were fearful for their lives at the hands of the Gestapo. When they visited the headquarters of OKW they found it chilling and aloof, with little knowledge of the conditions actually prevailing at the front and even less desire to learn. The atmosphere of distrust and suspicion corroded all sense of responsibility. The field commanders feared to exercise initiative and referred all important decisions to OKW. Orders emanating from OKW were seldom amended but were simply passed on to lower echelons with the remark "copy from OKW."

The disposition of command and decision in the person of one man, far removed from the practical considerations of the battle front, was evidenced in the late spring and early summer of 1944 by an almost complete abnegation of the principles of maneuver and mobility in the conduct of the war in France. From Normandy onward Hitler's *idée fixe* was that each German soldier in the West should stand his ground—even if this permitted the enemy to cut him

[36] The German term, "*Oberbefehlshaber West*," which may mean either the Commander in Chief West or his headquarters, has been rendered as "*OB WEST*" when it refers to the headquarters and as "C-in-C West" when it refers to the person.

off—until he was struck down or was victorious. Basically this concept seems to have been derived from earlier successes on the Russian front in which German formations had held fast, although surrounded, and then had blunted the Soviet thrust and cut their way free.

As a result of these Eastern Front experiences, Hitler had issued a long directive in September 1942 which contained the essence of the Hitlerian dogma on the unyielding defense and which still further stripped the German field commanders of authority and initiative. No army commander or army group commander, Hitler had written, could undertake any "tactical withdrawal" without the express permission of the Fuehrer. So far as the records show this order was never rescinded. In 1944 the precipitate German surrender of Cherbourg added to Hitler's innate distrust of the loyalty and courage of his commanders and provoked more diatribes on the "last ditch" defense. The results of this monomania were to deprive the German ground commanders of their chief operational concept—maneuver—at a time when Allied materiel superiority was stripping the German forces of the means of mobility in maneuver. Hitler's insistence on defending each foot of ground cost the German armies in the West dearly in men and materiel, but did not retard the pace of the August retreat across France. The German field commanders sought to protect themselves by a convenient formula, apparently first advanced by General der Infanterie Guenther Blumentritt, the chief of staff at *OB WEST*, which appears over and over again in dispatches to OKW: "Thrown back. Countermeasures are being taken." With the whole front in collapse Hitler could hardly single out the officers who ordered retreat.

At the beginning of September OKW sent a new Hitler "intention" for the conduct of the war in the West to Field Marshal Model, C-in-C West.[37] In it Hitler ordered that the retreating German armies must stand and hold in front of the West Wall in a battle to gain the time needed for rearming the West Wall defenses, which in the years since the conquest of France had fallen into disrepair, but which he regarded as potentially impregnable. The holding line designated by Hitler ran from the Dutch coast, through northern Belgium, along the forward positions of the West Wall segment between Aachen and the Moselle River, and thence via the western borders of Lorraine and Alsace. A successful defensive battle along this general line, so Hitler reasoned, would have several important results:

[37] MS #B–308 (Zimmermann); *OKW/WFSt KTB, Ausarbeitung Der Westen.*

(1) The Netherlands would be retained as an important center of German air and naval activity, while its industrial and agricultural production would continue to flow to the Third Reich.

(2) No German soil would be lost.

(3) The Allies would be unable to use the port of Antwerp, so long as the Schelde mouths were denied them.

(4) Allied air bases would be kept as far as possible from central Germany.

(5) The great industrial production of the Ruhr and the Saar would be protected.

This "stand and hold" order, like those issued earlier through OKW, showed little appreciation of the difficulties facing the German troops and commanders in the West. Field Marshal Model, who was now acting both as the C-in-C West and as the commander of the group of armies in northern France, *Army Group B*, had done what he could to convey to Hitler some sense of the crisis in the West, sending report after report to Jodl with the urgent plea that they be brought to Hitler's attention. On 24 August Model reported that the Allies had sixty-one divisions on the Continent, "all thoroughly motorized and mechanized," and that these ground troops were supported by 16,400 planes, of which a minimum of one-third to one-half could be considered operative at any given time.[38] Five days later Model reviewed the rapidly worsening situation. The retreating troops, he warned OKW, had few heavy weapons and were mostly armed with carbines and rifles. Replacements and new weapons were lacking. The eleven German panzer divisions would have to be refitted before they could equal the strength of as many regiments; few had more than five to ten tanks in working order. The infantry divisions possessed only single pieces of artillery. The panzer divisions seldom had more than one battery. The horse-drawn transport of the German formations made for an unequal struggle with a fully motorized enemy. The troops were thoroughly depressed by the Allied superiority in planes and tanks. Finally, there now existed a wide gap between the two German groups of armies, *Army Group B* and *Army Group G*.[39]

On 1 September Model asked OKW for three fresh infantry divisions to cover this gap between the two army groups in the Lunéville–Belfort sector. OKW acceded to his modest demand, after some haggling, but on 2 Septem-

[38] *Heeresgruppe B* (hereafter cited as *Army Group B*), *Lagebeurteilungen, Ia*. Actually the Allied strength was some fifteen divisions short of Model's estimate.

[39] *Army Group B*, *Lagebeurteilungen, Ia*.

ber Model reported that the Lunéville–Belfort gap was no longer the chief danger point; the entire Western Front must be propped up lest it give way completely. On the same day Model made an urgent plea that some of the Flak artillery concentrated in Germany against the Allied air offensive should be sent to the West for use against the Allied tanks. This request was denied. Model's request on 3 September for three panzer divisions from the Eastern Front met the same fate.

Finally, on 4 September, Model sent his last request to Jodl, this time urging that it be placed before Hitler "in the original." In this message Model painted a gloomy picture that must have been most irksome to Hitler, who at this stage in the war was prone to charge his field commanders with defeatism. In a detailed appraisal of the front held by the three armies under *Army Group B*, against which the bulk of the Allied forces were concentrated, Model estimated his "actual combat strength" as the equivalent of 3¾ panzer and panzer grenadier divisions, and 10 infantry divisions. *Army Group B* would need, he said, a minimum of 25 fresh infantry divisions and 5 or 6 panzer divisions.[40] These estimates, it will be noted, took no account of the dire situation of the shattered divisions under *Army Group G*, now ending a long and costly withdrawal from the Bay of Biscay and the Mediterranean coast.

Model received no answer, for he was about to be relieved of his unenviable dual post as "Supreme Commander" in the West and commander of *Army Group B*. On 1 September Generalfeldmarschall Gerd von Rundstedt had been ordered to leave the rustic watering spot at Bad Toelz, where he had been taking the cure, and to proceed at once to Hitler's headquarters in East Prussia. This was not Rundstedt's first visit to the *Fuehrer Hauptquartier*. At the end of June 1944 Rundstedt, then in command of *OB WEST*, had journeyed to the Berghof at Berchtesgaden in company with Generalfeldmarschall Erwin Rommel, then commander of *Army Group B*. What the two famous officers told Hitler will probably never be known. Rundstedt and Rommel seem to have warned Field Marshal Keitel against continuing the war and may have said as much to Hitler. In any event Rundstedt was allowed to plead ill health and retire from his post; even Hitler dared not touch a man with Rundstedt's distinguished record of fifty-four years in the German Army. Rommel had returned to the front and there been injured. Lacking officers

[40] *Ibid.*

of the experience needed to fill these two posts, Hitler had given both to Generalfeldmarschall Guenther von Kluge. Model, who had succeeded Kluge after the latter's "sudden" death, continued the dual command.

Rundstedt's recall in September ostensibly stemmed from this untenable command situation. Other factors, however, were at work. Rundstedt had a reputation as a great strategist. He was well known to the troops, and his return to the front might be expected to give some much-needed encouragement. He had many friends in high places and although outspoken had rigidly adhered to the divorcement from politics which had characterized the old German Army. Rundstedt, therefore, would be returned to his old command as C-in-C West. Model, much to his own satisfaction, would be relieved and would retain only his position as the commander of *Army Group B*. Generalleutnant Siegfried Westphal, a young, energetic, and skilled staff officer, would be named Rundstedt's chief of staff. Westphal had fought the Allies in North Africa and Italy; during the latter campaign he had been chief of staff for Generalfeldmarschall Albert Kesselring. His selection for the new assignment seems to have resulted from Hitler's conviction that General Blumentritt, the incumbent chief of staff at *OB WEST*, lacked the practical experience and ruthless energy necessary at this stage of the war.

From 1 to 3 September Rundstedt and Westphal were briefed by the OKW staff and cursorily by Hitler. Hitler expressed himself as unworried about the situation on the Western Front. He believed that the Allies were outrunning their supplies and would soon be forced to a halt. In any case the Allied advance was being carried by "armored spearheads." These could be cut off by counterattacks and the front would then be stabilized. The best opportunity to truncate these armored spearheads would be found in the vicinity of Reims, on the south flank of the northern Allied forces. Finally, like the OKW staff, Hitler stressed the importance and impregnability of the West Wall. His verbal orders to Rundstedt were brief: stop the Allied advance as far to the west as possible; hold Belgium north of the Schelde and all of the Netherlands; take the offensive in the Nancy–Neufchâteau sector by a counterattack toward Reims. The task assigned Rundstedt was formidable, but would be made somewhat easier by the fact that Westphal had succeeded in bringing Jodl to modify the "hold at all costs" concept which had so stultified all maneuver in the West.[41]

[41] MSS #T–121, T–122 (Zimmermann *et al.*); see also MS #B–308 (Zimmermann).

On the afternoon of 5 September Rundstedt assumed command in the main *OB WEST* headquarters near Koblenz. *OB WEST* was far from being a "supreme headquarters" in the sense of SHAEF. Nominally it represented a unified command, but jealousies among the men close to Hitler and the conventional totalitarian philosophy of "divide and rule" would allow only limited exercise of over-all command by an Army general. The Luftwaffe, the Navy, the *Waffen-SS*, and the party appointees holding political posts in areas behind the Western Front all possessed and would exercise a very considerable independence despite Rundstedt's "supreme command."

One of Rundstedt's first and most urgent problems—a problem he never completely solved—was the restoration of a collective strategy for the whole of the Western Front. (*Map IV*) Model had concerned himself almost entirely with hard-pressed *Army Group B*, on the German right wing, and had paid only cursory attention to the plight of *Army Group G*, on the left, or to the threat of a rupture along the thin security line that formed the only link between them. The counterattack ordered by Hitler against the south flank of the American Third Army might be expected to check the Allied thrust into this gap, but Rundstedt was none too optimistic of success in such a venture and warned that the forces needed could not be gathered before 12 September at the earliest.

In Rundstedt's opinion the Allied advance posed two additional threats to a collective defense on the Western Front. First, the Allies were pressing in the direction of the Ruhr industrial areas. Aachen and the sector of the West Wall covering the approaches to the Ruhr appeared to be particularly endangered. Second, the Allies possessed airborne forces that were not committed; Rundstedt agreed with Model's earlier estimate of the "acute threat" of an Allied airborne attack in the rear of the West Wall or east of the Rhine.

On 7 September Rundstedt forwarded his first estimate of the situation in the West to OKW, confirming Model's pessimistic reports. The C-in-C West estimated that the Allied forces in northern France and Belgium now numbered fifty-four divisions, "thoroughly mechanized and motorized." He predicted that there were at least thirty additional divisions in England—of which six were airborne. The German formations were extremely hard pressed and in considerable measure "burned out." They lacked artillery and antitank weapons. The Allied superiority in armor was tremendous—*Army Group B* had only about a hundred tanks fit for combat. Reserves "worthy of the name" were nonexistent. The sole reserves available were the "weak" *9th Panzer Divi-*

sion, one "weak" *Sturm* panzer battalion, and two assault gun brigades. These reserves were already en route to the Aachen sector. Reinforcements were needed at once, said Rundstedt, at least five "and better" ten infantry divisions, properly armed with assault guns and heavy antitank weapons, plus "several" panzer divisions. Tanks and tank destroyers, Rundstedt repeated, were needed desperately to defend the Aachen front against the Allied armor concentrating there.[42]

The immediate effects of Rundstedt's report were negligible. Hitler reiterated that the Western Front must be spiked down and held as far to the west as possible, the shattered divisions in the line must be withdrawn and reconstituted, and the counterattack against the southern flank of the American Third Army must be made as scheduled.

Enemy Dispositions in the Moselle Sector

During the first few days of September the German front in the West had begun to stabilize itself somewhat, although a co-ordinated and homogeneous defense still was lacking along the four hundred miles between Switzerland and the North Sea. Logistical difficulties were harassing and impeding the advance of the Allied armies. A few fresh formations had arrived to reinforce the tired and disheartened German divisions. Furthermore, the German forces had now been driven back onto a system of rivers, canals, mountains, and fortifications which, although far from impregnable, favored the defender.

When Rundstedt assumed command on 5 September the paper strength of the combined German armies in the West showed a total of 48 infantry divisions, 14 panzer divisions, and 4 panzer brigades. Of this number, 13 infantry divisions, 3 panzer divisions, and 2 panzer brigades were close to full strength, although 4 of the infantry divisions in this category were encircled in fortress positions behind the Allied lines; 12 infantry divisions, 2 panzer divisions, and 2 panzer brigades were greatly understrength but still usable; 14 infantry divisions and 7 panzer divisions were "fought out" and of little or no combat value; 9 infantry divisions and 2 panzer divisions were out of the line and in process of rehabilitation and refitting.[43]

The bulk of these German divisions were grouped under Model's *Army Group B*, whose front extended from the North Sea to a point south of Nancy,

[42] *Army Group B, Lagebeurteilungen, Ia.*
[43] *OKW/WFSt KTB, Ausarbeitung Der Westen.*

GERMAN GENERALS OPPOSING THIRD ARMY

Upper left: *General der Panzertruppen Hasso von Manteuffel*

Upper right: *Generaloberst Johannes Blaskowitz*

Lower left: *General der Panzertruppen Otto von Knobelsdorff*

Lower right: *General der Panzertruppen Hermann Balck*

in Lorraine. *Army Group B* commanded four armies, the *Fifteenth Army* (General der Infanterie Gustav von Zangen), the *First Parachute Army* (Generaloberst Kurt Student), the *Seventh Army* (General der Panzertruppen Erich Brandenberger), and the *First Army* (General der Infanterie Kurt von der Chevallerie), aligned from north to south. *Army Group G*, commanded by Generaloberst Johannes Blaskowitz, formed the exceedingly amorphic German left wing. It lacked a recognizable forward line in the first days of September, but was charged with the establishment of a front west of the Vosges mountains in the area between the Nancy sector and the Swiss border. Blaskowitz' command comprised only the independent *LXVI Corps* (General der Artillerie Walther Lucht), operating on the north flank of the army group in the Neufchâteau–Langres sector, and the *Nineteenth Army* (General der Infanterie Friedrich Wiese), a total of seven divisions.[44] The advance of General Patton's Third Army toward the Moselle would strike directly into the German *First Army* front, brush against the northern flank of the *Nineteenth Army*, and threaten to sever the extremely tenuous connection between the two. The *First* and *Nineteenth Armies*, therefore, would be the initial opponents of the Third Army in the battle for Lorraine.

Hitler had intervened directly to nominate a new commander for the *First Army*, writing a personal letter to General Chevallerie, who had led the *First Army* during the withdrawal across France, relieving him on the grounds of "ill health." Chevallerie had been an infantry officer, a veteran of the Eastern Front.[45] The new appointee, General der Panzertruppen Otto von Knobelsdorff, also was a veteran of the Russian campaigns but had an armored background. He had first commanded a panzer division on the Eastern Front and then had led three successive panzer corps. During the attempt to relieve the German *Sixth Army* at Stalingrad, Knobelsdorff's corps had won considerable distinction—which may explain his subsequent appointment in the West. He was reputed to be a brave officer, had received several wounds, and as a corps commander had been much in the front lines. Hard, forceful, "steady in times of crisis," and an "unflinching optimist," Knobelsdorff possessed the characteristics that Hitler valued most. But his military superiors had agreed that he was "no towering tactician" and that he lacked somewhat

[44] The German situation in the West at the beginning of September is taken from situation maps maintained by the *OKH, Gen. St. d. H./Operations Abteilung* and *OKW/WFSt.*

[45] This and subsequent biographical notes are taken from the *Personalakten* of the officers named. The German *Personalakten* correspond to the 201 files kept by the U.S. Army. They are now in the GMDS collection.

"in the realm of ideas." It should be noted in passing that when Knobelsdorff took command of the *First Army* on 6 September he was already physically weakened by the rigors of long months on the Eastern Front.

Friedrich Wiese, the *Nineteenth Army* commander, was an infantry officer. After fighting through the four years of World War I, he had become a police official and then, like many of the German police, had transferred to the Wehrmacht in 1935. Wiese made the Polish campaign in command of an infantry battalion and did not rise to division commander until the fall of 1942. A year later he was given command of an army corps on the Eastern Front, where he won a good reputation. In June 1944 Wiese was brought directly from the Eastern Front to assume command of the *Nineteenth Army*, then employed in watching the Mediterranean coast. During the retreat from southern France he had shown considerable talent as a tactician and was commended by his superiors for the dispatch with which he had oriented himself in the battle practices of the West.

Far superior in reputation to either Knobelsdorff or Wiese was Blaskowitz, the *Army Group G* commander. Since the *First* and *Nineteenth Armies* would be grouped under his command on 8 September, General Blaskowitz was to be the chief ground commander opposed to the Third Army in the first weeks of the Lorraine Campaign. An East Prussian, a stanch religionist, and avowedly nonpolitical in his affiliations, Blaskowitz, like his friend Rundstedt, represented the traditions of the old German Officer Corps. In October 1939 he had been promoted to command the *Eighth Army*. Subsequently he had spent the four years of occupation in France as commanding general of the *First Army*. On 10 May 1944 Blaskowitz had been raised, at Rundstedt's insistence, to command *Army Group G*. Actually Blaskowitz was already *persona non grata* at OKW, which attempted in various ways to limit his authority. This tacit antagonism seems to have stemmed from the fact that Blaskowitz was lukewarm toward the Nazi regime and had run afoul of Himmler in Czechoslovakia and Poland, provoking an enmity from the latter which would continually plague Blaskowitz in his conduct of combat operations. This old feud came to the fore again on 3 September 1944, when Blaskowitz protested a Himmler order, issued in the latter's capacity as chief of the Replacement Army, for the construction of a defense line that would be under Himmler's command immediately behind the battle front in the Nancy–Belfort sector. OKW in this case supported Blaskowitz' authority, possibly because of the imminent return of Rundstedt to the West. The latter regarded Blaskowitz as a top-flight organizer and an able commander, a judgment that Blaskowitz' successful withdrawal from southern France appeared to sustain.

In the last days of August the *First Army* had retreated across the Meuse with a force numbering only nine battalions of infantry, two batteries of field guns, ten tanks, three Flak batteries, and ten 75-mm. antitank guns. Advance detachments of two veteran formations from Italy, the *3d* and *15th Panzer Grenadier Divisions*, had arrived in time to see some action during the withdrawal from the Verdun–Commercy line. The main bodies of these two divisions finally came up on 1–2 September and took positions along the east bank of the Moselle. During the retreat from Châlons-sur-Marne the exhausted *17th SS Panzer Grenadier Division* ("Goetz von Berlichingen") had been withdrawn to the *First Army* rear for rest and refitting in the Metz area. On 31 August, however, the situation had deteriorated so markedly that two battalions of the *17th SS* hastily were gathered to form an outpost line west of Metz.

By 1 September the *First Army* had a battle strength in the Thionville–Nancy sector which *OB WEST* reckoned as the combat equivalent of three and a half divisions. Reinforcements, however, were close behind the *First Army* lines, with advance sections from two of the new volksgrenadier divisions and a panzer brigade in process of arrival on 1 September. East of Metz one regiment of the *559th VG (Volksgrenadier) Division* had unloaded. The *553d VG Division* was detraining at Saarbruecken, en route to Nancy. And the *106th Panzer Brigade* was moving its new Panther tanks off flat cars in the Trier rail yards.

The ensuing lull, as American pressure eased in the first days of September, permitted the *3d, 15th, 553d,* and *559th* to complete their assembly and assume positions along the *First Army* front. The lone armored brigade gathered its tanks and armored infantry west of Trier. The *17th SS* proceeded with the work of refitting and absorbing large numbers of replacements from the *49th* and *51st SS Panzer Grenadier Brigades.*

On 5 September the German *First Army* held a loosely formed front reaching from Sedan, in the northwest, to an ill-defined boundary south of Nancy. (*Map V*) Here the immediate problem was that of establishing a co-ordinated security line to meet the American attack. More specifically the *First Army* was charged with defending the mining and industrial area around Longwy and Briey, as well as that of the Saar, establishing secure bridgeheads west of the Moselle River at Metz and Nancy, and re-establishing firm contact with the *Nineteenth Army*.[46]

Although only a collection of weak "splinter detachments," individual regiments, and staffs without troops at the end of August, the *First Army* now was the strongest of all the German armies in the West, with a combat strength which *OB WEST* estimated as equal to 3 panzer grenadier divisions, 4½ infantry divisions, and 1 panzer brigade. On the extreme north wing the *LXXX Corps* (General der Infanterie Dr. Franz Beyer) was deployed between Sedan and Montmédy along a line echeloned somewhat forward of the main *First Army* front and facing the American V Corps. On 31 August a regiment of the newly arrived *15th Panzer Grenadier Division* had been put into line to reinforce the five weak battalions of police and security personnel with which the *LXXX Corps* was conducting a northeasterly retreat from the Reims area. No further attempt was made to reinforce Beyer's corps, which, at less than the strength of a division, could do no more than establish a chain of outpost positions.[47]

The *LXXXII Corps* (General der Artillerie Johann Sinnhuber) formed the *First Army* center, with the mission of defending the Moselle River position from north of Thionville to south of Metz and maintaining the bridgehead west of the latter city.[48] This corps faced the American XX Corps. Since there were several *Waffen-SS* units in this sector, control would pass on 7 September from the *LXXXII Corps* to the *XIII SS Corps*, the former staff moving north to assume command on the right wing. Generalleutenant der Waffen-SS Herman Priess, commander of the newly formed *XIII SS Corps*, had gained distinction on the Eastern Front while commanding the crack "*Death's Head*" *Panzer Division* (*3d SS Panzer Division*). The defense of Metz would be his first experience as a corps commander, but he was known to be a determined and resourceful leader. The *First Army* center had been considerably reinforced since the end of August and now existed as an organized front. The *17th SS Panzer Grenadier Division* and the *48th Division* were in the line, after having fought in late August as a covering force to permit the organization and deployment of fresh formations. The new *559th VG Division* and *Division Number 462*, which had just been reorganized at Metz, completed the *LXXXII Corps* order of battle.

[46] MS #B-222 (Knobelsdorff).

[47] MS #B-006 (Beyer).

[48] MS #B-002 (Sinnhuber), Hist Div files.

The left wing of the *First Army* was held by the *XLVII Panzer Corps*, whose sector extended along the Moselle from Arnaville to Bayon, roughly opposite the American XII Corps. North of Nancy the line was manned by the *3d Panzer Grenadier Division* and one regiment of the *15th Panzer Grenadier Division*. The new *553d VG Division* was deployed in and around Nancy. In addition a large number of replacement and school troops belonging to the *First Parachute Army* had been placed under the command of the *553d*. Some attempts had been made to extend the *XLVII Panzer Corps* front far enough south of Nancy to make a hard and fast connection with the *Nineteenth Army*, but on 5 September the German forces on the extreme left wing of the *First Army* consisted only of outposts and security patrols.

Although the staff of the *XLVII Panzer Corps* at the moment had no armored divisions under its control, word had already been given that it would take charge of the armor released by Hitler for use in the prospective counterattack against the right flank of the Third Army. The corps commander, General der Panzertruppen Heinrich Freiherr von Luettwitz, was a onetime cavalry officer and one of the expert horsemen of the German Army. With the introduction of mechanization he had turned to armor, had fought in Poland and in Russia, and then had returned to the West in command of the *2d Panzer Division*. Although his division had been almost completely destroyed in the Falaise pocket, Luettwitz' prestige had grown apace—even General Patton had referred to the *2d Panzer Division* as the best German armored division in the West—and on 5 September Luettwitz was promoted to command the *XLVII Panzer Corps*. Several times wounded in action, he had won a reputation for personal bravery. Although domineering in manner and harsh, he was considered one of the ablest of German field commanders and armored tacticians.

While the *First Army* was numerically stronger than its neighbors on the right and left, it possessed very limited means of antitank defense. There were only single antitank weapons for the army to give the corps. The volksgrenadier divisions had not yet received their allotment of assault guns. Not one of the panzer grenadier divisions had the tank battalion normally organic to this type of formation, and at best they retained only a few self-propelled guns. The chief defense against mechanized attack in the *First Army* area, therefore, would have to be the natural antitank barrier formed by the Moselle River. Artillery support also was limited, and for this reason the German guns were spread along the front in two- and three-gun sections, isolated batteries, and occasional battalions. The system of communications was extremely poor. The *XLVII Panzer Corps* had virtually no signal equipment and the *First Army* had only one signal battalion, which was run ragged repairing the wire breaks caused by Allied air attacks.[49]

The *106th Panzer Brigade* in Luxembourg constituted the sole *First Army* reserve. It was also the only armor at Knobelsdorff's disposal. Two divisions, the *19th VG* and *36th VG*, were en route to the *First Army* front by rail. Hitler had personally selected the *19th VG Division* as a replacement for the troops that were to be taken from the *First Army* for the projected counterattack against the American Third Army. The *36th VG Division* was slated to reinforce the inexperienced *553d VG* and *559th VG* on the Moselle line. However, forthcoming American attacks would divert the *19th* and *36th* to other uses.

The dispositions of the *Nineteenth Army* on 5 September are more difficult to trace than those of the *First Army*. Some parts of the long *Nineteenth Army* front had solidified and now presented an organized defense, but other sectors were completely bereft of troops or were held lightly by outpost detachments and roving patrols. In general the *Nineteenth Army* was extended along a wide, west-reaching salient. The southern shoulder of this salient—or bulge—rested on the Swiss frontier near Pontarlier, with a hastily organized line at the Doubs River facing the Allied advance from the south. Two weak corps, the *LXXXV* and *IV Luftwaffe Field*, held this sector, reinforced by the famous *11th Panzer Division* which had covered the *Nineteenth Army* retreat up the Rhone Valley.

The western sector, which extended from Autun to Chaumont, was not an organized line but rather a gap or "bridgehead" west of Dijon held open by the German forces on the north and south, through which moved the long march columns retreating from the Bay of Biscay and the Atlantic coast under the command of the *LXIV Corps* (General der Pioniere Karl Sachs). This hegira comprised about 80,000 men and some 2,000 women, mostly toiling slowly on foot toward the German lines. The retreat, which had begun in organized fashion on 20 August, could not be made in a straight line to the northeast because the Maquis held the Massif Centrale; therefore the German march columns were forced to move circuitously by way of Poitiers, Bourges,

[49] MS #B-363 (Emmerich); MS #B-214 (Mantey). The general condition of the *First Army* is outlined daily in *OB WEST KTB (Text)* (hereafter cited as *OB WEST KTB*) for the period. The *KTB* for the *First Army* during this period has been lost or destroyed, probably the latter.

and Nevers. On 1 September a liaison officer from *Army Group G* reached the *LXIV Corps* with a reprimand from Blaskowitz for the slow progress of the retreat and orders to send the combat elements of the *16th Division* and *159th Reserve Division* on ahead. By 5 September the main elements of these divisions had arrived in the "Dijon bridgehead," the *159th* moving south to support the *11th Panzer Division* and the *16th* going to the *LXVI Corps.*

The north shoulder of the German salient was held by General Lucht's *LXVI Corps*, which operated directly under General Blaskowitz and the headquarters of *Army Group G.* As early as 1 September Blaskowitz had reported to OKW that he was no longer worried about maintaining his left-wing anchor position on the Swiss frontier and that the *Nineteenth Army* possessed a cohesive front facing the Allied attack from the south. His chief concern was with the north flank of the *Army Group G* salient where there were very few troops and where a fast link with the *First Army* was lacking. Blaskowitz' immediate problem was to hold this north flank long enough to permit the escape of the *LXIV Corps*, but he also took occasion to warn OKW of a possible irreparable breach between *Army Group G* and the *First Army.*[50]

The men around Hitler were not unaware of this latter danger. Indeed, reports from secret agents working behind the Allied lines in France had led OKW to warn Blaskowitz that the American Third Army might turn southeast in the direction of Epinal instead of launching an attack on the Metz–Sarreguemines axis as had originally been anticipated. In addition Hitler was insistent that the prospective counterattack against the Third Army flank should jump off from the forward areas covered by the *Army Group G* north flank. However, Blaskowitz' request for a mobile, armored force to hold this blocking position went unheeded. Instead, Hitler sent a personal order that the *16th Division* would be thrown in on Blaskowitz' endangered north flank and there would "hold at all costs."

On 5 September the advance echelons of the *16th Division* had reached the important communications center at Langres and were preparing to deploy in the north and northwest. The *16th* constituted the only division under the *LXVI Corps* command. The German line along the north shoulder, Chaumont–Neufchâteau–Charmes, was manned in sketchy fashion by over-age

[50] *Armeegruppe G (Fuehrungsabteilung) KTB Nr. 2* (hereafter cited as *Army Group G KTB Nr. 2*) and *Anlagen,* 1. VII.–30. IX. 44; see also *Obkdo. Heeresgruppe G, KTB der Fuehrungsabteilung Nr. 3a* and *Nr. 3b* (hereafter cited as *Army Group G KTB Nr. 3a* and *3b*) and *Anlagen,* 1. X.–31. XII. 44. The retreat from the south and southwest has been recounted by several of the high-ranking German officers who took part. See *Army Group G*: Report of the Chief of Staff, MS #A–999 (Mellenthin).

police and security battalions, backed up by a mobile reconnaissance battalion and a small Kampfgruppe from the *21st Panzer Division.* Troops from the *21st* had joined with security patrols from the *553d VG Division* south of Nancy on 4 September, making the first tactical link between the *First Army* and *Army Group G* since 26 August; but this connection was most insecure and there were no reserves west of the Rhine River in position to do a quick soldering job if the need should arise. All of the German commanders on this part of the Western Front, therefore, looked with apprehension at the Nancy–Neufchâteau sector when, on 5 September, the Third Army finally resumed its attack toward the Moselle.

The Lull in Operations Comes to an End

The priority on gasoline which had been assigned the First Army, in consequence of General Eisenhower's decision to make the main Allied effort in the north, left the Third Army virtually immobilized from 1 to 5 September. During the period 26 August–2 September the gasoline received by the Third Army averaged 202,382 gallons per day.[51] Since Patton's tanks and trucks had habitually consumed between 350,000 and 400,000 gallons a day during the last phases of the pursuit, and since some 450,000 gallons per day would be needed east of the Moselle, there could be no real question of mounting a full-scale attack against the Moselle line until the supply situation improved. On 2 September the gasoline receipts at Third Army dumps reached the lowest figure of the entire arid period—25,390 gallons. But finally on 4 September the gasoline drought started to break, only a day later than General Bradley had predicted to General Patton. On this date the Third Army was issued 240,265 gallons; during the next three days 1,396,710 gallons arrived, and by 10 September the period of critical shortage was ended.[52] In the meantime, however, General Patton had been given permission to resume the Third Army advance.

The knowledge that the logistical situation was improving had an impact on each level of the Allied command. On 4 September General Eisenhower directed a letter to the Allied commanders which contained a confident ap-

[51] During this same period the First Army receipts had averaged 435,851 gallons per day.

[52] These figures have been compiled by R. L. Thompson of the Historical Division staff from daily reports prepared in the headquarters of the 12th Army Group, First Army and Third Army. See Thompson manuscript in Historical Division files.

praisal of the situation and a concise statement of his plans for the conduct of forthcoming operations. "Our best opportunity of defeating the enemy in the West," he wrote, "lies in striking at the Ruhr and the Saar, confident that he will concentrate the remainder of his available forces in the defense of these essential areas." Such a strategic concept would require a simultaneous attack both by the forces north of the Ardennes—the 21st Army Group and the First Army—and by Patton's Third Army. The directive of 4 September reiterated the original strategic assumption that the enemy would regard the Ruhr, with its greater resources, as more important than the Saar area and would concentrate more heavily in defense of the former. The Allied forces moving on the Ruhr (the 21st Army Group and First Army) would have as their mission securing Antwerp, breaching the sector of the West Wall (Siegfried Line) covering the Ruhr, and then seizing the Ruhr. The offensive mission assigned the Third Army by the letter of 4 September would serve in effect as the green light for General Patton's forces: "[The Third Army is] to occupy the sector of the Siegfried Line covering the Saar and then to seize Frankfurt. It is important that this operation should start as soon as possible, in order to forestall the enemy in this sector, but [the] troops . . . operating against the Ruhr northwest of the Ardennes must first be adequately supported." In addition the Supreme Commander ordered that the Third Army "take any opportunity of destroying enemy forces withdrawing from southwest and southern France."[53]

On the day following the issuance of this letter of instruction the Supreme Commander dictated an office memorandum explaining his employment of the Third Army:

> For some days it has been obvious that our military forces can advance almost at will, subject only to the requirement for maintenance. Resistance has largely melted all along the front. From the beginning of this campaign I have always envisaged that as soon as substantial destruction of the enemy forces in France could be accomplished, we should advance rapidly on the Rhine by pushing through the Aachen Gap in the north and through the Metz Gap in the south. The virtue of this movement is that it takes advantage of all existing lines of communication in the advance towards Germany and brings the southern force on the Rhine at Coblentz, practically on the flank of the forces that would advance straight eastward through Aachen. . . . I see no reason to change this

[53] Msg, Eisenhower to commanders, FWD–13765, 4 Sep 44, SHAEF file, Post OVERLORD Planning 381, I. The capture of Brest, earlier assigned as a Third Army mission, now was given to the new Ninth Army. The VIII Corps passed to General Simpson's Ninth Army at noon on 5 September. The Third Army retained the mission of protecting the Allied right flank.

conception. The defeat of the German armies is complete, and the only thing now needed to realize the whole conception is speed. . . . I now deem it important, while supporting the advance on eastward through Belgium, to get Patton moving once again so that we may be fully prepared to carry out the original conception for the final stages of this campaign.[54]

General Bradley and General Patton were ready and waiting for the order that would start the Third Army "moving once again." Indeed, on the afternoon of 4 September the Third Army commander had given General Eddy permission to start the 317th Infantry marching toward the Moselle north of Nancy. The following day, while the 317th was actually engaged in the fight for a crossing, the 12th Army Group commander met with General Patton and his corps commanders at the Third Army headquarters east of Châlons-sur-Marne and there outlined the plans for the Third Army attack. Gen. Wade H. Haislip's XV Corps had already been assigned to flesh out the Third Army but as yet had nothing but corps troops, since it had left its divisions with the First Army. General Bradley promised Patton that the 79th Infantry Division and 2d French Armored Division would be returned to the XV Corps. The 6th Armored Division and 83d Infantry Division—both still in Brittany—would be available as soon as the incoming 94th Infantry Division and 95th Infantry Division could relieve them. The addition of these divisions would give General Patton the three corps which the SHAEF operations staff had set as the necessary strength when, on 1 September, it had suggested to the Supreme Commander that "there may be an opportunity to breach the Siegfried Line by rapid, aggressive movement by the Third Army on the Saar and thence on Frankfurt."

General Bradley's verbal orders assigned the Rhine River as the Third Army objective—this barrier to be crossed as soon as the Third Army could breach the West Wall.[55] *(Map VI)* In point of fact nothing had happened during the period of gasoline shortage to alter radically the Third Army mission. A 12th Army Group order on 29 August already had directed General Patton to drive toward Frankfurt and cross the Rhine between Koblenz and Mannheim; now, with the addition of one corps, the Third Army front was broadened to take in the entire sector of the Rhine that lay between Koblenz and Karlsruhe.

[54] Diary, Office of the Commander in Chief, under date of 5 Sep 44. This diary was kept on instructions of General Eisenhower by Capt. Harry C. Butcher, naval aide (deposited in Adjutant General's Office, Department of the Army).

[55] TUSA Diary, 5 Sep 44.

At the conclusion of the meeting with General Bradley, late on 5 September, the Third Army commander ordered General Walker to begin an attack at once on the Third Army left with the XX Corps. Part of General Eddy's XII Corps was already in action on the right, but since this corps was charged with the protection of the south flank of the army General Eddy could not commit the entire strength represented in his three divisions until Haislip's XV Corps was in position to relieve the XII Corps of this responsibility. Therefore, Patton was forced to limit the XII Corps attack to the 80th Infantry Division and 4th Armored Division until such time as the 35th Infantry Division could be freed to join in the advance.

General Patton's written operational directive to his corps commanders foresaw two phases in the forthcoming advance.[56] In the first the Third Army would attack to seize a bridgehead east of the Moselle River. In the second the advance would be continued to seize a bridgehead east of the Rhine. Initially the XII and XX Corps would make an advance abreast, while the XV Corps covered the right flank of the army. Once the 79th Infantry Division and 2d French Armored Division had arrived, the XV Corps would join the Third Army attack. Patton planned to use the 6th Armored Division as his reserve, committing it with the corps which would have the greatest success or sending it, with the 83d Infantry Division, in a dash to capture Karlsruhe.

On the eve of this resumption of active operations General Patton, his staff, and his commanders showed no anticipation of any stubborn enemy resistance at the Moselle; nor is there evidence of unusual concern over the possible results of the enforced lull during late August and the first days of September. General Patton himself had expressed the opinion that the German forces in front of the Third Army might make a stand at or in front of the West Wall, but he was confident that this line could be breached by armored action. The Rhine seemed not too distant, at this period, and Patton's orders to the Third Army cavalry optimistically called for the squadrons to cross the Moselle "and reconnoiter to the Rhine River." [57] At the close of hostilities in Europe, however, General Patton was to express the opinion that the decision to give logistical support to the 21st Army Group and First Army instead of the Third Army "was the momentous error of the war." His memoirs add: "At first I thought it was a backhanded way of slowing up the Third Army. I later found that this was not the case, but that the delay was due to a change

[56] TUSA AAR II, 5 Sep 44.

[57] TUSA Diary, 7 Sep 44.

of plan by the High Command, implemented, in my opinion by General Montgomery."[58]

Actually General Eisenhower had not deviated from his original plan to make the primary effort in the northeast with the object of destroying the bulk of the remaining enemy forces, which he expected to be drawn into that area to defend the Ruhr. Nor had he surrendered to Montgomery any part of the responsibility for decision which was inescapably his own. And it is symptomatic of the problems and rivalries inherent in a great Allied command that Montgomery in his turn would question the wisdom of diverting supplies to support Patton's drive to the east.[59] The Supreme Commander's attitude, however, did not change: ". . . we must push up as soon as possible *all along the front* [italics by the author] to cut off the retreating enemy and concentrate in preparation for the big final thrust."[60]

[58] Gen George S. Patton, Jr., *War as I Knew It* (Boston, 1947), p. 119f. After the war and before his execution, General Jodl, Chief of the *WFSt*, told interrogators that he had feared a co-ordinated drive, supported by all of the Allied resources, straight toward Frankfurt. See interrogation by Maj. Kenneth Hechler in Historical Division files.

[59] Montgomery to Eisenhower, 7 Sep 44, SHAEF SGS File, Supply Problems of Allied Advance, 400.3/1.

[60] Eisenhower to Montgomery, 8 Sep 44, SHAEF SGS File, Supply Problems of Allied Advance, 400.3/1.

CHAPTER II

The XII Corps Crossing of the Moselle (5-30 September)

The XII Corps Plan[1]

The successful *coup de main* by Combat Command A, 4th Armored Division, at Commercy on 31 August and the establishment of a bridgehead east of the Meuse placed the XII Corps in position to continue the advance toward the Moselle River and Nancy. (*Map VII*) Thus far the retreating Germans had offered no real opposition, nor were there any signs that the Wehrmacht shortly would stand and fight. During the past sixteen days the XII Corps had made an eastward advance of 250 miles. The 80th Infantry Division was coming up fast on the left of CCA and on 1 September crossed into the bridgehead. On the same day CCB, earlier slowed down by the necessity of repairing bridges over the Marne, crossed the Meuse River and took position south of the 80th Division and CCA. On 2 September the bulk of McBride's 80th Division relieved CCA in the Commercy bridgehead, while the left-wing regiment, the 319th, crossed the river at St. Mihiel farther to the north. The 35th Infantry Division remained behind the rest of the XII Corps, guarding the right flank of the Third Army, and so far as General Eddy knew he had to make his future plans on the basis of one infantry and one armored division.

The quick successes won by speed and surprise in earlier river crossing operations prompted General Eddy to consider using the 4th Armored Division in a surprise attack at the Moselle, with the infantry following. Neither

[1] This chapter is based on the records and journals (including those at battalion level) of the American units concerned. Thus far only the 6th Armored Division and the XII Corps have published unit histories covering this period—see *Combat Record of the Sixth Armored Division* (Aschaffenburg, 1945) and XII Corps: *Spearhead of Patton's Third Army* (Baton Rouge, 1947). Diaries kept by Maj. Gen. Manton Eddy, commanding general of the XII Corps, and by Capt. Stedman Seay, Assistant G–3 of CCA, 4th Armored Division, have been used. The Historical Division Combat Interviews survey much of this operation; those covering the 80th Infantry Division (collected by 1st Lt. Theron Burts and Sgt. Carlos Angulo) are particularly detailed and valuable. The enemy materials for this sector and period are very sketchy. German records at the level of the division and corps are not available. However, MS #B–412 (Einem) gives the German story from the viewpoint of the Chief of Staff, *XIII SS Corps*.

General Wood, the armored commander, nor General McBride, the infantry commander, looked with favor on such a plan.[2] They reasoned that the Moselle presented a more difficult military problem than any river yet encountered, that the enemy strength and dispositions were unknown, and that the armor should not be risked in such a venture but rather conserved to exploit a bridgehead won by the infantry.

Actually, any planning for a surprise crossing by the armor was somewhat academic in view of the gasoline shortage which paralyzed the XII Corps, just as it did the XX Corps, waiting to cross the Moselle in the north. Fortunately the XII Corps had overrun a number of enemy rail yards. After scouring the area the corps G–4 found enough loaded tank cars to augment the limited gasoline issue and so allow the corps to concentrate east of the Meuse River. First call on the gasoline available was given to the armored patrols and the corps cavalry. But on the afternoon of 2 September even the armored reconnaissance elements were forced to halt, with fuel for only twenty miles left in their gas tanks. The XII Corps was immobilized.

General Patton visited the XII Corps commander on 3 September and with his customary optimism launched into a discussion of methods for attacking the West Wall, many miles beyond the Moselle. There was reason for optimism. Gasoline was already on its way to the Third Army front and the XII Corps could prepare to continue the advance east. That night the 4th Armored Division received 8,000 gallons as a token installment, and on the following day enough gasoline arrived in the Commercy area to permit resumption of the forward movement.

In midafternoon on 4 September, General Eddy outlined his general scheme of maneuver.[3] He had decided to commit one regimental combat team of his only available infantry division in a reconnaissance in force, such as had been so successful at the Marne and the Meuse. This first plan for negotiating the Moselle barrier and capturing Nancy turned on a quick thrust across the river north of Nancy. One regimental combat team of the 80th Division (the 317th Infantry and its attachments) was ordered to establish a bridgehead in the vicinity of Pont-à-Mousson, a crossing site since the days of the Romans. Through this bridgehead CCA, reinforced by a battalion of the 318th Infantry, was to make a wide sweep, circling to the south and attacking Nancy from

[2] Interv with Gen Eddy, Washington, D.C., Aug 47; Hist Div Combat Interviews (Col W. A. Bigby, CofS, 4th Armd Div); Ltr, Maj Gen Horace McBride to Hist Div, 25 Nov 46.

[3] XII Corps Rpt of Opns, 4 Sep 44.

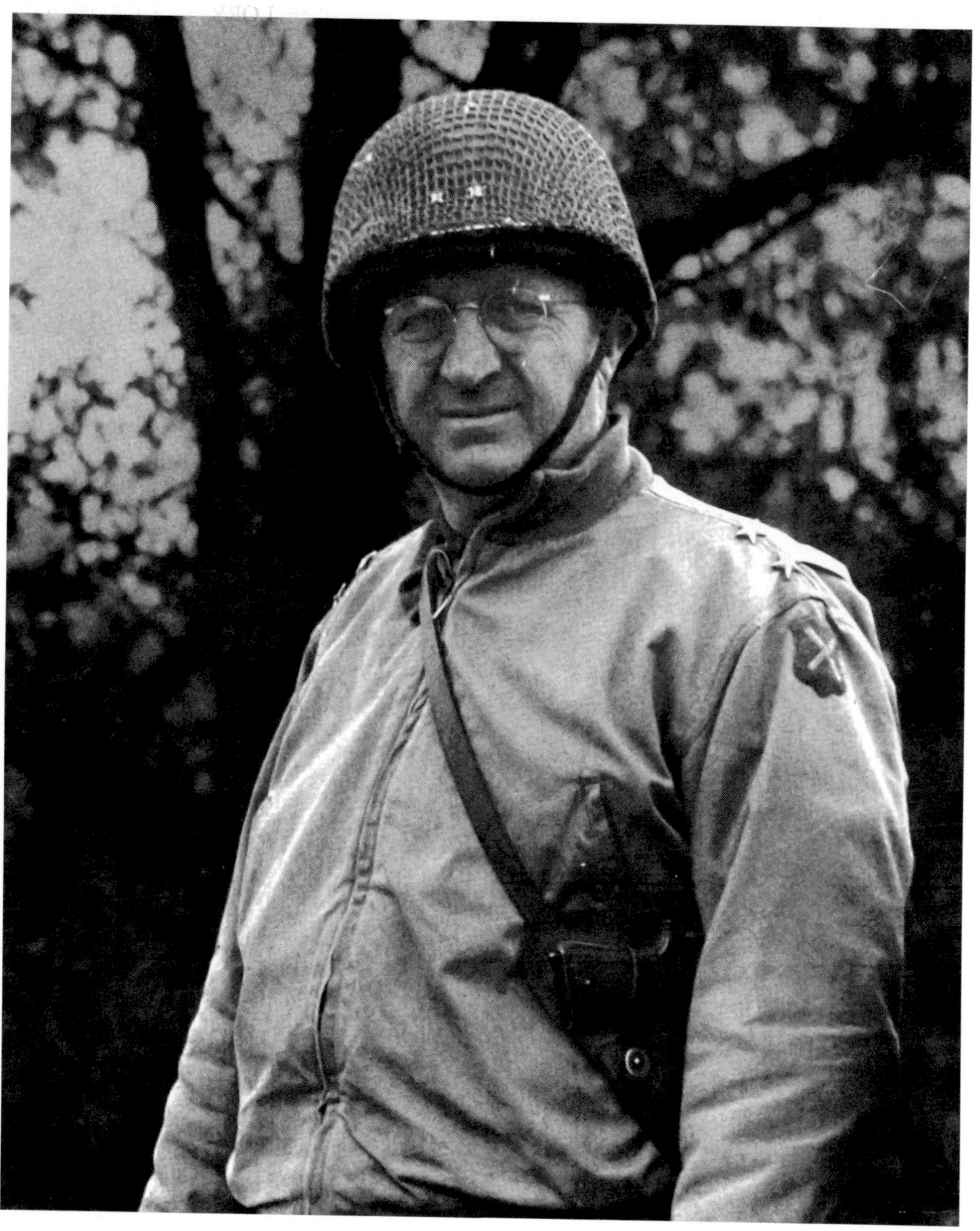

MAJ. GEN. MANTON S. EDDY, *XII Corps Commander.*

the east. The 319th Infantry had the mission of securing a bridgehead at Toul, where the Moselle River made its wide loop to the west, and attacking east toward Nancy in conjunction with the envelopment by the armor. The 80th Division reserve, the 318th Infantry (—), was designated by General McBride to force a "limited bridgehead" in the center of the division zone, by crossing east of the Belleville–Marbache sector. No specific time schedule was set for the execution of this corps maneuver, but even as orders were being drafted at the XII Corps headquarters the 317th was on the march to test the enemy strength at the Moselle line.

The Assault at Pont-à-Mousson

During the late afternoon of 4 September the 317th Infantry (Col. A. D. Cameron) moved along the Flirey–Pont-à-Mousson road toward the Moselle. (*Map 2*) There was no time for daylight reconnaissance across the river, and indeed very little was known of the terrain on the west bank from which the crossing attempt was slated to be made that same night. Emphasis now was on speed—hurry to the river and hurry across—the tactic which had kept the retreating Germans punch drunk for days past. The enemy, however, had used his respite to dig in on the east bank of the river and there establish a consolidated position which by this time extended from a point opposite Pagny-sur-Moselle south to Millery. The *3d Panzer Grenadier Division*, recently hurried to France from the Italian front and still clad in tropical uniforms, held the greater part of this sector. It could be given some help by elements of the *92d Luftwaffe Field Regiment* which were deployed on the left of the *3d Panzer Grenadier Division* opposite Dieulouard. The *3d Panzer Grenadier Division* (Generalmajor Hans Hecker) was an old and battle-tested Wehrmacht unit. Its morale was high and its ranks nearly full. The artillery regiment was intact, but much of the motorized equipment being of Italian make was only passable. The division engineers and the organic tank battalion, which normally characterized this type of division, had not yet arrived from Italy. The *92d Luftwaffe Field Regiment* was a temporary training regiment that had been hastily collected from antiaircraft gunners and Luftwaffe replacements stationed in and around Nancy.

Two days before, the Germans in this sector had been alerted to the threat of a crossing attempt by the activity of American cavalry in the vicinity of Pont-à-Mousson. In addition, enemy observers on Mousson Hill (382),

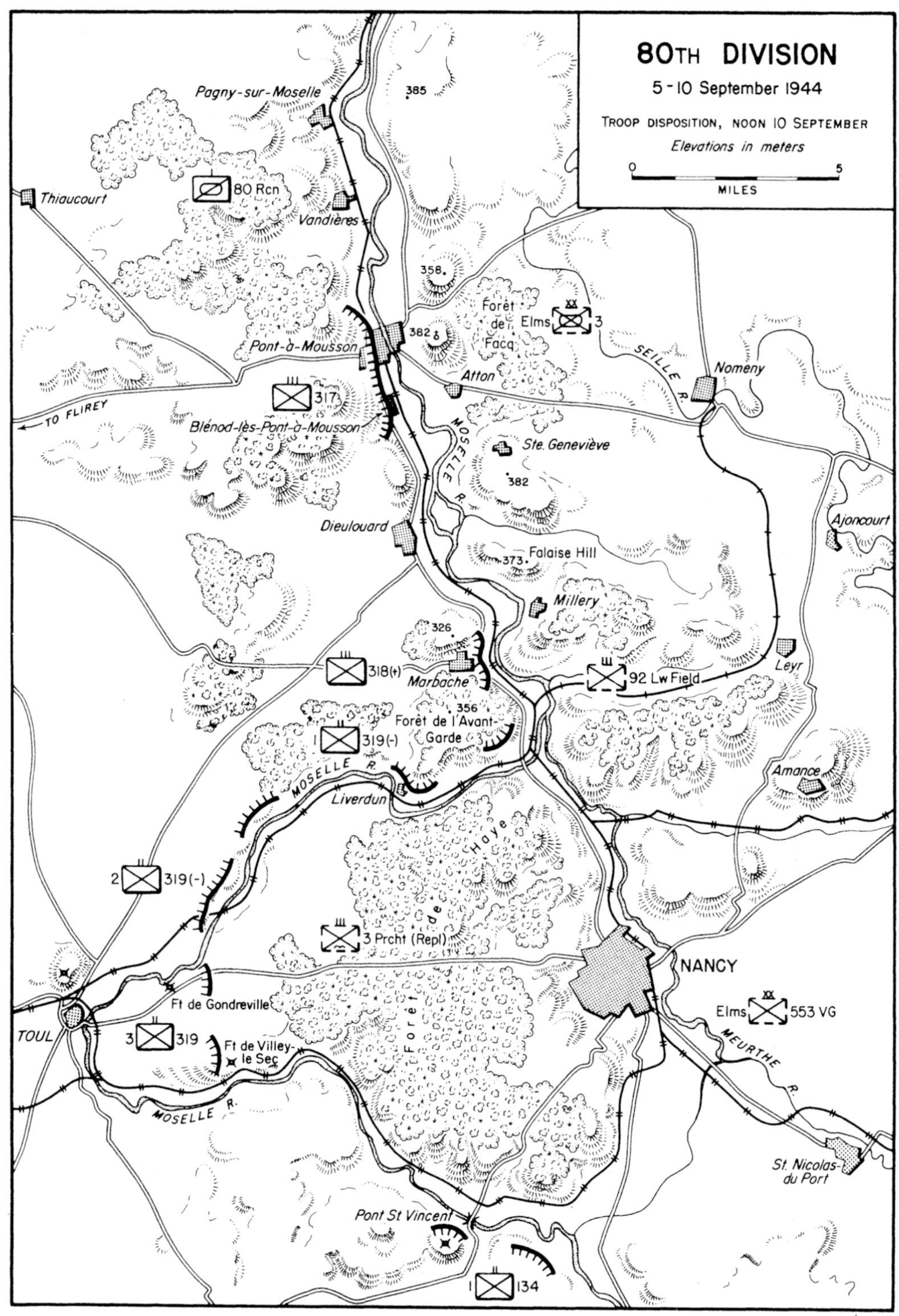
80TH DIVISION
5-10 September 1944
TROOP DISPOSITION, NOON 10 SEPTEMBER
Elevations in meters
0
5
MILES
Pagny-sur-Moselle
385
80 Rcn
Thiaucourt
Vandières
358
Forêt de Facq
Elms
3
382
Pont-à-Mousson
SEILLE R.
Nomeny
Atton
317
TO FLIREY
Blénod-lès-Pont-à-Mousson
MOSELLE R.
Ste. Geneviève
382
Dieulouard
Ajoncourt
373
Falaise Hill
Millery
326
318(+)
Marbache
Leyr
92 Lw Field
356
Forêt de l'Avant-Garde
1
319(-)
MOSELLE R.
Liverdun
Amance
Haye
2
319(-)
de
3 Prcht (Repl)
NANCY
Ft de Gondreville
Forêt
Elms
553 VG
TOUL
3
319
Ft de Villey-le Sec
MEURTHE R.
MOSELLE R.
St. Nicolas-du Port
Pont St Vincent
1
134
R. Hanson

MAP NO. 2

Ste. Geneviève (382), and the Falaise (373) were able to watch every movement of the 317th Infantry as it advanced along the Flirey road. The strength and location of the German force east of the Moselle were unknown to the Americans. Reports from FFI (French Forces of the Interior) agents, whose sources of information were becoming more unreliable as the Allied advance reached the 1914 boundaries of France, and from cavalry patrols operating west of the Moselle, indicated that the Germans were not in sufficient strength to make a stand on the east bank. These reports, coupled with the optimism engendered by the speed of the American advance in August, prompted the XII Corps G–2 to advise the 80th Division commander that there was nothing much across the river.[4]

In the early evening the 317th Infantry arrived in assembly areas on the wooded bluffs looking down on the Moselle. Patrols, working in darkness, discovered a possible crossing site near Pagny-sur-Moselle far over on the north flank, another south of Vandières, and a third in the vicinity of Dieulouard. The situation in front of the 317th was still obscure, and about 2200 General McBride decided not to risk a night crossing but instead to try a surprise attack on the following morning. The area across the Moselle in which the 317th Infantry expected to establish a bridgehead was dominated by Mousson Hill, rising sharply east of the ancient town of Pont-à-Mousson, and by Hill 358, three thousand yards north of Mousson Hill. Colonel Cameron gathered his battalion commanders shortly before midnight and outlined a plan of attack for the next morning based on the seizure of the two commanding hills. The 1st Battalion, on the right, was ordered to begin an assault boat crossing east of Blénod-lès-Pont-à-Mousson at 0930 on 5 September, swing south of Atton toward the Forêt de Facq, reorganize there in the woods, and then attack straight to the west and take Mousson Hill from the rear. At the same hour the 2d Battalion, farther to the north, was scheduled to ford the Moselle at the Pagny site, move directly east toward Hill 385, and then attack south along the ridge line and seize Hill 358. The two hills were about 6,500 yards apart. The 3d Battalion, in reserve, was to assemble behind the 1st Battalion and follow the latter across the river once a footing was secured. Colonel Cameron had been assured of air support and seems to have expected that the 80th Division artillery would fire concentrations on the regimental objectives before the infantry assault. Actually, the time necessary to effect co-ordination between

[4] 80th Div, G–2 Jnl, 4 Sep 44.

the infantry, artillery, and air was lacking. On 5 September the XIX TAC turned its entire striking power against the Brittany ports, sending no planes to the Moselle front. Artillery preparation for the 317th assault was fired only by the 313th Field Artillery Battalion on the right in direct support of the 1st Battalion.[5]

At daylight on 5 September—a bright, clear day—the assault battalions moved from the cover of the tree line on the western bluffs and down toward the Moselle. The 2d Battalion had progressed some distance along a draw south of Pagny-sur-Moselle when suddenly it was struck by artillery and mortar fire coming in from positions dug on the forward slope across the river. So intense and accurate was this fire that the battalion was paralyzed—nor did it again move forward. On the right the 1st Battalion reached Blénod and reorganized for the assault in the shelter of the houses bordering the river flats. In front of Blénod a small canal ran parallel to the river. The battalion found a partially demolished footbridge and crossed the canal without difficulty; it moved only about two hundred yards in the direction of the river when enemy machine guns began to sweep the flats from the north. Completely in the open, the 1st Battalion reorganized and tried to move forward again. This time heavy and accurate mortar fire broke in the American ranks, destroying most of the rubber boats intended for the river crossing. About 1500 the battalion fell back to the line of the canal and there took shelter behind a railroad embankment. The division commander made another attempt to put troops across and ordered the 3d Battalion to cross near Pont-à-Mousson by whatever means were at hand. However, no ford could be found and the battalion withdrew.

Late in the evening the 317th regrouped for another effort, a night attack in which all three battalions would take part. To the left the 2d Battalion marched south to Vandières, where a possible crossing site had been reported. The 3d Battalion, in the center, prepared to take Mousson Hill with a frontal assault across the river. The 1st Battalion moved across the canal to retrace its steps east of Blénod. But again the two exterior battalions were driven back from the river. The Germans on the opposite bank allowed the 1st Battalion to reach the flats between the canal and the river and then opened fire. Casualties were heavy and the badly shaken troops fell back to Blénod where the

[5] Hist Div Combat Interviews (Lt Col J. E. Shaw, Ex O, 80th Div Arty); XII Corps Arty Periodic Rpt, 5 Sep 44. For air missions on 5 September see XIX TAC, A Rpt on the Combat Opns of the XIX TAC, 30 May 45.

FRONTAL ATTACK ACROSS THE MOSELLE. *The 3d Battalion, 317th Infantry, prepares to take Mousson Hill, which may be seen across the river.*

survivors took refuge in a concrete factory building. Shortly after midnight the 2d Battalion began crossing the canal at Vandières using some barges found tied to the bank. Very slowly, in the pitch black, the rifle companies formed in a single file and began groping their way across the open space between the canal and the river preparatory to forming in line for the final crossing assault. The battalion was swung out in a wide loop when, about 0415, the silence was broken by a command shouted in German. This single incident saved most of the infantry, for they fell in their places a split second before the German machine guns across the river opened an intense grazing fire. Flares and mortar shells followed, pinning the troops where they lay. One company close to the canal was able to withdraw, but the rest of the battalion was not pulled out of its precarious position until the following afternoon.

The 3d Battalion had greater initial success in the central crossing attempt at Pont-à-Mousson. The 305th Engineer Combat Battalion, ferrying the infantry across the Moselle in rubber assault boats, landed about four platoons of infantry from I and L Companies on the enemy bank, although casualties were heavy and thirty-eight of the sixty-four assault boats were lost. The infantry dug in about one hundred yards east of the river, and there they were held by machine gun and mortar fire as soon as day broke. The available troops of the 2d Battalion now were ordered to march to Pont-à-Mousson and reinforce the 3d, while smoke was put on the opposite bank to cover the thin American line. But before aid could be crossed the German infantry left their foxholes along the river bank and closed in with bayonets, grenades, and machine pistols. The American position was wiped out by 1100, with 160 officers and men missing.[6]

Further river crossing attempts at this point were canceled by the XII Corps commander, and the 317th Infantry began a slow, piece-meal withdrawal into the woods west of Pont-à-Mousson. Insufficient time for daylight reconnaissance, a daytime attack, the decision to dispense with an artillery preparation in order to gain tactical surprise, lack of co-ordination, and intelligence estimates that minimized the enemy strength had all contributed to the initial failure to bridge the Moselle. But the most important explanation of this reverse must be found in the fact that the enemy held ground superbly adapted to the defensive and that he was prepared to fight for it.

The 80th Infantry Division Advance East of Toul

The remainder of the 80th Infantry Division also met toughening opposition and more difficult terrain as it drove east out of the Commercy bridgehead. West of Nancy the Moselle makes a wide loop, swinging out as far as Toul, one of the most historic of French fortress cities. In the XII Corps plan it was intended for the 80th to attack astride the northern segment of the Moselle River loop. When the 317th Infantry began the march forward on 4 September, two battalions of the 318th Infantry, forming the division center, moved up along the north bank of the Moselle toward Marbache, about three miles south of Dieulouard. One battalion of the 318th Infantry was attached to CCA, 4th Armored Division, which assembled behind the 317th Infantry ready to cross the river when a bridgehead was established. Late on 4 September the 319th Infantry, forming the right wing of the division advance, forced its way across the Moselle at the point where it touched on the eastern suburbs of Toul, and drove a re-entrant into the wide, enemy-held salient formed by

[6] 317th Inf S–1 Jnl, 6 Sep 44.

the river loop.[7] The terrain at the crossing site gave no advantage to the defender; therefore the Germans did not react in force.

Next morning the two regiments attacking astride the Moselle began a protracted battle to close up alongside the 317th Infantry, already at the main north–south river channel. In front of the 80th Division center the main body of the *92d Luftwaffe Field Regiment* was disposed on the heavily wooded hills and ridges surrounding Marbache. Despite its recent conversion to infantry the *92d* proved to be an able combat outfit. When the 3d Battalion of the 318th Infantry attacked to take Hill 326, which commanded Marbache and the road running east to the Moselle, the Germans contested every step through the woods. Progress was slow, but on the morning of 6 September the battalion was in position for the final assault against Hill 326. American guns sprayed the crest with high explosive and in the middle of the afternoon the 3d Battalion took the position. The enemy left seventy-five dead and wounded on the hilltop. The attackers also lost heavily and the battalion commander, Lt. Col. J. B. Snowden II, was mortally wounded. He refused to leave his men and died the following morning. On the right, the 2d Battalion of the 318th made a pre-dawn attack on 6 September against a battalion of the *92d Luftwaffe Field Regiment* entrenched on the west edge of the Forêt de l'Avant Garde. Although the first enemy position was quickly overrun after tanks and tank destroyers swept the tree line with fire, the Germans fought stubbornly as they were forced back through the woods, their retreat covered by twin 20-mm. antiaircraft guns and artillery firing from east of the river. A co-ordinated attack put the 2d Battalion astride Hill 356 on 7 September. Now the 318th Infantry commanded the high ground north and south of Marbache, as well as the roads defiling through the town from the west, and on the night of 7–8 September patrols entered and outposted Marbache. Later, German fire swept the area and the American hold was broken by a counterattack.

The drive out of the 319th bridgehead went more slowly than the attack north of the river. Here, in the Moselle salient, the *3d Parachute Replacement Regiment* held an outpost line barring the western approaches to Nancy. This German position lay about ten miles west of that strategic city, running north and south across the narrow tip of the Moselle tongue and anchored at the flanks by two old French forts which had once formed a part of the Toul fortress system. The northernmost work, at Gondreville, fell to the 3d Battalion

[7] For gallantry during the crossing attack, 1st Lt. Gottlieb Ruby, I Company, 319th Infantry, was awarded the DSC.

FORT VILLEY-LE SEC

of the 319th on 5 September, the day on which the battalion began to wedge its way into the river salient. But Fort Villey-le Sec, occupying the high ground on the southern flank, was stubbornly defended by a full battalion of the *3d Parachute* and proved tough to crack. The fort was surrounded by a deep, dry moat faced with stone. The inner works had reinforced concrete walls and ceilings, five feet thick, and steel cupolas housing automatic weapons and at least one 75-mm. gun. In the woods surrounding the fort the Germans had dug in machine guns, strung wire, and emplaced a few artillery pieces. A preliminary attack on 6 September[8] reached the fort but was broken up by cross fire from the German machine gun emplacements in the woods to the south. Company K led off a co-ordinated assault on the next day, accompanied by tanks and supported by fire from two towed tank destroyers. Lt. Col. Elliott B. Cheston, commanding officer of the 3d Battalion, led his men up to the moat, firing tracers from his submachine gun to designate targets for the tanks.[9] At the edge of the moat the infantry tried to force an entry, while the tanks beside them fired at the enemy embrasures. But the American assault failed to cross the moat: the tanks were forced to withdraw in the face of heavy antitank fire, and the infantry were beaten back by automatic fire and hand grenades pitched out of the port holes. Fort Villey-le Sec finally was occupied on 10 September when the German garrison withdrew toward Nancy.

The Germans launched a last series of counterattacks in the 80th Division zone north of the river on 8 and 9 September, using troops from the *553d VG Division* to reinforce the *92d Luftwaffe Field Regiment.* The recapture of Marbache was followed by sorties at Liverdun, where the 3d Battalion, 318th Infantry, was attempting to clear the north bank of the Moselle bend. This last flurry, apparently a rear guard action, soon was ended and by 10 September most of the enemy had withdrawn across the north-south channel of the Moselle or had fallen back toward Nancy.

The XII Corps Returns to the Attack

General Patton's order of 5 September, directing the XII Corps to cross the Moselle, seize Nancy, and prepare to continue the advance as far as Mann-

[8] During the approach to Fort Villey-le Sec on 5 September, 2d Lt. Hershel T. Hardin destroyed two German machine guns in a singlehanded attack. He received the DSC.

[9] Colonel Cheston was awarded the DSC in this action. Chaplain (Captain) Benedict A. Henderson, 319th Infantry, was awarded the DSC for evacuating wounded under fire.

heim and the Rhine River still stood.[10] Even while the 317th Infantry was engaged in the last-gasp attempt to cross the river at Pont-à-Mousson, General Eddy was considering new ways and means for carrying out the XII Corps mission. For a brief period on 6 September the corps commander thought of throwing in CCA, 4th Armored Division, to help the 317th, but after conversation with General Wood the idea was abandoned and General Eddy ordered the crossing attempt halted. On this date the corps commander still expected to make a major crossing in the 80th Division zone and wrote in his diary: "This time we will make sure it goes through."

Meanwhile the danger of a German thrust against the exposed and extended south flank of the XII Corps, which had caused General Eddy considerable concern, diminished day by day. The Seventh Army drive north along the Rhone Valley was pinching the retreating enemy, who now appeared to be more concerned with avoiding entrapment between the two American armies than with any counterattack operations aimed at the Third Army flank. The 2d Cavalry Group, scouting toward the Madon River southeast of the XII Corps, brushed against German columns retreating hurriedly to the east. On 6 September the 42d Cavalry Squadron and 696th Field Artillery Battalion blocked off one such column on the road between Xirocourt and Ceintrey, killed 151 Germans, captured 178, and destroyed 30 vehicles. On the following day the cavalry were on the Madon River and held a heavy bridge, still intact. In addition, the XV Corps had been returned to the Third Army and would shortly appear to take over the mission of protecting the open south flank. This meant that the 35th Infantry Division could be brought forward and used in mounting the new XII Corps attack.

On 7 September General Eddy mapped out a tentative new plan, much like his original scheme but this time shifting the main effort so as to use the 35th Infantry Division and the entire 4th Armored Division in a wide envelopment starting south of the existing corps front and swinging across the Moselle and Meurthe Rivers to gain the rear of Nancy. Once this limited-objective attack had been concluded, General Eddy expected to use his armor to spearhead a further advance toward the north and east, as part of the larger Third Army plan. Reaction to the proposed maneuver at headquarters of the 4th Armored Division was distinctly adverse; late in the afternoon General Wood phoned Col. Ralph Canine, the XII Corps chief of staff, and reported: "My people are appalled at this thing." He reasoned that beyond the Madon

[10] See Chap. I, p. 55.

River the armor would become involved in negotiating a whole series of water-courses, the Moselle, the Mortagne, the Meurthe, and the Marne-Rhin Canal, not to mention various small but impeding tributaries, before the rear of Nancy could be reached. General Wood pointed out that the advance on the southern flank would be "a terrific problem" even without enemy resistance. He urged that his division be allowed to make its attack in the north, where CCA was in position to knife in alongside the projected XX Corps crossing site and where the only immediate natural obstacle was the Moselle River.[11] General Eddy, however, regarded the Moselle headwaters as less difficult obstacles than the main river north of Nancy. Besides, the terrain in the north gave the enemy better observation than did that in the south. Reports coming in from the corps cavalry were building up a picture of German withdrawal south of Nancy. On the other hand it seemed likely that the enemy was still deployed in force opposite the XII Corps left. The solution finally adopted was this. The 35th Infantry Division would make the envelopment south of Nancy, and CCB, 4th Armored Division, at the moment deployed on the corps right flank in the neighborhood of Vaucouleurs, would add the armored impetus necessary to the sweep. The 80th Infantry Division would then be committed in the Moselle sector north of Nancy as the enemy attention switched south, and the combined corps effort would lead to a double envelopment of the initial objective, the city of Nancy. CCA, in corps reserve, would be available to exploit a crossing on either flank.

On 9 September the corps commander set 0500, 11 September, as H Hour for the attack on the south. The 35th Infantry Division was moving up into line, adequate stocks of gasoline were available, and all fuel tanks and auxiliary cans were full. The cavalry had established a screen along the Madon River and early that morning had begun a dash, fruitless as it proved, to seize the Moselle bridges between Gripport and Flavigny where the 35th expected to cross. On 10 September the corps heavy artillery moved south to support the initial attack. North of the XII Corps the sound of gunfire signaled the beginning of the attack to establish a bridgehead in the XX Corps zone.

The XII Corps Crosses the Moselle South of Nancy

On the morning of 10 September the 35th Infantry Division moved forward under scattered shellbursts to occupy the high ground west of the Mo-

[11] XII Corps G–3 Jnl, 7 Sep 44.

selle. Two regiments, the 137th Infantry on the right and the 134th Infantry on the left, were designated to make the crossing set for the following day. Engineer support would be given by the 1135th Engineer Combat Group (Col. Charles Keller). The north wing of the division advance rested on the Moselle River loop and the southern wing swung eastward in line with the town of Vézelise. (*Map VIII*) The enemy was not in evidence and limited his opposition to artillery fire from guns earlier emplaced east of the Moselle. Shortly after noon the tempo of the advance accelerated when word reached the 35th Division headquarters from the 134th that there was a bridge, mined but still intact, on the Moselle near Flavigny.[12] General Baade gave Col. B. B. Miltonberger, commanding the 134th Infantry, permission to push for this bridge. Colonel Miltonberger passed this information to his 2d Battalion, which reached the bridge after a sharp skirmish with German infantry and armored cars west of the river in the Moulin Bois, and about 1900 began the crossing. Three hours later most of the battalion was dug in on the east bank of the Moselle near the bridge exit. But for some reason the tank destroyers, ordered to hurry across the bridge and support the American infantry, did not arrive. Up to this point fortune had favored the Americans and the enemy had failed to react in any force. About midnight German planes dropped bombs near the bridge but without making a hit. Then the German field guns took over the job and with a few accurate salvos smashed the structure, leaving the 2d Battalion (Maj. F. C. Roecker, Jr.) stranded on the enemy bank. For two and a half hours enemy shells fell unremittingly on the American position and casualties mounted. At last the German counterattack, delivered by infantry from the *104th Panzer Grenadier Regiment* of the *15th Panzer Grenadier Division* and paced by tanks, swept in on the decimated and shaken battalion. Losses inflicted on the Americans were very high.[13] Those who could escaped through the night and swam or waded back to the west bank.

The reverse suffered by the 2d Battalion temporarily checked the 134th Infantry attack. But the co-ordinated attack by Col. Robert Sears' 137th Infantry, delivered as originally planned on the morning of 11 September, secured a toehold across the river. After firing for over an hour in a feint at an area five miles to the north of the 137th Infantry crossing site set at Crévéchamps, the entire 35th Division artillery, reinforced by heavier guns from the XII Corps,

[12] The bridge may have been discovered by patrols of the 2d Battalion. See 134th Inf Unit Jnl, 10 Sep 44.

[13] 134th Inf Unit Jnl, 11 Sep 44. The 2d Battalion was reduced to a total of 295 officers and men.

laid a half-hour barrage across the river in front of the 137th. Shortly after daylight the first waves of the 2d and 3d Battalions were across the Moselle, but here they were stopped by fire from concrete emplacements manned by four companies of the *104th Panzer Grenadier Regiment.* The American infantry dug shallow holes and held on grimly while fire swept back and forth along the bank, denying any movement and preventing reinforcement. Late in the afternoon the 1st Battalion was committed in a surprise attack to the south near Neuviller-sur-Moselle and put two companies across the river before nightfall. After dark the 1st Battalion pushed east to Lorey and General Baade ordered it to make contact with CCB, 4th Armored Division, which had crossed farther south during the day.

In the original XII Corps scheme of maneuver CCB (Brig. Gen. H. E. Dager) was to advance in two columns on the right of the 35th Infantry Division, the north column to cross the Moselle near Bayon, the south column to cross at Bainville-aux-Miroirs. Lunéville and Vic-sur-Seille were designated as objectives. When the armor attacked, on the morning of 11 September, the armored infantry leading the southern column became involved in a sharp fight in the town of Bainville-aux-Miroirs, were initially driven back from the river, but finally succeeded in crossing two companies. The northern column met less resistance in the Bayon sector. A platoon of tanks from the 8th Tank Battalion, led by 1st Lt. William Marshall, followed hard behind the infantry. At this point the main antitank obstacle was a steep-banked canal on the west side of the river channel. Although the German gunners had taken the American tanks under fire, Lieutenant Marshall proceeded to build his own causeway across the canal by firing into the banks until they caved into the water and then topping the earth with a ramp of rails and ties.[14] Marshall's platoon, followed by the rest of the 8th Tank Battalion, then successfully negotiated the four separate streams which here comprise the Moselle; bypassing Bayon, the left column of CCB seized the hills northwest of Brémoncourt which overlooked the 137th Infantry position.

During the night of 11–12 September the advance guard of the armor met the 1st Battalion of the 137th Infantry near Lorey. The engineers, meanwhile, had floated a 168-foot bridge over the Moselle at the Bayon site, and the remainder of CCB, with the 2d Battalion of the 320th Infantry, started to move across into the bridgehead. The Germans made a desperate attempt to throw

[14] Lieutenant Marshall was awarded the DSC.

TANK CROSSING CANAL NEAR BAYON

AMERICAN TANK DAMAGED BY GERMAN FIRE. *This tank of the 8th Tank Battalion was hit during the German counterattack to destroy the Bayon Bridge.*

the Americans back across the river, or at least to destroy the Bayon bridge, and early on 12 September sent a battalion through the outposts of the 8th Tank Battalion. This counterattack was suicidal. Tanks and infantry encircled the enemy detachment, killed many, and took about 150 prisoners. Meanwhile the 2d and 3d Battalions of the 137th Infantry fought their way out of the pocket at the river bank and during the morning swung south to join the main force. Tanks, tank destroyers, guns, and trucks by this time were pouring into the bridgehead. A few German tanks essayed a brief rear guard action east of Méhoncourt, but by midafternoon the remnants of the *104th Panzer Grenadier Regiment* were in full retreat toward the Meurthe River, harassed by fighter-bombers sent over by XIX TAC and closely pursued by CCB and the 137th.

The 35th Division attack had been planned as a two-regiment maneuver. After the disastrous fight at Flavigny, however, the 134th Infantry took no further part in the battle for the crossing, becoming involved in holding the anchor point for the division left flank at Pont St. Vincent, where the Madon

River runs into the Moselle and a series of bridges funnel rail and highway traffic southwest from Nancy. On the west bank a French fort looks down on the town and bridges. One company of the 134th had been detailed to hold this key position and thus secure the north flank while the 35th Infantry Division launched the crossing attack on 11 September. About 0800 that morning the American garrison was surprised by two companies of German infantry which had crossed the river from the Nancy side, circled quietly to the woods north of the fort, and crept in close enough to breach the walls with bazooka fire. The attackers took some prisoners and for a while held a corner of the fort. About this time more Germans were seen entering the woods and word was relayed to the 35th Division headquarters, which ordered the 1st Battalion of the 134th to march to the aid of the American garrison. Friendly artillery soon neutralized the enemy assembly area in the woods and no further attempts were made to seize the fort. But this German threat had been successful in subtracting weight from the 35th Division assault at the Moselle.

The XII Corps Crosses the Moselle North of Nancy

The successful attack by CCB, 4th Armored Division, on 11 September and the seizure of a foothold across the Moselle in the Bayon sector, dictated a prompt effort to cross the Moselle north of Nancy and start the left hook required by the XII Corps plan of concentric attack. Furthermore, the XX Corps had achieved a crossing at Arnaville, just north of the zone selected for the thrust by the left wing of the XII Corps, and it might be expected that this would attract considerable German attention. On the afternoon of 11 September, therefore, General Eddy gave orders for the 80th Infantry Division to start the Moselle crossing the following morning.[15]

After the failure of the reconnaissance in force that the 317th Infantry had undertaken on 5–6 September, General McBride, his staff, and his regimental commanders laid plans for a carefully co-ordinated assault and adequate support in the next crossing attempt. A new crossing site was selected in the neighborhood of Dieulouard, about four miles south of Pont-à-Mousson. (*Map IX*) In the new plan the 317th Infantry again would be responsible for seizing the river crossing and securing a hold on the enemy bank, its initial objective to be the series of hills and ridges immediately east of Dieulouard. Once the

[15] Records for the 80th Division crossing are good. In addition this operation is covered extensively by Historical Division combat interviewers.

LONG TOM MOUNTED ON SHERMAN TANK CHASSIS. *This 155-mm. gun was one of many that concentrated on targets across the Moselle before the assault.*

317th was across, two battalions of the 318th Infantry (Col. H. D. McHugh) were slated to follow into the bridgehead, wheel north, and capture Mousson Hill and the surrounding heights. The 319th Infantry (Col. O. L. Davidson) was engaged astride the Moselle east of Toul; therefore General McBride could count on only five battalions. CCA, 4th Armored Division, assembled behind the 80th Infantry Division, was prepared to cross through the infantry bridgehead four hours after the heavy bridges were in and strike for Château-Salins, a strategic road and rail center some twenty-three miles east of Nancy. To give added weight to the armored drive the 1st Battalion, 318th Infantry, was motorized and attached to CCA. Engineer support for the 80th Infantry Division effort would be given by the 305th Engineer Combat Battalion (Lt. Col. A. E. McCollam), assigned the task of crossing the infantry assault force, and the 1117th Engineer Combat Group (Col. R. G. Lovett), designated to put in the heavy bridges and act as a combat reserve.

The initial attack by the 317th Infantry had shown that the Germans were well organized for defense in the Pont-à-Mousson sector, and it was probable that this first American effort had alerted the enemy all along the river line in the 80th Infantry Division zone. Measures were therefore adopted to screen the direction of the new assault and assure at least some measure of tactical surprise. On 8 September patrols crossed the canal near Dieulouard and scouted as far as the river, selecting possible crossing sites and routes of approach. No further patrolling was allowed and all movement of troops or vehicles into the 317th area was prohibited. Each day the American artillery fired concentrations on the targets selected for special treatment on the day of the assault so as to forestall an enemy alert when the guns opened prior to H Hour. Counterbattery fire was laid on all known enemy gun positions but was none too successful. The winds generally blew toward the German lines, thus curtailing effective sound ranging, and the numerous hills and hollows east of the river offered flash defilade. Apparently the enemy interpreted this artillery activity as normal harassing and counterbattery work. No local reserves were moved into the Dieulouard sector and the daily German intelligence reports prior to 12 September concentrated exclusively on the signs of coming American attacks at Metz and south of Nancy.[16]

Although careful plans and preparations would increase the chances of a successful crossing, the Germans occupied a position so strengthened by the configuration of the ground that there was no easy route of penetration if they chose to defend. The heights of the Moselle Plateau, across the river from the 80th Infantry Division, were crowned by remains indicative of the historic military importance of the area. On Mousson Hill lay the vestiges of a medieval church-fortress, at Ste. Geneviève lines of Celtic earthworks could still be traced on the crest, and at Mount Toulon the ruins of a Roman fort were still evident enough to be shown on French General Staff maps.

The Moselle itself, as it winds through the Dieulouard sector, is no serious military barrier to any modern army. The average width of the river here is 150 feet, with a depth from 6 to 8 feet. Several fords are available for crossing infantry, but the river bottom is too muddy for tank going. East of Dieulouard the Moselle River and the Obrion Canal form two arms that wind around a flat, bare island, a little less than 2,000 yards across. A macadam road runs across this island and the approaches to fords and bridging sites, via the island, are good. Parallel to the western bank of the Moselle at this point is a barge canal, 50 feet wide and 5 feet deep, separated from the river by an 8-foot dyke

[16] See *Army Group G KTB Nr. 2* and *Anlagen* for this period.

that rises abruptly between the two. North and south of the island the Moselle meanders through a wide flood plain covered by marsh grass and dotted by a few scattered trees. But once off the river flats infantry and armor advancing toward the east are faced with a series of abrupt ascents leading to the hills that crop out of the Moselle Plateau—Mousson Hill to the north, Hill 382 in the center, and the Falaise to the south. Numerous draws, gullies and low ridge lines lead back to the heights, but all of these avenues of approach are dominated by neighboring hills and afford excellent corridors for counter-attacks directed down toward the river. This terrain limits tank maneuver, since the roads are often bounded by deep ditches on one side and cliffs or steep cuts on the other. Beyond the hill chain the ground to the northeast slopes gently into the Seille River basin, but any advance toward the southeast—that is, toward Château-Salins—must follow roads dominated by a second hill curtain at Mount St. Jean and Mount Toulon. In effect the enemy-held ground ahead of the 80th Infantry Division presented a tactical problem as difficult as any the Third Army would encounter in the course of the Lorraine Campaign.

As a preliminary to the 80th Infantry Division attack the IX Bomber Command sent fifty-eight medium bombers on 10 September to cut the bridge at Custines that spanned the Mauchère River and provided a quick route over which reinforcements might be moved from Nancy into the Dieulouard sector. The American bombers damaged the bridge, but it is problematical whether this hindered subsequent troop movement by the enemy. On the afternoon of 11 September other planes came over and began a feint at the Pont-à-Mousson area calculated to divert German attention from the intended crossing site. An air strike at Mousson Hill was successful and an artillery observer reported that "it looks like the top of the hill has been blown off"—an overly optimistic view as later events showed. The American artillery joined in this demonstration and continued to shell the Pont-à-Mousson sector during the night.

At midnight on 11 September the two assault battalions of the 317th Infantry moved through the trees covering the approaches to the Moselle and fell into line along the west bank of the barge canal. By 0400, H-hour for the crossing, the 3d Battalion had traversed the island and was at the Obrion Canal, where a ford had been marked by the engineers. On the left, at a crossing site about 500 yards north of the island, the 2d Battalion was hit by mortar fire and briefly disorganized while crossing the barge canal, but at H Hour the first wave was at the Moselle. Now nine battalions of field artillery opened fire on the road south of Loisy, and fifty machine guns emplaced on the Bois de Cuite during previous nights and manned by engineers put a curtain of fire over the heads of the assault waves. Thirty rounds of white phosphorus set the town of Bezaumont ablaze and provided a marker to guide the infantry advance through the darkness. The 3d Battalion forded the Obrion Canal and by 0530 had possession of its first objective, la Côte Pelée, south of Bezaumont. The 2d Battalion waded across the Moselle or crossed in plywood boats and at 0800 was in position on the heights at Ste. Geneviève.

Thus far the Germans had reacted only with occasional fire. Apparently the river line had been very weakly outposted and the high ground, seized by the 317th, was not occupied at all. A drizzling rain reduced visibility in front of the enemy OP's (observation posts), and the moving barrage laid ahead of the attacking infantry probably knocked out the German communications net and dispersed local reserves. However, when the reserve battalion began to cross by a footbridge put in behind the 2d Battalion the German gunners were on the target and succeeded in damaging the bridge. The engineers made repairs under fire and the 1st Battalion moved over the river to its objective, Hill 382, northeast of Bezaumont on the Ste. Geneviève Ridge. The arrival of the 1st Battalion between the 2d and 3d placed the 317th on its first objective, with a semiorganized front of some 3,000 yards. Just before noon the 318th Infantry (—) began crossing into the center of the bridgehead and took up positions on the reverse slope of Ste. Geneviève Ridge and west of Bezaumont. Later in the day the 318th Infantry tightened up the perimeter defenses of the bridgehead by road blocks near Ville-au-Val, Loisy, and Autreville-sur-Moselle. As night drew on the five American battalions dug in to await the inevitable counterattack.

All during the day the engineers had worked furiously to throw heavy bridging across the river and the canals. The original engineer plan provided that heavy bridge construction should be postponed until late on 12 September, when, it was expected, the German guns would be pulled back from direct ranging on the bridge sites. However, the speed and ease of the infantry advance during the morning led General McBride to order the heavy ponton companies immediately to work—a decision that had an important bearing on the events of the next day. By midnight of 12 September two companies of the 702d Tank Battalion, the 313th Field Artillery Battalion (105 Howitzer), some antitank guns, and a few towed tank destroyers were in the bridgehead, the heavy weapons and vehicles being assembled in the dark—

close to the exit from the main ponton bridge—near a small cluster of houses known as le Pont de Mons.

Little sign of enemy activity had been seen during the day.[17] As darkness settled, the German guns to the east began a sustained fire on the bridgehead, while enemy mortars methodically searched the reverse slopes on which the American infantry reserves lay. The 80th Infantry Division attack had struck a thinly manned sector of the *First Army* line. In front of the 80th extended the southern wing of the *3d Panzer Grenadier Division*, rated by OKW as being capable of limited offensive operations (*Kampfwert II*), a rating usually given only the best German divisions on the Western Front since virtually none could be graded at this time as capable of sustaining an all-out attack (*Kampfwert I*). The rifle strength of the *3d Panzer Grenadier Division* was still nearly complete, its artillery was good, and in addition it now had a complement of thirty-three assault guns—an unusual number for any German division at this stage of the war. Somewhat south of Bezaumont the sector of the *3d Panzer Grenadier Division* joined that of the *553d VG Division*. On 12 September there was something of a gap between these two German divisions, covered only by an outpost line. The greater part of the *553d VG Division* was concentrated in and around Nancy, about ten air-line miles to the south of the 80th Division bridgehead. The left wing of the *3d Panzer Grenadier Division* had been stripped to send reinforcements northward, where other elements of the *3d* were engaged alongside the *17th SS Panzer Grenadier Division* in the attempt to erase the XX Corps bridgehead.[18] Lacking local reserves in the Dieulouard sector the enemy had been unable to launch a prompt counterattack. But about 0100 on 13 September the Germans dealt the first blow at the 80th Infantry Division perimeter defenses. The initial counterattack was made by a battalian of the *29th Panzer Grenadier Regiment*, reinforced by at least ten assault guns,[19] which drove in on the road block north of Loisy held by F Company (Capt. Frank A. Williams) of the 318th. Captain Williams and his men fought bravely to hold the position until orders

[17] On the afternoon of 12 September some P–47's from XIX TAC were attacked near Pont-à-Mousson by sixteen to twenty German planes. The Americans destroyed five enemy aircraft and lost one during the ensuing battle—one of the very few aerial combats ever fought above the Third Army troops. The XII Corps commander had asked for extra air support on 12 September because he believed that the Germans were pulling out of the 80th Division bridgehead sector and he hoped to strike this retrograde movement. TUSA Diary, 12 Sep 44.

[18] MS #B–412 (Einem).

[19] 318th Inf S–2 Jnl, 13 Sep 44.

came for the company to fall back to the south. The main German counterattack developed from the Forêt de Facq as a tank-infantry thrust aimed at rolling up the north flank of the bridgehead and destroying the American bridges. This force (later estimated as two battalions and fifteen tanks) took the village of Ste. Geneviève, swept over the end of the ridge which extended south of the village, captured Bezaumont, and began a final assault in company with the Loisy combat group to reach the bridge sites. The small detachments of the 317th Infantry outposting the north tip of the Ste. Geneviève Ridge were driven back into the 318th Infantry positions. Communications were destroyed and command posts overrun. At the command post of the 318th Infantry a sharp fight briefly halted the German attack, but the regimental commander, Col. Harry D. McHugh, was wounded, part of the regimental staff was captured, and about 120 officers and men were killed.

Little co-ordinated resistance was possible as the scrambled units of the 317th and 318th were forced back toward the bridges.[20] Officers gathered small groups wherever they could locate a few men in the darkness, majors commanding platoons and captains commanding battalions. Near the bridge site the situation was further confused when American vehicles coming from across the river met the stream of trucks and infantry moving back toward the bridges. About 0500 a thin line of infantry firing from the ditches along the road between Loisy and the crossroad west of Bezaumont momentarily checked the enemy; but this position was quickly overrun by German tanks that left the ditches full of dead and wounded. However, the fight along the roadside had given time for Lt. Col. J. C. Golden, commanding officer of the 2d Battalion, 318th Infantry, to gather enough men and tanks at le Pont de Mons to meet the final German assault. While the infantry fought from the houses, B Company, 702d Tank Battalion, knocked out the leading enemy tanks and assault guns at ranges as close as two hundred yards. No Germans reached the bridges, although at one time the fight surged within a hundred yards of the eastern exits, where three companies from the 248th and 167th Engineer Combat Battalions defended the bridges with rifles and machine guns. The attack had spent itself, the German commander had no fresh troops to give the added impetus needed for the last few hundred yards, and with full daylight the attackers began to withdraw toward the north, harassed by

[20] The Cannon Company of the 317th Infantry was outflanked and very nearly cut off; but the gunners remained at their pieces and did much to check the German attack. For this and later actions in the bridgehead battle the Cannon Company received a Distinguished Unit Citation.

DIEULOUARD BRIDGEHEAD AREA

MOSELLE RIVER
LA COTE PELEE
FALAISE HILL

shells from the 313th Field Artillery Battalion—the only American artillery in the bridgehead.

Meanwhile CCA, 4th Armored Division, had begun to cross into the bridgehead and the head of the armored column cut into the retreating enemy. By 0800 the advance guard had fought its way into Ste. Geneviève and the armor was rolling toward the east, leaving the American infantry to recover its lost ground and hold the bridgehead. The troops around le Pont de Mons were hastily reorganized and at 0930 General McBride gave the order to counterattack. Many of the enemy left in the wake of CCA were captured, and at no point could the Germans stand and hold. Company A, 702d Tank Battalion, which led the 80th Division counterattack, lost five tanks, but the 80th regained Loisy, Bezaumont, and Ste. Geneviève. Two companies of the 317th had maintained their hold on Hill 382 throughout the night and at dawn on 13 September counterattacked and drove the enemy off the slopes. Infantry of the 317th also had repelled a number of sorties made against the outpost position at Landremont, the most advanced point reached the previous day. The 80th Division counterattack regained contact with these isolated positions and by the late afternoon of 13 September had restored the original bridgehead perimeter.

CCA, 4th Armored Division, Begins the Penetration

During the lull following the unsuccessful attack by the 317th Infantry at Pont-à-Mousson, CCA, 4th Armored Division (Colonel Clarke), lay in the rear areas of the XII Corps awaiting gasoline and further orders. The commander and staff of the 4th Armored Division were extremely anxious to continue the highly mobile operations that had characterized the work of the division in Brittany and across France, and they produced a new attack plan almost daily, most of which turned on the idea of a deep thrust by the entire 4th Armored north and east of Nancy. When the corps commander decided to execute a double envelopment, General Wood gave Colonel Clarke permission to choose his own crossing site on the north wing of the corps. The XX Corps attack to secure a crossing near Dornot, on 8 September, had prompted Colonel Clarke to suggest that CCA should cross the Moselle alongside the 5th Infantry Division. On 11 September the establishment of a bridgehead by the 5th Division, and the beginning of the XII Corps envelopment via the south wing, gave the opportunity General Wood and Colonel Clarke had been waiting for. Plans were made for CCA to cross the Moselle the following day over bridges to be thrown across the river near Pagny-sur-Moselle, immediately south of the 5th Infantry bridgehead.[21] On the night of 11 September the armored engineers moved down to the river with orders to put in a bridge before morning. Most of the steel treadway equipment had been given to CCB. Some large timbers and "I" beams were found at the site but these could not be manhandled into place. Finally the single bulldozer in use overturned and with this last bit of bad luck bridging attempts ceased. Colonel Clarke postponed further operations for twenty-four hours and sent a request to the corps headquarters for a Bailey bridge; but by this time the corps bridge parks were nearly exhausted, except for the large sections of Bailey equipment earmarked for future use at Nancy.[22]

In the interim the 80th Infantry Division made its quick, successful crossing at Dieulouard and on the afternoon of 12 September General Wood ordered CCA to cross through this bridgehead. Colonel Clarke dispatched D Troop, 25th Cavalry Reconnaissance Squadron (Capt. Charles Trover), to move to the bridgehead and establish liaison with the infantry. When Captain Trover and his armored cars arrived at the river the heavy bridges were already in place, but a regulating officer refused to allow the troop to cross.[23] The main body of the combat command began the move to the river about 0400 on 13 September. By this time the Germans were counterattacking all along the bridgehead perimeter and were driving through the north flank of the 80th toward the bridges. Shortly after 0615 the regulating officer gave Captain Trover permission to cross; with this the troop rolled over the bridge and into the midst of the battle on the east bank. Troop D fought its way through the German infantry, crashed through Loisy, and headed up the heights toward Ste. Geneviève. There enemy self-propelled guns proved too heavy for the light armor and Captain Trover pulled his troop off the road and into defilade on the rear slopes, where he and his men awaited the rest of Colonel Clarke's combat command.

[21] See Diary of Captain Seay, Asst G–3, 4th Armd Div, in 4th Armd Div G–3 Jnl (hereafter cited as Seay Diary).

[22] A shortage of engineer bridging equipment threatened the Third Army, and particularly the XII Corps, in the second week of September. On 12 September the Third Army was given a special allocation of 3,554 long tons of Bailey bridging, and this was moved by separate bridge trains directly from Normandy to the front. TUSA AAR II, Pt. 12.

[23] The American artillery was heavily engaged in fire to repel the German counterattack. The 80th Division regulating officer could not permit the cavalry to cross the river until the artillery had been alerted as to the route the cavalry would follow. See Ltr, Gen McBride to Hist Div, 31 Jan 49.

Back on the west bank General Eddy was holding a council of war with the commanders of the 80th Infantry Division, the 4th Armored Division, and CCA. The bridgehead area had been drastically reduced, and the risk entailed in crossing CCA was obvious. General Eddy asked Colonel Clarke if there was sufficient space left for CCA to deploy on the east bank, assuring him that he would receive no blame if he decided against the venture. The CCA commander turned to ask the opinion of Lt. Col. Creighton W. Abrams, at this time commanding the 37th Tank Battalion and already marked in the division as a daring combat leader. Pointing across the river, Abrams laconically remarked: "That is the shortest way home." Colonel Clarke, with the approval of the corps commander, ordered: "Get going!" [24]

Colonel Abrams immediately sent into the bridgehead the 37th Tank Battalion, comprising the bulk of the first of the three task forces making up the long armored column. Thus began a demonstration of daring armored tactics which the XII Corps commander later likened to Stuart's ride around the Union Army in front of Richmond. The road net leading out of the bridgehead was good and generally hard surfaced. Along these roads the armored column rolled, punching to break through the crust of German defense positions and road blocks encircling the bridgehead and fighting for control of the twenty-two feet of highway surface which in effect constituted the "front" for the combat command.

The 37th Tank Battalion had driven the enemy out of Ste. Geneviève by 0800, though this advance had resulted in some sharp fighting, and the remainder of CCA began to cross the river. Covered on both flanks by a screening force of light tanks, Task Force "Abe" continued along the highway toward Château-Salins, marked generally as the initial objective for CCA. About 1615 the head of the three-hour-long column was south of Nomény, while some elements of the command were still crossing the Moselle bridges. Thus far the advance had been halted repeatedly by enemy road blocks, small German tank detachments, and antiaircraft gun emplacements. These were quickly knocked out by the 75-mm. guns on the leading medium tanks or were blasted by fire from the armored artillery following close behind the head of the column. The last phase of the day's operations saw the beginning of the wheel to the southeast. The major part of the combat command coiled

[24] This phase of the operations of the 4th Armored Division has been well covered in a pamphlet prepared by some of the participants: *The Nancy Bridgehead* (Fort Knox, 1946). See also Ltr, Gen Eddy to Hist Div, 14 Feb 49.

for the night near Fresnes-en-Saulnois, only three miles from Château-Salins, after having "swept aside" enemy resistance in a penetration of some twenty miles. In this day of action CCA had lost only twelve dead and sixteen wounded. The damage inflicted on the enemy was very considerable: 354 prisoners had been taken; 12 tanks, 85 other vehicles, and 5 large-caliber guns had been captured or destroyed. The number of German dead and wounded is unknown, but must have been high.[25]

On the morning of 14 September CCA remained in laager waiting for the arrival of its trains, which had bivouacked during the night near Ste. Geneviève. Shortly after noon the division commander radioed Colonel Clarke and gave new orders. CCA would bypass Château-Salins and seize the high ground around Arracourt, north of the Marne-Rhin Canal, block any German move coming in from the east, and cut the escape routes from Nancy. In addition the combat command was to effect contact with CCB, coming up from the south, and use its bridge train at the Marne-Rhin Canal to help CCB, whose bridging equipment had been almost entirely expended on the supply route over the watercourses now behind it.

As on the previous day Task Force "Abe" led CCA, taking to the side roads and trails until the road center at Moyenvic was reached and then rolling south on the main highway. Now the armor was deep in enemy territory and the back areas offered good targets. Near Arracourt the American tanks caught up with columns of the *15th Panzer Grenadier Division*, moving out of the *First Army* zone to reinforce the German lines southeast of Nancy. By the end of day they had taken 409 prisoners and destroyed or captured 26 armored vehicles, 136 other vehicles, and 10 88-mm. guns. An American air observer, flying over the combat command, was able to report "a path of destruction" clear to the canal. Again the losses sustained by CCA had been relatively slight: ten men killed, twenty-three wounded, and two medium tanks destroyed.[26]

CCA assembled in the Arracourt–Moncourt area on the night of 14 September and set up a perimeter defense facing east. One task force took position astride highway N–74, the main paved road running from Nancy, and began

[25] These and subsequent casualty estimates for CCA are taken from Seay Diary.

[26] In the little village of Valhey, southwest of Arracourt, a detachment from the 37th Tank Battalion was halted by antitank fire which knocked out the lead tank, that of Sgt. Joseph J. Sadowski. Sergeant Sadowski was killed when, under direct machine gun fire, he attempted to get his bow gunner out of the burning tank. For this act he posthumously received the Congressional Medal of Honor.

snatching up small German detachments as they came down the highway serenely unaware that there were any Americans within miles. Colonel Clarke saw an opportunity to follow up the successes of the past two days by forcing an even deeper penetration straight to the east. He was in radio range of CCB and by midnight patrols from the two combat commands would meet at the Marne-Rhin Canal. The CCA commander therefore broached the matter by radio to General Wood: "Recommend capture Sarrebourg early tomorrow in order to get crossing over Canal [des Houillières de la Sarre] and thru lake region [east of Dieuze] while enemy is on the run."

General Wood passed this proposal to the corps commander, who refused the desired permission, pointing out that such an advance would take CCA outside the XII Corps zone, which was projected northeast rather than due east, and that the main corps mission at the moment was to destroy the Germans in the Nancy sector and incidentally to open a main supply road for the Third Army across the Marne-Rhin Canal. In this particular case, as so often in the operations of the Third Army, the corps commander was forced to concern himself with the necessity of providing infantry support close in the wake of the armored penetration. The Third Army commander and his armored leaders, accustomed to envision sweeping tank movements, seldom gave much thought to this tactical consideration. As early as the afternoon of 13 September Colonel Clarke had urged that the 80th Division send infantry forward to clear the Germans out of the Forêt de Facq, which bordered on the CCA line of supply, and on the night of 14 September he strongly urged that the 80th Division "rush men to Lemoncourt to follow up the advantage gained."

Back in the bridgehead, however, the infantry had been hit by counterattacks in considerable force on 14 September; every available rifleman was engaged in a bitter struggle to hold the ground already won and extend the bridgehead line out to the east and onto the last chain of hills, grouped around Mount Toulon and Mount St. Jean. On 15 September the situation in the 80th Division bridgehead had deteriorated so markedly that General Eddy ordered the CCA commander to release the 1st Battalion of the 318th Infantry, which had been attached to the combat command, and sent it back by truck to reinforce the 80th. Colonel Clarke dispatched a company of tanks to convoy the truck column and the following morning, after some sharp skirmishing along the road, the little task force arrived in the bridgehead—just in time to intervene in a fight then raging. CCA remained, as ordered, in the Arracourt area, shooting up the Germans on the Nancy road and patrolling toward the Marne-Rhin Canal, where, late on 15 September, CCB effected a crossing.

The Envelopment Southeast of Nancy Continues

After CCB, 4th Armored Division, and the 35th Infantry Division had forced their way over the Moselle River on 11 and 12 September, the enveloping wing south of Nancy began to gain considerable momentum.[27] The terrain between the Moselle and the Meurthe Rivers offered no natural obstacles to favor the defense; therefore, the few companies of the *553d VG Division* and *15th Panzer Grenadier Division* that had opposed the Americans along the Moselle fell back precipitately to the cover of the Forêt de Vitrimont, which borders the north bank of the Meurthe hard by Lunéville. (*Map VIII*) On 13 September a gap developed on the east flank of the retreating enemy,[28] and through this opening the American armor drove.

By the morning of 14 September the two columns of CCB had crossed the Meurthe at Damelevières and Mont-sur-Meurthe and were heading into the Forêt de Vitrimont. The enemy had not been given time to dig in and make any kind of stand. No real effort was made to hold the forest and only the muddy, narrow roads delayed the American tanks and supply trucks following. By that evening CCB had its left flank on the Marne-Rhin Canal near Dombasle and was astride the main road leading east into Lunéville. Some of the enemy fled across the canal toward Buissoncourt and Haraucourt; the rest fell back on Lunéville under cover of a thin screen of infantry and tanks. This important rail and road center was fast becoming a trap, since the 2d Cavalry Group had crossed the Meurthe southeast of the city and was busily engaged in blocking the highways into Lunéville, destroying bridges, and shooting up traffic on the roads. Late that night patrols from CCA and CCB met near the canal, here completing the concentric envelopment of the Nancy–Moselle

[27] During the advance by the 137th Infantry on 12 September, an American rocket-launcher team drove five German tanks to cover in a patch of woods. Sgt. Sherwood C. Lines, Company E, 137th Infantry, took a sound-powered telephone, entered the woods, climbed a tree from which to obtain observation—within thirty yards of a German machine gun nest—and whispered orders back to the American batteries. They brought down such accurate fire as to destroy three of the enemy tanks. Sergeant Lines received the DSC.

[28] See situation maps of *OKH, Gen. St. d. H./Operations Abteilung*. In part this gap had resulted from the withdrawal of the *First Parachute Army* units which had been sent north to rejoin that army in Holland.

position. What the 4th Armored Division columns had accomplished (*Map X*) was spectacular,[29] and, as the German records show, exceedingly worrisome to the *First Army*; but the XII Corps would endure weeks of costly fighting before the area now rimmed by the routes of the armored columns could be occupied by the Americans.

While CCB made its sweep toward Lunéville the 35th Infantry Division moved up fast on the left flank of the armored columns. Early on 13 September General Baade committed his reserves, two battalions of the 320th Infantry (Col. B. A. Byrne), to exploit the 137th bridgehead at Lorey, swinging the 320th through and to the east of the 137th and then sending the two regiments abreast in an oblique advance toward the Meurthe River. (*Map VIII*) The enemy harassed the infantry columns with fire from roving artillery pieces and isolated mortar and machine gun positions but could do little more. The *104th Panzer Grenadier Regiment* had been pulled back at right angles to the *553d VG Division*, which still held the Moselle north and south of Nancy, and the 35th Division attack hit directly at the weak joint between the two German units. About the middle of the morning the enemy artillery abruptly slackened its fire, apparently an indication of a general German withdrawal across the Meurthe River. By the evening of 14 September the two battalions of the 320th Infantry were on the enemy bank of the Meurthe, east of Rosières-aux-Salines, and the 737th Tank Battalion had patrols along the river at St. Nicolas-du Port, only six miles from Nancy.

On 15 September the entire southern wing of the XII Corps either crossed the Marne-Rhin Canal or closed along the near bank. On the right CCB began a fight for crossings at Maixe and Crévic, under orders from the division commander to push forward, hit the retreating Germans, and "cut them to pieces." General Dager replied aggrievedly, "We are cutting them to pieces," but ordered his combat command to spur on. At Maixe, on the right flank, the enemy made a determined stand, reinforced by artillery across the canal. Intensive counterbattery fire and smoke laid on the high ground north of the canal finally quieted the German guns, and at dark a platoon of armored infantry crossed the canal. Since the crossing at Crévic met little opposition the

[29] During this operation the 4th Armored Division had taken 1,269 prisoners and had destroyed or captured an estimated 50 tanks or other armored vehicles, 27 pieces of artillery, and over 400 miscellaneous vehicles. The 4th Armored Division itself had suffered 16 killed in action, 35 wounded in action, 10 missing in action; it had lost 3 armored cars, 4 M–4 tanks, 1 M–7 gun. (In addition a task force consisting of the 1st Battalion, 318th Infantry, and Company C, 35th Tank Battalion, under the command of Maj. C. L. Kimsey, had lost 3 M–4 tanks and a few men killed and wounded.) Seay Diary, 16 Sep 44.

tank units of the combat command were sent over at that point. General Dager had radioed word of the enemy concentration at Maixe to CCA, and the 37th Tank Battalion was sent down to strike the German rear; but when the 37th arrived on the morning of 16 September it found that the enemy had withdrawn from the Maixe sector during the night. This foray was not without result, however, for a tank company of the 37th Tank Battalion, detached en route to clear out the village of Courbesseaux, surprised a large force there, destroyed seven antiaircraft guns, and killed nearly two hundred enemy infantry. CCB assembled in the vicinity of Courbesseaux on 16 September and after a series of orders and counterorders was told to attack north toward Nomény with the object of easing the pressure on the 80th Infantry Division. Although the main body of the 4th Armored Division was now concentrated north of the Marne-Rhin Canal, the small division reserve, CCR (Col. Wendell Blanchard), which was seldom used on independent combat command missions in 4th Armored practice, was dispatched to Lunéville on 16 September and took up positions in the northwest quarter of the city. Meanwhile the 42d Cavalry Squadron, 2d Cavalry Group, entered from the southeast.

On the left of CCB the two regiments of the 35th Division continued to move men and equipment across the Meurthe River and the Marne-Rhin Canal. By 0800 the 320th Infantry (minus the 2d Battalion attached to CCB) was on the march toward Dombasle. The scattered units of the *553d VG Division* continued their retreat in front of the 320th Infantry, and in the afternoon the 1st Battalion of the 320th crossed the canal in a sharp attack[30] and deployed in defensive positions on the bluffs north of Dombasle and Sommerviller, closely supported by the 216th Field Artillery Battalion firing interdiction on the roads behind the canal. In the sector northwest of Rosières-aux-Salines the 137th Infantry met a stubborn German rear guard, and an attempted assault boat crossing over the Meurthe in the vicinity of St. Nicolas-du Port was checked by concentrated mortar and machine gun fire.

The enemy began to stiffen on 16 September, holding where he could and even turning to counterattack. The 3d Battalion, 320th Infantry, drove north toward Buissoncourt, but was slowed down by sharp skirmishes with the German rear guard. At dusk the battalion reached Buissoncourt, surrounded the village, and then made an assault that netted 115 prisoners from the *104th*

[30] The 1st Battalion, 320th Infantry, was forced to make a crossing on an improvised bridge under heavy small arms and mortar fire from the opposite bank. For gallantry in leading this assault Maj. William G. Gillis, Jr., was awarded the DSC.

CROSSING CANAL NEAR DOMBASLE. *Men of 320th Infantry (above) are supported by tank (below), which fires on village from across the canal.*

Replacement Battalion (15th Panzer Grenadier Division). During the night the 1st Battalion came up from the south and CCB released the 2d Battalion, thus allowing the 320th Infantry to concentrate for a further drive northward.

The 137th Infantry effected crossings at the Meurthe and the canal during the morning of 16 September; the 2d Battalion swung northwest in the direction of Nancy,[31] and a company of the 1st Battalion secured the village of Varangéville. In the meantime the tank destroyers and tanks attached to the regiment crossed over the bridges in the 320th Infantry zone and hurried along the Meurthe valley to support the 2d Battalion, now pushed out precariously on the left flank. Around noon a "Cub," flying observation for the division artillery, spotted a large German formation about a mile away from the 2d Battalion, which by this time was near the village of Chartreuse. The Germans, estimated to number at least 800 foot troops and some 16 tanks, were advancing in conventional attack formation, with a platoon of infantry accompanying each armored vehicle. Six battalions of American artillery opened very effective artillery fire, reinforced at closer range by the 105-mm. howitzers of the assault gun platoon, 737th Tank Battalion. This massed shelling broke the counterattack before it could reach the 2d Battalion lines. The *coup de grâce* was delivered by A Company, 737th Tank Battalion, and B Company, 654th Tank Destroyer Battalion, which closed with the German tanks and knocked out at least eight of them. The success at Chartreuse placed the left wing of the 137th Infantry within two miles of Nancy and in position to continue the advance northward alongside the 134th Infantry, now pushing out to the northeast after the occupation of Nancy.[32]

Task Force Sebree Occupies Nancy—15 September

The decision to take Nancy by concentric rather than frontal attack had resulted from the consideration of two factors: the strength of the German

[31] A platoon of G Company, 137th Infantry, was pinned down by enemy fire on the far bank of the Meurthe River during the crossing near Chartreuse. Sgt. Paul A. Fall crawled forward alone and destroyed one German machine gun, then led his men in an attack that destroyed two more. He was awarded the DSC.

[32] On 16 September the 2d Battalion of the 134th Infantry attacked in the direction of Lay-St. Christophe. Company G was stopped by machine gun fire coming from entrenchments on its right flank. Sgt. Junior J. Spurrier, a squad leader, left the company and manned the .50-caliber machine gun on an accompanying tank destroyer. He drove the enemy into their dugouts with fire from this weapon, then dismounted and closed with the enemy infantry, taking 22 prisoners and killing several Germans. He was given the DSC.

forces reported to be in and around the city, and a terrain which favored the defender. Unlike Metz, the other linchpin of the Moselle line, Nancy was not a fortified city. Its strength lay in the geographic features, like the Forêt de Haye and the heights of the Grand Couronné, which had made Nancy a natural bridgehead for centuries. French strategy had conceived of Nancy as a garrison center from which, in time of war, field armies would be deployed to defend the Lorraine bridgehead east of the Moselle and Meurthe Rivers. This policy had been adopted in reverse by the German conquerors, and in 1944 Nancy became a bridgehead facing west in which the *553d VG Division*, the *92d Luftwaffe Field Regiment* (attached to the *553d* on 9 September), and miscellaneous fortress, training, air force, and police units concentrated to halt the advance of the XII Corps. The most important natural barrier between the Americans and Nancy was the triangular massif of the Forêt de Haye. Through early September intelligence reports from the FFI gave repeated stories of large concentrations of enemy troops in the woods, of heavily mined roads, and of freshly dug field works, backed up by numerous antitank guns. The approaches to the Forêt de Haye were too well defended to permit reconnaissance by light armored elements; the extent of its tree covering likewise ruled out effective reconnaissance from the air. As a result the XII Corps commander was forced to make his plans with little knowledge of the strength or location of the enemy force concentrated west of Nancy. In the main, intelligence reports indicated that Nancy would be defended. On 9 September the FFI informed the XII Corps G–2 that large German forces were fortifying the Grand Couronné and that there were at least five thousand enemy troops and huge ammunition dumps in the Forêt de Haye. The FFI reports probably were fairly accurate, for on this same date General Blaskowitz, commanding *Army Group G*, ordered the *First Army* to hold Nancy at all costs as a sally port for the counterattack against the Third Army then in the planning stage.

General Eddy hoped to soften up the Germans in the Forêt de Haye and called for help from the air force. On 10 September the IX Bomber Command diverted seven groups of B–26's from the Brittany targets and they bombed the forest—with indeterminate results. Two days later four groups of medium bombers made an attempt to knock out the German observation posts on the wooded heights. Again there was no way in which the results of the air effort could be measured; General Eddy wrote in his diary: "Nobody knows what is in the Forêt de Haye."

On 12 September the corps commander gave the formal order for the XII Corps to "concentrate east of the Moselle River." No immediate move was made to enter Nancy, although a provisional task force, commanded by Brig. Gen. Owen Summers, Assistant Division Commander, 80th Infantry Division, was organized from the 134th Infantry and the 319th Infantry for this purpose. At the same time word was sent to a French intelligence team, operating behind the German lines under the command of a Major Crinon, that the enemy signal cables leading into the Forêt de Haye from the east must be cut. This task was accomplished on the night of 13 September. A few hours earlier, however, Blaskowitz had given the *First Army* commander permission to evacuate Nancy, "except for a small bridgehead garrison in the west part of the city," in order that the *553d VG Division*, already weakened by commitments on the flanks of the Nancy position, might be used in the concentration of forces with which it was hoped to erase the Dieulouard bridgehead.[33] On the American side the situation in the 80th Division bridgehead had called General Summers and part of the 319th Infantry north.[34] As a result the Nancy task force was reconstituted under Brig. Gen. E. B. Sebree, Assistant Division Commander, 35th Infantry Division. On the night of 14 September new intelligence from the French undercover agents indicated that the enemy had evacuated the Forêt de Haye. Next day Task Force Sebree, guided by three members of the Nancy FFI, marched down the Toul road and entered the city; one battalion of the 134th Infantry pushed straight through to the east edge, with no opposition. Nancy was now in the hands of the Third Army; it would become the army headquarters and the chief bridgehead for the main army supply routes leading into Lorraine. The deci-

[33] *Army Group G KTB Nr. 2*, 13 Sep 44.

[34] The 319th Infantry was regrouped prior to the advance on Nancy. The 1st and 3d Battalions assembled in the Gondreville area and the 3d Battalion later marched to Nancy. The 2d Battalion was left north of the Moselle loop to clear the Germans from the river bluffs along the bend between Liverdun and Pompey. Here on 14 September E Company engaged in a hot fight with the enemy dug in on the bluffs. Although this action was subsidiary to the main battles elsewhere—and is hardly mentioned in the records of the 80th Division—it was distinguished by several acts of personal heroism. The Congressional Medal of Honor was awarded to 2d Lt. Edgar H. Lloyd for leading his men through a deadly cross fire, knocking out the first German machine gunner he met with his fist, and killing the crew with a hand grenade. In this fight Lieutenant Lloyd personally accounted for five machine guns. Sgt. William B. Humphrey was awarded the DSC for action that took place at the same time when he killed numerous German machine gunners with bayonet and grenades. Pfc. Edward M. Winterbottom distinguished himself by going forward alone when his squad was stopped by a German machine gun. His rifle was shot out of his hand and he received a severe wound, but he continued on until he was within fifteen yards of the enemy weapon—then destroyed it with a hand grenade. He was awarded the DSC.

sion to isolate this important communications center by envelopment had paid good dividends, but the bulk of the Nancy garrison had escaped and would face the Third Army again.

The Battle for the Dieulouard Bridgehead

The news of the 80th Infantry Division attack on 12 September caused little concern in the higher echelons of the German command. But a considerable furor resulted at the *First Army* headquarters when, on the morning of 13 September, General Knobelsdorff received word that an American armored column had broken through the German force in the Dieulouard sector and was striking east. First, Knobelsdorff dispatched an infantry battalion, reinforced by assault guns and two batteries of antitank guns, to Bénicourt—apparently in the hope of stopping the American tanks on the main paved road leading to Nomény. (*Map IX*) At least a part of this task force was engaged by CCA, 4th Armored Division, in Bénicourt at midday and was beaten decisively. Next, the *First Army* commander sought permission from Blaskowitz to evacuate Nancy, since he reasoned that the Dieulouard bridgehead must be erased, even at the cost of endangering the south flank of the *First Army*. Blaskowitz gave grudging assent to General Knobelsdorff's request and three infantry battalions moved north from Nancy on the evening of 13 September. At the same time Knobelsdorff dispatched two battalions of the *17th SS Panzer Grenadier Division* from Metz as additional reinforcements for the *3d Panzer Grenadier Division*, bolstering these battalions with elements of the ill-fated *106th Panzer Brigade* which had only five operational tanks in the entire brigade.[35]

This move to reinforce the German troops containing the bridgehead, on the night of 13–14 September, required a ruthless weakening of the *First Army* line. Knobelsdorff had one division in army reserve, but this was the *15th Panzer Grenadier Division* (Generalleutnant Eberhard Rodt) earmarked by Hitler himself as a part of the *Fifth Panzer Army* being formed for the proposed counteroffensive against the south flank of the Third Army. The *15th Panzer Grenadier Division* had arrived piecemeal on the Western Front after ten months of continuous action in Italy. It had suffered heavy losses in Italy and from air attacks on the rail journey north; at this time it had about

[35] *Army Group G KTB Nr. 2*, 13 Sep 44.

50 percent of its normal combat strength. The organic tank battalion was en route from Italy, but the division had on hand about seventeen tanks and assault guns. Although understrength, the *15th Panzer Grenadier Division* still was rated as a "limited attack" unit.

In reality the actual strength of the *15th Panzer Grenadier Division* was not available to Knobelsdorff, since the division was already moving by serial out of the *First Army* zone en route to join General der Panzertruppen Hasso von Manteuffel's *Fifth Panzer Army* farther south. The leading regiment, the *104th Panzer Grenadier Regiment*, had become involved in the fight south of Nancy, where some of its rifle companies had been thrown in to cover the open flank of the *553d VG Division*. Other elements of the *15th Panzer Grenadier Division* had been pulled out of the Arnaville area and were passing through the rear areas of the *First Army* en route to Lunéville; during this journey they were set upon by CCA, 4th Armored Division. Although the *First Army* commander had strict orders to release the entire *15th Panzer Grenadier Division*, he succeeded in halting the departure of the *115th Panzer Grenadier Regiment* by making various excuses to his superiors, and this unit was added to the counterattack force being gathered to destroy the Dieulouard bridgehead.

General Hecker, the *3d Panzer Grenadier Division* commander, did not wait for the concentration of the units being hurried to his sector but instead began a series of local counterattacks, committing each additional reinforcement as it arrived on the scene. In the early hours of 14 September the Germans struck at the 80th Infantry Division positions, using the tactics that had been so successful in the initial counterattacks the day before—tactics that would be employed with varying degrees of success throughout the battle in the bridgehead. The complex of hills, ridges, valleys, and ravines gave an obvious invitation to such counterattack. The early morning fogs rising from the Moselle River extended the protection offered by hours of darkness and gave the attacker time to maneuver into position and drive the attack home. The compartmentalization of the bridgehead into alternating sectors of high and low ground isolated the American detachments at outposts on road blocks and made them fair prey to attack in detail. German infantry were consistently able to win at least temporary success by attacking under the cover of darkness or fog, blinding the American outposts with flares, pinning them in position with automatic weapon fire, encircling and then sweeping over the position. Once the road block was destroyed or the outpost position driven

LOISY

in, the German tanks or assault guns took the lead, reinforced by larger infantry units gathered from assembly areas in the Forêt de Facq or behind the hills to the southeast. While the enemy assault troops drove down the roads and paths into the bridgehead, German guns and mortars placed intense fire on the hills and ridges where lay the main American positions, in preparation for final attempts to recover the high ground by direct assault.

The German counterattacks on 14 September were made by small detachments, all that the *3d Panzer Grenadier Division* commander had at hand. One thrust was delivered against the center of the 317th Infantry, at Landremont, but failed to reach the ridge line. An attack to turn the 317th left was more successful. Here G Company, outposting the village of Ste. Geneviève, was hard hit just before dawn by an assault that forced the company to withdraw, inflicted severe casualties, and cost the Americans all their machine guns. An extension of this attack carried the enemy into the lines of the 318th Infantry (temporarily commanded by Col. M. C. Shattuck) at Loisy, the crossroads position commanding access to the left and rear of the 80th. This time the enemy sweep through Loisy was less successful than on the previous morning and the six 105-mm. howitzers of the 318th Infantry Cannon Company, firing at point-blank range, checked the attack although the town itself was lost.

These small-scale German sorties failed to make any decisive headway, and about 1000 General McBride ordered the 317th Infantry to begin movement to the east in an attempt to seize the last chain of hills barring the eastern exit from the bridgehead. General McBride and General Eddy hoped that the impetus of the 317th Infantry drive would carry it as far as the railroad spur between Nomény and Leyr. The 1st Battalion began the attack with orders to seize the village of Serrières and the commanding hills, Mount Toulon and Mount St. Jean, to the east of Serrières. At the same time the 2d Battalion, on the left of the 1st, recovered the village of Ste. Geneviève and this time outposted it more heavily. On the right the 3d Battalion advanced to the forward slopes of the Falaise and here met and drove back two companies of the *1119th Regiment (553d VG Division)* which had just detrucked after a move north from Nancy.

The main effort, made by the 1st Battalion, ran into trouble almost as soon as it was begun. As the battalion advanced in column, the lead company was brought under German artillery fire. Disorganized by the enemy fire and shelled by a platoon of American tanks, which had been rushed forward and in the confusion had blasted their own infantry, the battalion fell back and re-formed east of Landremont. This time it circled to the north of the small groups of enemy barring the eastward advance and succeeded in putting one company on Mount Toulon. Late in the evening, however, General McBride withdrew this company from its exposed position and the 1st Battalion dug in between Mount Toulon and Hill 340, which had been occupied earlier in the day.

While the 1st Battalion was leading off in the 317th Infantry attack to the east, the 3d Battalion of the 318th pushed out to the north in an advance calculated to widen the base of the bridgehead. The main objective in this later maneuver was Mousson Hill, which overlooked the 80th Division bridges and which had never been successfully masked, though constantly subjected to concentrations of smoke by the American guns. Driving north, the 3d Battalion recaptured Loisy and seized Atton, from which an assault was launched against Mousson Hill. Light tanks carried the first wave of infantry straight up the hill while medium tanks from the 702d Tank Battalion maneuvered to the east side and up the more gradual slope there, coming under fierce enfilading fire from the Forêt de Facq as they moved forward. By 1400 the old castle atop Mousson Hill was taken and the battalion dug in on the heights, here beating off the first in a series of small counterattacks mounted by the Germans in the Forêt de Facq.

During the night of 14 September the *3d Panzer Grenadier Division* received considerable reinforcement and General Hecker prepared a co-ordinated counterattack for the next day. On the south flank of the 80th Division a battalion of the *1119th Regiment* was in place, with four or five companies of the *92d Luftwaffe Field Regiment* and at least one replacement battalion to its right. In the Forêt de Facq, on the north flank of the bridgehead, were gathered elements of the *3d Panzer Grenadier Division*, the *115th Panzer Reconnaissance Battalion*, and the *49th SS Panzer Grenadier Brigade* from the *17th SS Panzer Grenadier Division*, amounting in all to some four or five infantry battalions. These troops were reinforced by thirty or forty tanks and assault guns.[36] As yet no large number of German forces were in position to seal off the easternmost sector of the 80th Division penetration and link the counterattack force on the north with that on the south. Just before dawn on 15 September the German counterattack started, covered by an intense concen-

[36] 80th Div G-2 Jnl, 15 through 17 Sep 44.

tration of artillery and mortar fire. The 3d Battalion, 317th Infantry, was driven back about one thousand yards on the Falaise by the left wing of the southern force. On the rear slope the battalion dug in and held while four battalions of American artillery laid time fire on the enemy infantry, lining the hill with corpses lying in even rows. In the afternoon the 3d Battalion counterattacked and drove the surviving infantry off the Falaise. On the east flank of the German southern group, however, the enemy made good progress toward the north, since there were only a few American outposts to bar the way, and here formed a tenuous connection with the German units moving down from the Forêt de Facq.

Hecker's northern force struck the American positions about 0500. A battalion drove west from the forest and recaptured Atton. Near Atton three 57-mm. antitank guns were brought to bear on the German column and knocked out the leading armored vehicles; however, the American gunners had only armor-piercing ammunition, and when it proved ineffective against the German infantry the guns and the position were lost. The German advance continued south along the river road toward Loisy, where sharp fighting continued all through the morning. Loisy, however, was still in American hands when a battalion of the 319th Infantry crossed into the bridgehead and moved up to reinforce the left flank of the 318th.

The village of Ste. Geneviève, a tactical focal point during all these days of fighting in the bridgehead, was lost to the enemy by a confusion in orders when, on the night of 14–15 September, the troops holding the town were withdrawn to the south on word that a battalion was coming to relieve them. Next morning the Germans marched in without a fight.

With Ste. Geneviève and Atton in their hands the Germans had succeeded in isolating the American troops on Mousson Hill. Now there followed a number of local and generally un-co-ordinated attempts to retake Mousson Hill, to drive through Loisy and seize the American bridges, and to clear the American troops from the key ridge between Ste. Geneviève and Landremont. For such tactics the German assembly area in the Forêt de Facq was admirably situated.

The confusion of the battle on 15 September is reflected in the fragmentary and often contradictory records of the American units participating. Apparently the initial German assault at dawn, aided by very heavy and accurate mortar fire, drove the American troops off Landremont Hill at the southeastern end of the Ste. Geneviève Ridge. The fight for Hill 382, in the center of Ste. Geneviève Ridge, was extremely bitter, the Germans massing their heaviest counterattacks against this position. Here the slopes were gradual but gave the attacker no cover except small garden patches, and the American fire sweeping this glacis stopped the first German assault waves.[37] Meanwhile, the 1st Battalion, 317th Infantry, and its attached tanks and tank destroyers had received orders at 0430 from General McBride to relinquish the advanced position at Mount Toulon and turn back to the west. While this force was en route, new orders reached the 1st Battalion sending it to aid the 2d Battalion at Hill 382. The 1st Battalion arrived just in time to strike a German counterattack forming at the base of the hill; caught in a cross fire the enemy broke and by noon the 1st Battalion was redeployed atop the center of Ste. Geneviève Ridge.[38] The tank destroyers attached to the 1st Battalion (1st Platoon, C Company, 610th Tank Destroyer Battalion) reached the heights about 1300 and were ready to unlimber when the Americans saw some fifteen German tanks rolling out of the Forêt de Facq toward Hill 382. An antitank gun on the hill opened fire prematurely, but the tank destroyers were able to "sneak" over the ridge line and knock out at least nine of the enemy tanks before they could return to cover.[39] The Germans formed one last counterattack in the middle of the afternoon to take Ste. Geneviève Ridge, but before it could be launched it was broken up by fire from the 155-mm. gun battalions west of the river and the prompt intervention of fighter-bombers from the 373d and 406th Groups of the XIX TAC.

The enemy also continued the battle at Loisy during the afternoon, apparently trying to penetrate the extreme left flank of the 80th Division and reach the bridges. Here the German assault was made with a very strong force. The American defenders—the 1st Battalion of the 319th Infantry and some combat engineers, supported by a few 105-mm. howitzers and tanks—held stubbornly, despite many casualties, and repelled the attack.

Although the main enemy attack was directed against the bridgehead defenses on 15 September, the Americans isolated on the top of Mousson Hill also were subjected to considerable pressure. Small parties of German infantry and tanks circled the hill, probing to find a way up the slopes. A few Ameri-

[37] Company E, 317th Infantry, held the center of the ridge for several days and repulsed a number of counterattacks. Company E received the Distinguished Unit Citation for its fight to hold this position.

[38] Pfc. Charles F. Simcox, A Company, 317th Infantry, was given the DSC for gallantry in this engagement.

[39] Pfc. Lester J. Lynch, C Company, 610th Tank Destroyer Battalion, here rescued and evacuated two wounded tank men under heavy fire. He received the DSC.

can tank destroyers were lost to the enemy because their prime movers could not tow them up the steep gradient. American casualties included Brig. Gen. E. W. Searby, artillery commander of the 80th, who was killed while in the firing line fighting off an enemy attack. However, fire from the machine guns and mortars on the hill, reinforced by a protective barrage laid down by the 314th Field Artillery Battalion in position at le Pont de Mons, held the enemy in check. Artillery Cubs kept the isolated battalion supplied with blood plasma and ammunition, flown over the German lines and dropped on the summit.

The hard-fought battle of 15 September left its mark on both the combatants. German prisoners taken during the day all told a story of mounting casualties and gradual demoralization. But the six infantry battalions of the 80th Division also showed evidence of decreasing combat effectiveness and lessening morale. The 317th Infantry Regiment, which had assumed the main burden in the fighting since 5 September, was seriously reduced in strength. Casualties among officers and experienced noncommissioned officers had been high throughout the division. Few reinforcements were reaching the firing line, and as losses mounted the available infantry, already overextended, was disposed along a rapidly thinning front. The broken terrain necessitated an isolation of companies and platoons, another factor lowering morale, and this sense of having to fight alone was heightened further by German success in shelling out the American communications. Throughout the bridgehead the troops were fatigued by constant fighting and sleepless from nightly alerts. Finally, the enemy had continued to hold the initiative, striking at his own chosen time and place, while the 80th, lacking reserves, had to depend on a static and linear defense.

The Germans returned to the assault on the morning of 16 September, this time throwing in the bulk of the *115th Panzer Grenadier Regiment (15th Panzer Grenadier Division)*, which had arrived in the Forêt de Facq the previous afternoon and evening. But General McBride also had received reinforcement. On the afternoon of 15 September the 4th Armored Division had received orders to return the 1st Battalion of the 318th, then with CCA in the Arracourt area, to reinforce the 80th Division. The CCA commander immediately dispatched the infantry battalion and the supply trucks of the combat command, loaded with approximately a thousand German prisoners. Company C, 35th Tank Battalion, was sent as convoy. Just before dark the column was brought to a halt by tanks and antitank guns of the *106th Panzer Brigade* blocking the highway near Nomény. About this time the American task force met a platoon from the 80th Reconnaissance Troop which was on patrol deep behind the German lines and was finding it difficult to make a return to the 80th Division bridgehead. Maj. C. L. Kimsey, commanding the task force, turned his trucks and prisoners over to the cavalry patrol and sent them back to the south. Then Kimsey led the medium tanks forward to clear the road, and through the night the column of tanks and infantry fought its way toward the west. Early on the morning of 16 September radio contact was made with the 80th Division headquarters and the 1st Battalion, 318th Infantry, was given orders to seize Ste. Geneviève, which was still in enemy hands. This surprise attack was successful and about 150 Germans were captured. While mopping up in Ste. Geneviève the battalion was directed to continue on to Loisy and deal with a German counterattack forming there; this was done and the enemy, hit in the flank, broke and fled. This intervention by Kimsey's column gave results out of all proportion to the size of the force involved, for these fresh troops, by attacking from the east, were able to take the enemy completely by surprise.

General McBride now ordered the 1st Battalion, 319th, and the 1st Battalion, 318th, to relieve the battalion on Mousson Hill and disperse the enemy on the north flank of the bridgehead. While the 1st Battalion, 318th, was being resupplied, the infantry from the 319th drove toward the hill, taking Atton en route, and at dark reached the isolated battalion.[40] The German troops in this sector were retiring to the northeast and a pursuit was pushed as far as Lesménils, north of the Forêt de Facq. On the right the 1st Battalion, 318th Infantry, moved into the Forêt de Facq and started to flush out the rear guard remnants of General Hecker's command. While the German penetration in the north was being erased, the 317th Infantry, holding the center and right, sustained three counterattacks but refused to be driven from its positions. Late in the day the German artillery shelled the Falaise heavily in preparation for a twilight counterattack from the valley to the east, but the enemy infantry broke and fled when eleven P–51's came over, bombing and strafing. The 80th Division artillery finished the job with time fire on the survivors. The German attempt to wipe out the Dieulouard bridgehead had come close to success, but had failed. The key terrain—Mousson Hill, the Falaise, and Ste. Geneviève Ridge—was in American hands. The remainder of the 319th Infantry, released from the Nancy operation, moved across the

[40] As a result of this attack, and the earlier defense of Loisy, the 1st Battalion, 319th Infantry, was given the Distinguished Unit Citation.

river, and for the first time the 80th had a bridgehead reserve. General McBride began to reorganize his regiments, which by now had little cohesion, preparatory to a co-ordinated drive toward the east.

The XII Corps Continues the Advance

The capture of Nancy on 15 September and the completion of the XII Corps concentration east of the Moselle required that new direction be given the corps advance. On the Third Army left the XX Corps had a bridgehead across the river and was preparing to exploit this lodgment with elements of two divisions. The right wing of the army, the XV Corps, was closing up to the Moselle. General Bradley had just approved a plan, suggested by General Patton, which would shift the axis of the Third Army advance somewhat to the northeast on a narrower front and thus permit the XII and XX Corps to mass for the attack in column of divisions. On 16 September General Patton informed his corps commanders of this revised scheme of maneuver; the XII Corps was ordered to attack in a zone that would bring it to and across the Rhine in the vicinity of Darmstadt. General Eddy at once issued a warning order which called for the 4th Armored Division and 35th Infantry Division to attack in column toward the northeast, while the 80th Infantry Division continued clearing its bridgehead. Eddy set 18 September as D Day for the resumption of the attack, but on 17 September he postponed this advance in order to give some help to the 80th, struggling to emerge from the confines of the bridgehead. The corps commander had already ordered CCB, 4th Armored Division, to continue north from the Marne-Rhin Canal and relieve the pressure on the 80th Division by a blow in the direction of Nomény.[41] The 80th Division successes on 16 September led General Eddy to cancel the proposed operation by CCB on the following morning, but by noon the situation of the 80th had once again taken a turn for the worse and CCB was ordered on to Nomény. The German units deployed along the roads were now fully alerted and met CCB with road blocks, mines, and all kinds of antitank fire. General Dager ruefully reported "some of the fiercest enemy resistance to date." Heavy rains had fallen, the fields were impassable, and the armor was unable to swing off the pavement in any flanking maneuvers. The advance on the afternoon of 17 September proved so slow that when CCB

[41] XII Corps Rpt of Opns, 16 and 17 Sep 44.

was about halfway between the canal and Nomény General Eddy gave word to desist from further efforts.

Meanwhile, General Patton had given the XII Corps additional armor: CCB of the 6th Armored Division (Col. G. W. Read). The remainder of this division also had been promised to General Eddy as soon as it could be released from Brittany. The 6th Armored Division, an AUS formation, was commanded by Maj. Gen. Robert W. Grow. A graduate in engineering at the University of Minnesota, Grow had been commissioned in the Regular Army in 1916 and sent to duty on the Mexican border. In the decade after World War I he served with the cavalry and field artillery; then, in 1930, he was assigned to the young Mechanized Force. In 1940 Grow joined the 2d Armored Division, to which General Patton had just come as a brigade commander, and subsequently acted as Patton's G-3 when the latter commanded the division. Assuming command of the 6th Armored in May 1943, General Grow completed its training in the United Kingdom during the spring of 1944 and took the division into action, as a part of the Third Army, in the breakout at Avranches.

After the 160-mile sweep across the Brittany peninsula the 6th Armored Division had been split up to contain the ports of Brest and Lorient. General Grow was anxious to turn his containing mission over to the infantry divisions of the VIII Corps and rejoin the main body of the Third Army in the drive to the east. On 26 August he made the long trip to the Third Army headquarters at Pithiviers and there urged that the 6th Armored be relieved from its assignment in Brittany. General Patton responded to Grow's presentation of his case by ordering one combat command to be "slipped" east along the north bank of the Loire River, mopping up the area as it came. On 28 August, therefore, CCB left Lorient. The command closed near Montargis on 1 September and the following day relieved the 35th Infantry Division of the responsibility for guarding the right flank of the Third Army in the sector between Orléans and Auxerre.

The rest of the 6th Armored remained in Brittany, passing with the VIII Corps to General Simpson's Ninth Army on 5 September, but under orders from General Bradley to return to the Third Army as soon as a relief by the 94th Infantry Division (Maj. Gen. Harry J. Malony) could be effected. This relief was completed on 16 September and the 6th Armored formations in Brittany started the long move east to the Third Army, where CCB already was preparing for action with the XII Corps. The 6th Armored would enter the Lorraine operations with a fine reputation. Its status as a veteran division had been won at the cost of some 900 dead and wounded, but this loss had not been excessive when set against the type of assignments successfully carried out by the 6th Armored in Brittany. The division had rolled so far and so fast that it needed new tank tracks and considerable vehicle repair. Such maintenance would be accomplished in stages on the way east, but would delay the commitment of CCA.

The imminent arrival of CCB, 6th Armored, on the XII Corps front promised sufficient additional strength to make a mopping-up operation east of the Moselle successful. The corps commander therefore decided on 17 September to form a task force, consisting of his new armored combat command and the 134th Infantry, place it under the command of General Sebree, the assistant division commander of the 35th Infantry Division, and send it northward with the mission of clearing the Bois de Faulx and the Bois de la Rumont in conjunction with the 80th Division. (*Map VIII*) CCB, 4th Armored Division, then would be regrouped with the rest of the 4th Armored and the whole division committed to lead the projected corps attack northeast toward the Rhine River and Darmstadt. The latter point replaced Mannheim as the new corps objective.

The 134th Infantry, forming the left wing of the 35th Division, was already attacking along a northerly bearing, and on 16 September its leading battalion had seized the high ground north of Essey-lès-Nancy, which formed one of the abutments of the plateau northeast of Nancy known to French military geographers as "the Nancy curtain." The center and right of the 35th Division, formed by the 137th and 320th respectively, had driven across the Meurthe River valley and the Marne-Rhin Canal on 16 September, thus putting General Baade's division along an east–west line and in position to make a wheel into column behind the 4th Armored Division.

The combat command from the 6th Armored Division had not yet arrived in the forward zone on 17 September, but late in the day Task Force Sebree—now consisting of the 134th Infantry, the 737th Tank Battalion, some tank destroyers, and strong artillery detachments—opened the attack to drive the *553d VG Division* from the plateau northeast of Nancy, the first large terrain barrier on the way to the 80th Division. This plateau was dominated by a high butte, the Pain de Sucre, which stood alone to the east and offered observation for four miles in each direction. In 1914 the Pain de Sucre had formed one of the bastions of the Nancy curtain and against it the German divisions had broken in the great battle of the Grand Couronné. The 1st Battalion, 134th Infantry, took the Pain de Sucre without much opposition on 18 September, but in the dark hours of the next morning elements of the *553d VG Division* counterattacked from Agincourt, under cover of furious mortar and artillery fire. They drove the battalion off the hill, inflicting some 150 casualties and destroying most of its heavy weapons.[42] To control the Pain de Sucre was imperative and General Eddy ordered an immediate counterattack. General Sebree gathered a small force of tanks to stiffen his own counterattack, and at 1330 the 3d Battalion wheeled across the front of the 1st Battalion and advanced up the eastern side of the shell-torn hill. All through the morning three battalions of field artillery shelled the Germans, and as the 3d Battalion came on the enemy broke and fled down the hill to Agincourt, which was taken by the 3d Battalion in the late afternoon.[43] This successful attack was co-ordinated with an advance by the 137th Infantry in the direction of Amance Hill, a height about 3,500 yards northeast of the Pain de Sucre. At the same time twelve P-47's from the 36th Fighter Group had contributed considerably to the 134th Infantry success by strafing the western slopes of Amance Hill, neutralizing a number of dug-in artillery pieces that had been firing on the 134th and the approaches to the Pain de Sucre.

The events of 18 September placed the 134th Infantry in position to debouch from the plateau north into the Bois de Faulx and thus squeeze the *553d VG Division* between the 80th and 35th Divisions. A further advance to the north was denied by the enemy mortars and field guns on Amance Hill, whose fire interdicted the draw separating the plateau and the Bois de Faulx. Until the 137th Infantry could take Amance Hill and clear the ground on the right of the 134th Infantry the latter could make little or no progress. The problem was complicated, moreover, by a wide gap between the two regiments.

On the afternoon of 19 September the 137th Infantry began an advance through the extensive Forêt de Champenoux, which afforded the most direct route for turning the flank of the Amance position and which had to be

[42] In this fight Sgt. Ralph F. Greeley, D Company, 134th Infantry, covered the American withdrawal with fire from a dismounted machine gun. He stayed at his post until killed. Sergeant Greeley was awarded the DSC posthumously.

[43] The fight for the Pain de Sucre is ably described in J. A. Huston's Biography of a Battalion (MS, New York University, 1947).

cleared before the 137th could maneuver with any freedom.[44] The 2d and 3d Battalions moved abreast astride the north-south road running through the southern section of the forest and encountered little opposition until about 1830, when the leading troops emerged into the opening where the Nancy–Château-Salins highway cut through the woods. Here the advance was abruptly checked by fire from machine guns and 120-mm. mortars which the enemy had trained on the clearing.

The 137th now was forced to begin a bloody slugging match for access through the forest to the Amance plateau, reminiscent of the bitter fighting over the same ground in the first days of September 1914, although with far smaller forces on both sides. Then the German divisions had debouched from the Forêt de Champenoux at zero hour each morning and attacked in closed waves to the west, only to be driven back each day by French 75's on the heights at Amance and the Pain de Sucre. But in September 1944 the Germans held the Amance position, as well as the thick forests flanking it on the east and west which barred any close-in envelopment. Even the American position on and near the Pain de Sucre was not secure so long as the Bois de Faulx and Amance Hill were held by the enemy; indeed, on 20 September Agincourt was lost to a German counterattack and the company which had held it was reduced to sixty-five men. Agincourt was retaken the next day but only after a bitter house-to-house battle.

The 137th Infantry took advantage of the early morning fog on 20 September to make an assault across the no man's land at the highway clearing. Infantrymen from three companies rode into the clearing on the decks of the medium tanks attached to the regiment, but only two platoons—one cut to pieces by small arms fire—were able to hold on north of the road.

Troops of the *1120th Regiment* of the *553d VG Division* (reinforced by some training units) had been stationed in the northern sector of the Forêt de Champenoux on 17 September to cover the withdrawal of the rest of the division. With the characteristic zeal of well-trained German infantry, they had entrenched thoroughly, building a line of log-covered dugouts and foxholes ten or fifteen yards inside the forest. Within the shelter of the woods a few tanks and self-propelled 88's backed up the infantry and covered still

[44] On 17 September the 320th Infantry, then east of the Forêt de Champenoux with the 4th Armored Division, sent a reconnaissance party back to the west through enemy territory. This daring patrol from Erbéviller to Champenoux was led by 1st Lt. Raymond W. Braffitt, S–2 of the 320th Infantry, who was killed during this reconnaissance. Lieutenant Braffitt was awarded the DSC posthumously.

FORET DE CHAMPENOUX
MAZERULLES
TO NANCY
CHAMPENOUX
FORET DE CHAMPENOUX

more entrenchments. Heavy-caliber mortars were sited so as to lay a barrage on the clearing at the slightest movement from across the road. Through 20 and 21 September all the American attempts to secure a firm hold in the northern half of the forest were thrown back, determined though they were. What the attacking infantry and accompanying tanks could not accomplish might have been effected by artillery fire had not the supply of ammunition at the guns failed during the night of 20 September. The shells gave out just after a series of terrific concentrations by six battalions of American field artillery had literally blown to bits the German carrying parties as they moved through the woods and had pulverized the log-covered entrenchments. This pounding left the enemy weak and shaken, but still able to serve his weapons.

The XII Corps commander was anxious to eliminate the resistance delaying the 80th and 35th Divisions. The 4th Armored Division had become involved in a large-scale tank battle in the exposed salient that it occupied on the right wing of the corps[45] and General Eddy wished to bring his left and center forward. Eddy gave orders for a combined attack on 22 September in which the 80th Division, the 35th Division, and CCB, 6th Armored Division, would join. His earlier intention to employ the 6th Armored combat command as a means of filling out the XII Corps attack had been thwarted by the German armored threat at Lunéville. CCB had briefly taken over the defense of this sector, but a shift in the direction of the German attack brought the enemy armor up against the main body of the 4th Armored, farther to the east, and left Read's command free for aggressive use. On the morning of 21 September Eddy attached CCB to the 35th Division. Read left Lunéville at once, moving north through the gap between the German forces engaged by the 35th Division and those fighting the 4th Armored. While the 80th Division held fast the elements of the *553d VG Division* on its front with a thrust into the Bois de la Rumont, CCB assembled in the Forêt de Grémecey and then, on 22 September, began a turning move to the southwest with the aim of taking Amance Hill from the rear and drawing a cordon tight around the Germans holding the 137th Infantry at bay. (*Map XI*)

Colonel Read's combat command was a battlewise unit, rested after the fighting in Brittany, and with its tanks now in good repair. Early on the morning of 22 September CCB moved out toward the Seille River, using radio to maintain contact with the 35th Division. Although the enemy forces were

[45] See Chap. V, pp. 221ff.

surprised by the appearance of the American tanks in their rear, they succeeded in blowing the Seille bridges. CCB halted briefly, and then a ford was discovered near Han. Read's tanks negotiated the muddy crossing, though with difficulty, and attacked in a serial of three columns. About 1015 the leading column brushed against Armaucourt, heavily occupied at this time by the enemy, and pushed on to the south, losing six tanks to enemy antitank guns. At noon the second column, numbering some 250 men (a light tank company, a platoon of tank destroyers, a platoon of armored engineers, and two sections of antiaircraft artillery), drove into Armaucourt behind an intense barrage laid down by the armored artillery of the combat command. Before the dazed Germans could recover, the little force was in the streets, firing at everything in sight. The Americans destroyed 162 vehicles, 310 of the enemy surrendered on the spot, and 182 were counted dead in the streets. The Germans who fled the town were engaged and cut up by the third column, which had circled north of Armaucourt.[46]

Before morning ended the German lines were cracking under the pressure exerted by the armored columns. General Baade had held up the 35th Division attack until the enemy could feel the weight of the American tank drive. At noon two battalions of the 134th Infantry jumped off under heavy enemy fire to take the hill mass in the Bois de Faulx, while the 137th Infantry pushed rapidly through the last stretch of the Forêt de Champenoux. There was no fight left in the forest defenders and those who were able fled north along the road to Létricourt, where a narrow gap still existed. A squadron of P–47's flushed the last of the enemy off the Amance plateau; then more planes from the XIX TAC arrived to bomb and strafe the four-mile-long column of infantry, horses, vehicles, and guns moving painfully toward Leyr. When darkness came the 155-mm. guns and 240-mm. howitzers took over the job and shelled the road all through the night. The following day the 35th Division cleared the German rear guard detachments from the Bois de Faulx, swelling the bag of prisoners taken by the 35th and CCB to more than one thousand.[47]

The main part of the *553d VG Division*, thus far successful in shuttling back and forth along internal lines which permitted counterattacks against either the 35th or the 80th Division, finally faced the danger of complete

[46] The fight at Armaucourt is given detailed treatment in the *Combat Record of the Sixth Armored Division*.

[47] 35th Div AAR, 23 Sep 44. The total losses of the *553d VG Division* in September 1944 are listed as 319 killed in action, 1,052 wounded in action, and 2,125 missing in action. *Army Group G KTB Nr. 3a (Anlagen)*, Oct 44.

AMERICAN TROOPS ENTER FORET DE CHAMPENOUX. *Shown here are members of the 137th Infantry on 22 September.*

encirclement. On 23 September the German commander, Colonel Erich Loehr, ordered a withdrawal calculated to bring his division west of Château-Salins. When word of this break in the *First Army* lines reached the army commander, he sent a formal reprimand to the *553d* commander (Loehr subsequently was tried by court-martial) and ordered that a counterattack be started at once to regain the former connection with the Moselle River along the Custines–Leyr–Ajoncourt line. But such countermeasures obviously were impossible, given only the weakened battalions of the *553d*.

While the 35th Division and CCB had been fighting to destroy the German force pressing against the southern flank of the 80th Division, the latter had begun a slow and costly drive to clear the bridgehead area. On 17 September the 80th erased the last vestiges of resistance in the Forêt de Facq. The *3d Panzer Grenadier Division* was already in process of withdrawing to a new position, which extended from the left flank of the *17th SS Panzer Grenadier Division* south of Sillegny, followed the Seille River as far as Port-sur-Seille, and then made contact with the *553d VG Division* just east of Landremont.[48] This change in the German line eased the pressure on the north wing of the 80th Division and allowed the 319th Infantry to advance with little trouble. On the right, however, the battle-weary 317th found rough going,[49] and the 318th, attacking in the center and echeloned slightly to the rear of the 317th, also met continuing and stubborn opposition. Small groups of the enemy kept up a bitter delaying action, holding their ground wherever the hills or woods gave cover for mortars and automatic weapons, and filtering back into the American positions at night through the draws and gullies.

The first phase of the 317th Infantry attack, begun on 17 September, aimed at clearing the enemy from the Landremont–Morey–Millery triangle, preliminary to the final assault to carry the wooded heights of the Bois de la Rumont. After some heavy fighting—and heavy losses—the 317th pushed into the Bois de la Rumont.[50] Here, on 21 September, two American battalions were cut off and had to be supplied by tanks, but the German hold on the wooded plateau

[48] *Army Group G KTB Nr. 2*, 24 Sep 44.

[49] During the attack near Landremont on 17 September, Sgt. Howard O. Wagner, A Company, 317th Infantry, was cut off by the enemy while manning a machine gun. Although wounded Sergeant Wagner refused to surrender and fought on until he was killed. He received the DSC in a posthumous award.

[50] East of the Bois de la Rumont elements of the 317th Infantry made an advance on 19 September toward Bratte. During this engagement Cpl. James A. Rapino, L Company, 317th Infantry, led his squad in an assault with fragmentation grenades which destroyed four German mortars and three half-tracks—under severe enemy fire. Corporal Rapino received the DSC.

was finally broken. The withdrawal by the *553d VG Division* on 23 September allowed the 80th Division right and center to extend eastward. The hill mass east of Serrières, and more particularly the heights at Mount St. Jean and Mount Toulon, still had to be wrested from the Germans.[51]

General Patton had been watching the progress of the 80th Division with much interest. On 24 September he met the XII Corps commander and relayed General Eisenhower's directive halting offensive operations by the Third Army; but General Patton added that "limited objective" attacks would be continued and that the 80th Division must push on toward the Seille River, where a proper defense line could be organized. The 80th Division commander concluded that this mission might best be accomplished by a turning movement, through the towns of Moivron and Jeandelaincourt, designed to outflank the formidable hill mass confronting his right wing. He ordered the 318th Infantry to sideslip farther south, so as to support the 317th Infantry along the new axis of attack, and asked for more artillery.[52] The corps commander moved the battalions of the 404th Field Artillery Group across the Moselle and into firing positions near Millery; from there the American gunners kept up an almost continuous fire. On 26 September the attack was resumed on the new axis. But the *553d VG Division* had turned back to the west, under strict and peremptory orders from the *First Army* commander, and was dug in to meet the Americans. The 2d Battalion, 317th Infantry, launched an assault to take Moivron, but, although supported by heavy artillery and fighter-bombers, and reinforced by fresh troops from the 6th Armored Division, the worn and decimated infantry could not take the town. Nor did the 318th attacks, which had been battering at Mount St. Jean, have any greater success.

The 80th Division drive now came to a halt short of the Seille River, but with its regiments in position for a future advance into the Seille basin. A bridgehead eleven miles wide (Custines to Lesménils) and four miles deep had been taken and held against continuous German onslaughts. One of the

[51] Capt. Frank A. Williams, F Company, 318th Infantry—who had already won recognition as an intrepid company commander—received the DSC for bravery during attacks at Mount St. Jean on 23–24 September. On 24 September Captain Williams was wounded in both arms, during hand-to-hand fighting, but stayed with his company. He received a third wound in the shoulder but refused to be evacuated until that night, when F Company was relieved.

[52] From 12 to 16 September the 313th Field Artillery Battalion had been the only American artillery in the bridgehead. The battalion had distinguished itself by close support of the infantry and had fought on occasion as infantry. The 313th Field Artillery was awarded the Distinguished Unit Citation.

enemy divisions earmarked for use in the projected counteroffensive against the Third Army's right flank, the *3d Panzer Grenadier Division*, had been contained in the bridgehead area. During the month of September the 80th Infantry Division had taken 1,905 prisoners and destroyed approximately 46 tanks and assault guns—but at heavy cost. Its own casualties numbered 2,851 officers and men—mostly incurred in the fight for the bridgehead—of whom 437 had been killed and 657 were missing.[53]

[53] XII Corps Rpt of Opns (Table No. 1), Sep 44. The total German losses at the hands of the 80th Division are unknown. During the month of September the *3d Panzer Grenadier Division*, which led off in the fight to erase the 80th Division bridgehead, listed only 585 killed, wounded, and missing. *Army Group G KTB Nr. 3a (Anlagen)*, Oct 44. See n. 47 for the losses of the *553d VG Division*. It is probable that the losses suffered by the Germans during this period were much smaller than those sustained by the Americans.

CHAPTER III

The XX Corps Crossing of the Moselle[1] (6-24 September)

Preparations for the Moselle Crossing

On 28 August the exhausted and disorganized enemy forces were reeling back to the east, leaving only a few small groups of isolated infantry and stubborn antitank gunners from the *17th SS Panzer Grenadier Division* and the *48th Division* to delay the American advance. But at the same time gasoline began to run low in the tanks, trucks, and armored cars of the XX Corps. By 29 August the shortage was acute. The 90th Infantry Division, on the north flank, came to a halt at Reims with hardly enough gasoline left to keep the field ranges on the kitchen trucks burning. By siphoning fuel from supply and transport vehicles, elements of the 7th Armored Division and 5th Infantry Division were able to make the last few miles to the Meuse River and establish a bridgehead there. Contact with the main rear guard of the fleeing Germans no longer existed, and shortly after noon on 31 August tanks from CCA, 7th Armored Division (Colonel Rosebaum), rumbled across the Meuse on a bridge which had been found intact in the ancient city of Verdun. The crossing at Verdun was close to the last step in the rapid 400-mile advance which the XX Corps had made since 6 August. Of the seventeen tanks in the task force dispatched to Verdun only three reached their objective; the rest had

[1] This chapter is based on the After Action Reports and unit journals of the XX Corps, 7th Armored Division, 5th Infantry Division, 90th Infantry Division and 3d Cavalry Group, including those of infantry regiments, rifle battalions, and cavalry squadrons. Important information at the level of command has been obtained from the telephone journals attached to the daily G–3 Journals of the 7th Armored Division and 5th Infantry Division as well as from postwar correspondence with several of the staff officers and commanders involved in this operation. The Historical Division Combat Interviews for this period are very detailed and extremely useful. See also The Reduction of Fortress Metz; XX Corps Operational Report 1 September–6 December 1944; *Pass in Review—the Fifth Infantry Division in ETO* (Atlanta, 1946) (hereafter cited as *Fifth Infantry Division*); *History of the Eleventh United States Infantry Regiment* (Baton Rouge, 1947) (hereafter cited as *Eleventh Infantry*); *Historical & Pictorial Review, 2d Infantry Regiment* (Baton Rouge, 1946). Enemy information is taken from the *KTB's* of *Army Group G, OB WEST* and OKW. In addition various *Anlagen* to these *KTB's* have been used, plus the operations maps (1:300,000) of the *OKH, Gen. St. d. H./Operations Abteilung.*

run out of gasoline. The 5th Division followed as far as Verdun, outposted the east bank of the Meuse, and with this bridgehead in hand the XX Corps eastward drive stalled. For five days General Walker waited for gasoline, rationing the few hundred gallons left so as to send his armor and cavalry out on scouting missions to the north and east.

On the morning of 1 September, CCR (Lt. Col. J. W. Newberry) of the 7th Armored Division moved east along the main Verdun–Metz highway and reached Etain, some twelve miles from the Meuse, where on the previous night a raid by the 3d Cavalry Group (Col. F. W. Drury) had captured 4,000 gallons of gasoline—enough to send cavalry patrols on eastward to the Moselle River. For the next few days the 3d Cavalry Group acted with the élan of the old mounted cavalry tradition. But its accomplishments could lead to no substantial gain and did little more than indicate what might have been the story had not the iron grip of logistics intervened to thwart a Third Army dash across the Moselle. A platoon of B Troop, 3d Cavalry Reconnaissance Squadron, commanded by 1st Lt. James D. Jackson and guided by a French Marine, made a seventy-mile foray deep into the enemy rear and on the afternoon of 2 September reached Thionville, the large bridgehead city north of Metz. For two hours Lieutenant Jackson's little force—three armored cars and six jeeps—shot up the town, and Jackson even succeeded in cutting the demolition wires on the main bridge spanning the Moselle River; but eventually the Americans were driven off, and returned to their command. Jackson, who had been wounded twice at the bridge, was awarded the DSC. On this same day a platoon from the 43d Cavalry Reconnaissance Squadron made a reconnaissance toward Longuyon, twenty-eight miles northeast of Verdun, and penetrated the outskirts of that town before the surprised Germans mustered enough tanks and artillery to drive the American cavalry out. Another platoon of the 43d, led by 2d Lt. R. C. Downs, reached the Moselle River on 2 September and set up an observation post on the heights at Haute Kontz, north of Thionville, reporting by radio: "No enemy visible on other side of the Moselle. Many good places for bridges, all undefended. Rolling ground back of river." So disrupted were the German forces west of the Moselle that Lieutenant Downs was able to retain his point of vantage by dodging about until 5 September, when the lowering level in the gas tanks forced the platoon to cut back to the west and rejoin its squadron.

Elsewhere the 3d Cavalry Group was forced to curtail scouting operations between the Meuse and the Moselle as the limited gasoline supply began to fail. By the morning of 3 September the 43d Cavalry Reconnaissance Squadron, which had pushed out on the left wing of the XX Corps zone of advance, had to report that it could operate neither its vehicles nor its motor-driven radios. The remaining squadron, the 3d, was able to maintain contact with the retreating enemy all through 3 September and as night fell was approaching the Moselle River south of the city of Metz. But already there were signs of stiffening German resistance in front of the cavalry patrols and the FFI reported that its informants across the river had seen enemy troops entering Metz and strengthening positions south of the city near Arnaville. Contrary to rumors that later circulated through the Third Army, no American cavalry were able to enter Metz or its environs.

Meanwhile General Walker decided to make what use of the stalemate he could in hopes of adding to the enemy confusion. On 2 September, as an indication to the enemy that the XX Corps intended to turn to the north and northeast and move in the direction of Luxembourg alongside the VII Corps of the First Army, two armored task forces from the 7th Armored Division were sent north from Verdun, advancing on both sides of the Meuse with orders to make a feint at Sedan. The task forces ran out of gasoline before reaching Sedan, and on the afternoon of 3 September General Walker ordered them to return to Verdun. Some gasoline was available the following day and the armor then rejoined its division. It appears that the enemy initially reacted to this demonstration as General Walker had hoped. On 4 September German intelligence reports prepared in *Army Group B* headquarters noted: "The Third Army appears to be regrouping for a further drive to the *northeast.* A great attack on the line Mons–Charleville–Montmédy is to be expected soon." But the failure of American reconnaissance to follow up these first probing efforts on a northeasterly axis quickly convinced the German higher staffs that the Third Army attack would take some other course, and no troops were shifted to the Sedan sector.

During these days of enforced inactivity the XX Corps commander and his staff were busy with plans for a drive that would reach Mainz, on the Rhine, 140 air-line miles east of the XX Corps forward positions, before the German West Wall could be manned. This scheme of attack had been discussed by General Patton and General Walker during March 1944, while the Third Army was in the United Kingdom. It had been promulgated as a written order from General Bradley's headquarters on 29 August and now remained on the planning maps for immediate use once the gasoline drought was ended. In the first days of September, however, there was little the XX Corps could do but commit ambitious future plans to paper, wait, make a sterile record of the optimistic and pleading messages radioed in by the cavalry, put out daily periodic reports with the dour phrase, "no change," engage in gunnery practice when German planes came over at night in fruitless attempts to destroy the Verdun bridges, and hope that gasoline would soon arrive. Even the foot soldiers of the two infantry divisions had to wait on the life blood of mechanized warfare, for without gasoline no artillery, bridging equipment, rations, or ammunition could be moved forward to support them in any extended advance.

In the meantime the 315th Engineer Combat Battalion of the 90th Infantry Division worked feverishly to repair a large airfield near Reims which had been badly damaged by German ground crews before its capture. By noon of 3 September the main runways were in shape to receive cargo planes; this, coupled with reports that there was a plentiful supply of gasoline on the beaches back in Normandy, promised an early end to the shortage.

By the afternoon of 4 September enough fuel was on hand to extend the radius of cavalry action and the 3d Cavalry Reconnaissance Squadron began to push its patrols toward the Moselle between Thionville and Pont-à-Mousson, the projected zone of a renewed advance by the XX Corps. General Walker ordered the squadron to seize any bridges over the Moselle still standing, but the German defensive positions west of the river were rapidly being manned and apparently were fairly well co-ordinated. The FFI told the American cavalry that some bridges south of Metz were still intact. When a cavalry patrol reached the bridge at Pont-à-Mousson, however, it found the structure demolished. Scouting north along the river the cavalry tried to pass through the defiles leading down to the west bank of the Moselle at Arnaville, which commanded another bridge site. Three separate attempts to get into the town were checked by the German infantry and artillery posted along the defiles, and when night came the XX Corps was still without a bridge, though scouts had heard of a fording site at Ars-sur-Moselle some five thousand yards south of the Metz suburbs. The following day brought no greater success and the five cavalry task forces probing toward Metz and the river met strong resistance at every point. In one brush with the Germans near Gravelotte, the commanding officer of the 3d Cavalry Group, Colonel Drury, was ambushed and captured. As reports came back from the cavalry indicating that a German line was beginning to form for the defense of the river and the Metz–

Thionville position, the corps commander had to consider whether he should commit his one armored division at the river line in the hope of forcing a quick passage and making immediate exploitation deep in the enemy rear, or whether a systematic infantry assault would be necessary before the armor could be put across the Moselle and started on a dash toward the Rhine. Alternate plans finally were formulated to allow either the 7th Armored Division or the 90th and 5th Infantry Divisions to initiate the attack and seize a bridgehead over the Moselle. General Walker favored the use of the armor, with the hope of securing a bridge in a quick stroke. General Silvester and his officers believed that the infantry divisions should be committed in advance of the 7th Armored Division.[2]

Late in the evening of 5 September, General Walker returned from the meeting at the Third Army headquarters with the long-awaited word to resume the offensive. He hurriedly phoned his divisions and relayed the news, adding that the orders from General Patton "will take us all the way to the Rhine." Early the next morning the XX Corps headquarters followed up his alert with instructions that Field Order No. 10, the most ambitious and far-reaching of the various plans considered during the waiting period, would be put into operation at 1400 that afternoon. This field order reflected the optimism so strongly felt in the Third Army. It defined the initial corps mission as the seizure of crossings on the Sarre River, some thirty miles east of the Moselle. Beyond this the field order provided that, on the receipt of additional orders from army headquarters, the XX Corps would continue its advance to Mainz on the Rhine River. The 7th Armored Division now was assigned the mission of making the Moselle crossing in advance of the infantry, apparently in the hope that the armor would find a bridge intact at the Moselle, as had been the case at both the Marne and Meuse. The corps commander specifically enjoined General Silvester to make the approach march to the Moselle on a wide front and in multiple columns, but no decision was made as to whether the division should fight for a crossing both north and south of Metz or confine its efforts to the establishment of a single bridgehead. Once the 7th was beyond the Moselle, the role envisaged for the armor was clearly defined, both by General Patton's customary use of armor in the exploitation of a breakthrough, and by General Walker's instructions that the 7th Armored Division must bypass Metz—"if it doesn't fall like a ripe plum"—striking straight for

[2] XX Corps G–3 Jnl, 4 Sep 44; Ltr, Lt Col C. E. Leydecker (then CofS, 7th Armd Div) to Hist Div, 29 Jul 47; Ltr, Lt Gen Walton H. Walker to Hist Div, 8 Oct 47.

the Sarre River and its bridges. The two cities that formed the anchor positions for the German main line of resistance in front of the XX Corps, Metz and Thionville, were labeled as "Intermediate Objectives" and assigned as targets for the 5th and 90th Infantry Divisions respectively. But here again, as in the case of the armor, details of any long-range scheme of maneuver would have to await the seizure of a bridgehead east of the Moselle and more exhaustive intelligence on the enemy and the terrain.

The XX Corps commander now faced much the same problem as that encountered by von Moltke during the westward German advance in August 1870. Von Moltke, famous for the detail and exactness of his planning, had waited for the situation to clarify before deciding whether to make his flanking movement north or south of Metz. The head of the German *First Army* was on the Moselle before von Moltke finally gave the order for the southern crossing. Later, at the turn of the century, von Schlieffen examined this problem in a series of staff exercises on the defense of Metz, then, as in 1944, in German hands. Three factors led von Schlieffen to conclude that an advance along the western approaches to Metz offered considerable operational freedom and initiative to the attacker. First, defending field forces moving from east of the Moselle to counterattack would find it extremely difficult to defile in any strength through Metz and across its bridges. Second, the road net west of the Metz–Thionville position would permit the attacker to shift his weight quickly and with reasonable ease. Finally, the terrain to the north and the south would give almost equal facility for an advance from west to east.

The Enemy Situation

The XX Corps headquarters and higher intelligence echelons had relatively little information about the strength and the dispositions of the German forces along the Moselle. Earlier messages from the cavalry had indicated that the Germans were scattered and confused, and as late as 3 September the XX Corps G–2 reported: "There is every indication of enemy withdrawal." But on the following day additional information from the reconnaissance units to the front changed this optimistic appraisal with word of a considerable movement to reinforce Metz. By the night of 5 September the corps cavalry had encountered enough enemy resistance to give a general idea of the main German concentrations A strong, close-in defense system was already evident west of Metz, and the Germans showed every indication of making a stand at the Thionville bridge site. Some withdrawal was still in progress between Conflans and Briey, opposite the north wing of the XX Corps, but even in this area there were signs that the Germans would fight a delaying action in the rugged terrain west and northwest of Thionville. Few prisoners were being taken and their attitude had changed considerably, as compared with the demoralized and submissive mien shown in preceding days. Most of the captured now displayed the old German arrogance.

On 6 September, D Day for the new offensive, the XX Corps G-2 drew up an estimate of the possible German strength in front of the corps. He cautioned that, since the Metz-Luxembourg area was probably the most important center for German troop concentration and regrouping on the Western Front, enemy units might be found temporarily in the sector en route from this way station to other parts of the line. The *17th SS Panzer Grenadier Division* was known to have troops opposite the XX Corps, and some clues pointed to the possibility that elements of the *Panzer Lehr Division* and *21st Panzer Division* also might be encountered. Two panzer grenadier divisions, the *3d* and *15th*, had been identified on the Western Front in August, and since scattered detachments of the *3d Panzer Grenadier Division* had been thrown against the XX Corps during the withdrawal toward the Moselle it was expected that one or both of these divisions might be committed when the Americans resumed the advance. In addition, numerous small units, such as training and fortress battalions, had been engaged in delaying actions at the end of August and might substantially increase the strength of the German forces ahead. Altogether the XX Corps expected to meet a maximum of 38,500 enemy troops and 160 tanks and assault guns.

Less was known about the type, strength, and precise locations of the fortifications around Metz and along the Moselle than about the enemy troops. Existing aerial photographs gave very little detail of tactical value.[3] Camouflage was excellent throughout this fortified zone, as the Americans later learned to their cost, and on many of the works it had been enhanced by the natural growth of sod, bushes, and cultivation during the four years past. French intelligence officers from the 1940 *Deuxième Bureau* were consulted, but they, of course, knew little about the changes the Germans had made since the seizure of the Metz forts in the spring of 1940. American cavalry had fought for information, but were too weak to penetrate past the outlying

[3] TUSA MII (Military Intelligence Interrogation) Rpt, 8 Sep 44.

German positions. Furthermore, the American divisions had long since run out of detailed terrain maps and now were operating on road maps of the Michelin variety which gave little information on the configuration of the ground. As a result, all appraisals of the Metz–Moselle fortifications were little more than guesswork. In general, the XX Corps staff believed that this fortified system was of an outmoded, World War I vintage, in whose works the Germans might not be willing to risk a stand. Both the Third Army and XX Corps headquarters at this time tended to assume that the German forces at most would fight a delaying action at the line of the Moselle and that the main enemy stand would be made east of the Sarre River behind the works of the West Wall.[4]

Contrary to American intelligence estimates, Hitler and his military advisers in the headquarters of OKW had no intention of permitting the forces in the Metz–Thionville area to withdraw to the West Wall—or even so much as retreat behind the Moselle. Any organized resistance in the Metz area, as part of the defense of the Moselle "position" ordered by Hitler, entailed the disposition of German forces on the west bank of the Moselle, since the fortified system at Metz extended west as well as east of the river. And ultimately, when the Germans had been forced to withdraw behind the river line elsewhere along its length, they would continue the battle to hold the Metz "bridgehead" on the western bank.

On 5 September *OB WEST* estimated that the German troops available in the Metz–Thionville sector were equivalent in strength to four and a half divisions. Some order had been brought out of the chaos current in the last week of August, stragglers had been returned to their proper units, and an organized front could be presented to meet a continuation of the American advance. But the forces arrayed opposite the XX Corps represented a hodgepodge of miscellaneous battalions, detached regiments, and understrength divisions, which varied greatly in training, armament, and combat value from very good to poor.

Between Longuyon and Thionville, disposed at right angles to the Moselle, lay remnants of the *48th Division*, which had taken a severe beating in the retreat from the Chartres area during the last part of August and was due to be relieved as soon as fresh troops could be procured. Southwest of Thionville the *559th VG Division*, one of the new volksgrenadier divisions created by Hit-

[4] See XX Corps G–2 Jnl for this period. See also TUSA G–2 Periodic Rpt, 3 and 8 Sep 44.

ler to replace the units destroyed in the early summer, had just come up from Germany and by the night of 5 September had two of its infantry regiments in the line.[5] On the left of the *559th*, a miscellany of school and fortress troops, brigaded together under the staff of *Division Number 462*, was charged with the defense of Metz. Actually this "division" was an organizational makeshift, commanded by the faculty and administrative personnel of the German military schools located at Metz, and lacking both the service units and heavy weapons organic to a regular division. However, the rank and file of the student troops, picked for the most part for further training as officers and noncommissioned officers after having demonstrated superior abilities in the field, were among the elite of the German Army.[6] West of Metz small units of the *17th SS Panzer Grenadier Division* formed a covering force deployed along the Abbéville–Mars-la-Tour road, on the left of the *462d*. Although the *17th SS* had been heavily engaged in the Normandy battles and had fought a running rear guard action against the Third Army during the August retreat, it was still one of the better German divisions on the Western Front. The gaps in its ranks had been partially filled by the absorption of two SS panzer grenadier brigades, the *49th* and *51st*, which had been hurried into France from Denmark during the latter part of August. Since *OB WEST* was anxious to reconstitute reserves, almost entirely lacking during the withdrawal across northern France, orders had been given that the *17th SS Panzer Grenadier Division* be pulled back across the Moselle into a reserve position south of Metz and there refitted. This move began on 2 September, with the *462d* taking over the major share of the security line west of the city, but a few of the SS troops still were west of the river when the XX Corps began its attack. Actually, the *17th SS* did not complete its reorganization until 12 Sep-

[5] MS #A–972 (Muehlen). The *559th VG Division* had been intended for the Eastern Front and was officered by young veterans of the Russian fighting. The enlisted personnel was of fairly good caliber—some 60 percent of the division were in their twenties. The *559th* had been activated on 31 July and had little training as a unit.

[6] MS #B–042 (Krause). Generalleutnant Walther Krause commanded *Division Number 462*. One regiment came from the 1,800 members of the *Fahnenjunkerschule* (Officer Candidate School), reinforced by Wehrmacht stragglers who had been apprehended as they fled through Metz in late August. Its artillery consisted of six captured Russian guns, drawn by sick horses from the veterinary hospital at Metz. The second regiment was composed of about 1,500 men from the *Unterfuehrerschule* (NCO School), plus one battery. The *1010th Security Regiment*, which had fled east in front of the American drive in August, filled out *Division Number 462*. It numbered six companies, totaling about 600 men—mostly over-age and poorly armed. The Metz garrison also included two replacement battalions, one machine gun company, one engineer battalion, one or two Flak battalions, one artillery battalion, four companies of the *Waffen-SS Nachrichtenschule* (Signal School), and a few Luftwaffe troops.

tember. Farther to the south the *3d Panzer Grenadier Division*, deployed around Pont-à-Mousson on the east bank, covered the flank of the Metz position. This division subsequently engaged the XII Corps and took part in the fighting around Metz only during the first few days of the battle.

The two German armored divisions (*Panzer Lehr* and *21st Panzer*), which American intelligence had predicted might be encountered by the XX Corps, were no longer in the Metz sector, having been moved to other endangered parts of the front during the lull in the first days of September. A few tanks and assault guns had been salvaged by the infantry divisions, particularly the *17th SS*, but the only armored reserve available to the commander of the *First Army* was the untried *106th Panzer Brigade*, assembling in Luxembourg behind the *48th Division*.

The total German strength facing the XX Corps made a fairly impressive showing when paraded on the map in order of battle. In reality, however, the enemy forces constituted one demoralized and burned-out division, one untried and incomplete volksgrenadier division, one battle-weary SS division —lacking most of its tanks and assault guns but still possessed of good morale —one scratch "division" of heterogeneous units varying from very poor fortress troops to the trained and determined men from the Metz schools, and one panzer brigade whose potential strength was hardly that of an American armored combat command.

The Metz forts, when compared with the works of more modern construction in the Maginot Line and West Wall, were hardly formidable; but the attackers would assume that they were as the Lorraine Campaign progressed and the Germans proved their will to resist. Little had been done to modernize these fortifications during the years following 1919. The French had concentrated on the Maginot Line, farther to the east; and the Germans, after 1940, had given priority to arming the Channel coast. Some guns and steel plate had been taken from the Metz works and sent to the Atlantic Wall. Steel cupolas and bombproofs had been moved bodily to the industrial areas of the Ruhr and Rhineland as part of an air defense program. In July 1944, a few hundred civilian laborers had been drafted to work on the Metz fortifications, but they lacked equipment, concrete, wire and steel, and had accomplished little or nothing by the time the American attack finally came. Most of the forts lacked usable guns, ammunition, and fire control apparatus. Only Fort Driant had its fixed batteries functioning properly by 6 September, and even here some of the pieces were under repair as the Americans approached.

Communications between the various works were poor. Some of the lesser forts had no occupants at all; others were manned by skeleton garrisons. In short, the Metz garrison could not hope to rely upon a purely static defense behind an organized, modern, and well-armed wall of steel and concrete, for "Fortress Metz" possessed no such defensive capabilities at the moment of the XX Corps attack.

The military value of the Metz position lay not in the size of its garrison nor in the intrinsic strength of its numerous fortified works. Instead the long defense of Metz must be ascribed to a combination of factors favorable to the Germans: the presence of elite troops during the initial stages of the battle; the moral and physical strength derived from steel and concrete, even in outdated fortifications; and the possession of ground that favored the defender.

The eastern face of the Meuse plateau, whose heights average some 380 meters, falls sharply away to the plain of the Woëvre and a mean elevation of not more than 220 meters. In this plain the Imperial German armies had deployed for the bloody frontal attacks against the Verdun salient in 1916. Beyond the Woëvre the Moselle Plateau rises gradually to command the western approaches to Metz. The western edge of the plateau coincides roughly with the Conflans–Mars-la-Tour–Chambley road. The eastern heights, averaging 370 meters, drop abruptly to the Moselle River. East of the river some blocks of the Moselle Plateau reappear, but these are dominated by the higher ground on the west bank. The main plateau, if measured from Conflans to Metz, is about ten miles in depth. The western half is moderately rolling; on some roads the ascent to the east is barely perceptible. The eastern half of the plateau is high, rugged, and wooded, grooved by deeply incised ravines and innumerable shallow draws. It would be hard to imagine a terrain more compartmentalized and conducive to defense by small tactical bodies.

The Metz salient, as it confronted the XX Corps at the beginning of the September operation, extended for some eighteen miles in a perimeter west of Metz and the Moselle. On the left the German position rested on the Moselle near Arnaville, about nine and a half miles from the center of Metz. On the right a western affluent of the Moselle, the Orne, marked the limits of the German line, which was anchored near the village of Mondelange, approximately ten miles due north of Metz.

At the southern end of this bridgehead position, three ravines cut obliquely through the wooded Moselle scarps and defile down to the river channel. The Rupt de Mad, farthest from Metz, is traversed by a road that angles from

Mars-la-Tour via Chambley and reaches the Moselle at Arnaville. The middle road riverward can be entered either at Mars-la-Tour or at Rezonville. It then passes through the village of Gorze, lying in the main throat of the gorge to which it gives name, and attains the Moselle bank at Novéant. The third and northernmost of these ravines, the Mance, forms an "L" whose upright runs from north to south through a small depression in the Bois des Génivaux. Near Gravelotte this shallow gully descends into a deep draw, finally turning toward the east as a sharp cut between the plateaus crowned by the Bois de Vaux and the Bois des Ognons. Just east of Gravelotte the main highroad between Verdun and Metz dips to cross the Mance, while a secondary road branches south at Gravelotte and follows along the bottom of the ravine to Ars-sur-Moselle and the river.

These three defiles would canalize any attempt to turn the Metz position on the south by a drive to and across the Moselle. But a close-in envelopment or a frontal attack in this section would be hampered chiefly by the ravine of the Mance. In effect, therefore, the natural anchor position on the German left was formed by the lower Mance ravine, the plateau of the Bois de Vaux north of the ravine, and the plateau of the Bois des Ognons to the south. On the eve of World War I the German governors of Metz had reinforced this natural abutment by the construction of a heavily gunned fort on the river side of the Bois de Vaux plateau about a mile southwest of Ars-sur-Moselle. This strong work, renamed by the French in 1919 as Fort Driant, was sited so that its batteries dominated not only the southwestern approaches to Metz but the Moselle valley as well.

North and west of the Bois de Vaux two villages, Rezonville and Mars-la-Tour, served as outpost positions for the southern sector of the German front. They blocked the main road to Metz and controlled passage from north to south through the Mance and Gorze ravines. Beyond Gravelotte the Bois des Génivaux and the wood-bordered Mance combined in a strong defensive line and masked the German forts farther to the east. These rearward positions lay on the open crest of a long ridge whose western slopes were outposted by a sprinkling of isolated but strongly built farms.

North of the Bois des Génivaux the forward German troops occupied a plateau marked by the villages of Vernéville and Habonville. The strongest position in the German center, however, was farther to the east. Here the village of Amanvillers, located on a tableland, lay under the guns of forts hidden on wooded ridges to its rear. The Amanvillers plateau continued northward on the German right. In this area the forward defense line included the villages of St. Privat and Roncourt. To the rear rose a welter of rugged heights and heavy forests, running diagonally northeastward to the Orne. This northernmost portion was held only lightly. The main German line was a kind of switch position extending from the Bois de Jaumont along the Bois de Fêves ridge. This switch position was strengthened by a series of forts and walls. In this sector, however, the Moselle scarps do not come clear to the Moselle, as they do south of Metz. Here, in the area of Semécourt and Maizières-lès-Metz, a wide, level flood plain offered a gateway to the Metz position, once an attacker had cleared the western escarpment.

In sum, the ground west of Metz gave very considerable advantage to the defender. Long, open slopes provided a natural glacis in front of the main German positions. Wooded crests and ravines screened the movement of troops and supply from the eye of the attacker. Broken terrain permitted the most effective use of small defending groups. Ravines, draws, and thick wood lots offered ample opportunity for counterattack tactics, both in force and in patrol strength. Finally, the German soldier had used this terrain as a maneuver area and was prepared to exploit every accident of the ground.

The XX Corps Advance to the Moselle

On 5 September enough gasoline reached the XX Corps, by truck and plane, to permit General Walker to begin a concentration east of the Meuse bridgehead. The 5th Infantry Division moved forward from Verdun with no opposition and assembled along the line Jeandelize–St. Maurice, in what would be approximately the center and right when the corps began the attack toward the Moselle. (*Map XII*) In this position the infantry now screened the assembly areas around Verdun and Etain occupied by the 7th Armored. Since only enough gasoline remained to move one regimental combat team of the 90th Infantry Division, the 357th Infantry and the 90th Reconnaissance Troop advanced from Reims to cover the left wing of the corps northeast of Verdun. Bridging equipment, scattered in immobile trucks along the roads to the rear, and the corps artillery, mostly still west of the Meuse, were brought over the Verdun bridges as fast as quartermaster trucks laden with five-gallon gasoline cans arrived. By midmorning of 6 September, the day scheduled for the XX Corps attack, all battalions of the corps artillery were east of the Meuse and most of the bridging convoys were on the move to forward areas.

The remainder of the 90th Infantry Division assembled near Etain on 6 September, echeloned to the left and rear of the 5th Infantry Division and the 7th Armored. This movement completed the initial disposition of the corps for the eastward advance.

General Silvester, commanding the 7th Armored Division, had recommended that elements of his division be dispatched toward the Moselle, because of the obscure situation ahead, to undertake a reconnaissance in some force before the commitment of the main armored columns.[7] General Walker also wished to reinforce the corps cavalry and screen the advance scheduled for the afternoon of 6 September. About 0300 on the morning of the 6th, a strong combat reconnaissance force, commanded by Lt. Col. Vincent L. Boylan, set out toward the Moselle in four parallel columns, with orders to seize any intact bridges in the neighborhood of Metz.

The small cavalry detachments which had pushed out to the wings and already were engaged to the east had rough going as Boylan moved forward to their aid. South of Metz a small task force of the 3d Cavalry Reconnaissance Squadron succeeded in getting a few vehicles into Arnaville, but was driven out by artillery fire. Another task force that tried to cross on a ford at Ars-sur-Moselle was also beaten back. North of Metz the 43d Cavalry Reconnaissance Squadron had no better luck. But the cavalry actions had located possible fording sites south of Metz, near Pagny, Arnaville, and Ars-sur-Moselle, and had finally determined that all bridges in this sector were demolished.

Colonel Boylan's columns found the German resistance west of Metz stiffening as the morning wore on. When the four columns struck the *Fahnenjunkerschule* (Officer Candidate School) security line along the Fléville–Abbéville–Mars-la-Tour road, the enemy outposts, carefully dug in and supported by antitank guns, poured in a heavy fire. Colonel Boylan decided that his separate columns were too weak to advance alone, and about 1400 he shifted those on the left to reinforce the two columns on the right in an attempt to push through and join the cavalry south of Metz.

At this same hour the rest of the 7th Armored Division moved forward to mount the main attack. Since it was anticipated that the combat reconnaissance force under Boylan would either secure a crossing site or determine the most feasible location for bridging, no precise point seems to have been

[7] Ltr, Col Leydecker to Hist Div, 29 Jul 47.

fixed for the main division attempt to cross the Moselle.[8] The armor moved on an axis along the main highway linking Verdun and Metz, with CCA (Colonel Rosebaum) in two parallel columns on the left, CCB (Brig. Gen. John B. Thompson) deployed in the same fashion on the right, and CCR (Col. George H. Molony) following CCB. Most of General Silvester's command was refueled in time to take to the road, though even now the gasoline shortage forced CCB to leave the bulk of the 23d Armored Infantry Battalion, a company of light tanks, and a company of armored engineers back in bivouac. In the first hours of the advance only scattered German outposts were encountered. It therefore appeared that after Boylan's initial attack the enemy had begun to withdraw from the Fléville–Mars-la-Tour position. But about 1800 CCA found the Germans entrenched and waiting for a fight near Ste. Marie-aux-Chênes. Here the enemy fought stubbornly and the battle continued through the night. CCA did not reach the Moselle until the next morning.

Over to the right, CCB in the late afternoon met part of Colonel Boylan's force engaged in a fire fight west of Gravelotte, near which the Germans had emplaced a battalion of 88's. General Silvester ordered General Thompson to swing his combat command to the south of Boylan and continue toward the river. The north column assembled near Rezonville and in the twilight fought to dislodge a considerable body of German infantry and machine gunners located in the ravine east of the town on the edge of the Bois des Ognons. Farther to the south General Thompson's right column, commanded by Lt. Col. R. C. Erlenbusch, met raking shellfire as it passed around elements of the combat reconnaissance force at Buxières and approached the village of Gorze, which blocked the entrance to one of the narrow defiles leading to the Moselle. (*Map XIII*) One medium tank company of the 31st Tank Battalion attempted to thread a path past the town but was stopped by mines and antitank fire. Colonel Erlenbusch withdrew the tanks and sent B Company of the 23d Armored Infantry forward in an attempt to reach and cross the river under cover of night. The riflemen reached the canal west of the river; but as daylight came on 7 September the enemy troops in Arnaville and Novéant, discovering the Americans between them, concentrated their fire on the exposed company, causing heavy casualties. The infantry finally were withdrawn under covering fire from the American tanks west of Novéant and mortars firing smoke shells.

[8] *Ibid. Cf.* 7th Armd Div G–3 Jnl, 6 Sep 44. Here a field order, issued by 7th Armored Division headquarters at 1100 of that day, gives the division mission as the seizure of a crossing *north* of Metz.

Nevertheless CCB did succeed in reaching the Moselle. Just as General Thompson's north column was driving the German rear guard detachments out of the draw east of Rezonville on 6 September and night was coming on, Lt. Col. Leslie Allison arrived with a part of the 23d Armored Infantry Battalion, which had finally obtained gasoline for its half-tracks. General Thompson at once ordered the 23d (—) to push on to the river. The main road from Gravelotte to the Moselle descended through a narrow gorge which was strongly held by the enemy and heavily mined. Allison's scouts discovered a parallel road running through the woods on the right, and under cover of darkness the battalion fought its way along this woods road. About 0400, on 7 September, the 23d reached a little cluster of houses, known as le Chêne, on the river just north of Dornot. Now the battalion found itself in a precarious position, for as daylight came the Germans opened up with mortar fire and bullets from both sides of the river, while Fort Driant rained in shells from the heights southwest of Ars-sur-Moselle.[9] Colonel Allison turned the battalion to clear out Dornot, from which the fire was particularly deadly, and late in the afternoon the 23d attempted to put a patrol across the Moselle. This patrol was driven back by direct machine gun fire; two of the three assault boats were destroyed and a large number of the men in the patrol were killed.

The 23d Armored Infantry Battalion had been the first unit of the corps to reach and hold a position at the river. Later in the morning the left column of CCA broke through to Mondelange, ten miles north of Metz, and turned south of the riverside highway leading to Maizières-lès-Metz with the intention of finding a suitable site for a crossing attempt.[10] Shortly after noon the right column of CCA, which had been held up by a fight at St. Privat,[11] met the left column south of Talange. All the bridges in the sector had been destroyed, but a crossing site was found near Hauconcourt. The command came to a halt and waited for bridging materials and further orders, all the while under artillery fire from across the river. Colonel Rosebaum still expected to fight for a crossing north of Metz, as did General Silvester, who advised the corps commander that CCA had found a possible crossing site.

[9] Both banks of the Moselle at this point were held by the two replacement battalions, the *208th* and the *282d*. The contingent on the east bank crossed by ferry just ahead of the Americans. MS #B–042 (Krause). The approach by the south column, CCB, is described in a letter from Lt. Col. R. C. Erlenbusch to the Historical Division, 9 April 1948.

[10] This sector was held by a thin outpost line, formed by troops of the *Unterfuehrerschule*.

[11] At this point a battery of four 105-mm. howitzers reinforced the *Fahnenjunkerschule* positions.

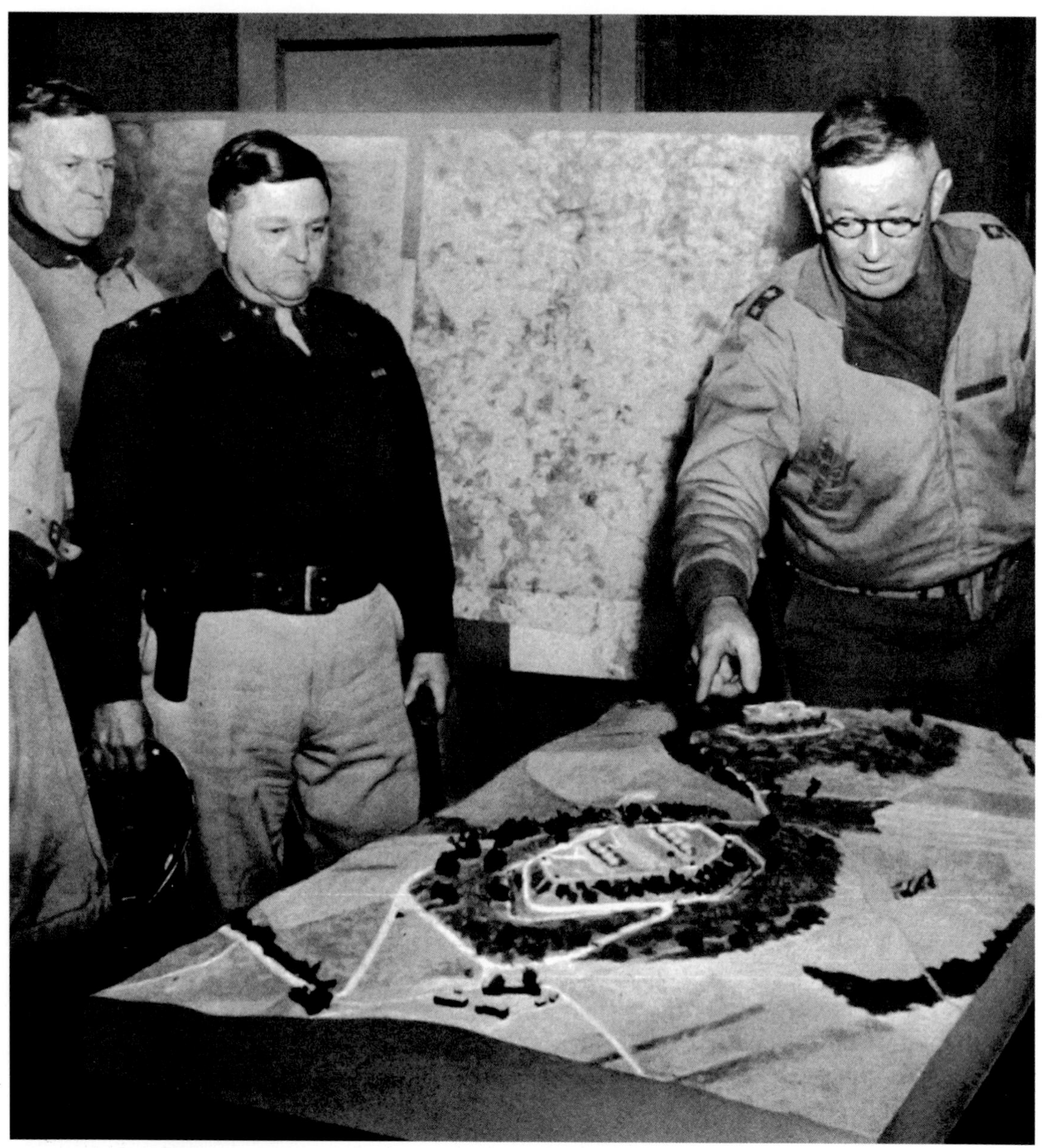

MAJ. GEN. WALTON H. WALKER, *XX Corps Commander (center), with Maj. Gen. S. Leroy Irwin, 5th Infantry Division, and Col. Paul O. Franson, General Irwin's chief of staff. Using a terrain model, General Irwin points out features of Verdun forts across the Moselle River at Dornot.*

On the morning of 7 September a part of CCB shook itself free from the Gorze defile and joined Colonel Allison's force on the river bank near Dornot. The combat command had no assault boats save the three with Allison and, indeed, was hard pressed to hold on the near bank as the German fire intensified and counterattack followed counterattack. Ars-sur-Moselle, north of Dornot, served the enemy as an assembly point for the most severe of these attacks. General Thompson, anxious to ease the pressure on the left flank of the 23d Armored Infantry Battalion and secure the crossing site, asked the division commander, who was at the combat command headquarters, to lend him CCR.[12] General Silvester agreed, and around 1120 CCR moved through Mars-la-Tour en route to launch an attack toward Ars-sur-Moselle. When the combat command was about halfway to the river the corps commander ordered the column to halt, in order to let the 5th Infantry Division through; CCR was then to return to corps reserve.

On the previous evening General Walker had told General Irwin to "pin onto" the tail of the 7th Armored Division and be prepared to fight for a bridgehead in the event that the armored attack failed. General Irwin was extremely concerned as to whether these orders called for the 5th to establish its own bridgehead on the corps' right, or pass through the 7th Armored elements already engaged. In the confused situation, with the corps headquarters meagerly informed as to the progress of CCB, no answer was forthcoming.[13] The 5th Infantry Division was somewhat dispersed on the morning of 7 September. General Irwin had expected to put its weight in an attack to the south of the 7th Armored elements and now found his division caught off balance. The 2d Infantry (Col. A. W. Roffe) had been brought forward behind the right wing of CCA with the mission of containing Metz by direct attack from the west. The 11th Infantry (Col. C. W. Yuill) was on the move east of Buxières, strung out along the roads behind and beside CCB. The 10th Infantry (Col. Robert P. Bell) remained in division reserve. Just before dawn twenty-two trucks rolled up with enough gasoline to fuel the vehicles of the 5th Division and mobilize it for the advance. At 0830 the 2d Infantry jumped off in a frontal attack with two battalions and moved past the Franco-Prussian War tombs and monuments. Three hours later, quite unaware of the enemy works ahead, the 2d slammed hard into a well-organized German defense line on the spur between Amanvillers and Vernéville held by the tough troops of

[12] Ltr, Col John B. Thompson (ret) to Hist Div, 17 Feb 47.

[13] 5th Inf Div G–3 Jnl, 7 Sep 44.

the *Fahnenjunkerschule* regiment. Losses were heavy, with fire from cleverly concealed machine guns and artillery sweeping across the front and flanks of the regiment. Here the 2d Infantry finally was checked in the first of a series of fruitless assaults on the western outworks of the Metz position.

At noon on 7 September, word reached General Irwin that he was to move through the 7th Armored Division and force a crossing at Dornot. He sent the 11th Infantry forward, CCR vehicles pulled over to the roadside to let the infantry through, and as night fell the regiment toiled slowly toward the high ground between Novéant and Dornot which was its objective. Mine fields and road blocks had to be cleared so as to bring up the trucks carrying assault boats, and the advance detachments were forced to break through the thin crust of German infantry that had re-formed in the wake of the American armor. Late in the evening General Walker told General Irwin to cross the Moselle on the following morning and use the 23d Armored Infantry Battalion to augment his own infantry. By midnight the 1st and 3d Battalions were about a thousand yards from the Moselle, and ready to cross the river to the south of CCB.

The Dornot Bridgehead[14]

Rain fell on the morning of 8 September and made the narrow and precipitous road through the Gorze defile slippery and treacherous. Troops and vehicles of CCB and the 11th Infantry were compressed on the narrow strip along the river between le Chêne and Dornot with enemy fire raking into the mass from the flanks, where the Germans still held on the west bank, and from across the river. Attempts were made to pull the armored vehicles out of the area, but this two-way movement resulted only in a traffic jam at Gorze. Orders were confused and, although General Walker verbally had given General Irwin command of all troops in the Dornot area, some time elapsed before a real co-ordination between CCB and the 5th Division troops could be introduced.

Around 0600 the 7th Engineer Combat Battalion reached the river's edge with some infantry assault boats, and the 2d Battalion of the 11th Infantry

[14] The history of the Dornot bridgehead is taken from Historical Division Combat Interviews obtained by 2d Lt. F. M. Ludden. The S–1 Journal of the 2d Battalion, 11th Infantry, is fragmentary; that of the 23d Armored Infantry Battalion has little for this period. See *Eleventh Infantry,* which derives most of its information from the Historical Division Combat Interviews.

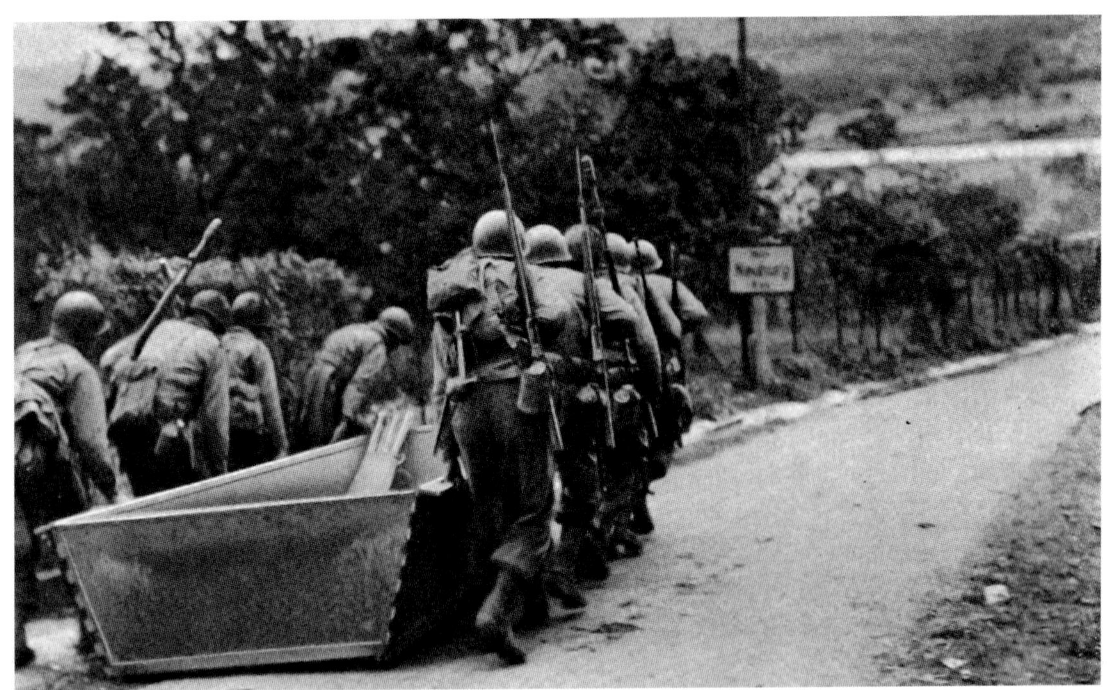

RIVER CROSSING AT DORNOT. *Infantrymen (above) carry assault boat down to the Moselle, and (below) members of 2d Battalion, 11th Infantry, cross the river at Dornot.*

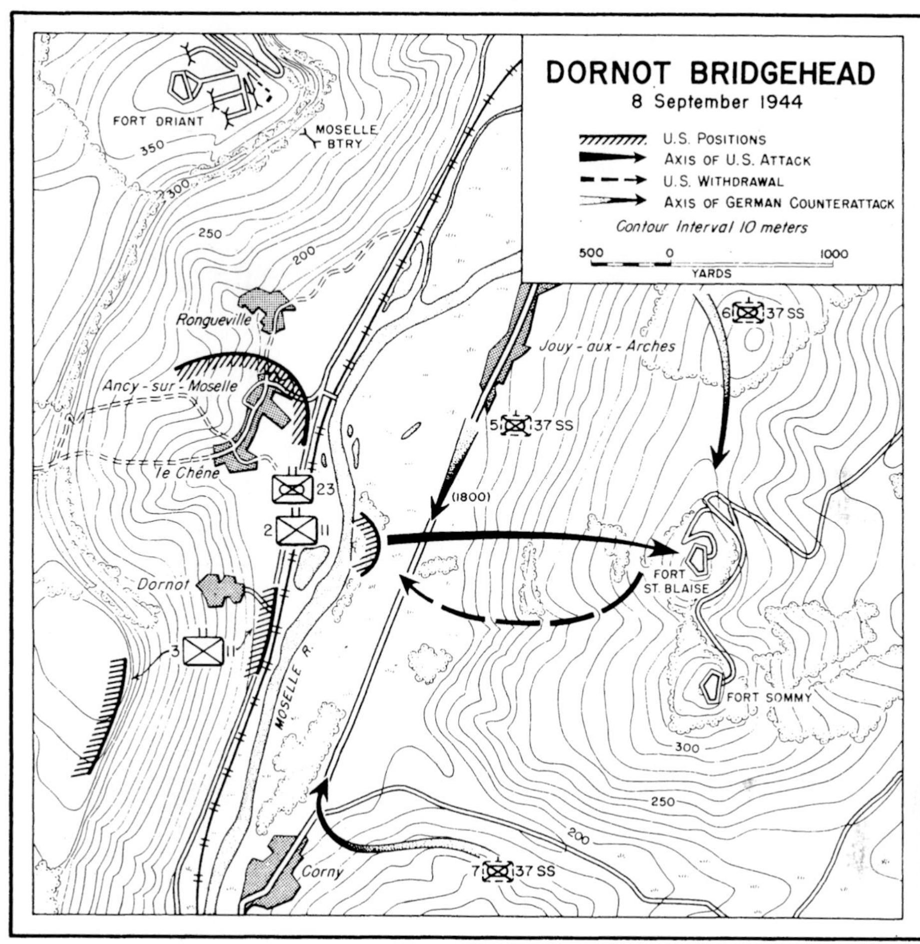

MAP NO. 3

(Lt. Col. Kelly B. Lemmon), chosen to make the first crossing, was in position to embark. During the previous night, General Thompson, the CCB commander, despairing of receiving the needed assault boats, had gone back in person and secured them. These boats, added to those brought down to the river by the infantry, seemed sufficient for the attempt. All chance of success by speed and surprise had long since vanished. This would be a frontal attack against what appeared to be a well-fortified position, with an enemy already engaging in continuous fire from *both* banks of the river. Under these circumstances General Irwin decided to postpone the attack until his artillery

TO JOUY-AUX-ARCHES

FORT ST. BLAISE
FORT SOMMY
TO CORNY

could displace forward to firing positions on the bluffs and some degree of co-ordination could be achieved between the armored infantry battalion and his own. Eventually the two commanders concerned made their own arrangements and General Thompson organized the crossing attack.[15] The 23d Armored Infantry Battalion by this time had incurred such losses as to reduce it to less than half its normal strength, and was further depleted when one company was committed to hold the left flank on the near side of the river. The 2d Battalion of the 11th Infantry, therefore, had to furnish the major share of the strength in the assault crossing.

Three battalions of 105-mm. howitzers finally were brought into position to support the assault, and about 1045 the crossing began just east of Dornot, where the river was only some hundred yards wide. The rest of the 11th Infantry and elements of CCB squared off to hold the position on the west bank. (*Map 3*) By 1320 Companies F and G, reinforced by a few armored infantrymen, were across the Moselle, together with heavy machine guns and 81-mm. mortars. Here the assault force re-formed in a patch of trees close to the river bank. German fire thus far was sporadic. But the American howitzers were strictly rationed in their use of ammunition, and whenever they ceased fire enemy mortars lobbed shells onto the crossing site, destroying several assault boats.[16] Little was known about the structure of Forts Sommy and Blaise, but they were obviously impervious to light artillery, and urgent requests for air support filtered back through higher headquarters all through the morning. At 1330 General Irwin was told that he could expect no planes because, as was so often the case early in that September, all available aircraft were being diverted far back to the west in an all-out attempt to smash the great fortifications at Brest.[17]

In the late afternoon the two assault companies, commanded by Capt. Ferris Church, S–3 of the 2d Battalion, moved out of the shelter of the trees and began a slow advance up the slope toward the forts, more than two thousand yards east of the river. The forts themselves were strangely quiet,[18] and the

[15] On this same date Brig. Gen. John B. Thompson was relieved, despite his personal efforts to restore some order in the confused situation at the crossing site. Lt. Col. A. J. Adams took command of CCB.

[16] Pvt. William E. Hall, 7th Engineer Combat Battalion, 5th Infantry Division, had two assault boats sunk under him by artillery fire on 8 September but continued to man a third all through the night and into the next day, when he was killed by a shell. He was awarded the DSC posthumously.

[17] See Chap. I, p. 20.

[18] The Germans had manned neither of the two forts and, when the American advance began, had only a small covering force along the east bank. MS #B–042 (Krause).

Americans suffered no loss until a sniper killed the commander of Company F near the top of the hill. Here the infantry came to the wire at the north fort (Fort Blaise), cut it, and then, faced by a moat and a causeway barred by an iron portcullis, drew back to radio for help from the artillery. While so disposed the two companies suddenly were hit by the *2d Battalion* of the *37th SS Panzer Grenadier Regiment* which swept in on both flanks and filtered through to their rear. Captain Church called for Companies E and K to come forward from the east bank, to which they had crossed during the afternoon; but they could not advance through the heavy enemy fire now traversing the slope, and the two forward companies began to withdraw, leaving dead and wounded marking the path. For nearly three hours the infantry crawled back through the gauntlet. The company aid men tried bravely to give help to the wounded left behind but were shot down at their tasks.[19] Most of the survivors did not reach the clump of woods near the river until 2300, here joining the rear companies in the defense of the minuscule bridgehead.

The four infantry companies, reinforced by forty-eight men of the 23d Armored Infantry Battalion whom Colonel Allison had brought across the river, dug a horseshoe line of foxholes just inside the edge of the woods and prepared to defend this narrow pocket, only 300 yards deep and 200 yards wide. East of the woods a highway paralleled the tree line and in the darkness enemy Flak tanks drove up and down, spraying the bridgehead with bullets and shell fragments. Fortunately, the German tanks, though protected by "bazooka pants," would not close with the Americans in the woods, and the attacks that followed through this night and succeeding days devolved on the enemy infantry.

The Arnaville Bridgehead

The precarious American foothold on the enemy bank east of Dornot was only nominally a bridgehead. There was no space for maneuver and no room through which additional troops could be passed to expand the line. In addition German 88's were sited for direct fire on the river segment west of the woods and made bridging impossible. General Irwin still had at hand the 10th Infantry, in the vicinity of Chambley, nearly two battalions of the 11th

[19] Cpl. William G. Rea, an aid man with the 11th Infantry, was awarded the DSC for heroic efforts to evacuate the casualties in front of his own lines. He carried one wounded soldier for three hundred yards under direct enemy fire.

Infantry, and the heterogeneous elements of CCB. On the night of 8 September he decided to bring up the 10th Infantry and commit it in a crossing about two and a half miles south of the 11th Infantry. Only vague reports filtered across from the 2d Battalion, 11th Infantry, during 9 September, and repeated requests for air support to ease the pressure on the bridgehead brought no help. General Irwin believed that the Dornot bridgehead was too rigidly contained to be of further value and wished to withdraw the troops there. But General Walker insisted that this foothold on the east bank would have to be maintained until another bridgehead was secured. Uncertain as to the exact situation across the river the division commander sent word for the 2d Battalion to push to the south and there link up with the 10th Infantry, whose crossing was set for the early hours of 10 September.

Preparations for the 10th Infantry assault crossing were carefully made. Artillery and tank destroyers were emplaced forward but found that the self-propelled guns across the river made difficult targets. The night before the attack the 84th Smoke Generating Company arrived on the scene. For some time past this company had been assigned to supply duties on the Red Ball Express route. The tactical employment of the 84th, now to be engaged in its first fight, would mark the initial attempt by the Third Army at large area smoke screening. Subsequently the use of smoke was to become standard procedure in Third Army river crossings. At this stage, however, the chemical troops were inexperienced and their use was not widely understood. But so long as the casemate artillery at Fort Driant had observation on the river from the west bank, and so long as the roving guns on the east bank could move freely within range of the river, all hope of throwing a bridge across, or of keeping it intact, rested with the smoke generators.

About 0200 that morning the 10th Infantry sent its first boatloads across the Moselle, choosing a site between Novéant and Arnaville. (*Map XIII*) The crossings were made quickly and easily, catching the enemy, whose attention was riveted on the 11th Infantry, completely by surprise. By 0720 the leading companies of the 1st and 2d Battalions were east of the river and astride the initial regimental objective. This objective had been chosen after a study of the only detailed maps available (the 1:50,000 sheets). These showed a partially wooded ridge line about a thousand yards from the river, running north from Hill 386, which rose in the midst of the Bois des Anneaux. Since no map sheets were at hand for the area east of this ridge line it was designated as an objective without knowledge of the fact that Hill 386, instead of being the key feature in the area, was commanded by Hill 396, a thousand yards farther to the east.

The 1st Battalion (Maj. W. H. Haughey) had little difficulty and occupied Hill 386 after dispersing a small enemy detachment in a short, sharp attack with marching fire and the bayonet. On the left the 2d Battalion (Maj. W. E. Simpson) took Hill 370 and the Bois de Gaumont in much the same way. The 1st Battalion was just in the process of deploying along an outpost line when the first German counterattack, made by tanks and infantry of the *17th SS Panzer Grenadier Division*, came out of Arry and struck the two companies on the right flank. A wild melee ensued, but the Americans finally beat off the tanks with bazookas, dispersed the German infantry, and gained a breathing spell in which to reorganize and entrench. About noon the enemy in Arry gathered a battalion of infantry, plus what the American outposts estimated to be a score of tanks or assault guns, and returned to the attack. This time the 1st Battalion was forced to give ground.[20] Eventually the German assault was smashed by the fire of American artillery and tank destroyers across the Moselle, reinforced by the machine guns and bombs of some P–47's which arrived on the scene late in the afternoon.

This intervention by the Third Army's old ally, the XIX Tactical Air Command, marked the beginning of nearly continuous air-ground co-operation in the fight to cross the Moselle and capture Metz. Early on 9 September the Ninth Air Force had turned down the Third Army request for support at the river, ruling that the XX Corps assault could be adequately supported by artillery. That evening the reports of a steadily worsening situation at the 5th Infantry Division crossing site convinced the G–3 air officer in 12th Army Group headquarters that help must be given or the shaky foothold east of the river lost. Thereupon, he authorized the Ninth Air Force to release as many of the XIX TAC fighter-bombers from the primary target at Brest as General Weyland, commanding the XIX TAC, should deem necessary for air support at the bridgehead.[21] General Weyland's command still had many responsibilities—bombing at Brest, attacking at Nancy, protecting the exposed southern

[20] Capt. William B. Davis, commanding officer of C Company, was wounded in both legs but strapped a radio on his back and continued to direct the American artillery fire. When the Germans were close to his company he dragged himself back to organize a defense. His men forcibly placed Captain Davis on a stretcher, but he was killed by a shell fragment as he lay there. *Fifth Infantry Division*. Major Haughey, commanding officer of the 1st Battalion, also distinguished himself by personal bravery and leadership in repelling the fierce German counterattacks. He received the DSC.

[21] Ninth AF Opns Jnl, 9 Sep 44.

flank of the Third Army, and flying cover for the heavy bombers over Germany.[22] But on 10 September the P-47's arrived opportunely to aid the troops in the Arnaville bridgehead.

Through the afternoon the enemy in Arry threatened to roll up the south flank of the 10th Infantry, launching attack after attack but to no avail, for across the river thirteen artillery battalions now were in position to support the bridgehead force. The few German tanks that managed to get through the shellfire were driven off by the infantrymen's bazookas. Late in the evening Colonel Bell sent two fresh companies of the 3d Battalion, which had just arrived in the bridgehead, to make a sortie into Arry. They took the town, but the 10th was spread too thinly to permit such a diminution of its rifle strength and the two companies were pulled out of Arry, shortly before midnight, to form a bridgehead reserve.

Back at the river a series of mishaps had occurred. About 1000 the winds over the Moselle valley had shifted, blowing the American smoke screen away to the west. German fire promptly searched out the generators, some of the green crews left their apparatus, and conflicting orders delayed reorganization. Eventually the 84th was shifted to new positions and by nightfall had a fog oil screen floating for a distance of between six to eight miles over the valley.

During the night of 10–11 September the 1103d Engineer Combat Group (Lt. Col. George E. Walker) began to put in a bridge, a task that had proved impossible in daylight, under constant enemy artillery fire accurately directed by forward observers close to the bridging site. A ferry was started and worked steadily during the night. By this means a smoke generator platoon was crossed to cover the operations at the river in the event of a shift in wind. All of the battalion 57-mm. antitank guns were ferried over, as well as extra bazookas and ammunition.[23] Evacuation of casualties had continued all through the day despite the German fire, and by dark 142 dead and wounded had been removed from the bridgehead—representing only a part of the day's losses.

The plan to sideslip the meager forces in the 11th Infantry bridgehead, opposite Dornot, and join them with the 10th Infantry was abandoned when

[22] This period is covered in outline in XIX TAC, A Rpt on the Combat Opns of the XIX TAC, 30 May 45.

[23] During the night German patrols infiltrated back to the river and attacked American carrying parties. Next day 1st Lt. Eugene Dille, who had crossed with extra bazookas, was found dead surrounded by thirty-five dead Germans. *Fifth Infantry Division*.

the regimental commander reported that "the men are all shot." Since the 10th Infantry now had a foothold on the east bank of the Moselle, General Irwin ordered the evacuation of the Dornot bridgehead. The withdrawal by the 2d Battalion and the little contingent of armored infantry on the night of 10–11 September ended an episode colored by countless deeds of personal heroism and distinguished by devotion to duty. Thirty-six separate assault attempts had been hurled against the men in the horseshoe without breaking the thin American line. Indeed, on the morning of 10 September, the Americans had the superb effrontery to send a demand that the Germans surrender, The War Diary of the *37th SS Panzer Grenadier Regiment* noting that the Americans promised such a concentration of fire as their enemies had never seen before if they did not capitulate forthwith. The determined infantry and their supporting artillery killed an estimated six hundred Germans in this bitter fight, and the toll of enemy wounded was probably very high. Detachments of at least four enemy battalions, reinforced by tanks and assault guns, were thrown against the bridgehead in the three-day battle, making their attacks with a ferocity and determination that astounded the Americans.[24] The American commander in the bridgehead, Capt. Jack Gerrie, passed word back to the 10th Infantry on the morning of 10 September: "Watch out for these birds, they are plenty tough. I've never run across guys like these before, they are new, something you read about. . . ." Time after time the German grenadiers came forward in close order, shouting "Heil Hitler" and screaming wildly, only to be cut down by small arms fire from the woods and exploding shells from the field guns on the opposite side of the Moselle. But each attack took its toll of the defenders in the horseshoe. The wounded were forbidden to moan or call out for aid, so that the Germans would not know the extent of the losses they had inflicted. The mortar crews abandoned their weapons, whose muzzle blast betrayed the location of the foxhole line, and took up rifles from the dead. A lieutenant operated his radio with one hand and fired his carbine with the other. Nearly all the officers were killed or wounded when they left their foxholes to encourage the riflemen or inspect the position. Each night volunteers carried the wounded to the river, crossed them in bullet-

[24] Enemy units identified here were: the *208th Replacement Battalion* (a stomach ulcer battalion); the *2d Battalion, 8th Panzer Grenadier Regiment (3d Panzer Grenadier Division)*; the *2d Battalion, 51st SS Panzer Grenadier Brigade (17th SS Panzer Grenadier Division)*; and the *4th SS Signal Battalion* (part of the *Waffen-SS Nachrichtenschule*). A detailed report of this action (as seen from the enemy side of the hill) was prepared by the *37th SS Panzer Grenadier Regiment, 17th SS Panzer Grenadier Division*. It may be found in the *Feldgericht* file of the same unit in GMDS.

ridden and leaking assault boats, then returned immediately to the firing line.[25]

The final evacuation of the bridgehead began at dark on 10 September, after two men swam the river to carry the order to Captain Gerrie, and was completed about midnight under cover of an intense protective barrage. Weapons and clothing were left behind as the able-bodied stripped to swim the river, leaving space in the assault craft for the wounded. Many drowned in the swift current. Others were killed by enemy fire sweeping the river. Company K of the 3d Battalion, which had reinforced the 2d Battalion in the horseshoe, came out of the three-day battle with fifty men and no officers. The three rifle companies of the 2d Battalion had only two officers among them and their total casualties numbered over three hundred.[26] The 23d Armored Infantry Battalion, which had fought on both sides of the river, likewise suffered severely and sustained two hundred casualties in its four days of action.[27]

The Fight to Expand the 5th Division Bridgehead

In the early hours of 11 September the 10th Infantry, in the Arnaville bridgehead, held the only footing the XX Corps possessed on the east bank of the Moselle River. East of Toul, in the XII Corps zone, the 3d Battalion of the 319th Infantry had a small bridgehead at the tip of the Moselle tongue. South of Nancy assault units of the 35th Infantry Division and the 4th Armored Division were forming up for a predawn crossing attempt between

[25] Pfc. George T. Dickey and Pfc. Frank Lalopa, both of K Company, 11th Infantry, were awarded the DSC posthumously for bravery in the fight for the bridgehead. The two soldiers volunteered to man a forward observation post during the night. When the Germans attacked, Dickey and Lalopa were warned to return to their lines. Instead they stayed at their posts and fired into the advancing Germans until they were both killed. Next morning twenty-two enemy were found by their bodies, some within three yards. Pvt. Dale B. Rex, G Company, 11th Infantry, also was awarded the DSC and was cited by his comrades as one of the leading figures in the bridgehead defense. For three days Rex manned a machine gun at an outpost. It was later estimated that he had killed some three hundred Germans. On the night of the evacuation Rex swam the river four times under shellfire in order to bring back assault boats to carry the wounded. Numerous deeds of heroism by other members of the little force in the bridgehead went unnoticed in this battle where personal bravery became the commonplace.

[26] 11th Inf Periodic Rpt, 11 Sep 44. The anonymous writer of *Eleventh Infantry* sets the casualty figures for the 2d Battalion and K Company at 363.

[27] 23d Armd Inf Bn AAR, Sep 44. Colonel Allison, commanding officer of the 23d Armored Infantry Battalion, was evacuated from the bridgehead on 10 September with a serious wound from which he died six days later. He had commanded the elements of B and C Companies, 23d Armored Infantry Battalion, that fought as a platoon of G Company, 11th Infantry.

ARNAVILLE CROSSING, *after bridgehead had become firmly established. On the left is fording site used during initial stage of the operation.*

Crévéchamps and Bayon, but success or failure on the army's right flank could not be expected to have any immediate repercussions on the enemy containing the 5th Division. Although the Germans had failed to engulf the Arnaville bridgehead, there was still no bridge to the east bank, nor adequate force across to expand the lodgment area.

On the night of 10 September General Irwin had given orders that "at all costs" a bridge must be put across the Moselle before morning. Much preparatory work was required, however, and no bridge was in position when daylight came. East of Arnaville the Moselle had a width of about eighty yards and a swift current. The bridging problem, moreover, was complicated by mud and swamps on both banks of the river, by a canal flowing parallel to the river on the west, and by an east-west tributary of the Moselle which bisected the 5th Division zone just opposite the 10th Infantry bridgehead. The engineers thus had to bridge the tributary, the canal, and a wide area of swampland before bridging equipment could be brought up to the main channel of the Moselle—all this under constant fire from the east bank. Furthermore, the river was too low in September to float a heavy ponton bridge. A partial solution was achieved by laying sections of a treadway bridge on the soft river bottom at a ford just north of the point where the canal briefly leaves the main river channel. This fording site was ready about 1100, but the depth of the stream, while permitting passage of dismounted troops, made it unusable for vehicular traffic.

On 11 September at dawn, a time favored by the enemy for local counterattacks, both flanks of the 10th Infantry were hit by infantry and tanks. The 1st Battalion suffered less than on the previous day and the Germans were driven back to Arry in short order, although the battalion antitank guns, posted to cover the approaches from Arry, were overrun by the enemy tanks. However, the 2d Battalion, deployed along the Côte de Faye, encountered a much stronger force and lost 102 men in a bitter fight during which the enemy managed to infiltrate into the American lines. But the attack faltered as rifle and machine gun fire continued to cut the Germans down, and they finally drew off, only to come under a shelling by the American batteries across the river.

Meanwhile reinforcements had crossed into the bridgehead and begun to expand the perimeter held by the 10th Infantry. Early in the morning General Irwin sent the 11th Infantry to make a crossing east of Novéant. His intention was to bring the 11th in on the left flank of the 10th Infantry and further stabilize the bridgehead by the seizure of the village of Corny, which the Germans were using as a sally port into the bridgehead area. Two companies reached an island, formed by the river and canal, and then found the opposite bank too steep to bring in heavy weapons. The companies retraced their steps and crossed directly into the 10th Infantry sector. But an antitank platoon, which had been ferried across at a more favorable point near the original site, was not alerted to this change of plans and went straight into Corny where it was cut to pieces and lost its 57-mm. antitank guns. By 1000 the 11th Infantry had the 3d Battalion and two companies of the 1st Battalion east of the river and ready to execute the plan for the advance to the north. All through the afternoon the 3d Battalion inched its way toward Corny under the fire of the German batteries at Fort Driant, some 4,500 yards distant. Casualties were heavy, but the battalion managed to reach the edge of the village and there reorganized as night came on.

The 10th Infantry sector remained rather quiet after the counterattacks in the early morning, probably because the 512th Squadron of the XIX TAC had descended on Arry and knocked out some ten German tanks and assault guns. Later in the day German artillery fire increased in tempo; artillery observers identified a total of forty German batteries firing on the Arnaville sector. Since the larger portion of the surrounding heights was still in enemy hands, American counterbattery fire was not very effective. Then, too, the shortage of artillery ammunition, chronic through all the Third Army in early September, was beginning to quiet the XX Corps artillery. On the two previous days the corps had fired about 20,000 artillery rounds per day, which had eaten heavily into its allotment and now forced a drastic curtailment in counterbattery and harassing fire. Again, as at the time of the gasoline shortage, the soldier fighting for his life found it hard to understand these logistical difficulties. One irate officer in the bridgehead, whose request for a fire support mission had been denied, asked sardonically, "Do they want us to come back, and duck, and throw stones?" Fortunately, air support was able to take over some of the artillery missions. Through the afternoon of 11 September more planes were diverted to support the 5th Division than in previous days,[28] bombing and strafing Arry and Corney, breaking up German formations as they moved up to attack positions, and by their very presence in the air periodically silencing the German batteries.

[28] XIX TAC flew 411 sorties on this date, about equally divided between Brest and the Moselle front of the Third Army. XIX TAC Morning Summary, 12 Sep 44.

A few tanks and tank destroyers were moved across to stiffen the American bridgehead line. Bombers had made a direct hit on a dam impounding the water near the fording site and so reduced the river level as to make vehicular fording possible. However, the continuous German fire made this ford hazardous. The treadway on the river bottom was literally blown out from under the first tank destroyers to cross, constant repairs were imperative, and at the end of the day only six tank destroyers and ten tanks were on the east bank of the river.

The Germans resumed their assault on the bridgehead at 0330 on 12 September, using troops from the *17th SS*, *3d*, and *15th Panzer Grenadier Divisions*. This time they came on in a co-ordinated attack striking at all sections of the American line, close behind a heavy barrage which rolled up the hills and ridge line and over onto the rearward slopes where lay the infantry reserves. On the right of the 10th Infantry, a battalion of German infantry and a company of tanks made the attack. American artillery mowed down the first waves, but two companies managed to break into the lines of the 1st Battalion; there most of the German grenadiers were killed in a hand-to-hand fight. Tanks led the enemy infantry against the extreme left flank of the bridgehead, where a composite battalion of the 11th Infantry had a slim hold on Corny. Four German tanks rolled through the darkness into the streets of the village: an American tank destroyer destroyed one, a 57-mm. antitank gun crew accounted for a second, and the others fled. Capt. Harry Anderson and eleven men of B Company killed twenty-two Germans and captured twenty-eight in a furious encounter at the company command post. But elsewhere in Corny the defenders suffered severely before artillery and tank destroyer fire repelled the German attack. When daylight came, the remaining enemy withdrew all along the line, leaving the Americans still in possession of the bridgehead perimeter. That night the *15th Panzer Grenadier Division* began a move from Arnaville south to the Nancy sector, leaving the *17th SS* to continue the battle.

During the night of 11–12 September the engineers had labored to complete a bridge, all the while under fire from Fort Driant and from German assault guns that had been run down close to the east bank of the river. Sections of the bridge were blown to bits as soon as they were completed and nearly a fourth of the two bridging companies were casualties in this single night. At noon on 12 September, the bridge was completed under fog-smoke and the 31st Tank Battalion, reinforced by a company of tank destroyers, both from CCB, 7th Armored Division, joined the troops in the bridgehead. The appearance of this reinforcement came opportunely, for the infantry were tired from constant alerts and shaky from the continuous pounding administered by the German guns. General Irwin, however, felt the need of more infantry before beginning a drive out of the bridgehead, and asked for additional reinforcements. The combat strength of the 5th Infantry Division was gravely reduced, short 35 officers and 1,300 riflemen. The 2d Infantry, attached to the 7th Armored Division, was closely engaged west of Metz; and CCB, which had been traded to General Irwin for the 2d Infantry, had lost much of its armored infantry in fighting at the river. The corps commander briefly considered a plan to aid General Irwin by stripping the central sector west of Metz, moving CCA south to the bridgehead, and gambling on the ability of the 2d Infantry to continue the holding attack in the central sector alone. But the 7th Armored Division commander advised that it would take more than one infantry regiment to contain the Germans west of Metz; therefore, General Walker turned to a plan for a wider reshuffling all along the XX Corps front which would free the forces needed to expand the bridgehead.[29]

The Battle West of Metz

When the battle began for a crossing site at the Moselle on 7 September, the center and north wing of the XX Corps were moving forward as part of the general advance ordered for the Third Army. General Patton's forces were still somewhat ahead of the other Allied armies driving across northern France and his northern flank hung in the air. The V Corps, the closest First Army unit on the left, had just begun to cross the Semoy River east of Sedan.[30] Therefore, the 90th Infantry Division, forming the north wing of the XX Corps, was forced to start the drive toward Thionville and the Moselle with its regiments echeloned to the left rear along a front of some twenty miles.

In the corps center, CCA of the 7th Armored Division led off on the south flank of the 90th and early on 7 September had thrust its way on a narrow front to the Moselle north of Metz. (*Map XIV*) Next in the line of battle to the south the 2d Infantry under Colonel Roffe pushed straight east toward

[29] 5th Inf Div G–3 Jnl, 12 Sep 44.

[30] FUSA Rpt of Opns, 1 Aug 44–22 Feb 45, p. 42. On 7–8 September a shortage of gasoline in General Gerow's V Corps forced the 5th Armored Division, which had led the advance north of the Third Army boundary, to slow down. *V Corps Operations in ETO* (Paris, 1945), pp. 236–238.

Metz, cavalry task forces and miscellaneous patrols linking it tenuously with CCA on the north and the main body of the 5th Infantry Division on the south. On 8 September General Walker took cognizance of the diverse missions in the corps and in effect created one command in the corps center and another in the bridgehead area on the right wing, by attaching the 2d Infantry to General Silvester's 7th Armored Division and giving CCB to General Irwin. This change in command did not alter the mission of the 2d Infantry. The regiment had to continue the frontal attack toward Metz and by constant pressure contain the German forces west of the city, forces that might otherwise be shifted to meet the American threat at Dornot and Arnaville. Nor could the 2d Infantry expect much help from the armor to which it was now attached, for the western approaches to Metz were far too heavily fortified to permit tank maneuver and could be tackled, if a frontal attack was employed, only by the foot-slogging infantry.

The 2d Infantry attack, initiated by two rifle battalions along the Amanvillers–Vernéville–Gravelotte line on 7 September, met mines, concrete bunkers and pillboxes, extremely accurate and sustained artillery fire, and repeated counterattacks by the *Fahnenjunkerschule Regiment* of *Division Number 462* and detachments of the *17th SS*. But at this juncture the regiment was not yet up against the main Metz outworks and had been given only a foretaste of what was to come. Ahead lay what once had been one of the most heavily fortified areas on the European continent. Limited intelligence information and inadequate ground and air reconnaissance, during the hurried drive to the Moselle, forced the 2d Infantry to attack blindly, groping in the midst of battle to feel out the contours of the German defense line. All the advantage was on the side of the enemy, who was fighting from steel and concrete, knew every yard of the ground, and held the main heights which gave observation over the area and facilitated counterattacks. Furthermore there was a hard core in the heterogeneous troops facing the 2d Infantry, tough products of the Metz military schools, now formed into special assault detachments and burning to distinguish themselves. These units were not content to fight a simple delaying action, but adhered rigidly to the German tactical doctrine of continuous local counterattacks designed to recover all lost ground and bar the approaches to the separate fortifications.

Early on the morning of 8 September a large German raiding party filtered into the lines of the 1st Battalion (Maj. W. H. Blakefield) and killed or captured two officers and sixty-six men before it could be driven off. Some time elapsed before the regiment could reorganize to continue the attack, and when its advance began, now with all three battalions in the line, the going became progressively tougher. At the end of the day the 2d Battalion (Lt. Col. Leslie K. Ball), in the center of the line, held Vernéville. The 1st Battalion reached the edge of Amanvillers but suffered such heavy losses from hostile artillery fire that it could not drive into the village.

General Silvester detached Task Force McConnell from CCA to support the infantry in the attack set for the following day. A new plan called for Task Force McConnell to turn the north flank of the German forces facing the 2d Infantry along the Amanvillers–Gravelotte line with a semicircular sweep out of St. Privat around to the east of Amanvillers and back toward Montigny. During the morning of 9 September American artillery, tanks, and tank destroyers blasted away at the known locations of German fortifications and batteries, and at 1330 the infantry and armor moved into the attack. Task Force McConnell proceeded only a short distance down the road east of St. Privat before coming under fire from the heights in the Bois de Jaumont and the guns in Fort Kellermann. The German batteries knocked out seven tanks and two self-propelled guns and forced the column to fall back through St. Privat. Here Colonel McConnell turned to execute a close-in thrust at Amanvillers from the north, with the intention of joining the 1st Battalion, 2d Infantry. The 1st Battalion, still fighting to enter the town from the west, had lost some ground to counterattacks coming in on its right flank and was pinned down by artillery fire from the Lorraine Forts.[31] When seven battalions of American field artillery opened up on these works, their fire subsided briefly; but field pieces had little effect on fortress batteries in steel emplacements, located on rear slopes and requiring high angle fire to reach them. The 3d Battalion (Maj. R. E. Conner), on the right flank of the regiment, attacked east of Malmaison toward Moscou Farm,[32] ran into a nest of pillboxes and bunkers, and came under cross fire from the draw southeast of Gravelotte. The 2d Battalion, driving east of Vernéville, made several hundred yards' gain through a weakly held section of the German line, but at the close of day was checked by fire coming from a sunken road to the west of Fort de Guise.

[31] Here 2d Lt. Frederick J. Giroux on two occasions went forward alone under withering German fire to rescue wounded men. He received the DSC.

[32] The heavy stone farm buildings formed a veritable *enceinte* in the center of the German field works. At this same farm the French repelled the assaulting columns of three German corps on 18 August 1870.

On the night of 9 September Colonel Roffe reported to General Silvester, told him that the 2d Infantry had lost 14 officers and 332 men, and protested against sending the infantry "uselessly" against "20 odd forts." The 1st Battalion was in very bad shape, had suffered 228 casualties in the bloody fighting around Amanvillers, and in spite of its efforts had made hardly a dent in the German positions. Artillery, argued Roffe, was futile in dealing with these enemy fortifications. Planes and heavy bombs were needed and without them the infantry could make no further progress.

The planes that General Weyland's XIX TAC could divert to the Third Army were spread thinly along a very wide front. The XX Corps G–3, faced with the dilemma of allocating the meager air missions allotted the corps, protested that the other divisions were "cutting my throat" for diverting missions to the 5th Division bridgehead. Nevertheless, on 10 September he secured three squadrons of fighter-bombers for use against the enemy holding up the advance near Amanvillers. The planes hit their targets, but the 500-pound bombs carried by the P–47's had little effect on reinforced concrete, and the ground attack begun at 1800 met as stubborn resistance as before. Despite mounting loses, the infantry pushed slowly forward, fighting to reduce each knot of pillboxes and every individual strong point in the way. Task Force McConnell meanwhile switched around to the south flank of the 1st Battalion, and at 2100 the tanks and infantry finally paused about a hundred yards from Amanvillers. In the center the 2d Battalion gained some ground and consolidated for the night on the high ground east of Vernéville.

The 3d Battalion continued a seesaw fight east of Gravelotte and Malmaison. Here the Germans could make ready use of their superior knowledge of the ground, gained by numerous exercises over this terrain when the Metz area had been a training center. East of Gravelotte[33] the Mance ravine runs north and south, fringed with thick woods that extend northward, as the draw tapers off, into the Bois des Génivaux opposite Malmaison. Since earlier combat patrols had been unable to push across the draw in the face of machine

[33] Gravelotte has given its name to the last and greatest of the three Franco-Prussian War battles fought prior to the investment and capitulation of Metz. The lines of the opposing forces on 18 August 1870 were almost identical with those of the opposing forces north and west of the Metz bridgehead in the second week of September 1944. But the machine gun and modern artillery had introduced a marked tactical change in 1944. Then the Americans committed one infantry regiment, one armored combat command, and about one squadron of mechanized cavalry, while the Germans employed approximately two understrength infantry regiments. On 18 August 1870, the combined French and Prussian forces totaled over 330,000 men; these engaged in combat on approximately the same frontage as that held by General Silvester's command.

FORTS
TO METZ
GRAV

GRAVELOTTE

BOIS DES GENIVAUX

[M]ELOTTE DRAW. *The area shown in the photograph is indicated on Map* XIV

gun positions on both banks and enfilading fire sweeping the bottom of the draw, the 3d Battalion tried to work its way around this trap by attacking through the Bois des Génivaux. But each attempt failed: whatever ground was taken was soon lost to small German detachments seeping back into the woods.

The 7th Armored Division commander could spare few additional troops to aid Colonel Roffe and the 2d Infantry. CCA was disposed so as to cover the flanks of both the 90th Division and the 2d Infantry, and was responsible besides for keeping a corridor open to the Moselle between Metz and Thionville. However, CCR, assembling at Ste. Marie behind the left flank of the 2d Infantry after extrication from the jammed road leading to Arnaville, could be used. A plan of maneuver was arranged with the 2d Infantry whereby CCR would make a hook from near Roncourt and attempt to close in behind the enemy positions holding up the 1st and 2d Battalions, while at the same time the infantry executed a frontal attack.

At 0630 on 11 September the armor moved east, through sporadic artillery and antitank fire, along the road to Pierrevillers. Near Pierrevillers the head of the column ran into concrete road blocks, covered by antitank guns, and swerved south toward Semécourt; there intense fire from the right flank of the Canrobert Forts checked its advance. Further progress into this fortified zone was impossible. Artillery fire was causing heavy casualties, and the enemy guns, skillfully camouflaged, could not be located. Colonel Molony, commander of CCR, Lt. Col. Robert B. Jones, commander of the 814th Tank Destroyer Battalion, and Lt. Col. Edmund L. Keeler, commanding the 38th Armored Infantry Battalion, all were wounded. Lt. Col. Norman E. Hart, on whom the command now devolved, faced CCR to the west and shortly after 1100 sent his dismounted troops up the rugged, wooded slopes northwest of the village of Bronvaux. The armored infantry won a toehold on the higher ground. But the hook designed to pierce the German flank had been blunted and deflected by the enemy fortifications, and could only glance back to the west, short of its objective.

The 2d Infantry assault, timed to follow the armor at 0800, was delayed by a series of successful counterattacks that disrupted the American lines and forced the battalions on the left and center to give ground. About 0400 two green flares were fired in front of the 2d Battalion and German infantry poured in on its right flank. In the bitter struggle that followed, the Americans were driven out of their positions and forced back southwest of Montigny, where they dug in and held. Pvt. Carlton C. Bates, H Company, 2d Infantry, remained alone in a position from which he could cover the broken flank and continued firing until his machine gun jammed. Then he resumed fire with another machine gun whose crew was dead or wounded. He was later awarded the Distinguished Service Cross for his part in breaking up the counterattack. Late in the day the 2d Battalion recovered much of the lost ground, under cover of artillery fire and exploding smoke shells laid on the German fortifications to the east; again the determined enemy counterattacked and drove back the battalion. About midnight one more German assault came in, but the 2d Battalion, which had lost half its men during this day of battle, stood fast.

The 1st Battalion, at the edge of Amanvillers, also was hard hit. Intense shelling and small arms fire made the American position untenable and the battalion pulled back about five hundred yards, making the withdrawal under a thick smoke screen laid down by its artillery support, but only with much difficulty and many casualties. Attempts to follow up an air strike on Amanvillers, made about 1400, were checked by a furious barrage.

Amanvillers had become the key to any further advance, just as it had been in 1870. It lay too snugly against the main German fortifications to permit a wide envelopment, and in any case the American forces were too weak to bypass and contain the town. General Silvester therefore altered the plan of attack on 12 September, bringing the 3d Battalion north from the Malmaison area, where it still was hung up on the draw east of Gravelotte, and using it to relieve the tired and battered 1st Battalion outside of Amanvillers. The gap thus opened on the right flank of the 2d Infantry was covered by a screen thrown out by the 87th Cavalry Reconnaissance Squadron, which General Walker had assigned to cover the left flank of the 5th Division while its main elements concentrated in the Arnaville bridgehead.

The first task was to straighten the 2d Infantry lines south of Amanvillers and retrieve the ground lost on 11 September; then the 1st Battalion could be recommitted at Amanvillers. Two days of bitter fighting redressed the 2d Infantry lines and brought the 2d and 3d Battalions up to the hedgerows around Montigny Farm, abreast of Amanvillers. Again the Americans had a long list of casualties, particularly in the 3d Battalion. The infantry were blind with fatigue after fighting for two days and nights without rest, their bodies so numbed that officers and men could no longer trust their sense of direction. Meanwhile, General Irwin sought to get the attack called off. Finally, on 14

September, orders to halt the attack reached Colonel Roffe from corps headquarters. The journal of the 3d Battalion noted thankfully: "Received warning order that we are to be relieved (which is good news, this is sure a hell hole)" —a feeling with which the entire regiment was in accord.

The Advance on the Left Wing of the XX Corps

After CCA, 7th Armored Division, had wedged its way to the Moselle River on 7 September, it had then fanned out along the west bank. (*Map XV*) General Silvester had been ordered to hold at this point, keep the Germans from recrossing the river, and protect the flanks of the 90th Infantry Division and the 2d Infantry, which were coming up on the north and south respectively. The 7th Armored Division commander, still expecting that he would be called on to make an assault crossing somewhere north of Metz, selected a site near Argancy, just outside the exterior ring of the Metz forts.

In order to contain the enemy in the north sector of the Metz "bridgehead," for such it had become, most of CCA concentrated south of Talange as a task force (Lt. Col. Richard D. Chappuis) composed of the 48th Armored Infantry Battalion, 40th Tank Battalion (—), 695th Armored Field Artillery Battalion, engineers, and tank destroyers. While the 2d Infantry battered away at the western line of the Metz forts, Task Force Chappuis engaged in an eight-day artillery duel with the guns of the German works on both sides of the river, the 695th Armored Field Artillery Battalion firing continuously around an arc of 270°. Here, as elsewhere, the German fortress batteries and roving guns returned the American fire with deadly precision, inflicting sixty-three casualties on the 48th Armored Infantry Battalion on 8 September and running up the tally daily until 15 September, when CCA was relieved.[34]

Unlike the narrow, rapid thrust made to the Moselle by CCA, the 90th Division began a deliberate advance on 7 September, moving northeast on a wide front and methodically clearing out the enemy in its zone, while the 43d Cavalry Reconnaissance Squadron scouted to the north and west. General McLain set the capture of the high ground west of Thionville as the division objective, preparatory to the capture of Thionville and the seizure of a crossing in its vicinity. Early intelligence reports indicated that the Germans were

[34] The 695th Armored Field Artillery Battalion fought not only as artillery but also as infantry and suffered heavy losses. The battalion was awarded the Distinguished Unit Citation for its part in this prolonged engagement.

prepared to fight only a delaying action, though it was expected that at least one division stood between the 90th and the Moselle.[35] Meanwhile, the 90th Infantry Division bore the responsibility of protecting the open north flank of the Third Army until such time as the V Corps of the First Army could draw abreast of the XX Corps. This would mean that General McLain could not concentrate his regiments initially in a power drive directly to the east.

On the morning of 7 September the 357th Infantry (Col. G. H. Barth) led off from Etain and moved toward Briey, a small mining town, but important as a main road center on the periphery of the rugged, wooded tableland rising west of the Moselle. Troops of the *559th VG Division* held Briey in some force and checked the 2d Battalion in a sharp fight. But the 1st and 3d Battalions, on the wings, executed a concentric attack which brought them together north of Briey. The following day the German commander, now completely surrounded, surrendered 442 men and the town.

The 358th Infantry (Col. C. H. Clarke), on the left of the 357th Infantry, met little resistance until the close of 7 September, when the two leading battalions became involved in a fight with a German rear guard detachment holding on some high ground west of Trieux. The advance by the 359th (Col. R. L. Bacon), echeloned to the left and rear of the 358th Infantry, was little more than a route march on this first day of the general attack and reached a point northeast of Landres. Just at twilight the division command post was set up west of the little town of Mairy, some four miles southwest of the 358th Infantry positions in front of Trieux. Here the division would meet its first large-scale counterattack.

On 7 September the new commander of the *First Army*,[36] General Knobelsdorff, decided to risk the *106th Panzer Brigade* against the left flank of the Third Army in a spoiling attack calculated to deflect the American advance toward the Briey mines. Hitler concurred in this decision, but tied a string to the *106th* with orders that it could be used for only forty-eight hours. In the late evening the panzer brigade moved south through Aumetz, slipped along side roads between the positions of the 358th and 359th, and about 0200 the following morning hit the 90th Division command post. Apparently the Germans did not realize what they had done, for some of the tanks continued on to the south, with the result that the *106th* soon was strung out in a disjointed

[35] The *48th Division* had been withdrawn from the German line and only the two regiments of the *559th VG Division* now opposed the 90th.

[36] See Chap. I, p. 45.

series of actions. The surprised Americans fought with whatever weapon was at hand: pistols, rifles, bazookas, and individual tank destroyers and antitank guns.[37] The artillery section of the division staff was encircled but fought its way out on foot. Tanks, tank destroyers, and three battalions of infantry rushed back to the scene at daylight and engaged the disorganized Germans, now almost completely surrounded by the 90th, wherever they could be located. The enemy had found it easy to break into the American lines but lacked the weight to exploit his gains or extricate himself. Very little of the armor that had formed the spearhead of the penetration succeeded in fighting its way back to the north. By the end of the day the 90th Division had captured or destroyed thirty tanks, sixty half-tracks, and nearly a hundred miscellaneous German vehicles. Many of the armored infantry escaped, but the *106th Panzer Brigade* returned to its lines hardly more than a name and number.[38]

This had been a day of good hunting in the 90th Division area. The German battalion pocketed in Briey capitulated in the late afternoon. The 1st Battalion of the 357th Infantry, occupying a wooded hill west of Neufchef, watched from cover as a German infantry battalion deployed and attacked straight toward an adjacent and unoccupied hill; then, in a matter of minutes, the 1st Battalion and supporting field guns cut down the enemy infantry. Earlier in the day, however, the 1st Battalion had run into its share of trouble during an enemy counterattack. The situation was precarious when a forward artillery observer, 1st Lt. Joseph R. McDonald, went alone to a hill from which he could direct the fire of the American artillery. The German counterattack was broken, but Lieutenant McDonald was killed. He received the DSC posthumously.

Because prisoners and enemy orders captured at Briey gave warning of another counterattack against the north flank of the 90th Division, General McLain held his troops in place until late morning of 9 September. Then, when this counterattack failed to materialize, the 90th resumed its advance to the northeast. The *559th VG Division* was in process of a general withdrawal. A few rear guard detachments holed up in towns and woods and

[37] Capt. Cud T. Baird, III, 358th Infantry, stopped one of the enemy columns by disabling the leading armored vehicle with fire from a bazooka. While the road was thus blocked Baird knocked out the second vehicle, all the while in the midst of a bitter return fire. Though wounded he later led a company in a successful counterattack. Baird received the DSC.

[38] The *106th Panzer Brigade* was reduced to a total of nine tanks and assault guns. *Army Group G KTB Nr. 2,* 9 Sep 44. Infantry losses also must have been substantial. *OB WEST* received reports that the *106th* had sunk to one-quarter of its normal combat strength. *OB WEST KTB,* 9 Sep 44.

were wiped out. Others were trapped on the roads. The 3d Battalion of the 359th cut cross-country to get east of a German column of horse-drawn wagons and infantry, ambushed the column, and killed and captured some two hundred in the trap. That night the leading battalions of the division bivouacked in the neighborhood of Fontoy and Neufchef, only eight miles from Thionville, and from the heights of Neufchef American outposts looked down on the Moselle.

On 10 September the *559th VG Division*, still lacking one of its regiments, continued the fight to delay the 90th Division advance through the gorges and defiles interlacing the tableland west of Thionville. The 357th Infantry attack carried from Neufchef through Hayange and then was checked by a German riposte. The 358th Infantry pushed its 3d Battalion into Algrange, commanding the large gorge running north from Hayange. Here the battalion deployed and attacked up the steep scarp behind the town. The fight raged at close quarters along the forward slope, but when darkness closed in the Germans still held along the crest. On the north flank the 359th took Aumetz and passed unhindered through a section of the old Maginot fortifications. In this sector the enemy was disengaging as fast as he could and the cavalry attached to the 90th Division swung out north on a reconnaissance that carried them several miles beyond the infantry outpost line.

General McLain made plans to close along the river on 11 September and strike for Thionville. The 5th Armored Division of the First Army now was abreast of the 90th Infantry Division and the latter could be fully committed in an attack eastward. Therefore, General McLain held the 359th in place, so that it would be intact for use in forcing a crossing near Thionville, and the other regiments continued the attack. The Germans had withdrawn from the scarp east of Algrange during the night and the 3d Battalion, 358th Infantry, moved over the crest, across a valley, and on toward the next scarp, southwest of Volkrange. Here the enemy chose to defend, but he was shortly ejected and the battalion stopped east of Volkrange, ready to descend into the plain in front of Thionville. The 1st Battalion found the Germans making a stubborn stand in the hills, even after an air bombing mission had been laid on them, but toward the close of day was on the down grade leading to Entrange and the plain. The German hold on the heights was broken and the 358th Infantry cheerfully reported: "Have lots of observation and can see halfway to Berlin from here." In the early evening Colonel Clarke dispatched his 2d Battalion through the corridor held open by the 1st and 3d, with orders to take Thionville; the going was slow and the enemy rear guard stubborn. On the division right flank the 357th Infantry succeeded in reaching the river at a few points south of Thionville and captured Florange, a railroad junction about five thousand yards outside of the larger city.

The next day German resistance west of the river ended, for General Knobelsdorff had ordered a general withdrawal behind the river line in the sector north of Metz. The 357th occupied Uckange and mopped up along the river bank. The 2d Battalion of the 358th climbed aboard tanks and rode into the western outskirts of Thionville, where it was reinforced by the 1st Battalion. The city streets were strewn with mines, and during the afternoon German sorties came in from across the river. But at dark the troops of the 358th held all of Thionville west of the river except a small sector barricaded by iron rails, concrete machine gun emplacements, and other obstacles at the western approach to the main bridge across the Moselle. The German demolition squads did not make the mistake, repeated in some instances later in the campaign, of waiting too long before blowing the bridge; it was destroyed during the night of 12 September.

General McLain was anxious to avoid a head-on attack across the Moselle straight into the enemy fortifications, clearly visible from west of the river. As an alternative he laid plans to swing wide, make a crossing north of Thionville, and close on the German river defenses from the rear. One battalion of the 359th Infantry already was en route to seize the heights at Basse Kontz, a key position on the north flank, when General Walker sent word that the 90th should prepare to seize a bridgehead at Thionville. General McLain alerted the 358th Infantry to lead the assault, gave orders to the 359th Infantry to put on a demonstration north of Malling, and set 15 September as a target date for the attack. These plans hardly were drafted when, about midnight on 13 September, the corps commander directed General McLain to hold up the scheduled assault and extend his south flank in order to relieve the elements of the 7th Armored Division and the 2d Infantry west and north of Metz.

Expanding the 5th Division Bridgehead

General Walker had not been insensible to the cost of the frontal attack west of Metz and to the fact that armor could not be usefully employed against the Metz fortifications. He was apprehensive, however, of exposing the corps' left flank and weakening its center in the face of revived German aggressiveness. He believed that his forces were disposed on too extended a front for further dispersion in a double envelopment of Metz, a maneuver which would put both the 90th and 5th Divisions across the river, but miles apart and separated by a heavily fortified area and a stubborn enemy.[39]

The 5th Infantry Division had a bridgehead. (*Map XVI*) But its troops were tired, holding on a wide front, and so closely engaged that it was exceedingly difficult to absorb the replacements coming into the bridgehead from the depots east of Paris. On 13 September the German batteries in Fort Driant destroyed a ferrying raft, partially demolished the treadway at the ford, and broke up the heavy ponton bridge then nearing completion. In addition, a critical shortage of artillery ammunition had developed in the XX Corps, burdening still further the infantry holding the bridgehead.

Early on 14 September the XX Corps headquarters issued a field order that called for the corps to regroup during the day in preparation for the execution of a new maneuver on the morning of 15 September.[40] This plan turned on reinforcing the corps' right flank. The 7th Armored Division would be assembled in the bridgehead and dispatched under orders to attack to the east, circle Metz from the rear by a left wheel, and "uncover" the Moselle line north of the city, thus permitting the 90th Division to cross unopposed in the Thionville sector. In the resulting shuffle the 43d Cavalry Reconnaissance Squadron was reinforced and given a twenty-three-mile front on the left wing of the corps, relieving the 90th Division piecemeal north of Thionville. At the same time General Walker asked for a "deception team" to simulate a stronger force in the cavalry sector. This team finally arrived from 12th Army Group headquarters and operated for some weeks in the area as an "armored division." (The Germans seem to have been well deceived for the *OB WEST* maps show the "14th Armored Division" in this area.)

The 90th Infantry Division was ordered to contain Thionville with a small force and relieve the 7th Armored Division and 2d Infantry north and west of Metz. Then, on 15 September, the bulk of the 90th would begin an attack to clear out the enemy west of the Moselle with a main effort on the south flank in the old 2d Infantry sector. During the night of 14–15 September the 90th completed the relief and arrived on its new positions: the 358th Infantry

[39] Notes on XX Corps morning briefing, 14 Sep 44 (Lt Ludden).

[40] XX Corps FO No. 11, 14 Sep 44. XX Corps G–3 Journal. This field order does not appear in The Reduction of Fortress Metz.

held a line from Uckange north to Garche; the 90th Reconnaissance Troop patrolled the river bank south to Talange; the 357th Infantry was deployed at right angles to the cavalry as far west as St. Privat (where a scratch task force covered the open ground northwest of Amanvillers); and the 359th Infantry relieved the 2d Infantry along the Amanvillers–Habonville road south to Gravelotte.

In the meantime the 5th Infantry Division had attempted to enlarge the Arnaville bridgehead by pushing to the south, as a means of establishing a firm and deeper base for future operations northward toward Metz. In the late afternoon of 13 September CCB tanks, newly arrived in the bridgehead,[41] began a drive to extend the bridgehead line south and east to Mardigny with the intention of seizing the enemy-held ridge on the 5th Division's right flank. Just as in earlier fighting, Arry proved to be the key position, and the armored column was stopped cold by the German antitank guns and artillery near the town. The new field order issued by the corps commander imposed what General Irwin considered to be an impossible mission on the 5th Infantry Division. But both General Walker and General Patton were now under pressure from the 12th Army Group commander, who in turn had taken responsibility for assuring the Supreme Commander that the Third Army would soon have a substantial footing east of the Moselle. By this order the division was to expand its existing bridgehead to the maximum on 14 September, and on the next day attack north toward Metz—thus permitting the 7th Armored Division to break out for the projected end run around the city. When 14 September dawned General Irwin decided to postpone the operations ordered for the day. A night-long rain had made the clay soil east of the river impassable for armor. Tank movement succeeded only in churning up the mire so badly that jeeps and supply trucks could not move. About three hundred replacements had just arrived to fill the depleted ranks of the 10th Infantry and some time would elapse before they could be absorbed in their proper units. In addition, the 2d Infantry was en route from the battle line west of Metz but had not yet joined the division.

At 0900 the next day, CCB and the 10th Infantry jumped off in the planned expansion to the southeast. Fog had closed in and much of the advance was by direction of the compass. In some of the low ground visibility was reduced to ten feet or less. Footing was slippery and the armored advance slow and

[41] CCB now was commanded by Brig. Gen. John M. Devine. Earlier, he had served as artillery commander of the 90th Infantry Division.

difficult. Targets could be seen only when they loomed out of the low-lying ground fog directly ahead, and the tank gunners were forced to use their weapons at point-blank range. Perhaps poor visibility hindered the enemy defense as well, for as the day progressed prisoners began to come through to the rear. Arry, so long a thorn in the flesh, was captured. The 3d Battalion of the 10th Infantry, supported by Company B, 735th Tank Battalion, took Hill 396 after a savage fight with the German troops manning the pillboxes that studded its slopes. Once on top of this key hill the infantry met a heavy concentration of artillery fire, for the summit was bare of trees and the German gunners were well ranged in. However, command of this nearly untenable point offered observation clear across the division front, weather permitting, and allowed the battalion to seize the crossroads town of Lorry, lying at its foot. Late in the afternoon CCB ended the day's operations by the capture of Mardigny and Vittonville, the latter marking the southernmost point of the advance. Then, receiving orders that it would be relieved by the 2d Infantry and revert to the 7th Armored Division, it halted.

Renewed American activity in the Arnaville bridgehead on 15 September and the presence of strong armored units east of the Moselle now forced Hitler to make a decision on the future tactical status of Metz and its garrison. On 8 September, while the American forces were beginning to probe vigorously at the Metz–Thionville position, the commanding general of *Army Group G*, General Blaskowitz, had put the question to his superiors as to whether Metz should be retained within the lines of the *First Army* or be abandoned to investment by the Americans when the *First Army* withdrew to the eastern side of the Moselle. Blaskowitz recommended on two counts that Metz be defended and that the field forces on either flank retain contact with the fortress: first, there were in the Metz garrison some fifteen hundred student-officers whom the German Army could ill afford to lose; second, Blaskowitz had no reserves to fill the gap that would result in the *First Army* line if Metz were encircled by the enemy.

Neither *OB WEST* nor OKW was prepared to take the responsibility for such a momentous decision, and when the situation in the Metz sector became more threatening on 15 September Blaskowitz's question was referred to the Fuehrer's headquarters.[42] By now Hitler was completely committed to the

[42] See *Army Group G* and *OB WEST KTB's* for these dates.

idea that every "strong place" should be garrisoned with second-rate troops (*Halb-Soldaten*) and left to wage a prolonged and lonely battle, with the object of containing as many American or Allied troops as possible.[43] In the case of Metz, therefore, Hitler's first reaction was to issue a mandate that the Metz garrison should submit to encirclement. But on 16 September the Fuehrer reversed himself, perhaps at the instigation of General Jodl and the operations staff of OKW, and sent a peremptory order that the *First Army* must reinforce the shoulders of the Metz salient with its field forces and thus prevent any encirclement by the Americans.

Early on 16 September the leading elements of the CCR column (Col. Pete T. Heffner) which had crossed on the previous day began an attack to break out to the east along the Lorry–Sillegny road. General Silvester intended to bring CCA in on the left of CCR, as it arrived in the bridgehead, and launch the two combat commands in attack along parallel routes. CCB was ordered to join the rest of the division, as soon as disengaged, and follow behind the artillery of the leading combat commands as a division rear guard. The line of departure for the 7th Armored Division attack was not marked too specifically on the ground, but generally followed the forward slope of the ridge line between Fey and Mardigny. In the plans prepared by the Third Army staff the 7th Armored Division would skirt the "known" forts south of Metz, cross the Seille River, then begin a wheel to the northeast in the neighborhood of Verny, cross the Nied River, and circle to the rear of Metz, with the inside column of CCA passing about three miles from the heart of the city. While this envelopment was in progress CCR, on the right, would be responsible for guarding the open flank, and would be covered in turn by a cavalry screen thrown out to the east. Such a scheme of maneuver was daring enough to suit even General Patton, but its successful execution hinged on numerous and unpredictable factors. Intelligence reports already carried information that the Germans were building a new line of defense across the Seille River, only six miles east of the Moselle. Once the Seille line was breached the 7th Armored Division columns would have to pass under the guns of the Metz exterior forts, clustered around Verny and Orny. If the weather continued poor, little help could be expected from the air force, and the armored columns would be unable to deploy across country off the main hard-surface highways.

[43] See MS prepared by General Blumentritt, CofS, *OB WEST* (MS #B–283). Cf. MS #B–308 (Zimmermann).

In any case the road net was limited, and it was known that the enemy had taken the precaution of emplacing much reserve artillery along the roads leading east.

CCR got a taste of the difficulties involved in this armored advance almost as soon as it began the attack. The Germans had dug in along the Lorry–Sillegny road and occupied a large woods astride the highway. One task force (Lt. Col. J. A. Wemple) of CCR, having fought its way through the woods and into the clear, was driven back to the shelter of the trees by accurate shelling from Sillegny. CCA, which had crossed the Moselle in the early morning, joined the attack at 1400 but was compelled to use the 48th Armored Infantry Battalion (Colonel Chappuis) instead of its tanks because of the fog and the slippery condition of the slopes on the line of departure. Some of the CCA tanks even had to be winched over the crest of the ridge in order to reach attack positions. As the armored infantry started down the slope toward the hamlet of Vezon, they were hit immediately by artillery fire plowing into the flank from the Verdun Forts in the north. Colonel Chappuis sideslipped his rifle companies behind a spur of the main ridge which jutted east between Lorry and Marieulles, and shifted the direction of the attack toward the latter town. Hill 396, taken by the 10th Infantry the day before, gave observation from which artillery officers directed a concentration of thirteen field artillery battalions on Marieulles preparatory to the assault. But, when the fire lifted, the Germans crawled out of cellars and foxholes, the guns behind the town opened up, and the 48th was beaten off.

Back in the bridgehead the 5th Division commander regrouped his battalions to join the battle with an attack alongside the armor. The 2d Infantry relieved CCB on the right flank of the bridgehead and the armor assembled in Vittonville. The 11th Infantry crossed an additional battalion and deployed along the north edge of the bridgehead, leaving the battered 2d Battalion (still minus helmets, automatic weapons, and even rifles, lost in the Dornot fight) to contain Fort Driant across the Moselle. In the center the 10th Infantry reformed its battalions, pushed patrols out toward Fey, and prepared to attack as soon as the 2d Infantry was in position and the situation in front of the armor cleared up. The Third Army commander was none too pleased with the day's operations and General Walker passed on his remarks to General Irwin: "General Patton is here and said if we don't get across [the Seille] he is going to leave us here and contain Metz while he goes across with the rest of the Army to the Rhine. Now that wouldn't do." General Irwin agreed that it wouldn't do, but noted privately: "The enemy is making a desperate stand, aided by his artillery, bad weather and poor observation."

Meanwhile the enemy had drawn heavily on his troops in the Metz area to check a further expansion of the American bridgehead. These reinforcements moved south during the late afternoon of 16 September and occupied positions in front of the 5th Infantry Division. In the early morning of the next day the Germans took advantage of fog and rain to launch an assault between the 11th and 10th Infantry. An enemy battalion, heavily armed with bazookas, burp guns, and antitank rifles, crept up the draw west of Vezon, struck the flank of the 11th Infantry and drove into the positions held by Companies I and L, 10th Infantry. Confused fighting raged here for most of the morning,[44] the German infantry pressing the assault regardless of losses. Company I later counted ninety-six dead Germans lying in front of its position. A platoon of L Company was engulfed and surrendered, but nearly all the men escaped when their guards were swept into the fight and shot down. The German counterattack ended abruptly when a platoon of tanks from the 735th Tank Battalion arrived on the scene and sprayed the draw with machine gun fire.

South of the 10th Infantry CCA continued the battle for Marieulles, where some five hundred enemy infantry fought stubbornly all day long.[45] In the first assault the 48th Armored Infantry Battalion (—), supported by the 23d Armored Infantry Battalion from CCB, was stopped at the edge of the town by emplaced 88's firing high explosive at point-blank range into the ranks of the attackers. In the afternoon two battalions of 155-mm. guns fired for one minute into Marieulles—all that ammunition rationing could permit—and the armored infantry returned to the assault, only to be repelled by a fusilade from the German antitank guns. Light American artillery joined in the fray and a final attack, spearheaded by tanks, carried Marieulles. Some 135 prisoners and the ubiquitous antitank pieces were captured. Even in the last moments of the battle, however, the German rear guard fought furiously, standing erect in the open streets to engage the American tanks and infantry with blasts from machine pistols. On the right, CCR spent the day removing road blocks and establishing a line of departure on the east edge of the Bois

[44] Pfc. Andrew A. Kalinka did much to repulse the Germans on the flank of the 11th Infantry, serving a light machine gun and maintaining a deadly, point-blank fire until he was fatally wounded. He was awarded the DSC posthumously.

[45] These were probably elements of the *1st* and *2d Battalions, 37th SS Panzer Grenadier Regiment.*

de Daumont before attacking to take Sillegny. German guns firing to cover the road blocks had good practice and inflicted several casualties. American counterbattery attempts proved futile in the fog and rain—an ominous introduction to the battle for Sillegny.

Troops and vehicles remained jammed together in the confined bridgehead area, and regrouping and assembly were a problem. General Walker, therefore, established a more precise boundary which gave the 7th Armored Division a definite zone on the right of the 5th Infantry Division. General Silvester ordered CCR, on the left, and CCB, now in position on the right, to continue the frontal attack until the Seille River was crossed and some freedom of maneuver was possible. CCA passed into reserve behind Marieulles, while the 10th Infantry took over its former section of the front. Elements of the 2d Infantry then drove ahead in the early evening and occupied Hill 245, a thousand yards to the east.

The plan of attack for 18 September turned on an advance along a somewhat wider front in which elements of both bridgehead divisions would participate. The immediate objectives were four towns strung along the lateral highway between Metz and Cheminot that followed the west bank of the Seille River. Pournoy-la-Chétive, the northernmost, was assigned to the 2d Battalion, 10th Infantry. Next in line the 1st Battalion, 2d Infantry, had the mission of taking Coin-sur-Seille. CCR already was poised in front of Sillegny, third in the series, and CCB aimed its attack at Longueville-lès-Cheminot, enfolded in a loop of the Seille. If these objectives were taken, the way to the Seille would be opened, with the 5th Infantry Division and 7th Armored Division properly aligned to execute the maneuver on and around Metz. *(Map 4)*

Weather along the front continued to be poor on 18 September. Much artillery had been brought into the bridgehead, but observation remained limited and fire not too effective. Tank maneuver was hampered by the sticky clay, and armored vehicles seldom could be used effectively except as supporting artillery. The burden of the attack fell largely on the infantry.

On the extreme right wing, patrols from CCB began the day's operations by occupying the town of Bouxières-sous-Froidmont, which had been evacuated but left strewn with mines. The rest of the morning was spent clearing a route through to the east. When the armored infantry (two companies of the 48th Armored Infantry Battalion and the 23d Armored Infantry Battalion) started on toward the loop in the Seille, they came under fire from German guns in concrete emplacements on Hill 223, about three thousand

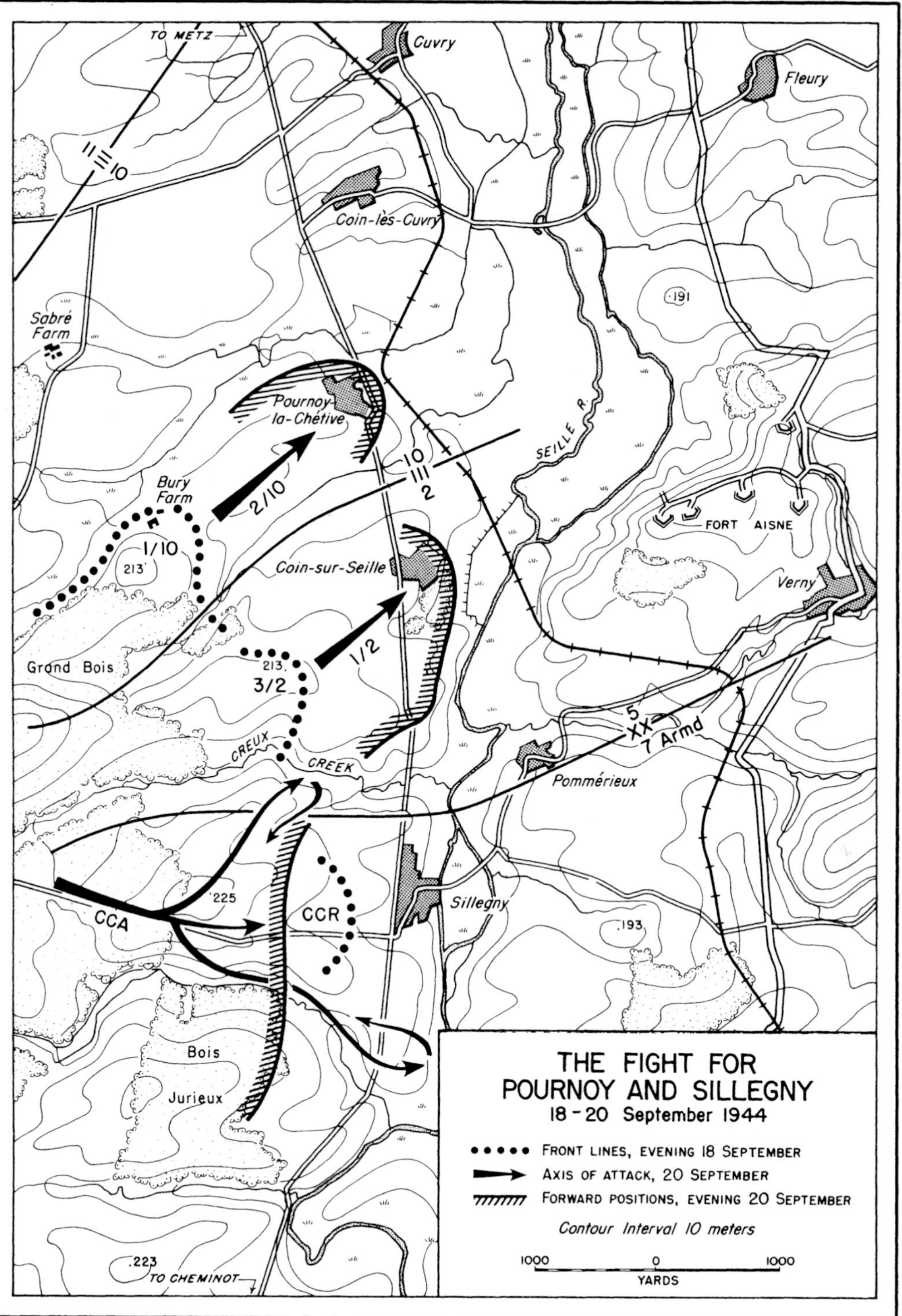
TO METZ
Cuvry
Fleury
Coin-lès-Cuvry
Sabré Farm
191
Pournoy-la-Chétive
SEILLE R.
Bury Farm
2/10
1/10
213
10
2
FORT AISNE
Coin-sur-Seille
Verny
Grand Bois
213
3/2
1/2
5
XX
7 Armd
CREUX
CREEK
Pommérieux
225
CCA
CCR
Sillegny
193
Bois
Jurieux
223
TO CHEMINOT
THE FIGHT FOR
POURNOY AND SILLEGNY
18-20 September 1944
FRONT LINES, EVENING 18 SEPTEMBER
AXIS OF ATTACK, 20 SEPTEMBER
FORWARD POSITIONS, EVENING 20 SEPTEMBER
Contour Interval 10 meters
1000
0
1000
YARDS
R Hanson

MAP NO. 4

yards ahead. Because the maps in use did not show the hill, the troops had trouble convincing the division staff that they had run into such opposition; but the incoming shells were real enough and the infantry halted.

On the opposite wing, the lead battalions of the 5th Infantry Division jumped off in the afternoon and, with little resistance to bar the way, advanced as far as the slight rise west of Pournoy-la-Chétive and Coin-sur-Seille. The 5th had begun to slow down. There was little drive left in the battalions. The troops had been fighting for eleven days and the ranks were filled with replacements still much in need of combat experience.[46] Since further progress would bring the advance under fire from the forts around Verny, planes were urgently needed to silence their guns—and any such help depended on the caprices of the weather. A few planes that managed to get through in the late afternoon dropped twelve napalm bombs on the forts, but their effort was only a gesture.

In the center CCR launched its first attack on Sillegny at 1515 with two companies of the 38th Armored Infantry Battalion (Lt. Col. W. W. Rosebro) and the three medium tank companies of the 17th Tank Battalion (Colonel Wemple).[47] As the infantry advanced out of the woods the enemy barrage opened up, the heavy guns in the Verny forts thickening the fire of the field pieces around the town.[48] Four artillery battalions supported CCR, but their forward observers could not locate the German guns and counterbattery was ineffective. Although the tankers advanced far enough to blast the town at ranges as close as five hundred yards, two companies of the mediums had to withdraw from the fight when their ammunition ran out and five tanks were lost. Nothing seemed to affect the German gunners; their shells poured into the American infantry line with such fury that the troops refused to move forward down the slope and fell back to the shelter of the woods. Colonel Heffner, commanding CCR, phoned the division headquarters and reported that he had thrown into the fight nearly all of his infantry[49] plus two platoons

[46] In the period 10–16 September the 10th Infantry alone is reported to have lost 24 officers and 674 men killed in action. See *Fifth Infantry Division*.

[47] The reports of the 38th Armored Infantry Battalion contain little on the battle for Sillegny. The action has been reconstructed largely from the telephone messages attached to the G–3 Journal, 7th Armored Division. A letter from Col. Pete T. Heffner to the Historical Division (29 May 1947) has helped to clarify the sequence of events.

[48] The Sillegny garrison seems to have been composed of the *3d Battalion* of the *37th SS Panzer Grenadier Regiment* and the *2d Battalion* of the *38th SS Panzer Grenadier Regiment*, reinforced by the bulk of the division artillery of the *17th SS Panzer Grenadier Division*.

[49] At this time Heffner had only two rifle companies of the 38th Armored Infantry Battalion.

of armored engineers, that he had only two platoons of infantry left in reserve, and that even if they were committed it was unlikely that the town could be taken with the weak force at hand. He was ordered to use the last two platoons and make another try for Sillegny. Again CCR formed up and went into the attack. This time the infantry broke under the steady fire, but were stopped by Colonel Rosebro, Colonel Heffner, and a few other officers, turned about, reorganized, and at dusk were sent in again. The tanks led off and the infantry "made a splendid come-back," as Colonel Heffner later reported, following the tanks right to the edge of the town, where small arms fire swept the line and brought the assault to a standstill. Colonel Wemple's tank battalion had performed valiantly through the day, but he was unwilling to risk his tanks in the town at night. The infantry dug in about fifty yards from the nearest buildings. In the early morning hours the 38th took a few houses in the town, but by daylight had lost even this slight hold. Meanwhile, prisoners reported that the German defenders had been reinforced during the night by two companies of infantry from Metz.

Through the morning of 19 September a confused and bloody battle continued at the edge of Sillegny. Colonel Rosebro was mortally wounded. The executive officer of the 38th, Maj. C. H. Rankin, was killed; and when Maj. T. H. Wells, the next senior officer, took command he too was lost.[50] Another battalion commander, Lt. Col. Theo T. King, was sent forward from the division headquarters and about 1100 withdrew the assault companies. Meanwhile, the third rifle company had been rushed up to the 38th from its post as division headquarters guard. The American artillery pounded the town while King reorganized the battalion, and at 1315 the infantry attacked once again. Although in the interim the German garrison had evacuated Sillegny, when the Americans entered the town they received a deadly shelling from enemy batteries on the high ground to the north and east looking down on the elliptical bowl in which Sillegny lay. The troops to the fore, unable either to move on through the town or to retire, took shelter in the nearest cellars. The enemy now moved to counterattack with infantry and tanks. Fortunately, American planes flying to attack the Verny forts were diverted by radio and struck at the German column. Though the bulk of the column was dispersed, a few German tanks reached the town and supporting infantry filtered in behind them. Two American tanks, which had come in earlier, knocked out

[50] Major Wells is carried on War Department records as missing in action.

the leading German tank; then, finding that their own infantry had taken refuge in cellars or left the town, they hurriedly pulled out to avoid the enemy bazookas. During this action Colonel King was wounded and evacuated. By 1830 the Germans once again held the town. An American captain and twenty-three men held on in a large stone house, though surrounded, but about 1900 radio contact with the encircled platoon was lost after a section of tanks had made a fruitless effort to come to its aid.

Lt. Col. R. L. Rhea, the new battalion commander, received permission to break off the engagement. The surviving infantry dug in on the slope east of the woods and Colonel Wemple deployed his tanks in an outpost line between the infantry and Sillegny, moving the tanks back and forth to diminish the target they presented. Colonel Heffner had been wounded and a number of the CCR staff killed or wounded. The 38th Armored Infantry Battalion was reduced to about one-fourth its normal strength and most of its officers were dead. General Silvester ordered CCA to relieve CCR, and on the following morning the badly shattered reserve command disengaged and withdrew into the woods. CCA took its place in front of Sillegny and prepared to resume the drive toward the Seille.

While CCR had been fighting desperately at Sillegny, CCB was moving slowly toward the river. On the morning of 19 September infantry from the 48th Armored Infantry Battalion drove the German gunners off Hill 223. With this threat removed the 23d Armored Infantry Battalion and a company of the 31st Tank Battalion drove on into the Seille loop toward Longueville. The enemy fought stubbornly in the shelter of the town and his antitank guns stopped the American tanks, but at dusk the Americans held Longueville. A subsequent attempt to capture Cheminot, on the southern bank of the Seille opposite Longueville, failed, and five tanks were destroyed by German antitank fire from across the river when they deployed to support the infantry. Cheminot remained as a potential threat to the whole right flank of the 7th Armored Division until 22 September, when the small garrison force from the *553d VG Division*, pinched between the 7th Armored Division and the XII Corps advance on the south, withdrew from this pocket.

By midafternoon of 20 September CCA was organized on its new position west of Sillegny, with the 48th Armored Infantry Battalion attached to give added infantry strength. CCA and CCB immediately jumped off in a coordinated attack to reach and cross the Seille River. CCA tried to maneuver around Sillegny to the north, but its tanks were stopped by Creux Creek, a small stream at right angles to the Seille. A second envelopment, swinging to the south and wide of the town, was abortive. The attack reached the river and then was stopped by antitank guns in reinforced concrete casemates on the opposite bank which proved impervious to direct hits by artillery and tank fire. CCB, advancing east under a continuous fire from Cheminot on the flank and enemy guns to the front, was no more successful. It, too, reached the river, but was forced to relinquish its gains and fall back.

Apparently the Germans reinforced the *17th SS Panzer Grenadier Division* at the Seille line during the night of 20–21 September,[51] for all American movement during the daylight hours of 21 September brought down intense and accurate artillery and mortar fire. After dark CCB forded two companies of armored infantry across the Seille south and east of Longueville. Since the enemy interdicted the river in daylight, engineer reconnaissance had been confined to hours of darkness and the first bridge site chosen proved unsuitable when actual work began. A second crossing site had to be abandoned when it was discovered that the equipment in the CCB bridge trains was insufficient to span the river, as a result of the loss of two truckloads of bridging materials which had received direct hits earlier in the day. At daylight the infantry companies withdrew, and the 7th Armored Division began to ready plans and bridging equipment for a co-ordinated crossing attack by both combat commands on the night of 23 September. This attempt was never made: on the afternoon of 23 September General Silvester received orders that his division was to leave the Third Army and go north to join the XIX Corps in the First Army zone.

The XX Corps had failed to make the dash to encircle Metz for which General Patton had hoped. The gasoline shortage at the end of August and the beginning of September had worked to the advantage of the enemy and allowed the German *First Army* to man not only the Metz fortifications but the line of the Moselle as well. The German plans for demolitions at bridges along the river were well co-ordinated and efficiently executed. The 7th Armored and 5th Infantry Divisions were thereby forced to fight for a bridgehead under conditions most unfavorable to an armored thrust, conditions that were less easy to meet because of the lack of an early co-ordination between elements of the two divisions at the initial crossing site. The amount of in-

[51] These German reinforcements probably came from a regiment of the *559th VG* Division which was withdrawn from the Thionville sector on 20 September, as American pressure eased, and assembled east of Metz.

fantry available to expand the bridgehead and support the armor in a breakout proved too small for such an undertaking. Bad weather, together with the clay soil prevalent on the east bank of the Moselle, also contributed to the difficulties faced by the armor. Finally, the German works on the periphery of the Metz fortifications extended well out from the heart of the city, interlaced and supported by entrenched field forces and a large complement of medium and heavy reserve artillery, the whole calculated to deflect any attempt at a rapid, close-in envelopment by armor. The losses of the 7th Armored Division during the September battles give some clue to the price paid for the use of the armor in frontal assaults against stubbornly defended and well-fortified positions: 47 medium and 8 light tanks destroyed, plus 469 men dead or missing and 737 wounded in the period of a fortnight.[52]

While the 7th Armored Division had been trying to bludgeon a path to the Seille, the 5th Infantry Division, on its left flank, also found the going slow. On 18 September, 10th Infantry patrols worked forward along the gentle slopes leading east to Pournoy-la-Chétive and troops of the 2d Infantry occupied Hill 213 in sight of Coin-sur-Seille. General Irwin called off the assault on the two towns scheduled for the following day in order to let the armor take Sillegny, from which fire was harassing his right flank, and to give time for the weather to clear. He hoped that the American air force could be used to silence the guns in the Verny forts behind Pournoy-la-Chétive and Coin-sur-Seille. The Germans took advantage of this pause on 19 September to gather a large counterattack force in Coin-sur-Seille. In the late afternoon, this force was caught en route to Sillegny by the P–47's and the 5th Division artillery. Late in the evening the 2d Infantry was hit by a similar counterattack from Coin-sur-Seille, but this was broken up by the American gunners before it could do any damage.

General Irwin ordered a co-ordinated attack by the 2d and 10th Infantry on 20 September and sent the assistant division commander, Brig. Gen. A. D. Warnock, to command on the spot. Since CCA, 7th Armored Division, had planned to take over the assault on Sillegny at 1100, the two regiments of the 5th Infantry Division were sent into the attack at this hour. As it turned out, the difficulties attendant on the relief of CCR so delayed the armored attack at Sillegny that the 5th plunged ahead alone. There had been some hope of air support, but during the morning a low overcast kept out the American

[52] 7th Armd Div AAR, Sep 44. CCR had eight different commanders during the period 1–21 September, most of whom became casualties.

planes. Furthermore, there was another cut in the ammunition allowed the supporting artillery, still further limiting the support on which the infantry could rely. Nevertheless the assault battalions fought their way forward through tank, mortar, and artillery fire. By early evening the 1st Battalion, 2d Infantry, held Coin-sur-Seille, though its flank had been under fire from the German batteries near Sillegny all during the advance.

In the north the 2d Battalion, 10th Infantry (Lt. Col. Paul T. Carroll), was roughly handled by the Germans in and around Pournoy-la-Chétive.[53] Having been filled out with replacements during a brief period in reserve, the battalion began its attack to take Pournoy-la-Chétive on the morning of 20 September with nearly its full complement. In addition the infantry was reinforced by Company B of the 7th Engineer Combat Battalion, Company B of the 735th Tank Battalion, and Company B of the 818th Tank Destroyer Battalion. Followed by tanks and tank destroyers, F and E Companies led off from Bury Farm, just outside of le Grand Bois, a sparse wood lot about two thousand yards southwest of Pournoy-la-Chétive. Company F, on the left, was hard hit by enfilading fire coming in from an enemy outpost position near Sabré Farm. But when the battalion wheeled east to strike Pournoy, the exposed company and Company G following in reserve found some shelter from the searching fire in a slight draw. As the infantry approached Pournoy, marching deliberately and firing as they moved, the enemy guns and mortars took heavy toll. Two of the rifle company commanders were killed (the third had been evacuated at the beginning of the assault). Companies E and F fought their way in and briefly held about a third of the town; in the early evening they were hit by tanks and driven back about three hundred yards from Pournoy, where they halted and dug in. Disorganized by the loss of its officers and shocked by continuous shelling from what seemed to be all points of the compass, one company began to straggle back toward the shelter of le Grand Bois. A few of the veterans sought to hold the new replacements, many of whom were under fire for the first time. Pfc. William A. Catri, from the reserve company, ran forward alone and drove off two of the German tanks with his bazooka.[54] Colonel Carroll, the battalion staff, and the few remaining company officers worked frantically to restore order and reorganize

[53] Information on this engagement has been obtained from Historical Division Combat Interviews, correspondence, and postwar interviews. The 2d Battalion reports and journals are of little value. A letter from Capt. Harry E. Arthars (then 2d Battalion S–3) to the Historical Division (21 February 47) gives a detailed story of the battle.

[54] Private Catri received the DSC.

the attack. Finally, in the early evening, the battalion returned to the assault, while the tanks swung to the east of the town and the tank destroyers swung around the west edge. This time the assault was successful. The German troops were driven from the streets and buildings, and Colonel Carroll deployed the battalion, still much disorganized, in an outpost line rimming Pournoy on the north, east, and south.

During the evening General Irwin visited his regimental commanders and concluded from their reports that a further advance would be impossible unless additional artillery ammunition could be provided. When the corps commander received this word from the 5th Infantry Division, he ordered General Irwin to hold his troops where they were. The 5th was deployed with the 2d and 10th Infantry on a north–south line in front of the Seille. At Pournoy-la-Chétive the front bent back abruptly at a right angle, with elements of the 11th Infantry stretched back to and across the Moselle so as to contain the outer Metz fortifications. This angle was now the key to the 5th Infantry Division position, whether the division held in place or resumed the advance. Against it the *17th SS Panzer Grenadier Division* directed all its available troops and guns, plus the remnants of the *106th Panzer Brigade.*

Through the late evening shells poured into the town from the heavy guns at Verny and Fleury, while at closer ranges the German 88's and 20-mm. cannon blazed away continuously. About 0100 on the morning of 21 September a sizable enemy force slipped into the American positions from the northeast. Incessant shellfire had disorganized communications, and before the 2d Battalion could get word back to the American artillery the enemy was in the streets and had sliced across the rear of F Company, deployed along the road and hedgerows east of the town. Most of the company were killed or captured, and only thirty-five men escaped to rejoin the battalion. Company E, on the south, was preparing to send patrols to cut the Metz–Château-Salins railroad line, a few hundred yards away, when the Germans struck. In beating off this attack, the company was badly cut up and reduced to two officers and sixty-four men. By daylight the Americans had redressed their lines close into the town. But the cost of the battle in its first phase had been very high; only some 450 men were left out of the 800 who had entered the engagement the previous day.

All during 21 September the Germans struck blow after blow at the 2d Battalion, forming their assault forces in Coin-lès-Cuvry, about 1,800 yards to the north, and striking in rapid succession around the peripheral defenses with tanks, armored cars, and motor-borne infantry. These attacks were made in considerable strength, one assault force being estimated by the defenders as approximating a regiment. Shells exploded continuously in the American positions. The sound of the German artillery, mortars, and "screaming-meemies" was "a constant roar." A tanker ruefully reported, "We were shelled just once at Pournoy, that was all the time." Men could not leave their cellars or foxholes even to get food and water, for any living thing in the open was cut down. As each attack came in, the tankers and tank destroyer crews served their guns and the infantry doggedly laid on fire with their rifles and machine guns. But the American artillery saved the beleaguered battalion,[55] sweeping across the German counterattack columns and blasting Coin-lès-Cuvry with heavy gun battalions and batteries of 240-mm. howitzers. Even this demonstration of American fire power failed to discourage the attackers and they stubbornly persisted in their efforts to recapture Pournoy. On 22 September the enemy counterattacks shifted in direction, perhaps because Coin-lès-Cuvry had been made untenable, and came out of an assembly area in a little wood southeast of Pournoy. These new assaults likewise were beaten off. The 2d Battalion was nearing the end of its strength, however, and on 23 September Colonel Carroll asked for relief. The corps and army commanders had new plans for the 5th Infantry Division, in which the project of a further eastward advance by the corps would be temporarily abandoned, thus robbing Pournoy of its tactical significance. On the night of 23–24 September the 1st Battalion, 10th Infantry, relieved its sister battalion, and subsequently Pournoy was abandoned as the division withdrew to a new main line of resistance back to the west. The battle for Pournoy had had no decisive result or far-reaching effect, but it ranks with Sillegny and the Dornot bridgehead among the most bitterly fought actions in the Lorraine Campaign.

The 90th Infantry Division Attack West of Metz

While the bulk of the XX Corps was trying without success to breach the German line at the Seille River, the 90th Infantry Division took over the holding attack west of Metz which had cost the 2d Infantry so heavily. The general regrouping in the corps zone on 14 September brought two regiments of the 90th south to occupy the 2d Infantry positions. (*Map XII*) The

[55] Participants in the fight for Pournoy pay special tribute to the 46th Field Artillery Battalion, which employed its 105-mm. howitzers in close support of the 2d Battalion.

357th Infantry, on the left, deployed so that its exterior flank lay along the Bois de Jaumont, east of St. Privat. The 359th Infantry, on the right, extended the opposite flank as far as the draw south and east of Gravelotte. By midnight of 14 September the last troops of the 2d Infantry were out of the line and the 90th Infantry Division was ready to join in the corps attack set for the following morning.

The earlier attacks by the 2d Infantry and probing by armored patrols provided the 90th with some intelligence as to the kind of enemy opposition to be expected. But the contours of the main German positions west of Metz were little disclosed. Again, as in the experience of the 2d Infantry, each new gain made toward the east would uncover camouflaged bunkers, pillboxes, and extensions of fortified lines previously unknown to the Americans. And again, as the artillery supporting the 2d Infantry had learned, American counterbattery fire would prove relatively ineffective so long as the enemy could move his self-propelled guns at will and so long as the Americans were denied observation covering the rear slopes where most of the German fortress guns were emplaced.

In front of the 357th Infantry lay two main lines of fortifications extending from either side of the St. Privat–Marengo–Metz road. North of the road the Canrobert works followed the ridge line of the Bois de Fêves obliquely northeast toward Semécourt. This line consisted of a continuous concrete wall, twenty feet high and thirty feet broad, reinforced by four forts, the whole covered on the west by an outpost line of foxholes, barbed wire, and machine gun positions. South of the St. Privat–Metz highway two detached groups of fortifications, connected by field works, flanked the Canrobert line. The northernmost, the Kellermann works, commanded the highway.[56] The Lorraine group of forts, echeloned to the southeast, lay astride a wooded hill looking down on Amanvillers. Across and beyond the front of the 359th Infantry the German line continued south until it reached its linchpin at Fort Driant, in the zone of the 5th Infantry Division. The portion of the line immediately south of Kellermann and Lorraine was composed of temporary field works, covered by permanent batteries to the rear and on the flanks. Beyond came the de Guise forts (east of Vernéville), more field works, the Jeanne d'Arc group of forts, and a line of small detached works known to the American troops as the "Seven Dwarfs." The last of the Seven Dwarfs,

[56] The Kellermann works were known to the Americans as "Fort Amanvillers," and this name appears in all the combat reports.

BOIS DE FEVES RIDGE. *Circles indicate positions of Canrobert forts.*

Fort Marival, covered the flank and rear of Fort Driant, just across the defile leading down to Ars-sur-Moselle. The western approaches to the Jeanne d'Arc group and the Seven Dwarfs were screened by the German hold on the ravine of the Mance, east of Gravelotte, which had proved so difficult to break during the early attacks by the 2d Infantry.[57]

On the morning of 15 September the 357th (Colonel Barth) and 359th (Colonel Bacon) opened the attack against the German line west of Metz. Both regiments were fresh, their losses during the advance to the Moselle had been slight, and their ranks were full. A series of relatively easy victories in recent fighting had done much to restore the self-confidence lost during the reverses suffered by the 90th in Normandy.[58] General McLain, the new commander, had had six weeks in which to acquaint himself with the division staff and influence somewhat the division *esprit*. Finally, the 90th Division was prepared to use the bulk of two regiments in this operation, whereas the 2d Infantry in its last assaults had been forced to work alone, and then much understrength.

In the initial attack on 15 September each of the two regiments committed its right-wing battalion. The 1st Battalion, 357th Infantry (Maj. B. O. Rossow), reinforced by an engineer platoon armed with flame throwers,[59] was given the mission of driving into the narrow gap along the St. Privat–Metz road where the highway cut between the Canrobert wall and the Kellermann works. The line of approach was somewhat protected by extensive undergrowth, but this also made control difficult and the advance was slowed down by the need for constant reorganization. The infantry drove in the German outposts south of the Bois de Jaumont, crossed a railroad track and seized a stone quarry west of Kellermann. At the close of day, with its right flank secured at the quarry, the battalion wheeled into position for a close-in assault on Kellermann from the north. Meanwhile, the 2d Battalion had sent patrols to test the northern end of the Canrobert line only to find that any advance

[57] The exact German dispositions in this line of fortifications are still uncertain. The western sector, from Fort Driant to Kellermann, was manned by the *Fahnenjunkerschule Regiment* and miscellaneous fortress units. Several of the works were not occupied, for example, some of the Seven Dwarfs. The *1010th* held the Canrobert line. See MS #B–042 (Krause).

[58] The story of the 90th Infantry Division fighting in Normandy is given detailed treatment in R. G. Ruppenthal, *Utah Beach to Cherbourg*.

[59] Flame throwers had been stocked in the Third Army depots in preparation for the anticipated assault against the West Wall. However, the flame thrower seldom was employed in the operations of the Third Army. Little training was given in its use, and most of the troops regarded this weapon with a very jaundiced eye.

there would have to be made across absolutely barren ground under direct fire from Fort Fèves. The idea of a flanking movement was therefore rejected.

Three-quarters of an hour after the 357th started its advance the 2d Battalion, 359th (Capt. O. C. Talbott), moved out from a line of departure southeast of Malmaison in an attack toward the Jeanne d'Arc forts, while a platoon of tank destroyers, dug in near Malmaison, supported the attack by firing over the heads of the infantry. Colonel Bacon apparently intended to bypass the most dangerous part of the ravine east of Gravelotte by pushing the right flank of the 359th around to the north through the Bois de Génivaux and across the head of the draw. At first the Germans offered little opposition, but about 1340 fire from a large pillbox in the woods directly east of Malmaison pinned the forward infantry to the ground and halted the advance. Since rounds from the American bazookas had not the slightest effect on the heavy reinforced concrete, a platoon of tanks and a platoon of engineers equipped with flame throwers were brought up to engage the pillbox. The German strong point was neutralized, but not taken, and the advance continued, making only a couple of hundred yards in "vicious fighting" (as reported that evening) at the edge of the draw.[60]

The story of this first day had been dishearteningly like that of earlier attacks by the 2d Infantry in the same area. That evening, after studying the reports from his two regimental commanders, General McLain concluded that a full-dress assault on the western defenses of Metz "was out of the question" unless additional troops could be secured. He therefore instructed Colonel Barth and Colonel Bacon to "nibble" at the German positions in limited-objective attacks, while maintaining harassing fire and heavy patrolling all along the front in order to keep the enemy constantly off balance.

The morning of 16 September opened with a heavy fog which clung to the ground through the forenoon and provided some cover for the American attacks. The 1st Battalion, 357th, formed up its three rifle companies and moved slowly toward the gap between Kellermann and the Canrobert line, under sporadic and aimless shelling by the German guns. However, the fog screen was not an unmixed blessing and the battalion lost its bearings. At 1000 the advance patrols found themselves about 150 yards away from the

[60] After the German attempts to cross the draw in 1870, one of the participants in the battle east of Gravelotte, General von der Goltz, wrote: "A stronger position in the open field can hardly be imagined." All of the Americans who fought over this ground in 1944 had reason to agree with von der Goltz' earlier estimate.

concrete wall that identified the Canrobert position. The battalion commander thereupon decided to send two companies through the gap at the end of the masonry where wire barricades and machine gun posts covered the St. Privat–Metz road. Colonel Barth then ordered the 3d Battalion to move in on the right of the 1st and block toward the south while the assault was made into the gap along the road. The two battalions were organizing for this maneuver when, a little after noon, the Germans struck hard at the two companies deployed for the assault. This counterattack, made by troops of the *Fahnenjunkerschule* regiment, was pressed with all of the determination and savagery that characterized these elite German infantry. But the Americans stood their ground and drove off the enemy, after losing seventy-two men in a bitter hand-to-hand fight. At 1700 the 1st Battalion again attempted to move forward but was stopped in its tracks by artillery and small arms fire that forced it to dig in.

In the 359th area the 2d Battalion resumed the effort to shake the Germans loose from the Mance ravine east of Gravelotte. This time the battalion turned its attack south, down into the draw. The enemy reacted at once with furious fire from mortars and automatic weapons concealed on the wooded banks and scattered the length of the ravine. By nightfall the battalion had advanced about two hundred yards and reached the Gravelotte–Metz highway, which here crossed the draw. This slight gain was made at the cost of severe casualties: 117 men and 15 officers (nearly half the officer complement of the battalion).[61]

The volume of German artillery fire brought to bear on the 357th and 359th increased abruptly on 17 September. General McLain and his staff were already perturbed by the width of the 90th Division front (some sixteen miles) and the numerous weak spots in the forward line. This new development, the division commander feared, might presage a major German counterattack against some thinly held part of his position.[62] Nonetheless, the two regiments west of Metz continued the attack, each using the single battalion which was all that could be committed to the assault without drastically denuding the extended American line. In the zone of the 359th Infantry the 3d Battalion relieved the 2d in the fight to clear the ravine, but the fresh troops had made

[61] Sgt. Donald E. Zweifel, G Company, 359th Infantry, was awarded the DSC for bravery in this action. When the 2d Battalion was halted by the murderous enemy fire Sergeant Zweifel went forward alone. Although wounded in the process he knocked out two machine guns and killed all but one of the German gunners.

[62] 90th Inf Div AAR, Sep 44.

little progress by the end of the day. The 357th Infantry also relieved its assault battalion, after an unsuccessful attempt during the morning to push a company through the wire and mortar fire at the south end of the Canrobert wall.

Gains made on 17 September could be reported only in terms of yards. The execution of even limited-objective attacks had proved too costly, and General Walker agreed with General McLain that the assault should be discontinued. New plans were already being made for the Metz operation, and the 90th Infantry Division would have ten days' respite before returning to the grueling task of battering a hole through the western German defenses.

CHAPTER IV

The XV Corps Advance[1] (11-20 September)

The Situation on the Southern Flank of the Third Army

From the time the Third Army poured out of Normandy through the Avranches gap and into Brittany, it had operated with an unbelievably long and attenuated south flank. With one army corps tied up in western Brittany, by what amounted to siege operations, and two corps driving pell-mell in the direction of Germany, General Patton could detach only a limited portion of his cavalry, tanks, and infantry to guard the line of the Loire. Although the Third Army commander often expressed a cavalier disregard for his flanks this attitude was perhaps more apparent than real. The Third Army would rely heavily on the additional flank protection provided by the XIX TAC and the irregulars of the FFI. General Weyland's planes maintained a constant lookout for any evidence of German troop concentration south of the Loire, swooping down to strike even small enemy columns. At General Patton's request General Koenig, chief of the FFI, had ordered the FFI irregulars to reinforce the Third Army units patrolling the Loire flank. Although poorly armed and loosely organized, these French bands were extremely valuable, guarding bridges and supply dumps, patrolling roads, and ferreting out isolated enemy groups left behind by the swiftly moving American columns. An exact statement of the strength of these irregulars is impossible. It is prob-

[1] The XV Corps After Action Report for the period covered in this chapter is unusually accurate and complete. The records of the 79th Infantry Division are in good condition, although the formal After Action Report is very inaccurate. The After Action Report prepared by the 2d French Armored Division (according to U.S. Army regulations) has been used, as well as the original unit journals, of which the Historical Division has photostatic copies. See also a semiofficial history, edited by Lt. Col. Repidon (G–2 of the 2d French Armored Division), entitled *La 2ème DB* (Paris, 1945). Historical Division Combat Interviews are available for the 2d French Armored Division, but there are none to cover the operations of the 79th Infantry Division, during this period. Maj. Gen. Ira T. Wyche, commander of the 79th Infantry Division, has permitted the Historical Division to use his personal diary. German sources for this chapter are particularly fine, both in the form of the *KTB* and in the personal reminiscences prepared for the Historical Division by the enemy commanders who directed the German operations.

able, however, that close to 25,000 of the FFI were co-operating with the Third Army II Special Forces Detachment (Lt. Col. R. I. Powell) by the end of August.

On 1 September the open flank of the Third Army extended from St. Nazaire, in Brittany, to Commercy and the Meuse River—a distance of 450 air-line miles. A further extension of this weakly guarded flank, as the Third Army approached the Moselle River and as the enemy stiffened, could not be undertaken with quite the same *sang-froid* that had marked General Patton's August drive. General Bradley had repeatedly expressed concern about this exposed flank, which was also the south flank for the entire group of American armies then in northern France. And General Eddy, the new commander of the XII Corps, had assumed his post with some misgivings as to the relatively scanty protection that could be given the XII Corps right and rear—although General Patton characteristically tended to make light of this problem.[2]

There was general agreement, however, that reinforcements were necessary if the Third Army was to continue east across the Moselle River and still carry out its mission of protecting the open Allied flank. For this reason General Bradley promised General Patton on 25 August that Maj. Gen. Wade H. Haislip and the XV Corps headquarters, which had been taken from the Third Army during the Seine crossing operations, would be returned to the Third Army, and that as soon as possible some of the divisions "borrowed" by First Army during the August advance would fill out the corps. During the first days of September the XV Corps headquarters and some corps troops assembled east of Paris near Rozay-en-Brie. General Patton gave orders on 5 September that when the XV Corps was fleshed out it would be put in on the right of the XII Corps and there take over the protection of the south flank of the Third Army from Montargis eastward—a distance of about 150 miles. On 8 September the 2d French Armored Division, leaving the scenes of its triumphal entry into Paris with the express consent of General de Gaulle,[3] joined the XV Corps and took over the sector between Montargis and the Marne River. Meanwhile the 79th Infantry Division, coming from Belgium, began to assemble to the east of the French combat commands in the vicinity of Joinville. The movement of these two divisions released the 35th Infantry

[2] Interv with Gen Eddy, 6 Aug 47.

[3] Smith to Bradley, 3 Sep 44, SHAEF Message File. Earlier General de Gaulle had insisted that General Leclerc's division be retained in Paris. Eisenhower to Bradley, 29 Aug 44, SHAEF Message File.

MAJ. GEN. WADE H. HAISLIP, *XV Corps Commander.*

Division, which marched by regimental combat teams into the Toul area preparatory to taking part in the XII Corps attack across the Moselle.

General Haislip and the XV Corps headquarters were well known to Patton and the Third Army staff. The XV Corps had trained in North Ireland as part of the Third Army and had entered combat under Patton's command. General Haislip, an infantryman, graduated from West Point in 1912. He took part in the Vera Cruz expedition, and during World War I served as a staff officer in the V Corps. After service in the peace years with the infantry and at the military schools, Haislip became G–1 in the War Department General Staff. There followed a tour of duty as a division commander; then, in February 1943, Haislip assumed command of the XV Corps.

General Haislip's divisions had both seen earlier service with the XV Corps. The 2d French Armored Division commander, Maj. Gen. Jacques Leclerc (a *nom de guerre*),[4] had won fame in the Free French forces and was held in high regard by the XV Corps commander as an aggressive and able soldier.[5] General Haislip himself was a graduate of the *Ecole Supérieure de Guerre* and by reason of this background was able to elicit a high degree of co-operation from the French general. The 2d French Armored Division had its origin in French Equatorial Africa, when, in August 1940, the Régiment de Tirailleurs Sénégalais du Tchad joined de Gaulle. In December of that year Colonel Leclerc took command in the Tchad. After a series of successful raids against outlying enemy posts in Libya, Leclerc's command made the long march north to join the British Eighth Army in December 1943. Additional Free French formations from Syria and Dakar, reinforced by loyal Frenchmen from all parts of the world, had increased the fighting strength of Leclerc's force. In April 1944, after campaigning in North Africa, Leclerc's command sailed for England as the 2d French Armored Division. It arrived on French soil during the night of 1 August and fought its first action in France under the XV Corps. The losses suffered by the 2d French Armored Division during the advance to Paris had been moderate and had been more than replaced by eager Frenchmen caught up by the patriotic fervor attendant on the liberation. The 79th Infantry Division was under the command of Maj. Gen. Ira T. Wyche. General Wyche was an artilleryman, a West

[4] This name had been adopted to protect Leclerc's family from retaliation by the enemy. After the war the French government accorded Leclerc the legal use of his *nom de guerre* and he became Vicomte Philippe François Marie Leclerc de Hauteclocque.

[5] Ltr, Gen Haislip to Hist Div, 17 Jul 47.

MAJ. GEN. JACQUES LECLERC, *2d French Armored Division Commander.*

Point graduate in the class of 1911. He had served with the Allied Expeditionary Force in the St. Dié sector during the summer of 1918, but then had been brought back to the United States to train new gunners. In the postwar Army Wyche had continued the career of an artillery officer. In May 1942 he was given command of the 79th Division, a Reserve formation. The 79th Infantry Division had received an estimated 7,500 replacements over several weeks to make up for the losses sustained since entering combat in June. It was now at nearly full T/O strength and endowed with a good reputation as a veteran division.

The two divisions of the XV Corps had barely assembled southeast of Troyes when, on 11 September, the corps began the advance to the east ordered by General Patton as part of the general Third Army offensive. Unlike the Third Army left and center the XV Corps had no orders to cross the Moselle River, but instead operated under instruction to close up to the Moselle between Epinal and Charmes and continue to cover the south flank of the army in the sector east of Montargis. This dual mission made a power drive straight to the east with both divisions out of the question. Instead, the first phase of the XV Corps attack would consist of a sequence of individual actions fought by separate combat teams or commands—irregularly echeloned back to the southwest so as to retain a continuing protective cover along the right flank of the Third Army.

The enemy forces confronting General Haislip's troops on 11 September were little more than a heterogeneous array of small Kampfgruppen, collected piecemeal during the German retreat from southern and western France, under the *LXVI Corps,* commanded by General Lucht. (*Map XVII*) In the first week of September the *LXVI Corps* had operated as a kind of task force, directly under the command of *Army Group G*, charged with keeping the escape hatch open north of Dijon for the thousands of Germans moving in weary columns from the Mediterranean and the Bay of Biscay back toward the Reich. When General Patton's rapid advance threatened to knife between the *First Army*, deployed along the Moselle line, and the *Nineteenth Army*, retreating north and east before General Patch's Seventh Army, the *LXVI Corps* received specific orders to maintain contact—"at all costs"—with the *553d VG Division* of the *First Army* along the east-west line through Toul and Nancy that formed the German interarmy boundary. An additional burden was laid on the harassed *LXVI Corps* on 7 September when General Blaskowitz issued orders that it would form a main line of resistance along the Marne-Saône Canal, between Langres and Chaumont, and extend its right flank so as to screen the Neufchâteau–Mirecourt area—all this to secure maneuver space from which to launch a powerful counteroffensive against the Third Army's exposed flank and rear. For this sizable task General Lucht was given permission to use the *16th Division* (Generalleutnant Ernst Haeckel),[6] which had marched clear across France from the Biscayan coast, shepherding a motley collection of smaller military detachments, customs officials, Todt workers and Luftwaffe ground personnel. The leading columns of this hegira, composed of the combat units, had just entered the Chaumont–Neufchâteau sector when the XV Corps attacked. In addition to having the *16th Division*, the *LXVI Corps* was composed of *Landesschuetzen* (Home Guard) battalions, organized under *Kampfgruppe Ottenbacher* and the *19th*

[6] On 16 August 1944 the *158th Reserve Division* and *16th Luftwaffe Field Division* had been reorganized as the *16th Division*. However, the division was not given the weapons of an infantry division and continued to appear on some German situation maps as a reserve division. The *16th Division* had very few heavy weapons and had lost two infantry battalions in fighting with French partisans during the retreat. *OKH/Org. Abt. Karteiblaetter.*

SS Police Regiment, whose battalions had been put in Andelot and Neufchâteau to cover the concentration of the *16th Division.* Politics had outweighed military necessity, however, and on 3 September Himmler began the process of moving the *19th SS Police Regiment* out of the area in order to provide "protection" for the French Chief of State, Marshal Pétain, and the Vichy administration now in Belfort.[7] The *LXVI Corps* was weak, but the build-up of the *XLVII Panzer Corps* in the Neufchâteau–Mirecourt area, as part of the projected German counteroffensive, ultimately would provide some stubborn resistance in the path of General Haislip's advance toward the east.

Hitler's Plans for a Counteroffensive

The planning and operations of the German high command, as related to the strategic problem posed by the rapid advance of the Third Army, give an illuminating picture of the way in which Hitler's "intuitive strategy" had come to supersede skilled professional operational planning and realistic appraisals of existing tactical conditions. In August 1944 Hitler studied the large-scale map in his headquarters at Eiche, near Berlin, and then ordered the counterattack toward Avranches designed to cut off the First and Third Armies, giving detailed instructions as to the way in which each division of the counterattack force should be employed.[8] Now Hitler again intervened in an attempt to destroy the Third Army, and again without reference to the advice of his field commanders or the capabilities of the weapon in his hands.

On 28 August General Jodl, who had weathered the command crisis following the attempt on Hitler's life and succeeded in retaining his post as chief of the operations staff in OKW, suggested a counteroffensive against the exposed flank of the Third Army, now extended from the neighborhood of Toul far back to the west. This attack was to strike in the Troyes sector and penetrate to the north between the Seine and the Marne. The project was abandoned as soon as it was proposed, for General Patton already was in force at the Meuse River. But on 3 September Hitler gave *OB WEST* new instructions for the over-all conduct of the war in the West which included

[7] The story of this retreat and regrouping is found in *Army Group G KTB, Nr. 2;* MS #A–000 (Mellenthin); MS #B–558 (Gyldenfeldt).

[8] During the Mortain counterattack Hitler sent General der Infanterie Walter Buhle to the front as his personal plenipotentiary, where Buhle had much the same status as that of Lt. Col. Hentsch at the Marne in 1914.

a plan for a large-scale counterthrust directed against the Third Army.[9] This scheme was the most ambitious to be advanced during the months between the Mortain counterattack and the Ardennes offensive. By Hitler's orders the German right wing and center would fight a defensive battle (but under no circumstances would any large units allow themselves to be encircled by the Allies). On the left wing a mobile force would be assembled west of the Vosges and given a dual mission: first, it was to cover the retreat of the *Nineteenth Army* and *LXIV Corps* while holding the terrain west of the Vosges necessary for freedom of maneuver; second, it was to attack in strength against the extended south flank of the Third Army, finally turning east to strike the American divisions in the back as they closed up facing the Moselle River. The *Fifth Panzer Army* staff, at the moment in Belgium, would be replaced by the staff of the *Seventh Army* and take over the direction of the counterattack.

This decision for a counterthrust at Patton's army was in part dictated by the strategic necessity of preventing a juncture of the Third and Seventh American Armies, and in part by the exigencies of the tactical situation. On 3 September the troops under Blaskowitz still held a very substantial bridgehead across the Moselle in the area south of Toul. Here, at Neufchâteau, was the western terminus of the road net leading through the Trouée de Charmes, and from Neufchâteau ran the most direct and easiest military route for turning the south flank of the natural defense line along the Meuse escarpment—a line already in American hands. Neufchâteau had been an important communications center since the Napoleonic Wars, and in 1914 the GHQ of the Second French Army had been located there, adjacent to the operations being conducted in western Lorraine and northern Alsace.

Hitler proposed to implement his grandiose scheme with considerable force, and he personally selected the units to carry out the maneuver. The initial counterattack group, as designated by Hitler, was to be composed of the *3d*, *15th*, and *17th SS Panzer Grenadier Divisions*. It would be augmented by three new panzer brigades (*111th*, *112th*, and *113th*), to be brought up from Germany, and would be reinforced "if possible" by the *Panzer Lehr Division*, the *11th Panzer Division*, the *21st Panzer Division*, and three more panzer brigades (*106th*, *107th*, and *108th*). In addition, a single division (the *19th*) would go to the *First Army* to replace the panzer grenadier units.

[9] *Army Group B KTB Anlagen*, 28 Aug and 3 Sep 44.

Several of the divisions named by Hitler were closely engaged on the *First Army* front at the time he gave his order, or were already in contact with American patrols pushing toward the Moselle. The three panzer grenadier divisions were in the Metz area, with one panzer grenadier regiment of the *15th Panzer Grenadier Division* engaged west of Arlon, in Belgium. The *11th Panzer Division* was fighting a rear guard action in the Besançon area, to cover the eastern flank of the retreating *Nineteenth Army*. The famous *Panzer Lehr* had been reduced to a shadow division and was still engaged. The *21st Panzer Division* was refitting. Of the panzer brigades only the *106th* had reached the front, detraining at the moment near Metz, while the rest were organizing in Germany. Model, aware of the true situation, begged for three armored divisions from the Eastern Front, but with no success.

Again, as at Mortain, the means were not available fully to carry out the plan. The Russian front was an ever-present consideration in all allocations of tanks and men.[10] Even while Blaskowitz was reading Hitler's counterattack order, his staff and service echelons were being stripped of "volunteers" to reconstitute the *49th VG Division* for use in the East. In Belgium the Allies had broken through every line the Germans had hoped to hold, and the very day after Hitler issued his counterattack order Field Marshal Rundstedt appealed to Berlin for twenty-five new divisions and an armored reserve of five to six divisions, without which, he said, the entrance to northwest Germany could not be defended. Finally, it was only a matter of hours until Patton, with his superior forces, would pin the *First Army* to the Moselle line.

Although the counterattack was the responsibility of General Blaskowitz and *Army Group G*, Hitler himself chose the commands to carry out this mission. Initially, the headquarters of *XLVII Panzer Corps* (General Luettwitz) would head the counterattack group; but as quickly as possible the headquarters of the *Fifth Panzer Army* would be brought back from Belgium, reorganized, and sent forward to assume the command.

Blaskowitz, at his headquarters in Gerardmer, west of Colmar, reacted to the *Fuehrerbefehl* with the promptness to be expected from a German commander not yet completely cleared of the suspicion that attached itself to all general staff officers after the 20 July putsch. On 4 September he finally reached Luettwitz by phone (all wires had been out), told him of the plan, and ordered the *XLVII Panzer Corps* headquarters down from Metz to take

[10] In August, however, Hitler had allocated most of the German tank production to the Western Front.

over in the Mirecourt–Neufchâteau area, the base for the proposed operation. The target date for the counterattack was set for 12 September—while Blaskowitz cast about for troops to give Luettwitz. On or about that date the offensive would open with a thrust to the northwest on either side of Toul; this was to be followed by a general advance toward the Marne River, with the left German wing covered by the Marne, the center pushing through Bar-le-Duc, and the right wing moving south of the Argonne Forest.

On 5 September Blaskowitz told General Wiese that his *Nineteenth Army* must now stand and hold on its right flank, designating the main line of resistance from the Langres Plateau east to Besançon as essential cover for the concentration of the counterattack group in the north. At the same time, however, the American XII Corps was becoming a threat east of Toul. After General Chevallerie had protested that his *First Army* dared not further extend its already weakened south flank by moving the line of the *553d VG Division* down to Neufchâteau, the *LXVI Corps* was assigned the stopgap mission. In spite of this regrouping, Allied pressure all along the Western Front made it difficult, if not impossible, for the German divisions earmarked for the big counterattack to disengage and move rapidly into the bridgehead being held open between Neufchâteau and the Moselle. General Blaskowitz reluctantly informed *OB WEST* on 7 September that the target date for the counterattack must be set back to 15 September. General Knobelsdorff,[11] menaced on the *First Army* front by the preliminary XII and XX Corps' attempts to put bridgeheads across the Moselle, asked for permission to shorten his left wing and free additional troops by a withdrawal behind Nancy to an anchor position on the Marne-Rhin Canal. Promptly, however, Blaskowitz appealed to *OB WEST*, reminding that headquarters, probably needlessly, of Hitler's express demands for a stroke against the Third Army. *OB WEST* replied on 8 September by transferring General Knobelsdorff's *First Army* from *Army Group B* to *Army Group G*, under Blaskowitz' command.

This addition of the *First Army*, from which many of the units tabbed for the counterattack were to be taken, did little to solve Blaskowitz' problem. General Knobelsdorff now had his hands full south of Metz where the XX Corps had begun crossing the Moselle, and the *XIII SS Corps*, defending that sector, could not release the *3d Panzer Grenadier Division* and the *17th SS Panzer Grenadier Division*. Knobelsdorff also held on to one regiment of the

[11] Knobelsdorff replaced Chevallerie as *First Army* commander on 6 September 1944.

15th Panzer Grenadier Division, in spite of repeated orders for its release, pleading that lack of gasoline prevented movement to the south. In addition, the *106th Panzer Brigade* had been thrown into a hasty counterattack against the 90th Division west of Thionville, on 8 September, and had come out of the fight with only nine usable tanks and assault guns—and no ordnance train to repair its damaged equipment.

Field Marshal Rundstedt had been sending daily reminders from his headquarters at Koblenz that the Hitler-inspired offensive must take place regardless of all difficulties. The Allied threat in the Aachen sector was growing more ominous hourly. On the German *Seventh Army* front the West Wall itself was in danger. At least six weeks, according to the calculations of the *OB WEST* staff, would be needed to put the West Wall in a state of proper defense. Rundstedt had a limited course of action. He could rush troops to the Aachen area and beg Hitler for new divisions. This he had done. He could hope to win time by seizing the initiative on another part of the front. This Hitler had decided, counter to Rundstedt's desire to mass all available armor in defense of the gateway to the Cologne plain. Therefore, on the night of 7 September, Rundstedt sent an appeal to Jodl asking that OKW support the *Fifth Panzer Army* with sufficient materiel, fuel, and planes to make the counterattack a success. On 9 September, however, Blaskowitz was informed that the *XLVII Panzer Corps* would begin the counterattack with only a Kampfgruppe (Colonel Josef Rauch) from the *21st Panzer Division* and the *111th* and *112th Panzer Brigades* coming up from Germany—a very considerable reduction from the scope of the original plan. Such a force was hardly calculated to inspire much confidence in any far-reaching success. The two panzer brigades were newly organized and equipped with a battalion of Mark IV's and a battalion of Mark V's (Panthers) apiece—a total of ninety-eight tanks per brigade—plus a two-battalion regiment of armored infantry. But the *21st Panzer Division* was woefully weak, for it had been broken up after the August fighting—one panzer grenadier regiment being assigned to *Army Group B* and the bulk of the remaining units being returned to Germany for refitting. Of the *21st Panzer Division*, Blaskowitz had at his disposal on 9 September only the *192d Panzer Grenadier Regiment* (with three companies totaling about 250 men and 10 light machine guns), the *22d Panzer Regiment* (with no tanks), seven batteries of artillery (five of which had no prime movers), and two 88-mm. antitank guns.

Before even this modest force could be committed the XV Corps began a drive on a forty-mile front toward the Moselle, overrunning the Mirecourt–Neufchâteau area. Yet even now Berlin remained far removed from the tactical situation and Hitler issued a Jovian decree that the *Fifth Panzer Army* would not be used in any frontal attacks against the advancing Americans, but would be kept intact for its main mission. Blaskowitz gave a very liberal interpretation to this last order (if he did not flatly violate it) and committed the *112th Panzer Brigade* against the XV Corps, with such disastrous results as to make that panzer brigade little more than a cipher in future operational plans.[12]

The XV Corps Advance to the Moselle

On the morning of 10 September the 313th Infantry (Col. S. A. Wood) arrived in the Joinville area, completing the movement of the 79th Infantry Division from Belgium to the south flank of the Third Army. The 315th Infantry (Lt. Col. J. A. McAleer) was already deployed and patrolling on the east bank of the Marne River. The 314th Infantry (Col. W. A. Robinson) had assembled on the west bank. The 79th Division, constituting the XV Corps left, lay forward of the 2d French Armored Division, which was echeloned back to the southwest as a screen for the corps and army. (*Map XVIII*)

The XV Corps had made no contact with the Germans in the Chaumont–Neufchâteau sector. Intelligence reports indicated that the enemy was holding a string of towns along the main highway leading from Chatillon-sur-Seine northeast to Neufchâteau, and from Neufchâteau to Charmes, on the Moselle. Earlier in September the 42d Cavalry had given the German high command a scare by sending small patrols toward Charmes. Indeed, Hitler had sent a personal order that Charmes be "retaken" at once, despite the fact that the Americans never entered the town. But the XII Corps cavalry had turned back to the north as the corps prepared to cross the Moselle, and ground observation of German troop movements into the Neufchâteau sector had ended. As a result the impending advance by Haislip's XV Corps would be a meeting engagement in the classical sense epitomized for American military students by the 1914 clashes at Virton and Longwy.

[12] Details of the German plan for a counteroffensive are found in the *Army Group G KTB*, in the *Panzer Armeeoberkommando 5 KTB* (hereafter cited as *Fifth Panzer Army KTB*) and *Anlagen*, and in the *XLVII Panzer Corps KTB* for the period.

The original mission given the XV Corps had been a relatively passive one. On 10 September, therefore, the troops were reconnoitering for defense positions, resting, taking hot baths in Joinville, and—in the 79th area—listening to Bing Crosby and his USO show. The 106th Cavalry Group (Col. Vennard Wilson) was moving through the 79th en route to take over a screening mission south of the infantry outposts. General Wyche, with Third Army permission, had just dispatched forty-eight of his 2½-ton trucks to the rear for supplies. Meanwhile the 35th Infantry Division, farther to the north and east, had begun the attack to carry the right wing of the XII Corps across the Moselle River. A little before 1500 a telephone message from the Third Army reached Haislip, alerting the XV Corps for advance to the east. This movement, set for the following morning, was intended to bring the corps to the west bank of the Moselle on a front extending from Charmes to Epinal. As yet, however, General Patton had given no orders for crossing that river in the XV Corps zone.

The main weight in this maneuver would have to be furnished initially by the 79th Division, since only a part of Leclerc's armor could be freed from the screening mission on the army flank. General Wyche selected the 314th Infantry for a stroke calculated to seize Charmes and gain a position on the Moselle. The corps commander immobilized two battalions of corps artillery to motorize the 314th. Only five medium tanks of the 749th Tank Battalion (attached to the 79th Division) were in repair; these tanks and a company of tank destroyers also were given to the 314th Infantry. About 0800 on 11 September the 314th Infantry entrucked and, preceded by the 121st Cavalry Squadron, began a semicircular sweep of some sixty-five miles around the enemy outposts and across the face of the *16th Division*, which was deployed fronting northward along the line Andelot–Neufchâteau–Charmes. The cavalry came within sight of Charmes around 1700 and engaged in a brief skirmish with the German outposts, but the 314th did not arrive in the Charmes neighborhood for another two and a half hours—too late to set up an attack against the town. The 313th Infantry had followed the 314th during the day, in trucks and on foot. In the late afternoon it wheeled south to get into position for an attack toward Mirecourt, possession of which would cut the main German line of communications leading from Neufchâteau to Epinal. The 315th Infantry meanwhile made twenty-two miles, also by motor and on foot, and as the day ended halted west of Neufchâteau, where patrols went forward to feel out the German positions.

While the 79th Division moved swiftly to strike at the north shoulder of the *LXVI Corps* salient, General Leclerc's armor attacked the German units farther west. Here *Kampfgruppe Ottenbacher* held a defensive position behind the Marne and Marne-Saône Canal at right angles to the *16th Division*, with its northern wing resting on Andelot and its southern wing abutting on the Langres Plateau. Generalleutnant Ernst Ottenbacher's command consisted mainly of over-age reservists, poorly trained and armed, who had been assigned to police duties during the German occupation of France. Just before the French attack General Ottenbacher lost his only well-equipped and mobile troops when the *100th Motorized Brigade* and the last two battalions of the *19th SS Police Regiment* were taken away and sent to Belfort, leaving the Kampfgruppe with only six *Landesschuetzen* battalions.[13]

General Leclerc began to probe the German positions on the morning of 11 September, using one combat command to make the developing attack while the rest of the division continued the screening mission along the Third Army flank. Combat Command L (Col. Paul Girot de Langlade) began a maneuver in front of Andelot but found the Germans strongly entrenched. General Leclerc, anxious to avoid premature and piecemeal entanglement on ground chosen by the enemy, ordered CCL to bypass Andelot and reconnoiter farther to the east. This order was carried out with dispatch. Colonel Langlade's command, advancing in two columns, struck sharply through Prez-sous-Lafauche, at the joint between the *16th Division* and *Kampfgruppe Ottenbacher*, and cut the Neufchâteau–Chaumont and Neufchâteau–Langres roads. When night put an end to the French advance one column was nearing Vittel and the whole of CCL was deep inside the German lines.

The XV Corps maneuver on the first day of the advance had brought its troops around the enemy or through the weak spots in the overextended lines of the *LXVI Corps*. Now, on 12 September, General Haislip's units came to grips with the Germans in a disconnected series of local engagements and surprise meetings extending all the way from Charmes back to Andelot. The 79th Infantry Division, spread over a forty-mile front, engaged the *16th Division*, whose troops had been concentrated in a succession of towns organized as strong points. At Charmes the 314th Infantry attacked in midmorning and after a day-long fight drove the defenders, approximately two battalions of the *225th Regiment*, out of the town and back across the Moselle. The re-

[13] MS #B–538 (Ottenbacher).

treating Germans blew the Charmes bridges, but General Haislip ordered General Wyche to cross and secure a bridgehead. After dark the 1st Battalion of the 314th found a ford and crossed to the east bank without mishap. North of the town the 106th Cavalry Group started to cross the Moselle, meeting no opposition. West of Charmes the 313th became involved in a fire fight with a strong force from the *221st Regiment* drawn up near the little village of Poussay just outside of Mirecourt. At Neufchâteau the 315th converged on the town from three sides, pushed the attack home late in the evening, and trapped a large part of the *223d Regiment.* Next day the German commander surrendered, turning over 623 prisoners and 80 vehicles and heavy weapons.

The 2d French Armored Division also was busily engaged on 12 September, cutting into *Kampfgruppe Ottenbacher* and driving almost at will through the German rear areas. CCL outflanked Vittel from the south and reported a bag of over five hundred prisoners, captured as they fled along the highways. CCV (Col. Pierre Billotte), committed at Andelot, had a brisk fight and not only killed or snared the entire garrison but also cut to pieces a German battalion, en route from Chaumont to reinforce Andelot. The reports of the 2d French Armored Division record that CCV killed an estimated 300 Germans and captured nearly 800 in this action.

Thus far *Kampfgruppe Ottenbacher* and the *16th Division* had fought alone, defending strong points in crossroads towns and villages, and meeting defeat in detail as the Allied troops cut through their lateral communications. General Blaskowitz, torn by the dilemma of obeying Hitler's orders to hold back the forces selected for the big counteroffensive without losing the Mirecourt–Neufchâteau area from which it was to be made, finally could delay no longer. On 12 September Blaskowitz ordered General Manteuffel to use elements of his newly arrived *Fifth Panzer Army* in a limited counterattack against the XV Corps. Manteuffel assigned this mission to General Luettwitz' *XLVII Panzer Corps*, which had been concentrated between Epinal and St. Dié. Luettwitz was given no time for reconnaissance and no opportunity to arrange a co-ordinated attack; he was simply instructed to attack toward Vittel, free the encircled troops of the *LXVI Corps*, and drive northwest into the Allied flank. This move would give the *Nineteenth Army* time and space in which to extend its right wing northward as a covering force for the deployment of the *Fifth Panzer Army.*

The forces General Luettwitz had under his command were relatively weak and widely separated. The *112th Panzer Brigade* furnished the bulk and the armored backbone of the *XLVII Panzer Corps.* If committed under different circumstances it might have been a formidable threat to the fragmentized XV Corps, since it had a full complement of new tanks: a battalion of 48 Mark IV's and another of 48 Mark V's. On 12 September the *112th Panzer Brigade* debouched from Epinal in two columns. The right column, consisting of the Panther battalion, mobile infantry, and artillery, moved directly west in the direction of Vittel while the left column, containing the Mark IV's, began a circular movement that carried it south toward Bains-les-Bains, in anticipation of an attack by advance units of the American Seventh Army which were already as far north as Vesoul. Late in the day the right column of the *112th Panzer Brigade* bivouacked near the village of Dompaire, southeast of Mirecourt. The left column, finding no American troops on its flank, had begun to wheel north toward Darney, from which a main road led to Vittel. General Luettwitz now decided to commit *Kampfgruppe Luck,* the weak infantry detachment belonging to his corps, and ordered it to march to Dompaire on 13 September.[14] Once this infantry reinforcement had reached the north column and the south column was in position, Luettwitz intended to throw the combined strength of the *112th Panzer Brigade* and *Kampfgruppe Luck* at Vittel, some eleven miles to the west. But this ambitious plan was doomed to failure.

After seizing Vittel on 12 September, CCL, 2d French Armored Division, continued east and laagered that night just short of Dompaire and Damas—the latter a village about two miles southeast of Dompaire. During the late afternoon French civilians had brought word to Colonel Langlade's headquarters that a large German tank force was moving on Dompaire. This intelligence was confirmed in the early evening when French outposts picked up the sound of heavy vehicles congregating in the area. Langlade ordered his artillery into position and prepared to engage the enemy on the morrow. His plans were simple: the right column (Colonel Minjonnet) of CCL would strike through Damas and cut the main road between Dompaire and Epinal; the left column (Lt. Col. Jacques Massu) would attack the enemy concentrated at Dompaire. The village of Dompaire lay in a narrow valley and most of the German tanks were assembled here on the low ground.

At dawn on 13 September a small reconnaissance party, headed by four tank destroyers, left Minjonnet's bivouac and rolled toward Damas. Just short

[14] *Kampfgruppe Luck* consisted of about 240 riflemen and a few assault guns from the *125th Panzer Grenadier Regiment (21st Panzer Division).*

DOMPAIRE

of the village it surprised some German Panthers, loosed a few rounds, knocked out a Panther, and hurriedly retired to the shelter offered by a small ridge. The German tankers made no move and soon the 12th Chasseurs was on the scene with its Sherman tanks. Colonel Langlade meanwhile had sent Massu's force around to the north of Dompaire. Here his observers reported the town and near-by fields "literally crawling" with enemy tanks. Langlade made a feint with his armored infantry and then, when the German Panthers started to deploy to counter this move, the French poured in a terrific fire from their tanks and field guns. But the French were not to engage the Panthers by themselves. The American air support officer with the 2d French Armored Division had succeeded in reaching XIX TAC by radio and General Weyland's headquarters dispatched the 406th Group from its base at Rennes, far back in Brittany. The fighter-bombers made four strikes at Damas and Dompaire during the day, lashing at the huddled Germans with bombs and rockets. After each air strike Massu and Minjonnet displaced forward, using the cover of neighboring apple orchards and pine groves and compressing the milling Panthers into a narrowing killing ground on the valley bottom. Eventually the French seized a cemetery, on a rise at the north edge of Dompaire, that gave them complete control of the battlefield. In the afternoon the leading tanks of the south column of the *112th Panzer Brigade* were discovered moving hurriedly toward Ville-sur-Illon, apparently intent on striking the French in the rear. CCL, however, was ready for this new threat and destroyed seven Mark IV's at the first encounter. As this action continued the German losses increased, and finally the southern column abandoned its rescue attempt. Late in the day the Germans in the Dompaire sector deserted their vehicles and fled on foot to the east, leaving the battlefield to the French.

This fight, characterized warmly by the XV Corps commander as a "brilliant" example of perfect air-ground co-ordination, not only was an outstanding feat of arms but also had dealt a crippling blow to Hitler's plans for an armored thrust into the Third Army flank. The *112th Panzer Brigade* had lost nearly all of its Panther battalion—only four of these heavy tanks escaped the Dompaire debacle. In addition the Mark IV battalion had sustained some loss, bringing the total number of tanks destroyed to sixty.[15]

[15] XV Corps G–3 Jnl, 14 Sep 44. *La 2ème DB*, 81. The 406th Group claimed 13 tanks destroyed and 15 damaged. A German report dated 16 September verifies the French claims. Some tanks had already been lost by the *112th* before it reached the battlefield, as a result either of air attack or of mechanical difficulties. The losses reported on 13 September totaled 34 Panthers and 26 Mark IV's. See *OB WEST KTB. Anlage 63. Army Group G KTB Nr 2* twice refers to these tank losses as "unbelievably high."

That day, 13 September, also proved to be an unlucky one for the Germans still fighting in the area west of Dompaire. CCD (Col. Louis J. Dio), the reserve combat command of the 2d French Armored, took Chaumont and ended the last organized resistance by *Kampfgruppe Ottenbacher*. The 315th Infantry captured its substantial bag of prisoners and weapons at Neufchâteau after a stubborn house-to-house fight in the town. The 313th Infantry experienced some difficulty in co-ordinating plans for its attack to take Poussay: companies had become separated and the supporting artillery was not in position. By late evening, however, the 2d Battalion was inside the village.[16] In the confusion and darkness the Americans bivouacked next door to the enemy, some—it was later reported—in the same buildings with the Germans. Elsewhere the German retreat turned into a rout, although here and there small detachments attempted a stand, or minute rear guard tank and assault gun detachments essayed fruitless counterattacks. The events of this day finally convinced Blaskowitz that he should withdraw the *16th Division* to the east before it was completely destroyed. General Lucht, the *LXVI Corps* commander, had advocated such a retirement many hours earlier. Now it was too late to make any co-ordinated withdrawal; the *16th* would make its retreat in a general *sauve-qui-peut.*

Nevertheless the 79th Division, having had word of the tank battles on the south flank of the XV Corps, proceeded cautiously on 14 September, as yet unaware of the summary manner in which the French had disposed of the German armor. At Charmes the 315th Infantry extended its outposts to the south, while patrols from the 106th Cavalry Group reconnoitered on the east bank of the Moselle. The 313th Infantry mopped up Poussay, where the 2d Battalion took seventy-four prisoners, and its 1st Battalion captured Mirecourt, thus cutting the Neufchâteau–Epinal road. That evening the 2d Battalion bivouacked in the village of Ramecourt, on the road west of Mirecourt, with the intention of blocking the Germans who were fleeing from the 315th Infantry after a rear guard fight at Châtenois. At midnight the head of a retreating German column marched unexpectedly into the village and without preamble began to bivouac in the streets and houses where the American infantry lay. Sudden mutual recognition precipitated a burst of "wild fighting." About two hundred prisoners were taken in the village itself and the

[16] On 13 September 1st Lt. Jonathan Hutchinson, F Company, 313th Infantry, took an enemy machine gun position and silenced two antitank guns with hand grenades in singlehanded attacks. He was awarded the DSC.

tail of the German column, still on the road, was riddled by the quick and accurate fire of the American gunners. By daylight over five hundred of the enemy had been killed or captured.[17]

The French, pursuing their victory of the preceding day, engaged *Kampfgruppe Luck* and some Mark IV's near Hennecourt. But General Luettwitz was unwilling to risk what was left of his command and on the night of 14 September ordered the *112th Panzer Brigade* and *Kampfgruppe Luck* to withdraw to the Canal de l'Est just west of the city of Epinal, there to hold open a route of escape for the fleeing troops of the *16th Division* and the remnants of *Kampfgruppe Ottenbacher*.

Although the XV Corps drive had been highly successful, General Haislip was restive under the compulsion of using one of his two divisions to protect the Third Army flank, and he therefore importuned General Patton for an additional infantry division. The Third Army commander had no infantry to spare. But on 14 September General Bradley released CCB of the 6th Armored Division in the sector west of Orléans and Patton sent it to take over the 2d French Armored Division security mission west of Troyes. On this same day the 2d French Armored met a Seventh Army patrol (from the 2d Spahis, 1st French Armored Division) near Clefmont. This connection between the Third and Seventh Armies remained very tenuous, however, and while the 79th Division closed on the west bank of the Moselle General Leclerc's combat commands remained strung out back to the southwest in position to guard the corps and army flank. Rumors of the movement of German armor in the Epinal area—which took on greater significance in the light of the big tank battle at Dompaire—had had enough weight to convince even General Patton that a continued watch toward the south and west was necessary, and on 14 September he gave verbal orders to the XV Corps commander to hold the balance of the 79th Division west of the Moselle and await crossing orders.[18]

Meanwhile, the enemy pocket between the Third and Seventh Armies was emptying rapidly. The remnants of the *16th Division* fled as best they could, in civilian automobiles and on foot, as single stragglers and in disorderly groups. By 16 September what was left of this ill-fated command had crossed the Moselle, and both the XV Corps and *Army Group G* wrote off

[17] *History of the 313th Infantry in World War II* (Washington, 1947), pp. 112–15.

[18] XV Corps AAR, 14 Sep 44. The original order to hold at the Moselle had been issued at General Patton's headquarters at 0045 on 13 September. See TUSA Diary.

the division as a combat unit. Following their usual practice the Germans subsequently re-formed the division under its old number, but American and German records both show that the *16th Division* had been reduced to a mere number on a troop list in the five-day battle.[19]

While the 79th swung into line on the west bank of the Moselle, the advance battalion of the 314th Infantry remained in position on the east side of the river opposite Charmes, with the XV Corps artillery sited to give fire support if necessary. Actually, only scattered security forces faced the 79th at this point since the German position on the Moselle had been unhinged by the XII Corps advance in the north. One troop of the 106th Cavalry Group had crossed the river in the XII Corps area and then turned south to screen in front of the Charmes bridgehead. More of the corps cavalry crossed on 16 September and began to reconnoiter toward the Mortagne River, believed to be the next enemy line of resistance. During this same day a combat team from CCV, the most advanced of Lerclerc's units, got into a sharp fight at Châtel, a village on the enemy bank of the Moselle about six miles south of Charmes to which the French had crossed during the previous night. Late on the afternoon of 16 September a large task force from the *111th Panzer Brigade* (estimated to consist of fifteen Panthers and two infantry battalions) suddenly struck Châtel in a pincers attack. General Leclerc hurried reinforcements to the scene and the Germans were beaten off—an officer prisoner later told his captors that the attackers had lost two hundred men and five Panthers. Nevertheless, the French general withdrew his men across the river in order to avoid involvement in a large-scale engagement while he was still charged with protecting the army flank *west* of the Moselle.

It was only a matter of days until the Third and Seventh Armies would be aligned more or less abreast, facing east and in position to give some mutual cover on their inner wings. The 2d French Armored Division cavalry (Col. Jean S. Remy),[20] patrolling near Bains-les-Bains on 17 September, made contact with their compatriots of the French II Corps (Lt. Gen. de Goilard de Monsabert) who had driven north along the valleys of the Rhone and Saône on the left flank of the Seventh Army. In the gap still remaining to the west CCB, 6th Armored Division, arrived to relieve CCD in the Chaumont

[19] XV Corps G–2 Jnl, 16 Sep 44, estimates that the *16th Division* had an original strength of about 7,000 men, of whom 4,000 were captured and 2,000 were casualties. See also *Army Group G KTB Nr. 2 (Anlage)*.

[20] The division cavalry consisted of four squadrons of the 1er Régiment de Marche des Spahis Marocains.

sector, whereupon General Patton relieved the XV Corps of responsibility for watching the Third Army flank, save in the narrow space between the Meuse and Moselle Rivers. By the night of 17 September all of the 2d French Armored Division was alongside the 79th on the west bank of the Moselle, except Langlade's combat command and Remy's cavalry, which remained echeloned to the right and rear of the division.[21]

The Advance to the Meurthe River

The XV Corps commander had expected to resume the attack east of the Moselle River on a somewhat narrower front, advancing in a column of divisions with the 2d French Armored Division in the lead so as to give some rest to the tired infantry of the 79th Division. On 18 September, however, German armor struck the XII Corps at Lunéville. About 1345 General Patton arrived at General Haislip's headquarters and after a conference with Haislip and the two division commanders ordered an immediate advance across the Moselle. The XV Corps mission remained the same—to furnish protection for the Army's south flank—but General Patton changed the axis of attack from east to northeast, consonant with the general shift toward the northeast by the entire Third Army. This maneuver would give the XV Corps an extended front and require the use of both its divisions in the first stages of the advance. The 79th Division, on the left, would move toward Lunéville and cover the exposed right wing of the XII Corps, which was being subjected to increasingly heavy enemy pressure. The 2d French Armored Division also would cross the Moselle and put some weight into the attack. The Seventh Army, however, had not yet pushed its northern flank as far as the Moselle and at the moment was in process of moving the 45th Division (Maj. Gen. W. W. Eagles) in to relieve the II French Corps on the army's left wing. Until the 45th Division could resume the offensive and draw abreast of General Haislip the 2d French Armored would have to make its attack a limited affair and concentrate heavily on screening toward the south and east.[22]

The German detachments facing the XV Corps were small in numbers and lacked heavy weapons. On the morning of 18 September the *Fifth Panzer*

[21] Information on this operation was slow in reaching the War Department. On 22 September General Handy cabled SHAEF on behalf of General Marshall expressing concern about the "deep [German] salient" west of Chaumont. Handy to Eisenhower, W–34664, 22 Sep 44, SHAEF Message File.

[22] Ltr, Gen Haislip to Hist Div, 17 Jul 47; Ltr, Gen Wyche to Hist Div, 2 Jan 47.

Army finally had begun the often-postponed counteroffensive against the Third Army. Strategic circumstances had whittled away both the force and the maneuver area envisaged in Hitler's original plans; the counteroffensive had dwindled in scope to what could more accurately be called a counterattack and its mission now was limited—at the most optimistic—to wresting the line of the Moselle away from the XII Corps. Luettwitz' *XLVII Panzer Corps* had a dual role in the undertaking. Most of it was thrown into an attack northward toward Lunéville. Part of the *21st Panzer Division* and the remainder of the *112th Panzer Brigade* were charged with guarding the exposed left flank of the *Fifth Panzer Army* along the Mortagne River, in which position these security detachments would meet the 79th Division attack. Farther to the south, in the Epinal–Rambervillers sector, the battered and broken *LXVI Corps* under the *Nineteenth Army* furnished a none too dependable anchor for Luettwitz in an oblique extension from the latter's left wing. Remnants of the *223d Infantry Regiment (16th Division)*, reinforced by a few of Luettwitz' tanks and the loan of two of the three 88-mm. guns salvaged by Ottenbacher during the recent retreat, still held a position on the Moselle River at Châtel, which had been reoccupied when the advance guard of the French armored division withdrew to the west bank.

In midafternoon of 18 September the 314th Infantry, which already had a battalion east of the Moselle, began the XV Corps advance, marching behind the screen thrown out by the 106th Cavalry Group as far as Moriviller, where the regiment bivouacked for the night. The 313th Infantry crossed the river and then moved by truck to Einvaux, thus taking position on the left of the division. The 315th Infantry, in division reserve, also crossed the Moselle during the night of 18–19 September and closed behind the 313th Infantry. Thus far the 79th had met no opposition, but the movement had started too late in the day to bring the division to the Mortagne River that same evening, as Patton had ordered.

The 2d French Armored Division began its advance in the late afternoon, under orders to drive no farther than the highway between St. Pierremont and Gerbéviller which followed the eastern bank of the Mortagne River. General Leclerc left CCL west of the Moselle as flank protection and brought Dio's combat command up from reserve to head the attack. Three bridges quickly were thrown across the Moselle and while CCV held the bridgehead Dio's tanks roared through the streets of Châtel, guided by the light of burning German trucks and the flashes of rifle fire from the houses where the enemy lay barricaded. By daylight CCD was clear of Châtel and racing toward the Mortagne River.

Both of General Haislip's divisions threw elements across the Mortagne on 19 September. The left regiment of the 79th, the 313th Infantry, put its advance guard across the river without opposition but ran into a sharp fight with some troops of the *192d Panzer Grenadier Regiment, 21st Panzer Division*, at the town of Xermaménil. The *21st Panzer Division*, however, was too dispersed in its role as a covering force to fight more than a delaying action at any point on the Mortagne, and the 313th quickly cleared Xermaménil—opening the road to Lunéville. The 314th Infantry, moving on foot, reached the river about 1800 and opened an assault on Gerbéviller, whose bridges led to one of the few good roads east of the Mortagne. At dark the American attack was called off, but during the night the German garrison withdrew to the east. Dio's French combat command reached the Mortagne about 1400; it found the enemy feeble and the crossing denied only by mines and blown bridges. During the evening the French made their way over the river near the village of Vallois, then dispatched reconnaissance troops to Vathiménil, on the west bank of the Meurthe River, which was taken around midnight.

The XV Corps breached the thin German line along the Mortagne at a half-dozen points on 19 September and during the night the *Fifth Panzer Army* commander ordered Generalleutnant Edgar Feuchtinger to pull his weak *21st Panzer Division*, which had been reinforced by the *112th Panzer Brigade*, back behind the Meurthe. But the detachments on the south flank were entrapped by the French raid to Vathiménil and were forced to flee on foot, abandoning over two hundred vehicles and some of the tanks belonging to the unfortunate *112th Panzer Brigade*. General Blaskowitz railed at the *Fifth Panzer Army* commander for relinquishing the Mortagne line, but this was no more than a "statement for the record" since *Army Group G* had no reserves with which to shore up the *Fifth Panzer Army's* threatened flank.

On 20 September the XV Corps made contact with the XII Corps in Lunéville, where the latter had been fighting since 16 September for command of the road and river complex dominated by the city. The leading battalion of the 313th Infantry passed through Lunéville, in which Americans and Germans still were battling, and wheeled southeast on the enemy bank of the Meurthe River in preparation for an attack designed to roll up the flank of the new German security line. To the south the 314th Infantry reached the Meurthe River but came under such heavy fire from the Forêt de Mondon, in which the Germans had taken cover on the east bank of the river, as to be prevented from an immediate crossing. In the meantime the 2d French Armored Division held in place and limited its activities to patrolling. CCL, which had been kept on the west bank of the Moselle to watch the German bridgehead at Epinal, was relieved during the day by the 45th Infantry Division. With the Seventh Army thus in position to start its left wing attacking across the Moselle, CCL moved east to rejoin Leclerc.

On 20 September General Patton altered the XV Corps left boundary, pushing it north to the Marne-Rhin Canal. This change allowed General Haislip more room for maneuver on his left flank. It also gave the XV Corps the responsibility for ejecting the remaining Germans from Lunéville and ultimately would bring the 79th Division into a bloody battle east of the city for possession of the Forêt de Parroy. The boundary shift had equally important implications in the XII Corps zone. When the German counterattack on 18 September hit the salient formed by the southern wing of the XII Corps, General Eddy's troops had been caught in a precarious position astride the Marne-Rhin Canal. Now the XII Corps commander could concentrate his forces to meet the main German attack north of the canal.[23]

[23] See Chapter V, pp. 222ff.

CHAPTER V

The German Counterattack in the XII Corps Sector (19 September - 1 October)

Plans for Employment of the Third Army

The Supreme Commander's decision to make a two-pronged advance in the direction of the Ruhr and the Saar, as set forth in the directive of 4 September,[1] had allowed the Third Army to launch its attack across the Moselle River and resume the push toward the Rhine. Logistical support for offensive operations by all the Allied armies was far from assured, however, and the question as to whether the subsidiary drive to the east could be maintained while the main effort was under way in the northeast remained a pressing one.

On 7 September the Combined Chiefs of Staff, representing the military staffs of the United States and Great Britain, requested General Eisenhower to state his intentions for the future conduct of operations on the European continent. The Supreme Commander's reply followed the line of reasoning advanced in the directive of 4 September but was somewhat less optimistic of quick success and noted that the enemy forces were beginning to stiffen. Eisenhower described the immediate operation as one

> to break the Siegfried Line and seize crossings over the Rhine. In doing this the main effort will be on the left. Then we will prepare logistically and otherwise for a deep thrust into Germany. . . . Once we have the Ruhr and the Saar, we have a strangle hold on two of Germany's main industrial areas, and will have largely destroyed her capacity to wage war whatever course events may take. During the advance to the Ruhr and the Saar we will be opening the deep water ports of Havre and Antwerp or Rotterdam which are essential to sustain a power thrust deep into Germany. I wish to retain freedom of action to strike in any direction so far as the logistical situation permits. At the moment and until we have developed the Channel ports and the rail lines therefrom, our supply

[1] See Chap. I, p. 52.

situation is stretched to the breaking point, and from this standpoint the advance across the Siegfried Line involves a gamble which I am prepared to take in order to take full advantage of the present disorganized state of the German armies in the West.[2]

The Combined Chiefs of Staff hastened to put their seal of approval on the "proposals" advanced by Eisenhower and further strengthened his hand by a cable from Quebec which called attention:

"(a) To the advantages of the Northern line of approach into Germany, as opposed to the Southern. They note with satisfaction that you appear to be of the same mind.

"(b) To the necessity for opening the Northwest ports, and particularly Antwerp and Rotterdam, before the bad weather sets in." [3]

All of these plans for the future obviously turned on a marked improvement in the logistical situation. By the second week of September supplies again were moving rapidly to the front from the Normandy beaches and the Channel ports; but this supply line was overextended, difficult to maintain, and, at the receiving end, subject to the caprices of the oncoming autumn weather. The stubborn German hold on Brest had prevented the use of that deepwater port, and in any case Brest was now too far removed from the main battle front. Supply over the beaches probably would be ended by the November storms. The great harbor at Rotterdam was off the axis of advance and undoubtedly would require enormous efforts to capture and rehabilitate. There remained the deepwater port at Antwerp. The city itself had been taken by Montgomery's forces on 4 September, but the enemy still held the islands and the Schelde mouths which barred ingress from the sea. Only a major Allied attack could hope to jar the Germans loose from this strangling position and open the much-needed port.

Although the supply lines from the beaches and coastal harbors would provide a daily average of 3,500 tons each to the First and Third Armies during the period of 16–22 September, this was not enough. Both of the American armies desired a daily supply tonnage double this figure; and the 12th Army Group, utilizing the logistical experiences since D Day, had arrived at the conclusion that in days of attack each division (plus its supporting corps and army troops) would require a minimum supply of 600 tons.[4] The

[2] Eisenhower to CCS, 10 Sep 44, SHAEF SGS File, Post OVERLORD Planning 381, I.

[3] CCS to Eisenhower, OCTAGON 16, 12 Sep 44, SHAEF SGS File, Post OVERLORD Planning 381, I.

[4] Rpt of conf on 14 Sep 44, Ltr, Gen Moses to Gen Crawford, 22 Oct 44, SHAEF SGS File, Supply Problems of Allied Advance, 400.3/1.

port of Antwerp, however, might be expected to meet the requirements of the field armies. The main supply center of the Third Army, Nancy, was 461 miles by rail from Cherbourg—but only 250 miles from Antwerp. The Cherbourg supply route, utilizing both rail and highway facilities, could provide adequate maintenance for only 21 divisions; the port of Antwerp, it was estimated, could support 54 divisions by rail alone.[5]

On 9, 10, and 11 September, General Eisenhower conferred with Bradley, Montgomery, and Admiral Sir Bertram H. Ramsay (Commander of the Allied Naval Expeditionary Force), following these meetings with a directive on 13 September which amplified that of the 4th:

> . . . the object we must now attain, one which has been foreseen as essential from the very inception of the Overlord plan, is the gaining of deep water ports to support major forces in the invasion of Germany. Inevitably the process of cleaning up the rear will involve some temporary slackening of our efforts toward the front. Nevertheless, without improved communications a speedy and prolonged advance by forces adequate in strength, depending on bulk oil, transport and ammunition is not a feasible operation. . . . The general plan, already explained, is to push our forces forward to the Rhine, securing bridgeheads over the river, seize the Ruhr and concentrate our forces in preparation for a final non-stop drive into Germany. While this is going on we must . . . secure the approaches to Antwerp or Rotterdam so that one of these ports and the lines of communication radiating therefrom can give adequate maintenance to the Northern Group of armies deep into the heart of Germany.[6]

The directive of 13 September restated in unambiguous terms that operations on the Allied left would "take priority in all forms of logistical support. . . ." The Third Army would be permitted to push only far enough "to hold adequate bridgeheads beyond the Moselle and thus create a constant threat to the German forces and prevent the enemy from reinforcing further north by tearing troops away from the Metz area." Once Montgomery's forces and the First Army had succeeded in seizing bridgeheads across the Rhine the Third Army would be given the green light for an advance through the Saar and over the Rhine. However, "if, at an earlier date, maintenance of the Third U.S. Army becomes possible, this advance will be initiated at that time." In this clause of the directive lay the permission General Bradley would need to continue the Third Army attack beyond the establishment of a firm bridgehead east of the Moselle.

[5] Estimates by the Chief of Transportation, ETOUSA, 19 Sep 44, AGO files (ETOUSA). See History of G–4, Com Z, ETO (MS), pp. 47ff.

[6] Directive, Eisenhower to Commanders, FWD–14764, 13 Sep 44, SHAEF Cable Log.

On 10 September General Bradley had instructed General Hodges to continue the First Army advance and secure crossing sites on the Rhine in the vicinity of Koblenz, Bonn, and Cologne, meanwhile providing cover for the right flank of the 21st Army Group. At the same time Bradley ordered the Third Army commander to continue the eastward advance with the object of making Rhine crossings in the neighborhood of Mannheim and Mainz.[7] Marshal Montgomery was quick to protest Bradley's directive as being contradictory to the strategy agreed upon for a main effort in the northeast, but Gen. Walter B. Smith, the SHAEF chief of staff, assured the field marshal that the weight of the 12th Army Group attack would be thrown on the left in support of the 21st Army Group drive toward Antwerp and the Ruhr, exactly as General Eisenhower had ordered.[8]

Actually the scheme of maneuver now taking form would cause General Bradley to re-examine his planned employment of the Third Army. The 21st Army Group was in process of shifting the axis of its attack from the northeast to due north.[9] The Ruhr remained the "real objective" but the execution of the new attack would be more intricate than that involved in a direct thrust northeast. Montgomery's plan called for the Second British Army to drive north and then eastward, thus circling around the northern face of the Ruhr. The initial penetration would depend upon an airborne operation (MARKET-GARDEN) carried forward by three Allied airborne divisions. D Day for the airborne attack was set for 17 September; its object was to secure the crossings over the Rhine and Meuse Rivers in the Arnhem–Nijmegen–Grave sector. Meanwhile the First Canadian Army would be committed in the west to clear the Germans from the seaward approaches to Antwerp. This turning movement *north* of the Ruhr would leave a considerable gap between Montgomery's forces and Hodges' First Army, as the latter pushed toward the southern face of the Ruhr. As a result Bradley was forced to employ one corps from the First Army to cover the gap; this move in turn required a general realignment from south to north on the First Army front and left the Luxembourg area, adjacent to the Third Army, only lightly held.

On the morning of 12 September the 12th Army Group commander met with General Hodges, General Patton, and officers from the headquarters of

[7] 12th A Gp AAR, V.

[8] Montgomery to Eisenhower, 11 Sep 44, SHAEF SGS File, Post OVERLORD Planning 381, I. Smith to Montgomery, 15 Sep 44, SHAEF SGS File, Supply Problems of Allied Advance, 400.3/1.

[9] 21st A Gp, General Operational Situation and Directive, M–525, 14 Sep 44.

ETOUSA (European Theater of Operations, U.S. Army) and the Advance Section of the Communications Zone. Hodges reported that the First Army had enough gasoline on hand to carry it to the Rhine, plus sufficient ammunition for five days of combat. Patton also had sufficient gasoline to reach the Rhine, plus a four-day supply of ammunition. Since the supply status in both armies showed signs of improvement and since both were committed, General Bradley agreed that the two armies should continue the general advance, the main effort, of course, being made by the First Army. Bradley attached a string to the Third Army and told Patton that if he was unable to cross the Moselle with the mass of his forces by the evening of 14 September the attack in this sector would have to be discontinued. If this happened Patton was to assume the defensive on his right wing and in the sector between Nancy and Luxembourg. The Third Army would not have to abandon all offensive operations, however, but would shift the axis of attack north of the Moselle gorge in close conjunction with the drive by First Army's V Corps.

Patton agreed that this alternative operation was sound, but he did not anticipate that it would be necessary. He reasoned that the German forces opposing the Third Army along the Moselle had no reserves or defenses in depth and that once a break-through had been made the way would be cleared for a rapid advance to the Rhine. Bradley himself was none too anxious to shift the Third Army to the north. The valley of the lower Moselle was tortuous in the extreme and far less favorable than the terrain on the Metz–Frankfurt axis. Some force would have to be left to hold the sector between the First and Seventh Armies. In addition, positions would have to be secured for feeding in the Ninth Army divisions which ultimately would be moved east from Brittany.[10] Even Montgomery was anxious for some continued activity in the existing Third Army zone, albeit limited in scope, and suggested that a deception plan be initiated with the object of making the Germans reinforce the Metz and Nancy sectors, at the expense of their northern front, during the period 14–26 September.[11]

On the morning of 14 September General Bradley was able to tell General Eisenhower: "The situation in front of Patton looks very hopeful [and] he has definitely crossed the river in strength. . . ." The next forty-eight hours, Bradley believed, would tell the story as to how fast the Third Army could

[10] Bradley to Eisenhower, 12 Sep 44, 12th A Gp File, Military Objectives 371.3, I.

[11] 21st A Gp suggestion cited in SHAEF to 12th A Gp, FWD–14837, 14 Sep 44, SHAEF SGS File, Post OVERLORD Planning 381, I.

go in the advance northeast from the Metz–Nancy base of operations, and whether or not Patton's progress would justify a continuation of the attack on the existing axis.[12] During the day the 12th Army Group commander visited the Third Army headquarters and there approved a plan set forth by Patton which called for a narrowing of the three corps' fronts in order to allow a power drive in column of divisions by each corps. The proposed shift still would bring the Third Army to the Rhine on the Frankfurt axis, but with a less extended zone of attack and a southern boundary running through Mannheim instead of Karlsruhe.[13]

Bradley's intended employment of the Third Army in a continuation of the advance toward the Rhine met with Eisenhower's approval and on 15 September the latter wrote: "We shall soon, I hope, have achieved the objectives set forth in my last directive [of 4 September] and shall then be in possession of the Ruhr, the Saar and the Frankfurt area."[14] General Eisenhower was optimistic. General Bradley was optimistic. But neither of the two was more optimistic than General Patton, his staff, and his division commanders. The Third Army left and center was across the Moselle. On the right the XV Corps was in the process of closing on the west bank of the river. At various points along the front the enemy continued to offer spirited and stubborn resistance; but the successful drive by the 4th Armored Division had penetrated deep into the German rear and had indicated that the enemy was not prepared to defend in depth once his linear defenses were broken.

Patton assigned objectives to his corps commanders on 16 September.[15] He ordered the XX Corps to continue the advance to seize Frankfurt, containing Metz, if necessary, with a small force. The XII Corps was directed to continue the advance "rapidly" to the northeast, take Darmstadt, and establish a bridgehead east of the Rhine. The XV Corps would remain echeloned to the right rear during the general advance but would be prepared, on General Patton's order, to capture Mannheim or move over the Rhine via bridgeheads belonging to one of the other corps.

Although the Third Army commander's order for a continuation of the advance applied to all three corps, he expected the XII Corps—in the center—to lead off in the initial deep penetration by a further use of line-plunging

[12] Bradley to Eisenhower, 14 Sep 44, 12th A Gp File, Military Objectives 371.3, I.

[13] TUSA Diary, 14 Sep 44.

[14] Eisenhower to Bradley, 15 Sep 44, 12th A Gp File, Military Objectives 371.3, I.

[15] TUSA Amendment No. 2 to Operational Directive, 5 September, dated 16 Sep 44.

tactics by the armor. The target date for the XII Corps attack was fixed as 18 September. The scheme of maneuver was as follows. The corps would move in column of divisions. The 4th Armored Division, already deep in enemy territory at Arracourt, would lead the column and strike hard to crack the German West Wall between Sarreguemines and Saarbruecken. If Wood's armor succeeded in punching a hole, Baade's 35th Infantry Division would follow through, sending one regiment to accompany the armor and using the remainder to hold and widen the gap. McBride's 80th Infantry Division, heavily engaged in the Dieulouard bridgehead, would remain behind and mop up the enemy in its area; then it would fall into the attacking column, take Saarbruecken and continue on toward the Rhine. The advance combat command of the 6th Armored Division, CCB, already was en route to the XII Corps front and General Patton promised General Eddy that this additional armored weight would be thrown into the attack.[16] Patton expected that Bradley would release the 83rd Infantry Division (Maj. Gen. R. C. Macon) from the Brittany area and assign it to the Third Army. If the 83rd arrived in time, Patton intended to use it in the XX Corps sector, sending the 7th Armored Division to reinforce the XII Corps attack. Actually, the Third Army commander had the intention of putting three full armored divisions into the XII Corps drive for a "break-through" to the Rhine. On 17 September he talked to General Grow, complimented him on the 6th Armored successes in Brittany, and ordered the remainder of the division to leave the Montargis sector at once for the XII Corps front.

Such was the ambitious scheme for a rapid advance to the Rhine. In the meantime, however, the enemy was on the march to launch a counterattack which would interrupt the execution of the Third Army plans and effectively contain the XII Corps.

The Dispositions of the Fifth Panzer Army[17]

In the summer of 1944 the Wehrmacht carried five panzer armies in its order of battle. The first four, by number, were operating on the Eastern and Southern Fronts. Only one, the *Fifth Panzer Army*, thus far had been com-

[16] XII Corps G–3 Jnl, 16 Sep 44.

[17] The American journals and After Action Reports for this period are uniformly good except for the 35th Division After Action Report, which has several errors in dates and hours. The Historical Division Combat Interviews have considerable value, particularly those obtained by Maj. Dello G. Dayton and 1st

mitted in the West. Actually it existed as a continuing organization only in name, and even the name was lost after reverses suffered in Tunisia. During the retreat through northeastern France the *Fifth Panzer Army* again appeared on the Wehrmacht rolls as successor to *Panzergruppe West.* But when the situation on the German right wing began to stabilize and the wrecked armored units were withdrawn from the line the *Fifth Panzer Army* headquarters was relieved from its operational role in Belgium and collected, with a few army troops, in Holland. Having determined to launch a counteroffensive against Patton's army, Hitler turned to the *Fifth Panzer Army* and ordered that its staff, and that of the *LVIII Panzer Corps* (General der Panzertruppen Walter Krueger), be brought to Strasbourg preparatory to assuming control of this operation. When the *Fifth Panzer Army* headquarters arrived from Holland, on 9 September, it consisted only of an operations staff and some communications troops. However, Hitler personally had selected a chief for the *Fifth Panzer Army* and two days later General Manteuffel appeared to assume the command, accompanied as was customary by his own chief of staff (Colonel Wolf von Kahlden). General Manteuffel was fresh from the Russian front, where he had last led an armored division. Small, energetic, a popular leader with a reputation for extreme personal bravery, Manteuffel had been named over many his senior to command an army. He was believed to be politically sound—an important consideration for any army commander after the events of 20 July—but his reputation as a prewar armored specialist, enhanced by service in North Africa and Russia, testifies that Manteuffel's assignment was not merely a political expedient.[18]

Before Manteuffel could exercise more than nominal command the maneuver space for the *Fifth Panzer Army* venture had been wiped out, and the *112th Panzer Brigade*, designated for employment in the counterattack, had been prematurely committed—with disastrous effect. By 14 September Blaskowitz had no choice but to tell Rundstedt that any assumption of the offensive

Lt. Gordon A. Harrison during and after the 4th Armored Division tank battles around Arracourt. Unfortunately, however, there are no Combat Interviews to cover the operations of the 79th Infantry Division. The German records are unusually complete. They include the *Army Group G KTB*, the *Fifth Panzer Army KTB,* and the *Gen. Kdo. LVIII Pz. Korps. Ia, KTB Nr. 3* and *Nr. 4* and *Anlagen* (hereafter cited as *LVIII Panzer Corps KTB*) for the period, as well as *Lage Meldung* from the *XLVII Panzer Corps.* The *OB WEST KTB* and *OKW/WFSt KTB Ausarbeitung, Der Westen,* are fragmentary, but do contain the most noteworthy orders issued by the *Fuehrerhauptquartier.* The manuscripts prepared by German officers for the Historical Division cover nearly every phase of the operations described in this chapter.

[18] *Personalakten* (Manteuffel). General der Panzertruppen Heinz Eberbach had commanded the *Fifth Panzer Army* in northern France but was captured by the British at the end of August.

by *Fifth Panzer Army* west of the Moselle and the Vosges was now out of the question. He protected himself, after a fashion, from the imputation that he lacked the "offensive spirit," by proposing a counterattack on a smaller scale east of the Moselle. (*Map II*) This operation by the *Fifth Panzer Army* would be mounted in the St. Dié–Rambervillers–Epinal area, co-ordinate with the arrival of the *113th Panzer Brigade*, which was on its way to Sarrebourg by rail. Thereafter, the maneuver would consist of an initial attack to secure Lunéville as a base, followed by a drive north toward Château-Salins with the intent to cut off the American armor moving east.

At *OB WEST* Field Marshal Rundstedt refused to take the responsibility for such a radical, though obviously necessary, change in Hitler's plans (perhaps he had already reached the point where, as he later explained, he could only give orders to the guards on duty in front of his headquarters) and referred Blaskowitz' request to OKW in Berlin. Twenty-four hours later OKW acceded to the new proposal. The *Nineteenth Army* was given permission to shorten its lines by a withdrawal on its right flank to a line through Epinal and Remiremont, in order to free the *XLVII Panzer Corps* for use in the *Fifth Panzer Army's* attack. The *11th Panzer Division* (Generalleutnant Wend von Wietersheim), licking its wounds near Belfort after the bloody rear guard actions during the *Nineteenth Army* retreat, should be brought up to strength, re-equipped, and handed over to General Manteuffel so as to give additional weight to the attack. Finally the *107th* and *108th Panzer Brigades*, whose tanks were still coming off the assembly lines, were ticketed for this new venture, with the provision that they would be given to General Manteuffel only when Hitler's intuition told him the right moment was at hand. The *Fifth Panzer Army* requested additional artillery, but Blaskowitz could only say that "as a possibility" one battalion *might* be taken from the *Nineteenth Army*. Manteuffel never received his guns, which is not surprising in view of the fact that the *Nineteenth Army* had lost 1,316 out of its 1,481 artillery pieces during the disastrous retreat from southern France. As a substitute Manteuffel was promised support by the Luftwaffe, after Rundstedt appealed to Hitler, but this promise proved empty indeed.

Some of the units originally designated for the operation already were moving into position. Feuchtinger's *21st Panzer Division* concentrated in the vicinity of Epinal, as infantry replacements came up from Germany. This division was virtually bereft of armor. Rundstedt and the inspector of armor on the Western Front (Generalleutnant Horst Stumpff) had met on 15 September and agreed that the *21st* and *Panzer Lehr* should receive priority on all available tanks, heavy weapons, and prime movers. Despite this, Feuchtinger would have to fight his division as an understrength infantry formation reinforced by a small tank complement. The *111th Panzer Brigade* moved into Rambervillers, after having lost eleven Panthers through air attack and mechanical failures. Both the Panther and Mark IV battalions were present, but the brigade had not received its company of mobile antitank guns. East of Sarrebourg, part of the *113th Panzer Brigade* was being reorganized for the march west, after having been scattered by an air attack while still entrained. On 16 September *OB WEST* gave detailed orders for the counterattack, hopefully enlarging the scheme submitted by Blaskowitz. The attack must begin not later than 18 September, not waiting for the arrival of the *11th Panzer Division.* The first objective would be to wipe out the American forces (from the XII Corps) which had just entered Lunéville. With this blocking position in German hands the American bridgehead at Pont-à-Mousson must be erased and the Moselle line restored north of Nancy.

To meet the deadline set by Berlin, Blaskowitz charged Manteuffel with a difficult scheme of maneuver requiring the concentration of his widely scattered forces in the very face of the enemy. This would be carried out as a concentric attack aimed at the 4th Armored Division, with the right wing of the *Fifth Panzer Army* attacking directly west along the north bank of the Marne-Rhin Canal, while the left wing advanced north to seize Lunéville, cross the canal, and strike into the American flank. The *LVIII Panzer Corps,* on the right, was assigned the *113th Panzer Brigade* and the troops of the *15th Panzer Grenadier Division* which had been able to make their way down from Metz to the Lunéville area before the American armor cut the roads east of the Moselle. The *113th* would move from the Sarrebourg railhead, cross to the north of the canal between Lagarde and Moussey (some fifteen air-line miles east of Lunéville) and strike due west against the American position—now held by CCA, 4th Armored Division. There the terrain between the canal and the Seille provided excellent tank going, with firm ground, gently rolling country—offering tank defilade—and an adequate network of lateral roads leading onto the main, hard-surfaced highway between Nancy and Château-Salins. However, there was little forest cover against air attack and observation.

The *15th Panzer Grenadier Division* held a thin line of pickets along the canal north of the Forêt de Parroy. This weak spot in the center of the *Fifth*

Panzer Army was effectively blocked by blown bridges at the canal and by the density of the forest, which precluded tank operations. According to the plan the *15th Panzer Grenadier Division* would make its initial contact with the *XLVII Panzer Corps*, as it came north, at Chanteheux—hard by Lunéville —and then be picked up by General Krueger as the *113th Panzer Brigade* rolled west.

The *XLVII Panzer Corps*, with the *111th* and *112th Panzer Brigades* and the *21st Panzer Division*, was given the mission of initially holding the left (or west) flank of the *Fifth Panzer Army* with a minimum force between Rambervillers and Lunéville (some twenty miles), while using its main force to drive north across the canal in company with the left wing of General Krueger's *LVIII Panzer Corps*. In this sector the Mortagne and Meurthe Rivers seemed to offer successive defense lines east of the Moselle; Lunéville, in its apex position at the head of a river complex, funneled the main roads leading across the canal. Finally, it was hoped that the *Nineteenth Army* could free enough troops to extend its right flank and take up the slack north of Rambervillers as the *XLVII Panzer Corps* moved to the attack.

General Manteuffel protested that the *Fifth Panzer Army* was not strong enough to attack on such a scale—but received peremptory orders that he *would* attack on 18 September. Manteuffel and his corps commanders may well have been dubious. General Luettwitz kept the phone busy with reports that the western flank of the *XLVII Panzer Corps*, on the Moselle, was "wide open." The day before the scheduled attack one panzer battalion of the *111th Panzer Brigade* and the few remaining tanks of the *112th Panzer Brigade* were still engaged against the French armor in the Châtel area, and it was questionable whether the *Nineteenth Army* could relieve them in any strength. The *21st Panzer Division* had just received twenty-four tanks, but was still minus much of its infantry. General Krueger's *LVIII Panzer Corps* was widely dispersed, with piecemeal commitment the only possibility. The *15th Panzer Grenadier Division* (Rodt), whose *Reconnaissance Battalion* was fighting in Lunéville, still had its rear columns in the *First Army* zone. The *113th Panzer Brigade* had assembled its battalion of Mark IV's, but was just in process of detraining the Panther battalion.[19]

[19] German plans for the counterattack are described not only in the *KTB's* of the various commands but in several manuscripts prepared by enemy officers who took part in this operation. See MS #A–916 (Blaskowitz); MS #B–589 (Gyldenfeldt); MS #B–037 (Manteuffel); MS #B–472 (Kahlden); MSS #B–137 and B–445 (Krueger); MS #B–473 (Triepel); MS #A–955 (Dingler); MS #A–871 (Feuchtinger); MS #B–364 (Wietersheim).

The Attack at Lunéville, 18 September

Despite Manteuffel's misgivings the *Fifth Panzer Army* moved in the early morning of 18 September to concentrate for the attack as had been planned. Krueger sent the *113th Panzer Brigade*, still minus some of its tanks, down the road to Blâmont and at the end of the day the brigade turned toward the canal. Luettwitz, after one last pessimistic prediction about his exposed western flank, moved northward along the Meurthe River toward Lunéville. This advance was made by seventeen tanks and the armored infantry of the *111th Panzer Brigade*, which had not been engaged on the Moselle. Meanwhile the *21st Panzer Division* remained echeloned apprehensively to the west of the Meurthe with its troops disposed on both banks of the Mortagne River.

The Germans and Americans were almost equally confused as to the strength and location of the opposing forces in and around Lunéville. On 15 September two troops of the 2d Cavalry Group (Col. C. H. Reed) had tried to enter Lunéville from the south but had been beaten off by the advance guard of the *15th Panzer Grenadier Division*. Next day the 42d Cavalry Squadron (Maj. J. H. Pitman) had returned to the attack, while CCR, 4th Armored Division (Col. Wendell Blanchard), circled into the city from the northwest. The Germans fell back from Lunéville to the shelter of the Forêt de Parroy, northeast of the city, but then returned to filter into Lunéville and there engage the FFI and the small American contingent. On the night of 17 September the *15th Panzer Grenadier Division* had so many men in the city that a German agent sent out a report that the Americans had left. This report was relayed to Luettwitz, who headed straight for Lunéville without thought of fighting for the town—and apparently with no idea that the 42d Cavalry Squadron had a line of outposts to the southeast.

Actually, the Americans still had a firm hold on Lunéville but had not taken cognizance of the armored threat now developing from the south. As early as 15 September the cavalry had learned from prisoners that tanks were being unloaded around St. Dié. Colonel Reed reported this information at XII Corps headquarters—with a request for additional antitank support—but was told that intelligence sources indicated that the German armor would be used against the Seventh Army.[20]

[20] Hist Div Combat Interviews (Reed). Third Army Intelligence had noted an armored build-up at Epinal as early as 12 September. TUSA Diary.

About 0700 on the morning of 18 September the advance guard of the *111th Panzer Brigade* hit the 42d Cavalry outposts manned by A Troop. The six 75-mm. assault guns from E Troop were rushed forward to meet the Panthers, but the American shells bounced off the heavy frontal armor of the German tanks and three of the guns were destroyed in as many minutes. The cavalry fought desperately, but armored cars and machine guns were no match for the Panthers. Dismounted action by small groups of cavalrymen was more effective against the German infantry following the tanks and held the enemy advance guard in check until about 1100. During the fight Major Pitman was killed. Colonel Reed was severely wounded and had to be evacuated.[21] The 42d Squadron executive officer, Captain W. E. Potts, had organized the initial defense and, as the enemy circled in a tightening noose around the squadron, finally led the 42d through the narrow gap remaining to the north and reached Lunéville. This gallant delaying action had won time for the remainder of the 2d Cavalry Group to retire through Lunéville and had alerted Blanchard's small armored force inside the city.

General Blaskowitz intervened about noon and ordered Manteuffel to press the attack and take Lunéville. A combined assault by the *111th Panzer Brigade* and *15th Panzer Grenadier Division* detachments forced CCR and the cavalry back into the north part of the city. In answer to this threat CCA, across the canal, rushed a task force to the scene while General Eddy detached CCB, 6th Armored Division, which had just closed to support the 35th Division east of Nancy, and started it for Lunéville. The first reinforcements arrived about 1600, including some tank destroyers from the 603d Tank Destroyer Battalion which distinguished themselves in a fire fight at close quarters; as the American artillery—now comprising two armored field artillery battalions and the 183d Field Artillery Group laid down an accurate and destructive fire, the enemy fell back behind the railroad tracks in the south quarter of the city. When night came Manteuffel ordered the *111th Panzer Brigade* to disengage and move piecemeal to an assembly area at Parroy, north of the canal, for a continuation of the general advance.

Meanwhile, *OB WEST* had sent additional orders to the *Fifth Panzer Army*. The direction of the main attack on 19 September now was to be changed from north to northwest, Nancy being substituted for Château-Salins as the initial army objective. This new maneuver aimed at freeing the hard-

[21] Colonel Reed was awarded the DSC. The citation issued by the Third Army credits Colonel Reed and his command with preventing the German occupation of Lunéville.

pressed *553d VG Division*, rapidly being hemmed in by the XII Corps, and at restoring the Moselle line—either by a future attack between Nancy and Charmes or a stroke north toward Pont-à-Mousson. Execution of the plan, however, was jeopardized by the XV Corps advance across the Moselle, which justified all of General Luettwitz' fears for the security of his weak left flank. So Manteuffel ordered a general regrouping. The *XLVII Panzer Corps* was given the *15th Panzer Grenadier Division* and told to defend on a line from the canal, at Einville, through Lunéville, and thence along the Meurthe River, west of which the *21st Panzer Division* and *112th Panzer Brigade* already were fighting French and American patrols. The *LVIII Panzer Corps*, in return, was given the *111th Panzer Brigade* to reinforce the *113th Panzer Brigade* in the drive for Nancy. At midnight Manteuffel phoned General Krueger and gave him instructions for the attack the following morning—with accompanying threats of condign punishment if his orders were not strictly carried out. By 0600 all of the *113th Panzer Brigade* had to be across the canal and in position at Bourdonnay, nine miles east of Arracourt, to start the drive west toward Champenoux, twenty miles away, where the armor would link up with the beleaguered *553d VG Division*. Further, General Krueger had to attack without waiting for the *111th Panzer Brigade* to cross the canal and come up on his left flank. This insistence on piecemeal and immediate attack is readily understood in view of the continuing pressure from Berlin, as well as of the marked German inability to pierce the American counterreconnaissance screen on the ground and in the air, precluding any real knowledge of the 4th Armored Division's strength and locations. But such piecemeal efforts were ultimately to play into the hands of the 4th Armored Division, standing between the *LVIII Panzer Corps* and Nancy.

The Arracourt Tank Battle, 19–22 September

On 17 September CCB, 4th Armored Division, had been sent north from the Marne-Rhin Canal to aid the 80th Division. By the end of that day the XII Corps commander had canceled further movement toward the 80th upon receipt of orders from General Patton alerting the corps for an advance northeast toward the Sarre River, to be executed in column of divisions with the 4th Armored Division in the lead. The optimism so prevalent in the Third Army in early September had abated somewhat, at least among the combat elements, and General Wood phoned the corps headquarters to warn that "this job of getting supplies across the river [the Moselle] and on the roads is getting to be a major problem. This will not be a very fast operation—no blitz." But at 0030 on 18 September, Wood gave orders for the resumption of the advance on the following day: CCB to move from Delme on Saarbruecken; CCA to move out from the Arracourt area along the center road in the XII Corps zone (Morhange, Puttelange) and by subsidiary roads on the south flank toward Sarreguemines. News of the German attack at Lunéville only partially deranged these plans for neither Eddy nor Patton was greatly concerned. CCA, after having sent a task force to aid CCR, was ordered to stand to until the situation at Lunéville was clearer and the task force had returned; but CCB continued planning for an attack toward Saarbruecken on the following day.[22]

On the night of 18 September the 4th Armored Division was deployed as follows: CCR had beaten off the Lunéville attack, with slight losses to itself, and was being relieved by the combat command from the 6th Armored Division. CCB was massed near Fresnes-en-Saulnois. The main body of CCA, somewhat reduced by the Lunéville mission, was assembled around Arracourt, about twelve miles to the southeast. (*Map XIX*) The extended CCA sector, reaching from Chambrey (south of Château-Salins) nearly to the canal, could be only thinly outposted on the night of 18–19 September since Colonel Clarke had a relatively small force at hand: two companies of medium and one of light tanks, a battalion of armored infantry, a battalion of engineers, a company of tank destroyers and three battalions of artillery.[23] The armored infantry and a company of medium tanks were deployed on the north flank between Chambrey and Arracourt. The combat command headquarters, the field artillery, and a platoon of tank destroyers were grouped in and around the town of Arracourt, while the bulk of the engineers held the south flank, withdrawn somewhat toward the west. One medium tank company, Company C of the 37th Tank Battalion (Capt. Richard Lamison), formed a combat outpost around the crossroads village of Lezey—between four and five miles northeast of Arracourt.

As yet there was no suspicion of the *LVIII Panzer Corps* advance from Sarrebourg, and though just before dark artillery observers had counted some

[22] Neither General Patton nor General Eddy took the German attack on 18 September very seriously. See Eddy Diary.

[23] The 37th Tk Bn (—), 53d Armd Inf Bn (—), C Co, 10th Armd Inf Bn, 166th (C) Engr Bn, C Co., 24th Armd Engr Bn, C Co 704th TD Bn, the 66th and 94th (—) Armd FA Bns, and the 191st FA Bn.

thirty tanks east of Lunéville (the second panzer battalion of the *111th Panzer Brigade* had now come up) this threat appeared to be checked by the American reinforcements at Lunéville.

Just before midnight the CCA outposts near Lezey heard tracked vehicles moving in the darkness to their front. They called for artillery fire and the clanking of the treads ceased. About 0730 on 19 September a liaison officer, driving down the road near Bezange-la-Petite, ran into the rear of a German tank column but escaped notice in the thick morning fog and radioed to his battalion commander, Colonel Abrams, who was at Lezey. At about the same time a light tank platoon had a brush with some German tanks in the vicinity of Moncourt.

The *113th Panzer Brigade*, with forty-two Panther tanks of the Mark V battalion and the *2113th Panzer Grenadier Regiment* in the lead, had moved from Bourdonnay in a successful night march, reorganized its advance guard near Ley, and now pushed through the heavy fog toward Bezange. In the meeting engagement which followed, as in the later tank battles, the morning fog common to this area played no favorites: it protected the German armor from air attack, but permitted the American tanks to fight at close quarters where the longer range of the Panther tank gun had no advantage. A section of M–4 tanks were in an outpost position south of Lezey when the first Panther suddenly loomed out of the fog—hardly seventy-five yards from the two American tanks. The Panther and two of its fellows were destroyed in a matter of seconds, whereupon the remaining German tanks turned hurriedly away to the south. Capt. William A. Dwight, the liaison officer who had reported the enemy armor, arrived at Arracourt and was ordered to take a platoon of the 704th Tank Destroyer Battalion to aid the tanks at Lezey. Just west of Bezange-la-Petite Dwight's platoon saw a number of German tanks moving through the fog. The tank destroyers quickly deployed in a shallow depression and opened fire at about 150 yards. In the short fight that followed, three of the four American tank destroyers were lost, but not until they had destroyed seven enemy tanks.

The *113th Panzer Brigade* attack developed in a series of consecutive jabs, generally made by a company of tanks and a platoon of infantry, as the enemy probed to find an opening in the CCA defenses. Meanwhile the American outposts had been drawn in, the company of medium tanks was hurried down from Chambrey, General Eddy sent the task force at Lunéville back to rejoin the command, and the armored artillery ranged in on the attackers. The superior mobility of the American tanks and self-propelled tank destroyers gave the defenders a decided advantage. When the Panthers turned away, after the abortive attack at Lezey, Captain Lamison took four tanks from C Company and raced the enemy some three thousand yards to a commanding ridge west of Bezange-la-Petite. Arriving on the position about three minutes before eight Panthers appeared, Lamison's tanks got set and knocked out four of the German tanks before they could return the fire; then they withdrew over the crest of the ridge, moved south a short distance, reappeared, and finished off the remaining Panthers. In the late morning the German attack turned west toward Réchicourt-la-Petite, attempting to drive around the town, first to the north, then to the south. Here again the American artillery, tanks, and tank destroyers inflicted severe losses on the enemy armor. A platoon of tank destroyers from the 704th netted eight Panthers and succeeded in driving the rest of an enemy tank company back in flight.

The company of medium tanks which had been sent to Lunéville returned in the afternoon and Colonel Clarke was ready to counterattack. A combined force from Companies A and B, 37th Tank Battalion, led by Maj. William L. Hunter, wheeled south through Réchicourt, caught the Germans in the flank, and knocked out nine Panthers with the loss of only three tanks. As the day ended, the 37th Tank Battalion turned its attention to mopping up the German infantry west of Moncourt, and finally, guided through the night by burning German tanks, assembled in the vicinity of Lezey.

The German armored attack appeared to have spent itself. General Patton, who had come to Arracourt from the Third Army headquarters at Etain, talked with General Wood and agreed that CCA should begin the push toward Sarreguemines the next morning, reinforced by CCR, which had arrived from Lunéville during the day. On the whole there appeared to be no reason for worrying further about a German threat in the Arracourt sector, since CCA reported that forty-three enemy tanks, mostly factory-new Panthers, had been destroyed,[24] and that its own losses had been only six killed and thirteen wounded; three American tank destroyers and five M–4 tanks had been knocked out.

[24] This was a fair estimate, for General Krueger reported that he had fifty tanks damaged or destroyed on 19 September—a loss he attributed mostly to artillery fire. Such a figure would seem to account for one of the two tank battalions in the *113th Panzer Brigade*, but German battlefield recovery and repair still approached the high standards set months before during the North African tank battles.

Elsewhere, the *Fifth Panzer Army* had been no more successful on 19 September. The *111th Panzer Brigade*, supposed to be north of the canal that morning, was misdirected along the way by a patriotic French farmer and did not make contact with the *113th Panzer Brigade* at Bures until late in the afternoon. The *111th Panzer Brigade* did not reach Krueger in full strength. Some of its tanks had not yet come up from the depots, and low-flying American planes had inflicted much damage on the column during the march north. Over to the west the security line set up along the Mortagne by the *21st Panzer Division*, and the remnants of the *112th Panzer Brigade*, had been pierced at several points by the forward columns of the XV Corps, and during the night of the 19th this defensive line was withdrawn to the east bank of the Meurthe. The *15th Panzer Grenadier Division*, in the north, was trying desperately to set up a blocking position between the Meurthe and the town of Einville, on the canal. With the *XLVII Panzer Corps* thus heavily engaged General Luettwitz had to tell his superiors that he had no troops to attack north of the canal.

General Blaskowitz was very dissatisfied with the day's showing and ordered Manteuffel to continue the *LVIII Panzer Corps* attack without regard to the losses already suffered or the crippled condition of the *113th Panzer Brigade*. Early the following morning the *LVIII Panzer Corps* made a gesture toward carrying out the army group commander's orders by sending some tanks from the *111th Panzer Brigade* out on patrol; but the rest of the corps remained stationary between Ley and Bures, while General Manteuffel tried hard to persuade Blaskowitz that the attack must be abandoned in its entirety. All he got for his pains was a sharp reprimand for not possessing "the offensive spirit" and further orders insisting that the drive toward Nancy must be continued.

On the morning of 20 September CCA began to move out toward the northeast,[25] leaving one company of the 35th Tank Battalion near Arracourt to cover the concentration of the 320th Infantry (—), CCR, and the 602d Tank Destroyer Battalion, which were moving in to take over the area. (*Map 5*) To the north CCB, which had initiated the scheduled attack on the previous day, was fighting in a thick blanket of fog to clear a road through Château-Salins, after attempts to bypass on miserable side roads had bogged down. At 1130 the head of one column of CCA had reached Hampont and

[25] Two companies of the 35th Tank Battalion and the balance of the 10th Armored Infantry Battalion had joined CCA during the night.

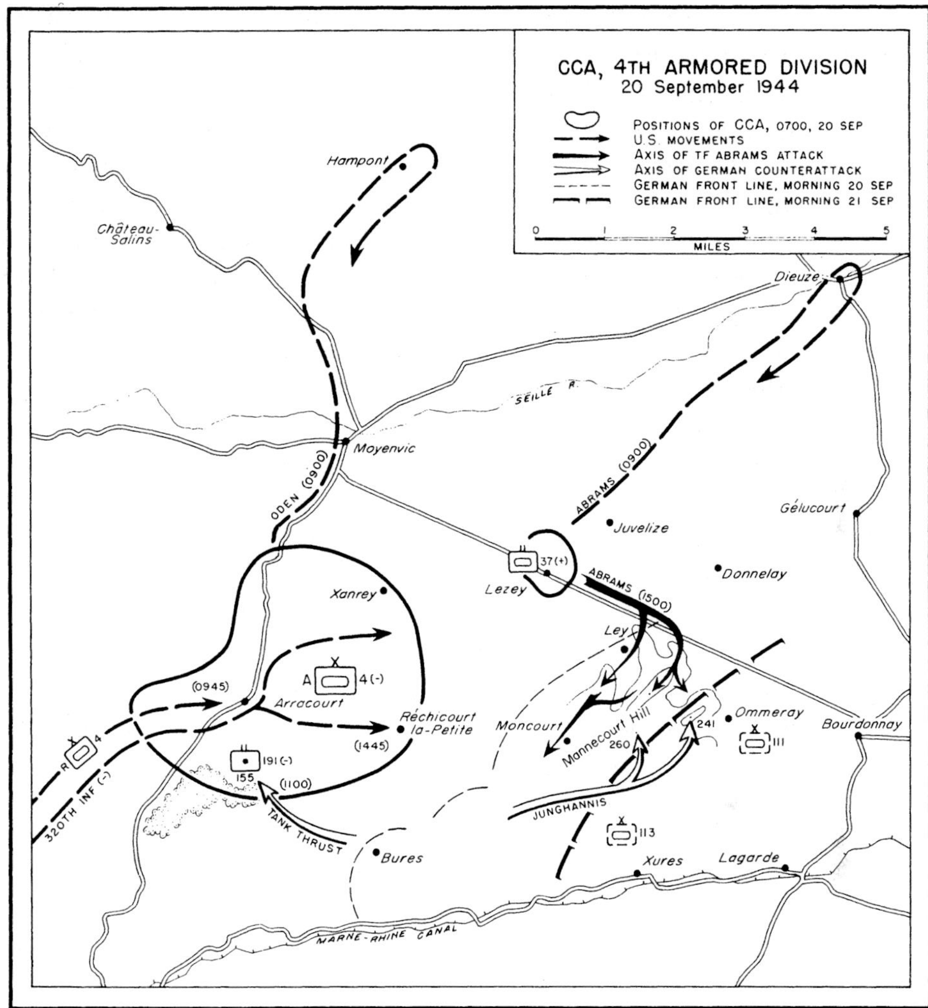

MAP NO. 5

another was closing on Dieuze when General Wood radioed that enemy tanks had returned to the attack near Arracourt and that a task force must be sent back to the scene at once. Actually, only eight German tanks were involved, having made a sortie toward the 191st Field Artillery Battalion just as it was ready to limber up and join the march column. This attack was readily handled by the 155-mm. howitzers, firing high explosive at one thousand yards, and by the appearance of the rear guard tanks and some tank destroyers, which allowed none of the attackers to escape. But Colonel Clarke led his whole combat command to turn back and sweep up the entire area "once and for all."

By midafternoon the sweeping operation was under way. Colonel Abrams assembled a force consisting of three medium tank companies of the 37th and two companies of the 10th Armored Infantry Battalion near Lezey, while the artillery adjusted its supporting fires, and then drove down on Ley. While Abrams had been gathering his people the Germans had moved to parry the coming blow by dispatching a Captain Junghannis and a group of Mark IV tanks and 88-mm. guns from the *111th Panzer Brigade* reserve to positions on Hill 260 and Hill 241 west of Ommeray. The main American force went through Ley with hardly a shot fired. But C Company, 37th Tank Battalion, which was covering Colonel Abrams' flank east of Ley, ran head on into the fire of Junghannis' tanks and guns. Between Ley and Ommeray rise two low hills with a narrow valley between: Mannecourt on the west and Hill 241, slightly higher, on the east. Company C, coming over Mannecourt Hill, met a fusillade from the Germans on the forward slope of Hill 241. In a fight lasting about three minutes C Company lost five or six tanks—but inflicted about the same number of tank casualties on the enemy. Then the Americans drew back from the crest and waited for Colonel Abrams to come up with B Company. When Abrams arrived the two companies maneuvered into new positions and engaged in a brief tank duel which brought the losses for both sides to some eleven or twelve tanks apiece.[26] Darkness was coming on and Colonel Abrams finally turned aside to complete the sweeping operation by a night attack southward, taking Moncourt[27] and then bivouacking with his main body back at Lezey. On CCA's south flank Major Kimsey and a small force had been sent during the afternoon to mop up along the canal. West of Bures five Panthers on patrol were destroyed, but when Kimsey tried to move into Bures the German tanks, fighting from cover, outranged the M-4's and the Americans had to give up the attack.

[26] Colonel Abrams was awarded the DSC for bravery in the fighting on 20 September. Junghannis and his detachment were cited in dispatches to Berlin for this action. As in most cases of this kind the estimates and reports of losses differ considerably with the headquarters. The 4th Armored Division After Action Report says that the 37th Tank Battalion lost 7 tanks and destroyed 18 of the enemy's. The CCA Operations Journal records: ". . . 37th lost 12 tanks and knocked out 8 enemy tanks." The *Fifth Panzer Army KTB* says that both sides lost 11 tanks.

[27] The night attack on Moncourt had been hastily organized and little co-ordinated. As a result some troops of the 10th Armored Infantry Battalion, which had entered the town first, were killed by the American fire.

Throughout the day CCA had held the initiative, but the additional armored weight given the *LVIII Panzer Corps* by the *111th Panzer Brigade* prevented any clear-cut decision.[28] General Blaskowitz, however, was far from satisfied by the events of 20 September and the *Army Group G* War Diary noted critically that "the Fifth Panzer Army shows a marked tendency to limit itself to defensive action." Again General Manteuffel was given a lecture on tactics and enjoined to regain his "operational freedom" by returning to the offensive and initiating counterattacks immediately after every American attack. Manteuffel's plea that the combat value of the two panzer brigades was "very limited" brought no reply from above. When Abrams took Moncourt, later in the evening, Manteuffel seized the opportunity to report that his lines had been broken at Ommeray, some two and a half miles farther *east.* He asked for permission to withdraw the *LVIII Panzer Corps* to a new and shorter line between Gélucourt and Lagarde, while redressing his southern flank, across the canal, by a general withdrawal in the *XLVII Panzer Corps* sector to a position east of the Forêt de Parroy and the Forêt de Mondon. Blaskowitz' only reply was a short homily on tactics and an order to counterattack.

Manteuffel's plea for a general withdrawal did not coincide with a new plan of attack which *OB WEST* had ordered with an eye to closing the gap opening between the *First* and *Fifth Panzer Armies* as CCB probed around Château-Salins and CCA pushed toward Morhange and Dieuze. Rundstedt instructed the *First Army* to gather reserves for an attack southeast from Delme. The *Fifth Panzer Army*, reinforced by the *11th Panzer Division* whose advance elements were just coming up from Sarrebourg, in turn was ordered to strengthen its right wing and attack to the north so as to meet the *First Army* drive near Moyenvic.

The failure to achieve an early and brilliant victory in the armored counterattack had provided Hitler with an excuse to get rid of Blaskowitz, who, although politically suspect, had not become involved in anti-Nazi intrigues and cabals. On 21 September Hitler relieved General Blaskowitz and gave the command of *Army Group G* to General der Panzertruppen Hermann

[28] The *LVIII Panzer Corps KTB* estimated that 18 American tanks were destroyed. The After Action Reports of CCA estimated that the Germans lost the same number. The events of this day resulted in one of the few recorded instances of pessimism on the part of General Patton. General Eddy phoned Patton to say that the Germans were determined to hold. Then, says the XII Corps commander, "Much to my surprise, Patton replied, 'It may be impossible to complete the mission which we started out on, but we could kill a lot of Germans trying.' " Eddy Diary.

Balck; Colonel Friedrich von Mellenthin replaced Generalleutnant Heinz von Gyldenfeldt as chief of staff.

Balck came from an old military family; his father had written a well-known textbook on tactics which had been translated and used for instruction in the United States. Balck had fought as a young officer through the four years of World War I and subsequently took part in the early mechanization of the Reichswehr. After winning recognition in the Somme campaign of 1940, he spent some months as a staff officer at OKH. Later, in the Russian campaigns, he commanded the famous *11th Panzer Division,* led the *XLVIII Panzer Corps* in the fierce battles around Lemberg, and briefly held the position of commanding general of the *Fourth Panzer Army.* Both Balck and Mellenthin came to the West with no experience against the Western Allies—a fact which Rundstedt always held against the new appointees. Politically, Balck long had held the reputation of being an ardent Nazi. His personal bravery was well established (he had been wounded six times), he was known to be an optimist, and he had a long record of successful offensive operations. On the other hand Balck already had been ticketed as an officer prone to take too favorable a view of things when the situation failed to warrant optimism. From his earliest days as a junior commander he had built up a reputation for arrogant and ruthless dealings with his subordinates; his first days in command of *Army Group G* would bring forth a series of orders strengthening the existing regulations on the enactment of the death penalty. He was, in short, the type of commander certain to win Hitler's confidence.

When Balck took over his new command on 21 September he immediately ordered the *First Army* to start its drive past Château-Salins, still in German hands, toward Moyenvic, and set 0700 the next morning as H Hour for an attack by the right wing of the *LVIII Panzer Corps.* This attack aimed at the seizure of the high ground southeast of Juvelize, preparatory to an advance on Moyenvic when the *11th Panzer Division* joined Manteuffel.

CCA made another sweep on 21 September, this time south to the canal past Bures and Coincourt, preceded by air raids over the sector and intense artillery fire. To their surprise the Americans met little opposition, except some infantry and a few dug-in tanks, for the *LVIII Panzer Corps* had refused its southern flank in conformity with the withdrawal by the right and center. Unaware of the impending German attack General Wood ordered the 4th Armored Division to take the next day for rest and maintenance, prior to an attack by both combat commands to clean out Château-Salins where the garrison thus far had defeated all attempts to take the town and had damaged seven American tanks the previous day. The 9th Tank Destroyer Group and 42d Cavalry Squadron were brought up to hold the ground between Ley and the canal.

The morning of 22 September was fogbound and murky, giving the German assault force protection from the dreaded Jabo's.[29] But the attack toward Juvelize began nearly three hours late because of the tardy arrival of an infantry battalion which had been sent forward by the *11th Panzer Division* to relieve the *111th Panzer Brigade*, the latter being intended for use in the subsequent attack against Moyenvic. (*Map 6*) In the first phase of the assault the blow was taken by the 25th Cavalry Squadron, which was screening CCA's left flank and observing the roads between Dieuze and Moyenvic. During the previous night German patrols had laid white marking tape up to the cavalry lines and now the advance guard of the main enemy force, circling around to the north of Juvelize, sneaked in on the squadron with tanks and infantry. In some instances the German tanks came within seventy-five yards of the cavalry pickets before they were observed. The thin-skinned cavalry vehicles were no match for the enemy and seven light tanks were lost in the melee. But C Company of the 704th Tank Destroyer Battalion, in hull defilade behind the center of the cavalry line, succeeded in destroying three of the German tanks.[30] This prompted the rest to turn back to the northeast, leaving the German infantry assault force stranded west of Juvelize.

The sun finally broke through and the XIX TAC flew into the area, strafing and bombing, while Colonel Abrams led the 37th Tank Battalion and the 10th Armored Infantry Battalion in a counterattack to take Juvelize and break up the German advance. Some of his tanks circled to the northwest and seized the hill at les Trois Croix looking down into the valley east of Juvelize along which German reinforcements were moving from the Bois du Sorbier. Fourteen enemy tanks were destroyed here by tank and artillery fire at ranges from 400 to 2,000 yards,[31] and Colonel Heinrich Bronsart von Schellendorf, commander of the *111th Panzer Brigade*, was mortally

[29] This term was the German soldier's argot for the American fighter-bomber.

[30] In the face of heavy fire Capt. Thomas J. Evans, C Company, 704th Tank Destroyer Battalion, mounted a disabled American tank destroyer, manned its gun, and knocked out one of the enemy tanks. During the fight Captain Evans distinguished himself by coolly walking about and disposing his troops, all the while under fierce enemy fire. Evans was awarded the DSC.

[31] This attack was led by Capt. William L. Spencer, A Company, 37th Tank Battalion, who had distinguished himself repeatedly during the fighting begun on 19 September. He was awarded the DSC.

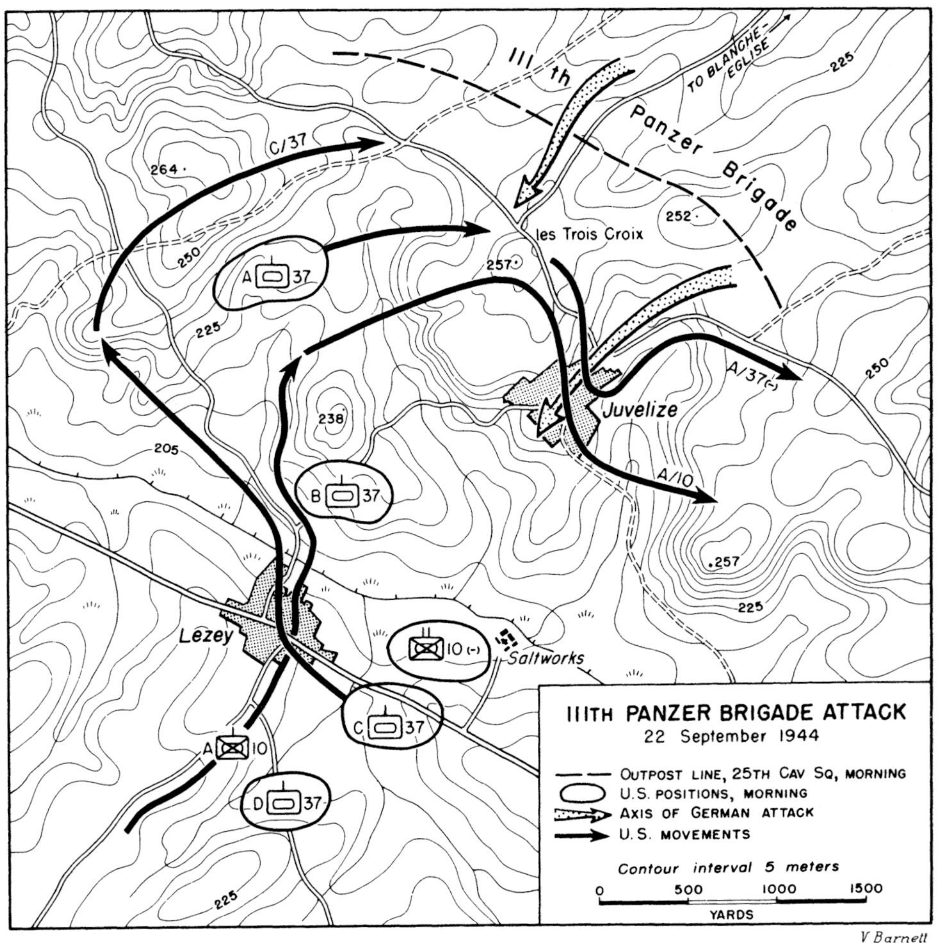

MAP NO. 6

wounded.[32] The P–47's broke up the remaining attackers, with the help of the armored field artillery, and cut them down as they straggled back to the northeast. Manteuffel's urgent pleas for help from the Luftwaffe remained unanswered and he reluctantly sent his last armored reserve, a few tanks from the *113th Panzer Brigade*, east of Lezey to hold astride the Moyenvic–Bourdonnay road. The German attempt to reach Moyenvic had ended in disaster. Only seven tanks and eighty men were left in the *111th Panzer*

[32] Colonel Seckendorff, commander of the *113th Panzer Brigade*, was killed the next day, apparently by an American P–47 from the 405th Group.

Brigade when night fell, and a scheduled continuation of the attack by the *111th Panzer Grenadier Regiment*, which was marching up from the *11th Panzer Division*, was called off as useless.

The tank battles fought from 19 through 22 September had cost CCA fourteen medium tanks and seven light tanks, totally destroyed, and a casualty list of 25 killed and 88 wounded. The German losses cannot be accurately determined, but two panzer brigades had been wrecked as combat units—without bringing the *Fifth Panzer Army* appreciably closer to the Moselle or the *553d VG Division.*

The XV Corps Advance to La Vezouse River, 21–24 September

The failure of the *Fifth Panzer Army* attack north of the Marne-Rhin Canal had a counterpart in the reverses suffered by the *XLVII Panzer Corps* south of the canal. General Luettwitz' security line hardly had been established along the lower Meurthe, after the withdrawal from the Mortagne, before the pursuing XV Corps attacked the new river position. The boundary changes between the XV and XII Corps gave General Haislip an opportunity to flank the Meurthe line by a turning movement through Lunéville, where the Meurthe bridges were held open by the XII Corps armor. (*Map XVIII*) The 313th Infantry, charged with executing this maneuver, detached one battalion at Lunéville, to aid the armor in the street-to-street battle for possession of the city, and the remainder of the regiment turned southeast to attack along the enemy bank of the Meurthe.

On 21 September the 313th (—) hit the outposts of Feuchtinger's *21st Panzer Division* at the village of Moncel, just outside of the Forêt de Mondon. Moncel was taken. But when the 313th reached the forest it was brought sharply to a halt by heavy fire from the main German position—a line of foxholes and trenches masked by the woods. General Wyche, the 79th Division commander, had planned a co-ordinated attack against the Forêt de Mondon on 21 September as a necessary prelude to an advance on the Forêt de Parroy. While the 313th probed the German positions on the north edge of the forest, therefore, the 3d Battalion of the 314th began a bitter fight to cross the Meurthe River and penetrate the forest from the west. Three companies succeeded in crossing the river near St. Clément, but were met by a hot fire when they moved forward onto the flat, bare plain which here extends some two thousand yards back to the forest. This narrow bridgehead, on the very edge of the Meurthe, could not be maintained and when night came the battalion fell back across the river.

On 22 September General Luettwitz attempted to ease the growing pressure on his north flank by local counterattacks around Lunéville. At Moncel three enemy tanks and a small party of infantry broke through the lines of the 313th Infantry and reached the northwest quarter of the town, where they were surrounded and killed or captured. Lunéville continued to be a sore spot for the Americans since it lay adjacent to the Forêt de Parroy, from whose recesses the *15th Panzer Grenadier Division* launched new forays on the city at will. Two battalions of the 315th, which had just been brought up from reserve to take over the city, were hit during the day by an attack that reached the stadium in the northeastern suburbs, but the enemy was again driven out.

The 79th Division continued its drive to dislodge the *21st Panzer Division* and the few remaining tanks of the *112th Panzer Brigade* from the Forêt de Mondon, but with little immediate success. Here, as elsewhere in Lorraine, the veteran German proved himself a skillful and tenacious forest fighter. At the northern edge of the woods, although the 313th Infantry inflicted heavy punishment on the German grenadiers, it could make no real headway. The 314th forded four companies across the Meurthe but found it impossible to move forward any heavy weapons without a bridge; nor could the infantry attack the German positions in the woods without close-up artillery and tank support. The drive halted until dark, when a bridge could be built.

The progress of the 79th Division had been slow on 22 September, but the situation of the opposing *XLVII Panzer Corps* was growing more precarious by the hour. On the north flank the *15th Panzer Grenadier Division*, still minus one of its regiments, was straining to hold between Lunéville and the canal as a cover for the left flank of the battered *LVIII Panzer Corps*. The *21st Panzer Division*, now hardly at regimental strength, held a line along the east bank of the Meurthe that already had been extended past the breaking point and was almost completely bereft of antitank weapons and assault guns. The few tanks left to the *112th Panzer Brigade*, after the debacle at Dompaire, had been reduced to one Panther and six Mark IV's. Furthermore the brigade had lost nearly all of its transport and was moving on foot. Harassed as it was by the evening of 22 September, the *XLVII Panzer Corps* received news of still another threat when *OB WEST* sent radio warning that an American airborne landing could be expected in the rear of the corps

—probably on the following morning. General Manteuffel asked for permission to withdraw the entire *Fifth Panzer Army*, but at midnight General Balck refused, citing "the clear *Fuehrerbefehl*" that the army must reach the *553d VG Division* east of Nancy. All the help Balck's headquarters could give was one battalion of Flak which was sent to Blâmont, in the rear of the *XLVII Panzer Corps*, for use against the anticipated airborne attack.[33]

This threat of vertical encirclement failed to materialize on 23 September. But the 79th Division began to close on the Forêt de Mondon in a series of hand-to-hand engagements and by noon the enemy was retreating to the east, under such cover as the German batteries in the Forêt de Parroy could provide. Although the Forêt de Mondon had been wrested from the German defenders and the area between the Meurthe and Vezouse Rivers freed, the battle had won some time for Luettwitz and had taken heavy toll among the American battalions taking part. The 3d Battalion of the 314th Infantry, which finally broke the German hold, suffered nearly two hundred casualties in the frontal assault across the Meurthe and lost most of its officers.[34]

The 2d French Armored Division, reinforced by the reserve combat command which had come up from the Moselle, crossed its armored infantry over the Meurthe between Flin and Vathiménil during the night of 22–23 September and sent tank patrols through the southern part of the Forêt de Mondon, reaching Bénaménil on La Vezouse River. There enemy tanks and infantry made a stand and drove off the French. One patrol did succeed in crossing the river on 23 September and chased the headquarters of the *112th Panzer Brigade* out of Domjevin. Late in the afternoon a battalion of the *15th Panzer Grenadier Division*, which had been rushed down from the north, retook the town and re-established the river defense line. That night the last German rear guard detachments crossed the river and the *XLVII Panzer Corps* organized to defend a new position which extended from the Forêt de Parroy to Croismare—on La Vezouse River—followed the river, turned south along the ridge between Ogéviller and Hablainville, and then tied in with the *Nineteenth Army* at the Meurthe River near Azerailles. Here Luettwitz' harassed troops entrenched, and awaited the resumption of the American advance.

[33] No evidence can be found that such an American attack ever was contemplated. Perhaps these German reports resulted from "sympathetic fears" induced by the Allied airborne operations which had just begun in Holland.

[34] The 3d Battalion, 314th Infantry, received a Distinguished Unit Citation for its part in this battle.

The Continuation of the Tank Battles, 24–29 September

After the German attack on 22 September the 4th Armored Division was given a day's respite, while the American cavalry scouted to the east and the XIX TAC continued to interdict the enemy-held roads and strafe isolated targets designated by the armor. However, prisoners reported that a new attack was in the offing and early on 24 September the blow came—this time delivered by the *First Army* in the CCB sector, west of Château-Salins.

Two days before, Hitler had repeated his orders that contact must be established with the *553d VG Division*, that all the enemy north of the Marne-Rhin Canal must be destroyed, and—specifically—that the *First Army* and *Fifth Panzer Army* must join in the Château-Salins–Moyenvic sector. To effect this junction Field Marshal Rundstedt took the *559th VG Division* from the sector north of Metz and assembled it at Morhange, with the *106th Panzer Brigade* in support. *Division Number 462* was left to cover the gap by extending its front to the north past Thionville. At the same time General Priess and the *XIII SS Corps* took command east of Nancy.

On the morning of 24 September, CCB was concentrated in the area between Château-Salins and Fresnes-en-Saulnois, screening in front of the 35th Division and awaiting orders to continue the offensive to the northeast. At dawn an unusually heavy concentration of artillery fire broke on the command, and enemy tanks and infantry were in on the American positions before the division artillery could be brought to bear. Two regiments of the *559th VG Division* attacked on three sides of the CCB perimeter in a mounting melee. Shortly after 0830 the main enemy effort was launched against the American right flank by a tank thrust from Château-Salins. This coordinated attack threatened to have serious results when, about 1000, the skies cleared and the P–47's came into the fight. In fifteen minutes the attack was broken and the Germans were in flight, leaving eleven wrecked tanks behind them and about three hundred dead. Although no further assaults were made, the German artillery, firing from the shelter of the Forêt de Château-Salins, continued a heavy shelling all through the afternoon, destroying an American aid station and spraying the area with fragments from time shells. CCB sustained 120 casualties in this action but at the end of the day still held its ground.

Now the *Fifth Panzer Army* prepared to return to the attack. On the night of 24 September Rundstedt appealed to OKW to abandon the *Fifth*

Panzer Army counterattack and send the remaining armor north to the Aachen front, where an Allied break-through seemed imminent. But Hitler brusquely ordered Manteuffel to continue the fight. General Manteuffel had asked for two new armored divisions to replace the crippled and decimated panzer brigades. There were no reserves at hand, however, and he had to be content with such elements of the *11th Panzer Division* (Wietersheim) as had reached his army. The *11th Panzer Division*, popularly known as the "*Ghost Division*," was one of the most famous armored units in the Wehrmacht. It had captured Belgrade and then had fought continuously on the Eastern Front, where it was cited three times in 1943 for distinguished action. In February 1944 the division was badly mauled during the Korsun encirclement and had to be transferred to southern France for rest and reorganization. In August it was given the difficult task of covering the retreat of the *Nineteenth Army*—since it was the only armored division south of the Loire. After the retreat from southern France the division took up position in the Belfort Gap, from which it moved on 18 September to reinforce the *Fifth Panzer Army*. Although the *11th Panzer Division* had lost heavily during the Rhone Valley battles it still had most of its artillery and infantry. However, a Kampfgruppe (consisting of a tank company, the assault gun battalion, and some infantry) had to be left behind in the Belfort region, and a few tanks were destroyed by air attacks on the rail journey to Sarrebourge,[35] where the division detrained. When the *11th Panzer Division* finally was committed on the *Fifth Panzer Army* front, General Wietersheim, an able and experienced commander, had only the *110th* and *111th Panzer Grenadier Regiments*, sixteen tanks, and two batteries at his disposal—hardly the force required for an advance to Nancy. All told, however, the *Fifth Panzer Army* had about fifty tanks when it resumed the attack.

The fate of the *111th Panzer Brigade* on 22 September had prompted General Manteuffel to seek for surprise on 25 September by moving the axis of his attack farther to the north. (*Map XX*) On the night of 24 September scouting parties reported that Moyenvic was unoccupied and that Marsal was only weakly held. The main attack by the *11th Panzer Division* jumped off the next morning at 0900—two hours later than scheduled—because of a steady downpour that slowed up tanks and guns as they moved into position. The thin cavalry screen on the American north flank was easily brushed aside

[35] Planes of the XIX TAC had made an air strike against the *11th Panzer Division* rail movement on 21 September.

and the Germans seized Marsal, where, under a smoke screen, they reorganized to fan out in attacks toward the south. One prong of the German drive continued through Moyenvic and by noon had come to a halt at Vic-sur-Seille—finally effecting the junction with the *First Army* which Berlin had decreed.

This quick success on the north flank dictated a widening of the attack and about 1000 General Manteuffel ordered a general advance along the whole *LVIII Panzer Corps* front, its object to be the seizure of a line reaching from Moncel-sur-Seille (some seven miles west of Moyenvic), diagonally through Bezange-la-Grande and Bathelémont, back to the canal at Hénaménil where the *XLVII Panzer Corps* still held. Manteuffel called on Luettwitz to support the attack from south of the canal with counterbattery fire on the American artillery massed behind the hills northeast of Bathelémont; but such an artillery duel could profit the Germans very little for it is doubtful whether Luettwitz had a score of guns available in his entire corps. The German attack corps had a fair number of artillery pieces (about two battalions), but, just as in the case of the relative armored strength, the American superiority was pronounced; at least six field artillery battalions were brought into play during the course of the battle.

At noon the enemy began to shoulder his way against CCA's north flank in an attempt to widen the corridor of assault. Ten tanks rolled down from the north and hit the 37th Tank Battalion, northeast of Juvelize, but were handily beaten off by the American M-4's—which outnumbered them and held positions on the slopes above the German line of approach. Next, infantry in about battalion strength, reinforced by a few tanks, tried to drive in the outpost lines manned by the 10th Armored Infantry Battalion (southeast of the 37th Tank Battalion), the 25th Cavalry, and the 53d Armored Infantry Battalion, the latter two holding on the north flank along a line running west. These attacks continued sporadically throughout the afternoon and evening in a steady rain which curtained off the battleground and left the decision to men, tanks, and guns. The enemy occupied Moncourt, but elsewhere the Americans held their ground and blunted the spearhead of the German drive by successful counterattacks.

During the night General Wood moved CCB down to take over the line of the 320th Infantry (—) between Réchicourt and the canal, on the right flank of CCA, while the 35th Infantry Division occupied the former CCB sector west of Château-Salins. On 26 September the 4th Armored Division reorganized its front with a slight withdrawal to the west, as part of the shift to the defensive which had been ordered for the Third Army. General Manteuffel seized the opportunity offered by the American withdrawal to report the uncontested occupation of Juvelize and Coincourt as "victories," and then prepared to resume the attack toward the west.

Manteuffel switched the direction of the *LVIII Panzer Corps* attack on 27 September so as to bring his main force to bear against the American south flank. An armored task force of about twenty-five tanks was scraped together from the *11th Panzer Division*, *15th Panzer Grenadier Division*, and the two panzer brigades. These tanks, reinforced by the *Reconnaissance Battalion* of the *11th Panzer Division*, which had just come up from the *Nineteenth Army* front, were given the mission of making an envelopment by a march along the narrow road between the canal and the Etang de Parroy—following this by an attack to take the camel back, at Hills 318 and 293, and Arracourt. Both Manteuffel and Balck were gravely concerned with the American possession of this camel-back plateau, east of the Arracourt–Bathelémont road, since its two hills rose to command long reaches of the ground held by the *Fifth Panzer Army*. The attack on 27 September, then, would be a fight to deny the Americans the observation which, coupled with their superiority in artillery, effectively barred the road to Nancy. General Wietersheim, the *11th Panzer Division* commander, opposed this new plan, for his experience with American planes and artillery during the retreat from southern France dictated the dispersal rather than the concentration of tanks in attack. Manteuffel, still thinking in terms of his experience with massed armor on the Eastern Front, was adamant—in addition he had been promised that fifty planes would fly cover over his tanks during the attack.

At 0800 the *LVIII Panzer Corps* (minus the armored task force) began a series of bitter diversionary attacks along the left and center of the 4th Armored Division perimeter. A battalion of grenadiers and a few tanks struck with particular fury against the 10th Armored Infantry Battalion (Lt. Col. Arthur West), which had been withdrawn to the new main line of resistance and had taken over the sector between Bezange-la-Petite and Réchicourt. Colonel West's battalion occupied a front of some 3,500 yards. Its left flank extended tenuously beyond the edge of Hill 265, west of Bezange; between its right flank and the 51st Armored Infantry Battalion a gap existed which neither of the battalions had the rifle strength to fill. The German assault bent the thin American line but could not break through.[36] At Hill 265 the enemy succeeded in gaining a foothold, but at this point 1st Lt. James H. Fields inspired his men to stand fast, though he had been rendered speechless by wounds in the head and throat. When two German machine guns caught the Americans in a withering cross fire, Fields took up a light machine gun from its dead crew and knocked out both of the German weapons. For gallantry in this action Lieutenant Fields received the Congressional Medal of Honor. On the north flank the *110th Panzer Grenadier Regiment* advanced as far as Xanrey. But while the Germans were reorganizing for a continuation of the attack some American tanks entered the town, under cover of smoke and artillery fire, and killed about 135 of the grenadiers —abruptly terminating this phase of the enemy maneuver.

About 1000, Manteuffel's armored task force began the main attack, but its advance guard had gone only as far as Fourasse Farm, some 1,800 yards west of Bures, when the American artillery brought the tanks to a halt. During the night General Wietersheim switched the *110th Panzer Grenadier Regiment* around from the north flank and put it in on his south flank to reinforce the tank group. One of its combat patrols filtered through to the north of the farm and captured Hill 318 after a sharp fight. Hill 318, and the plateau from which it projected, now became the focal point for the whole German effort. At daybreak on 28 September the 51st Armored Infantry Battalion retook the hill, but the fight continued through the morning, surging back and forth on the crest. About noon, the 51st got a firm hold. One last enemy counterattack was broken up by shellfire from American batteries to the northeast, raking the flank of the German assault column. In the center of the 4th Armored Division line German infantry and assault guns drove in close to the CCB positions under cover of a smoke screen. But by midafternoon the superiority of the American artillery began to tell, and the appearance of the Jabo's broke off the action.

When darkness came the Germans again sent a shock force, this time supported by a few tanks, up the forward slope of Hill 318. This assault drove

[36] Pfc. Clyde E. Workman, A Company, 10th Armored Infantry Battalion, was given the DSC for "conspicuous courage, many times displayed." When his squad leader was killed, Workman took command and in single combat destroyed an enemy mortar and killed ten German riflemen who were harassing his men. Later he engaged an enemy tank with a .50-caliber machine gun on a half-track and set the German tank afire.

the Americans back over the crest and onto the reverse slope, where they were caught by a well-executed barrage laid down by German guns. Just before midnight the 51st Armored Infantry Battalion regained the crest, after a preparatory shelling by four battalions of artillery had broken the German hold. The enemy retaliated promptly. CCB was hit by heavy-caliber artillery fire which continued for nearly one hour—causing thirty-five casualties in one company alone. Under cover of this fire the *11th Panzer Division* extended its hold on the camel back, took Hill 293, and drove on to seize the high ground at the eastern edge of the Bois du Bénamont. However, the infantry from the 51st, crouched in foxholes close to the crest of Hill 318, refused to give ground.

The German attack had made important gains during the night of 28–29 September, but the 4th Armored Division had added to its estimable record as an assault force and had proved to be equally tough and stubborn on the defensive. Here, as in previous engagements, the XIX TAC had given yeoman support to the American troops fighting on the ground. General Weyland sent 107 fighter-bombers to aid the XII Corps during 28 September. One squadron, the 23d, made a strike at Bures which nearly leveled the village and cut up the German reserves assembling there, thus weakening still further the ability of the enemy to exploit an attack that had been initiated successfully.

The morning of 29 September broke with a thick fog obscuring the battlefield. The exhausted German infantry tried to push on toward Arracourt but made no headway. Meanwhile, a platoon of medium tanks from the 8th Tank Battalion moved up Hill 318 in the fog, and when the haze finally lifted the tank commander directed the American planes onto the German tanks which had assembled under the screening fog in the valley below. After several mishaps—which included the dropping of propaganda leaflets instead of bombs[37]—the air-ground team began to close on the enemy. By the middle of the afternoon the Germans were streaming back through Fourasse Farm, and the rout was checked only when a few tanks were brought up to form a straggler line east of Parroy. Remnants of the *2d Battalion* of the *110th Panzer Grenadier Regiment* (Captain Schneider) and a few tanks from the *Reconnaissance Battalion, 11th Panzer Division*, held bravely to their positions in the Bois du Bénamont, all the while under heavy fire from American tank

[37] These leaflets had apparently been loaded for use at the Metz forts.

destroyers and cavalry assault guns. When night came the survivors filtered south through the American lines.[38]

The back of the *Fifth Panzer Army* attack was broken on 29 September; nor was there any further possibility of creating a new force for a continued effort to reach the Moselle River. During the afternoon, while the remnants of Manteuffel's armored task force were being hunted down around Bures by the fighter-bombers, General Balck made a personal visit to Rundstedt's headquarters at Bad Kreuznach. He told the C-in-C West that he still intended to wipe out the Pont-à-Mousson bridgehead and recover the Moselle defense line, but that he would need a "minimum" of three additional divisions, forty or fifty tanks, twenty or thirty assault guns, fifty antitank guns with prime movers, four battalions of heavy artillery, and four battalions of engineers. Rundstedt had no troops to give *Army Group G*, for Hitler and Jodl had decided to throw the few reserves still available on the Western Front into an attack against the Second British Army, at this time driving forward to surround the *Fifteenth Army* between the Rhine and the Maas. Balck, therefore, had no choice but to order the *Fifth Panzer Army* to go over to the defensive.

Both Balck and Manteuffel must have felt uneasy about giving up a project cherished by Hitler, for both hastened to go on record in their respective War Diaries. Balck wrote that *Army Group G* always had attempted to build up sufficient tactical reserves to make counterattacks possible, but that local commanders constantly had whittled away such reserves by committing them wherever a thin portion of the line was menaced by the enemy. He added, furthermore, that withdrawals had been made without permission of the *Army Group* headquarters, and that losses of towns and territory had occurred which were never reported to the higher headquarters. Manteuffel contented himself with repeating the report made by General Krueger on the battles fought in the previous days by the *LVIII Panzer Corps*. Said Krueger, the enemy had superiority in the air and in the artillery arm. There was no cover in this area for tanks and infantry; whenever the weather cleared the American planes descended on the corps—while all requests for the Luftwaffe were answered by reports that the German airfields were weathered in. American artillery was ceaseless, firing day and night—"a regular drum fire."

[38] The 405th Group claimed 11 enemy tanks destroyed and 2 damaged on this date. The 511th Squadron claimed an "assist" after flushing 6 German tanks into the open, where they were knocked out by the American artillery. The CCB After Action Report estimates that the three-day battle in this sector cost the enemy 700 dead.

Finally, the Americans held the high ground, looking deep into the corps area, and so long as Hill 318 was in American hands no success was possible.

The Lorraine tank battles had ended, except for a last American tank sweep on 30 September, and this sector relapsed into quiet. The 4th Armored Division took up stabilized positions north and east of Arracourt, while the German infantry dug in a few hundred yards away. On 12 October Wood's division was relieved by the 26th Division and went into corps reserve.

On the whole the September weather had been favorable to the superior speed and maneuverability of the American armor, with only a few days of mud to fasten the tanks to the highroads and with the sun burning through the morning haze in time for intervention by the XIX TAC. Through the earlier battles in Normandy and Brittany the division had developed a high degree of co-ordination among the various arms—as now shown in the losses which tank destroyers, artillery, and planes had inflicted on the enemy, and in the tenacity and skill with which the armored infantry and the tanks had repelled the desperate German attacks in the last days of September. Equally important, the division had learned much of the capabilities and limitations of the M–4 tank and its short-barreled 75-mm. gun, with which most of the medium tank companies were equipped. Maneuver had been the major tactic in Lorraine, with various types of the "mouse trap play" and surprise attacks from hull defilade, or under cover of the fogs rising from the Moselle and Seille bottoms, against German tanks whose high-velocity guns generally out-ranged the American tank weapon but whose turrets—traversed by hand—turned so slowly that four or five rounds could be fired into a Panther before its own gun could be brought to bear. The American tank losses usually had been sustained in frontal attacks against enemy armor fighting from cover, or over level spaces where the superior range of the long-barreled 75-mm. gun on the Mark V could make the kill.

The operations of the 4th Armored Division had been highly successful—even if the division had never been free to make the dash to the Rhine which its personnel, officers and men alike, had wished. Since crossing the Moselle it had destroyed or damaged an estimated 285 German tanks or other armored vehicles, at relatively small cost to the division.[39] As a result the 4th Armored

[39] The 4th Armored Division After Action Report, September 1944, records the losses of that division during the entire month of September as 181 killed in action, 394 wounded in action, and 51 missing in action. CCA, which bore the brunt of the armored clashes, lost 25 medium tanks and 7 tank destroyers totally destroyed.

would take the field in November as a veteran and successful division, with only a small admixture of untried replacements.

The Forêt de Grémecey Battle

General Patton's decision, on 20 September, to fix a new boundary line between the XII and XV Corps provided some protection for the south flank of the 4th Armored Division salient. But in addition the XII Corps commander was anxious to secure a firmer grip on the supply lines leading to the 4th Armored and suggested to Patton that the Forêt de Grémecey, commanding the main highway east of Nancy, should be occupied. The forest already had been used as an assembly area for CCB, 6th Armored, when, on 22 September, General Grow was sent with his armored infantry, some cavalry, and artillery to occupy this area and screen between the 80th Infantry Division and the 4th Armored. Grow's troops pinched out the 35th Division and threw a line north of the woods between Fresnes and the western angle of the Seille. The 6th Armored was in the midst of preparations for an attack north toward Delme when word arrived that the Third Army was to go over to the defensive. On 25–26 September the 35th Division relieved Grow's troops in the Forêt de Grémecy sector and CCB, 4th Armored Division, which had held a blocking position in the Fresnes area.

Since any continuation of the XII Corps advance appeared to be indefinitely postponed by General Eisenhower's order placing the Third Army on the defensive, the 35th Infantry Division settled down in anticipation of some respite from the interminable slogging that had marked the advance east of the Moselle. The 35th held a front some twelve miles in length, the Nancy–Nomény and Nancy–Château-Salins highways marking the left and right boundaries respectively. The larger part of this front (a distance of some eight miles) outlined a salient or bridgehead north and east of the Seille River. The apex of this salient was formed by the Forêt de Grémecey. (*Map XXI*) Following the edge of the forest as it did, the American front line bent sharply, almost at a right angle, in the northeast corner of the woods. The Germans would attempt to exploit this disposition, for the forest angle lay only about two thousand yards from the Forêt de Château-Salins, which was still in German hands, provided ample cover for large-scale troop concentration, and was the dominant ground in this area. The right wing of the 35th

Division was close to the junction of the two important enemy-held roads coming in from Morhange and Dieuze.

General Baade placed two of his regiments along the 35th Division main line of resistance, the 137th Infantry on the right and the 134th Infantry on the left. The 320th Infantry, which had returned from the 4th Armored Division, was assigned to the XII Corps reserve. The right regiment had hardly dug in when, on the evening of 26 September, the German guns opened fire from the Forêt de Château-Salins and a sharp attack drove in the American outpost line.[40] This was the prelude to a sustained and desperate enemy attempt to recover the Forêt de Grémecey.

The *First Army's* failure to brush aside CCB, 4th Armored Division, in the earlier attack to effect a junction between the *First Army* and the *Fifth Panzer Army*, had brought General Knobelsdorff into General Balck's disfavor, although this was somewhat mitigated by the reverses suffered in the *Fifth Panzer Army* attack. Knobelsdorff was anxious to avoid a repetition of the *First Army* failure and ordered General Priess, who, as commander of the *XIII SS Corps*, was directing operations in this sector, to throw everything he had into a resumption of the attack on 27 September. Priess selected the village of Moncel, on the Nancy–Dieuze highway, as the initial objective—apparently hoping to punch a hole in the 35th Division line through which Manteuffel's *Fifth Panzer Army* could roll toward Nancy. To make this attack Priess had available the *559th VG Division* (Generalmajor Kurt Freiherr von Muehlen), the *106th Panzer Brigade*—elements of which already had been used against CCB in the fight at Fresnes—and the *59th Regiment* of the *19th VG Division*. Both of the infantry formations were new and relatively untried as units; both were somewhat under regulation strength. The *559th VG Division* had a large number of veterans and, unlike many of the other VG divisions, most of its infantry came from the younger mobilization classes. The officers and noncoms were young and able veterans from the Eastern Front. The artillery regiment of the *559th* was at average strength, with two light battalions and one medium.[41] One company of tank destroyers replaced the conventional assault gun battalion as antitank defense. The *106th Panzer*

[40] Cpl. Harold J. Lange, Medical Detachment, 320th Infantry, was awarded the DSC (posthumously) for his gallantry in this initial engagement. Lange volunteered to go forward and aid the wounded. He continued his task, even after he himself was wounded, until he was cut down by machine gun fire.

[41] MS #A–972 (Muehlen).

Brigade had been re-equipped but did not yet have a full tank complement. Balck had tied a string on the *106th* by ordering Priess to send it to the *Nineteenth Army* the moment the combined *First Army* and *Fifth Panzer Army* attack reached the Moncel–Arracourt line.

The *559th VG Division* and *106th Panzer Brigade* launched their attack on the morning of 27 September as scheduled, although Priess had to be satisfied with a piecemeal commitment since some elements of both these formations had not yet arrived in the *XIII SS Corps* area. The *2d Battalion* of the *1127th Regiment (559th VG Division)* led off in an attack down the Chambrey–Pettoncourt road which took the Americans completely by surprise. The German tanks and infantry wiped out a road block east of Pettoncourt manned by troops of the 1st Battalion, 137th Infantry, overran four antitank guns, and drove on into the village of Pettoncourt, where the main American supply route crossed the Seille River. At Pettoncourt a scratch force made up of a battery of light antiaircraft artillery, some pieces from the 219th Field Artillery Battalion, and an antitank platoon from the 137th Infantry brought the German attack to a halt, although the enemy grenadiers were close enough to bring the gunners under rifle fire.[42] When reserves arrived from the 320th Infantry the German force withdrew slowly toward Chambrey, but lost the entire rear guard platoon when the American artillery located the range and began time fire. A second enemy column, with a few tanks and half-tracks, drove toward Grémecey, but was checked about a mile east of the village by artillery fire.

At the northeastern edge of the forest the enemy filtered in from the Forêt de Château-Salins during the morning and at some points broke through the position of the 3d Battalion, 137th Infantry. This attack drove as far as the regimental reserve line, where a company from the 737th Tank Battalion and the 752d Field Artillery Battalion—firing its 155's at point-blank range—helped the 3d Battalion to retake most of the lost ground. During this fight the Germans attempted to reinforce their assault force in the forest, but the 35th Division brought four artillery battalions into action to interdict the clearing between the Forêt de Grémecey and the Forêt de Château-Salins, and few of the enemy got through.

On 28 September German attacks hit all along the 35th Division front as more of Muehlen's infantry arrived in the sector. The bulk of the *559th*

[42] During this fight 1st Lt. Odie T. Stallcup, 1st Battalion, 137th Infantry, led his antitank platoon with such bravery that he received the DSC.

was thrown against the 137th Infantry in a concentric assault from the east and north. Again the Germans reached Pettoncourt with a thrust from the east, and again they were stopped by the American artillery and infantry. Toward the end of the afternoon two enemy columns marched out of Chambrey to make a last assault to the west but they were spotted at once and broken up by American planes. On the northeastern edge of the forest the German infantry and tanks were more successful in their attack against the 137th left flank. The woods screened the attackers from direct artillery fire and made it difficult for the defenders to maintain their contact with neighboring units. Early in the morning the Germans broke into the forest under cover of a barrage laid down by field guns and mortars. As the day progressed small detachments of tank-supported infantry worked their way to the rear of the 3d Battalion line, which had been reinforced on the right by the 1st Battalion of the 320th Infantry. The situation grew steadily worse and about 1500 the battalion of the 320th, hard pressed by the enemy who had circled around its left, started a withdrawal that carried it back about a thousand yards. As the infantry fell back, General Baade took countermeasures. At 1545 C Company of the 737th Tank Battalion began a sortie to mop up the enemy who had pierced through the rear. This tank drive, reinforced by infantry from the divisional reserve and supported by tank destroyers from the 654th Tank Destroyer Battalion, was successful. Most of the lost ground was retaken and shortly after dark contact between the front-line companies had been restored. All during this action L Company of the 137th (1st Lt. Rex Hopper) had been engaged in a lone and desperate fight at Hill 282, which rose midway between the village of Fresnes and the Forêt de Grémecey and overlooked the road leading into the woods. The German attacks, launched by small assault detachments equipped with automatic pistols, failed to break L Company; but the Americans finally were forced to fall back to the tree line at the northeastern edge of the woods.

The *559th VG Division* also struck at the western flank of the 35th Division during 28 September—with little success. In the early morning the 3d Battalion outposts of the 134th Infantry saw troops and tanks gathering for the attack in Jallaucourt, a village some thirteen hundred yards north of the forest. Before the Germans could do more than start their armored spearhead toward the wood line the American gunners were on the target and broke the attack. Then eleven American field artillery battalions sent the village up in flames with a TOT and the surviving enemy fled northeast.

Over on the extreme left flank of the 134th Infantry, where the 2d Battalion formed a link with the armored infantry of the 6th Armored Division deployed on the west bank of the Seille River, the enemy made a few minor attacks which were easily repelled. Actually, this sector of the 35th Division line never was seriously threatened. The enemy force opposite consisted of only a battalion of the weakened *553d VG Division* which had been gathered at Han, opposite Manhoué, to contain the American left flank while General Priess directed the main effort by Muehlen's *559th* against the American right and center.

By nightfall of 28 September, the position of the 134th Infantry was intact. The 137th Infantry had endured a day of confused and hard fighting, but had wiped out most of the Germans who had infiltrated to its rear and had reorganized and tied in the battalions in the forward positions. Nonetheless the enemy had finally succeeded in getting a foothold in this part of the forest. When the action waned the German and American foxhole lines lay hardly two hundred yards apart.

During the night prisoners taken by the 137th Infantry told their captors that a big attack from Fresnes was scheduled for 0500 the next morning. To forestall the enemy General Baade ordered the 3d Battalion, 320th Infantry, which had come up from reserve and was fresh, to attack at 0430 on a narrow front, spike down contact between the 134th and 137th along the north edge of the woods, and retake Hill 282 on the Fresnes road. The 3d Battalion counterattack jumped off at H Hour. Thirty minutes later the 1st Battalion, 320th Infantry, and the 3d Battalion, 137th Infantry, joined in the fight and started a counterattack to clear the eastern edge of the woods. Both of the American counterattacks were checked as soon as they hit the German positions inside the forest. The enemy attack from Fresnes was delivered as promised, the movement of the German infantry and tanks cloaked by a dense morning fog that blotted out all but the sound of tank treads and wheels. Company L of the 137th, deployed in the small neck of woods jutting out from the northeastern corner of the Forêt de Grémecey, took the full force of the first assault but stood its ground until surrounded, then fought a way back to the battalion. Lieutenant Hopper was wounded. His executive officer, Lt. Lawrence Malmed, was trapped in the German pillbox that served as the company command post, but during the melee persuaded twelve of his captors to go over to the American lines.

Inside the forest perimeter the fight turned into a confused succession of hand-to-hand battles fought independently by companies, platoons, and squads from the 137th, the 134th, and the 320th. As the day progressed the five American battalions slowly won the upper hand, while friendly artillery and the ubiquitous fighter-bombers isolated the forest battleground. By 1830 the 3d Battalion, 320th Infantry, behind a company of tanks which crushed and blasted the German machine gunners holding up the advance,[43] had regained the northern rim of the woods and stationed itself at the seam between the 134th and the 137th. But the latter regiment, harassed by a series of counterattacks from the east, could not drive the opposing infantry out of the woods. Over on the left flank of the 35th Division, F Company of the 134th advanced the American line by a sortie which took the town of Han, whose aged stone buildings had proved impervious to shelling by the divisional 105-mm. howitzers. Although the elements of the *1120th Regiment (553d VG Division)* in the neighborhood of Han were weak, the Germans followed their usual custom and counterattacked immediately, but with nothing except casualties for their pains.

During the afternoon of 29 September General Baade had visited seven of his battalion commanders. He found general agreement that the situation was tense, but not yet desperate. Each officer was of the opinion that the front was too wide and the American troops far too extended to prevent enemy infiltration. Furthermore, the woods were so dense, the trails so few, and the enemy knowledge of the forest so accurate that linear defense could hardly be successful. The only solution was to locate the infiltrating detachments and root them out of the woods.[44]

General Muehlen, commander of the *559th VG Division*, also had his problems. He struggled against a combination of factors unfavorable to his division in the fight for the Forêt de Grémecey. First, and perhaps most important, the *559th* and its attachments had been thrown into the battle piecemeal. The *559th* had received very little training as a unit, even by 1944 standards, and lack of training showed up very quickly in woods fighting. Artillery support was very limited—both guns and ammunition were in short

[43] Sgt. James A. Burzo and Pfc. Gerald D. Downing, both of L Company, 320th Infantry, received posthumous awards of the DSC for bravery in this action. When their squad ran into an ambush the two soldiers attacked the enemy machine gunners sweeping the American position. Both were mortally wounded but lived long enough to hurl their grenades and wipe out the German machine guns.

[44] See Ltr, Gen Baade to Hist Div, 18 Jan 49.

supply. Finally, the American troops fought most stubbornly and used the World War I trenches, which cut through the forest, to good advantage.

The difficulties besetting Muehlen as a division commander concerned with the performance of his single unit, however, reflected only a minor portion of "the big picture" pondered by his superiors. Late in the afternoon of the 29th, after a meeting with Field Marshal Rundstedt, General Balck sent word to the *First Army* that the attack to win the Forêt de Grémecey would have to be ended since the *First* and *Fifth Panzer Army* drive to the Moselle was now out of the question. The *XIII SS Corps* did not acknowledge the receipt of this order until the middle of the next morning—perhaps because Priess felt that success was within his grasp—and the fight for the forest continued. Priess had just received reinforcements: the *115th Fuesilier Battalion* of the *15th Panzer Grenadier Division*, and the *73d Regiment* of the *19th VG Division*, which had come down from Thionville. *OB WEST* already had ordered the immediate release of the *106th Panzer Brigade*, which was badly needed by the hard-pressed *Nineteenth Army*, but Priess found several convenient difficulties to delay the transfer and managed to send only one tank platoon out on the night of 29 September. With this accumulated strength the *XIII SS Corps* commander now ordered an all-out attack to take the Forêt de Grémecey, planning to send the fresh troops in against the 134th Infantry on the left of the American line.

Before first light on 30 September the *115th Fuesilier Battalion*, heavily armed with automatic weapons, struck the right flank of the 134th, where the 3d Battalion was deployed. The attack moved into the woods behind L Company and was pressed so stubbornly that the regimental reserve of the 134th had to be rushed into the fight. The *73d Regiment*, which had assembled behind the *115th*, followed up with an assault on a wider front, supported by continuous artillery and mortar fire. The fight inside the woods mounted in intensity as the day wore on and as more and more of the enemy infantry infiltrated on the right of the 134th.

Elements of the 137th Infantry and the two battalions of the 320th had begun a counterattack about 0630 to push back the enemy in the eastern portion of the woods. But the Germans had blasted trees across all the forest trails along which tanks might move; the American infantry, widely extended as the companies diminished in rifle strength, could neither move forward nor prevent the enemy from filtering in to the flanks and rear under concealment of the morning fog. German mortars and field guns kept up an incessant fire, and casualties from tree bursts mounted rapidly. One such burst killed Major W. G. Gillis, commanding the 1st Battalion of the 320th. By 1030 several enemy groups had worked around the left flank of the 2d Battalion, 137th, where a 700-yard gap had developed in the fog and confusion. They had wiped out a platoon of E Company and were moving south along the ravine in the middle of the forest. General Baade sent a tank platoon to aid E Company and then ordered the 133d Engineer Combat Battalion forward to occupy the high ground in the open north of Pettoncourt and seal off this penetration. But inside the woods the 35th Division continued to lose ground, and by midafternoon both the 137th and the 134th were fighting with extensive gaps in their lines.

General Baade had kept his sole remaining reserve, the 2d Battalion of the 320th Infantry and Company A of the 737th Tank Battalion, on the alert since 0850 that morning. His original intention was to use this reserve to bolster the right of the 134th, but the tough fight put up by L Company (Capt. F. S. Greenlief) had somewhat lessened the danger in this sector. The deep penetration behind the 137th presented a more serious problem and as the morning wore on threatened to turn into a large-scale break-through. At 1117, therefore, the reserve battalion was given fresh alert orders for an attack to clear the neck of woods that projected from the southeastern corner of the Forêt de Grémecey. At 1145, on attack orders, the 2d Battalion began the move to its line of departure.

The reserve battalion was assembled south of Grémecey village and would require some time to make the two-and-a-half-mile march, over rough ground, into position for the attack. Meanwhile, the corps commander had been kept informed of the German progress and sometime around 1400 called a conference in Bioncourt at the command post of the 320th Infantry. General Gaffey, the Third Army chief of staff, was present, as was General Grow, whose 6th Armored Division now constituted the Third Army reserve. All three regimental commanders of the 35th were there, plus General Baade, General Sebree, and members of the 35th Division staff. The officers had just gathered in the building which housed the command post when shellfire struck in the yard where the aides and orderlies were waiting. Several in the yard were killed or wounded, including some who had been with General Eddy since his days in North Africa. The officers inside the building gave what help they could, then returned to a consideration of the problem at hand. General Eddy was particularly concerned about the German penetrations in the 137th sector northeast of Grémecey and was prepared to order a general withdrawal from the Forêt de Grémecey, with the aim of making a stand behind the Seille River. Eddy was keenly aware of the danger to the 4th Armored Division in the event that the German attack broke through the lines of the 35th. In addition he was worried by the fact that the XII Corps positions were split by the Seille River, and by intelligence reports that the Germans were preparing to blow a large dam at the Etang de Lindre, southeast of Dieuze, so as to flood the waters of Seille and isolate the American troops that were on the north bank.

What now passed between General Eddy and the others in the command post is not clear. Eddy polled each of the regimental commanders present; they seem to have agreed that further German infiltration could not be halted. Whether General Baade was consulted is doubtful. Later he contended that he was not in favor of a withdrawal, but believed that General Gaffey and General Eddy were agreed on this course and so made no protest. In any case the corps commander appears to have taken Baade's concurrence for granted. The fact that General Baade already had given the order committing his final reserve was known to General Eddy. Whatever the considerations involved, the corps commander issued orders about 1420 for the 35th Division to retire behind the Seille River as soon as night came. General Grow was told to cover the withdrawal with his armor, and plans were made to alert the 4th Armored Division in preparation for a retrograde movement to the west.[45]

In the meantime General Gaffey had telephoned to General Patton, who immediately flew from Etain to the XII Corps headquarters in Nancy. The Third Army chief countermanded the order for the withdrawal of the 35th Division: "Counter-attack with the 6th Armored and take the thing. Go in right now with the 6th Armored, that is as soon as you can. Tell them [the 35th Division] to hang on." This order was passed on to General Baade at 1650. Then Patton gave the 4th Armored commander his instructions: "The 35th will stay and fight and you will not move back." Next General Patton and General Eddy visited the 6th Armored Division command post, east of Nancy, where plans were made for the division to attack on the following

[45] The story of the meeting at the 320th command post has been pieced together from sources which are fragmentary and often contradictory. The sources used are: 35th Div G–3 Jnl; 320th Inf AAR and G–3 Jnl; 134th Inf Jnl; TUSA Diary; Eddy Diary; Ltr, Gen Baade to Hist Div, 18 Jan 49; Ltr, Gen Grow to Hist Div, 23 Feb 49.

morning and where, as the Division Journal noted with some discreet expurgation, "Gen. Patton emphatically stated that he would not give up another foot of ground to the Germans."

General Baade hastened to carry out the Third Army commander's orders and threw in his last reserves, whose attack orders had been rescinded earlier in the afternoon. Their mission was to drive the Germans from the south edge of the woods and plug the gaps in the center of the thin line of weary infantry. As twilight came the tide began to turn and the 35th Division stiffened and held. During the night the enemy began a gradual withdrawal, in compliance with Balck's earlier order to Priess. When the German pressure eased, the 3d Battalion, 137th Infantry, which had suffered most heavily during the four days battle, was relieved—marching out of the woods with only 484 men of the 900 or more who had begun the fight.

Meanwhile General Grow had started his armor moving, preparatory to the attack slated for the morning of 1 October. The 6th Armored had become the XII Corps reserve on 26 September. In actual fact, however, Grow's division had been assigned a number of divergent missions. CCB was in the line, holding the Leyr corridor and linking the 80th and 35th Infantry Divisions. CCR (Lt. Col. A. E. Harris) spent a few days near Briey as XX Corps reserve and had just returned to the 6th Armored on the late afternoon of 29 September. CCA (Col. H. F. Hanson) was in billets about five miles east of Nancy. Grow's armored artillery was supporting the XII Corps as part of the corps artillery. General Patton had plans for using the 6th Armored to mop up the remaining enemy west of the Seille as soon as the 26th Infantry Division (en route to the Third Army) was available for infantry support. Therefore, he had tied a string to the 6th Armored, making it in effect his army reserve. The first German thrust at Grémecey, on 27 September, caused General Eddy to alert General Grow for the possible employment of his tanks in support of the 35th Division. The following day Grow's G–3, Lt. Col. M. J. Galvin, joined the 137th Infantry in the Forêt de Grémecey as the first step toward reinforcement or counterattack in this sector. Early on the morning of 29 September Grow moved CCA forward to Champenoux, about five miles—by road—south of Pettoncourt. Plans already were in the making for a counterattack to cover a possible retirement by the 35th across the Seille. Since the German successes in the forest on 30 September resulted in orders for the execution of this withdrawal, CCA and CCR were on the move toward the Seille when General Patton countermanded the withdrawal orders.

The new schemes of maneuver called for the two combat commands to make a co-ordinated attack with the 35th Division and drive the Germans out of the villages north and east of the Forêt de Grémecey which had served as sally ports for the attacks hurled against the 35th. CCR would attack from the lines of the 137th Infantry east of Pettoncourt with the mission of seizing the high ground north of the village of Chambrey. CCA would swing through the left wing of the 35th, clear the Germans from the northwest edge of the forest, and occupy the ridge between Lemoncourt and Fresnes which commanded the road net running into the woods. The 35th Division would mop up inside the forest, then relieve the armor.

Five nights before, the 25th Armored Engineer Battalion had completed a treadway bridge across the Seille in the vicinity of Brin-sur-Seille. Here Hanson crossed his command, bivouacking on the night of the 30th near Alincourt, about a mile south of the 134th Infantry positions. Harris crossed the main corps bridge at Pettoncourt and turned east. The movement of the two columns, favored by bright moonlight, went off without a hitch.

The attack on the morning of 1 October constituted what the 6th Armored Division commander later characterized as an example of "perfect teamwork." Jumping off at 0620, the two armored commands moved forward with such speed and drive that by 0900 they were on their respective objectives. CCR drew heavy casualties from mines and 88-mm. antitank guns as soon as it passed the American infantry lines; two tank company commanders were killed. By midmorning, however, CCR had cleared the high ground, secured it with engineers, tank destroyers, and antiaircraft artillery detachments, and turned to attack Chambrey. Although the Germans fought stubbornly in the half-burned town under orders to hold until the last man, in three-quarters of an hour the American tanks had command of the streets. Through the rainy afternoon CCR held Chambrey, in spite of constant shelling and repeated counterattacks, while infantry from the 137th moved into the village to relieve the armor. About 2000 Harris was relieved and the infantry had set up a combat outpost north of Chambrey.

CCA advanced rapidly in its zone, skirting close to the west edge of the Forêt de Grémecey in order to flush out the Germans there. Hanson's tankers had a field day with their .50-caliber machine guns along the northwestern fringe of the woods, literally strewing the ground with dead Germans. Some of the medium tanks mired down at Osson Creek and the attack was brought to a halt while the advance guard, under fire, built log bridges for the light vehicles. The infantry dismounted from their half-tracks and went on to the objective, the medium tanks following when a permanent bridge was found intact. In spite of the accurate counterbattery fire maintained by the American guns, the German artillery had kept up a ragged fire. The few enemy infantry left in this area, however, showed little inclination to fight and came forward with hands above their heads. The attackers encircled Jallaucourt, finding only a few Germans. When finally in command of the Lemoncourt–Fresnes ridge, CCA turned its guns back on the Forêt de Grémecey. But inside of the woods Americans and Germans were fighting at such close quarters that the 35th Division came under this tank fire and radioed word to the armor to wait until the Germans could be driven out of the woods—"and then kill them." During the afternoon and evening CCA turned over the ground it had taken to the 134th Infantry and reverted, with CCR, to the XII Corps reserve. The two combat commands had carried out General Patton's orders and restored the XII Corps main line of resistance, but the day of action had cost them over two hundred casualties and eleven tanks. Most of these losses were incurred after the armor had arrived at its objectives.

Within the Forêt de Grémecey the 35th Division had proceeded doggedly to win back its original positions. The enemy artillery kept up an intense and accurate fire as the Americans advanced; General Baade was wounded by a shell splinter. The German rear guard infantry, taking shelter in old entrenchments of World War I, fought savagely. By dark the 35th had reached the forest edge at several points. But elsewhere lone groups of enemy machine gunners and riflemen fought on through the night of 1–2 October to cover the main German withdrawal, while General Priess was organizing a new line of defense in the Forêt de Château-Salins and along the western slope of the draw running south toward Chambrey. The next day the fighter-bombers struck through the cloud banks and dispersed the Germans north of Chambrey while the 35th combed the forest. Americans and Germans now settled down for a long period of watchful waiting, beginning a lull in this sector which would continue until November.

CHAPTER VI

The October Pause in Operations

At the end of the third week in September Allied offensive operations again were feeling the pinch of an unfavorable logistical situation. The battles attendant on the Holland airborne attack, the First Army drive to crack the West Wall at Aachen, and the Third Army attempt to expand the bridgehead east of the Moselle all combined to strain to breaking point the existing port facilities and the supply and communications systems in northern France. The shortage of artillery ammunition had become a critical problem, and it was only a question of time until several combat divisions would have to be "grounded" for lack of transportation, gasoline, and essential equipment. Not only did the supply situation threaten to limit the scope of those operations already in progress, but, still more important, there could be no adequate logistical preparations for the support of a final drive into Germany.[1] The hope of a deep thrust across the lower Rhine and a quick drive on a narrow front into the heart of Germany had proved illusory, if, indeed, it had ever been seriously entertained by SHAEF. The fight for the Arnhem bridgehead obviously was going against the Allies.[2] It now appeared that a major offensive on a broad front would be required to put the Allied armies across the Rhine; such an offensive could be mounted, but it could not be sustained unless the port of Antwerp was in operation.

On the afternoon of 22 September General Eisenhower met with his top commanders. In forthright terms he announced that he "required general acceptance of the fact that the possession of an additional major deep-water port on our north flank is an indispensable prerequisite for the final drive deep into Germany." Priority, therefore, would be given to an attack on the north flank by Montgomery's 21st Army Group with the object of clearing the Schelde approaches to Antwerp (the latter had been captured on 4 Septem-

[1] See Ruppenthal, Logistical Support; see also 12th A Gp Rpt of Opns V and VI.

[2] On the night of 23 September the Second British Army finally authorized the withdrawal of the 1st British Airborne Division from the bridgehead; two nights later the survivors of the gallant division were brought back across the lower Rhine in assault boats.

ber). Furthermore, said the Supreme Commander: "All concerned [must] differentiate clearly between the logistical requirements for attaining objectives covered by present directives, including seizing the Ruhr and breaching the Siegfried Line, and the requirements for the final drive on Berlin." In other words the current Allied main effort, "the envelopment of the Ruhr from the north by 21st Army Group, supported by the First Army," would be regarded as the paramount Allied concern and as a "matter of urgency." [3]

The allocation of the supplies needed to support the 21st Army Group efforts and the First Army attempt to drive through the West Wall to Cologne and Bonn would not permit the Third Army to continue the attack east of the Moselle. The drive toward the Saar always had been subsidiary to that aimed at the Ruhr. Now the priority accorded the opening of Antwerp—a priority on which the Supreme Commander and the Combined Chiefs of Staff were agreed[4]—would reduce still further the importance attached to the Lorraine operation. Eisenhower therefore instructed the 12th Army Group commander that the Third Army and any units of the new Ninth Army that entered the line were to take "no more aggressive action than is permitted by the maintenance situation after the full requirements of the main effort had been met."

To open the port of Antwerp was now the order of the day. Eisenhower wrote a personal letter to Montgomery, who had not attended the meeting of 22 September, and after a discussion of the over-all situation—which included a statement that the First Army might be forced to abandon the thrust eastward from Aachen—concluded: "Of course, we need Antwerp." In this same message the Supreme Commander sought to quiet Montgomery's continued protests against the diversion of troops and supplies to the Lorraine area by a reference to the 4th Armored tank battles: "Bradley has been quite successful in keeping a lot of enemy strength to the south, as is clearly indicated by the enemy concentration of armor in the Lunéville area." [5] General Bradley, in turn, passed on the Supreme Commander's decision to General Patton in a personal letter apparently calculated to allay the latter's frequently expressed suspicion that he and the Third Army were the victims of subterranean maneuvers at SHAEF. After telling Patton, "It is apparent to everyone that no

[3] Minutes of meeting at SHAEF, 22 Sep 44, SHAEF SGS File, Post OVERLORD Planning 381, I. Field Marshal Montgomery was represented at the meeting by his chief of staff.

[4] For fuller discussion, see Pogue, Supreme Command.

[5] Eisenhower to Montgomery, 24 Sep 44, SHAEF SGS File, Post OVERLORD Planning 381, I.

major offensive by American forces can be undertaken until the port of Antwerp is opened," Bradley broke the news that only one of the American armies in the 12th Army Group could be supported in further major operations, that the Third Army would have to go over to the defensive, and that Patton would have to release the 7th Armored Division in order to reinforce the drive in the north.[6]

The scheduled attack by the 7th Armored to force a crossing over the Seille south of Metz was now perforce to be abandoned.[7] At the same time plans were in the making to take the XV Corps from the Third Army and give it to Lt. Gen. Jacob L. Devers' 6th Army Group. Here again the factor of supply ruled tactical assignments. General Devers' troops were being supplied from the great harbor of Marseille. He had assured General Eisenhower on 22 September that the southern line of communications could support two more divisions in the attack. Since the Supreme Commander had ordered the continuation of the 6th Army Group attack toward Mulhouse and Strasbourg —an attack made possible by the logistical independence of the southern group of armies—and since he desired to keep as many divisions as possible on the offensive, Eisenhower now assigned the XV Corps to Devers as "the simplest solution."[8] The transfer would be made on 29 September. This whittling process naturally tended to weaken the Third Army, even when on the defensive. A Letter of Instructions from Bradley's headquarters on 25 September, therefore, stated the intention to extend the Ninth Army front southward to include Metz when the Ninth Army arrived to take over a sector between the First and Third Armies.[9]

General Patton quite naturally was restive under the new orders forcing him to abandon the offensive. Logistical difficulties he found irritating, but in the past, when in command of smaller forces, he had shown uncanny skill in continuing his attacks despite meager supplies. Patton's unwillingness to be slowed down during the Sicilian campaign by terrain, communications, supply, Germans, or higher commands had caused Eisenhower to recommend him to General Marshall "as an army commander that you can use with [the] certainty that the troops will not be stopped by ordinary obstacles."[10] Now

[6] Bradley to Patton, 23 Sep 44, 12th A Gp File, Military Objectives 371.3, I.

[7] See Chap. III, p. 173.

[8] Eisenhower to 12th and 6th A Gps, FWD–15934, 26 Sep 44, SHAEF SGS File, Post OVERLORD Planning 381, I.

[9] 12th A Gp Ltr of Instructions No. 9, 25 Sep 44.

[10] Eisenhower to Marshall, 24 Aug 43, SHAEF Cable Log.

Patton expressed his impatience with what he considered to be "a defensive attitude" on the part of SHAEF and what he derided as the "big picture" problems arising from the over-all conduct of the war on the Western Front.[11] Although the Third Army would have to give up all thought of a general offensive for the time being, Patton saw a number of opportunities for continuing local attacks, and these he successfully put before General Bradley. At the same time, however, the Third Army commander hastened to carry out his new orders, moving the 7th Armored Division out of his area with the promptness which had constantly commended him to his superiors.

On 25 September General Bradley wrote a personal note to General Eisenhower and in passing set forth his agreement with the Third Army plans for local operations:

> In accordance with instructions I received at your headquarters the other day, I have ordered the Third Army to assume the defensive. At the same time, however, I have authorized George to make some minor adjustments in his present lines. There are about three localities just in front of his present position which he assures me he can take from time to time as ammunition becomes available on his present allotment, and which will save many casualties in the long run. One of these localities is a woods on his right flank from which many counterattacks have been launched. These woods make a good anchor for his right flank. A couple of other places are hills which look down on his present position and furnish such excellent observation of the enemy that George believes it will be economical in the long run to take them as opportunities present themselves. I am doing this in the belief that it complies with the spirit of your directive to assume the defensive in order to save supplies for the First Army.[12]

These "minor adjustments" were published to Patton's general officers on the same day as a series of priorities for immediate operations to secure "a suitable line of departure so that we can move rapidly when the Supreme Commander directs us to resume the offensive."[13] (*Map XXII*)

The first priority was to be the capture of the Forêt de Parroy in the XV Corps sector on the right wing of the army. Its seizure would bring the XV Corps abreast of the XII Corps salient east of Arracourt and reduce enemy pressure on the 4th Armored Division. The second priority was given to operations intended to drive a wedge into the concentric Metz fortifications by the capture of forts west and southwest of the city. Of these works Fort Driant

[11] TUSA Diary, 23 Sep 44. See also the author's notes taken at the time in the Third Army headquarters.

[12] Bradley to Eisenhower, 25 Sep 44, 12th A Gp File, Military Objectives 371.3, I.

[13] TUSA AAR, Ltr of Instructions No. 4. This letter ends with the typical Patton touch: ". . . We only await the signal to resume our career of conquest."

had been ticketed by the XX Corps as most important. A third priority was assigned to pushing the XII Corps main line of resistance to and beyond the villages of Donnelay, Château-Salins, and Fresnes-en-Saulnois. An advance in this area would place the XII Corps in position for a future attack toward either Morhange or Dieuze. It will be remembered, however, that on 25 September the enemy was counterattacking in this sector.[14] The last priority designated the capture of the high ground northeast of the Nomény loop in the Seille River as an object for local operations by the XII Corps. The objective was named as Moncheux, four miles northeast of Delme. As yet, of course, the 80th Infantry Division had not reached the Seille line.

The local operations outlined above would lead to limited-objective attacks by elements of the Third Army through the last days of September and well into October. Although there was now to be a pause in the Third Army offensive toward the Rhine, there would, nevertheless, be extremely hard fighting.

The Initial Attacks on Fort Driant

During the first phase of the XX Corps operation against Metz, air support had been available only sporadically and in a very limited quantity. Faced with the necessity of increasing the number of European ports available to the Allies, SHAEF had decided to take much of the air force normally allotted in tactical support of the ground forces and assign it to the operation at Brest. Although the XIX Tactical Air Command and IX Bomber Command did divert squadrons to the Third Army front, such missions generally were carried out by relatively small numbers of fighter-bombers and a few medium bombers. The air operations over Brest continued from 26 August until the capitulation of the fortress on 19 September. During that time the XIX TAC, usually assigned to co-operate with the Third Army, flew the majority of its missions at Brest on twenty-three of the twenty-six days involved. Whether the decision to divert tactical air power to Brest was the part of wisdom remains a debatable question. The modern fortifications around that port were very strong and the Ninth Air Force subsequently stated: "The reports of the bombing of modern reinforced concrete emplacements were negative. These structures proved practically impervious to air attack, and there appears to be no authenticated report of one being de-

[14] Chapter V, p. 236.

stroyed." [15] On the other hand, the most important works in the Metz fortifications subsequently proved to be quite as resistant to attack by air as the Brest forts. The ground commanders and the troops around Metz were nevertheless as one in their conviction that air support was essential if Metz was to be taken; this would be an overriding consideration in all thinking and planning, as it became more and more apparent that the infantry-artillery team could not breach the fortress ring alone. Therefore, as the Brest operation drew to a close and the hopes for a quick armored envelopment at Metz went glimmering, the Third Army prepared for a new operation against the fortress city based on an extensive and co-ordinated attack by the Ninth Air Force and XX Corps.

On 17 September, after agreement by the staffs at 12th Army Group and the Ninth Air Force, General Walker issued a tentative and highly secret plan under the code name "Operation Thunderbolt." This called for a combined effort by air and ground forces and set 21 September as a target date for beginning the operation. The attack would turn inward toward Metz, generally following the axis of the Moselle, with the river tentatively marked as the boundary between the 90th and 5th Divisions, the two formations selected to make the main effort on the ground. No change was made in the mission assigned the 7th Armored Division, which, in this plan, would continue its attempts to isolate the Metz area by envelopment to the east. The projected operation was divided into three phases, of which the seizure of Fort Driant would be the first. Each phase, in turn, consisted of three stages: preparatory attacks by heavy bombers; advance by the infantry to the line of departure under cover of a bombardment by medium bombers and artillery fire; then the final infantry assault, supported by direct-fire weapons and artillery. Fighter-bombers from the XIX TAC were to furnish continuous support to the ground forces as the operation developed.[16]

The "Air Support Plan," prepared for the Metz attack by the G-3 Air, 12th Army Group, contained one extremely important proviso: "The assault will be based on the attack of the medium bombers and will not take place until weather permits their use." But in addition to the highly problematical condition of the weather in late September the operation would be contingent also on the priorities which might be assigned the Ninth Air Force by headquarters above the Third Army. While it was true that SHAEF had erased

[15] AAF Historical Studies, No. 36 (Oct 45), pp. 222-231.
[16] XX Corps G-3 Jnl, 17 Sep 44.

the top priority given the Brest operation as early as 9 September, the limited number of planes diverted from Brest in mid-September generally had been allocated to support the First Army drive toward the West Wall. This air priority accorded the First Army was an integral part of the larger strategic plan to put the main effort on the north wing of the Allied armies. As a result the Third Army seldom could be given better than a second priority on air support from 18 September onward.

The first object in the proposed air-ground operation against Metz was the reduction of Fort Driant, a required preliminary to any further attempt to penetrate the Metz fortifications from the south or southwest. Col. Charles W. Yuill, the commanding officer of the 11th Infantry, had urged that Fort Driant could be taken by storm and seems to have been instrumental in selling this idea to the corps and army staffs. General Walker, who was not too impressed with the strength of the fortified works around Metz, made no special arrangements to reinforce the assault force earmarked for the Fort Driant attacks and proposed to use only the 2d Battalion, 11th Infantry, which had been left to contain the fort and its garrison while the main body of the 5th Division battled east of the Moselle. From 19 September onward the 2d Battalion was alerted almost daily to begin the attack. Numerous factors conspired to delay the operation, however: several days of bad flying weather; uncertainty as to the exact time when the American planes would arrive on those days when they were able to go aloft; and a continued shortage of artillery ammunition which made it impossible to support an attack east of the river and still conduct an intensive shelling at Fort Driant.

In the meantime the 90th Infantry Division had returned to the attack in the Jeanne d'Arc sector, roughly two and a half miles north of Fort Driant. In the 90th Division scheme of maneuver, planned originally as a part of "Operation Thunderbolt," General McLain intended that his division should execute a power drive to the east from positions south of Gravelotte, making the main effort toward the Jeanne d'Arc works. In order to shift the balance of the division and nourish this attack, the 358th was relieved on the north flank by Task Force Polk (the 3d Cavalry Group, reinforced) and on 27 September moved south around to the right flank of the 359th, where the 3d Cavalry Reconnaissance Squadron had been deployed. A day earlier the 3d Battalion of the 359th had commenced a fight to seize the road between Gravelotte and St. Hubert's Farm as a jumping-off point for the projected large-scale attack. Repeated attacks by the 359th made no headway, even after the entire regiment was committed. On the evening of 27 September it was clear that the 359th had shot its bolt. The stock of artillery ammunition which had been carefully husbanded for this attack was low, with little prospect of replenishment. General McLain called off the operation, and the front lines were thinned to a containing shell in order to rotate troops to rear areas for rest and further training. When the month of September came to a close the 90th Division front was quiet, but General McLain and his staff already had sketched out "a long-range plan" for future operations which provided that the 357th Infantry should push around the north flank of the German bridgehead and capture Maizières-lès-Metz. The outline plan provided also for an assault by the 358th and 359th against the Jeanne d'Arc positions, but it contained one important and limiting proviso: "Above all, the operation is based on the prior capture of Fort Driant and our subsequent occupation and utilization of it as a flank anchor, OP and base of fire."

The decision, in higher headquarters, to detach the 7th Armored Division from the XX Corps forced Patton to abandon the projected drive east of Metz. Although General Patton and General Walker disliked giving up any ground it was apparent that the 5th Division by itself could not hold the existing line east of the river and mount an assault on Fort Driant at the same time. Therefore, General Irwin was ordered to extend his right flank to take over from the 7th Armored Division, while shortening the extended front by a limited withdrawal back toward the Moselle. The relief was completed by the morning of 25 September. The 7th Armored Division began a move to Hasselt, Belgium, and the 5th Division withdrew to a new main line of resistance under a covering shell of infantry outposts. This reorganization was completed without incident, and on the night of 25–26 September the outpost line was pulled back to the main body. The new main line of resistance east of the river was held by the 11th Infantry (—) on the north wing, the 10th Infantry in the center, and the 2d Infantry on the south. The towns which had cost so much to take—Corny and Pournoy-la-Chétive—were abandoned while the line in the north and northeast was constructed. The 2d Infantry was thus freed to take over the sector formerly held by CCB, 7th Armored Division, on the high ground west of the Seille River—from Cheminot north to the Bois Jurieux. North of the 2d Infantry the 10th Infantry line swung in an arc back to the west. At Marieulles the 11th Infantry (—) sector began, following the ridges northwestward to a point opposite Novéant. The weary infantry dug in along this new main line of resistance and put out a strong outpost line.

Meanwhile the focus of attention shifted across the Moselle to Fort Driant, where the 5th Division faced a special and difficult task. By 26 September the static situation along the new main line of resistance in the 5th Division bridgehead promised a little more freedom in the use of artillery ammunition, and General Walker, more and more impatient with the delay at Fort Driant, ordered the attack to begin the following day—with or without support from the air.[17]

Virtually nothing was yet known of the detailed construction of Fort Driant, or the field fortifications around it. American patrols had made numerous attempts to work their way into the fort area only to be stopped each time by the enemy outposts and ranging fire from the main works. Air photos showed little but the outlines of the casemates, bunkers, connecting trenches, and the surrounding moat. However, operations both east and west of the Moselle had amply demonstrated the tactical importance of this particular fort. Fort Driant (or Kronprinz) held a dominant height from which the artillery in the other southern works of "Fortress Metz" could be directed and controlled. Its own guns covered the approaches along the Moselle and provided flanking fire in support of the Verdun group (Forts Sommy and St. Blaise) on the east bank of the river. Obviously, any attempts to wedge a way into Metz along the Moselle axis, a maneuver for which the XX Corps was now deployed, or any penetration east of Gravelotte must be contingent on capturing or at least neutralizing this fort.

Fort Driant belonged to the outer ring of the Metz fortresses, comprising the most modern and the strongest works in the system. (*Map XXIII*) Built in 1902, it had been modernized and further strengthened by both French and Germans.[18] The main works stood on a bald-topped hill, 360 meters in height, and fringed sparsely by trees. A supply road angled north to Ars-sur-Moselle. Below the hill a thick patch of woods reached out toward the southwest slope, and in these woods the Americans assembled for their first attacks. The main

[17] The XIX TAC began attacks against the Metz forts on 26 September and continued to attack daily until 30 September. However, the fighter-bomber efforts had little effect. XIX TAC Report on the Combat Operations of the XIX Tactical Air Command, 30 May 45.

[18] The fort had been renamed, when the French repossessed it after World War I, in honor of the heroic Lt. Col. Driant of the 56th Battalion of Chasseurs, who had met his death in gallant fashion at Verdun in 1916.

FORT DRIANT

defenses consisted of four casemates, with reinforced concrete walls some seven feet thick and a central fort in the shape of a pentagon, the whole connected by underground tunnels runing into the central work. Each casemate mounted a three-gun battery, of either 100- or 150-mm. caliber, while the southern side of Fort Driant was covered by a detached battery (Battery Moselle) of three 100-mm. turret guns.[19] The interior of the works seemed almost a flat, bare surface, for the casemate roofs were built flush with the surface of the ground, leaving only the gun turrets, four concrete bunkers (each providing shelter for 200 to 500 men), and some armored observation posts and pillboxes above the surface. The fort faced southwest, although its main batteries were sited so as to provide fire through 360°, with a frontage of 1,000 yards and a depth of 700. The central fort was surrounded by a dry moat, 60 feet wide and as much as 30 feet deep, with wings extending out to either flank. Barbed wire to a depth of 60 feet encircled the entire fort and was further interlaced between and around the interior works. Finally, the Germans had taken care to provide the defenders with adequate water, storage space for food and ammunition, and a system of artificial ventilation in the main bunkers and tunnels underneath the ground. It is not known how large the Fort Driant garrison was at the time of the first American assault. It probably was small, but could and would be quickly reinforced by troops from Ars-sur-Moselle.

Colonel Yuill was far from satisfied by the maps available to guide his assault troops. The 1:100,000 sheets in use at the time of the Moselle crossings had been replaced by a fairly accurate series of 1:50,000 maps, but even this scale was too indefinite and too sparse in detail for a battalion attack. Members of Colonel Yuill's staff, with the aid of corps and army intelligence officers, succeeded in locating in Paris a few 1:20,000 contour maps of the Metz area. Then followed a search for detailed plans of the fortification. The trail led from Verdun to Nancy to Lyons, where engraving plates, hidden by a French officer in 1940, were uncovered. These provided a wealth of detail on the works at Fort Driant. Unfortunately the detailed ground plans did not reach the 11th Infantry until 29 September, and the troops making the first assault received only a vague briefing on the basis of inexact sketch maps of Fort Driant and its surrounding terrain.[20]

On the morning of 27 September the skies cleared, and General Irwin, anxious to give his air support as much time as possible, ordered the assault

[19] MS #B-042 (Kittel).

[20] 5th Div AAR, Incl 10, Sep 44.

battalion to jump off at 1415.[21] P–47's from the XIX TAC dropped 1,000-pound bombs and napalms as a starter, coming in as low as fifty feet to make their strikes on the fort, but with negligible results. Other squadrons of P–47's followed in the early afternoon, dropping napalm and high explosive bombs on the trenches and bunkers, and strafing the interior of the fort. This effort failed to damage Fort Driant.[22] The artillery, which fired two concentrations prior to H Hour, seems to have had no better luck, for the enemy guns and mortars were quieted only briefly. Fire from the 155-mm. howitzers of the 21st Field Artillery Battalion and emplaced tank destroyers, when directed against the pillboxes dotting the forward slopes, failed to penetrate or destroy these outworks.[23]

At H Hour E Company moved out of the woods south of the fort under cover of a smoke screen which a company of 4.2 chemical mortars had laid on the fort and the wooded draw behind it. Company G and a company of tank destroyers from the 818th Tank Destroyer Battalion followed. Short of the fort the infantry came upon a moat, or ditch, and heavy wire entanglements, the whole covered by outlying pillboxes. The enemy in the fort had been relatively quiet during the American approach, but now he opened up with small arms, machine guns, and mortars. Two platoons worked their way around to the west side of the fort, where a causeway gave entrance to the *enceinte* itself, but were driven to earth some three hundred yards from the moat by a hail of small arms fire. The tank destroyers, which had driven onto the open ground close behind the infantry skirmish line, engaged the outer German pillboxes and the machine gun embrasures in the main works, but, despite what appeared to be accurate laying, could not put the enemy crews out of action. The mass of wire entanglements, fire from numerous and previously undiscovered pillboxes surrounding the fort, and the inefficacy of tank destroyer fire against reinforced concrete works forbade a continuation of the action; at 1830 General Irwin gave Colonel Yuill permission to with-

[21] The massed air attacks scheduled in the THUNDERBOLT plans had been abandoned on 25 September. General Bradley had given verbal orders to the 12th Army Group G–3 Air, Col. Sheffield Edwards, canceling the operation on the grounds that there was insufficient artillery ammunition to support an all-out ground attack against the Metz forts. Interv with Col Edwards, Washington, 21 May 47. Thereafter bomber support was allocated on a day-to-day basis.

[22] On the contrary, the morale of the German garrison was raised by these attacks, since it found that the concrete works gave adequate protection. AAF Evaluation Board, The Effect of Air Power in the Battle of Metz, 19 Jan 45.

[23] The 2d Battalion attack was supported by 3 battalions of 105-mm. howitzers, 3 battalions of 155-mm. howitzers, 1 battery of 8-inch howitzers, and 1 battery of 240-mm. howitzers.

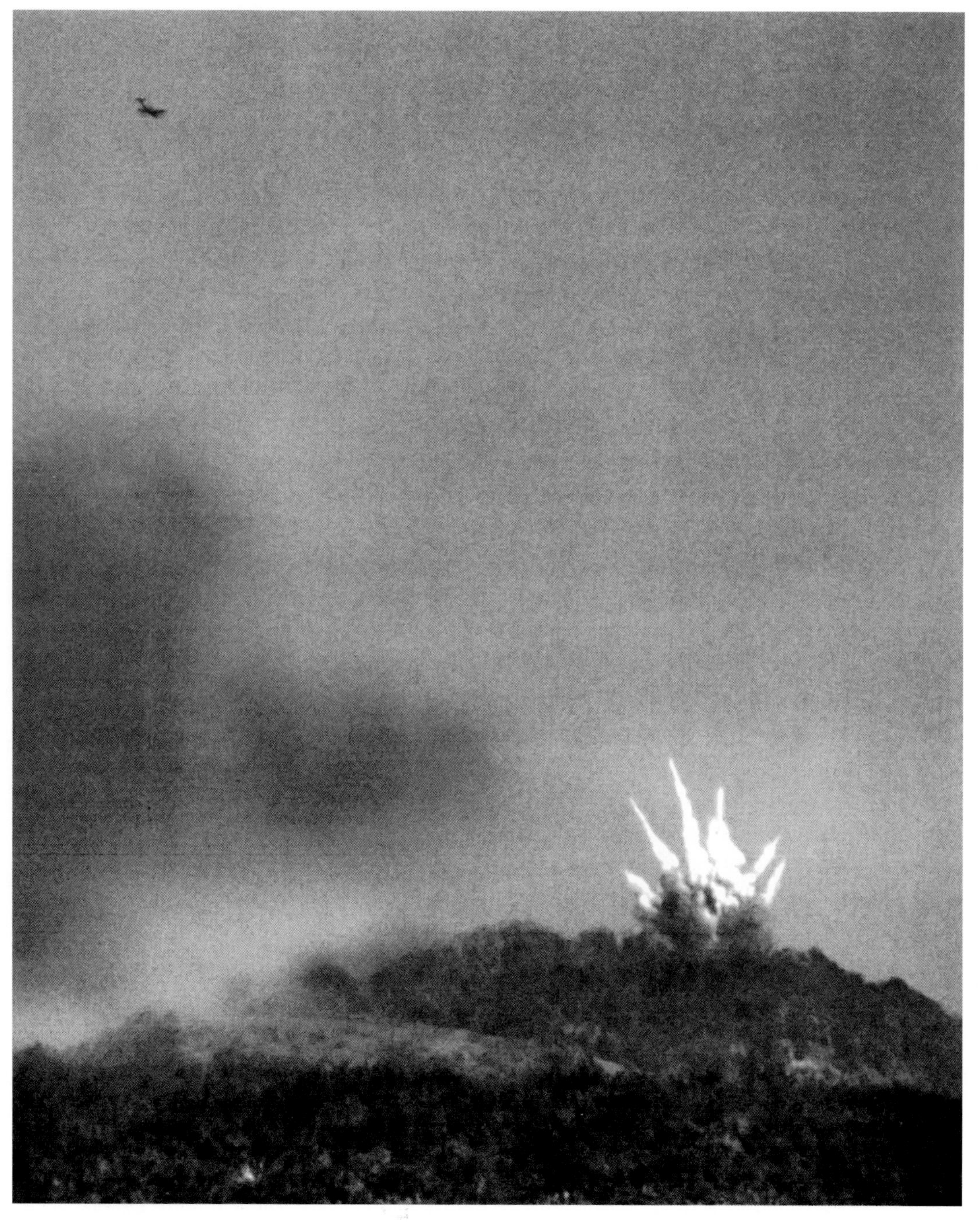

BOMBING OF FORT DRIANT *by P–47's from the XIX Tactical Air Command.*

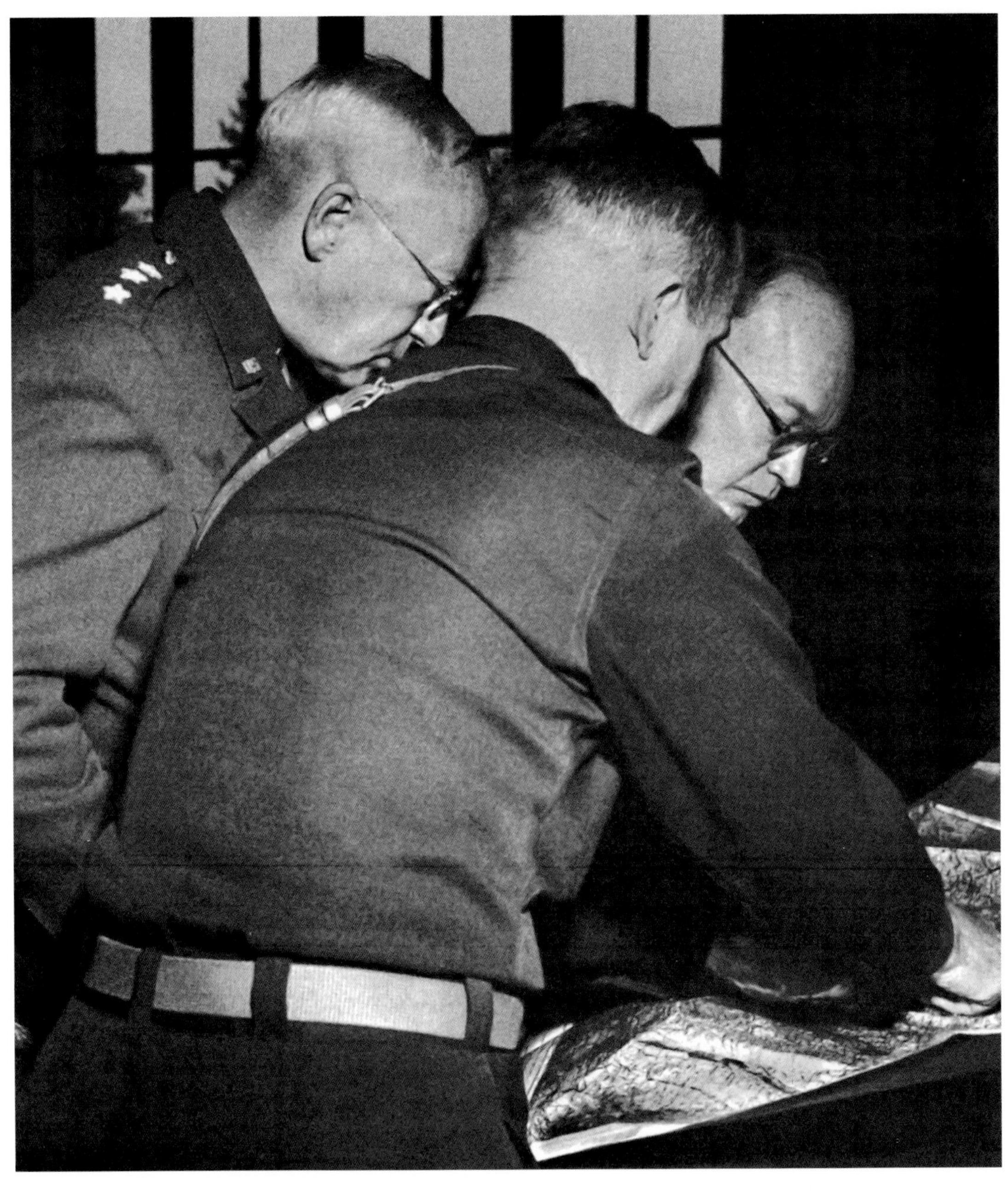

PATTON CONFERS WITH EISENHOWER *on plan for reduction of Fort Driant. On left is General Patton, on right General Eisenhower.*

draw the assault force to its original positions. Losses had been slight—only eighteen men in the two infantry companies.[24]

On the following day General Patton met with General Walker and General Irwin to consider the situation. The army commander himself did not press General Irwin to continue the Driant operations, but instead instructed the 5th Division commander to take advantage of the forthcoming lull in the army's operations to rotate and rest his tired division. General Walker was not so charitable. He sharply insisted that more aggressive personal leadership should have been shown by the regimental and battalion commanders responsible for the initial attack at Fort Driant. General Irwin, however, noted that the difficulties encountered by the attacking force had been greater than anticipated, and reminded the corps commander that the air photos had shown neither the intricate wire entanglements nor the large number of pillboxes around the fort.[25] There was as yet no talk of abandoning the Driant enterprise, and General Irwin and his staff continued with plans based on the experience of 27 September for a systematic reduction of the fort.[26] Final approval was given the operation by General Patton on 29 September, when the army commander invited a number of his ranking officers to meet General Eisenhower in the headquarters of the army at Etain. General Eisenhower here stressed the point that advantage was to be taken of the lull to get men and equipment in shape for future operations. Then General Patton directed that the plans for local operations would be carried out as supplies and artillery ammunition became available.[27] General Walker immediately gave orders for the 5th Division to continue the Driant operation and, further, to make preparations for a subsequent attack on the Verdun forts east of the Moselle.

General Irwin believed that his division needed rest and training,[28] and was convinced that the fort should be taken by encirclement—for which maneuver troops were lacking. Nonetheless he and his staff worked overtime to

[24] 11th Inf Jnl, 27 Sep 44. See also 11th Inf AAR, Incl 10, Sep 44.

[25] 5th Div Telephone Jnl, 28 Sep 44.

[26] The orders releasing the XV Corps from the Third Army had automatically erased the Forêt de Parroy attack as top priority of those listed by General Patton on 25 September. A new TUSA Operational Directive, issued on 28 September, gave the Metz fort first priority in the revised program for local operations.

[27] TUSA Diary, 29 Sep 44.

[28] The 5th Division losses during September are listed *tentatively* as 380 killed, 2,097 wounded, and 569 missing. 5th Div G–1 Jnl and AAR, Sep 44. These losses do not include sick and combat fatigue cases. The number of such cases was so high that on 26 September General Patton sent General Gay to make

make the next assault at Driant a success. They planned carefully, amassing ammunition and various types of new equipment which was just arriving at the army engineer depots. Two items seemed well adapted to an attack on a fortified position, the tankdozer and the "snake." The first, it was hoped, would be able to fill in the moat under fire, while the snake, a long pipe or tube filled with explosive, was designed to be pushed through barbed wire or mine fields and there exploded, somewhat in the manner of a bangalore torpedo. Both tankdozers and snakes were difficult to procure, but even more trying was the search for trained personnel to operate these machines and to make such modifications as were required for the task at hand. Although General Irwin's division was spread over a very wide front,[29] with little infantry left over for the Driant attack (now scheduled for 3 October), he had been given substantial artillery support both in front of the fort and across in the bridgehead; all the corps artillery had been moved into position to support the 5th Division, leaving the 90th and 83d to rely upon their own divisional guns. An incident on 2 October, however, indicated that modern artillery was not necessarily the solution to the tactical problem of reducing even a moderately modern fort, for an 8-inch howitzer got eight direct hits on one of the turrets at Fort Driant only to have its fire returned fifteen minutes later by guns in that same turret.[30]

The plan of attack for 3 October was carefully worked out. The 2d Battalion of the 11th Infantry again was designated as the assault force, but this time was reinforced by B Company of the 1st Battalion, a company of combat engineers, and twelve tanks from the medium companies of the 735th Tank Battalion. Company B would attempt to gain entrance at the southwestern edge of the fort, Company E would attack at the northwestern corner, and

an inspection. Gay's report was favorable to the 5th Division. He noted that morale was good, that the division had taken severe losses, and that it had been fighting hard for a considerable length of time. Gay added that in his opinion any student in a military school who "attacked" a position such as the 5th Division had attacked and held would have been graded "Unsatisfactory" on his solution. Furthermore, the 5th Division was in process of absorbing and training 200 officers and 3,773 enlisted replacements who had come into the division during September. Many of these replacements saw their first fighting at Fort Driant.

[29] The 5th Division held a line of approximately 19,000 meters, which, the 5th Division G–3 pointed out, was "no division front." So exposed was the 2d Battalion, 11th Infantry, that the 2d Battalion, 358th Infantry, was sent by trucks to Gorze on 3 October with orders to cover the left flank of the assault force. General Irwin asked for the use of "only" two companies of the 358th's battalion, but this request was refused by General Walker.

[30] What the 500- and 1,000-pound aerial bombs failed to accomplish by direct hits could hardly be expected of a 286-pound shell.

Company G, in reserve, would be used to exploit whichever penetration was successful. Tanks and engineers were equally divided among the three infantry companies. Air support had been promised by the IX Bombardment Division for the morning of 3 October but because of bad weather the bombers did not arrive,[31] and finally at 1200, unwilling to wait any longer, General Irwin gave the order for the attack to begin.[32] Corps and division artillery laid a barrage ahead of the advancing infantry, two companies of 4.2 mortars from the 81st Chemical Mortar Battalion spread a pall of smoke over the valley between Driant and Ars-sur-Moselle, and tanks ahead of the infantry line pulled and shoved to get the unwilling snakes into position against the German wire. The snakes broke almost immediately and the wire was finally cut by high explosive fired by the American artillery. The tankdozers were halted by mechanical failures. Company E was stopped at the wire by intense German artillery fire and entrenched enemy infantry.[33] Company B was more successful and at 1400 had fought its way around the end of the moat, through the wire, and into the fort.[34] Here the infantry and supporting tanks proceeded methodically to clear the Germans out of the ditches and bunkers, harassed the while by machine guns, mortar fire, and German riflemen who would pop out of tunnel entrances to give fire and then quickly retreat below ground. Engineer squads, working on the nearest casemates, tried again and again to blast an opening with demolition charges, but the heavy walls were as impervious to TNT as to shells and bombs.[35]

At dark the reserve company and its tanks came in through the gap made by B Company. Two platoons began to thread their way through the barbed wire and small arms fire to assault the two northernmost casemates, which lay clear across the fort surface. This first attack failed: the platoons were

[31] Ninth AF Summary of Opns, 3 Oct 44. However, about 1245 the 358th Group of the XIX TAC arrived and dropped napalm bombs in the Driant area. The P–47's continued to give support throughout the afternoon.

[32] The subsequent account of the Driant operation is taken from several sources: TF Warnock Jnl; 5th Div G–3 Jnl; 11th Inf Jnl and Inclosures; Hist Div Combat Interviews; and 5th Div AAR II, Oct 44.

[33] Company E dug in on the glacis and held there under constant fire for four days; when the company withdrew it numbered 85 officers and men.

[34] Pfc. Robert W. Holmlund, B Company, 11th Infantry, was awarded the DSC as a result of action at Driant during the 11th Infantry assault on 3 October. In the assault wave he drove the enemy from the first emplacements and knocked out a machine gun. When the enemy counterattacked he advanced to an exposed position and stopped the attack with his BAR. Holmlund later was killed while checking the positions held by his men.

[35] Company B had four flame throwers, but only one functioned. Flame throwers were little used throughout the operation.

badly shot up and forced to withdraw when the Germans came up from the tunnels and filtered into their rear.[36] All through the night small groups of the enemy continued forays into the American positions. Four American tanks were knocked out by bazooka men, and by dawn the Americans in the fort were badly disorganized.

In the morning General Irwin ordered Colonel Yuill to hang on and extend his hold on top of the fort area;[37] then he sent in Company K, 2d Infantry, to stabilize the line and plug up the holes left by the 110 casualties lost in the first twenty-four hours of the operation. Futile attempts were made during the day to break into the central fort, but the German snipers systematically picked off the men carrying flame throwers and explosives. The few who reached the large steel doors at the rear of the fort found them covered by protruding grillwork that made it impossible to put the charges against the doors themselves. When the second night came attempts were made to reorganize the troops who, during the day, had scattered wherever they could find shelter from the enemy fire—in abandoned pillboxes, ditches, shell holes, and open bunkers. During the night, however, the Germans again came out of the underground tunnels and threw the attackers into confusion.

As daylight came on 5 October the guns of the surrounding German forts opened a heavy fire on the troops in and around Driant. American artillery observers crawled forward and tried to locate the enemy guns, but a thick haze lay in the Moselle valley and counterbattery work brought few results. Although the stationary pieces in the casemates in Driant could not be brought to bear on the Americans in the fort area, two German howitzers finally were depressed so as to give bursts in the trees fringing the fort. Their effect was deadly. By midafternoon B and G Companies were reduced to a combined strength of less than one hundred men; K Company also was growing weaker.[38] General Irwin decided to strip the division front still further, and

[36] During 4 October the Third Platoon of G Company, 11th Infantry, made an assault to force one of the fort entrances. The platoon was driven back by a counterattack but was saved by the heroic action of 2d Lt. L. S. Dilello, who covered the withdrawal with fire from a BAR until he was killed by a hand grenade. Lieutenant Dilello received a posthumous award of the DSC.

[37] About this time General Patton told General Walker to take Driant, saying that "if it took every man in the XX Corps, [he] could not allow an attack by this army to fail." TUSA Diary, 4 Oct 44. Actually, the Third Army commander's subsequent actions as regards Driant all show a more reasonable attitude.

[38] In the late afternoon of 5 October the S–3 of the 2d Battalion, Capt. Ferris N. Church, sent back a message with a graphic report from an infantry captain on conditions at the fort: "The situation is critical a couple more barrages and another counterattack and we are sunk. We have no men, our equipment is shot and we just can't go. The trs in G are done, they are just there whats left of them. Enemy

organized a task force under the assistant division commander, Brig. Gen. A. D. Warnock, to continue the fight. During the night of 5–6 October the 1st Battalion, 10th Infantry (minus A Company), went in under Warnock's command and relieved B and G Companies on top of Driant. Fortunately, German fire was light, for the relief was difficult, many of the original assault force having to be carried down from the fort on stretchers. At 1100 more reinforcements from the 3d Battalion, 2d Infantry (minus Companies I and K), arrived to join Task Force Warnock. With these troops in hand, plus the entire 7th Combat Engineer Battalion, General Warnock gave orders for a resumption of the attack on 7 October, his intention being to drive the Germans out of the southeast section of the fort and force an entry into the main tunnel system. Colonel Yuill had not been furnished a plan of the underground maze, but such a plan had been prepared for Task Force Warnock and showed a tunnel running from the area held by the Americans, underneath the southernmost casemates, there connecting with the main tunnel system which branched out to all the casemates, the bunkers, and the central fort.

At 1000 on 7 October the 1st Battalion, 10th Infantry, opened the attack. One rifle company slowly worked its way east and in four hours succeeded in inching forward about two hundred yards, taking three pillboxes in the process. This advance brought the lead infanty into a deadly cross fire coming from the southern casemate and Battery Moselle. Orders were given for the company to reorganize and hold on to its gains, but the ground was too hard for digging and the captured pillboxes were open on the side now exposed to the Germans. About 1615 the Germans came to the surface and counterattacked. The company commander and the two forward platoons were cut off and lost. The survivors fell back to the original positions. One platoon had been sent into the tunnel, entering at a concrete bunker which was already

has infiltrated and pinned what is here down. We cannot advance nor can K Co, B Co is in same shape I'm in. We cannot delay any longer on replacement. We may be able to hold till dark but if anything happens this afternoon I can make no predictions. The enemy arty is butchering these trs until we have nothing left to hold with. We cannot get out to get our wounded and there is a hell of a lot of dead and missing. There is only one answer the way things stand. First either to withdraw and saturate it with hvy bombers or reinforce with a hell of a strong force. This strong force might hold here but eventually they'll get it by arty too. They have all of these places zeroed in by arty. The forts have 5–6 feet walls inside and 15 foot roofs of reinforced concrete. All our charges have been useless against this stuff. The few leaders are trying to keep what is left intact and that's all they can do. The trs are just not sufficiently trained and what is more they have no training in even basic Inf. Everything is committed and we cannot follow attack plan. This is just a suggestion but if we want this dammed fort lets get the stuff required to take it and then go. Right now you haven't got it. Gerrie, Capt., Inf." TF Warnock Jnl, 5 Oct 44.

in American hands. This passageway was very narrow (only three feet wide and seven feet high) and was barred close to the entrance by an iron door. Engineers blew a hole in the door, but found the other side blocked with pieces of machinery and some old cannon. This block could be moved only if the wrecked iron door was cut away, an operation that would require an acetylene torch. On such seemingly small items the fight now turned.

During the night an acetylene torch was brought up to the fort and the tunnel door cut down. Then the junk pieces were pulled out and laid on the floor of the tunnel, still further cramping the efforts of the troops in the tunnel confines. By the middle of the morning of 8 October the rubble and debris had been cleared away; it was believed that the next door ahead would lead into the southern casemate. The men in the tunnel had heard sounds of digging; fearing that the Germans were preparing to blow in the tunnel walls they rushed up a 60-pound beehive charge and exploded it. This detonation released carbide fumes and for the next two hours no one could re-enter the tunnel. Ordinary gas masks were tried but failed to protect the wearer. An engineer officer finally groped his way through the tunnel and found that the first charge had made only a small hole. When the fumes began to clear, more explosive was brought in, but the Germans opened fire with a machine gun and rifle grenades. There was nothing left to do except hastily erect a parapet of sandbags, mount a machine gun, and engage in a desultory exchange of shots.[39] The Germans next set off a counterblast in the tunnel, killing some men of Company C and driving the rest into the barracks.

General Warnock, having decided earlier that more troops were needed to clear the surface of the fort area, during the previous night had moved up the 3d Battalion, 2d Infantry, to the cover of the concrete barracks. The fumes from the tunnel, seeping up into the barracks, overcame some of the men and they were forced to take turns at the firing slits in order to fill their lungs with fresh air. With many of the troops *hors de combat* and a general state of confusion prevailing, the attack against the two southern casemates scheduled for the night of 8–9 October was canceled.

By 9 October the situation at Fort Driant was confused beyond belief. Cpl. C. F. Wilkinson, a messenger for the 284th Field Artillery Battalion, while wandering around in search of the American command post walked

[39] When the Germans opened fire, Sgt. Dale H. Klakamp, 7th Engineer Battalion, 5th Infantry Division, sprang forward and started to build the barricade. His comrades, who had been shaken by the sudden fire, then came to his aid. Sergeant Klakamp was awarded the DSC.

straight into the guard room of the central fort, but escaped before the astounded Germans could bring him down. Maneuver space atop the fort was far too limited to permit the full-scale and necessary reorganization of the heterogeneous units crowded into the bunkers or in such other scanty cover as could be found. Daylight attack had proved too costly in the face of the cross fire sweeping the surface, and night attacks had quickly become disorganized when the Germans erupted from the tunnels onto flank and rear. The American troops were jittery and in some companies their officers believed it questionable whether they would stick much longer. Losses thus far had been relatively high: 21 officers and 485 men killed, wounded, and missing.[40]

At noon on 9 October General Gay, representing the army commander, General Walker, General Irwin, and General Warnock met to discuss continuance of the operation. The task force commander candidly said that further attacks within the fort area would be far too costly and gave as his opinion that Fort Driant must be surrounded, the enemy all driven underground and there destroyed. Since this plan required an additional four battalions of infantry it was immediately rejected. General Gay ordered the fort to be evacuated and the operation abandoned, although he gave the corps commander permission to make one more attempt to blast a way through the tunnel.[41] This attempt was not made; on the night of 12–13 October the last American troops left the fort without a shot being fired by the enemy.[42]

All of the higher American officers involved in this operation were loath to bring it to an unsuccessful conclusion. It represented the first publicized reverse suffered by the Third Army. What made it particularly depressing was that it came at the beginning of a lengthy period of quiet in which General Patton and his troops could have no opportunity to distinguish themselves by new victories. However, much had been learned concerning attacks against modern-type fortified positions. These lessons were put to immediate use during the training period in October, and would be successfully applied during the November offensive which finally saw the reduction of the Metz fort system.

[40] This is a tentative estimate of losses for the period 3–8 October. See special report in XX Corps G–3 Jnl, 8 Oct. 44. The total casualties for the Driant operation numbered 64 killed in action, 547 wounded in action, and 187 missing in action. See *Fifth Infantry Division*.

[41] TF Warnock Jnl, 9 Oct 44; TUSA Diary, 9 Oct 44.

[42] Six tanks from the 735th Tank Battalion had to be left in the fort; they were destroyed by the American artillery.

The 90th Division at Maizières-lès-Metz

General Patton's desire to continue limited-objective attacks at certain points on the Third Army front was in part prompted by the necessity of securing an advantageous line of departure for a future general resumption of the offensive. In the XX Corps zone the seizure of Fort Driant would have put Third Army troops astride a direct route from the south into Metz. On the north, the shortest and most direct route into the city so far as the approaches on the west bank of the Moselle were concerned was offered by the main highway from Thionville to Metz which traverses the narrow plain between the river and the western heights.[43] The September operations of the 7th Armored Division and 90th Division had cleared this avenue of approach as far south as Maizières-lès-Metz, a mining and smelting town of some five thousand population only seven miles from the center of Metz. The capture of Maizières-lès-Metz would not only plant the American forces solidly on the southern section of the Thionville–Metz highway, but would also be of considerable tactical importance in any future operation to turn the right flank of the strong German positions west of Metz.

At the end of September the 90th Division had relinquished the plan to force a penetration east of Gravelotte. The 83d Division, newly assigned to the Third Army, had assumed responsibility for protecting the north flank of the XX Corps (with Task Force Polk), thus permitting a little more tactical freedom in the employment of the left-flank elements of the 90th Division. When the weight of the 90th shifted to the south, the 357th Infantry was moved to occupy an east–west line from Talange, on the Moselle, to St. Privat, hemming in the German defenses.[44] About 24 September General McLain, the 90th Division commander, suggested that the 357th make a limited-objective attack in the Maizières-lès-Metz sector for the purpose of training in assault tactics against fortifications and to secure a good line of departure for the coming Metz offensive. The XX Corps commander agreed to the

[43] Marshal Bazaine attacked north along this route in his last attempt, in October 1870, to break out of the iron ring forged by the German armies around the French at Metz. The French advanced as far as Woippy and were there defeated.

[44] Activity in this sector consisted of patrolling. For his part in one such patrol on the night of 29 September, Pfc. L. G. Zehner, G Company, received the DSC. Zehner was the point man in a patrol sent to cross a footbridge at the canal near Richemont. He was well ahead of the rest of his patrol when a German voice challenged him. Zehner ran straight across the bridge, firing his BAR. On the enemy bank he captured a machine gun, silenced German rifle fire by throwing grenades into the near-by houses, and then rejoined the patrol.

plan as one means of maintaining an "active defensive" in the quieter sectors of the corps front.[45]

At 0430 on 3 October, the same date on which the 5th Division launched the main assault at Fort Driant, two companies of the 357th Infantry led by Maj. Jack W. Ward made a surprise attack from the Bois de l'Abbé, west of Maizières-lès-Metz, and with only four casualties gained control of a long, high slag pile which overlooked that town from the northwest.[46] *(Map XXIV)* For three days the Americans occupied the slag pile without any serious contest, though under heavy artillery fire by the Germans. On 6 October Task Force Polk relieved some of the elements of the 357th Infantry on the division north flank, and with this limited reinforcement General McLain proceeded with his plans to capture Maizières-lès-Metz itself.[47]

The attack planned for the morning of 7 October called for E Company to make the initial penetration in Maizières-lès-Metz by thrusting from the west along the Bronvaux road. Company G, following on its heels, was then to swing south and begin mopping up the factory buildings west of the Thionville–Metz railroad tracks which formed a main point of enemy resistance. Fortunately, the Germans played into the hands of the 357th by making a predawn attack in force against the company on the slag pile. While these attackers were being cut down on the steep, barren slopes of the mound of slag, E Company jumped off, skirted the slag heap, and knifed through the town under cover of a concentration fired by two field artillery groups. The northern part of the town was quickly overrun and by dark the Americans had a foothold in the factory area, but further advance was stopped by S-mines (one of which caused fifteen casualties) covered by determined German riflemen and field pieces close behind them.[48] That night the Germans hastened to reinforce the troops in Maizières and sent elements of the *73d Regiment, 19th VG Division*, into the lines.[49] Strengthened by these new arrivals, the garrison settled down to a long-drawn-out fight, house to house and block to block, punctuated by sorties and artillery duels. The houses in Maizières were strongly constructed, generally of stone, and strengthened by

[45] Ltr, Gen Walker to Hist Div, 8 Oct 47.

[46] Major Ward was given the DSC.

[47] General McLain had hoped that seizure of the slag pile would make the town untenable to the enemy. XX Corps G–3 Jnl, 2 Oct 44.

[48] 2d Bn, 357th Inf, Jnl, 7 Oct 44.

[49] At the same time the *First Army* massed several field artillery battalions, since there was little American pressure elsewhere, and put very heavy fire on the Americans. See MS #B–214 (Mantey).

wire and sandbags so as to form a succession of miniature forts which had to be reduced one by one. The pivotal point in the Maizières *enceinte* was formed by the heavy masonry of the Hôtel de Ville, east of the railroad tracks, around which the fighting surged indecisively.

During the next days the 2d Battalion, 357th Infantry, continued to wedge its way slowly into the factory area and the center of the town, using demolition charges and flame throwers, while field guns and tank destroyers fired constantly to interdict the German supply route leading in from Metz. The 4.2 mortars maintained a haze of smoke at the south edge of town over the slag heap that served the enemy as an observation post. A platoon of tanks was brought in from the north after the roads were cleared of mines, but there was little room for maneuver in the narrow streets—down which German bazookas and antitank guns were sighted—and the tanks played only a minor role in the fight for the town.

By 11 October optimism engendered by the success of the initial push into Maizières was considerably dissipated.[50] Colonel Barth advised the division commander that two battalions of infantry should be used in the town. But although there had been some slight reshuffling of troops along the 90th Division front to take advantage of the general lull there were not two fresh battalions at hand: the best that could be done was to relieve the worn 2d Battalion by filtering the 3d Battalion, 357th, into the line on the night of 12–13 October. General McLain[51] still had some hope of taking Maizières, but a new order from Third Army headquarters freezing the allotment of all artillery ammunition above 3-inch caliber put an end to the idea of continuing a full-fledged assault. The 3d Battalion turned to using the town as a training ground, setting up attack problems in which a platoon, or a squad, took a house or two each day.

The Germans apparently were quite willing to limit the fighting to such a scale, although they retaliated with a bitter shelling on 20 October when an American 155-mm. self-propelled gun was run to within 150 yards of the Hôtel de Ville and slammed ten rounds into the building. Meanwhile the Third Army completed plans for a return to the offensive in November and granted the XX Corps a special dispensation for artillery ammunition to be

[50] XX Corps G–3 Jnl, 11 Oct 44.

[51] On 15 October General McLain was given command of the XIX Corps and Brig. Gen. James A. Van Fleet took over the 90th Division. Earlier General Eisenhower had credited McLain with making the 90th "a first class fighting outfit." Eisenhower to Marshall, CPA–90255, 25 Aug 44, SHAEF Cable Log.

AMERICAN INFANTRYMAN IN MAIZIERES-LES-METZ. *By the evening of 30 October the 357th held what was left of the town.*

used against Maizières, prior to the new attack on Metz. The new 90th Division commander, Brig. Gen. James A. Van Fleet,[52] ordered the 357th Infantry to take Maizières by 2 November, and Colonel Barth began to set the stage for a final assault by alternately probing and battering at the Hôtel de Ville. On 26 October K Company reached the lower floor of the building but was stopped by piles of burning mattresses in the hallways; it was then driven out by flame throwers. The next day four 10-man assault teams tried again. This time three of the assault teams were checked by mines and barbed wire. The fourth crawled through a gap blasted in the wall by the 155-mm. self-propelled gun and engaged in a hand-to-hand fight inside the building, in

[52] General Van Fleet had assumed command of the 90th Division on 15 October, after having spent about a month as commander of the 4th Division. Van Fleet was a West Point graduate. During World War I he had participated in the Meuse-Argonne offensive as a machine gun battalion commander and had been wounded in action. An infantry officer, Van Fleet took over the 8th Infantry Regiment in 1941, trained it for amphibious operations, and led it across Utah Beach on D Day. Subsequently he was awarded the DSC for gallantry in the action of 8 June. Before his promotion to division commander Van Fleet had taken part in fighting at St.-Lô and Brest as assistant division commander of the 2d Division.

which all but one man were killed or wounded. The survivors managed to escape while the unwounded soldier held off the Germans.[53]

On 28 October three companies of infantry moved into the cover afforded by the factory buildings, while a fourth company began a diversionary attack from the north. At 0730 the next morning, with no artillery preparation to herald the main assault,[54] the three companies attacked abreast across the tracks into the section of town south of the Hôtel de Ville, while two more companies swung in from the north.[55] In the face of this assault, with shells smashing the houses of the town to bits and detonating the mine defenses, the Germans gave way.[56]

The Hôtel de Ville was made a shambles by some 240-mm. howitzers which put down their fire with remarkable accuracy seventy-five yards ahead of the advancing infantry. When the building was entered the next day it was found occupied only by German corpses. By the night of 30 October the 357th held the town and the approaches to the south, although the enemy retained an observation post on a slag heap to the southwest. Colonel Barth, the regimental commanding officer, was wounded on the first day of the attack, but the total of American casualties in this last phase amounted to only fifty-five officers and men, as contrasted with the loss of an entire German battalion. Once again it had been demonstrated that a strong town, stubbornly defended by the enemy, could be taken with a minimum of loss to the attackers if the attack was carefully planned and co-ordinated, with sufficient infantry in the assault and marked superiority in the artillery arm.

Operations on the North Wing of the XX Corps

The shift in weight of the XX Corps during the last week of September to strengthen the right wing south and southwest of Metz was made possible by the assignment of another infantry division to General Walker's command.

[53] See 90th Div AAR for these days.

[54] Instead the American artillery fired counterbattery fire before H Hour. As a result the infantry assault met little fire from German guns.

[55] Lt. Col. John H. Mason, commanding the 3d Battalion, 357th Infantry, was given the DSC for gallantry displayed in this attack, as was the regimental commander, Col. George H. Barth, who was wounded while with an assault platoon.

[56] The town had been carefully mapped, even down to watering troughs and laundry sheds. Each platoon in the final assault was given a block of houses as an objective, each block carefully numbered on the town plan. The 1st and 3d Battalions, 357th Infantry, participated. The 2d Battalion, 357th, feigned an attack opposite Semécourt.

On 10 September the 83d Infantry Division (Maj. Gen. Robert C. Macon)[57] was relieved from the VIII Corps, with which it had fought in the Brittany campaign, and began the move east to the main battle front. At General Patton's request the 83d Division was attached to the XX Corps on 21 September and, as its regiments arrived on the front, took up positions on the extreme north wing of the corps, occupying territory in Luxembourg that had been held by armor and infantry of V Corps, and by the XX Corps cavalry. Although originally General Patton had intended to send the 83d Division across the Moselle at Remich, midway between Thionville and Trier, the stalemate south of Metz and the subsequent orders from SHAEF for the Third Army to assume the defensive canceled that operation.[58] General Macon's division was used only to strengthen the left wing of the XX Corps, opposite which the *36th VG Division* had appeared, and to make limited-objective attacks to the east. Particular orders were given the 83d for the defense of the city of Luxembourg.

Before the arrival of the 83d Division the left flank of the XX Corps had been so sparsely held as to have courted certain disaster if the enemy had possessed sufficient reserves on the Western Front to attack such weak points in the Allied battle line. The 43d Cavalry Reconnaissance Squadron, screening over twenty-three miles of open, rolling country, and theoretically "reinforced" by a simulated armored division, was given some limited reinforcements[59] as reports of new German forces across the Moselle came in. The reinforced detachment was constituted as Task Force Polk (from the name of the 3d

[57] General Macon was a graduate of the Virginia Polytechnic Institute. After his commissioning as an infantry officer in 1916, Macon served at various posts in China, the Canal Zone, and the United States. From 1940 to 1942 he trained armored infantry. During the invasion of North Africa Macon commanded the 7th Infantry Regiment. He had assumed command of the 83rd Division early in 1944.

[58] On 19 September General Gay, the Third Army deputy chief of staff, made a personal reconnaissance in the Thionville sector and advised General Patton that the terrain here favored a crossing. Patton at once asked Bradley to give him the 83d Division. The following day General Bradley granted him permission for the use of the 83d. However, the logistical situation did not permit such an extension of offensive operations; the Third Army was put on the defensive and General Macon was given orders to destroy the enemy in the Remich sector, patrol to the Moselle–Sauer line, and prevent the enemy from recrossing the rivers. TUSA Diary, 19 and 20 Sep 44; Ltr, Gen Macon to Hist Div, 29 May 47.

[59] The 43d Cavalry was reinforced by some artillery, the 135th Combat Engineer Battalion, a task force from the 6th Cavalry Group, and the 2d French Battalion. On 22 September, 259 men were sent to join the latter but only 22 had rifles. Colonel Fabian, liaison officer for these French forces, had great difficulty in equipping them. The men were members of the FFI, organized as a unit of the First Paris Regiment (Major Dax), and armed with French, Italian, Belgian, and German rifles. Units were attached to both the 90th Division and Task Force Polk. Used generally on patrol and security missions, the French seem to have given a good account of themselves.

Cavalry Group commander) on 19 September. By 25 September the 83d Division had a regimental combat team on the west bank across the river from Remich and Task Force Polk was enabled to shift south to the Thionville sector, freeing the 358th Infantry, in turn, for use on the right wing of the 90th Division. (*Map XXV*)

The mission of the 83d Division now was limited to clearing the salient west of Trier, formed by the Moselle and Sauer Rivers. This sector was not too strongly held, for the major part of the German forces in the area had withdrawn east of the Moselle and north of the Sauer; but rear guard detachments had been left in the little Luxembourg bridgehead towns to make a fight of it, particularly in Echternach on the north and Grevenmacher on the south.[60] General Macon's division had lost about half its original strength in the course of the drive out of the Cotentin peninsula, the fight for St. Malo, and the subsequent operation in the Brittany peninsula. The mass of replacements needed considerable training. Therefore, although General Macon placed two regiments in the drive east, the actual fighting was carried out by one or two companies at a time, allowing the bulk of each regiment to be rotated to rear areas for training in the abandoned Maginot Line. By 1 October Company C of the 329th Infantry reached the outskirts of Grevenmacher. Here the enemy held stubbornly in the stone houses and were not driven out until the night of 5 October, after artillery and fighter-bombers jarred them loose from the village. The 3d Battalion of the 329th fought for nearly a week outside Echternach on the Sauer, which, as shown later by the American experience during the Ardennes campaign, was extremely well adapted to defense. But on the afternoon of 7 October a co-ordinated assault by infantry, tanks, and artillery broke the German resistance and took the town. On the same day the 331st Infantry drove the enemy out of Wormeldange, north of Remich, thus erasing the last enemy foothold on the west bank of the Moselle in the Luxembourg sector. All three of these villages, Echternach, Grevenmacher, and Wormeldange, were on low ground exposed to German fire coming from heights to the east. General Macon had been loath to take them, since they could readily be neutralized by American guns on top of hills to the west, and the 83d Division withdrew its main forces at once, holding the towns with outposts only. The enemy were more than will-

[60] The Germans had been pushed back into the West Wall positions east of the Moselle and north of the Sauer by the First Army during mid-September. This sector, held by the *LXXX Corps,* was given to the *Seventh Army* about this time.

ing to consider this a quiet sector, and it so remained until the south wing of the great German counteroffensive swept through Echternach on 16 December.[61] On 11 October the 83d Division once again reverted to the VIII Corps, now with the Ninth Army, and the left boundary of the Third Army was brought south to Sierck-les-Bains. Task Force Polk took over the job of patrolling the west bank of the Moselle in this sector.[62]

Stabilizing the XII Corps Main Line of Resistance

When the Third Army advance was halted at the end of September, the XII Corps was generally in a position favorable to the defensive. Although the enemy breached the new main line of resistance in the 35th Division and 4th Armored sectors during the September attacks, the center and right wing of the corps were solidly re-established by 3 October. On the left wing, however, the 80th Division had been unable to close up to the natural defense line of the Seille River—on a sufficiently wide front—because the Germans held a re-entrant along the hill mass between Serrières and Moivron. (*Map XXVI*) General McBride's attempt to erase this salient by swinging the main weight of the 80th Division around the south, and so envelop the German positions by a drive through Moivron and Jeandelaincourt, had been frustrated by the stubborn defense put up by the *553d VG Division.*[63]

On 1 October, consonant with General Patton's orders, the 80th Division began a series of small local attacks to wipe out the forward centers of enemy resistance west of the Seille. Here the Germans had placed their infantry, in platoon to battalion strength, in the little Lorraine villages—particularly in those which lay athwart the roads leading to the Seille. In most cases these garrisoned villages consisted of only a handful of houses; but the houses were solidly built of heavy stone which proved capable of withstanding an immense amount of battering by artillery, and they gave shelter from the heavy autumn rains. The fight for observation had now yielded priority to the fight for cover.

[61] See the 83d Div AAR, Oct 44.

[62] On 14 October, 2d Lt. R. C. Downs, Troop C, 43d Cavalry, carried out a daring daylight reconnaissance on the enemy bank of the Moselle. Downs and a companion had orders to determine the location of enemy positions some 1,200 yards east of the river. They obtained the needed information but were brought under fire. The second man was lost, but Downs swam the river in full field equipment and reached his own lines. He was awarded the DSC.

[63] Chapter II, p. 115.

The 80th Division got a preview of what this fighting would be like when, on the evening of 1 October, a company of the 318th was dispatched to take Renaissance Farm. With the cluster of houses at les Quatre Fers, the farm controlled the Pont-à-Mousson–Nomény road—the boundary between the 318th and 319th. The Germans had turned the stone farm buildings into a small fortress, with port holes from which machine guns and 20-mm. anti-tank pieces covered all approaches. After futile attempts to work their way in close enough to engage the enemy gunners, the attackers withdrew and called for artillery; but before they could give fire direction twenty or thirty Germans, who had followed the Americans from the farm, slipped into the company area. In the melee which followed (labeled in an 80th Division message "Department of Utter Confusion") the company was disorganized and a further attack abandoned. The next morning several concentrations of artillery were laid on the farm, and a company of tank destroyers from the 808th Tank Destroyer Battalion was brought forward to blast the stone buildings at a point-blank range. A company of the 319th took the position with only slight opposition from the dazed defenders.

Most of the XII Corps front was quiet, but on 2 October the 80th Division continued to pry away at the German positions on the hill mass west of the Seille. Here a road ran across the saddle between Hill 340 and Mount Toulon, terminating in the little villages of Serrières in the north and Sivry in the south. An attack on Serrières by the 318th Infantry (Col. Lansing McVickar) was called off after heavy losses. But the 317th, which sent its 2d Battalion against Sivry, became involved in a long-drawn-out and desperate battle that cost half of the attacking force.[64]

The village of Sivry lay in a narrow valley close to hills that on the north were held by the Germans. Sivry therefore had to be taken by an attack from the open side, where maneuver space allowed deployment of only limited forces. Across the southern face of the town the enemy had laid a continuous mine field, still further restricting the possible avenue of advance. All through 2 October the 105-mm. howitzers of the regimental cannon company pounded Sivry, and late in the afternoon G Company (Capt. R. A. Ashbrook) began to work its way in a loop to the southwest around the mine field. By 0300 the next morning the company was in position to attack, and at 0555 the yellow flare went up signaling that the town had been reached. Early in the

[64] This battle may be followed in the 317th Infantry S–3 Journal. Command of the 317th Infantry passed on the afternoon of 3 October to Col. Warfield M. Lewis, who relieved Col. A. D. Cameron.

fight a part of the German garrison (the *2d Battalion, 1119th Regiment, 553d VG Division*) withdrew to the cover of an orchard just north of Sivry, but some of the grenadiers held on, retreating from house to house and finally falling back to the village church where they were surrounded and captured. On the morning of 4 October, about 0320, German guns in the hills opened up on Sivry, and the enemy infantry, collected for the counterattack from Serrières and Mount Toulon, swept into the town.

A platoon of Americans was gathered in the church; the rest were scattered in the houses. The company commander radioed for help but the regimental commander, Col. W. M. Lewis, dared not risk a night advance straight into Sivry across the mine field. When light came Company E went forward, circled around the mine field through a dense fog, and succeeded in reaching the houses on the edge of the village. But the enemy also was reinforcing his troops in Sivry; all through the day small groups of infantry braved the American artillery fire, interdicting the road from Serrières, to swell the counterattack (a battalion from the *8th Panzer Grenadier Regiment, 3d Panzer Grenadier Division*, and a battalion of the *1121st Grenadier Regiment* were involved). The American relief company could not reach the church—every street was enfiladed by machine gun fire—and General McBride finally gave the orders for withdrawal. Through the night the survivors straggled back to the regiment; 381 men had taken part in the attack but only 191 escaped from Sivry, one-half of them wounded.[65]

At this juncture General Eddy decided to throw in sufficient strength to win a decisive victory and firmly establish the main line of resistance on the XII Corps left wing by clearing the enemy from the area south and west of the Seille River, in accordance with Patton's orders on 25 September. The rest of the corps front was quiet and troops could be spared for such an operation. On 5 October a XII Corps Operational Directive set the date for the attack as 8 October, with the 80th Division, 6th Armored Division, and 35th Division participating. The 328th Infantry, from the 26th Division, now coming into the corps area, was also attached to the 80th Division, taking over the left flank and relieving the 319th Infantry so that the latter could take an active role in the operation. While the XII Corps was regrouping, the XIX TAC began a systematic bombing of the German strongholds, Moivron, Jean-

[65] Only forty men were left in G Company. These probably owed their escape to a rear guard action fought by Sgt. James L. Atkins. Sergeant Atkins was wounded but made his way back through the village after covering his comrades. He was awarded the DSC.

delaincourt, and Mount St. Jean. At the same time the American guns battered away at Moivron and Sivry, their fire reinforced by one of General Patton's favorite weapons, the 4.2 chemical mortar, firing white phosphorus. For once the XII Corps was in a position to fight an action according to a carefully prepared plan of maneuver—quite unlike the hasty improvisations common in the hurried operations of mid-September. The artillery fire plan was developed in meticulous detail, with forward observers posted only fifty yards apart in some sectors. So effective was this plan that on the day before the attack thirteen observed counterbattery missions were fired, neutralizing twelve enemy batteries. On the same day three squadrons of P-47's went to work on the German reserves and line of communications, dropping 864 fragmentation bombs on the Bois dit la Fourasse—the main enemy troop assembly area behind the hill mass—and bombing the Seille bridge at Nomény.[66]

At 0515 on 8 October all seventeen battalions of the XII Corps artillery reinforced by the artillery of the three attacking divisions and the 86th Chemical Mortar Battalion opened up, firing for sixty minutes prior to the armor-infantry attack. Jeandelaincourt, which had proved so tough a nut to crack in late September, received special treatment; three TOT's were fired on the town with an average of eleven field artillery battalions participating in each. When the three divisions jumped off in the attack at 0615, after fifteen minutes of artillery fire directly to their front, the massed guns raised their fire and for an hour and a quarter shelled the German battery and single-gun locations and battered the rearward enemy communications.[67] The P-47's also took part in the attack, bombing and strafing the heights between Moivron and Jeandelaincourt.[68] The main burden of the attack was carried by the 6th Armored Division, whose final objective was the plateau west of Létricourt.[69] Possession of this high ground would block off the salient formed by the looping Seille and would inevitably force the Germans to withdraw behind the river. CCB, organized with two-thirds of the division's combat strength, formed the spearhead of the first day's attack, striking out from Leyr toward the north in three combat teams, each supported by a battalion of field artillery. Combat Team 50, on the left, had its leading tanks inside Moivron a half hour after the jump-off. Here, as elsewhere during the day, the enemy's

[66] XII Corps Opns Rpt, Oct 44.

[67] The American artillery fired 17,588 rounds (or about 600 tons of shells). XII Corps Opns Rpt, Oct 44.

[68] The 510th Squadron of the XIX TAC did excellent work against the German battery emplacements.

[69] See the 6th Armored Division *Combat Record* for this operation.

artillery remained virtually silent. His infantry fought much less tenaciously than in the September battles, falling back when the attack was pressed home or surrendering in groups when a position was overrun or encircled. Nevertheless, the American infantry, from the 317th, had to fight to get into Moivron and relieve the armor there.[70]

Combat Team 15, forming the center column, had been ordered to seize Jeandelaincourt and clear the Bois de Brasquin and the Bois d'Ajoncourt, the line of departure for the next day's operations. Part of the combat team swept on to the edge of the woods but was checked there by mortar and small arms fire until late in the afternoon, when a company of armored infantry came up and cleared the woods. The main force encircled Jeandelaincourt from the east and north while the 80th Division infantry, which had pushed forward to the reverse slope of Mount St. Jean, fired into the town. The bulk of the German garrison attempted to make a stand in a large factory building. Tanks and tank destroyers shelled the factory at point-blank range, but the finishing blow was dealt by some P–47's that made a direct strike on the factory, setting it ablaze. When the survivors broke for the open they were met by a fusillade of machine gun bullets that left only a few to surrender. Over the open radio General Grow heard Lt. Col. Embry D. Lagrew, the commander of the combat team, saying: "This beats any Fourth of July I ever saw."

Combat Team 69, advancing on the right flank of CCB toward Arraye-et-Han, was retarded in the early morning by the fog rising from the near-by Seille, but by 1300 the town was taken. To the east the 35th Division brought up its left flank along the Seille, thus extending the American line to include Ajoncourt and Fossieux.[71] This squeeze play was so successful that Combat Team 15 went on to sweep the Bois de Chenicourt. The town of Chenicourt was left unoccupied, for the American armor had learned the inadvisability

[70] The 3d Battalion of the 317th Infantry had a hard time getting into Moivron and fought there most of the afternoon. 317th Inf Jnl, 8 Oct 44. However, the initial advance was made somewhat easier by effective overhead fire from the 633d Antiaircraft Artillery Battalion.

[71] On 8 October, 127 prisoners were taken in Fossieux. On the morning of 9 October, 7 enemy tanks and about 140 infantry got back into Fossieux and hit the two companies there. The tanks first took cover behind a heavy wall in the north part of the town. When they finally came out, the American tank destroyers knocked out four and crippled a fifth. The infantry were able to clear the town the next day. In the course of this action 1st Lt. Frederick L. Bach, L Company, 137th Infantry, went alone into a house from which the enemy were firing and captured a German officer and fifteen men. Bach was given the DSC. (In this operation the 35th Division identified troops from the *1120th Regiment,* remnants of the *73d Regiment,* and part of the *103d Panzer Reconnaissance Battalion* of the *3d Panzer Grenadier Division.*)

of outposting a town in a valley during hours of darkness so long as the enemy still held the surrounding hills.

The left wing of the XII Corps attack now was brought forward by the 80th Division and its attached tank battalion, the 702d, quickly overrunning the German defenses on the hill masses and along the valley roads. The Germans apparently had expected a continuation of the operation which had been begun at Sivry and Serrières; indeed, on the day before the corps attack, they had aimed a propaganda broadcast at the 317th Infantry facing Mount St. Jean: "Do not attack the hill in front of you if you want to get home. If you do you will surely die." But the strength put behind this attack and the weight of the metal turned against them on the early morning of 8 October seem to have demoralized the German infantry. The 319th Infantry had a battalion on Mount Toulon by 0655; by the end of the day it held Lixières and Sivry. In the 317th Infantry sector one battalion closed on Mount St. Jean from the west while another advanced from the south, the two driving the enemy survivors into the hands of the 6th Armored Division in the valley below. The 318th Infantry also pushed closer to the Seille[72] and by noon had troops in Manoncourt. This was the "black day" for the *553d VG Division*, which had stubbornly contested every mile of ground as it was forced back from the Moselle line.[73] The 80th Division ended the day's action with 1,264 prisoners, most of them from the *553d*. The casualties suffered by the 80th Division are not known.[74] The 35th Division had encountered little resistance; CCB had

[72] The village of Clémery was taken during this advance. Here Sgt. Watson W. Paine, B Company, 318th Infantry, while carrying a message to a platoon leader through heavy artillery fire, was wounded in the arms and hands by shell fragments. A machine gun nest blocked his way, but he assaulted the position with rifle fire and grenades and destroyed it, got through with his message, and helped destroy another machine gun before he was evacuated. Paine was given the DSC. During the 318th Infantry fight at les Quatre Fers, Sgt. Louis A. Antal, E Company, took command of his platoon after the platoon leader, platoon sergeant, and all the squad leaders had been killed or wounded. Antal reorganized the remnants of the platoon and led it in an assault which cleared the village. In the course of this action the sergeant personally knocked out a German antitank gun and captured the surviving members of its crew. Antal was awarded the DSC.

[73] On 5 October the *3d Panzer Grenadier Division* had been pulled out of line on the north flank of the *553d VG Division* to go to the Aachen sector. The *553d* was forced to extend its line to fill this gap and was badly outnumbered in the attack of 8 October. Late on 8 October Balck ordered an armored Kampfgruppe from the *11th Panzer Division,* held behind the right flank of *LVIII Panzer Corps,* to move during the night to Delme. On the afternoon of 9 October it started some counterattacks from Abaucourt, but these were broken up by American artillery. All free German tanks and guns were rushed to the *553d* sector, and plans were made to commit the *48th Division* in case the American attack continued. Balck also authorized a withdrawal to the line Port-sur-Seille–Nomény–Malaucourt. On 9 Oct *Army Group G KTB* reported that the mass of the infantry of the *553d VG Division* had been destroyed.

[74] The 80th Division losses for the month of October were 382 killed, 898 wounded, and 425 missing. Most of these casualties were sustained in the period 1–8 October. 80th Div AAR, Oct 44.

lost twenty dead, sixty-one wounded, and six medium tanks (five of which were reparable).

CCA, which had been brought up close behind CCB for this operation, attacked on 9 October through the center of CCB and then fanned out by combat teams for a thrust through the Bois du Haut des Trappes and the Bois d'Aulnois which screened Létricourt, the final 6th Armored Division objective. The Germans still were disorganized and dispirited, after the weight and speed of the first day's attack and their heavy losses. The left and center columns were through to the Létricourt side of the woods shortly after noon, having been impeded more by the narrow forest trails than by the enemy. But Combat Team 44 (Lt. Col. Lewis E. McCorison), advancing in the open on the exposed right flank of the combat command, came under the enemy guns in Chenicourt and received a terrific shelling. At 1310 Colonel McCorison reported that the combat team could not continue the attack toward Létricourt because of heavy casualties and disorganization. CCB was forced to rush up reinforcements to hold the gains already made. Through the day the 80th Division infantry had kept abreast of or followed very close on the heels of the armor but darkness intervened before the 317th Infantry could reinforce Combat Team 44 for the capture of Létricourt.[75] CCA's losses, mostly in Combat Team 44, had been 39 killed and 87 wounded. The 6th Armored Division had bagged 650 prisoners for the whole operation.

This action ended the XII Corps attack and the push to the Seille. The 80th Division relieved the armor, taking the high ground which overlooked Létricourt and clearing the woods, but leaving the village in German hands. During the next two days the enemy essayed small counterattacks, without gaining any success.

The Quiet Phase[76]

The establishment of a new main line of resistance on the XII Corps left wing began a period of quiet along the thirty-mile corps front that lasted,

[75] For his part in the fight for the Bois du Haut des Trappes on 9 October, 2d Lt. James G. Schwartze, F Company, 319th Infantry, was awarded the DSC. Schwartze was severely wounded while leading his platoon, but continued in action—personally accounting for a German machine gun—until ordered by his battalion commander to go to the rear. In this same action 2d Lt. W. E. Newing led a platoon of G Company, although so badly wounded that he could not stand without assistance. Newing was awarded the DSC.

[76] A detailed discussion of supply planning and problems during October and early November will be found in Ruppenthal, Logistical Support.

with only a few interruptions, until 8 November. At the beginning of October General Eddy received the new 26th Infantry Division as reinforcement for his corps. The 26th, a National Guard division, had reached the Continent on 7 September. The supply situation did not permit the immediate use of the division in combat; its vehicles were taken away to haul supplies and its troops were employed briefly as guards on the lines of communication. When the division finally reached the Third Army and was placed in the line it had neither a full troop complement nor all of its equipment. Maj. Gen. Willard S. Paul, the 26th Division commander, had entered military service as a private in the Colorado National Guard. After a Regular Army peacetime career in garrison and at the military schools, Paul served as G–4 with GHQ and the headquarters of the Army Ground Forces, and then activated the 75th Infantry Division. He had commanded the 26th since August 1943.

On 12 October General Paul's division relieved the 4th Armored Division, taking over the right wing of the corps. Thus far the 26th had experienced no combat as a unit. To remedy this lack, and extend the American salient east of Arracourt, a limited-objective attack was set up for 22 October. This brief but sanguinary interruption in the prevailing lull saw Paul's infantry supported by troops from the experienced 704th Tank Destroyer Battalion advancing over terrain which had been the scene of the fierce tank battles in September. The baptismal attack resulted in some very hard fighting, but at the end of the day the 26th Division had pushed forward on the rolling ground west of Moncourt. Those elements of the green division used on the 22d had fought well enough to call themselves to the attention of the Third Army commander.[77] The Germans paid a real tribute when Balck commended the units

[77] See TUSA Diary, 25 Oct 44. In the fight near Moncourt Woods, Pfc. Harry G. Gamble, Jr., Headquarters Company, 104th Infantry, volunteered to deal with a troublesome machine gun and advance alone, armed only with a demolition charge. Within a few feet of the German position he lit the charge and threw it, killing the 6-man crew and destroying the machine gun. He received the DSC. Cpl. Thomas J. Walsh of the 104th Infantry gave aid to the wounded under heavy fire until hit in both legs, then continued to drag himself about to give first aid to the critically wounded. Exhausted by loss of blood he finally crawled to a ditch where he lay for two days. He also was awarded the DSC.

Company A, 704th Tank Destroyer Battalion, was attached to the 26th Division during the attack near Bezange-la-Petite. Here 2d Lt. Charles Kollin, who was leading a platoon to reinforce the infantry attack, found himself and his platoon in a mine field under heavy artillery fire. He reorganized the platoon and went back and forth through the mine field directing evacuation of the wounded, then led the attack forward. Lieutenant Kollin was awarded the DSC. The A Company commander, 1st Lt. John J. Preneta, also was awarded the DSC. When the company was halted by the mine field he made a reconnaissance on foot, killed two snipers with his pistol, and captured two others in a pillbox. Capt. Elva Harris, 253d Armored Field Artillery Battalion, also received the DSC for his leadership near Bezange, where he rallied a rifle company that had suffered heavy losses and led it in the assault.

MARLENE DIETRICH, *entertaining front-line soldiers of the Third Army.*

who had opposed the 26th Division and the 704th Tank Destroyer Battalion for their battle against the American "shock troops."

The Germans were more than willing to leave the XII Corps front undisturbed—heavily involved as they were in the bitter fight at Aachen. With the exception of a few local sorties and the drafting of halfhearted and abortive plans for a counterattack against the north flank of the XII Corps, they contented themselves with digging and wiring and with rotating their troops through this new rest area. Earlier, on 24 September, General Eddy had begun to draw up a plan of defense and had issued instruction on the rotation of troops during the coming period of inaction. General Eisenhower, in a visit to the Third Army headquarters on 29 September, had set forth the policy of a continuing rotation of front-line and reserve battalions in order to rest the tired divisions and get them in shape for a future offensive. This policy was followed, except when the local attack program did not permit, to the extent allowed by the width of the front and the supply of billets. The

MAINTENANCE WORK IN MUDDY FIELDS. *During the October lull ordnance companies were put into buildings, with a consequent increase in efficiency.*

80th, 35th, and 26th were left in line—generally with two-thirds of the riflemen in battle positions. As troops came into reserve they were billeted in the shell-torn Lorraine towns and villages, given clean clothes, and—if they were lucky—trucked to Nancy, St. Nicholas, and other leave centers for a bath, a movie, or possibly attendance at Marlene Dietrich's USO show, which was even more popular than Bing Crosby's Third Army tour had been in early September. But the men in the line lived under continual rain and in seas of mud.

Quartermaster bakeries increased the issue of fresh bread and roasted green coffee to replace the bitter soluble variety in the K ration. Company cooks now found time and shelter for preparing the tons of German beef captured at Reims and Briey weeks earlier. Ordnance companies were taken out of muddy fields and put into buildings (greatly increasing their maintenance capacity), where they began overhauling vehicles and equipment that in many cases had received little or no repair since the start of the campaign in August. Also, a new type of grouser was improvised to give the American tanks flotation somewhat equivalent to that of the wide-tracked German tanks.[78] The October rains gave ample evidence of the mud slogging that would be required of armor in the next campaign, and the tankers pinned great faith on the grouser. Approximately eighty tanks per day were fitted with these "duck bills."

New tanks were brought up from the communications zone to replace those which had been destroyed or irreparably damaged. In the period between 1 September and 22 October the Third Army had lost 63 light tanks and 160 mediums. The most noticeable lag in replacements had come at the end of the third week in September, when the Third Army ordnance officer reported that the army was 130 tanks short of its scheduled strength. Light armored cars, 60-mm. mortars, BAR's, tires, and tubes also had fallen into short supply during the September operations and now had to be replaced.

Gasoline rationing continued through most of October; the MP's were kept busy apprehending jeeps and command cars without authorized trip tickets. Parenthetically, it may be noted that the MP's had their hands full, for General Patton used the quiet period to refurbish the "spit and polish" discipline which characterized his administration of the Third Army. Artillery ammunition was so severely curtailed that the XII and XX Corps finally were

[78] These grousers were 3½-inch pieces of reinforced 4-inch channel iron which were welded to the outer edge of the track connectors.

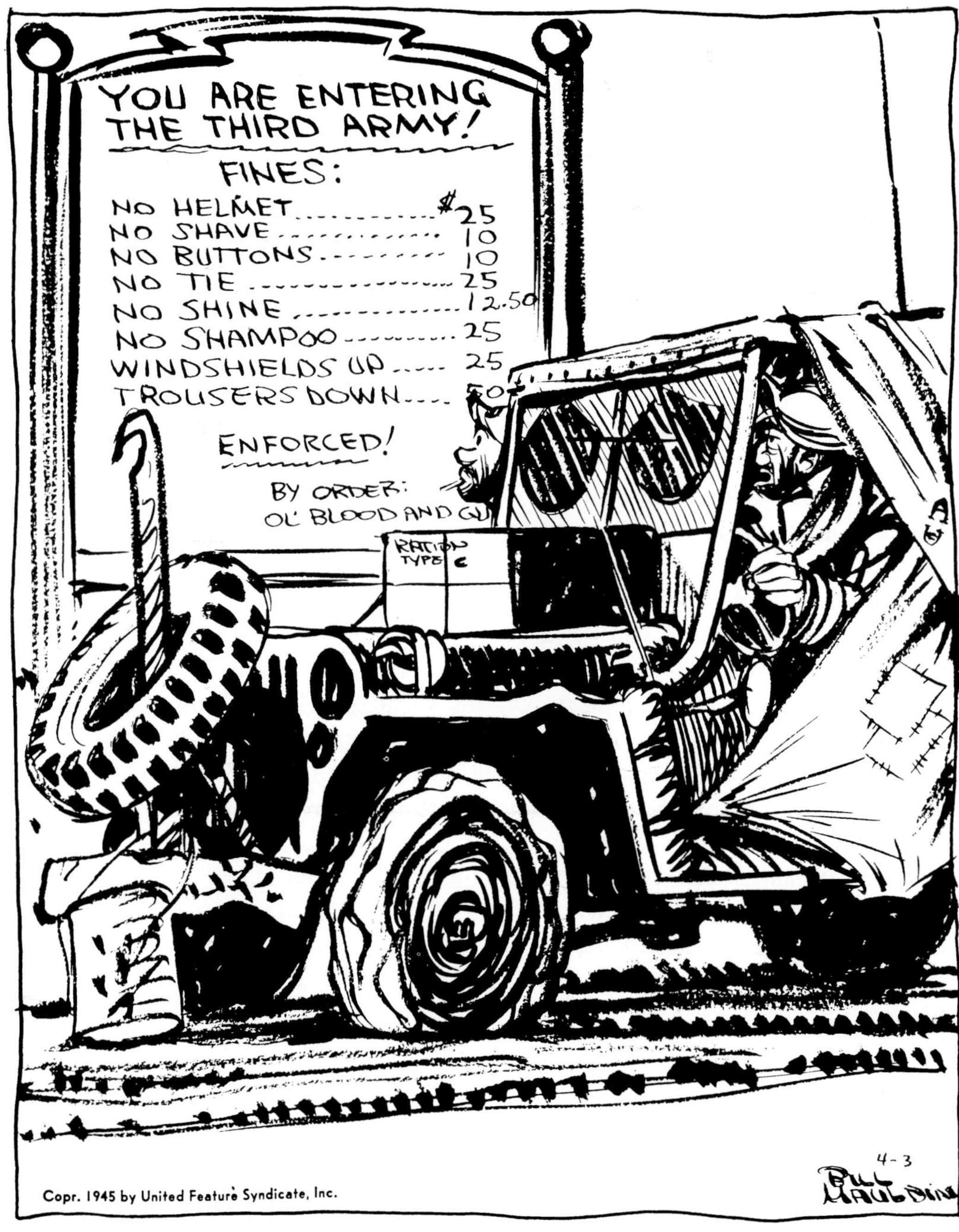

"Radio th' ol' man we'll be late on account of a thousand-mile detour."

reduced to firing only in retaliation against a German outburst, and to using tanks, tank destroyers, and chemical mortars, whose ammunition stocks were not so depleted as those of the field artillery battalions. The fighting in early October had drawn heavily on the Third Army allotment for the month; the total expended during October by the XII Corps alone was 12,700 tons of artillery and small-caliber ammunition. Some winter equipment came forward during October: blankets, overcoats, new-type sleeping bags, stoves, and other necessities. Most of the combat troops had three blankets and an overcoat. But in extremely wet or cold weather this issue would be insufficient to protect the soldier properly, especially in view of an acute shortage of waterproof ground sheets and raincoats. Rubber overshoes, a critical item as the Lorraine plains turned to mire in the constant fall downpour, were so scarce that they could be issued only on the basis of one pair for every four enlisted men.[79] Shelter halves, woolen clothing, and socks also were lacking in sufficient quantity.

Planning and preparation for the renewal of the offensive went on apace. Sometimes these preparations took unorthodox forms as the individual units attempted to build up gasoline reserves or increase their ammunition stocks, by "hook and by crook" as their commanders enjoined them. Planning and training aimed at what was believed to be the next great obstacle, the West Wall, and officers and men studied relief models and maps of this much-vaunted position. But General Patton and his commanders were looking beyond it to the Rhine; so a floating Bailey bridge school was added to the varied collection of "schools" functioning in the back areas.

The October pause also was used to remove a potential threat to any future Third Army advance in the XII Corps zone by the destruction of the earthen dam which impounded the waters of the Etang de Lindre, just south of Dieuze. The Etang de Lindre fed the Seille River, which ran through the American forward lines. The upper valley of the Seille was to form one of the most important avenues in the initial phases of an attack to the east. The military significance of this lake–river combination had been recognized by French military engineers of the seventeenth century, who had built the dam as a part of the Vauban system for the defense of Metz. In German hands the dam could be blown and the waters of the Etang de Lindre—about thirty-three feet above the level of the Seille River—released to flood the valley and

[79] This was the established War Department basis of issue. General Patton made numerous bitter complaints and finally got a more reasonable issue.

cut off the American forward units. Therefore, it was decided to anticipate the enemy and destroy the dam. Since the Etang de Lindre was swollen considerably by recent rains the XII Corps engineers expected a flash flood; they therefore built a regular flood control system. On 20 October two squadrons of P–47's,[80] using 1,000-pound bombs, made a fifteen-yard breach in the dam.[81] The American positions were not flooded out, and the threat was removed.

On the heels of the Maizières-lès-Metz operation one final tactical step was taken in preparation for the ensuing Third Army offensive. During the afternoon of 1 November the 319th Infantry attacked to erase the re-entrant (in the Abaucourt–Létricourt sector) formed by the loop in the Seille on the left front of the XII Corps. The attack gained complete surprise. In an hour and a quarter the two towns were cleared and the enemy was driven back across the Seille, leaving behind 162 prisoners and 148 dead.

Plans for the Resumption of the Offensive

The Supreme Commander's decision to halt the advance of the Third Army, in the last week of September, had stemmed from an untenable logistical situation. Bradley's 12th Army Group alone needed 20,000 tons of supplies per day in order to support a "secure" offensive for bridgeheads across the Rhine. The "expectations" for the delivery of supplies during the period 1 to 15 October summed up to only 12,000 tons per day.[82] Under optimum conditions the entire Allied logistical effort could support only twenty-five divisions on or at the Rhine in October. To accomplish even that much support all other troops would have to be immobilized and much of the Allied air strength would have to be diverted from strategic to supply missions.[83]

Faced with the apparent necessity of tailoring the suit to the cloth, General Eisenhower had continued the priority given to the attack in the north. During October Montgomery's 21st Army Group fought to clear the banks of the Schelde and thus open the water gates to the essential port of Antwerp. This crucial operation was handed over to the First Canadian Army. Montgomery's right, the Second British Army, was committed in an attempt to

[80] From the 362d Group, XIX TAC.

[81] The *Army Group G* reports say that the cut was 30 meters wide.

[82] Ltr, Gen Moses to Gen Crawford, 2 Oct 44, SHAEF SGS File, Supply Problems of Allied Advance 400.3/1.

[83] SHAEF G–3 Memo, Advance into Germany after the Occupation of the Ruhr, 24 Sep 44, SHAEF SGS File, Post OVERLORD Planning 381, I.

BOMBING OF ETANG DE LINDRE DAM *by P–47's on 20 October. The photograph was made fifteen seconds after the dam was breached.*

destroy the German bridgehead west of the Meuse, but on 16 October Montgomery decided to end the Second British Army attack in order to employ all his strength against the stiffening enemy opposition along the Schelde. Meanwhile the American First Army battered away at Aachen, drawing much of the German armor away from the British and Canadian front farther north. On 21 October the conquest of Aachen was completed and the First Army turned to preparations for its part in a general Allied offensive. In the days that followed, the Canadians continued the battle to clear the Schelde estuary. By 3 November most of Walcheren Island was in Canadian hands. The following day the first mine-sweeper ships reached Antwerp. The first seaborne convoy was not to anchor in that port until 28 November, but long-range plans of supply could now be elaborated in terms of Antwerp's great tonnage capacity.

Despite the hiatus in offensive operations induced on the Third Army front by the lag in supply, General Eisenhower had not abandoned his intention to drive toward Berlin on the direct northern route while at the same time moving his flanks forward, "all in one co-ordinated, concerted operation." At the very moment that General Patton received his orders to go over to the defensive, the SHAEF G–3 (Maj. Gen. H. R. Bull) and the SHAEF Planning Staff were putting the final touches on a scheme for an advance into Germany after the capture of the Ruhr and Frankfurt.[84] Admittedly this was planning for the long pull, but it was an important reaffirmation of the role intended for the Third Army—secondary though that role might be. Early in October the 12th Army Group planners drafted other proposals for a two-pronged advance to put the First Army (and the 21st Army Group) across the Rhine River in the north, while the Third Army attacked from the "Nancy salient" and crossed the river in the Frankfurt sector.

All of this planning in late September and early October was general in nature and set no precise date for reopening the Allied offensive. On 18 October, however, General Eisenhower met with his chief subordinates and issued a more detailed directive, complete with the "probable" dates on which the armies might expect to resume the attack. The top priority mission for 21st Army Group remained "the early opening of Antwerp." About 10 November the Second British Army would be ready to start a drive to the southeast, between the Meuse and the Rhine, with the mission of supporting an Ameri-

[84] *Ibid.*

can advance to and across the Rhine. The American First Army was charged with undertaking an offensive to secure a footing across the Rhine in the area south of Cologne. The probable date for the First Army attack, it was estimated, would fall between 1 and 5 November. The Ninth Army, in line between the British Second and the American First, would act initially to cover the north flank of the First Army during its push to the Rhine. Subsequently the First and Ninth Armies would have the task of encircling or capturing the Ruhr, the First Army operating south of the great industrial area and the Ninth Army operating north. No date was set for an attack by Patton's forces. The Third Army, it was agreed, would resume its advance "when logistics permit," driving in a northeasterly direction and covering the right flank of the First Army.[85]

On the day Aachen fell to Hodges' First Army—21 October—General Bradley dispatched detailed instructions to his army commanders, ordering preparations for an advance to the Rhine by all three armies. The target date for the attack by the First and Ninth would be 5 November; for the Third, 10 November. The axis for the Third Army drive lay in line with Frankfurt, as in previous plans. But provision was made for alternative missions: if the situation permitted, Patton was to cross the Rhine somewhere between Mainz and Worms; if a crossing could not be won immediately, Patton was to turn his army north and clear the west bank of the Rhine up to the point where that river met the Moselle.[86] The role of the Allied forces on the right of the Third Army was outlined in a personal letter from General Eisenhower to General Devers, the 6th Army Group Commander. Devers' forces, supported over their own Mediterranean line of communications, would act to protect the south flank of the 12th Army Group and deploy in strength across the Rhine. Eisenhower added that once the Third Army had succeeded in crossing the Rhine it probably would move on Kassel, in which case the 6th Army Group might anticipate that its own drive east of the Rhine would aim at Nuremberg.[87]

This suggestion of objectives and missions *east* of the Rhine was still a matter of hypothesis. When, on 28 October, the Supreme Commander issued what would be his last general directive prior to the November offensive, he

[85] Decisions reached at Supreme Commander's conference, 18 Oct 44, SHAEF SGS File, Post OVERLORD Planning 381, II.

[86] 12th A Gp AAR, V.

[87] Eisenhower to Devers, 23 Oct 44, SHAEF SGS File, Post OVERLORD Planning 381, II.

foresaw three phases in the forthcoming operations: a battle to destroy the enemy west of the Rhine, during which the Allies would take advantage of "any opportunity" to seize bridgeheads across the river; a fight to win bridgeheads and deploy on the east bank; and a continuation of the advance deep into Germany. But of these three phases only the first two were outlined in detail.[88]

During October new American divisions had been arriving on the Continent, complicating the supply system considerably, but giving promise of additional weight behind the future Allied drive to the Rhine. General Patton had been assured that his army would receive reinforcement, and on 10 October the III Corps headquarters (Maj. Gen. John Millikin), newly arrived in Normandy, was assigned to the Third Army. As yet the III Corps commanded only a few corps troops. On 19 October Patton wrote a personal letter to Bradley, setting forth Third Army plans for a drive up to the West Wall, "in not to exceed D plus 2 days."[89] Patton assured Bradley that the enemy on the Third Army front was disposed with all his strength in the front lines and that once these forces were destroyed or captured the Third Army stood a good chance of penetrating the West Wall and driving rapidly to the Rhine. Such an operation, Patton was careful to explain, would not digress from the secondary role assigned the Third Army, but would be timed so as to precede or follow an offensive by one of Bradley's other armies, thus "disjoining the German scheme of defense." The catch, as Patton saw it, was that the Third Army was the stepchild of supply. Therefore he carefully tabulated the tonnage which he and his staff reckoned to be necessary in mounting and maintaining the proposed attack.

In actual fact the Third Army had two plans for resuming the offensive, both of which were predicated on the ultimate employment of the new III Corps. Plan A called for a simultaneous attack by the XII and XX Corps in which the XII Corps would drive northeastward with Faulquemont as its objective while the XX Corps attacked from Thionville—bypassing Metz—with Boulay as its objective. The III Corps, starting from the Briey area, would advance in rearward echelon on the Third Army left. Plan B was a variant of the first scheme in which the III Corps would force the Moselle line in the Thionville sector while the XII and XX Corps advanced south of Metz.

[88] Directive, Eisenhower to A Gp Commanders, SCAF 114, 28 Oct 44, SHAEF SGS File, Post OVERLORD Planning 381, II.

[89] Patton to Bradley, 19 Oct 44, 12th A Gp File, Military Objectives 371.3, II.

The main problem as to the employment of the Third Army, given adequate supply, was that of timing its attack. The Supreme Commander had given no ruling except to say: "These operations will be so timed as best to assist the main effort in the north." By 1 November the logistical support of a general Allied offensive seemed assured. That afternoon Patton met with his corps commanders, representatives of the Eighth and Ninth Air Forces, and General Weyland (whose XIX TAC would co-operate with the Third Army as usual). The plans agreed on here would be the blueprint for the Third Army November offensive—except for timing. Following the First Army attack on D Day, the XII Corps would lead off for the Third Army on D plus 1. The XII Corps armor would follow up on D plus 2. In the XX Corps zone an attack would be launched on both sides of Metz. After a demonstration by the 95th Division on the afternoon of D plus 1, the 90th Division would begin to cross the Moselle north of Metz on D plus 2. The 5th Division would carry the attack south of Metz as soon as the left wing of the XII Corps had cleared some of the ground to its front. Ultimately the III Corps would be given some divisions and be set to mopping up the "Metz pocket." [90]

Meanwhile regrouping for the main Allied offensive in the north had been retarded by determined German resistance opposite the First Canadian Army and a series of spoiling attacks directed against the Second British Army. As a result two American divisions which had been loaned to Montgomery (the 104th Infantry Division and the 7th Armored Division) could not be released to reinforce the 12th Army Group as planned. Faced with this temporary diminution in the strength of his main effort, General Bradley visited the Third Army headquarters on 2 November and explained that the British were not yet ready to jump off and that the First Army was not prepared to attack until the two divisions were returned. Bradley posed the question: could the Third Army begin the offensive by itself? Patton answered that he would attack on twenty-four hour notice. It was agreed, therefore, that the Third Army should begin the offensive as soon as the weather permitted the air forces to soften up the enemy. If good flying weather failed, the XII Corps would attack on 8 November.[91] One further decision remained. What protection could the 6th Army Group give the right flank of the Third Army as the latter advanced to the northeast? General Eisenhower had already assigned General Devers the task of denying the pivotal Lunéville area

[90] TUSA Diary, 1 Nov 44.

[91] *Ibid.*, 2 Nov 44.

to the enemy. Now the 6th Army Group commander assured Patton that the XV Corps would be committed in the zone south of the Third Army within two days after the Third Army began its attack.[92]

General Patton's command was large and well equipped on the eve of the November offensive. It included six infantry divisions and three armored divisions, as well as a high number of nondivisional units:

1 ranger infantry battalion
22 antiaircraft artillery battalions
5 tank battalions
14 tank destroyer battalions
38 field artillery battalions
6 cavalry reconnaissance squadrons
3 engineer general service regiments
15 engineer combat battalions
4 engineer heavy ponton battalions
11 ponton and treadway bridge companies

By dint of strenuous efforts on the part of the supply services and considerable reallocation in the distribution to the three armies in 12th Army Group, the Third Army had been given the support needed to mount its offensive. On 7 November the Third Army had a four-day reserve of rations and a five-day supply of gasoline. The only items of artillery ammunition in short supply were white phosphorus shells for the 105's and 155's. It seemed likely that the daily maintenance requirements of the Third Army could be met: 1,000 tons of rations, 2,000 tons of gasoline and oil, 2,000 tons of ammunition, and 1,000 tons of other items. The countless pieces of engineer equipment required in assaulting fortifications or making river crossings were comprised in a 10,000-ton stock of engineer supplies. The Third Army armored formations had been brought up to their normal tank strength; however, there were very few medium tanks available as replacements in the army ordnance depots.[93] The troop status of the Third Army divisions was close to the assigned organizational strength; though the total casualties for the month of October numbered some 14,000, the army had received over 13,000 replacements. The *effective* strength of the Third Army was approximately a quarter of a million officers and men.[94]

[92] *Ibid.*, 5 Nov 44.

[93] TUSA AAR, II.

[94] TUSA G–1 Periodic Rpt, 4–11 Nov 44.

Morale throughout the Third Army was high despite the mud, the rain, and the tedium of enforced inactivity. Some of the optimism which had been so marked in late August and early September had gone. Nonetheless rumors floated through the army area that the war would be over by Christmas, and there was a prevailing sense that this would be the last big push. General Patton drove up and down the area adding his voice to the optimistic prophecies of private soldiers and division commanders. A speech to the new 95th Division expressed a belief which the army commander would repeat again and again: "It is 132 miles to the Rhine from here, and if this army will attack with venom and desperate energy, it is more than probable that the war will end before we get to the Rhine. Therefore, when we attack, go like hell!" [95] In the meantime army weather stations and air force liaison officers watched for a break in the seemingly interminable rains. They and the infantry who waited for the bomber planes to makes the advance easier would be disappointed. In the Nancy area, from which the Third Army attack was to begin, the month of November would bring a total of 7.2 inches of rain, as contrasted with a normal fall of 3.0 inches during this month. To the meteorologist in uniform this was merely an upward swing on a graph; to the foot soldier and tanker it meant a slow advance under enemy fire through sucking mud and over swollen, rushing streams.

German Defensive Preparations, October and Early November 1944[96]

While the Third Army made preparations during the October lull for a resumption of the offensive, the German forces opposite were busy with plans and preparations to meet the American attack which their intelligence predicted would begin sometime during the first half of November. General Balck and *Army Group G* could be given little aid and only trifling additions to the meager forces already available, since men and materiel were being shunted to the north in preparation for a great counteroffensive in the Ardennes region. In addition *Army Group B* was seriously menaced by the Allied operations in the north; during October a sizable part of Balck's very limited reserves was sent by OKW to the Aachen and Holland sectors. As

[95] 95th Div G–3 Jnl, 4 Nov 44.

[96] This section is based on the *KTB's* of *Army Group G* and *OB WEST* for October and early November, 1944. A number of situation maps in the GMDS collection show the planned defenses.

the result of these detachments a number of small-scale counterattacks which had been planned to regain the ground lost to the Third Army in early October were canceled. With minor exceptions the entire *Army Group G* front lapsed into quiet.

Twice during October Rundstedt suggested to Balck that further withdrawals should be made at those points along the front where the Americans had shown indications of aggressive intentions, in this way shortening the German lines and freeing troops for use as reserves. But Balck held firmly to the idea that no ground should be surrendered without a fight. To give ground unnecessarily under pressure, or the threat of pressure, meant only that the Americans would continue to push ahead in that same sector. Balck summed up his concept of the defensive about ten days before the opening of the Third Army November offensive when he told Rundstedt that he intended to counterattack "on the spot" against the point of any American penetration, that in the long run this would entail fewer losses and would give time to build up some defense in depth in the sector most endangered.

The relative strengths of the two armies under *Army Group G* gave all the advantage to the *First Army*. Balck estimated that of the nine divisions in the *Nineteenth Army* only three, by reason of strength and experience, deserved to be called divisions.[97] Each of the remaining six was at best no stronger than a regiment. In the *First Army*, also composed of nine divisions, five were estimated as equal to ordinary "defensive" divisions, while two of these five were adjudged capable of limited use as "attack" divisions. Since the terrain in the Vosges favored the defender, and since German intelligence sources indicated that the next American offensive would be thrown not against the *Nineteenth Army* but against the *First*, Balck decided to divert such replacements and weapons as he could inveigle from the higher commands to the *First Army*, while hoping that the forces in Alsace could continue to hold in static defense positions. Balck had no illusions about the weakened character of the forces under his command, particularly on the *Nineteenth Army* front where fighting continued throughout October. On 9 October the *Army Group G* commander sent a personal letter to Jodl at OKW, apparently in hopes of getting some help from the man who had

[97] Not included in these nine divisions was the *30th SS Grenadier Division* (Russian), which had mutinied in September and been sent to the Belfort area for reorganization. *Army Group G* was unwilling to use these *Ost troops* and had advised that they be disarmed and broken up into labor battalions. However, *OB WEST* refused this request—a good commentary on the dire condition of German resources in manpower at this stage of the war.

Hitler's ear. After enumerating the heavy losses sustained in the battles just past, Balck appealed for replacements on the ground that the individual soldier was the decisive factor in the "jungle fighting" in the Vosges mountains and the woods of Lorraine. Further, said Balck, "If replacements are not forthcoming the time will arrive when there is no longer any front to defend. The front is already strained to the breaking point and one wonders how the few tired men can ever repair the situation." Worst of all was the situation in the *Nineteenth Army.* "I have never commanded such jumbled up and badly equipped troops," said Balck, "as there." He seems to have lost most of the personal optimism that had earlier recommended him to Hitler as an army group commander, for he ended this appeal to Jodl with the dark conclusion that the only thing which had saved his armies thus far was "the poor and timorous leadership" of the American and French commanders who had failed to take advantage of the critical German situation. The only reply to Balck's urgent plea was a soothing note which implied that he was not fully cognizant of the over-all situation [98] and promised some replacements.

Instead of acquiring additional divisions in October, *Army Group G* continued to lose its best troops, receiving in return untrained infantry divisions of dubious quality.[99] Three crack headquarters staffs, those of the *Fifth Panzer Army*, *XLVII Panzer Corps*, and *LVIII Panzer Corps*, were detached and sent north to *Army Group B*. On 17 October the *LXXXIX Corps* came in to take command in the sector, originally under the *Fifth Panzer Army*, astride the Marne-Rhin Canal, thus filling out the southern wing of the *First Army*. The loss of these well-trained staffs and their communications equipment, always a critical item, was perhaps less important than the loss of the *3d* and *15th Panzer Grenadier Divisions*, which were still rated as capable of use in attack and in consequence were withdrawn to the strategic reserve being formed by OKW in the Ruhr–Westphalia area. This reserve, though in the *OB WEST* area, was not under Rundstedt's command.

By the first week of November the major reshuffling of units along the *Army Group G* front was completed; the German corps and divisions were disposed approximately as they would meet the Third Army attack and the

[98] Apparently Balck was informed about 1 November that a great German counteroffensive was being planned. He was not entrusted with the location of the German attack, but was told that it would not be in the *Army Group G* sector.

[99] On 9 October Balck reported to *OB WEST* that *Army Group G* had been reduced by about 28,000 men since the last days of September. Of this number 12,000 were casualties and 16,000 were in divisions which had been taken away from *Army Group G*.

later drive by the Seventh Army. The fronts of the German *First Army* and the American Third Army were nearly coterminous, although the north and south flanks of the *First Army* extended somewhat beyond the Third Army zone. With the addition of the battered *553d VG Division* from the *First Army*, which had been shifted to a sector just south of the Marne-Rhin Canal, the *Nineteenth Army* was aligned opposite the Allied 6th Army Group. German troop lists for 1 November showed a total strength of 136,161 officers and men in *Army Group G*. The estimated *combat strength* was much lower: 92,094 officers and men. Of the total strength listed, 86,622 officers and men belonged to the *First Army*. Between 1 and 8 November a few hundred replacements were brought up to reinforce *Army Group G*; most of these went to the *First Army*.[100]

Through most of October *Army Group G* had rationed artillery ammunition at the rate of one to one and a half rounds per gun per day, in an attempt to build up a sufficient stock to meet the coming attack. In this matter of resupply, as in others, priority had to be given to the needs of the embattled German troops on the Aachen and Holland fronts, while hundreds of trainloads were diverted to building up supplies for the Ardennes offensive.[101] As a result Balck was low on artillery ammunition when the American attack began, although he was to receive large stocks shortly thereafter. Assault guns and tank destroyers, so essential in German combat organization at this time, filtered slowly through supply channels, a half-dozen at a time. When battle finally was joined no single division had its full complement of these weapons; some divisions had none. The artillery regiments organic in the German division were in fairly good shape, although the number of field pieces in the artillery regiment generally was well below the complement of the American divisional artillery. New tanks arrived in some quantity, in view of the state of German tank production and the demands made by the creation of the OKW strategic reserve, with the result that *Army Group G* had some 140 tanks of all types and weights by the first week of November. The bulk of this limited armored strength, just as in the case of ammunition and infantry replacements, was earmarked for the *First Army*, which had a total of about a hundred tanks and assault guns when the Americans finally attacked.

[100] *OKH/Org. Abt. KTB, Anlage,* 1 Dec 44.

[101] The lack of fuel and the constant attacks by American planes slowed up all movement by supply trains. Trains were dispatched only on orders from *OB WEST* so as to use all poor flying weather and hours of darkness. This remote control from higher headquarters still further ensnarled the overloaded railway system.

Attempts to fill out the depleted ranks of the German infantry divisions had limited success. Only a few regular replacement battalions were available for Balck's command. In the main, the divisions were replenished with security and fortress battalions of indifferent worth, although the fortress machine gun battalions, whose equipment was generally good and whose personnel had been drawn from veterans of the Eastern Front, helped to stiffen the new cadres. The October lull did give occasion to regroup the German units and fit the fragmentary Kampfgruppen, some of which had not been reorganized since the invasion, into divisional frameworks. A rotation policy allowed some rest for the worn-out German soldiery and training for the green replacements, but replacement contingents came in so slowly that many received only a week or ten days of training, instead of the four- to six-week period which Balck and his commanders believed necessary. While the Americans across the line were being schooled in attacks against fortifications, the Germans concentrated on training in night fighting, since OKW had flatly ruled that *Army Group G* should receive no air support and since Balck's commanders were by now all too familiar with the futility of daylight operations so long as American planes held unchallenged sway over the battlefield.

The German decision to use an elastic defense on the *First Army* front and thus "hem in" the spearheads of the anticipated large-scale American attack required the construction of field fortifications in depth, for which neither sufficient time, manpower, weapons, nor construction materials were available. In view of the admitted American superiority in materiel, particularly in guns and planes, Balck fell back on a modified version of the World War I scheme of elastic defense used by Ludendorff in 1916. In this system the first line of defense was held by weak forces, which were to be withdrawn to a main line of resistance about two or three kilometers to the rear as soon as the Americans began an attack in strength. American guns and planes would dump their shells and bombs on the field fortifications in the first line —the "false positions"—or so it was assumed. Then, as the assault waves moved forward through the weakly held first line, the main German combat elements in the main line of resistance would be in position to hold and counterattack in the "maneuver ground" between the front line and the MLR. Lacking sufficient antitank weapons, the Germans were forced to rely mainly on land mines as the chief defense against tanks; these were laid by the thousands. Weak points in the main line of resistance were to be covered by the massed guns of stationary fortress antitank companies. Still further to the rear the German field artillery was ranged in on tactical check points prepared by each division, so that a minimum of one light and one heavy field artillery battalion could be brought to bear on any main penetration. (On 1 November Hitler ordered the build-up of an "artillery line" in depth behind the *First Army* front. As a result the *First Army* received a considerable amount of army artillery, fortress artillery, and other army troops between 1 and 10 November.)

Behind the existing German main line of resistance and in front of the West Wall, attempts were made to build up an intermediate position, the *West-Stellung*. This line of defense lay in the rear of the *First Army*, its right boundary in the neighborhood of Insming and Sarre-Union, and its left just south of the Marne-Rhin Canal in the vicinity of Dieuze. Work on the *West-Stellung* was entrusted to Generalleutnant Bernard von Claer and a special staff in late September. But as was so often the case in the autumn of 1944 the lack of skilled labor, interference from Nazi party officials, scarcity of concrete and steel, and a general lack of agreement as to how the line should be built nullified most of the efforts of *Stab General von Claer*. However, a number of antitank ditches were dug by the civilian population and the main roads were mined and strewn with obstacles for ten or fifteen kilometers in front of the *West-Stellung*—all of which delayed the American armored columns in November.

On 4 November General Balck began the final steps to align his troops for the long-awaited American offensive and ordered radio silence to cover the German movements, except for those units in the forward defense positions. Some troops and guns were still coming up; so it was not until 6 November that the final orders were given for the disposition of reserves in the *First Army* sector. Each division was told to create a tactical reserve of one infantry regiment, one antitank company and two battalions of light howitzers. Actually, the divisions had neither the strength to strip their extended fronts nor the time to carry out such orders; most divisional commanders were fortunate if they had so much as a battalion in reserve when the Americans attacked on 8 and 9 November.

On 19 October OKW, with its usual lack of appreciation of the hard tactical facts of life confronting the German commanders at the front, had "advised" Balck to create an operational reserve of four infantry divisions and three panzer divisions in *Army Group G*. But by the beginning of November *Army Group G* had been so denuded of mobile or semimobile troops that the only operational reserve free for immediate use was the *11th Panzer Division*, assembled in a more or less central position behind the *First Army* front in the area west of St. Avold. In addition the *21st Panzer Division*, holding a sector on the *Nineteenth Army* front, was scheduled for use as an additional mobile division for this operational reserve. Despite this plan OKW had so much trouble in finding an infantry division to relieve the *21st Panzer Division*, and such difficulty with its transport, that the armored division was still deployed on the *Nineteenth Army* front when the Americans attacked in the north. Finally, Hitler himself intervened to give Balck some additional fire power in the very last days of the lull, ordering the *401st Volks Artillery Corps* (apparently with five field artillery battalions) and a weak assault gun brigade to reinforce the *First Army*. These units were en route to the front when the American offensive began.

While it was clear to the German high command that General Patton would eventually resume the offensive and that this attack would be thrown against the *First Army*, there was somewhat less certainty as to which side of Metz the Americans would strike. After the deadly blow dealt the *553d VG Division* on 8 October *OB WEST* and OKW believed for a time that the Americans would follow up this success sometime before the middle of November with an onslaught south of Metz. However, intelligence reports from agents behind the American lines began to indicate unusual activity opposite Thionville about the middle of October, and for some time both the American 14th Armored Division and the 4th Armored Division were carried on German situation maps as tentatively located in this area. The appearance of a new American armored division in the Metz sector, reported by agents on 28 October as "possibly the 10th Armored Division," confirmed a conclusion that the American offensive would be mounted both north and south of Metz. With the paucity of mobile reserves in *Army Group G* little could be done to prepare for this threat aside from shifting some artillery to the north flank of the *First Army*. In any event, General Balck expected that the American attack would hit hardest against the south flank of the *First Army*, probably between Delme Ridge and the Marne-Rhin Canal, where the terrain offered fewer obstacles to a rapid advance than in the area north and northeast of Metz. Although the Allied forces opposite the *Nineteenth Army* continued to make local attacks through October and early November, activity on this front was viewed as incidental to the threat poised in front of the *First Army*. German intelligence gave little attention to the Alsace sector until 7 November, when increased Allied artillery fire and troop movements opposite the *LXXXV Corps* gave rise to the fear that the American offensive might begin simultaneously in both the Metz and Belfort sectors.

Although the deceptive devices used opposite Thionville had misled the Germans into erroneous identification of the 14th Armored Division (which in fact was not yet on the Continent when first "identified" by the enemy), most of their information on the divisions in the Third Army was quite accurate as to location and strength. Secret agents provided much of this useful information to the German headquarters. But the Americans themselves supplied German intelligence with most of it by extremely careless use of telephones and radios at the various traffic control points along the routes where troops were moving. No specific date was set by German intelligence as the day on which the American offensive would be likely to start, but it was generally anticipated that the Third Army attack would come not earlier than 3 November and not later than the second week of November. Troop movements behind the American lines on the nights just prior to 8 November had been carefully observed and apparently placed the German high command on something approaching an hour-to-hour alert. When General Patton did strike, on 8 November, Balck reported to his immediate superiors that the offensive had begun "as expected." Undoubtedly, higher German headquarters did expect the American attack about this time. But it is equally certain that the troops in the front line were taken by surprise on 8 and 9 November, and that "tactical" surprise, at the least, was achieved by the American divisions.

CHAPTER VII

The XII Corps Resumes the Offensive (8-17 November)[1]

Plans for the November Offensive

During the last week of October the XII Corps began to map plans for the day when the Allied supply situation would allow the Third Army to resume the offensive. On 3 November General Eddy issued Field Order No. 10 giving the general mission for the drive now scheduled to open between 5 and 8 November. Faulquemont, about twenty miles east of the front lines of the 80th Division on the main railroad between Metz and Saarbruecken, was designated as the first objective. Thereafter the XII Corps was to advance "rapidly" to the northeast and secure a bridgehead over the Rhine River, in the sector between Oppenheim (south of Mainz) and Mannheim. The first general objective east of the Rhine was indicated tentatively as the Darmstadt area.

General Eddy had a very sizable force under his command for this operation: three infantry divisions, including the veteran 35th and 80th—now brought up to strength by replacements—and the new 26th; two veteran armored divisions, the 4th and 6th; and seventeen battalions of field artillery, approximately nine engineer battalions, seven tank destroyer battalions, seven antiaircraft artillery battalions, three separate tank battalions, and two squadrons of mechanized cavalry.

American intelligence agencies estimated the German strength opposite the XII Corps as two complete infantry divisions (the *559th* and *361st VG Division*), plus a part of the *48th Division* and some smaller formations, giving a strength of about 15,000 men and twenty tanks or assault guns. In addition it was believed that the *11th Panzer Division* and the panzer regi-

[1] The American records have been discussed in the notes to Chapter V. German documents are adequate for this period, but the *XIII SS Corps KTB* has been lost or destroyed—as have most *Waffen-SS* combat records.

ment of the *21st Panzer Division* were re-forming in rearward areas within the XII Corps zone of advance. This G–2 appreciation was fairly accurate, although the *21st Panzer Division* actually was far to the south in the *Nineteenth Army* area.

The *361st VG Division* (Colonel Alfred Philippi) had come into the Moyenvic sector on 23 October, there relieving the *11th Panzer Division.* New and unseasoned, it was organized under a reduced T/O with two battalions per regiment and manned with a collection of sailors, Luftwaffe personnel, and a miscellany of other similar troops stiffened by a substantial number of veteran officers and noncoms. Artillery and train were horse-drawn—indeed the movement of the division from north Holland had been delayed for several days by an epidemic among its horses. Unlike other divisions, whose artillery had been left immobile by the shortage of automotive prime movers and gasoline, the *361st* was able to haul its full complement of guns. In addition the division had one battery of assault guns.

The *559th VG Division* (Muehlen), still in the Château-Salins area, had been roughly handled by the XII Corps in earlier fighting but could hardly be considered a weak division—at least in comparison with other VG divisions on the Western Front. However, it did lack tank destroyers and other heavy antitank weapons. The *48th Division* (Generalleutnant Carl Casper) had fought against Third Army troops at Chartres and then, in September, had taken extremely heavy losses in the fighting in Luxembourg. On 13 October the *48th* was sent in opposite the 80th Division to relieve the wrecked *553d VG Division,* although it too was far below strength. The *48th* had been rebuilt, but with over-age replacements, and now it was considered one of the poorest divisions on the *First Army* front. Two of its regiments had had some training, but the third (the *128th Regiment*) was not yet ready for combat.

During October the headquarters of the *Fifth Panzer Army* and the *XLVII Panzer Corps* had been withdrawn from *Army Group G.* On 1 November the *LVIII Panzer Corps* headquarters went north to the *Seventh Army* and was replaced by the *LXXXIX Corps* (General der Infantrie Gustav Hoehne), which took over the sector on the left flank of Priess' *XIII SS Corps.* On the eve of the American offensive the German order of battle opposite XII Corps was as follows: the *361st VG Division,* assigned to the *LXXXIX Corps,* disposed in the sector from the Marne-Rhin Canal up to a point just west of Moyenvic; the *559th VG Division,* deployed toward the west with its right boundary at Malaucourt; and the *48th Division,* holding a line from Malaucourt to north of Eply. These last two divisions were under the *XIII SS Corps.*[2]

Although General Balck had outlined a detailed defense plan to his subordinates, based on the collection of local reserves for immediate counterattack, the German divisions, understrength as they were, could not afford the luxury of large tactical reserves. Early in November the *48th Division* had one battalion in reserve at Delme Ridge; the *559th VG Division* was rotating its regiments in a reserve position in the Château-Salins area, and the *361st VG Division* had a battalion in reserve near Dieuze. Few, if any, changes were made in these allocations of reserves before the American attack. The *11th Panzer Division* remained the only division in operational reserve available to *Army Group G* in the area west of St. Avold. This division had been re-equipped after the September battles with the 4th Armored Division; on 8 November it had a complement of nineteen Mark IV tanks and fifty new Panthers, but not more than one or two tank destroyers. The reserve location of the *11th Panzer Division* had been chosen with an eye to meeting an attack from either Thionville or what the Germans still called the "Pont-à-Mousson bridgehead." But when the *First Army* commander had raised the question as to where the *11th Panzer Division* would counterattack in case the American offensive should strike in both these sectors, General Balck, with no other reserves at hand, could only defer an answer.

Hitler himself added another reserve component to *Army Group G* at the eleventh hour by sending it the *401st Volks Artillery Corps.* The five artillery battalions making up this new unit were detraining at St. Avold in the first week of November. Finally, the *243d Assault Gun Brigade*—really a battalion—was ordered to the Dieuze area and plans were made to relieve the *21st Panzer Division* from the *Nineteenth Army* and send it behind the *First Army* lines for needed rehabilitation. Both of these units, however, failed to arrive in the *First Army* zone before the Americans struck.[3]

During its first weeks in France, General Patton's Third Army had thrust deep into the Continent. In contrast to this swift campaign, the operations of XII Corps, begun on 8 November and continued through early December, took on the character of a far more conventional type of warfare. The offensive spirit had not changed—but the terrain and the weather had.

[2] MS #B–412 (Einem); MS #B–492 (Tippelskirch); MS #B–443 (Emmerich); MS #A–972 (Muehlen).

[3] *Army Group G KTB* and *Anlagen* for this period.

After passing the Moselle River and clearing the irregular scarps to the east, the right wing of the Third Army had debouched into the rich farming country of Lorraine. The territory east of the Moselle, called by the French "la Plaine," was gently rolling, interspersed with irregular watercourses and dotted with forests and hills. Military geographers and historians recognized this area as "the Lorraine gateway," since historically it had formed a natural route between the Vosges mountains to the south and the western German mountains in the north. But although it permits greater ease of entrance or exit between eastern France and the Rhine Valley than the mountains on either side, the Lorraine gateway also has its barriers. To the east the Sarre River and the lower Vosges act as a curtain connecting the bastions formed by the Vosges and the western German mountains. The Sarre River position in turn is strengthened on its southern flank by the maze of forests, swamps, and lakes in the triangle bounded by Dieuze–Mittersheim–Gondrexange, and on its northern flank by the Saar Heights which rim the Saar Basin.

West of the Sarre River and directly in front of the XII Corps lay two long, narrow plateau spurs paralleling the projected American line of advance. (*Map 7*) These two outcroppings are separated by the Petite Seille River. They are generally known by the names of the most important towns near them—the Morhange plateau in the north and the Dieuze plateau in the south. Perhaps a more accurate identification is furnished by the forests which cover them, since the Forêt de Bride et de Koecking runs nearly the entire length of the Dieuze plateau, and the Morhange plateau is outlined in its southwestern extremity by the Forêt de Château-Salins. Any advance eastward along the valley of the Seille would have to pass under the shadow of the plateau covered by the Forêt de Bride et de Koecking, and any move northeast toward Morhange would be constricted by the two plateaus. To the northwest lies an isolated military barrier known to the Americans as Delme Ridge (Côte de Delme). It has fairly abrupt slopes and dominates the Seille Basin. Delme Ridge has long been recognized as having a prime tactical importance: first, because the Seille River, at its foot, forms a local natural re-entrant running back into the Moselle position; second, because Delme Ridge itself affords observation over the entire area bounded by the Nied and the Seille.

In the years prior to 1914 the French General Staff, under the influence of the Grandmaison school of strategy, planned, in the event of war with Germany, to take the offensive in the first days and strike obliquely, into the

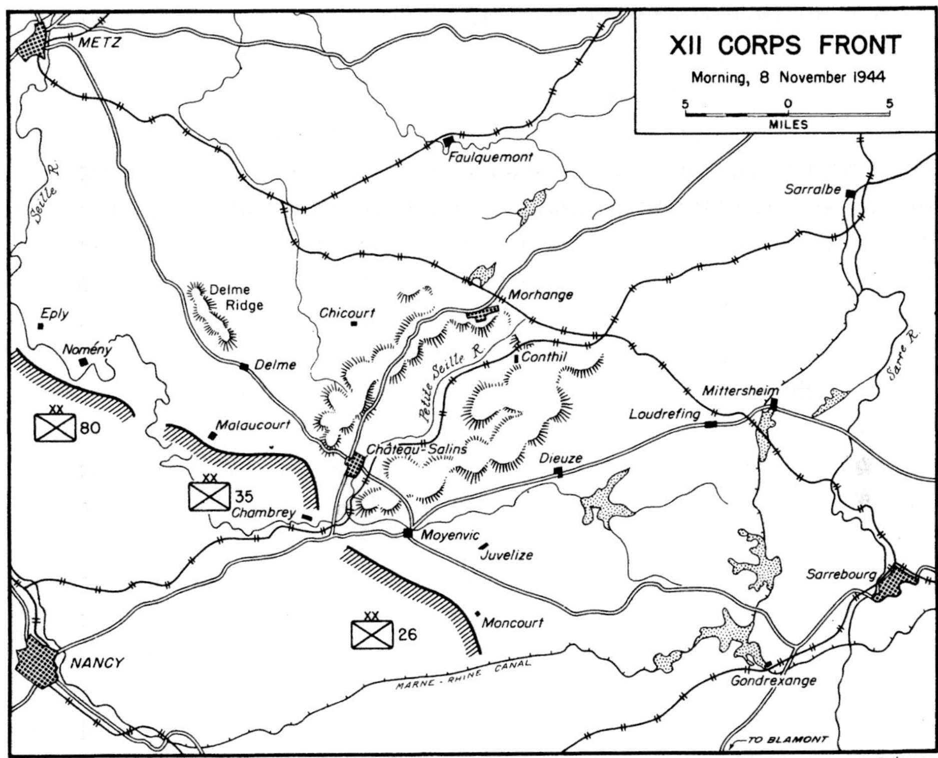

MAP NO. 7

flank of what the French thought would be the German route of advance, with a double-headed offensive through the Belfort Gap and the southern sector of the Lorraine gateway. On 14 August 1914 the French began this double attack. Four days later, after overrunning the forward German defense line which extended from Delme Ridge via Château-Salins and Juvelize (or Geistkirch) across the Marne-Rhin Canal to Blâmont, the French Second Army (Castelnau) and a part of the First Army (Dubail) were in contact with the main forces of the German *Sixth Army*, commanded by Archduke Rupprecht of Bavaria. The battle which followed, on 19 and 20 August, is generally known as the Battle of Morhange, although it covered much more terrain than just the approaches to that city. This battle is instructive since the French were faced with most of the tactical problems encountered on the same ground by the XII Corps in November 1944.

Because the Germans in 1914 held Delme Ridge in strength and could readily be reinforced from Metz, Castelnau made no attempt to take the ridge, leaving a reserve infantry division to contain the position and cover his left flank and rear. The 20 Corps, commanded by General Foch, advanced across the Seille between Chambrey and Moyenvic, took the valley route toward Morhange (with its ultimate objective as Faulquemont), skirted the Forêt de Château-Salins, and crossed the western tip of the Forêt de Bride et de Koecking. Initially the enemy opposition in the valley was none too strong and by the morning of 20 August the 20 Corps held a line from Chicourt to Conthil. On the right the 15 Corps attacked diagonally from Moncourt into the Seille valley and after bitter fighting reached Dieuze, which it held for a few hours. Farther to the east the 16 Corps advanced directly north, threading its way through the swamps and forests between Dieuze and Saarburg in an attempt to turn the German position by an attack along the east bank of the Sarre River. The terrain forced the 16 Corps to dissipate its strength in small detachments and the advance finally was brought to a halt in the neighborhood of Loudrefing. Then, as the German artillery began to play havoc with the attackers on the morning of 20 August, the 16 Corps was forced to fall back in a hurried retreat. Now the Bavarians counterattacked all along the front, leaving the cover of the forests and pouring down from the Dieuze and Morhange plateaus, while their heavier guns silenced the French 75's. Caught in the valleys below, the French could not hold. Castelnau's army fell back on Nancy and the Grand Couronné, covered by Foch's 20 Corps which fought a rear guard action near Château-Salins where the two valleys converged. In August 1914 the French were beaten by heavy field artillery, by the machine gun, and by the German possession of admirable defensive positions. In November 1944 the attacker possessed the superiority in materiel—as well as numbers—but the Germans again had the advantage of the ground and in addition were to be favored by the autumn rains.[4]

[4] In the autumn of 1918, Foch ordered Pershing and Pétain to lay plans for a great offensive in Lorraine. The Imperial German Army surrendered before the offensive could get under way, but even in its blueprint form this plan is worthy of notice: first because it repeats the categorical connection between terrain and tactics; second, because it gives an interesting comparison between the size of the force required in massed and slow-moving attacks (1918) and the force needed to cover the same ground in an era of greater mobility and fire power (1944). In the 1918 plan the front of the Allied advance was to extend from Metz to Dieuze. Six American divisions from the Second Army were to contain Metz with a drive east of the city. The French Tenth Army was to make the main effort, bypassing the Forêt de Grémecey on the north and driving to the Sarre River along the axis Delme–Faulquemont–St. Avold–Sarreguemines. On the right, the French Eighth Army would hook north from the Juvelize sector, clear the Forêt de

The XII Corps plan of attack was ready by 5 November. D Day would be set by General Patton. The scheme of maneuver was simple. Since the area ahead was so broken up by streams, woods, and isolated elevations as to make detailed tactical planning fruitless, General Eddy and his division commanders allowed a free hand to the subordinate leaders who would direct the action on the battleground.[5] The three infantry divisions would launch the attack, making a co-ordinated advance along the entire corps front. The two armored divisions, the 4th behind the right wing and the 6th behind the left, had orders to push into the van and lead the attack as soon as the German forward lines were broken and a favorable position for further exploitation was secured.

In this attack, as in the three-division operation a month earlier, the XII Corps could rely on its tremendous superiority in the artillery arm—a superiority which made initial success certain whether or not the American Air Force was able to support the offensive. The XII Corps artillery fire plan again was elaborate and detailed. Tactical surprise would be sacrificed in order to bring the greatest weight of metal against the forward enemy positions, on which the Germans had worked and sweated for a month past under the glasses of American observers. The seventeen battalions of corps artillery would fire a preparation for three and a half hours (H minus 60 minutes to H plus 150), with twenty battalions of division artillery strengthening the fire during the first thirty minutes. Of the 380 concentrations planned, 190 would be fired on enemy artillery positions; for the most important targets a concentration was charted every three minutes. To thicken this terrific fire the 90-mm. guns of the antiaircraft artillery battalions, the 3-inch guns of the tank destroyers, and the 105-mm. howitzers of the regimental cannon companies were pushed forward close behind the infantry's line of departure. By 5 November the artillery had completed its registrations, and only just in time, for torrential rains and low-hanging clouds grounded the artillery observation planes and blinded the American observation posts.[6]

These preparations were reminiscent of the tactics of 1916 and the close co-ordination then developing in the artillery-infantry team. There was less

Koecking, and take Morhange. The Allied forces allocated for this offensive numbered 28 infantry divisions, 3 cavalry divisions, 614 batteries, and 600 tanks. See *Les Armées Françaises dans la Grande Guerre,* Tome VII: 2ème vol. (Paris, 1938).

[5] Earlier, Foch came to this same conclusion—and for the same reason—in his 1918 plan for a Lorraine offensive.

[6] XII Corps AAR, Nov 44.

unanimity of thought, however, on the use of armor in the coming operation. General Patton believed, and stated this belief at every opportunity, that tanks could easily breach the West Wall, now the big obstacle athwart the route to the Rhine. But many of the veteran junior officers in the armored divisions were less sanguine and privately held the opinion that the armor would be cut to pieces in the maze of antitank defenses ahead. Of greater immediate concern was the problem of tank going in the November mud. Many believed that the campaign was beginning a month too late—a belief shared by infantry and armored officers alike. There was nevertheless considerable optimism among the troops and their leaders, though this optimism was less flaunted than it had been in August and September. Now it was tempered by the long period of inactivity, the mud and the rain, and their exaggerated estimate of the strength of the German West Wall.

Beginning on 5 November, the first date possible for the attack according to Third Army plans, rain fell with only brief intermissions. On 7 November a downpour began that lasted without a break for twenty-four hours. General Patton could wait no longer for flying weather and gave the code words, "Play ball," which were to begin the XII Corps advance on the morning of 8 November. At nightfall on 7 November the infantry slowly toiled through rivers of mud into position for the attack. So began the Third Army's education in Napoleon's "fifth element of war"—mud—bringing for some a personal appreciation of what other Americans had experienced in France a generation earlier. This November campaign would lack the dash and the brilliant successes of earlier operations by the Third Army, but it would record a heroic story of endurance and devotion to duty.

H Hour came at 0600 on 8 November with most of the elements of the three infantry divisions moving forward as had been planned. On the right the 26th Division advanced with the 104th, 101st, and 328th Infantry abreast (left to right). In the center the 35th Division, attacking on a narrower front, led off with the 137th and 320th Infantry in line (left to right) and the 134th Infantry in reserve. On the left the 80th Division attacked with the 317th, 318th, and 319th Infantry abreast (left to right). The XII Corps right flank, abutting on the Marne-Rhin Canal, was covered by the 2d Cavalry Group; its left flank was protected by the XX Corps, whose advance was scheduled to begin on the following day.

The opening bombardment by the massed field artillery battalions smashed the forward enemy positions, destroyed communications, and effectively neutralized most of the German guns. The XII Corps artillery fired 21,933 rounds in the twenty-four hours from 0600 on 8 November to 0600 of the next day, the gunners using time fire wherever possible because impact fuses often failed to detonate in the mud. Later, as the bad weather abated, planes from the IX and XIX TAC's swooped down to give close support by striking at woods, towns, and entrenchments.

The infantry advance, in its early hours, found little will to resist among the German grenadiers and machine gunners whose carefully prepared dugouts and trenches had received such a merciless pounding. As always, there were small islands of resistance where a few determined grenadiers held stubbornly in place and forced the attackers to recoil, necessitating the arduous business of outflanking the position or making costly and repeated frontal assaults. Mud, however, slowed the American infantry more than did the German line. The Seille River had flooded its banks, with the highest waters since 1919, and fields and woods along the river channel had turned to quagmires or veritable lakes. But in spite of the mud and cold the infantry moved steadily forward. Over a thousand Germans in the front-line positions were captured in the rapid advance of this first day and a large quantity of enemy equipment was taken or destroyed.

It is impossible to tell to what degree the German troops and commanders were caught by surprise on the morning of 8 November. German intelligence had reported unusual vehicular activity behind the XII Corps lines on the nights before the attack. But the top intelligence officers at *Army Group G* believed that in all probability the next major American thrust would come in the Thionville sector or between Metz and Pont-à-Mousson. This opinion was reinforced by the continued activity on the XX Corps front, and by the American destruction of the Etang de Lindre dam, which was interpreted as an indication of a purely defensive attitude in the XII Corps sector. *OB WEST* did not share the view that Patton would make the prospective drive with his left. On 2 November the G–2 at Rundstedt's headquarters predicted that the Third Army would launch a general attack all along its front—but he did not hazard a guess as to the date. Apparently the enemy front-line troops did not anticipate any immediate danger, for those taken prisoner on the first day said that their positions were regarded as a "winter line," in which they were to sit out a lull in operations until spring arrived. Possibly there was a division of opinion in the higher German headquarters. There is evidence that at least a few German intelligence officers predicted that General Patton would launch an attack on 8 November in commemoration of the Allied landings in North Africa on that date two years before; but no last-minute changes were made in the German order of battle to indicate that such a prediction was given any weight.[7] In any case it is unlikely that the limited German forces opposite the Third Army could have done more than they did in the face of the first crushing blow of men and metal thrown against them. Most of the German officers who faced the attack of 8 November later agreed that careful preparations and excellent camouflage had won tactical surprise for the Americans.[8]

The First Phase of the 26th Infantry Division Advance

On the night of 7–8 November the 26th Infantry Division moved up to its attack positions, prepared to carry forward the right wing of the XII Corps in the drive scheduled for the morrow. (*Map XXVII*) The 104th Infantry assembled opposite Salonnes and Vic-sur-Seille, the assault companies of the 101st concentrated near the "Five Points" on highway 414, which led to Moyenvic, and the 328th faced east toward Moncourt and Bezange-la-Petite. The right flank of the division was covered by a cavalry screen thrown out by the 2d Cavalry Group, which General Eddy had attached to the 26th to cover the gap between the Marne-Rhin Canal and the main forces of the division. South of the canal the dispositions of the Seventh Army assured a solid anchor on the right of the Third Army base of operations. The left boundary for the 26th Division zone ran from Chambrey through Château-Salins, thus placing Dieuze and the eastern Seille in the division sector, as well as the eastern half of the valley of the Petite Seille which offered a natural route to the town of Morhange. The zone of advance would require that the commanders of the smaller units be given a free hand. The 328th Infantry (Col. B. R. Jacobs), on the right flank of the division, was ordered to make a feint toward Moncourt and Bezange-la-Petite—the obvious route toward Dieuze and the one taken by the French troops in 1914. In the center the 101st Infantry (Col. W. T. Scott) was given the mission of seizing the Seille crossing at Moyenvic. Once across the river the regiment would attack Hill 310 (Côte St. Jean), about 2,400 yards to the north, which formed the forwardmost bastion of the 8½-mile plateau-wall covering Dieuze. The main

[7] See *Army Group G KTB* for this period and *OKW/WFSt KTB Ausarbeitung, Der Westen.*
[8] MS #B–078 (Mellenthin).

DIEUZE
TO MOYENVIC
MARSAL

COTE ST. JEAN

TO SALIVAL
BOIS ST. MARTIN

assault would be made by the 104th Infantry (Col. D. T. Colley), crossing at Vic-sur-Seille and advancing east of Château-Salins so as to swing into the attack on the north side of the Koecking ridge. Two small task forces, made up of tank destroyers, tanks, and engineers, were added to reinforce the 104th Infantry.[9]

On the morning of 8 November the 26th Division attack began, moving with speed and élan much as had been planned. At 0600 the American gunfire lifted.. The 104th Infantry drove into Vic-sur-Seille and after a short, sharp fight seized some bridges which the outposts of the *361st VG Division* had not completely demolished.[10] At the same time the 2d Battalion of the 101st Infantry (Lt. Col. B. A. Lyons) jumped off to take the Seille bridge at Moyenvic, while the 1st Battalion (Lt. Col. L. M. Kirk) made a diversionary attack toward the east near Xanrey. The Moyenvic assault gained complete surprise. Just before dawn the 101st Field Artillery Battalion opened fire on Hill 310 and then "rolled back a barrage" through Moyenvic as the 2d Battalion attacked. The dazed German garrison yielded 542 prisoners. Company E, stealing forward from house to house, managed to reach the bridge over the Seille before the enemy demolition crew could blow it and crossed the river at once to begin the fight for Hill 310, there joining riflemen of F Company who had swum the river.

This dominating ground was held by troops of the *953d Regiment* and *361st Engineer Battalion*, reinforced by six infantry howitzers as well as mortars and machine guns. The forward slopes extended for some fifteen hundred yards, mostly open but dotted here and there with lone trees and small clumps of woods. Company E moved up the slope to the assault, but about five hun-

[9] Hist Div Combat Interviews; 26th Inf Div AAR, Nov 44. *OKW/WFSt KTB Ausarbeitung, Der Westen* gives some of the German reactions to the XII Corps attack on 8 November. The German officers reporting the start of the American offensive noted that deception was excellent: radio silence, lack of air activity, a short artillery preparation, the late movement of infantry to the line of departure, and the concentration of tanks well to the rear—each was singled out as effective.

[10] The commanding officer of the 104th Infantry, Col. Dwight T. Colley, was awarded the DSC for personal bravery in leading the attack on 8 November. During the action at Vic-sur-Seille Sgt. Charles J. Yestramski, E Company, 104th Infantry, saved a comrade at the cost of his own life. Sergeant Yestramski, although himself wounded, volunteered to carry a wounded man back across a footbridge which was under fire. A German shell broke the bridge and threw both men into the river. Sergeant Yestramski kept his companion afloat until help arrived, but was then swept away and drowned. The sergeant was awarded the DSC posthumously. In the house-to-house fight inside the town 1st Lt. Max M. Fitzpatrick of C Company distinguished himself by advancing ahead of his platoon and destroying a German machine gun crew. Fitzpatrick was killed while searching out the enemy in a house from which fire had been directed against his men. He received the DSC posthumously.

dred yards from the top of the hill was stopped by the murderous fire delivered from the German entrenchments on the crest and field guns firing from the village of Marsal. This fusillade cost E Company its commander and several men. Company F, following on the left, lost all of its officers. The two companies crowded together, seeking shelter where they could, and tactical organization soon was lost. All heavy weapons had been left behind to enable the troops to move quickly up the slope; sporadic and uncontrolled rifle fire could not pin the enemy down.

About 1100 G Company was committed, but its commander was hit while crossing the Moyenvic bridge and the company remained on the slope below E and F. An hour later two companies of the 3d Battalion arrived on the slope in accordance with the timetable earlier arranged for an attack by column of battalions, but the assault could not be started forward again. Here the infantry huddled through the afternoon, the clumps of trees where they sought cover continually swept by cross fire and by German guns on the crest. As dusk came on the enemy guns blasted the slope with a 20-minute concentration, causing heavy casualties and still further disorganizing the American assault force.[11] During the night the engineer battalion of the *559th VG Division* arrived to reinforce the German hold on the hill.

Although the initial attack at Hill 310 had failed, the 26th Infantry Division generally had been successful in the first day of the new offensive. The 101st and 104th had the Seille bridges securely in hand, while the demonstration toward Dieuze by the 328th Infantry had pushed the American lines past Bezange-la-Petite and Moncourt, pinning at least six companies of the *952d Regiment* to the defense of this sector, although with heavy cost to the attackers.[12]

[11] Hist Div Combat Interviews; 101st Inf Jnl; Ltr, Col Walter T. Scott to Hist Div, 14 Jul 47. These items cover the entire fight for Hill 310. The action at the hill on 8 November, although unsuccessful, was marked by numerous deeds of heroism. Pfc. Roy W. Smith, G Company, 101st Infantry, was acting as an ammunition bearer when he saw a machine gunner fall wounded. He crawled forward under direct fire, took over the gun and manned it, although wounded, until he was killed. Private Smith received the DSC in a posthumous award. Pfc. George R. Meyer, L Company, 101st Infantry, was awarded the DSC for attacking alone with his BAR, killing eight of the enemy, wounding four, and knocking out two machine guns.

[12] For his heroism during the fight near Bezange-la-Petite on 8 November Cpl. Alfred L. Wilson, an aid man with the 328th Infantry, received the Congressional Medal of Honor. Despite his own wounds, Corporal Wilson worked his way under fire to dress the wounds of others. When he could no longer move Wilson gave instructions until his wounds made it impossible for him to speak. He died refusing aid for himself. Pfc. Henry F. Howington, D Company, 328th Infantry, received the DSC as a result of the same action. At the edge of the village of Bezange-la-Petite, A Company was halted by fire from a German

Now the 26th Division began a three-day battle to maneuver around Hill 310 and pivot onto the Koecking ridge. The weather suddenly had turned cold; snow and rain fell on 9 November. The 101st Infantry, whose men had shed even their field jackets in the assault on Hill 310, suffered particularly, and exposure started to reduce the already weakened rifle strength on the slopes. Carrying parties could reach the 101st only through a deadly cross fire, and food had to be sacrificed for ammunition. Cold, hungry, with its ranks thinned and many of its officers casualties, the 101st tried to envelop the enemy positions on the crest. On the morning of 9 November the 1st Battalion, which had skillfully disengaged at Juvrecourt and come up through Moyenvic during the night, attempted a double envelopment but was stopped in its tracks by the German fire and by the mud which bogged down its supporting tanks at the base of the hill. The 3d Battalion finally dispatched two companies in an attack north up the ravine toward Salival, a little hamlet from which enemy machine gun fire enfiladed the western slope. At dark Salival was taken and the American infantry passed into the woods beyond, where German trenches, strongly manned, covered the flank and rear of the *953d* positions atop Hill 310.

Meanwhile the 104th Infantry, which had moved to flank Château-Salins in conjunction with the 35th Division attack toward the Forêt de Château-Salins, fought its way into this key town. On 9 November the troops from the *559th VG Division* which were holding Château-Salins were ejected by the 104th, and the right flank of the regiment was extended to Morville-lès-Vic in an attempt to put troops on Koecking ridge behind Hill 310. Morville was taken about 1500 by one of the task forces (Task Force A) attached to the division. Company K, 101st Infantry, cleared the town in a house-to-house fight, after the lead tank of a platoon from the 761st Tank Battalion was knocked out by a bazooka, blocking the narrow road into the town and forcing the infantry to go it alone. Then the little task force continued on toward Hampont, its progress slowed by mud and antitank fire. Capt. Charles F. Long, the K Company commander, was killed and half of the infantry company was lost in this fight.

The infantry had borne the burden of the attack on 9 November. Visibility was poor for the supporting gunners. Many of the artillery liaison planes

machine gun. Private Howington charged the gun, destroyed it, and killed three of the crew. At Moncourt Pvt. Melvin A. Cross of G Company was awarded the DSC for standing alone with his BAR and covering the withdrawal of his platoon during an enemy counterattack.

were grounded, some of them standing in water up to their wings. Not only was the artillery blinded to the point where it could give only limited support, but the air co-operation which had played such an important role in earlier operations also was drastically curtailed. The IX Bombardment Division sent 110 bombers to attack Dieuze, but because of the murky weather only 29 aircraft arrived over the target.

Nonetheless the left wing of the 26th Division had driven far enough to clear the way for intervention by the armor and, without realizing it, had forced a wedge between the left wing of the *559th* and the right wing of the *361st*.[13] On the night of 9 November General Eddy ordered CCA, 4th Armored Division, to attack on the following morning. At 1055 CCA (now commanded by Lt. Col. Creighton W. Abrams) began crossing over the Seille bridges en route to Hampont. But the appearance of the American tanks had no immediate effect on the battle still being fought for the possession of Hill 310.

The 1st Battalion of the 101st Infantry continued to work its way around Hill 310 on 10 November. About 1610 Colonel Scott gave the order to assault the ridge behind the hill. This assault was the turning point in the fight for a foothold on the Koecking plateau. Company C, attacking with marching fire behind a curtain of shells, succeeded in pushing the Germans off the ridge northeast of Hill 310. A company of enemy infantry counterattacked immediately, but C Company beat off the attack, although it was badly mauled; it then dug in while the German gunners took over the fight and tried to shell the Americans out of the position. The rest of the 1st Battalion swung around to the left, into the Bois St. Martin, and reached out to meet the 3d Battalion, which the day before had wheeled in a wider arc to move onto the Koecking ridge. The 3d Battalion literally blasted its way out of the thick, dark woods and on 11 November reached a road junction south of Hampont, where about a hundred Germans were captured.[14] Then the 3d Battalion turned back on the main ridge line to meet the 1st Battalion. On the same day, the 1st had finally driven the enemy off Hill 310 and from this vantage point was now directing the American batteries in counterfire against the German guns at Marsal and Haraucourt-sur-Seille in the valley below. Firmly astride the Koecking ridge, the 26th Division could begin the slow and costly process of fighting step by step to clear the Koecking woods, dis-

[13] MS #B-443 (Emmerich).

[14] The 3d Battalion used marching fire and expended two full bandoleers per man.

place the enemy on the plateau, and seize the villages in the valleys and on the slopes. The 26th Division, however, already was understrength. The fight for Hill 310 alone had cost 478 officers and men, dead and wounded.[15]

Initial success in the penetration by CCA, 4th Armored Division, in the Hampont sector offered some possibility for maneuver by the 26th Division's left. On 11 November, therefore, General Paul switched the 328th Infantry to the center of the division zone—on top of Koecking ridge—sent the 104th Infantry in on the left to support CCA in the drive toward Rodalbe, and turned the 101st to the east in an advance along the southern slopes of the Koecking ridge.

The CCA Attack along the Valley of the Petite Seille

The 4th Armored Division entered upon the November campaign as one of the crack armored divisions in the American armies in Europe. It was now a thoroughly battlewise division, imbued with a high degree of confidence as a result of the successful tank battles in late September, with relatively few green replacements, and with nearly a full complement of tanks and other vehicles. However, the 4th Armored, as well as General Patton's other armored divisions, was faced with a combination of terrain and weather which promised very bad tank going and which would inevitably restrict the mobility that had distinguished American armored formations in preceding months. During the final phase of the November operation the 4th Armored Division would be handicapped also by the fact that the right boundary of the Third Army continually was subject to change, making it necessary for the division constantly to alter its axis of advance in order to stay within the proper zone, and even, on occasion, to double back on its tracks.[16]

General Wood appears to have suggested that his entire division be used in an attack through the Dieuze defile, along the Moyenvic–Mittersheim road. General Eddy did not favor this plan because reports from the corps cavalry indicated that a considerable German force had been gathered to hold the narrow avenue through the Dieuze bottleneck.[17] Furthermore, Mittersheim, the Dieuze road terminus, lay inside the projected Seventh Army zone. Gen-

[15] Figures cited by CO, 101st Inf, Col Scott, in ltr to Hist Div.

[16] The 4th Armored Division operations during November are unusually well covered in Historical Division Combat Interviews.

[17] Interv with Gen Eddy, 6 Aug 47. See Hist Div Combat Interviews with officers of 4th Armd Div staff; see also 37th Tk Bn Jnl, Nov 44.

eral Eddy and his staff considered putting the 4th Armored Division through north of Château-Salins as the spearhead of the XII Corps advance. But General Patton's decision to add the 6th Armored Division to the XII Corps for the November offensive necessitated a regrouping of Eddy's armored strength. In the final plan the 4th Armored Division was given a "goose egg" on the map, covering the Morhange area, as an initial objective. Its additional and very tentative assignment was to continue the offensive in the direction of Sarre-Union and the Sarre River crossings there. In this plan it was intended that CCA would advance on the right, pass through the 26th Division, attack northeast along the valley of the Petite Seille, bypass Morhange, and strike out along the Bénestroff–Francaltroff road. CCB meanwhile would circle to the north of the Morhange plateau, in order to free the one good road through the valley of the Petite Seille for CCA, and capture the vital road center at Morhange. Both combat commands would have to contend with the lack of hard-surfaced roads in the area. As a result the routes finally followed consisted of a series of zigzags and cutbacks—the whole further complicated, as events showed, by the movement of supply and transport for the infantry divisions on these same roads.

On 9 November CCB (Brig. Gen. H. E. Dager) jumped off through the 35th Division bridgehead.[18] The following day CCA entered the attack, Colonel Abrams[19] passing his lead column (Major Hunter) through the 104th Infantry, which was fighting the rear guard of the *559th* near Morville. Hunter's column moved slowly, since even the limited enemy resistance encountered at road blocks along the way caused delay and confusion. Maneuver generally was impossible. Tanks and trucks that went off the black-top surface of the main highway had to be winched out of the quagmire. Hunter's tanks drove through Hampont before dark on 10 November, but CCA's second column (Lt. Col. Delk M. Oden) was unable to make a start along the crowded roadway and did not reach Hampont until the close of the next day.

Hunter's column fought its way toward Conthil on 11 November but ran into serious difficulty south of the village of Haboudange, where a battalion of the *361st VG Division* and the *111th Flak Battalion* had assembled in preparation for a counterattack to regain contact with the retreating *559th*.[20]

[18] The CCB attack is treated in the section on the 35th Division.

[19] Col. B. C. Clarke, who had led CCA during the September tank battles, had been assigned to the 7th Armored Division.

[20] *Army Group G KTB Anlagen*, 10 Nov 44.

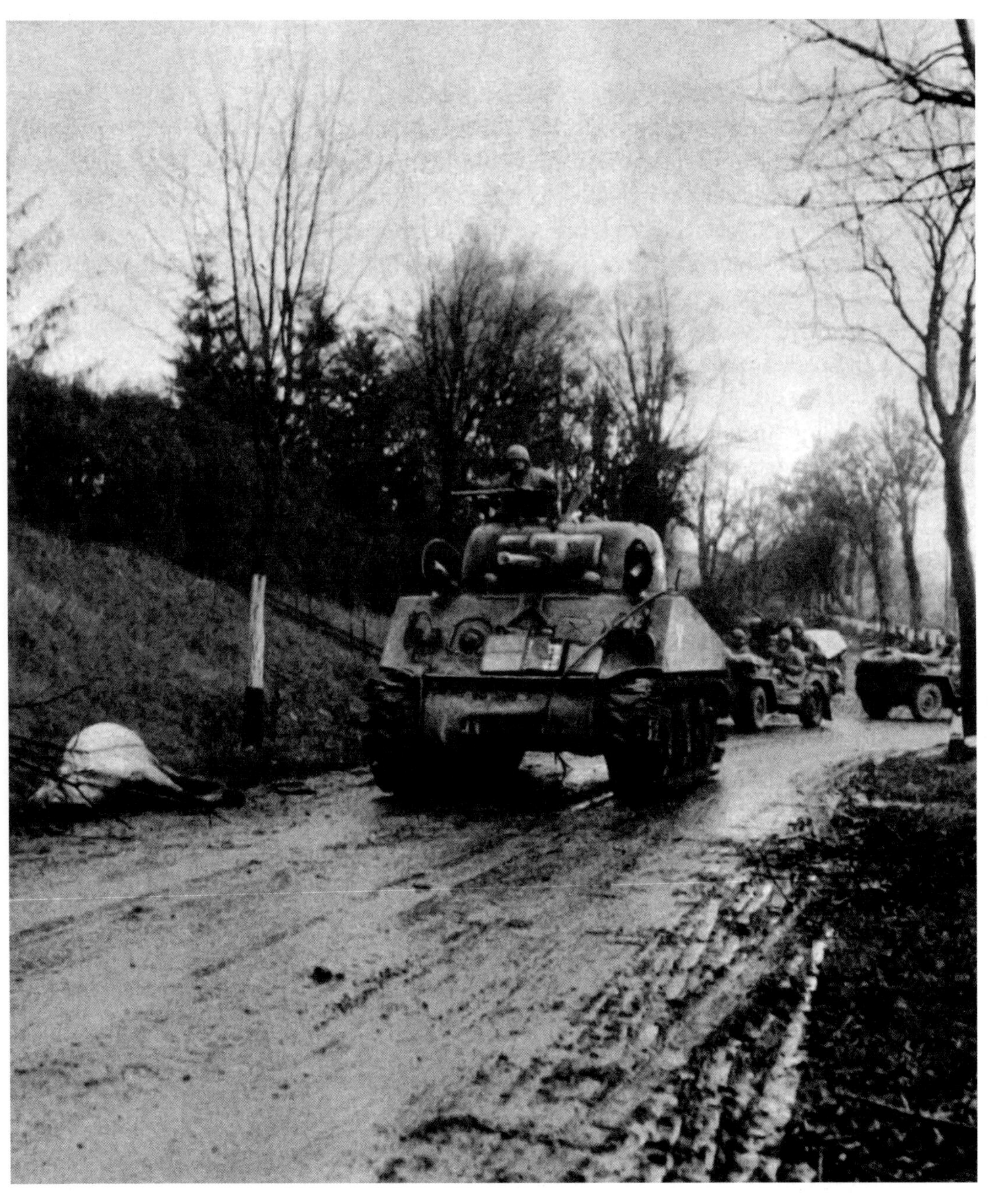

TASK FORCE ODEN LEAVING CHATEAU-SALINS, *on the morning of 11 November.*

At this point the road passed through a narrow defile formed by the river on one side and a railroad embankment on the other. As the column entered the defile hidden German dual purpose guns opened fire. The leading tanks were knocked out, blocking the road and bringing the column to a halt. Four American officers were killed, one after another, as they went forward to locate the enemy gun positions. Finally Hunter turned the column back and continued the move by a side road, bivouacking that night between Conthil and Rodalbe, while two companies of the 104th Infantry outposted the latter village. Progress had been slow this day, impeded by the German antitank guns and minor tank sorties, but Hunter's column had destroyed fourteen enemy guns and three tanks—although at considerable cost in American dead and wounded.[21]

The next morning Oden's column drew abreast of Hunter, with the 2d Battalion of the 104th Infantry (the regiment was now commanded by Lt. Col. R. A. Palladino) following in support. Oden turned off the main road and took Hill 337, southeast of Lidrezing, a commanding height that overlooked the enemy positions along the path of advance eastward. About noon Hunter's column reached Rodalbe, which had been occupied the previous evening by K and L Companies of the 3d Battalion (Lt. Col. H. G. Donaldson), and started north toward Bermering with the intention of cutting off the troops of the *559th VG Division* now retreating in front of CCB and the 35th Division. However, the enemy had had enough time to prepare some defense and the road north of Rodalbe had been thoroughly mined. While the tanks of the 37th Tank Battalion were trying to maneuver off the road in order to avoid the mines, a number became hopelessly mired and an easy target for the German guns which opened up from the north and from the Pfaffenforst woods. Hunter's column was forced to fall back under the rain of shells and took cover in the Bois de Conthil, about a thousand yards west of Rodalbe.

The enemy was ready to capitalize on the thin, elongated outpost line held by the 104th Infantry. On 10 November Balck finally had committed his armored reserve, the *11th Panzer Division*, against the left and center of the XII Corps, and by 12 November the German tanks were in action along a 12-mile front. The width of this front made any linear defense impossible and Wietersheim was forced to rely on a mobile defense, counterattacking wherever

[21] 4th Armd Div AAR, 11 Nov 44.

TO BERMERING
TO CONTHIL
RODALBE

opportunity availed. Wietersheim had sent his reconnaissance battalion, ten Panther tanks, and a battalion of the *110th Panzer Grenadier Regiment* to support the elements of the *559th VG Division* in the Rodalbe sector and restore the connection between the *XIII SS Corps* and the *LXXXIX Corps*. This combined force unleashed a full-scale counterattack on the heels of Hunter's withdrawal. The American artillery broke up the first attack aimed at Rodalbe on the afternoon of 12 November; but back to the west the enemy surrounded two companies of the 1st Battalion of the 104th in the neighborhood of Conthil—only to lose his intended prey when the Americans fought their way out of the trap.

The next morning the Germans launched an infantry attack against the 3d Battalion troops in Rodalbe but were repulsed. Just before dusk the enemy returned to the attack after extremely accurate counterbattery fire had effectively neutralized the American artillery. The German grenadiers pushed into the town from all sides and their tanks followed down the Bermering road. A 28-man patrol from the 2d Battalion, 104th, succeeded in entering the town with orders for the 3d Battalion troops to withdraw, but it was too late. The 2d Battalion patrol became engulfed in the fight and only one officer and three men returned to report the fate of the Rodalbe force. Company I, the regimental reserve, by this time reduced to twenty-three men, tried to force a way through to relieve the trapped companies; but the German tanks now held all the entrances to Rodalbe. West of the village Panther tanks, mines, and antitank guns barricaded the highway against an attack by the American tank battalion in the Bois de Conthil. Actually the mud and the darkness prevented any such intervention. Inside the village the American infantry took refuge in cellars and attempted to make a stand, but civilians pointed out their hiding places to the enemy tankers who blasted them with high explosives at short range. A few Americans escaped during the night; two officers successfully led thirty men of M Company back to the American lines. But some two hundred officers and men were lost in Rodalbe, although a handful of survivors were found in hiding when the village finally was reentered on the morning of 18 November.[22]

The reverses suffered on 12 November brought CCA and the 104th Infantry to a halt. Hunter's force was placed in reserve, while waiting for new

[22] 4th Armd Div AAR, 12 Nov 44; Hist Div Combat Interviews; 26th Div G–3 Jnl. The 104th regimental journal for this period is missing. Much valuable information has been supplied by Col. Ralph A. Palladino in a letter to the Historical Division, 20 September 1947. See also CCA AAR, 12–13 Nov 44.

tanks to replace those lost by the 37th Tank Battalion, and Oden detached a task force which recaptured Conthil and opened the main supply route back through the valley. The 104th Infantry, now badly understrength, took up positions along the arc made by the Conthil–Lidrezing road. This whole line formed a salient in which the weakened 104th Infantry "stuck out like a sore thumb," with CCB and the infantry of the 35th Division on the left flank stepped back along the railroad line between Morhange and Baronville, and the balance of the 26th Division advancing slowly and painfully to the right and rear along the Koecking ridge.

The Fight for the Koecking Ridge[23]

Since the 101st Infantry had been badly cut up during the fight for Hill 310, General Paul committed the 328th Infantry in the center of the division zone to carry the main burden of clearing the forest atop the Koecking ridge. He added the 3d Battalion of the 101st Infantry to the left flank of the 328th in order to strengthen the attack. The woods ahead were mostly beech, still covered with leaves that gave the forest a dark and somber aspect even during the light of the short November days. Dense copses of fir trees within the forest formed cover for machine gun positions and for snipers. Mines, booby traps, barbed wire, and concrete pillboxes reinforced the old zigzag trench positions of World War I. Nor had the attackers escaped the mud; even on this plateau the forest floor had turned into a bog under the constant rain. There were numerous trails and clearings, but the most important avenues of advance were a steeply banked east-west road, which traversed the entire length of the forest, and a lateral road running from Conthil to Dieuze, which had been prepared by the Germans as a reserve battle position. The enemy force there deployed to meet the 328th was small, consisting of the *43d Machine Gun Battalion* and the *2d Battalion* of the *1119th Regiment* (some elements of the *553d VG Division* had been taken over by the *361st VG Division*). Nevertheless, these units were veterans, skilled woods fighters, and well entrenched on ground with which they were familiar.

The 328th Infantry started east through the forest on the morning of 12 November and at first encountered little opposition. Shortly after noon the advancing skirmish line reached an indentation in the woods made by a large

[23] Historical Division Combat Interviews for this series of actions by the 26th Division are very complete. See also 26th Div AAR, and regimental journals.

clearing around Berange Farm. Here small arms fire from German pillboxes, reinforced by a very accurate artillery concentration, brought the advance to an abrupt halt and wounded the regimental commander, Colonel Jacobs. The 2d Battalion, which had reached another large quadrangular opening in the woods southeast of Berange Farm, was hit by a sudden hail of mortar fire as it entered the clearing. Many were killed, including the battalion commander, Maj. R. J. Servatius, who had taken over the battalion only the night before. The Americans rallied all along the line, however, and by 1530 the German defenders had been driven back. The strong point at Berange Farm was cleared after 120 rounds of artillery were poured in on the farm buildings.

Now the night turned cold and snow fell on the foxholes in the sodden forest. The infantry had left their blankets behind during the attack. After the day of severe fighting, exposure also took its toll.

South of the woods the 1st Battalion of the 101st embarked on an attack to take St. Médard. Here the open ground was swept by cross fire from the edge of the forest and from the enemy guns at Dieuze, which for three hours shelled the attack positions of the 101st and inflicted severe losses. General Paul then called off the 101st advance until the 328th could outflank the St. Médard position from the north.

On 13 November the German batteries in Dieuze became even more active, and the 328th, advancing along the east-west road, found itself under almost constant shelling. Early in the day the advance was slowed down by fire from automatic weapons sited in the underbrush. Tanks and tank destroyers advancing along the east-west road gradually blasted the Germans out of the woods on either side and by nightfall the skirmish line was abreast of the lateral highway. The progress of the 328th had carried it well ahead of the 101st (—), still held up at St. Médard and Haraucourt, and the 328th found enemy pressure increasing on its exposed right flank. The 26th Division was slowing down, with its rifle companies much below strength and its flanks contained by a stubborn enemy. The 101st Infantry had just received some 700 replacements, but it would require time for so many new officers and men to learn their business. The 328th Infantry had lost many battle casualties in the forest fighting, but exposure had claimed even more victims: over five hundred men were evacuated as trench foot and exposure cases in the first four days of the operation. The 104th was even weaker. Its rifle companies averaged about fifty men; in the 1st Battalion some company rosters showed only eight to fifteen effectives. Said an officer of the 104th: "All through this I think we were taking a worse beating than the Jerries. They fought a delaying action, all the way. When things got too tough they could withdraw to their next defense line. And when we sat for awhile, they pounded us."

This bitter fighting had been done at high cost to the enemy as well. The weak German battalions, although reinforced by the *2d Battalion* of the *953d Regiment* and a Luftwaffe engineer battalion, could hold no position for any great length of time. On 14 November CCA made a sweep through the Bois de Kerperche, the northeastern appendage of the Koecking woods, and this pressure on the German flank and rear helped pry loose the enemy grip on the Koecking ridge. The 328th, reinforced by the 3d Battalion, 101st, put its weight into an attack on 15 and 16 November which drove straight through to the eastern edge of the woods. Little fighting was involved, for most of the enemy had withdrawn on the night of 14–15 November. At the same time the 101st Infantry and 2d Cavalry Group pushed toward Dieuze, following the enemy who were now in full retreat. On 17 November the 26th Infantry Division regrouped, parceled out new batches of replacements to the 104th Infantry, issued dry clothing, and prepared to attack the next German position.

Meanwhile the enemy undertook a general withdrawal in front of the 26th Division; concurrently Balck shifted the bulk of the German artillery, which had played so important a role, northward for use against the XII Corps left and center. The new enemy line, facing CCA and the 26th Division, followed the railroad spur between Bénestroff—an important railroad junction east of Rodalbe—and Dieuze. This position had little to offer in natural capabilities for defense, except on the north where woods and hills masked Bénestroff. But solid contact had again been established on the right with the *11th Panzer Division.*

Task Force Oden Attacks Guébling

Colonel Oden's column, CCA, 4th Armored Division, made the initial attempt to penetrate the new German position between Bénestroff and Dieuze. Oden's objective was Marimont-lès-Bénestroff, a crossroads village about one and a half miles southeast of Bénestroff. A passable road led out of the

GUEBLING. *Circles indicate wreckage of German tanks.*

Koecking woods through Bourgaltroff to Marimont, avoiding the hills and woods around Bénestroff. This road intersected the German line at the village of Guébling, about four miles north of Dieuze, which would be the scene of the first American assault.

Leaving Hunter's column to cover the exposed flank and rear of CCA, Oden's column, divided into two task forces, struck out from an assembly area near Hill 337 at first light on the morning of 14 November. Task Force West skirted the Bois de Kerperche and moved by a secondary road southeast toward Guébling. Task Force McKone took a route directly through the woods, which had not yet been cleared of the enemy by the advance of the 328th Infantry, but found the forest road so heavily mined that it was forced to turn back. About 0845 Major West's force encountered six Panther tanks which had taken position among the buildings at Kutzeling Farm on the road to Guébling. These tanks belonged to a detachment of ten Panthers that General Wietersheim had dispatched from the *15th Panzer Regiment* as a roving counterattack formation. For nearly six hours the German tanks fought a stubborn rear guard action along the road to Guébling, using the long range of their high-velocity 75-mm. guns to keep the Americans at bay. After much maneuvering at Kutzeling Farm, West's tanks closed in and disabled three of the Panthers. The rest escaped under a smoke screen. Later in the day five Panthers made a stand just west of the railroad, where a corkscrew road out of the forest dipped abruptly toward Guébling. Again the Panthers showed themselves impervious to long-range fire from the American M-4's and supporting 105-mm. howitzers, and again maneuver was used to bring the Panthers within killing range. Fortunately, the German tanks were so closely hemmed in by their own mine fields as to be virtually frozen in position. Snow and rain precluded an air strike by the fighter-bombers, but finally an artillery plane managed to go aloft and adjust fire for the 155-mm. howitzers of the 191st Field Artillery Battalion. This fire forced the Panthers to close their hatches, and A Company of the 35th Tank Battalion charged in on the flanks of the partially blinded Germans. Leading the attack, 1st Lt. Arthur L. Sell closed within fifty yards of two Panthers and destroyed them, although two of his crew were killed, two seriously wounded, and his own tank was knocked out.[24] Sell's companion tanks finished off the remaining Panthers, and as the afternoon drew to a close Task Force West rolled into Guébling.

[24] Lieutenant Sell subsequently received the DSC.

The village itself was quickly secured, but the short November day gave no time for the armored infantry to take the high ground and the German observation posts that lay beyond.

Next morning about 0300 three gasoline trucks came into the village to refuel the task force. The sound of movement inside Guébling reached the enemy observation posts and brought on the worst shelling the American troops had yet experienced. The gasoline trucks were destroyed and several tanks and other vehicles were damaged. Early in the morning Task Force McKone arrived to strengthen the detachment in Guébling, and at daylight the 10th Armored Infantry Battalion was thrown into an attack to clear the high ground beyond the village. The armored infantry pushed the attack with vigor and determination but were beaten back by the German gunners. American counterbattery fire failed to subdue the enemy batteries, the guns shooting blindly into a curtain of snow and rain.

About noon the 4th Armored Division commander ordered Colonel Oden to withdraw from the precarious position in Guébling and return to the original assembly area at Hill 337. Oden evacuated his wounded, destroyed his damaged vehicles, and gave the order to withdraw. By this time the German guns had ranged in on the exit road running back to the west and the Americans were forced to run a 1,500-yard gauntlet of exploding shells, with only the cover provided by a smoke screen. Oden's command finally extricated itself, suffering "severe losses" in the process, and rejoined the 26th Infantry Division. This venture had cost the armor heavily—the 35th Tank Battalion had only fifteen tanks fit for battle—and on 16 November General Wood gave orders putting an end to independent attacks by elements of the 4th Armored Division.[25]

The Attack by the XII Corps Center

On the eve of the November offensive the 35th Infantry Division was deployed with the 134th Infantry (Col. B. B. Miltonberger) on the right, holding the Forêt de Grémecey, and the 137th Infantry (Col. W. S. Murray) on the left, aligned along the ridges running from the Forêt de Grémecey to the 80th Division boundary northwest of Ajoncourt. At H Hour on 8 November the 320th Infantry (Col. B. A. Byrne) was scheduled to pass through

[25] See CCA Jnl, for this action. Seventeen members of the 10th Armored Infantry Battalion won the Silver Star for their part in the Guébling fight.

the lines of the 134th Infantry, the latter going into division reserve while the 320th made the attack. (*Map XXVIII*) As elsewhere in the XII Corps no detailed plan had been laid down for the division scheme of maneuver except to set a line through Laneuveville-en-Saulnois, Fonteny, and the southwestern section of the Forêt de Château-Salins as the initial objective. Once the 35th Division had achieved a hold on the terminus of the Morhange plateau and the 26th Division had broken through the enemy on the right, the entrance to the valley of Petite Seille would be open for a thrust by CCA, 4th Armored Division. CCB, assigned to work with the 35th Division, was to pass through the attacking infantry as quickly as possible and advance toward Morhange, while the infantry followed to take over successive objectives softened up by the armor. General Eddy also foresaw some possibility that the 6th Armored Division, teamed with the 80th Division on the left, might find a weak spot in the German line and ordered General Baade to put his reserve regiment in trucks, prepared to exploit a break-through by either the 6th Armored Division or CCB of the 4th.

The rain had been pouring down steadily for five hours by 0600 (H Hour) of 8 November, flooding the roads and footpaths along which the 320th Infantry was moving to its line of departure. Before day broke and the line of departure was reached, the assault troops on the right already were tired and gaps appeared in the ranks as stragglers fell behind. However, most of the formations slated to make the attack were able to jump off close to schedule.

The 137th Infantry, on the division left, had as its mission to establish a bridgehead across the Osson Creek and make a quick jab at Laneuveville, some four miles distant, in order to cut the main highway between Château-Salins and Metz. In September, when the 35th Division had fought along its banks, the Osson had been no more than a small stream. Now the flood waters of the sluggish Seille had backed into the creek, increasing its width to about fifty yards and making it a real barrier. The engineers had prepared for this obstacle, however, and by 1040 the attackers had put a prefabricated bridge across south of Jallaucourt. Two hours later the 1st Battalion of the 137th, supported by tanks of the 737th Tank Battalion, was in the shell-torn village itself. The enemy soldiers froze in their places at sight of the tanks and surrendered. A second bridge opened the road into Malaucourt, and shortly after 1600 two companies of the 2d Battalion, supported by tanks, took the village. By midnight the 137th Infantry was in position on the ground rising east of the two villages, having taken some two hundred prisoners (mostly from the *1125th Regiment* of the *559th VG Division*) at a cost of eighty-two casualties.[26]

On the right wing of the 35th Division the 320th Infantry attacked to secure a foothold in the Forêt de Château-Salins on the Morhange plateau, in conjunction with the 26th Division attempt to gain a position on the Koecking ridge. The only road that led from the 35th Division area into the Forêt de Château-Salins was blocked by the German possession of Fresnes, about 1,200 yards north of the 35th Division lines. Until Fresnes was taken and the road eastward cleared, no tanks could be used in support of the 320th Infantry attack on the forest, and supply had to be made by carrying parties wallowing up to their knees in mud. Apparently the Americans had hoped to clear Fresnes by a quick stroke and thus open the vital roadway in time to send the tanks into the forest edge in conjunction with the infantry assault. But the German hold on Fresnes was far more tenacious than on the villages in front of the 137th Infantry. Fresnes had been an important supply and communications center for the enemy in earlier operations and had received constant and heavy shelling by the American artillery. As a result the German garrison, estimated to be a battalion, had dug in deep and was little disturbed by the heavy shelling on the morning of 8 November. When the fire lifted, the garrison rose to meet the American attack. The 3d Battalion, 320th Infantry, and a company of tanks succeeded in entering Fresnes after a bitter fight; but all during the night and for part of the next day the German defenders fought on, barring the road into the forest.

While the 3d Battalion hammered at Fresnes, the 2d Battalion, on its right, began a frontal attack toward the western extension of the Forêt de Château-Salins known as the Bois d'Amélécourt—only to suffer a series of costly mishaps in this first day of the offensive. The assault troops of the 320th Infantry had had to pass through the lines of the 134th Infantry during the night of 7–8 November. This move, difficult enough under favorable conditions, was further complicated by the seas of mud, and the two companies leading the attack arrived on the line of departure at the northeast edge of the Forêt de Grémecey a half hour late, their rifle strength already depleted by stragglers who had fallen out along the way or been lost in the woods.[27]

[26] 137th Inf AAR, Nov 44. See also Hist Div Combat Interviews and 35th Div AAR, Nov 44.

[27] Interv with CO, 2d Bn, 320th Inf (Hist Combat Interviews). The 2d Battalion had to march nearly a mile to reach its line of departure.

When the 2d Battalion finally moved into the attack, daylight already had come and the smoke screen which had been fired for ten minutes before daylight was beginning to dissipate—leaving little cover as the companies started to cross some two thousand yards of muddy ground. The Bois d'Amélécourt was held by a battalion of the *1127th Regiment*, whose northern flank in turn was covered by a battalion from the *1125th Regiment*. The Germans in the woods held a strong position on the higher ground and were supported by three infantry howitzers that had been wheeled forward to the tree line so as to cover the open ground over which the Americans had to attack. In addition the highway passing in front of the woods had been wired and mined as a forward defense position, and was further strengthened with machine guns sited in enfilade.

The Americans crossed the first few hundred yards of open ground without drawing much fire. Company G, on the left, reached the enemy outpost line, which here followed a railroad embankment, and took some forty Germans from their foxholes. Beyond the railroad F Company drew abreast of G Company and the two started toward the woods. When the first assault wave reached the wire along the highway the guns and mortars in the woods opened fire, while the German machine guns swept the American right flank. Under this hot fire Company F fell back, until rallied by a battalion staff officer. Company E, the reserve, attempted to intervene but also was repelled by the German fire. Company G, somewhat protected by a slight rise, reached the edge of the woods and hurriedly dug in. During the afternoon the two rifle companies still outside the woods made a second effort. In the midst of the assault the American batteries firing smoke in support of the infantry ran out of smoke shells, and as the smoke screen blew away a fusillade poured in from the German lines. Again the attack was brought to a halt and the two companies withdrew to the cover of the railroad embankment. The 2d Battalion had suffered severely but was saved from complete destruction by the mud, which absorbed shell fragments and in which the German shells, fitted with impact fuses, often failed to explode.

In the late afternoon Colonel Byrne ordered the 1st Battalion of the 320th Infantry up from reserve to close the gap between Fresnes and the Bois d'Amélécourt. Mine fields slowed down the battalion, however, and when darkness fell it halted at the Fresnes road. During the night of 8–9 November the 3d Battalion mopped up the enemy still holding on around Fresnes. The

2d Battalion sent carrying parties back to evacuate the wounded and bring up ammunition, which had run low during the fire fight in the afternoon. This still further depleted the rifle strength opposite the enemy; indeed it is characteristic of most of the woods fighting in November that a considerable part of the roster of every unit had to be detached from the fire line to keep communications to the rear functioning over terrain where vehicles could not be used.

When morning arrived on the second day of the battle the engineers cleared the mines from the road east of Fresnes and the 1st Battalion marched to the aid of the 2d Battalion. Company C, 737th Tank Battalion, which had played a major role at Fresnes, followed behind the infantry, although it was seriously crippled and had lost six of its tanks in the fight for the village. Meanwhile the 2d Battalion resumed the attack on the Bois d'Amélécourt. Two of the troublesome German howitzers had been knocked out by the American artillery, but the enemy machine guns still were in position to rake the American flank. Once again the attack was broken by the withering fire and this time the dispirited infantry could not be induced to return to the assault. About 1000 the tanks from Fresnes arrived on the scene. Their appearance abruptly shifted the balance against the enemy. The tank gunners quickly destroyed the German machine gun nests and drove the enemy back from the edge of the woods, putting the 1st and 2d Battalions inside the tree line.[28]

Once inside the woods, however, the infantry found the enemy cleverly entrenched and determined to fight for every yard of ground. Barbed wire, prepared lanes of fire, dugouts roofed with concrete and sod, foxholes, and breastworks improvised from corded wood provided an intricate net of field works facing the attackers wherever they turned. Once again the German grenadier proved himself an experienced and resourceful woods fighter, clinging obstinately to each position and closing to fire rifle grenades and even antitank grenades point blank at the American infantry. Significant of the stubbornness with which the defense was conducted, the enemy left more dead than prisoners in American hands.[29]

On the north flank of the 35th Division the rapid advance made by the 137th on the first day of the attack offered an opening for armored exploita-

[28] The account of the fight to gain a footing in the woods has been taken from interviews with the commanding officers of the 1st and 2d Battalions, 320th Infantry (Hist Div Combat Interviews). See also 320th Inf AAR and Jnl.

[29] The advance by the 320th Infantry is covered fully by the regimental journal and Historical Division Combat Interviews.

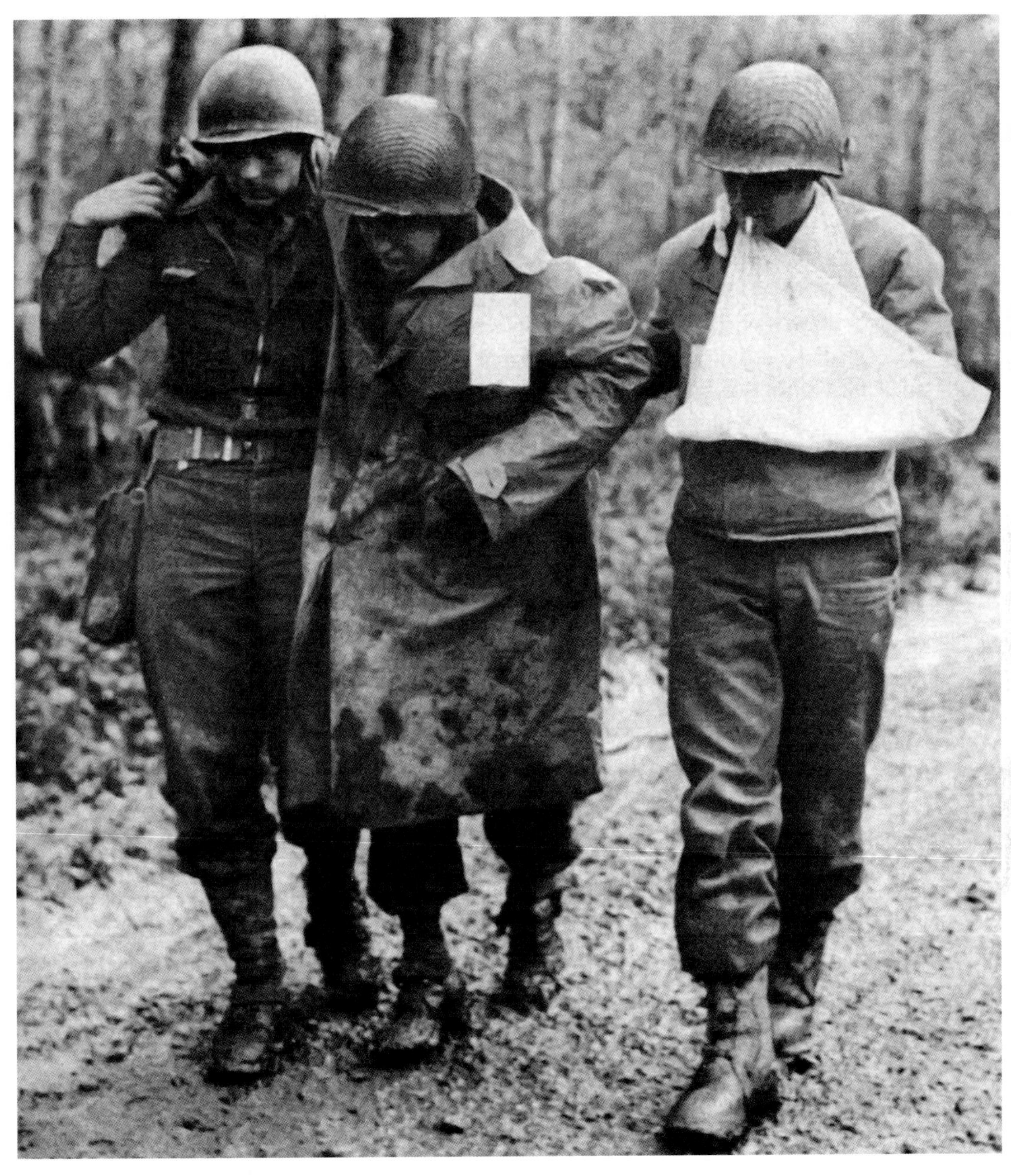

WOUNDED SOLDIER HELPED TO AID STATION, *after fighting in the Forêt de Grémecey.*

tion. General Eddy committed CCB, 4th Armored Division, on the morning of 9 November, sending it wheeling north of the Forêt de Château-Salins in a drive toward Morhange. General Dager, CCB commander, followed the usual practice of the division and attacked in two columns: the left column (Maj. Thomas G. Churchill) passed through the 137th near Malaucourt; the right column (Lt. Col. Alfred A. Mayback) struck into the open near Jallaucourt. The enemy had not recovered from the brusque attack made by the American infantry on the previous day and could present little in the way of a co-ordinated defense against the armored columns. Churchill's column was able to stick to the highway, though five medium tanks were lost to mines, and reached the village of Hannocourt. Here the enemy had emplaced a few antitank pieces to cover the road, but the 510th Squadron of the XIX TAC, flying cover over the American tanks, blasted the German gun positions with fragmentation bombs and napalm. Churchill's advance uncovered the southern flank of the *48th Division* position at Delme Ridge—directly in front of the 80th Infantry Division—and enabled the 137th Infantry to capture the village of Delme, an attack made in conjunction with the 80th Division assault against the ridge itself.[30]

On the right Colonel Mayback's column met much stiffer opposition but moved speedily ahead despite concrete road blocks, antitank gunfire, and the necessity of having to halt and clear German foxhole chains alongside the road. At first the troops of the *559th* were slow to react to the appearance of the American armor deep inside their lines. At Oriocourt the 1st Battalion of the 137th Infantry, following close behind the tanks, bagged a battery of field guns and 150 prisoners. At Laneuveville the American tanks overran the enemy guns before the startled crews could get the covers off their pieces. The supporting infantry captured 445 prisoners with only slight losses in their own ranks. While the infantry mopped up in Laneuveville Mayback's armored column moved east toward the village of Fonteny. In midafternoon the American advance guard had just begun to descend the road into the draw where the village lay when suddenly enemy guns opened fire from positions on a hill northeast of Fonteny and from the Forêt de Château-Salins. The Americans had run into a hornet's nest: this was a prepared secondary position which had been heavily armed in early November by guns from the *9th*

[30] Captured German officers later cited the operations around Delme Ridge as an example of fine co-operation between armor and infantry.

TASK FORCE CHURCHILL CROSSING THE SEILLE RIVER

Flak Division.[31] Having brought the column to a halt the enemy struck with a detachment of tanks against the American flank. A lieutenant and a small party of armored infantrymen equipped with bazookas drove off the German tanks, though nearly all of the little detachment were killed or wounded during the fight.

Meanwhile, Colonel Mayback sent forward C Company, 37th Tank Battalion, to help the advance guard. The main body of the column had been somewhat protected by a small rise of ground, but the moment the company of medium tanks crossed the sky line three tanks were knocked out. When C Company attempted to deploy off the road the tanks bogged down, presenting more or less a series of sitting targets for the German gunners. Nevertheless C Company inflicted considerable damage on the German batteries (it was later estimated that the tanks had put thirty German guns out of action) and continued the duel until the ammunition in the tanks was expended. As night

[31] MS #A-972 (Muehlen).

fell Colonel Mayback ordered his forward elements to withdraw behind the ground mask southwest of the village. The American losses, mostly sustained in the fight outside of Fonteny, had been heavy: fifteen tanks, ten half-tracks, and three assault guns. But the column had made an advance of some four miles into enemy territory and had broken a way for the infantry.[32]

When word of the fight at Fonteny reached General Dager the CCB commander ordered Mayback to hold up his advance and wait for reinforcements from Churchill's column, bivouacked near Hannocourt. The marching American infantry was still about five miles behind the armored columns. During the night of 9–10 November enemy infantry and tanks from the *11th Panzer Division* cut in behind Churchill's force and occupied the village of Viviers, thus severing the only usable road to Fonteny. This German force was fairly strong, including troops of the *43d Fortress Battalion* and the *110th Panzer Grenadier Regiment*, as well as a large number of self-propelled guns. The fight to clear the enemy from Viviers on 10 November developed into a series of confused actions. The 22d Armored Field Artillery Battalion, located on Hill 260, halfway between Viviers and Hannocourt, entered upon an old-fashioned artillery duel with some batteries of the *401st Volks Artillery Corps* to the north which were harassing Churchill's column. The American tanks attempted to open the road to Viviers but were forced off the highway by the enemy antitank guns and mired down in the boggy fields.[33] The 2d Battalion, 137th Infantry, which had come up from the west, then carried the attack into Viviers in a battle that continued through the entire afternoon.[34] At dusk the infantry secured a firm hold on the village, after a heavy shelling had somewhat softened up the enemy garrison. More than one hundred dead Germans were counted in the streets and houses and some fifty surrendered, but a small and desperate rear guard detachment held on in the burning village through most of the night.

The 35th Division fought a punishing battle all along its front on 10 November and only slowly eased the enemy pressure on CCB. While the 2d Battalion of the 137th Infantry attacked at Viviers, other elements of the regiment pushed past Laneuveville and joined Mayback's column west of

[32] CCB AAR, Nov 44.

[33] However, the Germans let an American ambulance pass through Viviers without a shot being fired.

[34] Sgt. Vernon L. Allison, F Company, 137th Infantry, was awarded the DSC for destroying two German machine guns, which were firing on his platoon, and for the capture of thirty prisoners.

Fonteny, there extending the flanks of the 51st Armored Infantry Battalion which had been thrown out as a screen for the armor. During the day the Germans directed one small tank attack against Mayback's command, but this was repelled handily by the American tank destroyers.

In the center of the division line the 320th Infantry passed from the Bois d'Amélécourt and continued the fight in the mazes of the Forêt de Château-Salins, its men soaked to the skin and harassed day and night by enemy detachments that slipped through the woods like Indians in raids on the flanks and rear. German reinforcements were coming in from the *1126th Regiment* and the *110th Panzer Grenadier Regiment*, bringing the numbers on each side to something approaching equality. The 3d Battalion relieved the 2d Battalion, as the fighting strength of the latter diminished, but even when placed in reserve the tired American infantry had to battle heavily armed German patrols sneaking through the fragmentary front lines. General Baade had put the 134th Infantry in on the right of the 320th Infantry, on 9 November, with the mission of clearing the eastern edge of the Forêt de Château-Salins and covering the division's flank. Here, too, the Germans stubbornly contested the ground; by the night of 10 November the regiment still was short of Gerbécourt, only a third of the way alongside the forest.

Resistance in the Forêt de Château-Salins began to slacken on 11 November, and during the afternoon the *559th* commenced a general withdrawal toward a line between Frémery and Dalhain, giving the fighter-bombers an appetizing target as the columns of infantry and horse-drawn artillery debouched into the open. The 365th Squadron destroyed fifty-eight guns and vehicles in a single sweep. No continuous front line remained—only German rear guard detachments holding out grimly at points of vantage. Their stand, coupled with the miserable conditions of the roads and early darkness, made the 35th Division advance a slow affair. Both the 320th and 134th Infantry made some progress, but both were beset by the difficulty of getting food and ammunition forward through the rivers of mud.[35]

On the left of the division, resistance briefly increased in front of CCB and the 137th Infantry, and shellfire poured in as the German artillery sought to halt the American advance long enough to permit the troops in the Forêt de Château-Salins to escape. Early in the day a counterattack was thrown at

[35] Carrying parties taking rations to the 1st Battalion of the 320th, for example, started forward at ten o'clock in the evening but did not reach the battalion until nine hours later.

Churchill's force, which had been ordered to continue toward Morhange, only to be dispersed by the armored artillery. During the day the column destroyed fourteen antitank guns yet was unable to fight its way clear of the Bois de Serres, through which the main roads to Morhange passed. The Mayback column made an attempt to drive straight through Fonteny but was beaten back by direct antitank fire at close range. Meanwhile the 1st Battalion, 137th Infantry, and a tank company had come up to aid in the assault and another attempt was made with an attack in deployed order. Shortly after noon the Americans entered the little village, and the fight continued from house to house all during the afternoon and through most of the night. During this action Colonel Mayback and Lt. Col. William L. Shade, commanding officer of the 253d Field Artillery Battalion, were mortally wounded; command of the column passed to Maj. Harry R. Van Arnam. In the early morning hours of 12 November the *11th Panzer* detachment evacuated Fonteny, saving most of its guns and infantry but abandoning three Panther tanks.

The 3d Battalion of the 137th Infantry came up to relieve the 1st Battalion in Fonteny, the 2d Battalion of the regiment seized Faxe—thus reopening contact between the north and south columns of CCB—and the armor and infantry struck east to secure the entrance into the valley of the Nied Française, through which passed the route to Morhange. Before the day ended the American tanks reached the village of Oron, there seizing a bridge across the Nied Française. The retreating Germans had offered little co-ordinated or effective resistance, and over six hundred surrendered to CCB and the 137th Infantry.[36]

The German withdrawal on 12 November placed the 35th Division and CCB in position for a final drive against the outpost villages guarding the western approaches to Morhange. In the center the 320th Infantry finally cleared the Forêt de Château-Salins. The regiment was placed in reserve and the shivering, weary men given fresh clothing—the first dry apparel for most of them since the fight for the forest began. On the east flank the 134th Infantry advanced almost without opposition. General Baade finally ordered the regiment to a halt at Bellange, about three and a half miles southwest of Morhange, so that warm clothing and dry socks could be issued to the attacking troops. The week-long rain had come to an end, but this brought no relief to the soldier, for bitter cold followed. The XII Corps commander ordered

[36] CCB AAR, 12 Nov 44.

PRISONERS BEING MARCHED TO THE REAR, *after surrendering to Combat Command B on 12 November.*

that overshoes be returned to the troops—they had been discarded at the beginning of the offensive[37]—and extra blankets and heavy clothing were issued as quickly as they could be brought into the front lines. Winter warfare was about to begin.

The Drive toward Morhange

Any military map of Lorraine will show the importance of Morhange as a road center. In 1914 the control of Morhange gave the German armies a sally port from which to debouch into the Seille Basin. In November 1944 the forces driving northeastward out of the Seille Basin were forced to funnel, at least in part, through Morhange. But a map will reflect the difficulty of reaching Morhange in force except by an attack along the chain of ridges leading in from the west.

The drive toward Morhange began on 13 November. On the left CCB moved east along the valley of the Nied Française with the 137th Infantry close behind. Van Arnam's column, south of the river, though advancing slowly in the face of successive mine fields and blown bridges, at dark was astride a ridge north of Achain and less than three miles from Morhange. Churchill's column, which had crossed to the north bank of the Nied Française at Oron, advanced by road as far as Villers-sur-Nied. At this point the enemy had mined the highway so thoroughly that Churchill decided to take his command cross country. In the course of this maneuvering Company A of the 8th Tank Battalion worked its way to the rear of some German batteries covering the Villers-sur-Nied–Marthille road. The light tanks of the battalion pointed the target with tracer bullets; then the company of mediums rolled over the gun positions with its own pieces blazing. Taken completely by surprise the German crews were unable to bring their guns to bear, and in one blow the American tankers destroyed seven 88-mm. and eleven 75-mm. field pieces. Churchill's column laagered on a ridge north of Marthille not far from Van Arnam's column during the night of 13–14 November, and the engineers undertook the difficult and dangerous task of clearing the mines from the road to the rear.

[37] The XII Corps commander had ordered all "walking troops" to remove their overshoes at the beginning of the 8 November offensive. The infantry generally preferred to go into action without overshoes since they gave uncertain footing.

The next day CCB and a battalion of the 137th attacked the villages of Destry and Baronville, preparatory to flanking Morhange from the north in conjunction with a drive from the south and west by the bulk of the 35th Infantry Division. The attack was successful, although the enemy fought back doggedly until well into the night. Fresh German replacements, just arrived from Poland, here had entered the *559th VG Division* line with orders to hold until the last man. The journals of the American troops who opposed them at Destry and Baronville all speak of "extremely bitter resistance" ending only with the death or capture of the German grenadiers.

However, the plans for CCB to close on Morhange from the north and continue the drive to Sarreguemines were doomed by the weather, rather than enemy resistance. The rains resumed, the armor was road-bound, and the left flank of CCB was left hanging in the air along the Metz–Sarrebourg railroad. While engaged in futile attempts to maneuver off the roads CCB received orders from XII Corps headquarters on 15 November to hold up the attack. Two days later CCB moved south to join the rest of the 4th Armored Division in a drive through the Dieuze gap, thus ending seven days of what the combat command would later recall as a "heart break action." [38]

The pressure applied in the Morhange sector by the American armor had helped to render the new German defensive line untenable and may have weakened the enemy will to resist. But the final phase of the operation, that is, the frontal attack by the 35th Division in the direction of Morhange, cost the American infantry heavily. After a night of snow and bitter cold the 134th Infantry moved out on the morning of 13 November to clear the natural causeway along which the Château-Salins–Baronville road led into Morhange. The 3d Battalion, on the left, was ordered to take the section of the ridge line known as the Rougemont (later known to the Americans as "Bloody Hill") and then drive astride the highway to the northeast. The 3d Battalion was roughly handled, losing its commander, Lt. Col. Warren C. Wood, when he was wounded and suffering severe losses during the advance across the valley floor and up the slopes of Bloody Hill, an advance in which each rifleman was outlined as a perfect target against the fresh white snow. Nonetheless the

[38] German intelligence believed that the 4th Armored Division had been withdrawn from the Third Army front because of crippling losses. *Army Group G KTB*, 17 Nov 44. Although the XX Corps was closing in on Metz at this time, Rundstedt was not particularly concerned about an American break-through in the Metz sector but instead feared an American penetration via Sarreguemines. *Army Group G KTB*, 15 Nov 44.

battalion took the objective and wheeled toward Morhange, bypassing Achain where the 2d Battalion was heavily engaged.

The 2d Battalion had jumped off at Bellange on the morning of 13 November and there begun an advance up the open valley with Achain as its objective. Three rifle companies took part in the 1,800-yard advance, under heavy fire from guns on Bloody Hill. The American casualties were severe; one company lost every officer before Achain was reached. About noon the assault wave hit the edge of the village, beginning a bitter fight that lasted for nearly ten hours. The American attack was pushed relentlessly, and ultimately the last of the German defenders were killed, captured, or driven in flight from the village. During the engagement Sgt. Junior J. Spurrier of Company G distinguished himself by making a lone sortie west of Achain while his comrades attacked east of the village. In the course of this one-man advance, Sergeant Spurrier killed twenty-five of the enemy and captured twenty-two. He subsequently was awarded the Congressional Medal of Honor. A total of 150 Germans surrendered in Achain, but the advance up the valley and the fight for the village cost the 2d Battalion 106 officers and men.

At Morhange the enemy troops—mostly from the *1127th Regiment*—found their position increasingly precarious as the American infantry and armor closed in on 14 November.[39] As early as 11 November the American 155-mm. guns and 8-inch howitzers had brought the town under fire, and on 14 November the 240-mm. howitzers joined the bombardment. During the night of the 14th, the 105-mm. howitzers were brought into play; one battalion (the 216th Field Artillery) fired 999 rounds into the town. On the morning of 15 November the *1127th* withdrew from the battered town and filed toward the northeast, blowing bridges and strewing mines in its wake.

In midafternoon the 35th Division reached the Metz–Sarrebourg railway. Here General Baade halted his troops to await new orders. The division had advanced twelve miles in eight days of hard fighting and had captured or destroyed fifty-three pieces of artillery—of 75-mm. caliber or larger—as well as twenty-six vehicles. The 137th Infantry, which had been in position to bag the most Germans, had taken over one thousand prisoners.[40] The 35th was given little rest, however, for on 17 November the corps commander ordered a resumption of the advance toward the Sarre River.

[39] In the advance near Pévange, south of Morhange, Pfc. Wilbur C. Pyle, C Company, 134th Infantry, made a lone attack in which he killed or captured the occupants of four successive foxholes. For this singlehanded battle he was awarded the DSC. Private Pyle was killed shortly after this action.

[40] 35th Div AAR, Nov 44.

The XII Corps Advance on the Left

At the beginning of the November offensive the 80th Infantry Division front extended from the XX Corps boundary line, west of Cheminot, southeast to Chenicourt, where the 35th Infantry Division sector began. The left and center of the 80th was posted along the west bank of the Seille River. But on the right wing the Germans still retained a foothold on the American side of the Seille in the re-entrant formed by a loop in the river north of Létricourt. (*Map XXIX*)

The regiments of the 80th Division, all committed on 8 November, were drawn up with the 317th, 318th, and 319th Infantry left to right. The main formations of the enemy force opposite the 80th Division were from the *48th Division*, whose zone ran from north of Malaucourt to north of Eply. In addition the left flank of the *17th SS Panzer Grenadier Division* abutted on the *48th Division*, with the result that some elements of the *38th SS Panzer Grenadier Regiment* faced the 317th Infantry.[41]

The 80th Division position placed it on the shortest and most direct axis for a drive toward the important communications center at Faulquemont (Falkenberg, as it is called in the XII Corps Field Orders). Therefore, the XII Corps plans for the 8 November offensive provided that the 80th Division should establish a bridgehead over the Seille, through which the 6th Armored Division could be passed, and that the armor should then attack toward Faulquemont. Once across the Seille River the 80th Division was scheduled to follow the armor, relieving the 6th Armored Division somewhere in the vicinity of Faulquemont.

The terrain in front of the 80th Division was somewhat less difficult than that in the center and on the right of the XII Corps zone of advance. The road system running northeast to Faulquemont was adequate, though the main highway—via Luppy and Han-sur-Nied—lay well off center in the division zone and confusingly close to the XX Corps boundary. However, the 80th Division did face a number of terrain obstacles, made more difficult than usual by the November rains and the mud. The first barrier was the Seille River, swollen grossly out of its ordinary channel. Next, the Delme Ridge rose to command the Seille Basin, covering so wide a portion of the 80th Division front that direct assault could hardly be avoided—although the ridge

[41] These dispositions are taken from the XII Corps After Action Report and the *OKH Gen. St. d. H.* situation maps.

could be turned from the 35th Division zone or by a narrow thrust along the XII Corps north boundary. Beyond lay the Nied Française, another flooded watercourse, which angled across the axis of advance. Southwest of Faulquemont this channel divided into the Nied Française proper and the Rotte; the latter stream then turned into an east-west channel. Of all these natural defense lines the Delme Ridge was believed by American intelligence to be most heavily fortified; for a month past 80th Division observers had watched the Germans busily digging and wiring on the heights.

At 0500 on 8 November the XII Corps artillery began firing in preparation for the Seille crossing, and shortly before H Hour the divisional artillery, tanks, tank destroyers, and infantry cannon companies joined to swell the barrage from positions about 3,000 yards west of the river.[42] At 0600 the main attack echelons of the three regiments jumped off and the battle for a bridgehead east of the Seille was begun.

The 319th Infantry, on the right, used its 1st Battalion to clear out the Seille loop between Abaucourt and Létricourt, and to take a crossing at Aulnois-sur-Seille—which was in American hands two hours after the attack began. In the center the 318th Infantry experienced some delay in crossing the river. Infantry footbridges, thrown across the Seille by the engineers early in the morning, were washed away in the flood waters and the bulk of the assault echelons had to be ferried across in assault boats. Once across the river the two leading battalions swung either side of Nomény, meeting sharp mortar fire as soon as they began the advance away from the river.[43] The 2d Battalion, on the left, sent troops into Nomény, which the Germans had fortified as a strong point at the river line. These elements of the battalion immediately became engaged in a hot fight which continued on into the following morning and cost over a hundred American casualties.[44] By that time supporting tanks were moving forward over heavy bridges and a company of mediums rolled into Nomény, ending the struggle for the village. The 317th Infantry, making the attack on the left on 8 November, put two bat-

[42] A very complete description of the 80th Division fire plan is contained in the Historical Division Combat Interviews.

[43] Capt. John B. Kelly, G Company, 318th Infantry, received the DSC for gallantry in this fight. He had received severe abdominal wounds while leading his company, but nonetheless went forward to an exposed position to direct artillery fire. Captain Kelly died shortly after from his wounds.

[44] For gallantry in this action Capt. Raymond G. Roy, 318th Infantry, received the DSC. Captain Roy had already distinguished himself as a daring combat leader during the fighting near Ste. Geneviève in mid-September.

talions across the Seille by footbridges, rubber assault craft, and fording. Using tactics similar to those employed at Nomény, the 1st and 3d circled Eply on the north and south, leaving the 2d Battalion, which was crossed behind the rest of the regiment, to clear the village itself.[45]

Late in the afternoon of 8 November the enemy began to react with artillery and small local counterattacks, this activity becoming most pronounced in front of the 317th Infantry whose advance had struck hard against the seam between the *38th SS Panzer Grenadier Regiment* and the *48th Division*. North of Eply field artillery brought up from the *17th SS* caught a company of the 317th just as it was digging in on the forward slope of Hill 237. During the shelling the company suffered many casualties and all of the company officers were killed. But the 317th got its revenge when, just at dusk, a company of German infantry—apparently moving to attack the 3d Battalion —unwittingly marched straight across the front of the 2d Battalion and was cut to pieces.

At dark on this first day the 80th Division had ten bridges across the Seille River and a sure footing on the enemy bank. Tactical surprise had been achieved, the enemy communications destroyed, and in the first hours of the attack the German artillery had been successfully neutralized. The American advance had carried far enough east of the Seille to roll back the south flank of the *38th SS Panzer Grenadier Regiment* in the direction of Metz and had cut through the forward lines of the *48th Division*. At Nomény the entrapped *1st Battalion, 126th Regiment*, was destroyed during the night of 8 November. The *1431st Fortress Battalion*, which had held the sector north and west of Nomény, also was overrun and almost completely erased.

On the morning of 9 November the *48th Division* rallied on Delme Ridge to stop the advance of the 80th Division. Delme Ridge was naturally a strong position and loomed large as a tactical problem for the Americans. General McBride's first intention had been to make a hook to the north end of the ridge with his center regiment, the 318th, which then would drive from north to south along the crest of the ridge and meet the 319th on the southern tip. The progress of the 318th on 9 November was impeded by the mud; as the morning advanced it appeared unlikely that the regiment would reach

[45] Sgt. Coleman S. Rogers, a medical aid man attached to the 317th, was wounded by artillery fire. Disregarding his own condition he dragged himself through the mud to another wounded man, then tried to carry the soldier out on his back. Rogers collapsed from loss of blood and was found some time later. He was awarded the DSC.

its objective. McBride decided to release his division reserve, a battalion of the 319th, and throw the right regiment into a frontal attack against the enemy defending the ridge. The 319th Infantry, supported by tanks that had crossed the river during the night and early morning, stormed up the heights, through little villages and terraced vineyards, sweeping past mine fields and over gun positions in which two battalions of captured Russian artillery had been emplaced. Fortunately the slopes were dry and provided good flotation for the American tanks, which easily disposed of the dug-in batteries.[46] The German mines, however, inflicted numerous casualties among the troops that moved on foot.

On the left the 317th Infantry took very heavy losses. Here the Germans made a stubborn stand and threw in the *1st Battalion* of the *37th SS Panzer Grenadier Regiment* to reinforce the line on the high ground north of Delme Ridge proper. In addition the 317th was forced to attack with its northern flank exposed, since the 5th Infantry Division of the XX Corps had not yet come up abreast of the XII Corps advance. During the day the 1st Battalion, 317th, advanced in front of the other battalions by a matter of some three thousand yards and ran into bitter fire from its front and flanks. By the following morning each of the three rifle companies in the 1st Battalion had been reduced to an average strength of fifty-five men. The 3d Battalion also was cut up badly during this attack. Nevertheless the 317th Infantry succeeded in taking all but the northern tip of the ridge line to its front.

Late in the afternoon of 9 November the 357th Squadron of the XIX TAC intervened in the battle at Delme Ridge and struck at the enemy on the reverse slopes and in the woods to the east. Meanwhile the three American battalions of medium and heavy artillery which had earlier pounded the enemy works on the ridge lifted their fire and began to beat the German rear areas. During the evening the 137th Infantry, attacking from the 35th Division zone, took the village of Delme, unhinging the German left and spiking down the right flank of the 80th Division advance. By this time the 5th Infantry Division had come up on the left, and the 80th was in position to mop up the last of the Delme line and continue the attack. The second day of the offensive had been highly successful. Most of the Delme Ridge position was in American hands. The *48th Division* had been badly beaten, as German reports show,

[46] 80th Div G–2 Jnl, 9 Nov 44.

and more than a thousand prisoners had been taken by the 80th Infantry Division.

The successes won by the infantry had made room for the armor, and while the 80th Division still was fighting at Delme Ridge, on 9 November, General Eddy ordered General Grow and his 6th Armored Division into the attack. The division was a veteran formation, at full strength, and highly confident as the result of its earlier successes in the Brittany peninsula and east of Nancy.[47] In late October some thought had been given to a maneuver in which both the 4th and 6th Armored Divisions would drive between Château-Salins and Delme Ridge. General Wood and General Grow had viewed this proposal with a skeptical eye. Later the XII Corps commander had considered using the 6th Armored to turn the north flank of the Delme Ridge position. But General Patton's decision for a rapid advance to cross the Sarre River and breach the West Wall had widened the scope of the 6th Armored mission. In the final plan—the result of much careful work in the corps and division headquarters—the 6th Armored was to attack from the 80th Division lines with two combat commands abreast, each with two columns, crossing the Nied River on a ten-mile front. The objective given the 6th Armored Division in the XII Corps plan was the high ground overlooking the town of Faulquemont. CCA, now commanded by Col. John L. Hines (Colonel Hanson had been injured), would have the mission of seizing the hills southeast of Faulquemont, in the vicinity of Guessling-Hémering; the objective for CCB (Col. G. W. Read) was the rising ground northeast of the city.

About noon on 9 November Combat Team Brindle (86th Cavalry Reconnaissance Squadron Mechanized (—) plus D Company, 15th Tank Battalion) jumped off at the head of CCB and succeeded, though with great difficulty, in crossing its light equipment at Port-sur-Seille. Moving on side roads the cavalry advanced to a point west of Alémont, where German antitank guns brought the thin-skinned light tanks and armored cars to a halt. Here again the autumn mud nullified a tactical plan based on speed and surprise. The lightweight armored vehicles of the cavalry combat team had less flotation than the medium tanks and could neither deploy off the road nor readily bypass the guns and road blocks which the German defenders had sited for

[47] The 6th Armored Division's *Combat Record,* one of the best unit histories of World War II, gives a good account of the November operations. It is augmented and in part corrected by the extensive coverage given in the Historical Division Combat Interviews.

RIVER CROSSING AT PORT-SUR-SEILLE. *The 15th Tank Battalion crosses its light equipment with considerable difficulty.*

a defense in depth. A lightning cavalry dash was no longer possible. The 6th Armored Division would have to fight its way to and across the barrier of the Nied Française.[48]

While Lt. Col. Harry C. Brindle's cavalry probed toward the east, elements of the 318th Infantry and armored infantry from the 6th Armored mopped up the rear guard enemy detachments in the neighborhood of Nomény. Nomény and Port-sur-Seille at this moment offered the only bridge sites suitable to crossing heavy armor; approaches to the other bridges in the 80th Division zone were under water and could not be used by medium tanks or artillery. Before the day ended both CCA and CCB had advance guards across the Seille. The remainder of the division passed over the river on 10 November, and the two combat commands struck out toward the Nied Française.

Meanwhile the 80th Infantry Division advanced rapidly on 10 November, working closely with the armor and driving nearly eight miles eastward despite mud and congested roads. The *48th Division*, decimated as it was, made its withdrawal toward the next line of defense at the Nied in surprisingly good order. General Balck had no troops to throw in for a counterattack. His armored reserve, the *11th Panzer Division*, had been dispatched from the Morhange assembly area on 9 November to make a counterattack and restore the lines of the *48th*. American fighter-bombers had checked this move before the German columns could engage in force in the Delme sector. Subsequently most of the *11th Panzer* was diverted southward to meet the attack by the American 4th Armored.[49] During the day, however, the 318th Infantry encountered a few troops from the *951st Regiment*, *361st VG Division*, which had been rushed north by bus and thrown into the line piecemeal to fight a holding action. Although the 80th Division made a very substantial advance on 10 November, the total number of prisoners taken was only about 350.

The 6th Armored Division attack was complicated by the fact that there was only one hard-surface road in the division zone. It ran from Pont-à-

[48] Historical Division Combat Interviews give the 6th Armored plans for a dash toward the east and tell the story of this initial stalemate. At noon on 8 November Read ordered the cavalry to advance in front of CCB toward the division objective. 86th Cav Unit Jnl, 8 Nov 44. The CCB commander expected the cavalry to seize crossings over the Nied Française which could be used by the main body of the command. CCB AAR, Nov 44. General Grow, however, did not count on the cavalry for this mission. Ltr, Gen Grow to Hist Div, 23 Feb 49.

[49] See *Army Group G KTB* for these days. See also rpt by General Wietersheim, the *11th Panzer Division* commander, in MS #B–416.

Mousson, via Vigny and Luppy, to the Nied Française crossing at Han-sur-Nied. Although CCB had the initial running rights on the Han-sur-Nied road, both combat commands finally would swing astride the road, entering at different points. Furthermore the 5th Infantry Division also had to use this road in order to support the advance on the right wing of the XX Corps. That this congestion did not act to halt the armor was a tribute to excellent—albeit unplanned—traffic control.

CCB, moving on the left, and CCA, on the right, swung obliquely to the northeast so as to get astride the Han-sur-Nied road at different points. Mud and mines on the side roads and trails provided the chief barriers during the early hours of this move. However, when the leading combat team of CCA reached Luppy a detachment from the *11th Panzer Division* contested the possession of the highway and the combat team spent the remainder of the day clearing the village. Back to the west, CCB fought its way onto the road at Vigny and Buchy. Again the enemy used the cover offered by the villages to make a fight for the road, but CCB, aided by the 2d Infantry which had come up from the XX Corps, cut off and captured both villages. Such German rear guard tactics would often delay the American advance during November; yet in sum these tactics could result only in progressive attrition as the enemy lost village after village and garrison after garrison.

General McBride and General Grow pressed their commanders to continue the attack—now really a pursuit—to the limit that men and equipment could endure. Both armor and infantry strained to keep the retreating Germans off balance and deny them time and opportunity to dig in for defense of the Nied Française. On the heels of the advance, corps and division artillery displaced forward with such speed as the mud and crowded roads allowed. On 11 November the 6th Armored Division celebrated Armistice Day by driving east on a ten-mile front and advancing about five miles to the Nied Française. Here, with the help of the 80th Division, the armor secured two bridgeheads in a series of bold and lucky strokes, and threw across a treadway bridge to support a third.

Early that morning CCA found its road blocked by an extensive mine field outside the town of Béchy. Here the left-wing elements of the *17th SS Panzer Grenadier Division* reinforced the *48th* and the German resistance was well organized. Entrenched riflemen, covering the mine field, fought a tenacious delaying action for over two hours. Meanwhile, the 1st Battalion of the 317th Infantry, which had been leading the regiment along the highway behind the armor, arrived at Béchy. Lt. Col. Sterling S. Burnette, commanding the battalion, intended to seize the bridge at Han-sur-Nied and therefore made arrangements with Colonel Hines to combine forces for the drive to the river. The augmented column moved toward Han-sur-Nied with a platoon of light tanks forming the point, followed by five half-tracks carrying troops of the 9th Armored Infantry Battalion. Company A, 317th Infantry, marched behind the half-tracks. The remainder of the infantry were strung out along the road to the rear, while the medium tanks and tank destroyers moved cross country on the flanks of the column.

Shortly after noon the head of the column reached a patch of woods which looked down a slight slope onto the bridge and the village of Han-sur-Nied, a little cluster of some twenty buildings on the east bank of the river. Here the Americans saw a truck-drawn field artillery battalion moving across the narrow bridge, while beyond the river what seemed to be "hundreds of vehicles" were streaming along the roads running east and south from the village. An artillery observer in a light tank radioed for time fire to be put on the bridge and its approaches. Perhaps this shelling drove off the German bridge guards, perhaps they were waiting for orders; in any event the wooden structure, already prepared with explosives and wiring, was not blown.[50]

Colonel Hines ordered an immediate assault. The 1st Platoon of B Company, 68th Tank Battalion (1st Lt. Vernon L. Edwards), led, firing at the Germans in foxholes on the west bank and engaging the antitank guns across the bridge as it advanced. Behind the tanks the 9th Armored Infantry Battalion (—) deployed in a thin skirmish line and started down the slope. Capt. James A. Craig and A Company of the 317th, now reduced to some sixty rifles by the fighting of the past few days, followed about two hundred yards to the rear. When only three hundred yards from the bridge, the armored infantry skirmish line was hit by high explosive shells from a detachment of sixteen 40-mm. antiaircraft guns posted on a hill northeast of the village. The armored infantry froze in their places or tried to reach the shelter of the ditches alongside the road to the bridge, while projectiles from the German guns, fired with almost sniperlike accuracy, swept up and down their ranks. The 231st Armored Field Artillery Battalion turned its howitzers on the enemy batteries, but as the German gunners were blasted—arms and legs flying into the air—others ran forward to serve the weapons.

[50] The account of the fight at Han-sur-Nied is based on exhaustive Historical Division Combat Interviews obtained soon after the action. See also Ltr, Col John Hines to Hist Div, 17 Sep 46.

TO REMILLY
TO BECHY
TO VITTONCOURT
TO HERNY
TO VATIMONT
TO LUCY

HAN-SUR-NIED

About this time Lieutenant Edwards' platoon of medium tanks started across the bridge. The first tank crossed successfully. The second stalled on the bridge when the platoon commander was hit; for a brief while the tank stood there, Lieutenant Edwards' body dangling from the open turret.[51] The third received a direct hit and burst into flame, but was backed off the wooden bridge by its commander after he had ordered his crew to leave the blazing tank. During this effort by the tankers 1st Lt. Daniel Nutter and Cpl. Charles Cunningham, B Company, 25th Armored Engineer Battalion, ran forward to cut the wires leading to the demolition charges. Lieutenant Nutter, at the enemy end of the bridge, was killed just as he completed his task. Corporal Cunningham, who had cut the wires at the western end, saw the lieutenant fall, raced across the bridge, and returned with the body of his commander.

Meanwhile Captain Craig's company of the 317th moved in single file down around to the right and crept toward the bridge, under the shelter of a railroad embankment paralleling the river. Who gave the order for the final charge probably never will be known. Perhaps it was Colonel Burnette, who had been standing erect in the open urging his lead company on and who received a mortal wound as he neared the bridge. Craig and a few men rushed the bridge, crossing the 100-foot span "faster than they knew how" amidst a hail of shell fragments and tracer bullets. Fourteen men from A Company and four of the armored infantry reached the enemy bank and took cover among the houses close to the bridge; there they were joined shortly by three of the tanks. Captain Craig disposed his little force as best he could and through the afternoon held the approach to the bridge against German tanks and riflemen.

In the meantime the American artillery engaged the German guns, now reinforced by heavier calibers farther to the east. The enemy gunners did not succeed in smashing the bridge structure, but their constant fire blanketed the bridge and its approaches. About 1715 Colonel Hines, who had been wounded, led a handful of men through the shellfire and across the bridge. Hines then returned a second time, leading Companies B (Sgt. Joseph Wercholuk) and C (Lt. Lacy B. Wheeler) of the 317th Infantry. No additional tanks had been committed, beyond the three already with Craig, because of the danger to the wounded lying on the narrow bridge. At dusk, however, the bridge was

[51] Lieutenant Edwards had been standing in the open turret firing a submachine gun. Before he was shot he succeeded in disposing of two German rocket launcher teams. Edwards was awarded the DSC posthumously.

cleared and tank reinforcements crossed to the east bank, followed by some two hundred armored infantry.[52] The crossing site now was held securely, and at 2130 Colonel Lewis sent the 2d and 3d Battalions of his 317th Infantry over the river to drive the Germans off the high ground beyond Han-sur-Nied.

On 11 November Combat Team 68 (Davall), the southern column of CCA, had worked its way in company with the 318th Infantry over the muddy secondary roads which led to the Nied. During the night the armor threw a treadway bridge over the river near Baudrecourt (two miles south of Han-sur-Nied), pushing across with the infantry on the following day. This crossing, however, had less immediate tactical significance than the one at Han-sur-Nied, for south of that village the Rotte Creek branched away from the Nied, leaving one more river barrier for the infantry to negotiate. Although the fight for a crossing in this southern sector had been successful and opposition light, cumulative losses were beginning to tell; the 2d Battalion, 318th Infantry, for example, was so reduced in numbers that on the night of 11 November it had to be reorganized as a rifle company.

The success at Han-sur-Nied on 11 November was enhanced through an equally important coup by CCB. Colonel Read's combat command had struck east in two combat teams with the intention of seizing bridges over the Nied Française at Ancerville and Remilly. At both these points, however, the Germans were more alert than their fellows at Han-sur-Nied and the bridges were blown in the faces of the American advance parties. At Remilly, where Combat Team 50 (Wall) was stymied, corps artillery fired a "serenade" on the town, as the CCB Journal remarks, "to commemorate Armistice Day, and for tactical purposes as well." Colonel Read secured permission from General Grow to swing farther to the north, although this move would take him out of the zone set for the 6th Armored. An engineer reconnaissance party, commanded by Lt. Frederick E. Titterington, 25th Armored Engineer Battalion, led the way north through the enemy lines. This party discovered a causeway and bridge near Sanry-sur-Nied. The structure was under eighteen inches of water but still intact. Lieutenant Titterington took a half-track onto the

[52] Colonel Burnette and Lieutenant Nutter were awarded the DSC posthumously for bravery in this action. Colonel Hines, Captain Craig, and Corporal Cunningham also received the DSC; Captain Craig was promoted to the rank of major. Company B, 68th Tank Battalion, was given a Distinguished Unit Citation for its part in the fight. Both the armor and infantry sustained heavy losses in the action at the bridge. The 6th Armored Division After Action Report gives its casualties as 21 killed and 239 wounded. The 317th Infantry S–3 Journal reports an effective 1st Battalion strength of 7 officers and 100 men on the night of 11 November.

bridge, dismounted, and in a fury of small arms fire walked the rest of the distance, cutting the demolition wiring.[53] The lead rifle elements of Combat Team 15 (Lagrew) promptly stormed the bridge, wiped out the defenders on the opposite bank, and established a bridgehead. This position, however, was not too advantageous for further exploitation since it lay under the guns of the outer Metz forts on the high ground around Sorbey. The troops in the bridgehead continued to receive artillery and mortar fire through the rest of the day and the night of 11–12 November.

CCA and the 80th Infantry Division rapidly exploited the Han-sur-Nied crossing on 12 November. The previous night the 69th Tank Battalion (Lt. Col. Bedford Forrest) had been attached to CCA in order to give added weight to the drive out of the bridgehead. Forrest's combat team led off on 12 November in an attack along the Faulquemont road. At Herny, about two miles east of Han-sur-Nied, the column encountered a battery of 88-mm. anti-tank guns, heavily supported by German infantry. Here a five-hour engagement ensued, the enemy clinging stubbornly to his position astride the highway. Finally one of the 69th's headquarters tanks, a new and heavily armored model, made a frontal assault on the German guns, taking seven direct hits without pausing, and enabled the medium tanks and tank destroyers to flank the position and destroy the battery.[54] Farther south, in the triangle between the Nied Française River and Rotte Creek, the Germans made a last effort to hold back the advancing infantry of the 318th and 319th, but withdrew when Combat Team 9 (Stablein) intervened from the north with tanks and armored infantry, outflanking the Rotte position. By the night of 12 November three bridges were in place across the Rotte and the infantry were moving across to support the armor in the advance toward Faulquemont. On this date, however, the XII Corps commander put a new plan of operations into effect. In this plan, aimed at the seizure of crossings on the Sarre River, the 35th Infantry Division would be pinched out by an advance on both wings of the corps. Of necessity, therefore, the 6th Armored Division zone was widened to the south and the division objective altered to include only the high ground south of Faulquemont. General Grow was caught somewhat off balance by this change in the corps scheme of maneuver since a part of CCB

[53] Lieutenant Titterington received the DSC for his part in securing the bridge.

[54] This tank was the M4A3E2, a Sherman medium tank to which more armor had been added. Only a few of this model reached the European Theater of Operations before the end of 1944. It was intended as a stopgap until the heavier Pershing tank could be put into production.

TANKS IMPEDED BY MUD *slow the advance of the XII Corps left wing.*

was across the Nied, well to the north of the original division sector. Fortunately the 2d Battalion of the 2d Infantry had crossed into the Sanry bridgehead during the morning of 12 November. This freed Colonel Read's troops, and Grow ordered him to maneuver CCB to the southeast so as to fall in behind CCA.

The advance on the left wing of the XII Corps was beginning to lose momentum. Rain and mud slowed the forward movement of armor, infantry, and supplies. Casualties sustained in the fighting since 8 November had been heavy. The enemy had reorganized and reinforcements were coming into the German lines west of Faulquemont. Repercussions of the American success at the Nied on 11 November seem to have resounded as far as the headquarters of *OB WEST*. In any event Rundstedt reluctantly released troops to reinforce *Army Group G* and ordered the *36th VG Division* to move from the *Seventh Army* to the *First*. Late on the night of 11 November General Balck issued a field order designed to rectify the situation created on the *First Army* front by the impact of Patton's Third Army offensive.

Balck was worried particularly by the collapse of the *48th Division* and the threat in the *XIII SS Corps* sector. The *XIII SS Corps* was in a precarious tactical position, attempting to hold with its right wing on the Moselle River —at Metz—and with its left at the Seille River line. A breach in the Seille position might conceivably crack the entire corps front. In addition the American success in the Han-sur-Nied sector posed a threat to one of the most important German supply roads, the Han-sur-Nied–Faulquemont–St. Avold highway. Balck therefore ordered General Priess, the *XIII SS Corps* commander, to counterattack at once with the object of restoring the Seille line. Priess had no reserves for such an undertaking, and when, on 12 November, the main body of the motorized regiment from the *361st VG Division* came up from the *LXXXIX Corps* to aid the crippled *48th Division* these fresh troops could do no more than retard the American advance.

The *XIII SS Corps* received more substantial reinforcements on 13 November when advance elements of the *21st Panzer Division* (General Feuchtinger) and the *36th VG Division* (Generalmajor August Wellm) arrived in the sector. The former had been carried on paper as part of the armored reserve of *Army Group G*, but because of the shortage of infantry divisions on the *Nineteenth Army* front it had not been able to move north as planned to meet the American offensive begun on 8 November. When the *21st Panzer Division* finally arrived in the *First Army*, Balck sent it to wipe out the bridgehead east of the Nied which CCB, 6th Armored Division, had won in the Sanry-sur-Nied sector. It will be recalled that the *21st Panzer Division* already had engaged the Third Army, fighting as infantry during the September battles. Actually the *21st* hardly merited the appellation of a panzer division, though it had been partially reconstituted during the October lull. Such was the paucity of armor on the Western Front that the German high command constantly overvalued this division and demanded that it carry out missions normally expected of a full-strength armored formation. Feuchtinger's division had been caught and roughly handled in the American Seventh Army attack in the Saverne area, while in process of leaving the line. When the *XIII SS Corps* commander threw the *21st Panzer Division* into line against the 6th Armored Division, Feuchtinger had about nineteen tanks, three assault guns, and four armored infantry battalions—the latter having only sixty to seventy riflemen in each.[55]

[55] MS #B–223 (Wellm); MS #A–871 (Feuchtinger); *Army Group G KTB* and *Anlagen*.

CCB, 6th Armored Division, had proceeded slowly after the seizure of the Nied bridge on 11 November. This command not only was responsible for holding the Sanry bridgehead but also had the mission of maintaining the tenuous contact between the XII Corps and the south flank of the XX Corps. Its proximity to a boundary between two corps whose main axes of advance were tangential resulted in confused orders and considerable delay. Lagrew's column widened the Sanry bridgehead on 12 November by attacks in which A and B Companies of the 15th Tank Battalion, A Company of the 50th Armored Infantry Battalion, and a few tank destroyers pushed out to the north, south, and east. Antitank fire, large craters, and mine fields made the advance difficult. On the north flank the B Company tanks were checked by direct fire from German guns sited to cover a mine field which extended between two woods. Capt. C. E. Prenevost, the B Company commander, dismounted and led the accompanying infantry to find a clear path. Prenevost was shot through the chest, but refused help for himself until the infantry detachment and its wounded had been withdrawn. He subsequently was awarded the DSC. During the course of the day the attack to the south and east had extended the bridgehead by some fifteen hundred yards. Elements of the 2d Battalion, 2d Infantry, which had worked hand in glove with CCB during the advance to the Nied, joined to mop up east of the river.

CCB was still straddling the Nied when the advance guard of the *21st Panzer Division*, which had assembled in the Forêt de Remilly, struck on 13 November. During the previous night Colonel Lagrew had dispatched a small cavalry detachment, commanded by Capt. James Bridges, to establish a blocking position at the main road junction between Bazoncourt and Berlize. Lagrew intended to expand the Sanry bridgehead by driving south and east with the bulk of his combat team while Bridges' task force gave cover on the north. Bridges' command consisted of D Troop, three platoons of 75-mm. self-propelled guns from E Troop (both troops of the 86th Cavalry Squadron), and a section from the 603d Tank Destroyer Battalion. Moving into position just before midnight on 12 November, the cavalry set up their outposts about six hundred yards south of Berlize. Bridges had been told that this village was held by troops of the 2d Infantry. Early the next morning the Americans saw considerable movement in Berlize, but it had been snowing and visibility was too poor to make out whether the village was occupied by friend or enemy. Suddenly the Germans attacked, leading with tanks and assault guns. Although the Americans gave a good account of themselves, in thirty minutes they had lost thirteen vehicles and suffered twenty-nine casualties. Requests for artillery support brought no immediate answer, and Bridges withdrew about a thousand yards to a hill which sloped down into Bazoncourt. Enemy shellfire inflicted more casualties, but the Germans could not push the assault home into the bridgehead.

Lagrew's main force had been checked during the day by road blocks and deep craters. Late in the afternoon General Grow ordered CCB to turn the Sanry bridgehead over to the troops of the 2d Infantry and move its left column back to the southeast in anticipation of further exploitation east of Herny. CCA continued the attack toward Faulquemont on 13 November, with the help of the 317th Infantry, driving a salient some two miles in width and about five miles in depth during a day of hard fighting. At Arraincourt, on the north bank of the Rotte, the enemy made a desperate stand to hold the river line so necessary to the protection of his flank. The village fell to the Americans, but Maj. Milford F. Stablein, who had taken command of the 9th Armored Infantry Battalion only two days before, was killed while leading the assault.

The *48th Division*, reduced to less than regimental strength and almost completely lacking heavy weapons, had fought stubbornly to bar the way to Faulquemont, but the events of 13 November showed that the division was at its last gasp. That evening General Balck gave orders to withdraw it from the line and lump it with the remnants of the *559th VG Division*, which had taken very severe losses in the Morhange sector. During the night of 13–14 November the main body of the *36th VG* moved in to relieve the *48th*. This fresh division was at full strength; its artillery regiment was well trained and equipped with new guns. Most of the infantry were recruited from the younger classes and the officers were veterans of the Eastern Front. During the early fall the *36th VG Division* had fought on the *Seventh Army* front, but had not taken part in any large-scale engagements or suffered heavy losses. The move south from the Trier sector had been accomplished in record time by motor and rail, a feat made possible partly by the bad weather which had grounded the American fighter-bombers.

The weakened condition of the *48th Division* indicated that a continuation of the American attack might make an irreparable breach in the German line. Therefore the *XIII SS Corps* comander hurried the detachments of the

36th VG Division to the front piecemeal as they arrived in the sector. One rifle battalion had been thrown in to reinforce the *48th* during the fight on 13 November. By the early morning of 14 November elements of all three regiments of the *36th VG Division* were facing the Americans, and the division's complement of antitank guns was in place at Many, astride the Han-sur-Nied–Faulquemont road.

General Wellm, commanding the *36th VG Division*, had gained considerable reputation as a tactician. Without prior reconnaissance, however, and without sufficient time to assemble or deploy his division properly, he was forced to abandon a co-ordinated linear defense. Instead he established a series of separate strong points as his companies and battalions moved into the sector. The position of the *36th VG Division* on 14 November leaned in the north on the Forêt de Remilly, where Wellm had been forced to take over a part of the front opposite the American XX Corps held by the *719th Division*. The German position then angled southeast, through Mainvillers and Chémery, to Landroff on the Rotte Creek. Here the *36th VG Division* hastily dug in—there was little time to wire in the position or lay mine fields—and awaited the American attack toward Faulquemont.[56]

General Eddy issued a new operational directive on 14 November which called for a continuation of the attack by the 6th Armored Division and the 80th Infantry Division. The latter, however, was given the limited mission of seizing the high ground south of Faulquemont from which the road and rail communications through the town could be interdicted. The XX Corps was still engaged in the battle for Metz, and until that operation could be successfully concluded and the XX Corps be brought east of the Nied Française General Eddy would have to limit the advance of the 80th Division so as to provide protection for the north wing of the XII Corps. Since the bulk of the 80th Division had not yet crossed the Rotte Creek the continuation of the attack devolved on the armor. CCB, disposed in echelon on the left, was ordered to drive east from Herny. CCA, already hard against the enemy positions, was given the mission of seizing a favorable line of departure on the right from which the infantry could close on Faulquemont. However, the combat troops of CCB were not all assembled east of the Nied until 1645 on 14 November. As a result Read's command did not join in the first armored attack.

[56] MS #B–223 (Wellm).

The objective selected for the CCA attack was the Côte de Suisse, a ridge which extended from Landroff northwest to Thicourt. Colonel Hines, the CCA commander, decided to execute a narrow thrust along the road bordering the Rotte and attempt to seize the village of Landroff, the anchor point for the German left flank and a pivot for any flanking movement against the Côte de Suisse. On the morning of 14 November Combat Team Davall (composed of the 68th Tank Battalion (—), a company of the 9th Armored Infantry Battalion, and some tank destroyers) led off in the attack along the river road. By noon the Americans had taken Brulange and Suisse and were poised for the final assault on Landroff.

German artillery interdicted a two-mile section of the highway west of Landroff, and the advance down the road was made under shellfire that took a high toll and left no officers in the leading tank company (A Company, 68th Tank Battalion). In the late afternoon the town was cleared of the enemy, and a staff officer, Capt. D. E. Smith, was sent in to take command. He had at his disposal the company of medium tanks, two platoons of infantry from the 44th Armored Infantry Battalion, and three tank destroyers. This little force was posted to meet the inevitable German counterattack, with the tanks at the edge of town watching the roads and covered by a few riflemen, while one platoon of infantry and the tank destroyers were located in the center of Landroff as a mobile reserve.

General Priess, the *XIII SS Corps* commander, feared that the whole Rotte Creek position would collapse with the capture of Landroff and its bridge. So he ordered Wellm to extend the left flank of the *36th VG Division* to the south and retake the village at once. Because the approaches to Landroff were flat, devoid of cover, and whitened by snow, Wellm held up his counterattack until dusk. Then he sent the *1st Battalion* of the *87th Regiment* and four assault guns, covered by the fire of the *268th Artillery Regiment*, to attack southward from Eincheville. The first assault, led by two self-propelled guns, succeeded in reaching the middle of the town before the lead gun was crippled and its gun crew cut down by small arms fire. The gun following turned tail. Deprived of their support the infantry fled. A second and stronger assault force attacked at midnight but was stopped at the edge of the village by the defenders' fire and a heavy artillery barrage. An hour later a third attack met the same fate.

In the meantime a company of armored infantry had come in to reinforce the American garrison and other troops had formed a corridor along the

Suisse road, there beating off German attempts to encircle Landroff.[57] About 0200 the enemy guns opened up, preparatory to a last assault. The leading wave of this attack was allowed to come within three hundred yards of Landroff, and then a concentration fired by eight battalions of field artillery cut the Germans to pieces. Succeeding waves pushed the attack home, however, and reached the streets of the village. There in the darkness a melee ensued with the combatants fighting hand to hand with rifles, pistols, bazookas, trench shovels, and grenades.[58] Slowly the Americans regained control of the southern half of the village. About 0500 a company of the 319th Infantry came in to take a hand, and the surviving Germans in the north part of the village were hunted down and captured or killed. A hundred or more German bodies outside the village gave mute testimony of the efficacy of the American artillery fire and the desperate nature of the German assault.

Lt. Col. Harold C. Davall's combat team was in no condition to continue the advance on 15 November, but with Landroff securely held it was possible to strike directly at the Côte de Suisse. At noon Combat Team 44 (Brown) went over to the attack with tanks leading the assault cross country from Brulange up the slopes of the Côte de Suisse, firing as they went, and followed by armored infantry and a battalion of the 319th Infantry. By dark the Côte de Suisse was taken and held in force. The *2d Battalion* of the *87th Regiment* was almost completely erased in this action.

The next morning CCA, together with the 318th and 319th Infantry, started a carefully co-ordinated and highly successful infantry-armor thrust in the direction of Faulquemont. Tanks, artillery, and tank destroyers, massed on the Côte de Suisse, provided a base of fire. The infantry, intermixed with the tanks, swept east in a concentric attack which cleared five enemy-held towns and put the 80th Division on the high ground south of Faulquemont.[59]

[57] A message entry in the CCA S–3 Journal, at 0415 on 15 November, is typical of countless messages sent out by armored units during the autumn campaign: "When will Doughs be up? We need them and need them bad."

[58] During the fight in Landroff Sgt. Herbert S. Latimer, B Company, 44th Armored Infantry Battalion, took command of a platoon whose officers and NCO's all were casualties. Sergeant Latimer led the platoon with such gallantry as to receive the DSC. Capt. Daniel E. Smith, the American commander in Landroff, also was awarded the DSC for bravery in the hand-to-hand battle for the village. In the course of rescuing two of his wounded men, he himself was wounded and had to be taken to the rear. Company A, 68th Tank Battalion, received the Distinguished Unit Citation for its part in the Landroff action. The company suffered ninety-seven casualties.

[59] Near the town of Thonville the infantry were brought under accurate artillery and mortar fire. Cpl. Otis M. Redd, C Company, 305th Medical Battalion, went alone to care for the most seriously wounded. Redd treated some twenty-seven of the wounded, all the while under German fire. He was awarded the DSC.

The speed and the weight of this envelopment so demoralized the weakened *87th* and *118th Regiments* that resistance generally was unorganized, wavering, and at points nonexistent. North of Thicourt, Forrest's tanks charged over Hill 337 and onto the enemy foxhole line on the reverse slope. Stunned by the American shelling and the presence of the tanks the Germans froze in their foxholes, in some cases permitting the tankers to dismount and kill them with Tommy guns. Brown's combat team, CCA, took Eincheville, after a TOT and direct tank fire had been laid on, and counted some two hundred and fifty enemy dead. CCA and the 80th took about twelve hundred prisoners during the day and killed a very large number of the enemy, tearing a gaping hole between the *36th VG Division* and *Kampfgruppe Muehlen*.[60]

The successful attack on 16 November placed the 80th Division in position to interdict enemy movement on the road and rail complex at Faulquemont. The advance by the left wing of the XII Corps was ordered to a halt, and the troops turned gratefully to dry clothes and hot meals. General Eddy and his commanders already had prepared new plans for a resumption of the offensive in which the 26th and 35th Divisions would drive to the Sarre River, and on 16 November a general shift of boundaries within the XII Corps zone signaled the change in the scheme of maneuver.

[60] Hist Div Combat Interview; 80th Div AAR, Nov 44. The *36th VG Division* commander estimates the German losses as around two thousand, including three battalion commanders. MS #B–223 (Wellm).

CHAPTER VIII

The November Battle for Metz

XX Corps Preparations for the November Offensive[1]

Prior to the November offensive the XX Corps was strengthened by the arrival of two new AUS divisions, one infantry, the other armored. The 95th Infantry Division had arrived on the Continent in September, coming by way of the United Kingdom. Elements of the division entered the 5th Infantry Division lines east of the Moselle on 18 October, but the combat experience of the 95th in the days that followed was limited to affrays between its own and German patrols.[2] Maj. Gen. Harry L. Twaddle, the division commander, had activated and trained the 95th. General Twaddle had come into the Army in 1912 as a university graduate. After a career as an infantry officer, he was posted to the War Department General Staff in 1938, later serving as G–3 of the War Department. His command of the 95th Division dated from March 1942. The 10th Armored Division had come to the Continent directly from the United States, debarking on 23 September. Its armored infantry entered the lines on 2 November in the Fort Driant area; however, this sector had lapsed into quiet and most of the division was to see its first combat during the November offensive. The 10th Armored was commanded by Maj. Gen. W. H. H. Morris, who had held his post since July 1944. General Morris

[1] The American records for both the planning and the operational phases of the battle for Metz are quite complete. The 90th Division After Action Report for November is particularly useful. The telephone journal attached to the 5th Division G–3 Journal and the unit histories published by the 5th Infantry Division, the 2d Infantry, and 11th Infantry add considerably to the journals maintained by the 5th Division. The records of the 95th Division and 10th Armored Division leave something to be desired since both of these units were new to combat. The casualties cited by the 95th Division are probably excessive inasmuch as loss reports from three battalions, which were isolated for several days, are admittedly inaccurate. Ltr, Maj Gen H. L. Twaddle to Hist Div, 17 Jan 49. However, extensive Historical Division Combat Interviews provide a check on the records of these two divisions. Several manuscripts have been prepared by German officers who took part in operations north of Metz—and these are valuable—but the *Army Group G KTB* has only incidental information on events in this sector.

[2] In one such action on the night of 6 November, Sgt. R. M. Schuller, L Company, 379th Infantry, led a patrol toward Fort Jeanne d'Arc. A hidden machine gun opened up on the Americans, one burst wounding the sergeant. Schuller picked up his submachine gun, which had been jarred from his hands, and fired a full clip, silencing the enemy weapon. He continued to direct his patrol until he collapsed from loss of blood. Schuller was awarded the DSC.

graduated from West Point in 1911. During World War I he commanded an infantry battalion in the St. Mihiel and Meuse–Argonne operations, was wounded, and received the DSC for gallantry in action. Morris had had much experience in training, holding successive commands with an armored infantry regiment, an armored division, and a training corps.

In addition to three infantry divisions (5th, 90th, 95th) and one armored division (10th) General Walker had the promise of "operational control" over the 83d Infantry Division (Maj. Gen. R. C. Macon), although with numerous strings attached. As it turned out, the 83d Division would give only artillery support after its transfer to the XX Corps on 8 November. The corps artillery numbered 19 battalions: 5 light battalions, 6 medium battalions, and 8 heavy battalions, this total reinforced by 2 battalions of the 422d Field Artillery Group attached to the 83d Division. The allotment of other corps troops had also been increased and now included: 5 tank destroyer battalions (plus 2 battalions attached to divisions); 3 separate tank battalions (attached to divisions); 4 antiaircraft artillery battalions (plus 4 battalions attached to divisions); the 3d Cavalry Group, with 2 squadrons; and 2 engineer combat groups, totaling about 8 battalions. In sum, General Walker had at his disposal 30 battalions of infantry, nearly 500 tanks, and over 700 guns when the long-awaited offensive began.

The plans for the coming operation had been prepared during days of the most exacting and detailed study; the air support plan, for example, contained a map showing each building in the city of Metz known to be occupied by Germans. On 3 November the XX Corps headquarters issued Field Order No. 12 to the top commanders, outlining the broad scheme of maneuver to be followed. An earlier statement of the XX Corps mission had given the idea that the corps would encircle and *reduce* the Metz fortifications as the initial phase in the resumption of the Third Army offensive toward the Rhine. But this final field order set the "primary mission of all troops" as "the destruction or capture of the Metz garrison, without the investiture or siege of the Metz Forts." Therefore, the plan called for the XX Corps to attack, encircle, and destroy the enemy in the Metz fortified area, reconnoiter to the Sarre River, seize a bridgehead in the vicinity of Saarburg, and finally, on orders from the army headquarters, resume the attack toward the northeast.

The initial envelopment of the Metz area was assigned to the 90th Division, forming the arm north of the city, and the 5th Division, encircling the city from the south. The 95th Division was to contain the German salient west of the Moselle. Then, as the concentric attack closed on Metz, the 95th Division was to drive in the enemy salient and, it was planned, cross the Moselle and capture the city proper. The 10th Armored Division, after crossing the Moselle behind the 90th Division, was to close the pincers east of Metz by advancing parallel to and on the left of the 90th Division, while simultaneously pushing armored reconnaissance columns east toward the Sarre River preliminary to making a crossing in the neighborhood of Merzig. Finally, the 3d Cavalry Group (Lt. Col. J. H. Polk) had the mission of following the 10th Armored Division across the river, swinging northeast into the triangle formed by the Moselle and Sarre Rivers, there probing toward Saarburg and screening the flank and rear of the forces engaged farther south and east.[3] It will be seen that the plan envisaged two phases: (1) the destruction of the German forces in the Metz area; (2) a quick shift in the axis of advance to the northeast. The establishment of a firm bridgehead across the Sarre River would be the objective of this second phase. From there the attack could be continued toward the Rhine along the Metz–Saarlautern axis. The speed and success of the concentric attack at Metz would in part determine the character of the subsequent advance across the Sarre; but the timing in the German *First Army* disengagement and withdrawal from the Metz bridgehead would be equally important.

The XX Corps Begins the November Offensive

Through the first days of November the XX Corps staff put the finishing touches on plans for the new offensive, while the troops finished their brief training schedules and convoys moved huge quantities of supplies up from depots in the communications zone. Rain and snow flurries persisted day after day, grounding the American planes and slowing traffic on the roads to a

[3] General Patton planned to send the 83d Infantry Division (minus the 329th Infantry) through the 90th Division bridgehead behind the 10th Armored Division. The 83d was then to attack northward, clear the Sarre–Moselle triangle, and establish a bridgehead over the Sarre at Saarburg. General Bradley, however, terminated the "operational control" exercised by the Third Army over the 83d Division before the latter could be committed. Ltr, Maj Gen R. C. Macon to Hist Div, 29 May 47; Ltr, Lt Gen W. H. Walker to Hist Div, 8 Oct 47; Ltr, Maj Gen H. R. Gay to Hist Div, 23 Nov 48. See also XX Corps AAR, 4 Nov 44. The Third Army staff had given much time and care to plans for the use of the 83d Division in mopping up the Sarre–Moselle triangle, despite the fact that General Bradley had written to General Patton on 30 October limiting the employment of the 83d. This question of the use of Macon's division was one of the very few, in the entire European campaign, which found General Bradley and General Patton in serious disagreement.

crawl. More important, the smaller streams that fed into the Moselle River reached torrential proportions and the Moselle itself began to rise ominously.

In general, the XX Corps already held the ground from which the attack would take off, but one slight readjustment in the lines had to be made in the vicinity of Berg-sur-Moselle, west of the Moselle, where the enemy still maintained observation posts on the heights overlooking the American north flank. (*Map XXX*) On the night of 3 November General Walker dispatched the 3d Cavalry Group to clear the enemy from the town of Berg. By 0800 the following morning dismounted troopers held the hill overlooking Berg, but in the afternoon the Germans counterattacked and retook the hill. The American cavalry unit returned to the attack on the morning of 5 November after Berg and the commanding hill had been subjected to a heavy shelling; this time it took and held both the town and the hill.[4]

On the night of 7 November the 90th Division began to shuttle its troops into assembly areas on the west bank of the Moselle across from Koenigsmacker, six miles northeast of Thionville, where the division would make its crossing. The 95th Division, on the right of the 90th, had its left regiment on its designated line of departure in position to lead off in the corps attack. Its original mission, that of making a demonstration on the west bank of the Moselle, was altered in the last hours before the jump-off. The 95th now would make a crossing, under orders to establish a bridgehead in the Uckange–Bertrange area three and a half miles south of Thionville.[5] Only a limited force, however, was assigned for use east of the river, and General Walker still expected the division to co-ordinate its efforts on both sides of the Moselle so as to give the impression of a major attack—while in fact the 90th Division made the main effort farther north. The 5th Division, which had returned to its old positions in the bridgehead south of Metz on 1 November, relieving the 95th Division there, was aligned facing the Seille River. Since the XX Corps plan of attack called for the 5th Division to make its main effort initially in the south beginning on 9 November, co-ordination of the 5th Division and XII Corps attacks was considered. However, on 4 November General Walker decided that the 5th Division would not attack simultane-

[4] Maj. George D. Swanson, executive officer of the 43d Cavalry Squadron, led the dismounted attack into Berg. For gallantry in this action he was awarded the DSC. During the attack 1st Lt. A. B. Minn, A Company, 135th Engineer Combat Battalion, advanced with his platoon to clear a mine field at the edge of the town. When the platoon was pinned down by automatic weapons fire, Lieutenant Minn rushed the enemy position and killed the defenders with grenades. Minn was given the DSC.

[5] XX Corps AAR, 8 Nov 44.

ously with the XII Corps.[6] The 10th Armored Division, intended for use with the 90th Division in the wide envelopment north of Metz, had been given a narrow front west of Metz during the first week of November. The final relief of the 10th Armored Division by the 95th Division was delayed until 8 November in the hope of misleading the enemy, but by that time the main columns of the 10th Armored were already on their way north.

On the night of 7 November, when General Patton gave the order that would set the Third Army attack in motion, the XX Corps assault troops began the move into assembly positions, guns were displaced forward to support the advance, and bridging and smoke generator equipment was trucked and manhandled as close to the Moselle as camouflage precautions permitted. Early on the morning of 8 November the dull sound of massed artillery fire to the south signaled the start of the XII Corps attack. All through the day the XX Corps troops lay quietly in woods and other bivouac areas. Then, as darkness came, the assault units took up attack positions and the 95th Division moved forward the troops assigned to carry out the demonstration and initial crossing preliminary to the main corps attack.

The Uckange Bridgehead

General Twaddle, the 95th Division commander, selected the 377th Infantry (Col. F. E. Gaillard) to make the D-day demonstration on the north flank of the 95th Division. This deceptive operation, called aptly enough by the code name CASANOVA, was intended as a limited-objective attack. Part of the 377th would cross the Moselle in the neighborhood of Uckange and extend a bridgehead about three-quarters of a mile inland to the little town of Bertrange, just short of the main highway between Thionville and Metz, thus giving some cover to the right flank of the 90th Division. The remainder of the 377th was given the task of erasing a small enemy salient on the west bank of the Moselle, which had been left south and east of Maizières-lès-Metz at the close of the 90th Division capture of that town. This attack was to be made in conjunction with the Uckange crossing. The rest of the 95th Division was

[6] 5th Div G–3 Jnl, 9 Nov 44. General Eddy had requested that the 6th Armored Division be given running rights on the road at the boundary between the XII and XX Corps. This necessitated putting the 5th Division onto the road some hours after the XII Corps attack began. See Chapter VII, p. 358. General Walker geared the corps attack to that of the 5th Division. Ltr, Gen Walker to Hist Div, 8 Oct 47. General Irwin, however, did not receive a formal order to attack on 9 November until the day preceding. XX Corps AAR, 8 Nov 44.

to take no part in this first phase of the attack. The 378th Infantry (Col. S. L. Metcalfe) and 379th Infantry (Col. C. P. Chapman) were disposed so as to contain the German forces in the larger Metz bridgehead west of the Moselle.

Just after dark, on the night of 8 November, a small detachment of engineers from the 320th Engineer Combat Battalion crossed the Moselle south of Uckange in assault boats, crawled onto the east bank, and there blew a gap in the German wire and mine field with bangalore torpedoes, returning to the American side of the river without casualties. At 2100, H Hour for "Operation CASANOVA," the 1st Battalion of the 377th Infantry (Lt. Col. Joseph E. Decker) dispatched C Company across the river. The first wave received no small arms fire while in the boats. The *73d Regiment*, *19th VG Division*, responsible for this sector, had no outposts at the river and required some time to move troops into the threatened area. But the "bouncing Betties" along the bank took their toll as the company debarked. The Americans passed through the gap in the German wire and advanced about four hundred yards to the east, then halted to await daylight and the arrival of the remainder of the battalion.

In the meantime the enemy artillery, located inland, had opened up, apparently firing on check points earlier fixed along the river. Company B of the 135th Engineer Combat Battalion, assigned as part of the 1139th Engineer Group to support the 95th Division crossing, tried desperately to throw a footbridge across the river, but the German guns were too accurate. Three bridge sections were destroyed, twenty-four men became casualties, and work on the bridge halted until a new and less vulnerable site could be found.[7]

The attack launched by the 2d (Lt. Col. Robert L. Walton) and 3d (Lt. Col. Ross Hall) Battalions to reduce the Maizières pocket on the near side of the river was less successful than the river crossing. In this sector the *1215th Regiment* of the *462d VG Division* had been forewarned by the 90th Division attack in late October and had laid a dense mine field in front of its lines. The three assault companies which were sent off at 2100 to drive the Germans from the small woods north of Semécourt, the slag heap outside Maizières, and a wood lot beyond Brieux Château ran into trouble immediately. Scouts stumbled onto trip wires that set off whole sections of the mine field and inflicted many casualties on the troops following. One platoon was reduced to a strength of one officer and five men. The Germans, alerted by

[7] 135th Engr (C) Bn AAR, Nov 44. Smoke was used here but apparently with little success. 161st Cml Smoke Generator Co AAR, Nov 44.

TRANSPORTATION OF BRIDGING EQUIPMENT *over flooded roads was a difficult problem.*

the exploding mines, poured in mortar and artillery fire, adding to the losses as the assault companies groped their way through the "vast mine fields." When the morning of 9 November dawned F Company held the woods north of Semécourt, but elsewhere the initial attack had been repelled.[8] Late in the afternoon the companies were re-formed, some tanks and additional infantry were put into the attack, and by dark the 377th had driven the enemy off the slag heap and away from Brieux Château.[9] A small German pocket still remained around the town of Hauconcourt, which lay beside the river northeast

[8] During the fight to take the woods the 2d Battalion commander, Lt. Col. R. L. Walton, led elements of F and G Companies forward through heavy German fire. A machine gun killed a sergeant and several men. Colonel Walton deliberately advanced on the machine gun and, although he was hit three times, shot the enemy crew and destroyed their weapon. Walton was awarded the DSC. Sgt. Harry H. Hunt, G Company, 377th Infantry, received the DSC for his gallantry in throwing himself across a wounded comrade to save the latter from a hand grenade. Hunt was seriously injured in the explosion. Pfc. John W. Metych, E Company, 377th Infantry, made a singlehanded attack near the woods and silenced two hostile machine guns with fire from his BAR. He was wounded while attempting to knock out a third position. Metych received the DSC.

[9] 95th Div AAR, 9 Nov 44. 2d Bn, 377th Inf, Jnl, 9 Nov 44.

of Maizières, but no attempt was made to clear it. By 10 November the Moselle had flooded the streets of Hauconcourt, and the 377th Infantry sector west of the Moselle therefore remained static for the next few days.

During the early morning hours of 9 November the 1st Battalion of the 377th shuttled more assault craft across the Moselle and by daybreak had two companies of infantry and a heavy weapons platoon on the flood plain east of the river. Sporadic mortar fire harassed the advance, but the lead troops bypassed Bertrange and moved onto a low hill about four hundred yards east of that village without meeting enemy infantry. Here the small force halted and dug in. Back at the river the rising flood waters and intense German gun fire made further crossings in daylight extremely hazardous, despite a smoke screen laid down by two sections of the 161st Smoke Generating Company, and Colonel Decker was ordered to hold the remainder of the battalion at Uckange.

The Moselle had risen steadily since the previous night. During the day it reached flood proportions, swamping its banks, inundating the road approaches and swirling along at a speed that made the flimsy assault boats unmanageable. By the night of 9–10 November the river torrent had nearly isolated the American troops on the enemy bank and it was problematical whether they could be reinforced and provided with heavy weapons before the Germans gathered enough strength to wipe them out.

Fortunately the *19th VG Division*, in whose area the troops from the 377th had landed, made no counterattack in any strength, the Germans contenting themselves with patrol action and desultory fire from field guns and mortars.[10] For the next three days supplies were flown across the river by small liaison planes, which dropped medical supplies, sleeping bags, socks, gloves, ammunition, and other necessities almost into the American foxholes.[11] Attempts by the engineers to build and launch an infantry support raft were frustrated by German gunfire and the turbulent river.[12]

[10] The Germans first regarded all of the American attacks north of Metz as "containing attacks" *(Fesselungsangriff)*. MS #B–443 (Emmerich).

[11] One pilot reported: "The troops were really happy when the first plane came over dropping supplies. We could see right down into their foxholes and they looked sort of hungry, wet and cold, but they were smiling when we saw them."

[12] A curious event took place on 10 November when Sgt. Ervin Bluhm and an assault boatload of unarmed medical aid men attempted to reach the troops across the river. Twice the boat was swept onto parts of the east bank held by the enemy, and twice the Germans courteously gave Bluhm directions as to where the Americans might be found. On the third attempt Bluhm landed at the right spot. 95th Div AAR, 10 Nov 44.

On the night of 11–12 November the waters began to recede, and during the next night the remainder of the 1st Battalion, 377th Infantry, crossed to join the troops in the tiny bridgehead opposite Uckange.[13] This crossing was made without loss, though the enemy artillery was still ranged in on the river, while the engineers made a feint to distract the German forward observers by running a battery of outboard motors at full speed on the American bank south of the actual crossing site.

The 90th Division Crossing in the Vicinity of Cattenom

When General Walker made his decision to put the 90th Infantry Division and 10th Armored Division into a wide envelopment north of Metz and Thionville, three points on the Moselle were considered as possible crossing sites: Rettel, Malling, and Cattenom. General Van Fleet, who had taken command of the 90th Infantry Division during October, ruled out the Rettel area because it lay under German observation from the heights to the northeast, and the 90th could spare neither the troops nor the time to seize or contain this ground. The terrain south of Rettel was more favorable. Here the Moselle flowed through a broad flood plain with low banks. Beyond lay one-half to one mile of flat land, terminating in abrupt slopes leading onto long, wooded ridge lines that on the far side extended perpendicularly back from the river valley. On the right of the zone assigned to the 90th Division the Cattenom crossing site lay under the guns of Fort Koenigsmacker, perched on the terminus of a ridge line. The tactical effectiveness of its location forbade that Fort Koenigsmacker be bypassed; it had to be taken, and quickly. Through the center of the division zone of advance ran the heavily wooded, rugged ridge lines on which the French had constructed some of the main fortifications of the Maginot Line. Here the initial obstacle was a group of bunkers and field works clustered around the little village of Métrich which blocked the main road south from the crossing site at Malling. The northern part of the division zone had natural features that favored the establishment of a blocking position on the left flank of the 90th Division while allowing the main attack to pivot toward the southeast. A long ridge line stretching southeast from Sierck-les-Bains through Fréching, with its highest point—Mount Altenberg—hard by Sierck, provided a natural defensive position for

[13] Resupply and reinforcement by boat came just in time, for the weather had turned colder and the small liaison planes were grounded by icing on their wings.

the exposed left wing of the 90th Division advance. This position would cover the two important approaches by which the enemy might strike at the American crossing sites: the Saarburg highway from the northeast; and the Merzig–Kerling road from the east.

General Van Fleet planned to put his division across the Moselle before daylight on 9 November in sufficient strength to overrun quickly the German forts at Koenigsmacker and Métrich and secure a firm hold on the tips of the ridges extending southeast. Remaining elements of all three infantry regiments were scheduled to take part in the follow-up on 9 November. The 358th (Col. C. H. Clarke), on the right, was to cross near Cattenom. Once on the east bank the right battalion (the 1st) would launch a direct assault to take Fort Koenigsmacker and the village of Basse-Ham lying at its foot. At the same time the 3d and 2d Battalions of the 358th were to bypass the fort to the north and strike to secure lodgment on the main ridge line extending southeast from the fort. The 359th Infantry (Col. R. E. Bell), using the Malling crossing site, was to carry the attack on the left wing of the division. Its objective, in the first phase of the maneuver, was the high ground between Mount Altenberg and the village of Oudrenne. The reserve regiment, the 357th Infantry (Col. J. H. George), was scheduled to cross behind either one of the two assault regiments at the earliest moment and thrust down along the Maginot Line through the gap left between the 358th and 359th. Since the large town of Koenigsmacker lay between the axes of advance for the two assault regiments, plans were made to neutralize the town and its hinterland by artillery and chemical mortar fire until such time as the 357th Infantry could arrive east of the river and seize Koenigsmacker.

The final object in the wide-swinging offensive by the 90th Division was the seizure of the southern terminus of the long, rough ridge line extending from Koenigsmacker to Charleville-sous-Bois. Once in position on this high ground northwest of Boulay-Moselle the 90th Division would dominate the main roads leading east out of Metz, and the northern half of the XX Corps pincers grip around the Metz–Thionville position could be considered closed. The distance to be covered by the 90th Division drive was some sixteen miles. The road net in the division zone east of the Moselle was hardly adequate, even in good weather. Furthermore, the main axial road, running southeast from Koenigsmacker beside a little stream known as the Canner, was unusable unless the Americans held the ridge lines on either side. These two ridge lines, in the right and center of the division zone of advance, were serious obstacles, heavily forested and broken across the grain at frequent intervals by streams and gullies. They were made more difficult as military barriers by the Maginot Line, which had been built as a system facing Germany but whose individual works could be used to defend against an attack lengthwise along the ridge chains.

General Van Fleet planned to break through the German defenses overlooking the Moselle and quickly push down the ridge in a power drive, using two battalions in each of the assault regiments. One battalion of corps engineers was attached to each assault regiment, with the initial mission of ferrying the infantry across the river; the 315th Engineer Combat Battalion, the divisional engineer unit, was assigned to handle the bridging of the Moselle. The 90th Reconnaissance Troop (reinforced) had the task of screening the right flank of the division during the drive to the southeast; it was anticipated that this unit would eventually make contact with elements of the 95th Division on the east bank of the Moselle. The 10th Armored Division would cross the Moselle behind the infantry and then come abreast of and protect the left flank of the 90th.[14]

The success of the 90th Division attack would turn to a considerable degree on surprise and the prompt seizure of its initial objectives. During the week before the Third Army resumed the offensive, the division was withdrawn from the line confronting the series of forts west of Metz and dispatched, ostensibly for training, to the Audun–Aumetz area behind the corps north flank, where both the 5th and 90th Divisions had conducted training during October. The final assembly area for the attack was the Forêt de Cattenom. Although this forest offered ample cover and lay close to the Moselle, it was on a forward slope under observation from the German side of the river and therefore could be entered only during hours of darkness. In the last quiet days the 3d Cavalry Group, screening this sector, extended its patrolling. Then, on two successive nights, the 90th Division artillery displaced to positions on the rear slopes behind the forest. The guns were followed on the night of 7–8 November by the infantry, moving by truck through the rain along slippery, narrow roads.[15] By daybreak the entire 90th Division, 6 battalions of supporting artillery, 2 battalions of tank destroyers, 1 battalion of tanks, 3 battalions of engineers, and 3 bridge trains were in position inside the forest and behind the hills. Each man who would take

[14] The plan is given in detail in the 90th Division After Action Report.

[15] The average distance for this move into position was fifteen miles.

TANKS AWAITING SIGNAL TO CROSS MOSELLE, *as 712th Tank Battalion near Sentzich moves up to support 90th Infantry Division. Antiaircraft gun is shown in foreground.*

part in the assault now was briefed. The artillery registered with one gun in each battalion. Assignments already had been given in the assault boats, and even the reserve regiment and supply troops had been given assault boat training in case there should be difficulty in bridging the Moselle. Telephone wires, strung during the past several nights, were at the river bank, and officers of the 90th, using 3d Cavalry Group vehicles and insignia, had completed reconnaissance on the west bank. During the early evening of 8 November the 3d Cavalry Group stepped up its harassing fire, a feature of previous nights, in order to mask activity on the American bank. Trucks moved bridging equipment down the roads leading to the demolished Moselle bridges. Mortars and machine guns were placed in position close to the water's edge so as to give direct support to the assault troops; tanks, assault guns, and infantry cannon moved to comparable positions at daybreak.

A little before midnight the assault battalions of the 358th and 359th began the 400-yard carry to bring their boats to the river. The ground they traversed was swampy, interlaced with irrigation ditches and barbed wire fences partially submerged by the Moselle waters—formidable obstacles at night. Meanwhile, the 95th Division had begun the demonstration at the Uckange crossing site, and at 0330 the first attack waves of the 90th Division pushed out onto the rising waters. Only the left battalions of the two assault regiments reached the river in time to shove off as planned, the 1st Battalion, 359th (Lt. Col. L. R. Pond), making the crossing at the Malling site and the 3d Battalion, 358th (Lt. Col. J. W. Bealke), leading off at the Cattenom crossing. Although the flood waters of the Moselle increased the difficulties of the crossing they acted also to lessen the dangers on the enemy bank. The extensive mine plots prepared weeks before by the Germans were flooded and the American assault craft passed over them with impunity. The foxholes and rifle pits dug along the east bank were water filled and untenanted. The scattered outposts of the *416th Division* in this sector, caught completely off guard, offered little opposition to the initial assault waves and were cut down with grenades, Tommy guns, and bayonets. By 0500 the two leading battalions were on the east bank, followed shortly by troops of the 1st Battalion, 358th, and the 2d Battalion, 359th. The latter two battalions, the right assault battalions in their respective regimental bridgeheads, were brought under fire by the enemy, recovering from his initial surprise, but losses were slight.

Now the main obstacle was the raging Moselle, rising with extreme rapidity. The right-wing battalions in each regiment had been forced to load into their assault boats in waist-deep water. Engineer boat crews had to be doubled in order to buck the current. Many boats on the eastern bank were lost when their crews, under galling enemy artillery fire, abandoned their craft, allowing them to float away after debarking the infantry. In the 358th sector, the eighty assault boats rapidly dwindled to twenty, although some of those lost were subsequently retrieved. The engineers working to put in footbridges found it impossible to anchor their cables securely. At the Cattenom site shellfire directed from armored observation posts in Fort Koenigsmacker made the bridge site untenable and destroyed the first five truckloads of bridging apparatus. At Malling a support raft was launched into the swirling waters and then capsized with its very first load.[16] All the while the river continued to swell.

[16] Hist Div Combat Interview; 358th Inf AAR; 359th Inf AAR. The 179th Engineer Combat Battalion supported the 358th Infantry, the 206th Engineer Combat Battalion the 359th.

On the east bank, however, the first phase of the attack was executed swiftly and according to plan in the midst of a drizzling rain. In the 359th zone the 1st Battalion was east of Malling by daybreak and had cut the main highway to Thionville and Metz in two places. The reserve company entered Malling before the sleeping German garrison could man its positions and in a matter of minutes seized all of the town but two fortified houses, which fell later in the morning when a section of 57-mm. antitank guns was ferried across and laid on these buildings. By noon 133 prisoners had been rounded up in Malling. As the day progressed the 1st Battalion pushed out to the east and north, driving isolated groups of Germans before it. The 2d Battalion extended the bridgehead area southward, taking Petite-Hettange and Métrich with little trouble. At dark the battalion was within 1,500 yards of Oudrenne but had been brought to a halt by large mine fields planted by the *LXXXII Corps* to fill the gaps in its weak infantry line. The reserve battalion, the 3d, following hard in the wake of the assault battalions, marched almost without opposition to the crossroads village of Kerling; there it linked up with the 1st Battalion on the north and occupied a section of the ridge line which had been designated as the 359th Infantry objective. On this high ground north of Kerling the Germans elected to make a stand, but the lead company of the 3d Battalion, attacking straight toward the flashing muzzles of a battery of four German antitank guns, took the position.

Across the river from Cattenom, in the zone of the 358th attack, the leading platoons of the 3d Battalion also moved speedily forward. They slipped past Fort Koenigsmacker before daylight and started the advance toward the high ground between Kuntzig and Inglange which marked the initial objective for the right wing of the 90th Division. The 1st Battalion (Lt. Col. C. A. Lytle),[17] on the right of the 3d, threw C Company into Basse-Ham before the enemy could react and dispatched Companies A and B to make the *coup de main* at Fort Koenigsmacker. On the success of this blow the 90th Division maneuver turned.[18] Before daybreak the two companies were disposed in the woods in front of the hill on which the fort stood. About 0715 the Americans attacked, rushing up the steep hill, cutting and smashing through the

[17] Earlier, on 20 September, Colonel Lytle had distinguished himself by the daring rescue, under fire, of some exhausted survivors of a patrol who were stranded on the ice breaker of a demolished Moselle bridge. Lytle, then a major, was awarded the DSC.

[18] The story of the fight at the fort is taken from very detailed Historical Division Combat Interviews.

wire entanglements around the fort. Apparently the defenders were unaware that any Americans were in the vicinity: no alarm was given until A Company (Capt. E. J. Blake) was already in sight of the unmanned, open trenches which lay inside the wire. Both companies were in the trenches before the Germans could loose more than a few rifle shots. At this point the enemy mortar crews began to fire into the trenches, while observers in the concrete observation posts on top of the fort gave the range. Although the main casemates housed a battery of four 100-mm. guns, these could not be depressed to bear on the attacking 1st Battalion and during much of the subsequent fighting they continued to be fired on the 3d Battalion as it worked its way forward in the draw to the north. As at Fort Driant the chief works lay below the surface, formed as a series of tunnels and underground rooms which were entered by way of steel and concrete observation posts and sally ports at the ground level. The fort was garrisoned by a battalion of the *74th Regiment, 19th VG Division*, which during the morning erupted from the tunnels in small-scale counterattacks that cost A Company some thirty-five casualties. In the midst of bursting mortar shells and small arms fire from the superstructures a platoon of engineers from the 315th Engineer Combat Battalion, led by 1st Lt. William J. Martin, and two assault teams, under 1st Lt. William Kilpatrick and 1st Lt. Harris C. Neil, Jr., of A Company, began the systematic reduction of the observation posts and sally ports.[19] Satchel charges, placed against steel doors, cleared a path to the stairways leading below. More charges demolished the stairs and cut off access to the surface. Ventilating ports were liberally doused with gasoline and then touched off by a thermite grenade or a string of threaded TNT blocks. On one occasion a German was blown to the surface by the force of the explosion. All this quickly used up the stock of explosives, and as the day ended additional charges were flown in by an artillery liaison plane and dropped by parachute near the fort. By nightfall the Americans were well established on the west side of Fort Koenigsmacker, but the fortress artillery and heavy machine guns still commanded the roads to the east and harassed the advance by the main body of the 3d Battalion which was moving through the draw north of the fort.

[19] The 358th Infantry After Action Report specifically singles out 1st Lt. Harris C. Neil, since he distinguished himself by personally placing the charges against the steel doors leading to the tunnels. He was awarded the DSC for especially daring action on 11 November, but was severely burned on that day when throwing a thermite grenade into a ventilator drenched with gasoline.

Meanwhile the 2d Battalion, 358th, had crossed the river, mopped up the remaining Germans near the river, and assembled west of the town of Koenigsmacker. The reserve regiment, the 357th, crossed its 2d and 3d Battalions, using both the Malling and Cattenom sites in order to speed its deployment. The 3d Battalion, using the few assault boats salvaged from the earlier crossings, took three hours to negotiate the swollen river, all the while under bitter fire from heavy-caliber German mortars. A few power launches that had been rushed by truck to aid the 90th Infantry Division were used to carry the 2d Battalion.

By midnight General Van Fleet had eight battalions of infantry on the enemy bank and a few light antitank guns. Seven towns had been taken and at a few points the bridgehead had been extended about two miles to the east. But the bag of prisoners had been small during this first day of the attack —only about two hundred—and it was apparent that the main enemy force had yet to be encountered.

The Enemy Situation North of Metz[20]

The *LXXXII Corps* (General der Infanterie Walter Hoernlein) formed the right wing of the *First Army*, holding a sector which extended from just south of Metz, through the Metz bridgehead, and north along the Moselle as far as the left boundary of *Army Group B*, in the neighborhood of Grevenmacher. The three infantry divisions comprising this corps were arrayed with the *462d VG Division* occupying Metz and its environs, the *19th VG Division* deployed in the corps center along the Moselle from Hauconcourt north to a point between Koenigsmacker and Métrich, and the *416th Division* holding a thirty-five-mile front along the river which took in nearly all of the western side of the triangle formed by the confluence of the Moselle and the Sarre.

The two German divisions north of Metz were far from first-class fighting formations. The *416th Division* (Generalleutnant Kurt Pflieger), like many another division on the Western Front in the autumn of 1944, had been beaten to fragments on the Eastern Front and then returned to Germany for reconstruction. After a brief stay in Denmark as a security division, it was dispatched to the *First Army* in early October, relieving the *48th Division* in the quiet

[20] This section is based on the *KTB's* of *Army Group G* and *OB WEST*. See also MS #B-079 (Kittel); MS #A-000 (Mellenthin); MS #B-527 (Britzelmayr).

sector on the army's north flank. The *416th* was filled with replacements from the older classes (the average age was thirty-eight years) who had never been in combat, although some had fought Russian partisans as guards on the line of communications. Known in the *First Army* as the "Whipped Cream Division," the *416th* was catalogued as a division capable at best of very limited use as a defensive formation. When additional replacements arrived in late October the *416th* was reorganized into three infantry regiments, each of two battalions. Its total strength was about 8,500 officers and men. However, the divisional artillery remained very limited: one battalion of outmoded fortress guns and a field artillery battalion equipped with captured 122-mm. Russian pieces. The *19th VG Division* (Colonel Karl Britzelmayr) also was rated as a defense division but was in better shape than the *416th* and already had been in combat. The *19th* had three field artillery battalions, and in addition received eleven new assault guns just before the American attack. The division strength was about the same as that of the *416th*.

In early November the *LXXXII Corps* had no tanks at all. General Balck made a gesture at strengthening the right flank of the *First Army* by sending the *486th Antitank Battalion*, equipped with forty or fifty antitank guns, to Dalstein. But in the absence of tanks and any substantial complement of antitank weapons the *LXXXII Corps* was forced to depend on the natural barrier provided by the Moselle to stop an American tank thrust north of Metz, supplementing the river obstacle with a series of huge mine fields. Balck recognized the importance of such a defense and divided most of the antipersonnel and antitank mines in his depots between the *LXXXII Corps*, for use behind Thionville, and the *LXXXV Corps*, defending the Belfort Gap. The *19th VG Division* alone planted some 40,000 mines along its front. The total number used to impede the progress of the American divisions in the attack north of Metz must have been tremendous.

About three weeks before the Third Army offensive Balck ordered General Knobelsdorff to group the five field artillery battalions of the *416th Division* and *19th VG Division* along the boundary between the two divisions so as to provide massed fire against any thrust in the Thionville sector. Further, Balck forbade Pflieger to commit his indifferent infantry against the first wave of American infantry and prescribed that in the initial phases of an attack the riposte should be made only by long-range, observed artillery fire and heavy infantry weapons, sited to cover mine fields and obstacles. German intelligence did not anticipate that the American attack would come in the sector held by the *416th Division*, but instead believed that the flank north of Metz would be hit by a penetration on both sides of Thionville, possibly supported by an advance on Trier, just across the interarmy group boundary. As a result General Pflieger's *416th Division* was allotted a very wide front, so extended that all its battalions were in the line doing outpost and security duty on 9 November except for one battalion of the *714th Regiment* which was held as corps reserve near Saarburg. The *19th VG Division*, holding a narrower sector, had two regiments in line. Its *59th Regiment*, assembled southeast of Distroff, was held on a string as *Army Group G* reserve for commitment on the right flank of the *First Army*. In theory the *11th Panzer Division* constituted a mobile armored reserve for the *LXXXII Corps*. But when Balck had raised the embarrassing question at *OB WEST* headquarters as to where the *11th* should be committed in the event of a synchronized attack both north and south of Metz, he was given no answer. Subsequently the *11th Panzer Division* was thrown in to stop the XII Corps offensive the day before the XX Corps advance started.

The initial American crossing east of Uckange on the night of 8–9 November had no immediate repercussions at the higher German headquarters. It seems probable that the limited strength used in the crossing led the Germans to diagnose this maneuver correctly as merely a demonstration. The enemy reaction to the subsequent attack by the 90th Infantry Division was slow, for undoubtedly the troops on the spot were caught by surprise. Later, local commanders attributed their slowness in launching counterattacks to the activity of American planes and the fierce concentration of artillery fire from the west bank of the Moselle. Actually, the east side of the river was only weakly outposted and during the first hours of 9 November the enemy was forced to rely on the fire of the artillery groupment, concentrated as Balck had directed, and the mortars supporting the infantry outpost line. In addition the attack by the 90th Division struck directly at the seam between the *416th Division* and the *19th VG Division*, further delaying the initiation of planned defense measures. The *416th Division* particularly was dispersed and unwieldy in the face of the American advance. At Malling, where the 359th Infantry made its crossing, there were only one and a half companies of infantry.[21] The nearest German support not already engaged was one company of the *713th Regiment* about five miles to the rear. Pflieger ordered his reserve bat-

[21] MS #B–090 (Pflieger).

talion around from the right flank to the endangered southern flank about 1000 on the morning of 9 November, but it did not arrive until late in the evening. Meanwhile Balck wrangled with OKW all through the day in attempts to get some help for his north flank. Finally, a little before midnight, General Jodl's headquarters at OKW gave way and freed two infantry battalions of the *25th Panzer Grenadier Division* for an attack from the northeast against the 90th Division bridgehead.[22] But once more the German poverty in trucks and gasoline worked to the advantage of the Americans and caused this Kampfgruppe to be held immobile at the Baumholder training area, fifty miles to the east, until the night of 11–12 November.

The only troops in the *First Army* free for use in an immediate counterattack were those of the *59th Regiment, 19th VG Division.* At dark on the night of 9 November a reinforced company, supported by three assault guns, was shuttled north. Shortly before 0300 on 10 November this force struck at Kerling, which had been taken a few hours earlier by elements of the 3d Battalion (—), 359th Infantry. The Germans overran the American outposts and captured two antitank guns blocking the road east of the village. Apparently civilian sympathizers had mapped out the American positions, for the enemy drove head-on in the darkness without any attempt at preliminary reconnaissance. The forward platoons of Companies L and K held on until their machine guns were out of ammunition, and then the battalion fell back to the high ground northwest of Kerling. This movement uncovered the Kerling–Petite-Hettange road, the main highway through the center of the regimental zone, but the few German survivors were in no condition to continue any drive to the Moselle. The 90th Division artillery massed its guns on Kerling and, as day broke, Companies I and G moved up and blocked the road west of the village.

The Continuation of the 90th Division Attack

During 10 November there was little activity in the zone of the 359th Infantry, on the north wing of the division, but opposite the center and right of the 90th enemy resistance began to stiffen as the American attack hit the Fort Koenigsmacker and Métrich positions held by the *74th Regiment.* The 357th Infantry had occupied the town of Koenigsmacher without a fight the

[22] These elements of the *25th Panzer Grenadier Division* were part of the OKW reserve for use in the event of an airborne attack by the Allies.

night before, and now the 3d Battalion marched under cover of the morning fog to attack the Métrich works, about a mile southeast of Koenigsmacker, which constituted the initial objective for the regiment. The leading company made the assault up the western slope of the heights on which the Métrich works were located, advancing with marching fire, killing some thirty Germans in the open trenches on the summit, and driving the remaining enemy back into the concrete fortifications. Meanwhile, the 2d Battalion moved one company from the town of Métrich in an attack against the eastern fortifications. Here the Germans, using intense cross fire from machine guns in pillboxes, killed the company commander and executive officer and repelled the assault. When artillery fire failed to neutralize this strong point the 2d Battalion moved around the heights to join the 3d Battalion, the two forming up to face down the Maginot Line ridge as the day ended.

On the right the 358th Infantry also found the Germans reacting more stubbornly on 10 November. After repulsing a stiff counterattack in Basse-Ham where it had been covering the regiment's open right flank, Company C was moved to Fort Koenigsmacker in an endeavor to take the fort by assault from the south. There it ran into a wide and deep moat faced with stone and concrete and filled with twenty-five rows of barbed wire. Company C then was shifted to the west to link up more closely with the remainder of the 1st Battalion and to knock out a German assault from the fort which had temporarily cut off one platoon of Company A. On top of Fort Koenigsmacker Companies A and B, now reinforced by C, blasted away at the ferro-concrete works jutting above the surface.[23] However, the enemy guns on the fort were not silenced and machine guns covering the roads below still were active. Concealed by the early morning fog two companies of the 3d Battalion passed the fort successfully and dug in on the Bois d'Elzange ridge, the regimental objective, where they waited for the remainder of the battalion to advance through the fire laid down by Fort Koenigsmacker. The 2d Battalion tried to swing around north of the fort and join the troops of the 3d Battalion on the ridge, but was badly cut up and halted by flanking fire from the fort.

As the second day of the attack ended, the situation in the 90th Division bridgehead seemed most precarious. Unaware of the weakness of the German

[23] Supplies were badly needed at the fort and 1st Lt. Lloyd A. Watland, an artillery liaison pilot with the 90th Division Artillery, was sent to discover the best approach by air. He deliberately drew the enemy fire, flying as low as ten feet from the ground, and so charted a reasonably safe course for other planes. He was awarded the DSC.

ENGINEERS WORKING IN CHILL WATERS *to span the Moselle at Cattenom, where the flooded river was 1,000 yards wide.*

forces opposing the division, General Van Fleet and his troops expected a full scale counterattack, since this was the obvious moment for retaliatory action. No armor or tank destroyer support was across the river as yet and covering fire depended on the batteries sited on the west bank, whose gunners, working in mud to their knees, fired around the clock. The infantry were tired, soaked to the skin, and numbed with cold. What few blankets were to be had were used for the wounded. Rations were slim and ammunition was becoming scarce. Battle casualties had mounted, but fatigue and exposure threatened to take an even greater toll in the ranks. The supply routes back to the river were still under fire. The rapidly dwindling medical supplies in the aid stations on the far side, plus the considerable hazard involved in the laborious three-hour crossing of the torrent, now under heavy fire from German artillery, forced the decision that evacuation across the Moselle would be limited to the severely wounded who were expected to die unless they were rendered more extensive medical attention than was possible there. Lacking their own vehicles, supply parties were forced to carry what they could in abandoned baby buggies and rickety farm wagons. The Moselle continued to rise and at Cattenom was nearly a thousand yards wide. Actually the inundated area measured one and a half miles in breadth, water standing in the streets of both Cattenom and Gavisse. At dark the long supply trek started. A few power launches and engineer rafts were able to battle their way across the river; other craft were sunk by submerged fence posts or swept downstream. The 1st Battalion of the 359th, the last reserve on the west bank, loaded into motor boats and attempted to cross, but all the boats except one were forced to return to the point of embarkation. Everything now depended on bridging the roaring current, for without an uninterrupted service of supply the 90th Division could not hope to drive far out of the bridgehead. The engineer ponton companies, working in the chill water and under constant shelling, did their best. But the work went slowly. Finally, about midnight, the bridge structure at the Malling site was completed. Even so, it would be some hours before trucks, tanks, and tank destroyers could start rolling across, for the causeway leading to the west end of the bridge now lay under five feet of water.[24]

Despite the weather and the river some resupply reached the troops across the Moselle, and a few 57-mm. antitank guns were ferried over to reinforce the infantry. Early on the morning of 11 November the three regiments swung into an advance, the tired and miserable "doughfeet" moving forward with surprising speed and drive. In the center the 2d and 3d Battalions of the 357th launched a predawn attack, moving abreast in column of companies down the main Maginot ridge line, which here rose between two little streams, the Canner and the Oudrenne. One company of the 3d Battalion was detached to clear the enemy from the remaining works of the Métrich position. Before daybreak the company was in the pillboxes surrounding the last large casemate—but something had been learned from the Fort Driant experience and no attempt was made to force a way through the tunnel entrances leading into the casemate. Instead, a small detachment was left behind to seal in the German garrison with small arms fire. The main body of the 357th moved swiftly over the rugged, wooded ground, following the few narrow trails that passed for roads, or maneuvering cross country to assault

[24] 90th Div AAR, 10 Nov 44.

or bypass the Maginot Line pillboxes that dotted the ridge. Those pillboxes which could be taken readily were blasted with demolition charges. At points where the Maginot works had a wide field of fire, or were stubbornly defended, the attackers circled wide and dropped off a few men to mop up the position. By the evening of 11 November the leading infantry of the 357th were in possession of the high ground northwest of Breistroff-la-Petite, forming a salient well in advance of the regiments on the flanks.[25] But both battalions of the 357th found themselves deployed in very great depth; only a few troops were on the forward line, the remainder being strung out rearward to cover the exposed flanks or to contain the bypassed enemy pillboxes.[26] Supply again was a problem. The 357th interdicted the valley roads below the ridge but could not use them itself, and through the night carrying parties stumbled across the transverse draws and gullies that chopped up the 4,000-yard supply route.

On the north wing of the division the 359th briefly was thrown off stride by local counterattacks during the morning hours—probably made by troops of the reserve regiment of the *19th VG Division*. Just before daylight a rain of artillery shells exploded among the 1st Battalion infantry holding the left flank of the regiment. Behind this concentration about one hundred fifty Germans and three assault guns advanced from the forest cover of the Videmsbusch toward the American lines. Two of the enemy guns were disabled at the first shock,[27] but the 1st Battalion was being driven back; then a platoon of only ten men, from A Company, charged in on the German flank and disorganized the attackers. By this time the American artillery was on the target and the enemy had no stomach for continuing the fight. At 0900 the lost ground was retaken and the battalion moved forward to the attack.[28]

On the opposite flank the 3d Battalion had just occupied the high ground directly north of Kerling when German assault guns and infantry counter-

[25] The 90th Division After Action Report says of the 357th Infantry (—): "The day's attack was a brilliant performance. . . ." The most advanced elements of the 359th Infantry were 4,000 yards to the rear of the forward line of the 357th; the 358th was 2,000 yards behind.

[26] No serious attempt had been made to man the Maginot Line in the *LXXXII Corps* sector prior to this American attack because guns and troops simply were not available. A German report gives the strength of the security forces in this sector of the line as 58 officers and 218 men. However, there were 51 machine guns and 16 guns in the fortifications.

[27] Probably by fire from the four battalion antitank guns which had been sent across the river to reinforce the 1st Battalion.

[28] Capt. Albert L. Budd, G Company, 359th Infantry, led a platoon from the reserve battalion in a counterattack into the German flank. Although he was seriously wounded, Captain Budd continued to lead his men until the enemy fell back. He was awarded the DSC.

attacked. Bazookas, the only antitank weapon at hand, failed to stop the oncoming assault guns. As a last desperate measure the American guns using indirect fire from across the river were told to continue their fire, even though the Germans were already in the 3d Battalion lines and casualties would be suffered by the Americans from their own shells. Capt. Frank Neuswanger, commanding I Company, and Capt. Henry Bauschausen, leading K Company, were both killed as they rallied the troops to make a stand, but their example gave heart to their men and the Germans finally were repelled.[29]

By midmorning the 359th attack had gained full momentum all along its front. The ridges ahead were taken after a stiff fight, Kerling was outposted, but Oudrenne remained in German hands. The American troops seized and blocked the crossroads southeast of Rettel, thus cutting the main highway entering the regimental zone from the north, and the left flank of the division was stabilized along a relatively defensible line.

Over on the south flank of the 90th Division the 358th Infantry had what the divisional After Action Report called "an exceptional day" on 11 November. Early in the morning the elements of the 3d Battalion which had filtered past the guns at Fort Koenigsmacker and taken up positions on the Bois d'Elzange ridge captured a three-man patrol coming along the back road that led to the fort. The Germans told their captors that a relief party of about 145 men was following, en route to reinforce the garrison. Thereupon, 1st Lt. Frank E. Gatewood deployed K Company and his five machine guns in an ambush and, when the German column was only fifty yards away, gave the order to fire. Over half of the enemy were killed. The rest fled.[30]

Before daybreak the 2d Battalion slipped past the machine guns and artillery on the north side of Fort Koenigsmacker, which had checked its advance the day before, mounted the ridge, and took its assigned position on the right of the 3d Battalion. While the 1st Battalion, reinforced by G Company, continued the fight at the fort, the balance of the regiment drove ahead along the ridge under continuous mortar fire. In the late afternoon the 3d Battalion attacked and took Hill 254, whose field fortifications overlooked the road between Valmestroff and Elzange, killing or capturing "its considerable gar-

[29] Captain Bauschausen, S–3 of the 3d Battalion, took over K Company when the company commander and executive became casualties. He reorganized the company and then led a counterattack, in which he was killed. He was given the DSC posthumously. Capt. Oral G. Nelson, L Company commander, also distinguished himself by reckless bravery during this action. Captain Nelson was awarded the DSC.

[30] The date of this action is uncertain. The 3d Battalion Journal gives it as 11 November. Historical Division Combat Interviews record it as a day later.

rison." [31] Back at Fort Koenigsmacker G Company, led by the regimental commander, Col. C. H. Clarke, made a close envelopment arriving at the rear of the fort just as the German battalion there decided to call it quits and evacuate the position.[32] Ringed in completely and trapped by fire on the tunnel exits to the east, the garrison commander put out the white flag. The Germans had lost at least 301 captured or killed in defending the fort.[33] The losses of the attacking battalion numbered 111, killed, wounded, and missing.

At the end of 11 November the 90th Division was in a far more advantageous situation than twenty-four hours earlier. The left flank, which was also that of the corps and army, was fairly secure. The first German main line of resistance had been broken at Forts Métrich and Koenigsmacker, and was cracking at spots along the ridge lines in the sectors of the 357th and 358th. Over five hundred prisoners had been taken. The area of penetration had nearly doubled. Finally, the flooded Moselle had begun to recede. At midnight the first tractors snaking trucks loaded with jeeps and supplies splashed through the flooded causeways and over the Malling bridge. Ferries, now more manageable, crossed vehicles and antitank guns. With the flood waters ebbing at the rate of about three-fourths of an inch per hour, however, it would still be a matter of hours until the 90th Division drive could be supported in proper fashion.[34]

The enemy fight thus far had been carried by the *416th Division*, reinforced by infantry of the *19th VG Division*. But at long last the Kampfgruppe of the *25th Panzer Grenadier Division*, earmarked earlier for use in counterattack, had procured some gasoline and trucks. During the night of 11–12 November this Kampfgruppe moved south to assembly areas opposite the 359th Infantry. Rundstedt's headquarters had ordered specifically that the counterthrust be made just south of Sierck, apparently with intent to roll up

[31] This attack was made with bayonet and grenade. During the assault against the hill 1st Lt. Max Short of K Company led his depleted platoon into the German positions, killed one of the enemy with a blow from his rifle butt, another with his trench knife, and then fell mortally wounded. He was given the DSC posthumously. Capt. Charles L. Bryan, L Company, 358th Infantry, also was awarded the DSC for heroism on this and the preceding day.

[32] Earlier in the day Pfc. Warren D. Shanafelter, B Company, 358th Infantry, volunteered to silence a particularly troublesome pillbox. Although all the while under fire he blew a gap, then coolly exploded another charge to widen the opening, entered the pillbox, and finished off its occupants He received the DSC.

[33] This figure is given in the 358th After Action Report. The 90th Division After Action Report estimates the German losses as 372 prisoners, plus "many dead."

[34] Brig. Gen. H. R. Gay, Third Army Deputy Chief of Staff, was awarded the DSC for personal reconnaissance in the 90th Division bridgehead on 11 November.

the 90th Division front by unhinging the American north flank. However, the subordinate headquarters, more familiar with the terrain, shifted the axis of the attack so as to avoid the deep ravine extending south from Sierck, and thus brought the assault up against the center and right of the 359th.

At 0300, on 12 November, the *25th Panzer Grenadier* Kampfgruppe, composed of the *35th Panzer Grenadier Regiment* and reinforced by some ten tanks and assault guns, struck the lines of the 359th.[35] The initial German assault drove the 3d Battalion outposts out of Kerling and forced the battalion back to the high ground northwest of the village. There, after much confusion, it re-formed on the right of the 1st Battalion. Shortly before 0600 the main attack developed, one enemy force thrusting along the Kerling–Petite-Hettange road, another striking at the junction of the 1st and 3d Battalions south of Hunting.[36] The attack down the road was made in force, with the obvious intention of seizing Petite-Hettange and from there launching a blow against the Malling bridge site. Led by assault guns and tanks, the German infantry marched in single file on both sides of the road—straight toward Petite-Hettange and the reserve positions manned by the 2d Battalion. The first clash came when the enemy hit G Company (1st Lt. A. L. Budd) and two platoons of the 2d Battalion heavy weapons company (Capt. S. E. McCann) deployed in the woods south of the road. A part of the German column turned aside to deal with these forces; a part continued on toward Petite-Hettange. The mortar and machine gun crews supporting G Company especially distinguished themselves in the action which followed. Sgt. Forrest E. Everhart, who had taken over the machine gun platoon when the platoon commander, 1st Lt. William O'Brien, was killed, led his men with such bravery as to be awarded the Congressional Medal of Honor.[37] Pvt. Earl Oliver stayed with his machine gun when the other guns had been knocked out, and maintained a continuous fire until he was killed by a mortar shell. When day broke twenty-two enemy dead were found in front of his position—some only fifteen feet away.[38] So close had the Germans pressed the assault that a sergeant in the mortar platoon had uncoupled the bipod of his mortar and used it at

[35] MS #A–000 (Mellenthin).

[36] The story of this fight is taken from Historical Division Combat Interviews, 359th Infantry and 90th Division After Action Reports. See also Ltr, Capt S. E. McCann to Hist Div, 14 Aug 47.

[37] Sergeant Everhart broke up an enemy counterattack with a one-man charge. The War Department General Orders that contain Everhart's citation state that he personally killed or wounded fifty of the enemy.

[38] Private Oliver was awarded the DSC posthumously.

point-blank range. Although G Company was cut off, the attackers could not overrun its position, and they finally were driven off when the American gunners west of the river laid down a box barrage.

Farther down the road toward Petite-Hettange two American antitank pieces were knocked out by the assault guns in the van of the attack column. But a third antitank gun continued to fire in the darkness up the Kerling road and succeeded in immobilizing the enemy point. Meanwhile, Lt. Col. Robert Booth, the 2d Battalion commander, gathered a mixed force of cooks, clerks, and an intelligence and reconnaissance platoon, at the crossroads southeast of Petite-Hettange. This scratch force momentarily checked the German column with fire from small arms and bazookas. By now all of the twenty artillery battalions available to give support were busy shelling the road. Then, as a last crippling blow, two American tank destroyers that had been able to make their way across the Malling bridge, just before it was destroyed by enemy artillery fire, came rolling through the half-light up to the crossroads and before stopping destroyed two German assault guns and immobilized a third. The American infantry, artillery, and tank destroyers had taken the heart out of the Germans and they began to fall back; only one enemy assault gun got away.[39] Later, some two hundred enemy bodies were counted lying alongside the cratered road.

The secondary attack against the south flank of the 1st Battalion, disposed in the woods north of Hunting, was equally unsuccessful. Here the enemy infantry crept forward through the darkness until they were only fifty yards from the woods and then charged, firing and yelling. Although the American riflemen were driven back, Pfc. Lloyd F. Harbaugh, of D Company, bravely manned his heavy machine gun and held back the attackers while his own infantry reorganized. When his ammunition gave out Private Harbaugh was killed, but he had won time for his comrades and the German attack finally was repelled with heavy loss to the enemy.

The main body of the enemy already was in retreat toward Kerling when Colonel Booth and Lieutenant Budd led Companies E and G in a wild charge into the German flank, turning the withdrawal into a rout. In sum, the counterattack on which the German command had counted so heavily cost the

[39] Not expecting any such aid the 2d Battalion bazooka teams were ready to blast away when a quick-witted sergeant intervened to save the two tank destroyers. Just after the pair of TD's had crossed, the German artillery hit the Malling bridge and broke loose a section which floated 800 yards downstream.

enemy over 400 dead, about 150 prisoners, 4 tanks, and 5 assault guns. By late afternoon the 359th had restored its lines and was ready to attack. The 2d Battalion led off along the road to Kerling, where the enemy attacks had been formed. It was slowed down by mines, however, and finally forced to halt short of the village at dark.

Progress along the ridge in the center of the 90th Division zone was rapid on 12 November, but the stubborn enemy made the 357th Infantry pay heavily for its gains. The reserve battalion had been brought across the river, though with much difficulty, and with this reinforcement available to mop up the troublesome pillboxes in their rear the 2d and 3d Battalions were free to continue the advance. As the 3d Battalion emerged from the Bois de Koenigsmacker and into the draw below, it came under fire from a line of trenches on the forward slope of the next ridge southeast of Breistroff-la-Petite. For some hours the battalion maneuvered to close with the Germans in the trenches. Finally, Pfc. Foster J. Sayers, of L Company, wormed his way through the wire strung along the glacis in front of the German trench line, leaped into the trench, and poured an enfilading fire from his light machine gun down its length. Private Sayers was killed.[40] But his company poured through the breach he had made and the position was taken. The 2d Battalion had circled around the Germans on the slope and when the day ended held a spur overlooking the village of Inglange.[41] On the left the 3d Battalion lay with its open flank refused, waiting for the situation in front of the 359th to clarify. This day of battle had seen the enemy forced to relinquish another segment of the long ridge chain; but the ranks of the two assault battalions were rapidly thinning.

The 358th Infantry likewise found the Germans on its front determined to stand and hold. The 1st Battalion was placed in reserve, covering the right flank of the division and resting after the hard battle at Fort Koenigsmacker. The 2d and 3d Battalions launched a co-ordinated attack against Valmestroff and Elzange. These villages were taken after bitter fighting during which

[40] Private Sayres accounted for twelve of the enemy before he was killed. He was awarded the Congressional Medal of Honor posthumously.

[41] During this advance 1st Lt. Claude E. Lovett, G Company, 357th Infantry, saw a detachment pinned down in the open by German machine gun fire. He charged through a wire entanglement and knocked out the enemy position. Lieutenant Lovett received the DSC. In a similar feat of arms Sgt. Joe T. Rutherford, also of G Company, destroyed a machine gun position, killing five and capturing four of the enemy. He was awarded the DSC.

the enemy not only stood his ground but counterattacked, firing bazookas into the trees to get tree bursts over the Americans. Beyond Valmestroff the 2d Battalion was checked by a cluster of field fortifications and pillboxes.[42] Worse than the enemy fire above ground, however, was a new and dangerous German weapon, met here for the first time—the plastic and wooden box mine—against which the conventional mine detector was useless.

Back at the river, prospects were a little brighter at the close of 12 November. A bridge was under construction at the Cattenom crossing. The Malling bridge was in process of repair, after a lucky hit by German gunners.[43] Both crossing sites were fairly well covered by a smoke screen. The Moselle had ebbed to a point where heavy rafting could be done, and by midnight two platoons of tank destroyers, two platoons of tanks, and a number of jeeps fitted as litter carriers had been ferried across. But in the forward positions there was little to cheer the foot soldier. There still were no dry clothes or blankets in which he might warm himself during the cold November nights. Each company had gaping ranks; and in six of the nine battalions the rifle strength was now only half the original complement.[44] Moreover, the events of 12 November gave no indication that the German will to resist was weakening.

On the enemy side of the hill the *LXXXII Corps* had only a gloomy story to relate to the *First Army* and *Army Group G*. As early as 10 November *OB WEST* started an investigation to determine the causes for the American penetration south of Sierck. The explanations proffered were: the lack of combat experience in the *416th Division* and its dispersal along an overextended front; the accurate and heavy American artillery fire, ably adjusted by low flying observation planes; and the intervention of the American Jabo's, which prevented the movement of troops into counterattack positions. There was little answer that Rundstedt's headquarters could make when presented

[42] While acting as a company runner Pvt. Earl F. Gormley, H Company, 358th Infantry, discovered a German artillery piece being brought into position. He attacked alone, killed or wounded three of the crew, and forced the rest to surrender. He received the DSC.

[43] The gallant work of the 991st Engineer Treadway Bridge Company at the Malling site was later recognized by the award of a Distinguished Unit Citation. When enemy fire destroyed their first bridge, the engineers constructed a ferry out of the fragments and manned it while building a second bridge.

[44] 90th Div AAR, 12 Nov 44. During these crucial days at the river General Patton was briefed on every single vehicle or gun that crossed to the east bank. The TUSA Diary for 11 November contains an excellent eyewitness account of conditions in the bridgehead in a report by the deputy chief of staff, General Gay.

with such an explanation. The picture became even more somber when a captured American officer told German interrogators that the XX Corps intended to make a double envelopment around Metz.[45] *OB WEST* warned Balck not to underrate the American threat north of Thionville. But, again, advice was all that the higher headquarters could spare—plus two battalions of artillery which were dispatched from *Army Group B* to the north flank of the *First Army*. On 11 November the *LXXXII Corps* pulled all security troops, except one battalion, away from the Moselle north of the 90th Division bridgehead and threw them in to face the American attack. The failure of the counterattack by the Kampfgruppe of the *25th Panzer Grenadier Division* on 12 November ended all hope of erasing or containing the American force north of Thionville—if, indeed, Balck and his lower commanders had ever had the illusion of success. German intelligence reported that the American 83d Infantry Division and an unidentified armored division were yet to be committed in the bridgehead.[46] Metz was being threatened from the south, the American XII Corps was widening its penetration in the center of the *First Army*, and the American Seventh Army was massing to launch an offensive in front of the Saverne Gap. Therefore, at 1720 on 12 November, Balck ordered the right wing of the *LXXXII Corps* to go on the defensive, adding extravagant promises that a new division would shortly be available for use as a counterattack force.[47]

The 90th Division Advance Continues—13 November

By 13 November the advance of the 357th Infantry had carried the regiment almost beyond range of its artillery support. The regiment paused and cleared out the remaining knots of Germans in its rear with explosive charges and flame throwers, while the regiments on either flank moved up abreast. The 359th Infantry reoccupied Kerling without a fight. But when the 2d Battalion attacked, late in the afternoon, to effect a juncture with the 357th outposts near Oudrenne, the leading company hit squarely into a large mine field. Three tanks, leading the advance, were destroyed in quick succession. After futile attempts to find the limits of the mined area, the infantry were

[45] *Army Group G KTB*, 10 Nov 44.

[46] German intelligence believed that this was probably the 14th Armored Division. The 10th Armored Division was still carried, by *OB WEST* situation maps, in reserve behind the XII Corps.

[47] The *First Army* commander had argued that further counterattacks would be suicidal in view of the American artillery strength. *OB WEST KTB*, 12 Nov 44.

forced to attack straight through the mines, taking their losses. (Later, over twelve thousand plastic and wooden box mines were taken from this one mine field.) The 358th Infantry also was slowed down by mines as it continued along the ridge chain, but the enemy infantry gave little opposition and apparently were retiring to a new line of defense.[48] The bridge at the Cattenom site was finally completed during the morning by engineer parties building from both sides of the river under a very elaborate smoke screen—laid down by smoke generators, 4.2 chemical mortars, and two battalions of field guns—which did not break once during the entire day. Just as the last section of the 645-foot steel treadway was moved into place a DUKW struck a mine near the far exit. Then it was found that the eastern end of the bridge lay in the midst of a mine field which had been covered by the flood waters, now receding. Five hours were lost while the engineers went about the hazardous task of probing under water for the mines, and at 1645 the bridge was ready. One gun from each light artillery battalion was rushed across to register at new ranges before darkness set in. The 90th Reconnaissance Troop and light tanks also pushed into the unending stream of bridge traffic and swung south to establish contact with the 95th Division bridgehead at Uckange. By dawn of 14 November all regimental transport, three battalions of 105-mm. howitzers, a tank destroyer battalion, and the vehicles of the division's engineer battalion were across the river. Using this single bridge, for the Malling bridge still was damaged, the 90th Division had crossed all of its organic units and attachments, plus four battalions of supporting artillery, by 1500 that same afternoon.[49] For the first time in six days and nights the troops in the bridgehead had overcoats, blankets, and dry socks.

During the day the 359th occupied Oudrenne and joined its right flank firmly to the line held by the 357th. The 358th continued its push and placed the 3d Battalion astride the Inglange–Distroff road. Then, when the German garrisons in the two villages were denied mutual support, the attack forked out to take them. The 2d Battalion captured Distroff in some very hard fighting and rescued a twenty-four-man patrol, belonging to the 3d Battalion, which had entered the village but had been driven to seek shelter in the

[48] During the first day the 1st Battalion cleared some woods called le Quart en Réserve—a name which for obvious reasons particularly pleased the American infantry.

[49] 90th Div AAR, 14 Nov 44. See also 179th Engr Bn Jnl, 13 Nov 44; 206th Engr Bn Jnl, for the whole period.

cellars when the streets were found alive with the enemy. Around Inglange the German artillery kept up a heavy shelling on the 3d Battalion, and patrols sent out toward the town reported that it was strongly defended. Capt. J. S. Spivey, commanding the battalion, therefore decided to withhold his assault until there was sufficient artillery and tank support forward. This support was on its way despite deep mud on the tops of the ridges, and not only the leading formations of the 357th, but the rest of the division as well, were shortly in position to resume a co-ordinated advance.

The Expansion of the 95th Division Bridgehead

On the night of 10 November General Walker ordered General Twaddle, the 95th Infantry Division commander, to expand his operation on the east bank of the Moselle, where the 1st Battalion of the 377th Infantry had its foothold opposite Uckange. General Walker was still seeking to establish a firm bridgehead, with adequate heavy bridging, through which to cross the 10th Armored Division in accordance with the XX Corps scheme of maneuver. The corps commander therefore instructed General Twaddle to commit the 2d Battalion, 378th Infantry (Lt. Col. A. J. Maroun), acting as corps reserve, in a reconnaissance in force to determine the feasibility of seizing a bridgehead at Thionville, about three miles north of the tiny lodgment area held by the 1st Battalion, 377th.

Two companies of the reserve battalion, supported by the 135th Engineer Combat Battalion, crossed the Moselle, which here separated the American- and German-held districts of the city, and by midday on 11 November had cleared a small area in the eastern section. Stronger resistance was encountered at the edge of the city, where the Germans were holed up in Fort Yutz, a large, old, star-shaped fortification of the Vauban type. This fort was separated from the city proper by a canal which served the fort as a forward moat. Fortunately, the canal was narrow enough at two points to be crossed without boats; F and G Companies made their way across and into the fort under heavy mortar fire. Here the German garrison stood its ground with flame throwers and small arms, but by noon of 13 November the 2d Battalion overpowered it and held Fort Yutz. North of Thionville the Americans quickly expanded the bridgehead perimeter. One artillery shell fired into Basse-Yutz produced a fluttering of white towels and sheets—the Germans had withdrawn. East of Thionville the battalion pushed out as far as Haute-Yutz before dawn of 14 November, and then took the village with little trouble.[50]

The story changed when the 2d Battalion switched to the southern sector of the Thionville bridgehead perimeter on the afternoon of 14 November. On the northern end of the Illange plateau were clustered four works of the Driant type, small but rather modern, and a fixed battery, grouped to give mutual support and to cover the main Metz–Thionville highway, along which the 2d Battalion had to advance in order to relieve the 1st Battalion of the 377th Infantry, isolated on the east bank of the Moselle opposite Uckange. As the 2d Battalion approached Fort Illange an apprehensive German soldier put out the white flag. Colonel Maroun dispatched 1st Lt. James Billings to demand a surrender, promoting Billings briefly for prestige purposes with an extra pair of captain's bars. Although the garrison consisted of only one company of the *74th Regiment*, the enemy commander nevertheless refused to negotiate and prepared to defend his position. A call from the 2d Battalion brought the artillery across the river into action and shells from the 155-mm. guns and 240-mm. howitzers poured in on the fort. When the fire lifted, the three rifle companies debouched from the woods surrounding the fort and went up the slope at a run in front of the German works. At the top the infantry took shelter in a fringe of trees encircling the fort area and waited while artillery and mortar fire again was concentrated on the enemy. The final assault was made through twenty yards of barbed wire under severe shelling by the German mortars, whose crews had returned to their weapons as soon as the American concentration ended. By dark a third of the *enceinte* was cleared.[51] All through the night a fire fight raged, but next morning the Americans "buttoned up" the reinforced concrete works above ground with machine guns and mortars, and then proceeded systematically to blast them open with shaped charges. Their occupants were finished off with threaded charges of ten-pound TNT blocks dropped in through the vents. At 1040 the German survivors surrendered to Colonel Maroun, who had been twice wounded during the action. The capture of the Illange forts ended all organized resistance in the northern sector of the 95th Division zone east of the Moselle. On the previous day the cavalry reconnaissance troop of the

[50] 95th Div AAR. See also a letter from Colonel Maroun to the Historical Division (16 June 1947), which gives detailed plans of the fort and describes the action.

[51] Sgt. Robert G. Bussard, F Company, 378th Infantry, was later awarded the DSC for his part in this action. He assaulted a pillbox alone—although wounded in the knees as he approached—killed four of the enemy, and captured twelve. Sergeant Bussard again was wounded before he could return to his platoon.

90th Division, reinforced by a light tank company, had struck out of the 90th Division bridgehead and reached the 95th Division troops in the Thionville sector, finally establishing a protected corridor along the east bank of the Moselle through which the 10th Armored Division could move.

At 1015 on 15 November, while Colonel Maroun's battalion still was fighting at the Illange forts, Col. Robert L. Bacon[52] was given command of the 95th Division troops east of the river, provided with some cavalry, engineers, and tank destroyers, and ordered to attack south with this task force toward Metz, clearing the enemy from the east bank of the Moselle as he went.[53] In actuality, Task Force Bacon at this moment did not exist as a homogeneous command, for the 2d Battalion, 378th Infantry, and the 1st Battalion, 377th Infantry, were not yet in contact. Indeed, the 1st Battalion now was so hard pressed by the enemy that the other troops composing Task Force Bacon were compelled to launch an immediate attack south for its relief.

On the morning of 13 November the last company of the 1st Battalion, 377th Infantry, crossed the Moselle to join the little force already in the Uckange bridgehead. General Twaddle had ordered the 1st Battalion to attack at once and push north past the towns of Bertrange and Imeldange, take Illange—which lay on the edge of the dominant plateau south of Thionville—and make contact with the drive southward by the 2d Battalion of the 378th Infantry. (*Map XXXI*) Company A debarked from its assault boats straight into the attack and took Bertrange and Imeldange without much fighting. The remainder of the 1st Battalion swung north and was just in the process of setting up defenses in the two villages, preparatory to bivouacking for the night, when a task force from the *73d Regiment* of the *19th VG Division* and a mobile unit from the *485th Antitank Battalion* counterattacked. The American forces in the two towns were separated and both were hard beset by mobile columns of infantry. In their armored personnel carriers the Germans dashed up and down the streets, firing into the houses where the Americans had taken shelter, and spreading disorder and confusion in their wake. The tank destroyers emplaced west of the river as direct support for the 1st Battalion did not have the range to reach the counterattack. Communication

[52] Colonel Bacon had previously commanded a regiment in the 90th Infantry Division.

[53] Task Force Bacon finally included the 1st Battalion of the 377th Infantry, the 2d Battalion of the 378th Infantry, the 95th Reconnaissance Troop, two companies from the 807th Tank Destroyer Battalion, one company from the 778th Tank Battalion, the 920th Field Artillery Battalion (105-mm. howitzer), and two self-propelled 155-mm. guns.

between the battalion and the artillery fire control center across the river was quickly lost. About 0830 on 14 November radio contact was re-established and the American artillery opened up, with the first sergeant of A Company acting as forward observer. All during the day the enemy, supported by light armored vehicles, pressed the attack. At 2200 Colonel Decker reported that the position of his battalion was "desperate." Once more contact with the battalion was lost. Patrols sent back to the river to carry messages and obtain supplies were cut off. By the morning of 15 November the two villages were wrecked and gutted by the bitter fighting, but the 1st Battalion, its ranks much reduced by severe losses, held on.[54] The relief force moving south from Illange arrived on the scene in the nick of time and, after a short sharp fight, Bertrange, on the main road, was freed.[55] Then a platoon of tank destroyers turned toward Imeldange and shelled the enemy out of that village.[56] By 1300 the Germans were routed and the 1st Battalion joined Task Force Bacon in the advance on Metz.[57]

The 10th Armored Division is Committed

On 9 November the 10th Armored Division assembled around Molvange and Rumelange, which were far enough west of the Moselle to be safe from enemy observation. There it waited for General Walker to give the order committing the division east of the river. On receipt of the order from the corps it was supposed to cross the Moselle in two columns, pass through the 90th Division bridgehead wrested from the Germans north of Thionville, and strike quickly to effect a deep penetration. Once the division sliced through the enemy crust the 10th Armored plan of maneuver called for the left column to advance to the east and win a bridgehead over the Sarre River, somewhere near Merzig. This bid for a Sarre crossing site was particularly important in

[54] Hist Div Combat Interviews; 377th Inf Jnl and AAR; MS #B-527 (Britzelmayr). During this fighting Cpl. Edward J. Stepanik distinguished himself as an aid man with C Company, 377th Infantry, bravely assisting the wounded under direct enemy fire. He received the DSC.

[55] Colonel Maroun received the DSC for bravery in directing the assault by the 2d Battalion, 378th Infantry, despite his wounds. Maroun's battalion was awarded a Distinguished Unit Citation for its battles between 11 and 15 November. During this period the battalion lost over two hundred casualties.

[56] The capture of Fort Illange and Imeldange broke the last connection between the *19th VG Division* and the Metz garrison.

[57] A check made by Colonel Bacon showed that the strength of the 1st Battalion, 377th Infantry, had been gravely reduced: Company A had only 1 officer and 42 men; Company B had 1 officer and 39 men; Company C had 4 officers and 107 men.

light of General Patton's plans for continuation of the Third Army offensive. The second column, advancing on the right of the first column and at the same time protecting the left flank of the 90th Infantry Division, was given the task of taking the division objective. This objective included Bouzonville—the center of arterial highway and railroad traffic running northeast out of Metz—and a stretch of high ground extending for about six miles north of Bouzonville on both sides of the Nied River valley. Capture of the sector would give the Americans command over one of the main corridors through which German reinforcements might be sent to Metz, or through which a retreat from that city might be made.

The terrain in the zone assigned for the 10th Armored Division drive had little to recommend it to an armored force. The road net was limited. One good paved highway did exist, running from Kerling, through Laumesfeld and Bibiche, to Bouzonville. The only other through road which could be used for tanks stretched from Oudrenne (via Lemestroff, Monneren, and Dalstein) to Freistroff. However, this route had not been used by the Germans during the occupation and had fallen into disrepair. Any cross-country movement would be most difficult, particularly after the autumn rains had beaten into the clay soil characteristic of this country.

For five days General Morris, commander of the 10th Armored, waited for the word to send his division across the Moselle. The five days were marked by orders and counterorders, new plans and estimates—all contingent on the caprices of the flooded river and the degree of success achieved by the enemy gunners shelling the American bridge sites. The assault crossing at Thionville by Maroun's battalion gave the possibility of a new and successful bridging operation, just as the corps commander had intended. At this point the flood waters of the Moselle were constricted by two relatively high retaining walls, and the stone piers of an earlier bridge still stood. The 1306th Engineer General Service Regiment (Lt. Col. W. C. Hall) set to the task of building a Bailey bridge on 12 November, under orders from General Walker to continue on the job regardless of enemy fire. German mortars and field guns threw in one concentration after another. Once, during the late afternoon of the 12th, work had to be suspended for a couple of hours. On the morning of the 13th the wind shifted, blowing away the covering smoke. German gunners laid their shells within a hundred yards of the bridge but could not get a direct hit. This time work on the Bailey continued, the engineers climbing into the superstructure clad in flak suits. Finally, at 0930 on 14 November, the Thionville bridge was ready—the largest Bailey bridge in the European Theater of Operations.[58] On the afternoon of that day CCB (Col. William L. Roberts) began the move across the Moselle, the head of the column winding along the east bank northward to the 90th Division sector. Before daylight on 15 November, the whole combat command had assembled near Kerling behind the screen formed by the 359th Infantry. Furthermore, CCA (Brig. Gen. Kenneth G. Althaus), which was dispatched over the Malling bridge, had two companies across before dark and subsequently took position south of Colonel Roberts' column. The 3d Cavalry Group also used the Malling crossing and moved forward one squadron to relieve the north flank battalion of the 359th Infantry, preparatory to a screening and reconnaissance mission in the Sarre–Moselle triangle.

CCB began the 10th Armored Division drive on the early morning of 15 November, advancing under flurries of rain and snow along the road east of Kerling. Progress was slow. The reconnaissance units and the platoon of medium tanks at the head of the column were forced to halt again and again to deal with German road blocks, antitank guns, and pillboxes blocking the highway. CCA pushed out of the bridgehead late in the afternoon and, as day ended, entered Lemestroff at the left of the line held by the 357th Infantry. General Althaus originally had intended to keep a provisional reconnaissance squadron at the head of his combat command, in conventional fashion, but the German guns blocking the route were too effective against light armor and these reconnaissance elements were deflected to the flanks of the heavier column.[59]

The enemy forces, mostly from the *416th Division* and the *25th Panzer Grenadier* Kampfgruppe, stood their ground where they could on 16 November, but the armored columns now were well into the German positions and about 250 prisoners were bagged.[60] CCA attacked in two task forces. Task Force Chamberlain (Lt. Col. Thomas C. Chamberlain) switched through Kerling and attacked southeast along the main paved highway, bivouacking for the night east of Laumesfeld. Task Force Standish (Lt. Col. Miles L. Standish) continued along the meandering, indifferent road east of Lemestroff

[58] Colonel Hall has given his own story in the *Military Engineer*, April 1948.

[59] CCA AAR, 15 Nov 44.

[60] The appearance of the 10th Armored Division prompted *OB WEST* to give *Army Group G* permission to withdraw its north wing. *OB WEST KTB*, 15 Nov 44. The following day *OB WEST* predicted that the 10th Armored Division was engaged in a concentric attack to join the 6th Armored Division in the vicinity of Faulquemont.

and took Ste. Marguerite. CCB got as far as Kirschnaumen. Losses in tanks and men in both commands thus far had been very small.

To make maximum use of the few poor roads, on 17 and 18 November the 10th Armored Division fanned out in splinter task forces. The Germans no longer had much cohesion, but a few small groups tried to check the American armor with bazooka fire and antitank guns. More than six hundred of the enemy surrendered to the tankers and the armored infantry. For the first time in days the skies had cleared, permitting the XIX TAC to go aloft in force. General Weyland put the 405th and 406th Groups on the columns retreating before the 10th Armored—with disastrous results to the enemy. On 18 November one detachment from CCA reached the Nied River, just across from Bouzonville, but found the bridges blown. A few tanks and infantry discovered a bridge near Filstroff, damaged but still usable, and crossed the Nied north of Bouzonville; night came before the rest could cross. In the meantime the north column of CCB took Launstroff, six miles west of Merzig. One task force drove as far as Schwerdorff, only four and a half miles from the junction of the Nied and Sarre Rivers, on 18 November.[61]

CCA established a shallow bridgehead across the Nied River the following day, although the enemy (rear guard detachments of the *73d Regiment*) showed more fight than in the days past and succeeded in killing fifteen of the combat command and wounding twenty-one—a relatively high loss for this operation. Likewise, CCB was moving very slowly as the enemy stiffened to hold the approach routes leading to the Sarre River; apparently there would be no dash to seize the Sarre crossings. But the 10th Armored Division had completed its mission, insofar as the XX Corps envelopment of Metz was concerned; the infantry divisions on the inner rim of the circle had clamped tightly around the city by the morning of 19 November, and there was little probability that the enemy had the reserves available for an attack from the east to relieve the Metz garrison. Therefore, with General Patton's injunction that the Sarre must be crossed ringing in his ears, the XX Corps commander ordered General Morris to pull CCA back from the Nied River and send it north to join the rest of the division. On the night of 19–20 November the combat command blew the Nied bridges and began rolling in black-out back through the 90th Infantry Division en route to take part in the attack toward the Sarre.

[61] See 10th Armd G–3 Jnl, of these dates.

The 90th Division Continues the Attack, 15 November

When the 10th Armored Division passed through the lines of the 359th Infantry on 15 November and struck out to the east, the 90th Division bridgehead had attained a width of eleven miles and a depth of seven. Although the *416th Division* and the *19th VG Division* were giving way, and the roads behind the German lines were filled with vehicles heading east, there was still a reserve force capable of making a serious counterattack. The Kampfgruppe of the *25th Panzer Grenadier Division* had been reinforced by a battalion from the *74th Regiment* after the reverse suffered at the hands of the 359th Infantry in the fight west of Kerling; now the *First Army* commander was given permission to use it in another riposte, this time at the southern flank of the 90th Division. The German records do not reveal the reasoning behind the decision to recommit this Kampfgruppe. Probably the enemy commander merely hoped to delay the American advance and cover the withdrawal of his own troops. In any event the Kampfgruppe of the *25th Panzer Grenadier Division*, composed at this time of three battalions of infantry, field artillery, tanks, and assault guns, was sent around the open right flank of the 358th Infantry to an assembly area in the Bois de Stuckange.[62]

At daybreak on 15 November the Kampfgruppe struck east at Distroff in what the 90th Division After Action Report later called "the most violent counter blow of the campaign." Distroff was held by the 2d Battalion, 358th Infantry, its position blocking the main road net leading into the rear of the regimental sector. In addition a platoon from Company A, 712th Tank Battalion, was bivouacked in and around the village, and a platoon from the 773d Tank Destroyer Battalion was in position back of Distroff. A little before 0700 enemy shells suddenly burst in the village. This preparatory fire continued for about twenty minutes. Then the Germans were seen coming along the road from Metzervisse, a few tanks and assault guns leading the attack, and the infantry marching or riding in armored carriers. Two German battalions seemed to be involved in this assault, one hooking into Distroff from the south and one circling to the east of the village. A third battalion, apparently marching to envelop the American position from the north, was checked by the fire of the 90th Division artillery and took no part in the main fight. Close to Distroff the German tanks and assault guns were hit by fire from

[62] MS #B–527 (Britzelmayr).

DISTROFF. *The area shown in the photograph is indicated on Map XXX.*

the village. Those crews able to remove their tanks and assault guns from the danger zone did so, leaving the grenadiers to close with the Americans. The first assault waves were repelled, but the German infantry closed their ranks and returned doggedly to the attack, finally breaching the 2d Battalion outpost line and sweeping into the streets of Distroff. Another German infantry force cut the road behind the beleaguered battalion. The American tanks, tank destroyers, and infantry, under the command of Maj. William Wallace, executive officer of the 2d Battalion, held grimly to the village. As the Germans spread out, the fight broke into a series of isolated actions to hold a house or a shop. The Americans fought from doors, windows, and roof tops with pistols, rifles, and bazookas. With his battalion pressed back into the buildings by swarms of German infantry and armor, Major Wallace called down 4.2 chemical mortar fire and all available artillery fire on the streets of the town. About this time Colonel Clarke, the regimental commander, sent his remaining platoon of tank destroyers and a platoon of tanks to reinforce the 2d Battalion. The tank destroyers succeeded in getting into the north edge of Distroff, under cover of the 4.2 mortar fire which provided a smoke screen, and there entered the battle. Colonel Clarke was reluctant to commit the 1st Battalion—his only infantry reserve—because heavy German artillery fire directed at the 3d Battalion, facing Inglange, seemed to threaten an attack against the left flank of the regiment. He therefore ordered the reserve battalion to move up from Fort Koenigsmacker to the Inglange–Distroff road, so that it could go to the aid of either the 2d or the 3d Battalion—whichever would need it more. By the time it reached that road, however, the 2d Battalion already had broken the back of the German attack. After four hours of fighting the Germans broke off the engagement and retired along the road to Metzervisse, taking several prisoners with them. The charred hulks of four tanks, four assault guns, and sixteen half-tracks were counted in and around Distroff; the German dead in one field adjacent to the town numbered over one hundred and fifty.[63] American losses though not recorded were heavy, for the 2d Battalion had been hard hit; they were substantially less, however, than those of the attackers.[64]

[63] 358th Inf AAR, 15 Nov 44; Hist Div Combat Interviews.

[64] In the first seven days of this operation the 90th Infantry Division had lost 2,300 in dead, wounded, and missing. 90th Div AAR, Nov 44. This figure is probably accurate, for the combat losses of the 358th Infantry totaled 748 (358th Inf S–1 Jnl, Nov 44) and the three infantry regiments all had approximately the same casualties.

The Distroff counterattack was the last to strike the 90th Division during the envelopment of Metz, though organized and stubborn German resistance continued a while longer. During 15 November the 357th Infantry maintained its uphill and downdale advance with an attack to take the ridge between Budling and Buding. About 0645 the 2d and 3d Battalions moved out of the woods astride the ridge where the regiment had halted three days earlier. As the troops came down the forward slopes overlooking the valley road toward Budling, enemy shells began dropping at an estimated rate of one round per second. At first the guns could not be discovered. Finally the American forward observers ascertained that the fire was coming from Maginot Line casemates on top of the Hackenberg, a promontory jutting out from the east end of the enemy ridge. From there belt-fed French 75's enfiladed the whole valley and the forward lines of the 357th. Since the 3d Battalion, nearest the Hackenberg, could not advance in the face of this quick fire without unnecessarily high losses, Col. J. H. George, the regimental commander, brought the 1st Battalion up from reserve to aid the 2d Battalion in making an envelopment of the enemy's left flank. At the same time American guns began hammering away at the Hackenberg works with counterbattery fire. A platoon of tank destroyers opened up at 2,750 yards and immediately scored direct hits on the German casemates—with no discernible results. Then the heavy pieces took a hand in the action, but neither the 8-inch guns nor the 240-mm. howitzers were able to still the enemy artillery.

The day ended with the 357th still held in check. During the night, however, some self-propelled 155-mm. guns were moved to within 2,000 yards of the Hackenberg and on 16 November they neutralized the German guns, allowing the two right-wing battalions to cross the valley and take the steep, wooded ridge beyond. Next day the attack continued on its up-and-down course, only to be checked in the second valley ahead when the 2d Battalion unexpectedly ran into a determined enemy detachment barricaded in the village of Klang. In the meantime the 3d Battalion occupied the Hackenberg. There they found that the American self-propelled guns had already given the quietus to its defenders, whose bodies lay heaped around the demolished quick firers. Hastening on to pass between the two leading battalions the 3d Battalion arrived just in time to take part in a squeeze play at Klang. The appearance of some American tanks rolling down the road toward Klang had discouraged the enemy in the town and precipitated a general exodus, but the Germans had delayed their retreat just long enough to permit the 2d and 3d Battalions to close a pincers beyond Klang. The regimental dispatches on the evening of 17 November reported laconically: "Slaughter was appalling."

While the 357th was busy cracking the last resistance in front of the division left wing (the 359th was now in reserve), the 358th wedged its way forward on the right. After waiting twenty-four hours outside of Inglange for the situation at Distroff to emerge clearly from the smoke of battle, the 3d Battalion struck down into Inglange on 16 November in a co-ordinated assault with tanks and tank destroyers. Most of the defenders had evacuated the spot during the earlier lull and only thirty prisoners and two antitank guns were taken. The 2d Battalion followed up its hard-won victory at Distroff in an attack co-ordinated with the 1st Battalion, both using marching fire. The 2d Battalion took Metzervisse, after the village had been subjected to a heavy shelling by division and corps artillery, and a flanking attack had turned the German position along the railroad embankment on the north. On 17 November the 2d Battalion continued on to Metzeresche with tanks leading. By now the enemy was withdrawing everywhere. Metzeresche was quickly overrun and the 1st Battalion leapfrogged ahead to a position astride the Dalstein–Metz road.

The events of 17 November, both north and south of Metz, greatly worried General Balck, the *Army Group G* commander. He saw that unless the north flank of the *First Army* was withdrawn to the east, and quickly, a gaping hole would be torn in the German front which might never be mended. At 1930 Balck gave orders for the *First Army* to pull back its right and center, the *416th Division* and *19th VG Division* withdrawing in this move to the line Borg–Launstroff–Bouzonville, while the *XIII SS Corps* redressed its right wing to link up with the left of the *LXXXII Corps*. During the night of 17 November the German guns began barrage fire and the enemy infantry abandoned their positions in front of the 90th Division and the southern column of the 10th Armored Division.[65]

On 18 and 19 November the American forces pursued the retreating German columns. General Van Fleet threw the 359th Infantry into the chase and

[65] Balck had received permission to make this withdrawal two days before but was afraid that an abrupt withdrawal could not be co-ordinated and would leave a gap between the *LXXXII Corps* and *XIII SS Corps* east of Metz. Knobelsdorff argued that his *First Army* could carry out a withdrawal only in slow stages because communications were so poor. *Army Group G KTB* and *Anlagen*, 17 Nov 44.

relieved the 358th, which was badly in need of a rest, as soon as it reached the town of Luttange. Specific objectives were no longer assigned. The general mission, however, remained the same: to close the gap east of Metz and join hands with the 5th Infantry Division advancing from the south. The infantry moved forward in trucks when they could, and marched when trucks were lacking or when blown bridges and craters cut the roads. Often the speed of the advance overran the rear guard German demolition details before they could blow the bridges. At the end of the first day of this pursuit the 359th Infantry had troops across the Nied at Condé-Northen, twelve miles east of Metz, and the 90th Reconnaissance Troop held Avancy, blocking one of the main escape routes from Metz. Through the night the Americans fired on the exit roads with every weapon they could bring to bear. The cavalry alone counted thirty enemy vehicles destroyed and took more than five hundred prisoners. On 19 November the 359th cut still another of the Metz exit roads at Les Etangs, after an advance in which planes of the XIX TAC worked directly with the infantry, swooping down as close as one hundred yards in front of the American patrols to strafe the fleeing enemy.[66] For most of the enemy who were trying to find a way out of the Metz pocket all hope of continuing the battle was gone; pounded by planes and guns, they surrendered willingly. About 1030 the 90th Reconnaissance Troop met the 735th Tank Battalion, supporting the 5th Infantry Division, and the envelopment of Metz had been successfully completed.[67] Just as the 357th Infantry, on the division left wing, wheeled to face east and was moving to launch an assault across the Nied River toward Boulay-Moselle, General Van Fleet received orders from the XX Corps headquarters to hold the 90th Division in place, preparatory to a general regrouping within the corps for a full-dress attack toward the Sarre River.

This eleven-day operation by the 90th Infantry Division shows how far it had come since its initial performance in Normandy. While the enemy forces opposing the 90th in the November operations often were poor,[68] elements

[66] From the 17th through the 19th good flying weather prevailed; General Weyland was able to commit all of his five groups. As usual, the presence of the fighter-bombers cheered the American ground troops. The Third Army Diary notes on 18 November: "This was the best and biggest Air day that the Third Army has had for a long time. The enemy was in retreat. . . . The rapidity of the attack of the Third Army caused them to take to the roads. God in all His wisdom having given us a clear day, the fighter-bombers caught them on the road."

[67] Chapter IX, p. 444.

[68] General Pflieger, who was commander of the *416th Division*, is of the opinion that the American advance north of Metz could have been completed in half the time actually taken. MS #B–090 (Pflieger).

of the division had met and defeated troops from one of the crack German divisions on the Western Front, the *25th Panzer Grenadier Division*, and had fought through terrain of considerable natural difficulty, made worse by the autumn rains. The seizure of a bridgehead over the Moselle in particular had been ably executed and had so impressed General Patton that he termed it "one of the epic river crossings of history." [69] The demonstrable losses inflicted on the enemy during this operation totaled 2,100 prisoners, some 40 tanks and assault guns, 75 artillery pieces, over 200 vehicles, and an unknown but high number of dead and wounded.[70] However, the 90th Division itself had lost some 2,300 officers and men in the first seven days which marked the hardest fighting.

[69] In a personal letter of commendation to the 90th Division on 12 November 1944. The 90th Division commander was promoted to major general on 15 November 1944.

[70] 90th Div AAR, Nov 44.

CHAPTER IX

The November Battle for Metz (Concluded)

The Enemy Situation in the Metz Area[1]

The wide envelopment made by the 90th Infantry Division and the 10th Armored Division north of Metz did not bring these troops into conflict with the German forces in the Metz area proper until the final hours of the operation, when elements of the two divisions were at last in position to cut off the enemy fleeing the city. On the other hand, the 5th Infantry Division and the 95th Infantry Division, attacking close in, fought the Metz garrison forces from 9 November onward. Before tracing the operations of these two divisions, a look at what the Germans were doing on their side of the barricades is in order.

When the September offensive against Metz tapered off into the October lull, OKW instructed General Balck to begin at once to set the Metz salient in a state of defense in anticipation of the resumption of the American attack. However, Generalfeldmarschall Wilhelm Keitel and the OKW staff gave with one hand and took away with the other. *Division Number 462*, which had defended Metz so ably in September, was upgraded to the status of a volksgrenadier division and given a normal complement of divisional engineers and artillery, plus an additional infantry regiment. At the same time the officer and NCO trainees, who had given the heart and sinew to the defense in September, were graduated on 9 October and sent as replacements to other divisions on the Western Front.[2] The gaps in the ranks of the *462d VG Division* now were filled with over-age and poorly trained troops from fortress battalions, sick battalions, and the like, derisively known in the argot of the Wehrmacht as "*Halb-soldaten*." Some attempt was made to replace the elderly

[1] Source materials for American units have been discussed in notes to Chapter VIII. The German sources for the present chapter generally are manuscripts prepared by officers taking part in the operation. The *Army Group G KTB* contains much on the decision to defend Metz, as does the *OB WEST KTB*.

[2] Colonel Joachim Siegroth's Kampfgruppe, consisting of the trainee detachments and school troops, was awarded a special arm band with the words METZ 1944 in recognition of its battles in September.

and rather academic headquarters that Generalleutnant Vollrath Luebbe had inherited, when he took over the *462d* on 18 September, with veteran commanders and staff officers.

Early in October a special program for building obstacles and mining was instituted in the *462d* sector, although there was no effort to build defenses on the east side of the city, or to supply its garrison against a siege. Considerable indecision existed as to the role Metz should play in future operations: *Army Group G*, *OB WEST*, and OKW carried on a three-way debate while the *462d* was left to shift for itself. Rundstedt was skeptical about the tactical value of the Metz bridgehead. Twice during October he suggested that Metz be abandoned, as part of his scheme for a general withdrawal by *Army Group G* back to the West Wall. Keitel, probably speaking for Hitler, refused to allow a withdrawal from Metz; but not until the day before the start of the American November offensive did Hitler specifically order the Metz garrison to hold its ground and submit to encirclement. Balck, on the other hand, wanted to make the Americans fight for Metz; yet he was afraid that if the *First Army* was ordered to hold the city until its garrison was surrounded a gap would be torn in the *First Army* front which could not be closed. Contending that the Metz fortifications were "out of date," Balck, his staff, and commanders wanted to evacuate the city as soon as the remainder of the Moselle line fell to the Americans.[3] Balck must have anticipated that Hitler would eventually sacrifice the force in Metz, for he refused to send any of his precious tanks or assault guns to reinforce the garrison. The troops added to the garrison during October were mostly fortress units, generally poorly armed and of indifferent combat value. Furthermore, Balck did not divert any large stores of mines and barbed wire to Metz, despite the orders he himself had given for strengthening its defenses.

Originally OKW believed that the American Third Army offensive would be resumed in the form of an envelopment south of Metz. On 22 October German intelligence issued a new appreciation and predicted a double envelopment in which it was estimated that the Americans could use three infantry and two armored divisions, with a total of 1,850 tanks. This analysis seems to have impressed OKW, for shortly thereafter Balck was given orders to

[3] General der Infanterie Kurt von Tippelskirch, who had arrived on 30 October to take over the *First Army* while Knobelsdorff went on leave, advised that Metz be abandoned at once, citing his personal experiences as commander of the *Fourth Army* on the Eastern Front. MS #B-491.

free both the *11th Panzer Division* and the *21st Panzer Division* for use as a mobile reserve, and the *11th Panzer Division* was moved to an assembly area west of St. Avold in a direct line behind Metz. At the end of October Rundstedt asked for a report on the state of the Metz defenses. Balck answered that the forces in Metz were so weak that they could not be expected to contain any large number of the enemy in the event they were encircled. In addition, he said, the *21st Panzer Division* could not be relieved from the *Nineteenth Army* without suitable replacement, and in any case the division could not reach the Metz area before 12 November at the earliest. Balck posed two questions. Where should the *11th Panzer Division* be committed in the event of a general American attack against the *First Army?* Should the Metz garrison allow itself to be surrounded? The first question was answered when the XII Corps began the November offensive a day ahead of the XX Corps stroke at Metz, forcing Balck to throw the *11th Panzer Division* in against the XII Corps armor. The second question was answered by Hitler when, on 9 November, he strongly reaffirmed his order that Metz should be held "to the last man." [4]

When the XX Corps finally launched its attack the Metz fortifications were in little better repair than they had been in September. For example, the water systems, built by the French, were nearly all out of order; had it not been for the heavy rains in November and December, some of the separate forts might have been driven by thirst to capitulate some days before they did. The only works with wide fields of fire, Forts Jeanne d'Arc (12 guns) and Driant (14 guns), remained the key permanent defenses. Some of the other forts had been strengthened by mine fields, wire, and other obstacles, but at best were only strong points on which the infantry defense could turn.[5] Field fortifications in depth were well developed only in the sector south of the city, a fact which would have considerable bearing on the 5th Infantry

[4] The policy of defending all fortified areas, even when cut off and surrounded, seems to have been outlined by OKW about the time Field Marshal Kluge replaced Field Marshal Rundstedt as commander on the Western Front. Hitler had already formulated such a general policy for defense on the Russian front. The theory was that fortifications should be manned with poor troops and arms, prior to the withdrawal of the main field forces, and then held as long as possible so as to contain large numbers of the enemy. Many German generals disagreed with this doctrine. General Zimmermann estimates that some 200,000 German troops were lost in this manner, without equivalent gains. On the other hand there were numerous cases in which the Allied advance was considerably delayed by such tactics. Metz certainly is one such case. See MS #T–121 (Zimmermann *et al.*).

[5] MS #A–000 (Mellenthin).

Division attack in this area. No orders had been given General Luebbe as to the conduct of the Metz defense, except that he was to hold, even though surrounded, and counterattack at all points where the Americans threatened to break through.

The strength of the Metz garrison at the beginning of the attack was probably not much over 14,000 officers and men. Its combat strength was somewhat lower, between 9,000 and 10,000. The *462d VG Division*, forming the bulk of the garrison, numbered approximately 7,000 officers and men. It is impossible to re-create precisely the German order of battle, for all of the pertinent records were destroyed just before the German capitulation. The *1215th Regiment* (Colonel Stoessel) was deployed on the north flank in the neighborhood of Maizières-lès-Metz and connected with the *19th VG Division* at the Moselle. The *1010th Security Regiment* (Colonel Anton) continued around the bridgehead perimeter to the west in the Norroy–Amanvillers sector. On the left flank of the *Security Regiment* the *1217th Regiment* (Lieutenant Colonel Richter) was deployed in a thin line reaching as far south as Ars-sur-Moselle, on the west bank of the Moselle River. The *22d Fortress Regiment* held a small sector astride the river and linked up with the *17th SS Panzer Grenadier Division* a few hundred yards in from the east bank. Other fortress units to the strength of about three infantry battalions and one heavy machine gun battalion were scattered in the various forts and in the city itself. General Luebbe's mobile artillery was limited to the *761st Artillery Regiment*, the *1311th Fortress Artillery Battalion*, and a few batteries of Flak. The only troops available as reserves in the Metz area on 9 November were one regiment of the *462d VG Division* (the *1216th Regiment*),[6] the *462d Fuesilier Battalion*, a crack outfit that distinguished itself in the later fighting, and a reconnaissance battalion on loan from the *17th SS Panzer Grenadier Division*.[7] To sum up, the *462d VG Division* began the defense of the Metz bridgehead in November with second-rate troops, inadequate artillery, and a force too small properly to man all of the permanent works around the city. On the other hand, the two divisions guarding the flanks of the *462d VG Division* (the *19th VG Division* and the *17th SS Panzer Grenadier Division*) were counted among the better fighting organizations in *Army Group G*.

[6] The *1216th Regiment* had been attached to the *19th VG Division* in early November. It occupied positions on the east bank of the Moselle, just north of Metz.

[7] MS #B–079 (Kittel); *OB WEST* situation maps; *Army Group G KTB*, 4 Nov 44.

The 5th Division Begins the Southern Envelopment

The XX Corps operation against Metz in November 1944 can be broken down, tactically, into four parts: the preliminary demonstration by the 95th Division (which had little effect on the enemy); the wide envelopment north of Metz by the 90th Division and 10th Armored Division; a close-in envelopment south of Metz by the 5th Division; and a containing action west of the Moselle by the 95th Division, culminating in a final assault on both sides of the river. For the sake of clarity these phases of the Metz operation are treated separately, leaving the mind of the reader to make the necessary co-ordination in point of time. Since it has seemed logical to deal first with both envelopment phases of this operation, the scene now shifts from the attack in the northern sector to the 5th Division thrust on the southern wing of XX Corps. The 95th Division, in the center, did not begin any sustained attempts at penetration west of the Moselle until 14 November.

On 1 November the 5th Division completed the relief of the 95th Division and once again occupied the bridgehead south of Metz which it had fought so hard to win in September.[8] During the interim there had been only very minor changes in the American main line of resistance. The 2d Infantry Regiment moved into the salient projecting east to the Seille River, thus taking position as the right wing of the 5th Division. The 10th Infantry was deployed in the center and the 11th Infantry held the left wing, facing both north and east. (*Map XXXII*) The ranks of the 5th Division, much depleted by the September battles, had been brought back to strength by replacements and by veterans of the division who had returned to their units from the hospital.

The general mission assigned the 5th Division in the XX Corps scheme of maneuver was to attack toward the east and make contact with the 90th Division, as the latter circled around Metz from the north, while at the same time maintaining touch with the XII Corps on the southern flank. As planned, the main effort in the attack would be made on the right wing of the 5th Division, aiming at the seizure of an objective (outlined only as a "goose egg" on operations overlays) astride the Nied Française River in the neighborhood

[8] The shuttling of the 5th, 90th, and 95th Divisions in and out of the XX Corps lines seems to have caused some confusion among the Germans. A prisoner taken by the 95th Division reported that the Germans knew that both the 90th and 5th Divisions had been so crippled as to necessitate their combination in one division, the new 95th. (At least, as General Twaddle commented, the Germans were correct in concluding that 90+5=95.) Ltr, Gen Twaddle to Hist Div, 17 Jan 49.

of Sanry-sur-Nied and Ancerville. This direction of attack would permit the 5th Division to swing wide of the outer Metz works in the early phases of the advance. The center of the division objective was some ten miles east of the 5th Division bridgehead lines. Although the target for the attack was designated as the moderately high ground on both sides of the Nied Française, the chief tactical object of the 5th Division attack would be the seizure of the communications complex running through this area.[9] An advance to and across the Nied would cut four of the main roads leading in and out of Metz, including one of the most important enemy military routes, namely, the Metz–Château-Salins–Strasbourg highway. Moreover, the 5th Division would be placed in position to block the double-track railroad line between Metz and Strasbourg and could deny the enemy the use of the junction line running to Saarbruecken.

The most important natural obstacles in the path of the attack were the Seille and the Nied Française Rivers. Normally, neither of these rivers would have presented much of a bridging problem, but in November both were swollen considerably by the fall rains. The underlying clay common to this country had caused the 7th Armored Division much trouble in September and might be expected to slow down the infantry and their supply vehicles. The numerous wooded areas scattered through the zone of advance were generally small in size. A few of the outer-ring Metz forts were located on and near the division objective, but the main works would not be encountered until the 5th Division turned inward to advance on the city itself.

Opposing the 5th Division was the *17th SS Panzer Grenadier Division* (Generalmajor der Waffen-SS Werner Ostendorff), which at this time constituted the north wing of the *XIII SS Corps* (Priess). The Cheminot salient, projecting west into the American lines at the boundary between the 5th Division and the 80th Division, was held by a few troops of the *48th Division*. The *17th SS Panzer Grenadier Division* was overstrength in early November (15,843 officers and men) but had received so many replacements, to compensate for its earlier losses, that it was no longer rated as an "attack" division and was considered fit only for defense. Like the majority of the panzer grenadier divisions on the Western Front, the *17th SS* did not have the mobile and armored equipment to distinguish it from the ordinary volksgrenadier division. When the 5th Division began its attack the *17th SS Pan-*

[9] Irwin Diary; Ltr, Gen Walker to Hist Div, 8 Oct 47; 5th Div G–3 Jnl, 9 Nov 44.

zer Grenadier Division carried a complement of only four Mark IV tanks and six assault guns (an additional fourteen assault guns were promised but these subsequently were sent to the Aachen front). However, the artillery regiment had all its guns, and the division could rely on support from the concentration of army artillery being built up behind the *XIII SS Corps*.[10] Part of the *38th SS Panzer Grenadier Regiment* was held in reserve between Courcelles-Chaussy and Han-sur-Nied so that it could be employed in support of its own division or the *462d VG Division* in Metz. This left the German line in front of the 5th Division rather weak and with little deployment in depth, although field works had been constructed for defense in depth. Balck had given strict orders that the *XIII SS Corps* should employ an elastic defense, in view of the lack of easily defended terrain in its zone. After an inspection of the *17th SS* lines on 5 November he reprimanded Ostendorff for the failure to man an adequate outpost line far enough forward. Apparently, however, little change was made in these dispositions prior to the American advance, except to bolster up the line with a few weak fortress companies of infantry and machine gunners.[11]

On the night of 5–6 November the 2d and 10th Infantry began to remove the mines and booby traps which had been placed in front of their positions during the long period of inactivity. Patrols scouted for a bridge site near Longueville-lès-Cheminot, and the 774th Tank Destroyer Battalion moved up behind the infantry.[12] Meanwhile the rivers in front and rear of the 5th Division began a rapid rise. By 8 November the Seille River had washed over its banks and at some points was two hundred yards wide. The Moselle flooded the supply roads in the rear of the division, but fortunately did not wash out any of its bridges until the day of the attack.

The XII Corps attack on 8 November had jumped off with only such air support as the XIX TAC fighter-bombers could fly late in the day. The weather was slightly better on 9 November, however, and the AAF was able to intervene on the scale originally planned for the Third Army offensive. The chief targets for the medium and heavy bombers were the Metz forts, but the air plan called for some attention to be given to the Thionville defenses and the marshaling yards at Saarbruecken and Saarlautern. The Eighth Air

[10] MS #B–412 (Einem); MS #B–491 (Tippelskirch).

[11] The *17th SS* commander was in process of moving troops to make a limited counterattack, with the objective of retaking the high ground southeast of Corny, when the American offensive struck.

[12] The 818th Tank Destroyer Battalion and the 284th Field Artillery Battalion had already been attached to support the 5th Division attack.

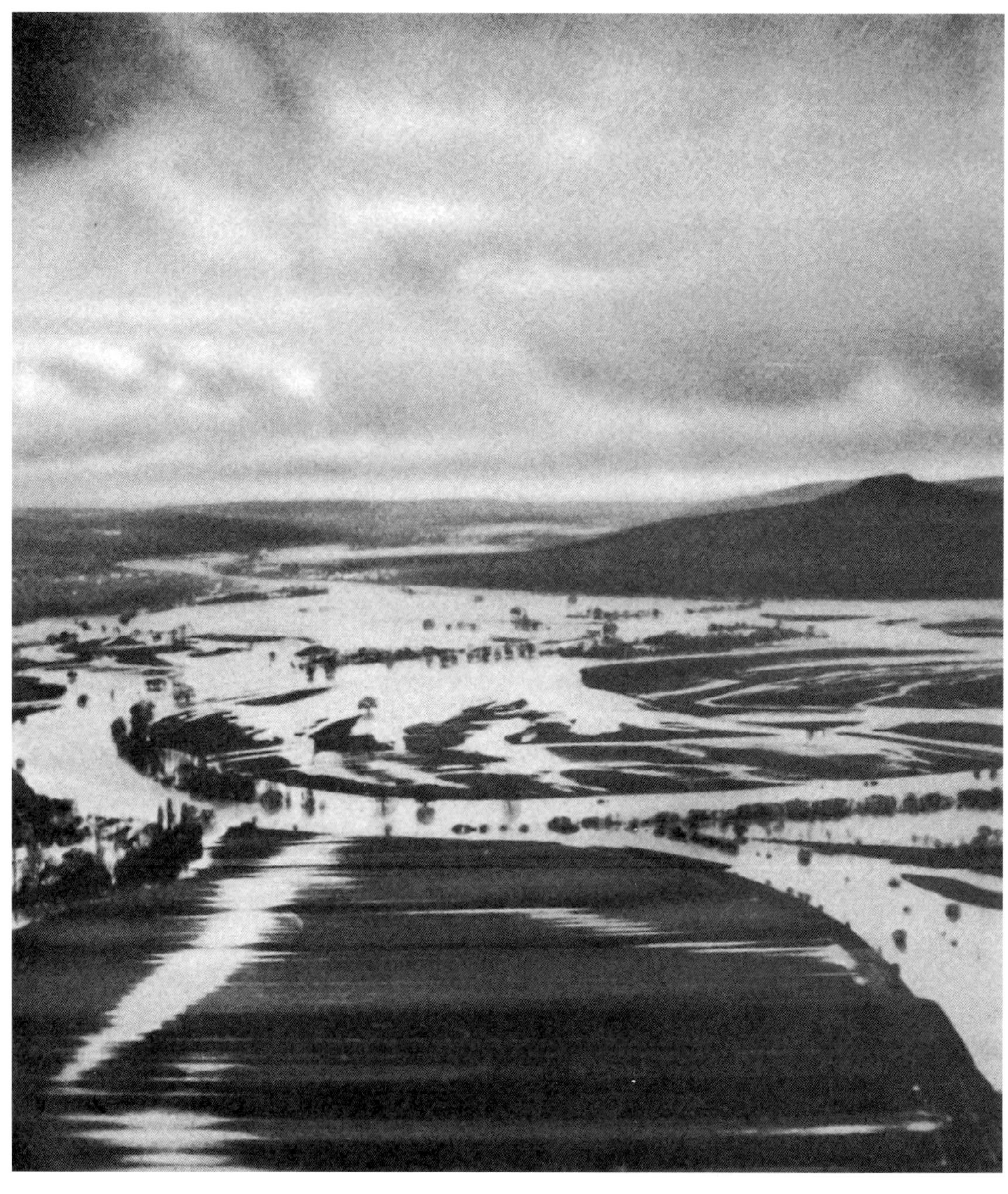

SUPPLY ROADS FLOODED BY THE MOSELLE, *in rear of the 5th Infantry Division. Mousson Hill appears on the right.*

Force put 1,299 planes (B-17's and B-24's) into the operation on 9 November, 1,223 of them reaching the target zones and dropping a total of 3,753 tons in the form of 1,000- and 2,000-pound bombs. Most of the heavy bombers released their loads from a height of more than 20,000 feet. The targets were often invisible through the clouds. At Metz, 689 of the heavies struck at seven forts which the Third Army had marked as priority targets. None of the forts were hit, although some damage was done to the enemy works, wire, and communications. The 432 planes sent against the Saarbruecken marshaling yards also returned with pessimistic reports, while at Thionville the air attack missed all the targets. The IX Bombardment Division dispatched 514 medium bombers to join in the aerial attack, but cloudy weather prevented all except 74 from actually taking part in the operation. Four of the Metz forts had been assigned as targets for the mediums; clouds intervened and these planes were turned to hit the German road centers at Dieuze and Faulquemont. The air effort on 9 November was marked by volume of bombing, rather than by accuracy; it did little to shake the enemy and had relatively small effect on the course of subsequent ground operations. However, the old ally of the Third Army, General Weyland's XIX TAC, better fitted than the bombers to operate in this kind of weather, gave close and effective support to the attacking divisions all along the army front on 9 November, intervening with such marked effect as to delay the movement of the main German reserves for nearly twenty-four hours.[13]

Although General Irwin had been told that the 5th Division would not attack at the same time as the 80th Division, General McBride had not been so informed. He launched the 80th Division attack on 8 November with the expectation that the 5th would join in immediately. This lack of co-ordination across the boundary separating the XX and XII Corps would continue to plague the wing divisions of both corps for some days. At 0600 on 9 November the 2d Infantry began the 5th Division attack along the line of the Seille,

[13] On the air attack of 9 November see: AAF Evaluation Board, Effectiveness of Third Phase Tactical Air Operations in the European Theater, Aug 45; Eighth Air Force Report (MS), pp. 85–94; IX Bombardment Div Daily Summary, 9 Nov 44; Eighth AF Int Opns Summary, 9 Nov 44. Einem, chief of staff of the *XIII SS Corps,* says that the bombing struck the right flank of the corps but did little damage. MS #B–412. However, General Irwin, 5th Division commander, expressed himself as being "highly satisfied with the bombing and results obtained." Ltr, Gen Irwin to XX Corps, 19 Nov 44, in XX Corps G–3 Jnl. Lt. Col. I. P. Murray, G–3, Air, Third Army, later reported his opinion that one bomb had struck Fort Yser. German records give considerable attention to the Jabo's (fighter-bombers).

crossing the river, now nearly two hundred yards wide, by footbridge and by assault craft. A squad and a half pushed into Cheminot, whose guns had held the southern Seille crossing sites in enfilade during September, but the Germans already had fled in order to escape the trap formed by the advance of the 80th Division. The 10th Infantry launched its assault conjointly with that of the 2d Infantry, but its 3d Battalion met real resistance as soon as it deployed on the east bank. Here, in a cluster of stone buildings called Hautonnerie Farm, a German company determined to make a fight for it. When the American infantry surrounded the farm the enemy captain sent out word that he intended to die for the Fuehrer—an exaggerated statement. Within a matter of hours he surrendered.

While the 3d Battalion was checked at this position the 2d Battalion pushed through to continue the advance. The speed of the 2d Infantry advance, coupled with very effective co-operation from fighter-bomber planes of the 362d Group, almost immediately disrupted the German communications and drove the enemy in disorderly retreat north into the zone of the 10th Infantry. By nightfall all battalions of the 2d Infantry, plus the two from the 10th Infantry, were east of the Seille, and the new bridgehead was extended to a depth of 6,000 yards and a width of 5,000. Northeast of Louvigny the two regiments joined their inner flanks, and the 10th Infantry (—) dug in to hold and cover the continuation of the main effort by its sister regiment on the right. Most of the enemy escaped to the north and east; about two hundred were captured. American losses on this day were fairly light, for the enemy had stood his ground at very few points.[14]

On the second day of the attack the German troops still showed little sign of recovering their balance, and the left wing of the *17th SS Panzer Grenadier Division* remained in a state of "collapse."[15] The three battalions of the 2d Infantry advanced on a narrow front to the left and rear of CCB, 6th Armored, moving fast. Shortly before noon Lagrew's tanks and armored infantry drove the enemy out of Vigny, after a cross-country march through the mud. The 2d Battalion (Lt. Col. L. K. Ball) of the 2d Infantry arrived about 1320 to take over the village, beginning a hand-in-glove association with the armor which would have a marked effect on the Nied River operation. Mean-

[14] The 5th Division G–1 Journal gives these losses: 3 officers and 117 men in the 10th Infantry; 1 officer and 37 men in the 2d Infantry (the latter figure is incomplete).

[15] MS #A–000 (Mellenthin). The failure of the *48th Division,* on the left of the *17th SS,* explains the manner in which the latter folded on 9–10 November. See Chap. VII, pp. 354–55.

while the 6th Armored cavalry cut the Vigny–Buchy road. In midafternoon Lagrew's combat team took Buchy, which was turned over to the 3d Battalion (Lt. Col. R. E. Connor) of the 2d Infantry just as dusk came on. The seizure of the two villages opened up the main supply road along the intercorps boundary. The 1st Battalion passed through the lines of the 2d Battalion, then wheeled north, captured Pagny-lès-Goin in a sharp fight, and in a "costly but successful attack" took Silly-en-Saulnois and the road junction to the east. Over four hundred prisoners were taken during the day. On 11 November the 2d Infantry maintained its rapid pace in a drive eastward along the road opened at Silly-en-Saulnois, which was greatly aided by the operations of the 6th Armored Division. At twilight the advance guards of the 2d were in Aube and Dain-en-Saulnois, only a short march from the Nied Française. The 50th Field Artillery Battalion went into position and opened fire on Courcelles-Chaussy, due east of Metz, an important junction point on the great highway running from Metz to Saarbruecken.[16] During the day the left column of CCB had swung outside the 6th Armored zone to seize the bridge at Sanry-sur-Nied, thus putting Lagrew's advance guard across the river at a point some two and a half miles northeast of the 2d Infantry lines.

The successful drive by the 2d Infantry necessitated a regrouping on 12 November to secure the attenuated line of communications back to the main body of the 5th Division. In the 11th Infantry sector the enemy had shown no disposition to make any move against the thin American line, and the 11th extended its right flank as far as the Seille, freeing the 10th Infantry to deploy on an east-west line facing the Bois de l'Hôpital. Meanwhile the 2d Infantry swung to the north and Colonel Ball's 2d Battalion crossed the Nied Française River early on the morning of 12 November at Sanry-sur-Nied, passing into the 6th Armored Division bridgehead. While Lagrew's armor pushed out to extend the confines of the bridgehead, the 2d Battalion mopped up around Sanry-sur-Nied and deployed to defend the village and the surrounding high ground. During the night of 12–13 November strong combat patrols from the *17th SS* forced their way into the village. Before they could reach the Nied bridge they were beaten off by the 2d Battalion, reinforced by a platoon of tanks and one of tank destroyers. Elsewhere along the 5th Divi-

[16] At 1710 the *48th Division* was ordered to retire behind the Nied. Three hours later the *17th SS*, which no longer had contact with the *48th*, received orders to retire to an east-west line generally north of Corny–Pouilly–Sorbey. This withdrawal ultimately placed the *17th SS* at right angles to the *48th*. *Army Group G KTB*, 11 Nov 44.

sion front the *17th SS* took advantage of the cover of night to withdraw to the north.

Meanwhile part of the 1st Battalion, 2d Infantry, made a night crossing south of its sister battalion and early on the morning of 13 November took Ancerville without meeting any organized resistance. This day brought rain and snow, increasing the incidence of trench foot which was beginning to cripple the 5th Division. As yet General Irwin had been given no orders about continuing the 2d Infantry drive east of the Nied. The elements of the five companies already across the river made up the largest force that the 5th Division commander could spare: though the enemy facing the 5th Division line back to the west showed no aggressive intentions the division was much overextended.[17] During the day the division engineers put a treadway bridge over the Nied near Ancerville, thus strengthening the American hold on the east bank. The German troops in the vicinity continued attempts to erase the bridgehead, and on the night of 13 November a composite force from the *38th SS Panzer Grenadier Regiment* and the *21st Panzer Division* drove into Sanry. It was repelled, however, before it could destroy the bridge[18] —to the great disappointment of the *17th SS* commander, who had counted very heavily on the success of this attack. The 10th and 11th Infantry continued to reorganize the new forward line, meeting little more than token resistance and generally finding that the enemy had abandoned the positions immediately ahead of the advance. The 10th occupied two works (Forts Aisne and Yser) in the outer ring of Metz forts south of the Bois de l'Hôpital, and the 11th recovered the ground around Fey, Pournoy-la-Chétive, and Coin-lès-Cuvry which had been abandoned by the 5th Division when it took over the 7th Armored Division sector in September.

In the early evening General Walker phoned General Irwin, complimented him on the performance of the 5th Division, and told him that the boundary between his division and the 95th was being changed to permit the 5th to capture Metz. Further, General Irwin was instructed to decide for himself whether or not to hold the troops of the 2d Infantry across the Nied. The losses suffered by the Germans in the fruitless counterattacks against the bridgehead and the tactical value of the Nied bridges for any future operation to the east convinced General Irwin that the bridgehead was too valuable to relinquish. Orders were therefore sent to Colonel Roffe telling him to hold

[17] Irwin Diary.

[18] *Second Infantry Regiment;* MS #A-871 (Feuchtinger).

the reinforced 2d Battalion in its positions east of the Nied. It was not too risky a venture since the 5th Division artillery was in position to cover the battalion.[19]

The 10th and 11th Infantry moved north through the cold rain on 14 November against the new German line of defense, while the 3d Battalion of the 2d Infantry marched forward to an attack position near Sorbey. The 11th Infantry cleared the enemy out of the woods southwest of Fort Verdun and farther to the right took Prayelle Farm in bitter fighting. The 10th Infantry made good progress during the day and cleared the southern half of the extensive Bois de l'Hôpital. Since the 11th Infantry was meeting fairly stubborn resistance on its left flank and the leading troops of the 10th now were only four thousand yards from Metz proper, General Irwin gave orders for the 10th Infantry to make the main effort and attack straight toward the city. The 5th Division commander was anxious to add more strength to the right wing of the advance toward Metz and free the entire rifle strength of the 10th Infantry for the final frontal assault. This would leave only the diminished 2d Infantry to cover the right and rear of the division; so he asked for permission to bring the reinforced battalion of the 2d Infantry back across the Nied. General Patton refused this request, perhaps because he was chary of further exposing the left wing of the XII Corps which already was much in the air.[20]

On 15 November the 5th Division lines were straightened and units regrouped for the drive into Metz. The 10th Infantry, advancing with its left on the Seille and its right battalion echeloned to the rear, drove the last Germans out of the Bois de l'Hôpital[21] and entered the town of Marly, where the *48th Fortress Machine Gun Battalion* was dug in. Much of the fighting was more severe than in the days preceding. In the middle of the afternoon a battalion of the *38th SS Panzer Grenadier Regiment* debouched from the fortifications north of Sorbey and started a sortie along the west bank of the Nied with the intention of seizing the Sanry bridge from the rear. Checked

[19] Two more counterattacks were thrown against the 2d Infantry bridgehead on the morning of 14 November. Prisoners later said that 750 troops had been used and that only one-third of this number remained as effectives when the German effort was finally halted. *Second Infantry Regiment.* The following units that were engaged in the defeat of the initial German attacks were awarded the Distinguished Unit Citation: E Company, 2d Infantry; 1st Section, 3d Platoon, H Company; 1st Platoon, A Company, 735th Tank Battalion.

[20] Irwin Diary, 14 and 16 Nov 44.

[21] The capture of these woods forced the southern enemy artillery groupment to displace to Fort Queuleu and curtailed German observation.

by the 2d Infantry reserve the German battalion retired to the north, leaving the Sorbey works unmanned. On the west flank of the 2d Infantry the 3d Battalion jumped off from the line of departure won on the previous day and drove another battalion of the *38th SS Panzer Grenadier Regiment* out of Mécleuves.[22] The 11th Infantry, opposed bitterly by fortress machine gun detachments (the best of the fortress troops), captured Augny and during the night pushed on as far as the edge of the Frescaty airport.[23]

The Enemy Situation in Metz

On the night of 11 November the *First Army* evacuated Metz, leaving the defense of the city to General Luebbe, the *462d VG Division*, and the hodgepodge of fortress units grouped under Luebbe's command. The code word for evacuation was passed to the Nazi party members and officials, a sizable group inasmuch as Metz had been an important administrative center, and they began an exodus toward Germany in their commandeered Citroëns and Renaults. The *17th SS Panzer Grenadier Division* pulled back still farther from the Moselle, leaving the gap south of the city to be filled by fortress machine gun units. Hitler, now taking a very personal interest in the defense of Metz, reiterated the order to hold to the last man and passed down word that the garrison must be reinforced, provisioned for a long seige, and provided with *Panzerfausts* and other antitank weapons for close combat.

Apparently higher German headquarters were dubious of General Luebbe's fitness for the Metz command; in any case, he had just suffered a stroke. Keitel told Balck to submit the names of nominees for the doubtful honor of becoming the Metz commander. After much teletyping Generalleutnant Heinrich Kittel, commander of the *49th Division*, was given the post and bound by a special oath to defend the city to the last man and cartridge. He arrived in Metz and assumed command at noon on 14 November, while Luebbe took over the *49th Division*. Kittel was fresh from the Eastern Front, where he had won considerable distinction as a military governor and a spe-

[22] An artillery forward observer with the 5th Division, 2d Lt. Lee R. Jamison, here called for artillery fire on his own observation post in order to break up a German counterattack which threatened a weak portion of the American line. He was awarded the DSC.

[23] On this date Sgt. Richard L. Marnell, E Company, 11th Infantry, displayed valor for which he received the DSC. When his platoon was checked by fire from antiaircraft and machine gun positions Sergeant Marnell crawled along a fire-swept ditch and destroyed two of the German positions with hand and rifle grenades.

cialist in the tactics of city fighting. On at least two occasions he had successfully defended a city encircled by the Russians and then withdrawn his command in orderly fashion. Naturally, Kittel was not too pleased with this new assignment. He protested to Knobelsdorff against the injustice of linking his name in military history with "Fortress Metz," which, in Kittel's opinion, was no fortress. Later, with the advantage of hindsight, Kittel charged that the high command never fully comprehended the differences inherent in the defense of a prepared position on the Eastern Front and one on the Western Front where the attackers possessed control of the air and superior mobility on the ground.[24]

Although the new commander received daily messages exhorting him to hold "each work and each strong point" to the last, there was little interference with his tactical dispositions. After all there was little choice as to the manner of defending the city. Kittel determined to hold on to the west bank positions as long as possible, thus protecting the bridges leading into Metz proper; as a last resort, he would defend Forts Jeanne d'Arc, Driant, Plappeville, and St. Quentin, all of which were fairly strong works and so sited as to deny the use of the Moselle crossings in their vicinity.

Kittel found his new command with less than two days' rations, but on the night of 14 November a train got through to the Metz station with sufficient provisions for two or three weeks. The same train brought in forty-eight pieces of German and Italian artillery, mostly the 70-mm. infantry howitzer type, with ammunition. There was sufficient small-caliber ammunition for rifles and machine guns, but only 4,000 rounds all told for the fortress artillery. The divisional artillery of the *462d* had enough shells for three days of heavy fighting. Kittel sent out a hurry call for a labor force of 12,000 civilians to work on the defenses, but higher headquarters refused to take a single worker from the West Wall. Requests for mines, barbed wire, and a small armored assault force were equally fruitless. The plans for the forthcoming Ardennes offensive loomed too large in OKW calculations, and Kittel would have to defend with what he had.[25]

No sooner had Kittel taken over the command in Metz on 14 November than he ordered a general counterattack to be made on the following day

[24] See Kittel's *Personalakten* for his earlier history. His views on "Fortress Metz" are expressed in MS #B–079.

[25] At 1750, on the day Kittel took command, *OB WEST* noted "a sudden and appreciable deterioration" all along the *Army Group G* front—hardly an auspicious introduction for Kittel's defense of Metz.

with a main effort west of the city. Because the *1216th Regiment,* originally the Metz reserve, was heavily engaged south of Thionville, General Balck loaned Kittel the *38th SS Panzer Grenadier Regiment,* now reduced to a strength of about eight hundred men after days of bitter fighting.[26] In order to regroup and concentrate for this new effort a number of the smaller works around Metz were evacuated on the night of 14–15 November, and in others the garrison was reduced to a skeleton force. Actually, the German commander expected very little to be gained by the countereffort set for 15 November since by now the Americans were pressing in at so many points that the limited reserves in Metz could gain little advantage from their position on interior lines.[27] The *38th SS Panzer Grenadier Regiment,* holding astride the Nied, was not able to disengage from its positions in front of the 10th Infantry on 15 November. The counterattack from its own lines (described earlier) achieved no success. The *Fuesilier Battalion* of the *462d VG Division,* acting as the division reserve, attempted to organize a counterattack in the western sector around Fort Jeanne d'Arc, but failed. In the north the Americans were driving forward so vigorously on both sides of the river that the *1216th* and *1215th Regiments* could not catch their breath or gain their balance for any co-ordinated riposte. By the night of 15 November it was all too obvious that any general counterattack was impossible. Balck ordered Kittel to prepare new positions in the rear and hold as long as possible at the existing main line of resistance. But, for the record at least, Kittel was told to counterattack locally and wipe out the American penetrations on the north flank near Woippy and on the south flank at the Frescaty airfield. Kittel, however, knew full well how desperate his situation was and during the night sent the last supply convoys to those forts which had been designated for a last-ditch defense. Symbolic of the hopeless state of the Metz defenses, 400 men of the *Volkssturm,* wearing brassards in lieu of uniforms and armed with old French rifles, were marched by police officials through the night and put into the lines between Fort St. Privat and Fort Queuleu. After one night in the rain and snow these *Volkssturm* troops were finished.

[26] The force under Kittel's command on the evening of 14 November was composed of the *462d VG Division,* the regimental staffs of the *22d* and *25th Fortress Regiments,* three fortress machine gun battalions, two SS machine gun battalions, one fortress engineer battalion, five fortress infantry battalions, two fortress artillery battalions, and two Flak battalions from the *IV Flak Corps.*

[27] As an example, the *462d Fuesilier Battalion* had been sent to retake the Bois de l'Hôpital but, before it could attack, was recalled and sent across the Moselle to the Fort Jeanne d'Arc area.

The 95th Division Attack West of the Moselle

After the 95th Division attack to reduce the Maizières salient on 8–9 November, the main part of the division remained in position along the lines hemming in the German bridgehead west of Metz. Large combat patrols were sent into the enemy lines each night, but no further operations were initiated west of the river until 14 November. By that time the flanking movements north and south of Metz were well under way and the 95th Division could be released from its inactive containing mission in the XX Corps center.

Earlier attempts by the 2d Infantry Regiment and 90th Division to break through the fortifications west of Metz by frontal assault having proved far too costly, General Twaddle and the 95th Division staff evolved a scheme of maneuver by which the 379th Infantry (Col. C. P. Chapman) would execute a penetration north of Fort Jeanne d'Arc. At the same time it would attempt to overrun the minor works in the Seven Dwarfs chain linking the main German fortifications at Fort Jeanne d'Arc and Fort Driant. (*Map XXXIII*) The final objective for this attack was designated as the eastern slopes of the heights bordering the Moselle in the sector between the town of Jussy and the edge of the Bois de Vaux. Once the 95th Division had command of this ground, only the river would separate it from the city of Metz.[28]

Before dawn on 14 November the 359th Field Artillery Battalion opened up on the German works with its 105-mm. howitzers and all battalions of corps artillery within range joined in. After thirty minutes of this artillery preparation the 2d Battalion, on the regimental left wing, moved into the assault along the road between the de Guise works and Fort Jeanne d'Arc. Fifteen minutes later the 1st Battalion jumped off in an attack to cross the deep draw east of Gravelotte, the scene of so much bloody fighting in September, which lay directly in the path of the advance to the Seven Dwarfs. The 3d Battalion, holding the right flank of the regiment, extended its line to the north but took no part in the initial attack.

Both assault battalions came under shellfire from Fort Driant and the Moselle Battery during the early stages of the advance, but the German infantry in front offered only slight resistance. By 1100, Companies E and F of the 2d Battalion had worked their way around Fort Jeanne d'Arc and

[28] Hist Div Combat Interviews.

were on the wooded high ground about five hundred yards northwest of Rozerieulles, well to the rear of the fort. Here they were immediately counterattacked. The enemy, beaten off, stubbornly returned to the assault twice in the course of the afternoon, only to be driven back with considerable loss.

On the right, Companies A and B of the 1st Battalion found the going slow and difficult. First, the German outpost line on the west bank of the draw had to be cut through. Then the attackers climbed down into the draw and up the opposite side, all the while under a merciless flanking fire from the guns at Fort Driant. The Seven Dwarfs had not been completely garrisoned, however, and shortly after 1400 the three northern works, Fort St. Hubert and the two Jussy forts, were taken. Company A swung south and about 1600 launched an assault at Fort Bois la Dame. Some of its men reached the top of the enemy works, but were driven off by fire from Fort Driant and a counterattack before they could pry the garrison loose.

By late evening, however, the situation of the 379th Infantry was critical. The two companies of the 1st Battalion were cut off by a large party of the *462d Fuesilier Battalion* that had filtered back into the draw east of Gravelotte. The force from the 2d Battalion was somewhat disorganized as the result of the loss of the battalion commander, Lt. Col. J. L. Golson, who was seriously wounded. Both battalions had incurred a high number of casualties during the day. The only supply road leading to these forward units was interdicted by Fort Jeanne d'Arc, and although artillery liaison planes had dropped ammunition and supplies just before dark such air service provided a very thin link with the rest of the regiment.[29]

During 14 November the Germans had been able to concentrate their reserves in the west bank sector to meet the singlehanded attack of the 379th Infantry.[30] But on 15 November the 95th Division committed elements of the 378th on the west bank in a co-ordinated advance against the north and northwestern sectors of the Metz bridgehead, easing slightly the pressure on the two isolated battalions of the 379th. At 0900, companies C and L, led by Lt. Col. Tobias R. Philbin, began to fight their way across the draw in an effort to pass through the two companies of the 1st Battalion. Once more the enemy took advantage of this natural defensive position to make an obsti-

[29] 379th Inf AAR, 14 Nov 44.

[30] On 14 November the *462d Fuesilier Battalion* was committed in the Jeanne d'Arc sector. Elements of the *1010th Security Regiment* cut off the American 2d Battalion. It is probable that the *1217th Regiment* opposed the 1st Battalion.

nate stand, but just after midday Company C reached the 1st Battalion. An attempt to push on to the final regimental objective was held in check. Company G, the 2d Battalion reserve, was less successful when it attempted to resupply and reinforce the troops southeast of Fort Jeanne d'Arc. While moving along the road north of the fort the column was brought to a halt by small arms fire from concrete field works commanding the road. No approach to these works could be made in daylight without high losses. After dark, demolition details tried their hand but the charges failed to blast open the concrete. However, this experience seems to have shaken the German lieutenant in command, for he allowed the Americans to talk him into surrendering.

The supply situation still was uncertain on this and the following day. The weather grew progressively worse as snow alternated with rain. The only road to the forward companies, that between Fort de Guise and Fort Jeanne d'Arc, was impassable for wheeled traffic—even if it had not been still under interdictory fire. Air supply was increasingly difficult and each time a pilot took off in one of the flimsy liaison planes he risked his life. Furthermore, the entire area was a rabbit warren of tunnels connecting the forts and outworks; the Germans could constantly reappear to block the paths and trails leading to the forward companies of the 379th.[31] It was increasingly apparent that the 379th could not push on to its final objective until a main supply road was cleared. Therefore, on 16 November the 3d Battalion was committed in the zone of the 2d Battalion, where it captured the large bunkers at St. Hubert Farm and Moscou Farm, then blew the tunnels leading back to the main forts.[32] South of Fort Jeanne d'Arc the *462d Fuesilier Battalion* continued the fight to hem in the 1st Battalion of the 379th. General Walker sent word to the 95th Division commander, as well as to his other commanders, to step up the attacks toward Metz.[33] But the 379th had been badly mauled, still lacked sufficient supplies, and could not yet reassemble for a final co-ordinated assault. On the early morning of 18 November a convoy of thirty jeeps churned through the mud and reached the 3d Battalion. Contact was established between the 3d Battalion and the 1st Battalion and the 379th struck out toward Moulins-lès-Metz, where a main highway bridge led across the Moselle and into Metz itself. At noon the advance patrols reached the bridge, only to find

[31] The November After Action Reports of both the 378th and 379th continually speak of the difficulties involved in bypassing fortifications during a *slow* advance.

[32] Pfc. Elmer A. Eggert, L Company, 379th Infantry, advanced alone against a machine gun, during the 3d Battalion attack, killed five of the enemy with his BAR, and captured four. He received the DSC.

[33] This took place on the afternoon of 17 November. 95th Div AAR, 17 Nov 44.

that the Germans had done a thorough job of destruction. Poised on the bank of the Moselle, the 379th had left enemy troops at Fort Jeanne d'Arc and at most of the Seven Dwarfs in the rear. However, those German detachments were surrounded and lacked the resources to constitute any real threat to the American line of communications. On the night of 18–19 November the first large convoy of jeeps and 2½-ton trucks reached Moulins-lès-Metz, opening the main supply road necessary to support a further advance.

The Attack by the 377th and 378th

The attack begun by the 379th Infantry in the Fort Jeanne d'Arc sector on 14 November was only the first in the series of attacks initiated by the 95th Division to erase the Metz bridgehead and to destroy the German forces west of the Moselle. On 15 November the 377th and 378th, each minus one infantry battalion attached to Task Force Bacon on the east side of the river, started a co-ordinated maneuver, the 378th leading off with a flanking attack on the Canrobert line and the Fêves ridge. The 377th, on the left, followed up to make the main effort of the division with a push south along the west bank of the Moselle.

Col. Samuel L. Metcalfe, commanding the 378th Infantry, had planned a daring operation in which the regimental front would be stripped of all but a tiny containing force in order to put real weight into the envelopment of the German right flank. On the night of 12–15 November the 1st and 3d Battalions moved north to an assembly area near Pierrevillers, leaving Capt. William M. St. Jacques, commanding officer of the regimental service company, to hold the old 8½-mile front with three rifle platoons, an antitank platoon, an intelligence and reconnaissance squad, and a few service troops. Immediately ahead of the old regimental front the enemy still held the ridge line of the Bois de Fêves, along which ran the Canrobert line with its four interlocking forts; the southern flank of this line was covered by the Amanvillers fortifications. Earlier action by the 90th Division had partially uncovered the northern flank of the Canrobert line by the push into the Maizièreslès-Metz sector. In later fighting the Americans had driven forward along the valley east of St. Hubert as far as Marange-Silvange, which now would serve as a point of departure for the attack by the 378th.

At 0800 on 15 November, after a fifteen-minute artillery preparation, the 1st Battalion and B Company, 778th Tank Battalion, moved forward to attack

Fort le Fêves, the northernmost work in the Canrobert line. The morning was foggy and wet, and smoke placed on the Canrobert forts clung persistently over the German positions. Company A (Capt. G. W. Hunter), leading the assault, was briefly checked when its commander was hit; but a wounded officer, Lt. Leo Prough, led a platoon, firing as it marched forward, up onto the tip of the main ridge line south of Frémecourt Farm and around to the rear of Fort le Fêves. By 1100 this key work, commanding the approaches to Metz from the north and northwest, was in American hands, and the attack rolled on toward the high ground southwest of the Bois de Woippy which was the regimental objective. During the afternoon troops of the *1010th Security Regiment* and the *1215th* made several furious but fruitless attempts to wipe out the American penetration in the rear of the Canrobert line. As each wave debouched from the German works it was cut down by fire from the lines of the 1st Battalion. By midafternoon the *1010th* and *1215th* had had enough and were evacuating the line of fortifications in disorderly fashion. At 1600 the 3d Battalion passed through the gap made by the 1st Battalion and when night fell its troops were on the regimental objective.[34]

The main effort launched by the 95th Division on 15 November began at 1000 when the 377th Infantry drove south of Maizières-lès-Metz into the positions of the *1215th Regiment*—now at only half strength. The infantry attack, spearheaded by medium tanks of the 778th Tank Battalion, made steady progress. At twilight the 3d Battalion held la Maxe and the 2d Battalion, to the west, was fighting hard in the town of Woippy—less than three miles from the heart of Metz—where the enemy had elected to make a stand with a battalion of the *1215th Regiment* reinforced by the reserve company of the *38th SS Panzer Grenadier Regiment.* The battle for Woippy continued until the afternoon of the following day, when the last Germans were captured or driven from the town.[35] During the night of 15 November patrols from the 377th and 378th made contact, and the next day the bulk of the two regiments pushed on to the south.[36]

[34] Hist Div Combat Interviews; 358th Inf AAR, 15 Nov 44.

[35] Cpl. C. J. Smith, C Company, 778th Tank Battalion, was awarded the DSC for his part in the fight at Woippy. Inside the village his tank received a direct hit. Smith continued to fire the tank gun, while his crew left the tank. Then he dismounted the .30-caliber machine gun and fought on alone until help arrived.

[36] Part of the 3d Battalion, 377th Infantry, attacked at Fort Gambetta on 16 November. Here Capt. Samuel T. Pinckney, K Company, 377th Infantry, led the assault until he was wounded and physically incapable of continuing. Even then he rallied his men and encouraged them to continue the attack. He was killed by a mortar shell before he could be evacuated. Captain Pinckney received the DSC posthumously.

The American successes on 15 November not only turned the north flank of the German bridgehead west of the Moselle but also threatened to cleave a corridor straight to the Metz bridges. Furthermore the enemy had been deprived of his observation posts on the Fêves ridge and had lost much of the artillery in the northern groupment around Bellevue and St. Rémy. General Kittel sent what reinforcements he could find to aid the force fighting to hold Woippy, but all he could disengage from the battle along the Metz perimeter was one rifle company of the *38th SS Panzer Grenadier Regiment.* Kittel sent orders to the *1010th Security Regiment* to fall back to an east-west line through Leipzig Farm and Fort Plappeville. This order was no longer possible of execution, for the *1010th* was so badly demoralized and disorganized that it no longer existed except as a hodgepodge of little groups retreating to the east in a general *sauve-qui-peut.* Fort Lorraine, which formed a second defense position behind the Canrobert line, was evacuated without a fight. Late on 16 November the two reinforcing companies of the *38th SS Panzer Grenadier Regiment* pulled out of the Woippy sector, and with their withdrawal all resistance by the *1215th Regiment* collapsed. During the night of 16 November the attack of the 377th and 378th had turned into a pursuit along roads strewn with abandoned equipment, half-loaded trucks, and artillery pieces. The following day the two regiments mopped up in the German works which had been bypassed, although Fort Gambetta was merely contained after the failure of an initial assault by troops of the 377th. The regiments then reorganized in preparation for the last stage of the advance into Metz.[37]

Early on the morning of 18 November the Germans blew the demolition charges on the Moselle bridges west of the city, destroying all but one, which apparently was left intact for the troops retreating from the bridgehead.[38] The 377th, having reached the suburb of Sansonnet the previous evening, rushed a company of infantry and a few tanks across the one bridge over the Hafen Canal, which at this point turned west from the river to form a small island. The Americans took some 250 prisoners on the island. A patrol from the 3d Battalion of the 378th Infantry rushed the bridge in its zone, but the structure

[37] Company K of the 377th made an assault at Fort Gambetta on 17 November. The company commander was killed and Sgt. F. M. Peterson, a squad leader, took charge, rallying and reorganizing the company. Peterson continued the assault, in which he personally accounted for two automatic weapons positions, and then led the company in a successful withdrawal. He was awarded the DSC.

[38] The BBC had broadcast to the Metz FFI to seize these bridges, but the Germans noted no extensive French activity until late on 18 November.

ENTERING THE OUTSKIRTS OF METZ, *men of the 378th Infantry are shown on the morning of 17 November in pursuit of the enemy along roads strewn with abandoned equipment.*

was blown while the Americans were crossing. Eight men who were on the bridge were killed and five who had already crossed were stranded. Later the five were rescued. The 1st Battalion, meanwhile, made a full-dress assault against Fort Plappeville, which lay about three thousand yards west of the river. Fort Plappeville was a well-constructed work with large tunnels and guard rooms below ground, and only casemates, pillboxes, and the like above the surface. Around and in the fort huddled the remnants of the *1010th Security Regiment* which had been unable to make their way across the river. About 1600 the 1st Battalion made a rush which carried it up and onto the fort, but the Germans were able to beat off this assault. A second American attack was more successful and all the defenders above ground were captured or killed. However, the battalion commander was unwilling to expose his men to the risk of a counterattack from the tunnels during the hours of darkness and the force withdrew at nightfall leaving its supporting artillery to work on the casemates and pillboxes.

The next day General Walker sent orders that all of the holdout forts were to be contained and not subjected to direct assault. Fort Plappeville was left to the 379th Infantry. The 378th, the 377th, and Task Force Bacon all entered Metz proper on 19 November.[39]

Operations of Task Force Bacon, 15–22 November

While the 90th Division and 10th Armored Division were making the wide envelopment north and east of Metz, the 1st Battalion of the 379th Infantry and the 2d Battalion of the 378th Infantry, combined as Task Force Bacon, began the short jab from positions on the inner flank of the 90th along the east bank of the Moselle toward the heart of Metz. Task Force Bacon began its operation on 15 November, timed to coincide with the parallel attack by the 377th and 378th west of the river. Since the fight to free the 1st Battalion of the 377th in the Bertrange sector consumed most of the day, the drive south did not begin until the next morning. Colonel Bacon's tactics were simple but effective.[40] The advance was made in two columns, moving along parallel roads on a narrow front, with tank destroyers and tanks—later reinforced by two self-propelled 155-mm. guns—at the head of each column,

[39] 95th Div AAR, 19 Nov 44; 377th Inf S–3 Jnl, 20 Nov 44; 95th Div G–3 Jnl, 18 and 19 Nov 44.

[40] Detailed explanation is given in Historical Division Combat Interviews.

and with the infantry following in trucks and on foot. The fire power in front blasted enemy strong points along the road. Then the infantry stepped in to mop up, or launch an assault, according to the degree of stubborness shown by the German grenadiers and gunners after they had been subjected to concerted tank and tank destroyer fire. When the terrain and the enemy combined to slow down one column, the second column hooked around the position into the German flank and rear. Occasionally these tactics were varied by a concentric attack in which both columns swerved to make a close-in envelopment of some center of resistance.

On 16 November Task Force Bacon made an advance of four and a half miles at the expense of the *1216th Regiment*, whose connection with the *19th VG Division* on the right now had been broken. The German regiment was thus forced to fight an independent delaying action with only such strength as it could muster after the reverses suffered in the Bertrange sector. Task Force Bacon was advancing on the west side of a huge mine field, and east of it the 90th Division was advancing. Colonel Bacon, believing that his left flank was exposed and that the screen originally provided by elements of the 90th had not been pushed south to keep pace with his task force, halted the advance with the open flank of his columns resting on the village of Trémery. The task force continued south on 17 November pushing its self-propelled guns forward to engage defended road blocks and bunkers at ranges as short as two hundred yards. At dark the task force columns converged along the main river road within sight of Fort St. Julien, less than four thousand yards from the center of Metz. Colonel Bacon decided to send the 2d Battalion of the 378th up against Fort St. Julien, whose strength and controlling position on the main highway made an assault imperative. At the same time he planned to switch the 1st Battalion of the 377th Infantry around past the fort in an attempt to keep the advance moving.

Under cover of the early morning fog on 18 November, the assault battalion moved silently off the road and circled into the sparse woods west of the suburbs of the town of St. Julien-lès-Metz. About 0700 the battalion began the attack east toward the rear of the fort. However, a fortress battalion, which had been sent north the day before, was in the houses and along the streets intervening between the woods and the fort. A sharp fight raged up and down the streets during the rest of the morning; but by noon the Germans had been driven back into Fort St. Julien and the Americans closed in with tanks, tank destroyers, and the ubiquitous self-propelled guns for the assault against the fort itself. For an hour the heavy weapons of the task force, their fire thickened by 240-mm. howitzers brought into play by the corps artillery, shelled the fort. Under cover of this shelling the infantry surrounded the German position. When the fire lifted, the first assault was launched in an attempt to breach the rearward wall. Fort St. Julien was an outdated work with high, thick walls surrounded by a moat some forty feet wide. From the west, or rear side, the moat was bridged by a walled causeway leading into an open areaway. The first men across the causeway were hit by fire from the loopholes in the *enceinte* which overlooked the causeway. Two light tanks then were run up to the causeway to provide covering fire for a tank destroyer which mounted a high velocity 90-mm. gun. The tank destroyer crew took their gun to within fifty feet of the great iron door in front of the areaway, but their fire could not breach it. At dusk one of the self-propelled 155-mm. guns was run forward. This did the job, ending most of the enemy resistance. Next morning the engineers sent in to blow up the works with TNT took two hundred docile prisoners out of the network of tunnels below the fort.[41]

While its sister battalion was fighting its way toward Fort St. Julien on 18 November, the 1st Battalion of the 377th had bypassed to the west and marched through the suburbs of St. Julien-lès-Metz. Barring the northeastern entrance to the older portion of Metz lay another large but outmoded work, Fort Bellecroix. Just as the battalion started forward to form for the assault a column of about one hundred German infantry came hurrying out of the fort with white flags in their hands. The reason for this hasty evacuation soon became evident. About 1400, as the battalion was moving along the street by the fort, two terrific blasts shattered the heavy masonry walls bringing the debris down on the startled Americans and leaving fifty-seven dead and wounded in Company C, which at the moment was closest to the fort.[42] The rest of the battalion threaded its way through the rubble. As the day ended, patrols from the task force began to mop up the scattered centers of resistance at the northern edge of the city. Task Force Bacon continued to take part in

[41] *Ibid.* During the action on 19 November Pfc. Walter Low, G Company, 378th Infantry, observed fire coming from a large pillbox. He ran to the pillbox under bitter cross fire, threw in a grenade, and routed thirty-two of the German occupants. Low received the DSC.

[42] 95th Div AAR, 18 Nov 44.

the rather desultory street fighting of the next few days and was dissolved on 22 November when resistance in Metz officially ended.[43]

The 5th Division Drive into Metz

After a general regrouping south of Metz the 5th Division continued its attack toward the city on 16 November. The whole operation was slowed by the inability of the 10th Infantry to make a rapid forward move while the bulk of the 2d Infantry was held at the Nied River. (*Map XXXII*) In the afternoon the 3d Battalion of the latter regiment pushed north toward Frontigny and came abreast of the right-flank battalion of the 10th, which thus far had been echeloned to the rear. The forward lines of the 10th came within sight of Magny; Marly, the scene of bitter fighting on the previous day, was finally cleared of the last enemy. The 11th Infantry found itself in a hornet's nest at the Frescaty airfield, where a fortress machine gun battalion was deployed, and both the 1st and 2d Battalions were thrown into the battle to drive the Germans from the hangars and bomb shelters surrounding the field.[44] In the meantime, the 3d Battalion was left behind to contain the Verdun forts, manned by the *48th Fortress Machine Gun Battalion.* These works were finally encircled on the night of 16–17 November.[45] As the day ended the left and center of the 5th Division were only about four thousand yards from the center of Metz. The bag of prisoners was swelling rapidly, but thus far the determined troops of the *38th SS Panzer Grenadier Regiment* and the fortress machine gun units showed no signs of abandoning their attempts to hold at each step of the way.

[43] The losses suffered by the 95th Division in the November fighting prior to the capitulation of Metz cannot be accurately stated. Since the division was new to battle all of its regimental reports tended to overestimate their losses. (This is stated by the divisional G–1 in the After Action Report for November 1944.) Estimated casualties for the period of combat up to 22 November are given in the 95th Division AAR as 281 KIA, 405 MIA, and 1,503 WIA: a total of 2,189 casualties. Enemy losses for this period are estimated as 6,082 prisoners, 1,577 KIA, and 3,546 WIA. The last two figures cannot be taken as reliable and the first is open to question.

[44] The 11th Infantry lost 4 officers and 118 men on this date. Although not excessive, these losses indicate the stubborn character of the German fight for the airfield. The 11th Infantry was also suffering badly from trench foot. Company F had only 14 men available for duty. 5th Div G–1 Jnl, 16 Nov 44. See also 5th Div AAR and *Eleventh Infantry Regiment.*

[45] The 11th Infantry After Action Report for November notes that the regiment made its greatest gains by night operations and says that the enemy did not like to fight at night. This latter allegation, incidentally, is constantly made against the American infantry in German documents.

With the withdrawal of the *38th SS Panzer Grenadier Regiment*, however, German resistance weakened on 17 November. The 10th and 2d Infantry Regiments, minus the battalion across the Nied, were able to move more rapidly. The minor forts lying in the path of their advance were quickly overrun or found unoccupied, and by midafternoon patrols from the 10th were at the Metz city limits. The general advance was stopped by Fort Queuleu, which the enemy apparently intended to defend. This was one of the old works on the inner ring of forts. The two battalions of the 11th Infantry, aided by tanks of the 735th Tank Battalion, continued the fight at the airfield. At the end of the day only a few Germans were left to defend the hangars on the northeastern edge of the field and the fight shifted toward Fort St. Privat, whose fire checked a further advance on the right. The reinforced battalion holding the bridgehead east of the Nied River began a withdrawal to the west bank on orders from General Patton, leaving CCR (Lt. Col. A. E. Harris) of the 6th Armored Division to hold the bridges while the 5th Reconnaissance Troop patrolled along the west bank. Patrols from the 5th Division had reported earlier that the Germans were escaping "in droves" through the gap still open east of Metz, and this may explain why the Third Army commander decided to assemble the entire 2d Infantry west of the Nied.

All through the night the 2d Infantry fought its way toward the north, prompted by exhortations from General Patton and the XX Corps commander to speed up the advance. On the morning of 18 November the key road and rail center at Courcelles-sur-Nied fell into American hands. General Irwin thereupon ordered the 2d Infantry, now with all three battalions in line, to push hard on its left so as to aid the advance of the 10th Infantry into Metz. This attack had reached and captured Ars-Laquenexy when, about 1945, General Walker phoned General Irwin and ordered him to press straight to the north and there meet the 90th Division, thus cutting the last escape routes to the east. Colonel Roffe, the 2d Infantry commander, detached his 1st Battalion (Lt. Col. W. H. Blakefield), reinforced by a company of tanks, for the mission. About 1030 on 19 November, these troops of the 5th Division joined hands with cavalry elements of the 90th Division north of Retonfey—so completing the encirclement of Metz.[46]

Over in the 10th Infantry sector on 18 November the 1st Battalion bypassed the 2d Battalion—which was deployed around Fort Queuleu—and entered

[46] 735th Tk Bn AAR, 19 Nov 44; 90th Rcn Tr Jnl, 19 Nov 44. The first detachments to meet came from the assault gun section of the 735th and a cavalry platoon.

MEN OF 5TH INFANTRY DIVISION ENTER METZ *on 18 November (above) and the next day (below) conduct a house-to-house search in this city.*

Metz.[47] At 1140 the next morning the 10th Infantry met patrols from the 95th Division near Vallières, just south of St. Julien-lès-Metz. The 11th Infantry also crossed the Metz limits on 18 November and by the night of 19 November had mopped up most of the streets and houses between the Moselle and the railroad loop in the southwest quarter of the city. The 2d Battalion, however, continued to be held in check by the stubborn defenders at Fort St. Privat.[48]

The Capitulation of Metz

On 16 November Kittel committed the last of his sparse reserves to defend on the north, south, and west of Metz. The eastern side of the city was undefended, except by the few troops maintaining a tenuous connection with the field forces of the *First Army.* Now General Knobelsdorff sent word to the beleaguered commander that on 17 November the *First Army* would detach itself from the Metz garrison and begin a withdrawal to new positions farther east, thus ending the drag of what one German general had called "the leaden weight" around the neck of the *First Army* command. The last of the German civilian population was escorted from the city by four motorized companies of *Feldgendarmerie* sent from Darmstadt, and Kittel's command was left to its fate. On the night of 16–17 November the *38th SS Panzer Grenadier Regiment* made its move east through the narrowing escape route, apparently acting on Hitler's earlier order that no part of the *17th SS Panzer Grenadier Division* (already on the roster of units for the Ardennes counteroffensive) should be entrapped inside of Metz. No word of this withdrawal reached Kittel until the morning of 17 November when he suddenly was informed that the *38th* had deserted the Metz garrison.[49]

Pleas for help from all the forts and sectors of the Metz front flooded General Kittel's headquarters on 17 November. There was nothing left for the German commander to do, however, but give orders that the Moselle

[47] The 2d Battalion captured Fort Queuleu on 21 November. 5th Div AAR, 21 Nov 44.

[48] The estimated losses for the 5th Division during November, nearly all incurred in the first three weeks, are given by the 5th Division After Action Report as follows: 13 and 172 KIA; 39 and 1,005 WIA; 4 and 143 MIA. The sick and nonbattle casualty rate of the 5th Division was very high. Figures for the entire division are not available, but the 11th Infantry, with a total of 380 battle casualties, had 1,081 sick and nonbattle casualties (mostly trench foot). 5th Div G–1 Jnl.

[49] The *38th SS Panzer Grenadier Regiment* appears to have suffered fairly heavily in this withdrawal. See MS #B–487 (Simon).

bridges be blown and make preparations for a house-to-house defense of the city itself.[50] The remnants of the *1215th Regiment* were hemmed in around the St. Quentin works. The *1010th Security Regiment*, which no longer had any semblance of organization, clustered around Plappeville. The *462d Fuesilier Battalion*, having given a good account of itself, had withdrawn to Fort Jeanne d'Arc, where it was joined on 17 November by most of the staff of the *462d VG Division*. The *1217th Regiment*, its ranks depleted, formed a new line of defense around Fort Driant. The *22d Fortress Regiment* had splintered into fragments with detachments in and around the forts at St. Privat, Queuleu, and St. Julien. About four hundred stragglers had been gathered to defend the old barracks on the Ile Chambière.

These last dispositions of the broken units under Kittel's command were based on no thoroughgoing plan, nor was further co-ordination between units possible. On the evening of 17 November the central exchange for the underground telephone system, located on the Ile Chambière, ceased to function and Kittel's over-all command ended.[51] A few of the Germans outside the forts tried to make a fight for it in these last hours, but most were content to fire a few shots and then march into the American lines with their hands in the air. No real house-to-house battle was waged in the city of Metz, despite futile attempts to defend some of the headquarters buildings. By the night of 19 November American mopping-up operations were well along. On 21 November a patrol from the 95th Division found General Kittel in an underground field hospital, badly wounded (he had been fighting in the line) and under morphine. The next afternoon hostilities formally ceased—although a number of the forts continued to hold out.[52] The *462d VG Division* no longer existed. German sources later estimated that the actual casualties in the defense of Metz had been four hundred dead and some twenty-two hundred wounded, about half of whom had been evacuated before the city was encircled.[53] But to these losses must be added those inflicted on the *416th Division*, the *19th*

[50] The *First Army* estimated on 17 November that the heart of the city could be held for three or four days and that the main forts could be defended for fifteen days. *Army Group G KTB*, 17 Nov 44.

[51] MS #B–079 (Kittel).

[52] Resistance ended officially at 1435 on 22 November. XX Corps AAR, 22 Nov 44.

[53] MS #B–079 (Kittel). The XX Corps estimates of the German losses in the defense of Metz are: 14,368 prisoners, 3,800 KIA, and 7,904 WIA. See 5th Div G–3 Jnl, 24 Nov 44. It is probable that the German estimates are too low; certainly the American estimates are too high. The formations written off by the Germans after the fall of Metz include: the *462d VG Division*, the *45th* and *53d Fortress Machine Gun Battalions*, the *811th Fortress Infantry Flak Battalion*, the *1311th* and *1519th Army Fortress Artillery Battalions*, and the *55th Fortress Engineer Battalion*. See *OKH/Org. Abt. KTB*, 2 Dec 44.

FORT PLAPPEVILLE, *as it appeared on 7 December, the day it surrendered to the 11th Infantry.*

Division, and the *17th SS Panzer Grenadier Division*, during the fight to envelop Metz. No casualty figures for these units are obtainable.

Since General Walker had forbidden direct assault against the holdout forts, and since artillery ammunition had to be carefully conserved to support the projected XX Corps drive to the Sarre River, the German garrisons were left to wither on the vine. One by one the isolated German forts succumbed. Fort Verdun surrendered on 26 November. Fort St. Privat capitulated with its garrison of five hundred on 29 November, after four American field artillery battalions and three 155-mm. self-propelled guns had shelled the fort.[54] At the end of November Forts Driant, Jeanne d'Arc, St. Quentin, and Plappeville still held out, forcing General Irwin to use most of the 2d Infantry and one battalion of the 11th Infantry to contain them. To this extent at least the Metz garrison carried out the orders given by Hitler. Short rations and general

[54] General Irwin credits the fall of St. Privat largely to the personal efforts of the 11th Infantry commander, Col. P. J. Black, who had relieved Col. C. W. Yuill on 21 November. Irwin Diary.

demoralization eventually took their toll even in those forts where determined German officers were able to keep their men in hand. On 6 December Fort St. Quentin surrendered with a sizable garrison. Fort Plappeville followed the next day. Then, by one of the fortunes of war, Fort Driant capitulated to the 5th Infantry Division at 1545 on 8 December—about fifteen minutes before the incoming 87th Division relieved the 5th.[55] Fort Jeanne d'Arc, probably because it was officered by the *462d VG Division* staff and garrisoned by the *Fuesilier Battalion*, was the last of the Metz forts to fall. Its garrison surrendered to the III Corps, which by then had taken over the Metz area, on 13 December.[56]

The credit for the envelopment of Metz and the final reduction of its defenses must be given to the combined ground forces which took part in the operation, since continuous bad flying weather had permitted only occasional intervention in the battle by the air arm. This operation, skillfully planned and marked by thorough execution of the plan, may long remain an outstanding example of a prepared battle for the reduction of a fortified position. However, determined enemy resistance, bad weather and attendant floods, plus a general tendency to overestimate the strength of the Metz fortifications, all combined to slow down the American offensive and give opportunity for the right wing of the German *First Army* to repair the tie between the *LXXXII Corps* and *XIII SS Corps* in time for an organized withdrawal to the Sarre River.[57]

[55] The total number of prisoners taken from these three forts was 59 officers and 1,516 men. The credit for the surrender of Fort Driant was claimed by both the 5th and 87th Divisions. However, the weight of the evidence confirms the 5th Division claims. The 345th Infantry had begun the relief of the 2d Infantry but had not officially taken over the area. See TUSA AAR, I; XX Corps AAR, 8 Dec 44; 2d Inf AAR, 8 Dec 44; Irwin Diary. Cf. 87th Div AAR, 8 Dec 44. General Walker had done his best to hold on to the Fort Driant sector so that the 5th Infantry Division could have credit for its capture. This was much appreciated by General Irwin and his division.

[56] The surrender was made actually to the 26th Infantry Division.

[57] German commanders who took part in the Metz campaign are generally of the opinion that the November operation should have been concluded by the Americans in less time than that actually taken. Such testimony, in part at least, is suspect as being proffered to bolster up the thesis common to many defeated commanders, namely, that their own forces were so lacking in materiel and so heavily outnumbered that naught but failure was possible. However, it is true that the events of September and early October had made the Americans wary of high losses and dramatic failures, such as the first attempt to take Fort Driant, and prompted a widespread use of cautious and slow-moving tactics in which crushing superiority in men, guns, and tanks was concentrated wherever the enemy showed signs of standing his ground. It must be added that mud and rain contributed greatly to slowing the American advance.

CHAPTER X

The XII Corps Drive Toward the Sarre (18-30 November)

The XII Corps attack toward the northeast had slowed perceptibly at the beginning of the second week of the November offensive. The left wing of the corps had advanced some twenty miles; however, Darmstadt and the Rhine River crossings, the ultimate corps objective, lay approximately 110 miles beyond the farthest point attained by the American forward line. Weather and terrain hampered General Eddy's armored columns, throwing the burden of the attack more and more on the infantry and the rifle elements of the armored units. At the same time that replacements were bringing the ranks of the infantry divisions back to strength, the incidence of loss from exposure and combat fatigue was on the rise. The enemy divisions facing the XII Corps generally were weak—even the newly arrived *36th VG Division* had taken a severe beating in the last American attacks west of Faulquemont. Nonetheless, the ground and the weather unquestionably favored the defense. Furthermore, the Germans now had been pushed back into rearward positions which had been given a measure of preparation during the October lull.

During the night of 17–18 November, the south wing of the *First Army* undertook a withdrawal to a new position roughly marked by the line Faulquemont–Bénestroff–Bourgaltroff, thus anticipating the renewal of the XII Corps attack by a few hours. The German formations in front of the XII Corps remained the same. The *LXXXIX Corps*, with two divisions, held a front which extended from the Marne-Rhin Canal to a point northeast of Morhange. The *361st VG Division*, on the left, confronted the 26th Infantry Division and the 2d Cavalry Group in the Dieuze–Bourgaltroff sector. The *11th Panzer Division*, which had sustained severe tank losses, held the *LXXXIX Corps* line on the right, with its armored infantry and remaining assault guns pushed to the fore.[1] The *XIII SS Corps*, relieved of responsibility

[1] The *11th Panzer Division* must have been reduced to a mere handful of tanks, for the *First Army* "collective tank strength" on 15 November totaled 5 Mark IV's, 18 Mark V's, 4 Mark VI's, and 26 assault guns. *Army Group G KTB* and *Anlagen*, 15 Nov 44. On 14 November the *11th Panzer Division* had an effective strength of only 800 men. *OB WEST KTB*, 14 Nov 44.

for the Metz defenses, faced the XX Corps with the bulk of its forces, while its left wing was drawn up west and south of Faulquemont.[2] The Faulquemont position, based on the old works of the Maginot Line and a recently excavated series of antitank ditches, was manned by the *36th VG Division* in the north and *Kampfgruppe Muehlen* in the south, the latter representing not more than the strength of one weak regiment. The only enemy reserves in the immediate neighborhood consisted of a small armored group drawn from the *11th Panzer Division.*

After a brief reorganization, the XII Corps resumed the attack on the morning of 18 November. General Eddy had determined to use his infantry and smash straight through to the Sarre River on a relatively narrow front. Once bridgeheads were secured across the Sarre, the entire corps might then be put in motion to carry the drive on toward the Rhine. In this first phase the 26th Infantry Division and 35th Infantry Division were to advance abreast, while the 80th Infantry Division would be left to contain Faulquemont and block on the exposed north flank. According to the corps plan, the two armored divisions were to be used as opportunity offered, the 6th Armored on the left and the 4th Armored on the right.[3] In actual fact, however, the armor was to have no respite but would continue the advance with the infantry.

The 26th Division Attack at the Dieuze–Bénestroff Line

On the south wing of the XII Corps the 26th Infantry Division started the new operation by launching an attack against the Dieuze–Bénestroff line, which Colonel Oden's 4th Armored column had penetrated briefly on 14 November.[4] (*Map XXXIV*) The 101st and 104th Infantry, the assault regiments, had received nearly a full complement of replacements and had been given a brief recess during which the men had slept, dried their clothes, and cleaned their weapons. After an hour-long artillery preparation on the morning of 18 November the 101st and 104th began the new attack. The 101st (Col. W. T. Scott) passed through the 328th and drove at Guébling and

[2] On 16 Nov Generalleutnant der Waffen-SS Max Simon assumed command of the *XIII SS Corps*, relieving Priess, who had been selected for an armored command in the forthcoming Ardennes counteroffensive. MS #B–412 (Einem).

[3] XII Corps Operational Directive No. 38, 17 Nov 44. CCB, 4th Armored Division, was designated as the XII Corps reserve.

[4] See Chap. VII, pp. 333–36.

Bourgaltroff as the armor had done. The 104th (Col. R. A. Palladino), advancing on the left, started in the direction of Marimont-lès-Bénestroff and Bénestroff but was brought to a halt almost immediately at the Bois de Bénestroff, just east of the Bénestroff railroad line. The 101st was thus exposed to flanking fire as it attempted to fight its way across the rail embankment west of Guébling. Undoubtedly the earlier attack by Oden's column had alerted the enemy, who was dug in along the railroad. The 3d Battalion, on the left, hampered by a large number of raw replacements, faced the strongest section of the German line. Here the enemy had sited his machine guns on the embankment and in culverts along the right of way so as to furnish a wall of fire up and down the track. A short distance to the east German artillery observers and more machine guns were located on Hill 273, overlooking the approaches to the track. Farther north the Germans held a strong post among the rock piles surrounding a quarry on the southern edge of the Bois de Bénestroff. Against this position the 3d Battalion launched assault after assault, only to be repelled each time with heavy losses; L Company, more exposed than the other companies, lost its commander, Capt. D. D. Donahue, and all the rest of its officers.

The 2d Battalion, 101st, advancing on the right of the main road leading down into Guébling, was more successful, since it could be supported by tanks and tank destroyers. The Dordal Creek again was an obstacle, as it had been for Oden's tank column, but the engineers, working under artillery and small arms fire, were able to put in an infantry support bridge and a steel treadway. Company A, 761st Tank Battalion, essayed a direct attack but took severe punishment from the German guns and was forced to withdraw. Within an hour of the jump-off, however, the infantry were fighting at the northern edge of Guébling. Subsequently a platoon of tank destroyers and five tanks joined the infantry inside the village, where the fight continued through the afternoon.

While the body of the 2d Battalion fought at Guébling, F Company, commanded by a replacement officer in his first battle, had circled the town and forged far ahead of the other companies. About noon the battalion lost radio contact with F Company, after a last report that the company was being hit by flanking fire. The 2d Battalion was unable to shake itself free in Guébling until 1630; then the 1st Battalion took over the fight and the 2d launched an attack to reach the area where the lost company had been last reported. This attack reached the edge of Bourgaltroff early in the evening[5] but F Company was not heard from again, although an artillery plane reported American troops being marched to the rear of the German lines.[6]

Late in the day the 104th Infantry succeeded in breaking through the Bois de Bénestroff, thus easing the pressure on the 3d Battalion of the 101st. As darkness fell, Sgt. Sam A. Longbottom led the survivors of L Company in a desperate charge up Hill 273, knocking out the German machine gun crews with hand grenades and bazooka fire at close quarters.[7] Meanwhile, the two companies on the left of the battalion fought their way forward past the quarry and sent patrols to meet the 104th in the southeastern part of the Bois de Bénestroff.

On 19 November the 104th and 101st continued the attack in an envelopment from north and south intended to encircle the road center at Marimont and seize Marimont Hill (Hill 334), lying just west of the village and overlooking the route along which the left wing of the 26th Division would have to advance.[8] The brunt of the attack was borne by the 2d Battalion of the 104th, advancing in column of companies on the right flank of the regiment, and the 3d Battalion of the 101st, pushing toward the Bois de Marimont. Little progress was made this day because the Germans had retired from the railway line in good order and now were fighting stubbornly to cover a general withdrawal on the *First Army* front which had been ordered for the night of 19–20 November. About 1000 the 104th was briefly checked by a detachment of tanks from the *11th Panzer Division.* The 3d Battalion of the 101st, already much weakened by the losses incurred the previous day, suffered heavy casualties from an accurate artillery shelling as it attacked with marching fire toward the Bois de Marimont. By 1100 the entire strength of the battalion was less than three hundred, and still more casualties were suffered in clearing

[5] During the attack at Bourgaltroff four German tanks opened fire on E Company. Sgt. Albert E. McPhee left his already depleted platoon and advanced alone with a bazooka. He hit two of the tanks and forced all four to retire. Sergeant McPhee was awarded the DSC.

[6] A subsequent investigation, cited in the 101st Infantry Journal, reported eight dead on F Company's last position. Apparently the company had taken cover in some farm buildings, had been blasted out by direct artillery fire at very close range, and then had surrendered *en masse.*

[7] Hist Div Combat Interviews; 101st Inf Jnl, 18 Nov 44.

[8] Pfc. Augustine Silva, G Company, 101st Infantry, on this day killed the entire crew of a German tank with only hand grenades and his rifle. He received the DSC. Cpl. John L. Farrell, aid man with the 101st Infantry, also was awarded the DSC for the rescue, under fire, of a wounded officer. Corporal Farrell himself was wounded in reaching the officer.

the Bois de Marimont. By the time the 3d Battalion entered the next woods, about 1,400 yards to the east, one rifle company numbered only nine men and another had been reduced to ten.[9]

About noon the 2d Battalion, 104th, reached Marimont and one rifle company entered the village, only to be driven out by an intense concentration of artillery and mortar fire. Actually the German artillery was engaged in covering the general withdrawal which had begun even before darkness came. During the night of 19–20 November the enemy in front of the 26th Division took up new positions between Mittersheim and Albestroff. The Americans re-entered Marimont on the heels of the retreating Germans and the 3d Battalion of the 104th Infantry Regiment occupied the important road center at Bénestroff.

During 19 November the 328th (Col. B. R. Jacobs), which had received some eight hundred replacements the previous day, moved south to take Dieuze and crack the hinge of the German line, thus opening the way for the 4th Armored Division to drive to the east. A German rear guard formation from the *361st VG Division* held on stubbornly and halted the 3d Battalion, leading the assault, in the muddy plowed fields north of the town with accurate small arms fire and artillery air bursts. In the late afternoon tanks from the 761st Tank Battalion, pushing forward in support of the infantry, were checked by antitank fire from Dieuze. During the night the German garrison withdrew toward Mittersheim, and the 2d Cavalry Group and 328th Infantry, reinforced by the 51st Armored Infantry Battalion, 4th Armored Division, moved into the battered town. Raids by the American air force and last-minute demolitions by the German rear guards had destroyed most of the bridges in Dieuze, but one remained intact and would provide quick passage for any pursuit to the east.[10]

The Drive to the Honskirch–Altwiller Line

The collapse of the Dieuze–Bénestroff line enabled the 26th Division and the 4th Armored Division to drive ahead some six miles during the next few days. The enemy fought delaying actions in a few villages where terrain was

[9] Hist Div Combat Interviews; WDGO No. 109 (1945). In recognition of its performance in the fighting between 18 and 21 November the 3d Battalion of the 101st was awarded the Distinguished Unit Citation.

[10] 26th Div AAR, 19 Nov 44; 3d Bn Jnl, 19 Nov 44; 26th Div G–2 Jnl; 2d Cav Gp S–3 Rpt, 20 Nov 44; 328th Inf AAR, 20 Nov 44.

JEEPS DRIVING THROUGH DIEUZE *with troops of the 4th Armored Division on their way to the front.*

in his favor, but made no attempt to hold on a continuous front.[11] Indeed, at many points the 26th Division completely lost contact with the enemy.

The main German force made its retreat in the northern part of the division zone of advance, using the road complex that ran toward Munster and Sarre-Union. On the night of 20–21 November the 3d Battalion, 101st Infantry, made a forced march in the rain to cut into the road net at the village of Torcheville, west of Munster. The battalion, which had received about one hundred replacements on the previous night, took the village and eighty-one surprised Germans.[12] On the left the 104th Infantry attacked during the morning of 21 November to take the village of Montdidier, situated on a long, narrow ridge overlooking the northern sector of the 26th Division zone. The 3d Battalion fought to get onto the ridge while the 1st Battalion bypassed to the south and continued in the direction of Albestroff. Mud, mines, and blown bridges slowed the Americans, and the German 88's and machine guns on the ridge maintained a constant and deadly fire. Even worse, liaison between the American artillery and the 3d Battalion failed, with the result that American shells poured in on the attacking infantry. Despite all this the 3d Battalion took Montdidier and organized a holding position in the woods to the northeast.[13]

The village of Albestroff presented a knotty tactical problem for the 26th Division. Five roads centered at this point and the village had to be taken in order to insure a firm hold on the approaches to the Sarre River. South of Albestroff the 101st Infantry was nearing the end of its strength and required additional replacements before it could be committed again in a major action. In any event further progress in the zone of the 101st would be most difficult. The road east of Torcheville was useless; the Germans had mined it thoroughly and blasted trees across it to form barricades. To the southeast the road via Lohr and Insviller was flooded by the waters of the Rode Creek, released when the Germans blew a dam in the valley. General Paul ordered the 328th Infantry into trucks and dispatched it from Dieuze to reinforce the 101st, but this move would take some time to complete and the outlook for a speedy advance along the Lohr–Insviller route was unfavorable. For these reasons,

[11] 26th Div AAR, Nov 44.

[12] *Ibid.*, 20 Nov 44.

[13] 104th Inf Jnl, 21 Nov 44. The reports on this action are confused: the 26th Division After Action Report even cites "the well co-ordinated maneuver and heavy artillery concentration" as notable.

the weight of the 26th Division attack shifted to the left wing, where the 104th Infantry faced Albestroff.

About 1625 on 21 November the 1st Battalion (Capt. L. D. Gladding) of the 104th reached Albestroff. During the early hours of the march eastward the battalion had been supported by B Company of the 761st Tank Battalion, but when four tanks were lost in a mine field the armor halted and the infantry went on into the village alone. The subsequent story of the 1st Battalion cannot be determined with any degree of accuracy: contact between the battalion command post, west of the village, and the three rifle companies inside Albestroff was cut off shortly after midnight. Apparently the leading company got as far as the eastern edge of the village before meeting the Germans in any force. Then troops of the *361st VG Division*, reinforced by mobile assault guns and tanks, swept into Albestroff along the converging roads and closed on the Americans. Early the next morning Captain Gladding took the remaining troops of the 1st Battalion and made an attempt to reach the companies inside the village; but he met only Germans and had to abandon the effort in the face of superior numbers.

Colonel Palladino, commanding the 104th, immediately made plans to capture Albestroff by encircling the town. At 1000 on 22 November the 3d and the 2d Battalions jumped off on 500-yard fronts to bypass Albestroff on the north and south respectively. The 3d Battalion advance came under the German guns at Réning, a village some 2,500 yards to the north of Albestroff in the 35th Division zone. Enemy observers in the church spire at Réning and atop Hill 275 quickly brought down accurate artillery and rocket fire on the battalion, wounding the commander, Lt. Col. H. G. Donaldson, and inflicting a serious number of casualties.[14] The 2d Battalion met less resistance, but when one company wheeled in toward Albestroff it met a storm of fire from the outlying buildings and had to fall back. Next, attempts were made to maneuver tank destroyers into positions from which the German tanks inside the town could be engaged, but no cover was to be had.[15] The 104th

[14] During this action a platoon from L Company, led by 2d Lt. Howard E. Myerle, was immobilized by heavy fire and could not evacuate its large number of wounded. Lieutenant Myerle, although painfully wounded himself, ran forward alone and killed a German machine gun crew that had brought the platoon under direct fire. He received the DSC.

[15] The American pressure on Albestroff diverted the attention of the German defenders and allowed nearly all the members of the 1st Battalion to escape from the cellars where they had barricaded themselves and return to the 104th lines. During the day about 60 men from A and B Companies got out.

was in a precarious position and at 1305 General Paul ordered the regiment to hold where it was. During the night, however, the Germans evacuated Albestroff and the following day patrols from the 2d Battalion reoccupied the village.[16]

The 26th Division success in penetrating the German line on 18 November offered an opening for the tanks. The 4th Armored Division was in good shape for the attack. The troops had had a brief rest in dry billets, new tanks had replaced those lost in the fighting just past, and a few mine-roller tanks had arrived to head the armored columns.[17] The plan now adopted called for Combat Command A (Col. W. P. Withers) to lead off in two columns, one advancing on the north flank of the 26th Division, the other following the infantry through Dieuze and striking out for the town of Mittersheim on the Canal des Houillières de la Sarre. Combat Command B (Gen. H. E. Dager) would be committed to support the southern column in the drive toward Mittersheim—the axis of attack advocated by the 4th Armored Division commander in September.

CCA jumped off on 19 November: Task Force Abrams returned to the Rodalbe sector, on the north flank of the 104th Infantry, and attacked in the direction of Insming; Task Force West moved up to Dieuze, waiting there for the 328th Infantry to force a passage. Abrams' column took Rodalbe, the scene of an earlier American reverse, but then was held up for some hours on the road north of the village while the engineers removed mines—911 were taken out in this one section. Toward the close of day the column swung over into the 35th Division zone to help the 3d Battalion of the 320th Infantry take Virming, a little village that controlled the roads forking out to the east. After a fierce shelling had set Virming ablaze, Task Force Abrams moved through and laagered on the road leading to Francaltroff. At Dieuze the in-

followed by 17 men from C Company who had reached the eastern edge of Albestroff. The bulk of the battalion reached the American lines during the night and the following day. In one such withdrawal Sgt. Algy C. Shameklis led most of B Company, which he had taken over two days before when all the company officers had become casualties, out of the village—despite severe wounds suffered when a German tank blew in the walls of a house he and his men were defending. Sergeant Shameklis was awarded the DSC. For executing a successful withdrawal from the eastern edge of the village with his platoon 1st Lt. Michael V. Kravontka, C Company, 104th Infantry, also was awarded the DSC. He had earlier received three severe wounds.

[16] For the Albestroff fight see the 104th Infantry Journal. See also 26th Div AAR; Hist Div Combat Interviews; and Ltr, Col R. A. Palladino to Hist Div, 20 Sep 47.

[17] The increased use of the wood-box mine made detection difficult; in addition the muddy roads allowed the enemy to plant mines in the tracks made by their own vehicles.

fantry attack had been checked during the day and General Wood ordered the southern column to switch to the north and follow Abrams. CCA continued toward Francaltroff on 20 November over a muddy road cluttered with mines and road blocks, and interdicted by rocket and artillery fire. Late in the day the armored infantry took Francaltroff in a dismounted assault and turned the village over to the 320th Infantry.

The general withdrawal by the left wing of the *First Army* and the obvious weakening of German resistance in front of the XII Corps on 20 November gave General Eddy the opportunity he sought to commit both of his armored divisions. The XII Corps Operations Directive[18] issued that day ordered CCA, 6th Armored Division, to seize Sarre River crossings in the 35th Division zone, while CCB, 4th Armored Division, advanced in the 26th Division zone—via Mittersheim. Such a scheme of maneuver might permit concentration of the entire 4th Armored in one telling blow. Therefore General Wood recalled CCA and sent it into an assembly area near Conthil, preparatory to a shift to the south in support of CCB. This was a fortunate respite for Task Force Abrams, which now had come into a semiflooded area and was forced to spend 21 November winching two companies of medium tanks out of a miry tank park near Francaltroff. CCA did not close at Conthil until the following afternoon.

Meanwhile CCB was involved in a confusion of orders and counterorders, dictated in part by the lack of usable roads in the zone assigned the command on the right of the 26th Division, and in part by changes in the objective.[19] Originally General Dager had been told to take his combat command by way of Dieuze and attack Mittersheim, which, by reason of its location at the apex of the impassable Dieuze–Gondrexange–Mittersheim triangle, was the anchor for the left wing of the German line facing the XII Corps. The enemy at Dieuze had delayed this move, but by the night of 21 November the head of the leading column (Major Churchill) was at Loudrefing, which had been reached without much opposition. Since there was no highway within the XII Corps zone going northeast out of Mittersheim, General Dager sent another column (Lt. Col. G. L. Jaques) into the 26th Division zone to seize

[18] Operational Directive No. 41. This order apparently was more a statement of ultimate intentions than anything else. At noon on the 20th General Grow warned the corps commander that a "blitz" was out of the question, but added that the armor could keep going by making short envelopments, punching ahead, and using plenty of artillery. Ltr, Gen Grow to Hist Div, 23 Feb 49.

[19] Orders for the 25th Cavalry Squadron were changed *eight* times during the day. 4th Armd Div AAR, 21 Nov 44.

the road net centered at Munster. The roads in the region were rapidly deteriorating—and could handle only limited traffic in any case. A traffic jam occurred at Guinzeling, just as the 328th Infantry was coming up from Dieuze to aid the 101st Infantry, and the 26th Division commander ordered the armor to leave his area. The problem of armored movement was solved in part on 22 November when the 8th Tank Battalion, CCB, drove the German rear guard out of Mittersheim and crossed the Canal des Houillères de la Sarre.

The zone of attack assigned to the XII Corps narrowed as it approached the Sarre River. This fact, coupled with the successful operation just carried out by CCB on the right flank of the corps, induced the corps commander to conceive a new maneuver in which the 6th Armored Division and 80th Infantry Division, on the left, and the 4th Armored Division, on the right, would gradually pinch out the 26th and 35th Divisions. The order, issued on 22 November, did not foresee the future independent operation by the 4th Armored Division east of the Sarre River and called for that division to wheel north, rolling up the enemy in front of the 26th and 35th Divisions with an advance along the narrow corridor between the Canal des Houillères de la Sarre and the Sarre River.

Neither of the two infantry divisions that had been carrying the attack was taken from the line immediately. The 26th Division still had to close up to the canal. In front the enemy were deployed in strong positions on the west bank, with large field fortifications facing the 26th Division left and center at Honskirch and Altwiller, while the extensive Bois de Bonnefontaine provided a natural area for a stand opposite the American right. The unlucky battle at Albestroff had disorganized one battalion of the 104th Infantry and had immobilized the entire regiment. The last phase of the 26th Division advance, therefore, turned on the efforts of the 328th Infantry and the 101st Infantry, tired and depleted as the latter was. The 328th, committed between its two sister regiments on 22 November, quickly captured Munster.[20] The following day, instead of relieving the 101st as had been planned, the fresh regiment took over the 104th sector and began a drive northeastward against the Vittersbourg–Honskirch–Altwiller line. This position consisted of bunkers and entrenchments in and around the three key villages, reinforced by large

[20] Pvt. B. F. Brogdon, E Company, 328th Infantry, was awarded the DSC for bravery in this action. When his squad leader fell Brogdon took charge, although he had been hit in the leg by a shell fragment. He led the squad, all but himself replacements, in the entire fight for the village. Twenty-eight hours later he was evacuated despite his protests.

mine fields and further strengthened by an extensive antitank ditch across the draw between Honskirch and Altwiller. Actually this German line was held rather weakly since the main enemy forces had withdrawn to the east side of the Sarre River. On 25 November the 328th broke through the north end of the line and took Vittersbourg. The next day a rifle company and eleven tanks attacked Honskirch. This first assault failed, with heavy cost to the Americans. A second assault, made in strength by the 1st Battalion, reached the double apron wire at the edge of the village but was checked there by strong small arms fire and the battalion withdrew under cover of a smoke screen.[21] The fight at Honskirch proved to be a last rear guard action. On 27 November the 328th Infantry occupied Honskirch without opposition; the 101st Infantry finished the operation and entered Altwiller without a fight.

While the 328th fought in the north, the 101st Infantry had been driving slowly through the woods to its front, using the 2d Battalion to lead the advance. The Bois de Bonnefontaine was far too large for the efforts of one battalion, and the Germans had dug in with trenches, concertina wire, mines, and emplaced 20-mm. antiaircraft guns. During the night of 24 November E Company fought its way into a large château in the center of the Bois de Bonnefontaine which had been fortified as a strong point by the Germans; the lead platoon was cut off inside the château and forced to surrender. When G Company was sent in to support E it became disorganized, under fire from the woods, and was driven back. The next day tank destroyers were brought up and G Company returned to the attack, driving the enemy from the château. On 25 November Colonel Scott, the 101st Infantry commander, attached Company K to the 2d Battalion in order to make good the losses sustained in the fight for the château. Company K was dispatched to clear the northern edge of the Bois de Bonnefontaine, where it immediately encountered disaster. The Americans had just deployed to charge some self-propelled guns on Hill 262, about a half mile south of Altwiller, when a company of grenadiers from Altwiller appeared on the scene. The Germans caught Company K by surprise and in a quick charge with the bayonet drove the Americans back into the woods, killing the company commander and leaving about half the Americans as casualties.[22] This was the last action in the 101st

[21] Sgt Stanley A. Davis, C Company, 328th Infantry, led his squad in knocking out three machine gun positions. At the third enemy position he received a severe wound, but refused to be evacuated and died an hour later—still in action. Sergeant Davis was awarded the DSC posthumously.

[22] Hist Div Combat Interviews; 26th Div AAR, 24 and 25 Nov 44.

zone and the main body of the regiment closed up to the Canal des Houillères de la Sarre. By 28 November the 328th Infantry was mopping up west of the canal in its area. Meanwhile the 4th Armored Division had widened the scope of operations and the XII Corps commander ordered the 26th Division to extend its front northward to take over most of the ground held by the 35th Division. At the same time he dispatched the 101st Infantry to Burbach, there to support the 4th Armored Division—east of the Sarre River—in an attack on the vital road center at Sarre-Union now scheduled for 1 December.

The 26th Infantry Division had suffered severely in its first major operation. The November drive by the XII Corps in the final analysis had devolved on the individual rifleman—88.8 percent of the total casualties in the corps were from the infantry[23]—and the 26th Division had lost more killed and missing than either of the other two infantry divisions. The 26th Division battle casualties for November totaled 661 killed, 2,154 wounded, and 613 missing, while nonbattle casualties from exposure, trench foot, and fatigue reached the high figure of 2,898 officers and men.[24] In part the 26th Division casualty rate may be attributed to the fact that both officers and men were inexperienced. In the main, however, the losses taken by the division must be explained in terms of the rugged and readily defended terrain over which the 26th Division had to advance in the early phases of the offensive, a period during which the enemy morale still was high and his means of resistance still adequate.

The 4th Armored Division Operations on the Sarre

The mission given the 4th Armored Division when it crossed the Canal des Houillères de la Sarre on 22 November was originally limited by the canal on the west and by the Sarre River on the east. The area between formed a corridor about four miles across at the southern end, but this corridor narrowed so severely at Sarre-Union that little space was left for maneuver north of that point. The plan had been for the armor to drive north through the triangle and roll up the enemy line holding in front of the 26th Division. However, although two good roads cross the area laterally, only a few narrow logging trails run north through the triangle. These trails were bogged by the November rains and hardly could be used by heavy armored vehicles.

[23] XII Corps Opns Rpt, Nov 44.

[24] 26th Div AAR, Nov 44.

Instead of turning north, CCB headed straight east from Mittersheim, overrunning the weak security line manned by the *953d Regiment* of the *361st VG Division*. The enemy infantry, supported only by 20-mm. Flak guns, were in no wise prepared to meet an armored attack, and on 23 November Task Force Ezell captured Fénétrange on the west bank of the Sarre in a surprise assault. The 25th Cavalry Reconnaissance Squadron quickly turned south and crossed the Sarre at Bettborn, meeting there patrols from the 44th Infantry Division (Maj. Gen. R. L. Spragins) of the XV Corps.[25]

The 4th Armored Division now was entering the Seventh Army zone of operations, for the interarmy boundary separating the XII and XV Corps extended diagonally northeast from Fénétrange. Subsequently this situation was regularized when General Eddy requested and received permission from General Haislip, the XV Corps commander, for the 4th Armored to operate inside the XV Corps area.[26] At the moment, however, the 4th Armored plans were tentative and opportunistic. General Wood intended to attack to the north, in the rear of the enemy holding the east bank of the Sarre, and then re-enter the XII Corps zone of advance. Early on the morning of 24 November, therefore, Task Force Jaques began crossing the Sarre in force near Gosselming, while Task Force Churchill made a second crossing about six thousand yards to the north at Romelfing. The details of the scheme of maneuver could be none too definite, but in general the CCB commander intended to make an advance to the northeast in two separate columns, uniting his command in the vicinity of Bining—eleven miles northeast of Sarre-Union—in which position he could cut in on the German lines of retreat from Sarre-Union and Sarreguemines.[27] Partly by accident and partly by design this plan of maneuver would benefit the XV Corps, whose left flank lay between the Sarre River and the Vosges mountains, and whose northernmost elements were disposed along a blocking position between Rauwiller and Bettwiller.

In a large-scale attack on 13 November the Seventh Army had thrown the XV Corps, which formed its left wing, into a drive to reach and cross the Vosges mountains in the vicinity of the Saverne Gap.[28] This operation marked the beginning of a full-dress offensive in which General Devers' 6th Army

[25] 4th Armd Div AAR, 23 Nov 44.

[26] XV Corps AAR, Nov 44.

[27] Hist Div Combat Interviews; 4th Armd CCB AAR, 23 Nov 44.

[28] The operations of the Seventh Army will be discussed in detail by Major Hamilton in his forthcoming volume, Southern France and Alsace, of this series.

Group would attempt to breach the Vosges line, drive the German *Nineteenth Army* out of Alsace, and reach the Rhine River. General Haislip's XV Corps made a rapid advance south of the Marne-Rhin Canal. On 21 November its 2d French Armored Division broke out to the east, thrusting past the German forces concentrated around the cities of Sarrebourg and Phalsbourg. That same afternoon one of the armored columns outflanked the Saverne Gap by way of a secondary pass and descended into the Alsatian Plain.

The successful attack by the XV Corps had driven straight into the joint between the *First* and *Nineteenth Armies*. The maneuver on 21 November threatened to isolate and destroy the *553d VG Division* and the weak Kampfgruppe of the *11th Panzer Division* which constituted the extreme left-wing elements of the *First Army* and alone barred the westward approaches to the Saverne Gap. There were no reserves whatever behind the seam between the two German armies. Once the Americans and French had overrun the weak German forces in the Sarrebourg–Saverne area the tactical connection between the *First* and *Nineteenth Armies* would be broken—as in fact it was broken on 23 November. General Balck, who as commander of *Army Group G* was responsible for the two armies, had already begun fervid pleas for armored help on the morning of 21 November. Field Marshal Rundstedt and the staff at *OB WEST* could give no aid—reinforcements in any strength would have to come from the strategic reserve of OKW. Field Marshal Keitel and General Jodl were far removed from the needs of the battle front and greatly concerned with the necessity of maintaining intact the armored formations scheduled for the Ardennes counteroffensive. At noon OKW refused Balck's request. Meanwhile reports of the XII Corps advance in the sector west of Sarre-Union posed a new problem, leading General Westphal, *OB WEST* chief of staff, to predict an additional break-through on the left flank of the *First Army*. Finally, at 1545, OKW released the *Panzer Lehr Division* to the *First Army*, promising that the division would be concentrated in the vicinity of Sarralbe on the morning of 23 November and ordering that it be used to attack directly south against the American flank in a blow to "annihilate" the force advancing east of Sarrebourg.[29]

The *Panzer Lehr Division* had once been among the top-flight armored units of the Wehrmacht, although it was one of the last to be formed. Generalleutnant Fritz Bayerlein, who commanded the division, had won fame as

[29] *Army Group G KTB* and *Anlagen* for this period. The detailed story of the *Panzer Lehr* attack is given in MS #D–322 by General Bayerlein.

Rommel's chief of staff in North Africa and was an able and experienced soldier. The *Panzer Lehr Division* had been bled white during the Normandy campaign and, after fighting in the withdrawal across France, had been sent back to Germany for refitting under the *Sixth Panzer Army* in preparation for the Ardennes counteroffensive. The replacements there received by the division were of indifferent caliber; the new tank crews in particular lacked training. On 21 November the formation stood at about half its authorized strength in armored infantry and artillery; the tank regiment had approximately thirty-four Mark IV's and thirty-eight Panthers.[30]

The *Army Group G* commander counted on Bayerlein to make his armored thrust "deep" into the American (XV Corps) flank.[31] But both Balck and the staff at OKW realized that additional support would be required to make good the *Panzer Lehr* effort and re-establish the connection between the *First* and *Nineteenth Armies* west of the Vosges. Bayerlein was ordered to make a co-ordinated attack with the *361st VG Division*, which already was in position on the proposed axis of advance; and OKW temporarily assigned four artillery battalions of the *401st Volks Artillery Corps*, in reserve near Sarre-Union, to support the two divisions. On the night of 22 November Balck dispatched a few of the *Volkssturm* to reinforce the *361st VG Division* troops and cover the right flank of the *Panzer Lehr* attack—but these pitiable oldsters failed to halt the American crossings south of Fénétrange. In addition OKW ordered the *245th Infantry Division* to start at once by rail from Holland, where it had been doing garrison duty, and released the main body of the *25th Panzer Grenadier Division* for Balck's use. These two infantry divisions, it was planned, would take over the ground won by the armor and restore the breach in the *Army Group G* lines west of Saverne.

The *Panzer Lehr Division's* 300-mile march from the Munster training ground brought the division into the Sarre-Union area on the morning of 23 November according to plan, despite gasoline failures along the way and green tank drivers who persisted in blocking the columns.[32] Balck, who had reported to his superiors that he was "very happy" about this armored reinforcement, addressed a special order of the day to the *Panzer Lehr Division* saying that

[30] The entire tank complement may not have been employed. An *OB WEST* situation map dated 25 November gives the *Panzer Lehr* strength as 33 Mark IV's and 20 Mark V's.

[31] *Army Group G* believed that the XV Corps was so thinly spread that *Panzer Lehr* could knife through. Also it held that the Third Army and 6th Army Group had no "operational reserves."

[32] The telephone journal attached to the *Army Group G KTB* gives an hourly recital of the difficulties encountered in this move.

"the fate of Alsace" depended on its efforts. The road net leading south to Sarrebourg was adequate for a tank attack, the American forces in the sector appeared to be only weak infantry detachments, the *Panzer Lehr* had a reputation as an elite armored unit (it had once been known as the "Parade Division"), and the *Army Group G* commander promised OKW that its intervention in the Saverne battle would bring "decisive results." The *First Army* commander, General Knobelsdorff, put himself on record, however, as predicting that the *Panzer Lehr Division* would recover none of the lost ground and probably would be fortunate to hold the sector north of Sarrebourg still in German hands.

Bayerlein formed his command into two columns south of Sarre-Union and by midafternoon of the 23d was ready to launch the attack, although two armored infantry battalions, two batteries of assault guns, and part of his reconnaissance battalion had not yet arrived at the concentration point. The easternmost column—the stronger of the two—had orders to attack via Eywiller and Schalbach. The route for the western column ran through Wolfskirchen, Postroff, Baerendorf, and Rauwiller. Its initial object was the seizure of the highway between Sarrebourg and Phalsbourg east of the former city. Bayerlein intended that the two columns would continue south to Hazelbourg, at the edge of the Vosges, and then turn north to free the troops around Phalsbourg. By dark the *Panzer Lehr* was driving in the cavalry outposts of the 106th Cavalry Group, north of Hirschland and Weyer, which screened the positions held by elements of the 44th Infantry Division. Balck instructed Bayerlein to continue the advance through the night, and at the same time ordered the *LXIV Corps*, which held the right flank of the *Nineteenth Army*, to send a Kampfgruppe north from the St. Quirin sector, some ten miles southwest of Hazelbourg, to implement a "concentric attack" against the American forces in the vicinity of Phalsbourg and Saverne.

During the night of 23–24 November the leading elements of Bayerlein's eastern column engaged part of the 114th Infantry and a few tank destroyers at Ischermuhl, just southwest of Weyer. The Americans held their ground against the first onslaughts and beat back the enemy. About 0400 the advance guard of the western column drove the American cavalry out of Hirschland, and an hour later the Germans were fighting the 2d Battalion of the 71st Infantry and a small force of cavalry and tank destroyers in Rauwiller. When the enemy main body came up, Rauwiller was quickly enveloped, but the 71st Infantry (Col. E. D. Porter) re-formed its lines south of the village. The

Panzer Lehr attack at this moment loomed large as a threat to the attenuated left flank of the XV Corps drive and General Haislip ordered the 114th Infantry (Col. R. R. Martin) to fall back on Schalbach, thus covering the exposed right of the 71st Infantry. In the threatened sector Haislip had the two regiments of the 44th Division, the 106th Cavalry Group, and three tank destroyer companies, plus the 157th Infantry of the 45th Division in reserve. The main body of the 45th Division was en route to the Saverne Gap, but General Haislip temporarily canceled this movement in order to provide additional reinforcements north of Sarrebourg if they should be needed.[33]

Two new factors, introduced on 24 November, radically altered the situation and wrested the initiative from the *Panzer Lehr Division.* General Eisenhower made a visit to the XV Corps headquarters at Sarrebourg and, after some study of the Seventh Army plans, directed that the XV Corps mission be changed from an advance eastward to an advance generally northward *astride* the Vosges mountains.[34] This shift ultimately would permit General Haislip to go over to the offensive in the Sarrebourg sector. But intervention by CCB, 4th Armored, would provide a more important and immediate counter to the *Panzer Lehr* attack.

The Sarre River crossings through which CCB moved on the morning of 24 November lay approximately abreast of the forward points reached by the advance elements of Bayerlein's two columns. However, the eastern bank of the river was so weakly manned by the *361st VG* as to permit the American armor some room for maneuver. Task Force Churchill, which crossed at the northern site, rolled with little opposition northeast to some high ground west of the village of Postroff. In this position the column could block while Task Force Jaques made the longer move up from the south. Jaques' command ran into a short, sharp fight at Kirrberg and then headed north to get onto the main road at Baerendorf—striking straight into the *Panzer Lehr* flank. The 53d Armored Infantry Battalion made a human chain to cross through the chilling waters of a stream west of the village and then, under cover of fire from the tanks and assault guns, took the high ground surrounding Baerendorf. Meanwhile a few tanks had been put across the stream and the assault force descended on the village, clearing it in a house-to-house battle with the *1st Battalion* of the *902d Panzer Grenadier Regiment*, reinforced by some engineers and reconnaissance troops. The enemy battalion had been

[33] XV Corps AAR, Annex No. 2, Nov 44.
[34] *Ibid.*, 24 Nov 44.

ordered to hold on until reinforcements could be brought back from the head of the German column. Later Bayerlein reported "very high losses" in the defense of Baerendorf. Actually the German armored infantry, most of whom were fighting in their first battle, did not offer much resistance—a symptom of the lack of training and poverty of personnel which at this time plagued many of the top-ranking German divisions. The fight at Baerendorf was characteristic of the ensuing engagements between the 4th Armored Division and the *Panzer Lehr Division*. The November mud limited tank maneuver to the roads—which soon went to pieces when used by two armored divisions. Slugging matches between tanks, like those which had taken place around Arracourt during September, seldom would occur. The armored infantry and engineers would be the final arbiters of the field, while the tanks would be relegated more and more to the role of accompanying artillery.

Bayerlein employed his strong eastern column to continue the main attack southward on the early morning of 25 November, at the same time turning his western column from its course in an attack toward Fénétrange designed to catch the American armor in the flank. Just before dawn the German tanks and infantry launched a counterattack from the north and east against Baerendorf. Here the 53d Armored Infantry Battalion had been disposed in a perimeter defense around the village, while beyond the eastern edge of Baerendorf a tank company from the 8th Tank Battalion held an outpost position guarding a bridge across a small creek. The enemy surprised one of the platoons east of the bridge, and a few of the American crews deserted their tanks. But when the Panthers incautiously came down to the bridge they were met by direct fire from other American tanks, several were destroyed, and the rest were forced to turn back along the road to Hirschland. On the north side of the Baerendorf perimeter the 53d engaged in a bitter melee in the dark. Although both sides lost heavily, the heavy machine guns manned by the 53d finally checked the assault and the enemy retired.[35]

While Task Force Jaques fought at Baerendorf the 2d Battalion of the 114th Infantry and the 106th Cavalry Group were hit by the eastern column of the *Panzer Lehr Division* advancing against Schalbach. An Alsatian deserter had given warning of the impending attack, but the troops in Schalbach were uncertain as to the whereabouts of the 4th Armored Division, and their supporting artillery had orders to withhold fire. The enemy attack was

[35] 53d Armd Inf Jnl, and 8th Tk Bn Jnl, 24 and 25 Nov 44. See also Hist Div Combat Interviews.

almost in the 2d Battalion lines when Lt. Col. Charles L. Haley, commanding the 17th Field Artillery Battalion, gave orders, on his own initiative, to open fire. This act broke up the first German attempt. About ten o'clock an air observer saw a long line of tanks and vehicles coming down the road from Hirschland. This time the American artillery was free to intervene. The 17th and 961st Field Artillery Battalions poured in a withering fire which continued for nearly an hour and a half. So deadly was this shelling that many German crews deserted their tanks and sought shelter in ditches and farm buildings, others ran their vehicles into defilades in front of the 2d Battalion positions, and the main body turned hurriedly back to Hirschland. At least seven enemy tanks and four armored cars were destroyed in this fight. The losses sustained by the German armored infantry probably were high.[36]

The events of 25 November blasted the optimistic hopes which the higher German commands had pinned on the *Panzer Lehr Division*. That evening Rundstedt gave orders halting the attack and Bayerlein was told to go over to the defensive. The *Panzer Lehr Division* immediately began to withdraw northward to positions along the lateral road linking Wolfskirchen, Eywiller, and Durstel, which Bayerlein had selected as his main line of resistance.

The American attack to reduce this position would be made by the 4th Armored Division, while the body of the 44th Infantry Division carried the advance forward on the right and the 121st Cavalry Squadron threw out a protecting screen in the northeast. On 25 November General Wood sent the 51st Armored Infantry Battalion, from CCR, and all of the 4th Armored Division artillery to reinforce CCB. General Dager reorganized his command, grouping the 51st with the tank companies of the 8th Tank Battalion which Churchill held at Postroff, and in the late afternoon resumed the advance toward the north—the armored infantry leading through the mud. Next morning CCB began a co-ordinated attack in which Task Force Churchill struck at Wolfskirchen and Task Force Jaques attempted to disrupt the new German line by seizing Eywiller. Scant gains were made in this first day of attack. The ground in front of the Americans was interlaced with small streams—now flooded—and slowed all maneuver to the foot soldiers' pace. The German artillery, using the massed fire of the *Panzer Lehr* batteries and the *401st Volks Artillery Corps*, maintained extremely heavy shelling to curtain the approaches to the new line of defense. Additional American troops were arriving, how-

[36] XV Corps AAR, Annex No. 2, Nov 44.

ever, to add weight and some flexibility to the 4th Armored drive. CCA moved east of the Sarre River on 26 November, passed across the rear of CCB, and then fanned out in an extension of the American line toward the right, opposite the left flank of the *Panzer Lehr Division.*

The attack on the second day was pushed home by the entire 4th Armored Division and broke through the *Panzer Lehr* positions. Wolfskirchen, the western anchor for the German line, was wrested from a detachment of the *25th Panzer Grenadier Division* which had been sent in to strengthen Bayerlein's division. The 51st Armored Infantry Battalion initiated an attempt to bypass to the east of the village but received such a hot flanking fire from Germans in the village that it became necessary to direct an assault into Wolfskirchen. A company of light tanks accompanied the armored infantry and the combined force quickly cleared the village, inflicting severe punishment on the German garrison. Eywiller was harder to crack. During the morning the 53d Armored Infantry Battalion, maneuvering to flank the village on the west, was checked by fire from a small wood. American fighter-bombers eventually neutralized the wood by an air strike, but a detachment of German Panthers continued to hold Eywiller until late afternoon when the capture of Gungwiller by a task force (West) from CCA made their position untenable. Gungwiller was taken after several hundred shells were fired into the village. The tanks then bypassed on one side and the tank destroyers on the other, while the infantry went through the main street clearing houses and cellars with grenades and flame throwers. The Germans had stripped Gungwiller in order to reinforce their flank at Durstel, where Task Force Oden, employing most of CCA, had begun an attack in mid-morning. The approaches to Durstel were mined and covered by a large number of antitank guns, making armored maneuver most hazardous. The enemy infantry fought stubbornly, and during the afternoon were reinforced three times by additional tanks coming in from the north. When night fell the Americans gave up the contest and withdrew to the south.

The next three days were spent in a slow and difficult operation to clear the villages on the hill mass which lay east of the Drulingen–Sarre-Union highway, and which had to be wrested from enemy hands before the 4th Armored Division could continue the advance to the north and east. Numerous small watercourses made a jigsaw puzzle of the ground. Visibility during the day was increasingly poor. The roads, churned up by both American and German armor, had become almost impassable. The enemy relied chiefly on his artillery during this period, but the *25th Panzer Grenadier Division* (Colonel Arnold Burmeister), which had relieved the *Panzer Lehr Division*, fought a succession of small delaying actions.[37] On 28 November CCB took Berg, overlooking the main road, and with it some bridges over a small stream that earlier had held up the advance. On the right CCA was forced to build its own bridges under artillery fire, but on 29 November Durstel finally fell. Next day the Americans captured the high ground overlooking Mackwiller, ending the fight for the hills and putting 4th Armored patrols from the south within four miles of Sarre-Union.[38] The XII Corps commander now gave orders that on 1 December the 4th Armored Division was to attack Sarre-Union in conjunction with an advance on the city from the west by the 26th Infantry Division.

The 35th and 6th Armored Divisions Advance Toward the Sarre

The target date for the resumption of the drive toward the Sarre River, in which the 35th Division and 26th Division would lead off for the XII Corps, was set as 18 November. In accordance with this new plan the 35th Division would extend its front to the north, pinching out the 80th Division —which remained in position to contain Faulquemont—and advancing northeast with its left flank initially covered by the XX Corps. The main weight of the 35th Division attack would be put on its right wing. The division objective was designated in general fashion as the high ground on the eastern side of the double loop made by the Sarre River south of Sarreguemines.[39]

The XII Corps commander intended to support the two-division attack by sending in a part of his armor at the earliest possible moment. The initial plan provided for the concentration of the entire 6th Armored Division south of the Rotte; then CCB would join the 35th Division in the Morhange area and CCA would revert to corps reserve. But congestion was so great on the few usable roads that only CCB (Col. G. W. Read crossed over the Rotte,

[37] Elements of the *25th Panzer Grenadier Division* began to arrive in the Sarre-Union sector on 25 November. Finally, on the night of 27 November, the balance of the *25th* was in the line and *Panzer Lehr* was relieved. *Army Group G KTB* and *OB WEST* situation maps.

[38] The 25th Cavalry (—) had completed its move northward between the river and the canal. On 29 November the assault gun troop and the 22d Armored Field Artillery Battalion opened fire on Sarre-Union from the west. Then D Troop essayed a sortie from Harskirchen into Sarre-Union but was repelled. 4th Armd G–3 Jnl, 29 Nov 44.

[39] 35th Div AAR, 17 Nov 44.

moving on 17 November toward Morhange, where the 137th Infantry was clearing the roads and where the further development of the drive eastward would begin. Meanwhile, on the same day, General Grow conferred with General Baade, the two arranging for CCB to give direct support to the 137th Infantry. CCB, hard against the flooded tributaries of the German Nied, could in no event advance directly to the east.

On the morning of 18 November the 35th and 26th Infantry Divisions swung into the attack. (*Map XXXV*) After the supporting artillery had fired for seventy-eight minutes the 35th Division jumped off. The first hours of the advance east of the Metz–Sarrebourg railroad met little opposition, for the left wing of the *XIII SS Corps* had been withdrawn during the previous night. The 320th (Col. B. A. Byrne) and 137th (Col. W. S. Murray), on the right and left respectively, advanced at marching speed. Late in the morning the 3d Battalion (Lt. Col. A. M. Butler) of the 137th Infantry came under fire from Bistroff, a village that lay at the southern end of an impassable area marked by lakes and flooded streams. By this time the marching infantry had outdistanced their supporting heavy weapons. Nonetheless, the battalion forded an icy stream and attacked straight into the village, clearing it after a sharp house-to-house battle. The enemy made several attempts to retake the village and so check the American advance around the flooded area. Lacking antitank guns or tank destroyers the battalion had to rely on the mines it carried, but these proved sufficient to cripple the German tanks; rifle and machine gun fire accounted for the enemy infantry.[40]

At the close of the 18th the right wing of the 35th Division was east of Vallerange and the left was near Bistroff. General Eddy decided that the moment was opportune to commit the armor and ordered Grow to put CCB through the left wing of the 35th Division. Since resistance seemed to be light, the corps commander told Grow that he should be prepared to pass the entire 6th Armored through Baade's division, in accordance with a plan on which the three commanders had agreed earlier. General Grow promptly ordered Colonel Hines to ready a combat team for dispatch from CCA to CCB, preliminary to switching CCA to the south and onto the left of CCB when the bottleneck northeast of Morhange was broken. Meanwhile Colonel Read moved CCB into position to carry the attack from the 137th Infantry lines on 19 November.

[40] The 3d Battalion, 137th Infantry, subsequently received a Distinguished Unit Citation for this action.

On the second day the attack reached the main German positions, a series of fortified villages strengthened by antitank ditches and sprawling mine fields, the whole supplemented by much antitank and medium artillery. The German troops were an ill-assorted mixture: the remainders of the *48th Division* and *559th VG Division*, plus fortress units and a handful of armored vehicles from the *1559th Tank Destroyer Battalion*, all now organized as a Kampfgruppe under the commander of the *559th*, General Muehlen. Although a motley force, *Kampfgruppe Muehlen* was still capable of a determined fight and small groups of defenders held grimly to the villages and any high ground.[41] Mud made cross-country maneuver virtually impossible and forced the American attack into channels previously prepared for defense. On the north wing Combat Team Lagrew from CCB, followed by the 1st Battalion, 137th Infantry, attempted to move via the Morhange–Gros-Tenquin road, but found the going very difficult. West of Bertring the armor was brought to an abrupt halt by an antitank ditch, beyond which were deployed antitank guns, infantry, and tanks. A brisk engagement ensued in which Combat Team Lagrew lost seven medium tanks and incurred sixty-five casualties, while five German Panthers were knocked out. Time fire finally drove off the last defenders; the American infantry crossed the ditch and began the reduction of the block houses on the edge of Bertring. About 1400 the antitank ditch was bridged and a tank platoon entered Bertring, ending the fight for the village. Progress thus far had been slow; the daylight hours were running out and plans were hastily made for a co-ordinated attack on Gros-Tenquin, a crossroads village a thousand yards to the northeast. At 1630 nineteen battalions of field artillery fired a TOT, fighter-bombers flew over to strafe and bomb, and mortars set the village ablaze with white phosphorus. Then the tanks moved in with the infantry attack to give direct fire support. There was no fight in Gros-Tenquin. The survivors—"quaking with fear," as the Americans reported—surrendered, and the infantry passed to the east, clearing the mortar crews and machine gunners off the hills. Muehlen's Kampfgruppe was about at the end of its tether, but during the night the *17th SS Panzer Grenadier Division*, which had been pulled out of the Metz sector, began to arrive in the German line opposite the 35th Division.

[41] Simon, the new *XIII SS Corps* commander, was worried about Muehlen's ability to hold and requested that a new unit replace Muehlen's shattered command. The *First Army* commander agreed to use the *17th SS Panzer Grenadier Division* for the relief, but this could not be accomplished before the night of 19 November. MS #B–487 (Simon).

ANTITANK DITCH WEST OF BERTRING *on Morhange–Gros-Tenquin road.*

During 19 November the 4th Armored Division had switched some of its tanks north into the 35th Division zone and there had lent a hand to the 320th Infantry in the capture of Virming. On 20 November the 320th followed CCA of the 4th Armored while the latter attacked and took Francaltroff. On the left of the division the 137th Infantry added its weight to the 6th Armored column, which had been reinforced by a combat team from CCA. This combat team, built around the 69th Tank Battalion (Lt. Col. Bedford Forrest), led the advance along the road to Hellimer. The Germans were deployed in and around the Bois de Freybouse, astride the highway. Their force was composed of a number of Panther tanks and self-propelled tank destroyers which had been dispatched early in the morning from the *11th Panzer Division* to halt the American drive on Hellimer. Forrest lost six light tanks and four mediums in the fight for the section of highway in the woods, but claimed a total of ten German tanks, three armored cars, and three antitank guns destroyed. The 2d Battalion, 137th Infantry, which had helped to clear the way through the woods, received a sudden and violent shelling when it emerged on the eastern edge, there losing six officers and a score of men. The resultant disorganization among the infantry and the tank losses suffered by Forrest halted the advance for the remainder of the day.[42]

The attack in the 35th Division zone had slowed to what the armored officers ruefully reported as "an infantry pace." Progress was limited to a slow advance on a narrow front, in which each successive village had to be assaulted and reduced. Such frontal and bludgeoning tactics inevitably would result in an inordinate rate of attrition. On 21 November, therefore, the American armor and infantry began to widen the front preliminary to attempting envelopment tactics. On the left wing Combat Team Wall and the 3d Battalion of the 137th turned north to take Frémestroff. Mines, mud, and antitank fire made a speedy move impossible. At the edge of the village a blown bridge forced Wall's armored vehicles to deploy off the road—where they promptly bogged down. The infantry, dismounting, continued the assault and took the village despite very strong resistance.

In the meantime Combat Team Forrest and the 2d Battalion, 137th, fought to capture Hellimer. The commitment of the *11th Panzer Division* Kampfgruppe on the previous day had been only a stopgap measure. Balck wished to re-form the *11th Panzer Division* as his army group reserve and had therefore sent in a part of the *15th Panzer Grenadier Division* (Colonel Hans-Joachim Deckert) to bolster the line. These fresh troops held the Hellimer crossroads. Early on the morning of 21 November, American field guns, close behind the 2d Battalion, struck the German artillery positions and pillboxes around Hellimer with very accurate shelling. At 1000 two companies of infantry began the assault under cover of a smoke screen laid down by mortars but, when about five hundred yards from the town, were driven back by a withering fire. Five German tanks now came forward, took cover behind some houses in the northwest part of the village, and proceeded to engage the American tanks and tank destroyers in a long-drawn fire fight. About 1500 an infantry platoon made a dash across the open and reached the shelter of a couple of houses; from this position the Americans worked their way toward the German tanks, disabling one by firing antitank grenades, killing the tank commander in another, and driving the rest out of Hellimer. Once freed of the enemy armor the town was quickly cleared.[43]

[42] 6th Armd CCB AAR, 20 Nov 44.

[43] 2d Bn, 137th Inf, Jnl, 21 Nov 44.

The lengthy battle for Hellimer had repercussions on the right, where the 320th Infantry was moving cross country in the direction of Grening. The left flank of the regiment came under fire from the German guns positioned near Hellimer and as a result was held immobile until that village was taken. The next morning the artillery set to work to soften up the enemy in Grening. Seven TOT's were fired on the village, followed by a salvo of "Safe Conduct" pamphlets. The German garrison, estimated to be an infantry battalion and five or six tanks, was apparently not impressed. When the 2d Battalion moved in to attack, enemy fire met and checked every advance. Colonel Byrne brought up his regimental reserve, the 3d Battalion, but the German tanks, supported by riflemen, counterattacked and held the Americans at bay. When tank destroyers were brought forward to engage the enemy tanks they found them sheltered in defilade and protected by extensive mine barriers. Attempts to guide the tank destroyer crews to their targets with low-flying artillery observation planes were unsuccessful. But toward the middle of the afternoon a patrol from L Company penetrated inside the village and seized a building next to the church. This building was held through the night, and with the Americans inside the village the enemy finally evacuated Grening.[44]

The armor-infantry attack in the north had continued on 22 November, CCB still maneuvering to widen the front and avoid the heartbreaking business of a headlong advance on the main road. Beyond Hellimer, CCB and the 1st Battalion, 137th, swerved north and made a surprise flank attack in which Leyviller[45] and St. Jean-Rohrbach were captured, the latter in what the journal of the 137th Infantry called "a vicious battle." Once the tide had turned, the Germans took to the open and fled across country to the east, giving the American artillery and tank gunners a field day.

That afternoon General Baade received new instructions from the XII Corps.[46] The 35th Division would close up to the Maderbach, a stream about eight miles west of the Sarre River, and there—with the neighboring 26th Division—would be pinched out by General Eddy's two armored divisions and the 80th Infantry Division. The successful armored thrust on the 35th Divi-

[44] 320th Inf Jnl, 22 Nov 44.

[45] Again the fight for observation had turned to the fight for cover. Any village whose houses still had roofs was regarded as a prize. Leyviller had been a German Army installation and offered real shelter. During the attack, Colonel Lagrew, whose combat team was back in the fight after a two-day rest, ordered: "Don't make holes in those beautiful barracks."

[46] XII Corps Operational Directive No. 41, 22 Nov 44.

sion left had driven a narrow salient into the German position west of the Maderbach, but the American center and right still had about six miles to go. General Grow ordered CCA, 6th Armored, to come south into the 35th Division zone,[47] and General Baade brought up the 1st and 3d Battalions of the 134th Infantry (Col. B. B. Miltonberger) from reserve to provide the additional infantry increment for the armor so necessary in this late autumn fighting.

While the 6th Armored Division was regrouping on 23 November, the 1st Battalion, 137th Infantry, advanced on Hilsprich, just southeast of St. Jean-Rohrbach, to widen the salient extending toward the Maderbach and secure a forward assembly area for CCB. Hilsprich was held by infantry from the *38th SS Panzer Grenadier Regiment* and a few tanks. This German force was deployed with strong outpost positions sited to give cross fire on any approach to the village. About 0900 the attack jumped off with A Company on the right and C Company on the left. When the infantry reached a small hill north of Hilsprich they could see five German tanks and numerous anti-tank guns. In response to the 1st Battalion's call four tank destroyers were sent forward but were driven back by the enemy guns. The two companies making the attack suffered considerably in the first phase of the advance and the commander of one company was killed. After their tank destroyer support had withdrawn, the infantry re-formed and made a final assault—across some eight hundred yards of open ground. The drive carried them into the northeast corner of Hilsprich, but at high cost. In the early evening five German tanks and about fifty riflemen blocked off both ends of the main street and methodically began to reduce the houses held by the Americans. The one remaining American officer, 1st Lt. Merrill H. Lyon, gathered about sixty survivors and led them through the enemy and back to St. Jean-Rohrbach.[48]

Possession of Hilsprich was essential to the success of the 6th Armored Division attack. General Grow intended to use CCB to capture Puttelange and the knot of roads and bridges it controlled; the seizure of Hilsprich would provide room for the CCB maneuver and cover the exterior flank of the combat command during the drive to the Maderbach. CCA, on the left of CCB, was to be employed farther north in an attempt to extend the American front and outflank the Puttelange crossings. Hilsprich was finally taken

[47] CCA had been trying to cross the Nied Allemande but had been held in check by difficulties with bridging, the flooded lowlands, and intense enemy artillery fire.

[48] Hist Div Combat Interviews; 35th Div AAR, 23 Nov 44.

late on the afternoon of 24 November after a terrific shelling had nearly demolished the village, the successful attack being made by the 1st Battalion of the 134th Infantry and the 737th Tank Battalion.

On 25 November the 6th Armored Division and its attached battalions from the 134th Infantry were in position to begin what was expected to be the last phase in the attempt to reach and cross the Maderbach. The weather had become progressively worse and the armor was roadbound in consequence. Indeed, even the roads presented a problem. Near the frontier they were more poorly constructed, cratered by demolitions, and interdicted at frequent intervals by antitank ditches. In addition the advance was entering the old fortified zone of the Maginot Line, which though no longer a first-class military barrier provided gun emplacements, pillboxes, and antitank obstacles to slow down the attack. Under these conditions the armor could do little toward carrying the assault. In slow and painful progress the infantry, both armored and attached, had to fight to clear every foot of road, as well as to establish "bridgeheads" wherever an antitank ditch intervened. As a result the number of sick and combat fatigue cases mounted rapidly, even though officers did all that they could to provide dry socks and warm clothing for their men. Rifle strengths dwindled; as one example, Combat Team Britton (the 9th Armored Infantry Battalion reinforced) lost only four killed and two wounded on 25 November, but found it necessary to evacuate twenty-six sick and ninety-three combat fatigue cases.

On the night of 24–25 November armored infantry and engineers threw a bridge across an antitank ditch intersecting the west road into Puttelange, along which CCB intended to attack. Next day the 15th Tank Battalion crossed the bridge. It had hardly started rolling on the opposite side when a huge crater halted the move. The leading tankers took their vehicles off the road to circle around the crater—and sank into the mud. Five medium tanks were lost here to the German antitank guns, and the 15th fell back. Farther to the south the 737th Tank Battalion (Lt. Col. F. M. Kroschel), which had been attached to CCB, also failed to make headway against mud, mines, and artillery fire. However, two rifle companies of the 134th Infantry, attached to the 737th, managed to reach the flooded Maderbach at Remering, where they were joined by armored infantry. CCA, not yet abreast of CCB, likewise found itself involved in a foot-slogging infantry battle on the left flank. At Valette fighter-bombers from the 377th Squadron dropped 500-pound bombs close to the German positions. Then the 9th Armored Infantry Battalion

(Britton) charged up a slippery slope with fixed bayonets and cleared the German position in a hand-to-hand fight reminiscent of warfare thirty years earlier. On the following day the 69th Tank Battalion attacked through the Forêt de Puttelange in an effort to bypass the main enemy force. All went well until the tanks debouched from the eastern side of the woods. Then the enemy opened up from positions in the Maginot Line works to the east. The tanks could not maneuver through the mud and the combat team commander, Colonel Forrest, withdrew his troops to forestall any attempts at ambush in the woods. Colonel Forrest was killed by a mortar shell while checking his positions for the night.

CCB now was in position facing the Maderbach. General Grow ordered the left to hold and sent Colonel Miltonberger's 134th Infantry to clear the west bank by an advance from Hilsprich. This mopping-up operation was successful, but attempts to move the tanks forward through the mud were of no avail. Finally, on 27 November, the 80th Infantry Division, again in motion on the north wing of the XII Corps, forced the enemy to begin a wholesale withdrawal across the Maderbach. So the month of November ended, with the 6th Armored Division deployed along the west bank of the Maderbach[49] and the 35th Infantry Division—now in corps reserve—resting and training replacements.[50]

The 35th Division and the 6th Armored Division had driven the enemy lines back twenty-seven miles during the November operation. The 35th had taken 2,309 prisoners; its own losses totaled 349 killed, 1,549 wounded, and

[49] On 30 November a strong German patrol attacked an outpost of the 86th Cavalry Reconnaissance Squadron, 6th Armored Division. Cpl. Jesse V. Davis sent the three men under his command back to alert the main body and remained alone, engaging the enemy with his submachine gun and hand grenades. He continued his lone battle until his ammunition was gone and he was killed. Corporal Davis was awarded the DSC posthumously.

[50] Certain units of the 35th Infantry Division, however, were still slogging away. On 27 November A Company of the 320th Infantry fought an action at the little village of Uberkinger which was so successful as to be the subject of special commendation in the After Action Report prepared by the regimental commander. Just before daylight Capt. Charles W. Bell, the company commander, led his men through a flooded stream that denied access to Uberkinger. As the company approached the village daybreak came, revealing the Americans to the Germans who were deployed outside Uberkinger. Bell's company rushed into the village and took cover in its buildings. Using bazookas, the only antitank weapons available, the American infantry immobilized a Tiger tank which had rolled into the streets and then set it afire with gasoline from a captured German jeep. Next the enemy drove into the village with five tanks and three infantry half-tracks. The American bazooka men went into the streets and onto the housetops and their fire, coupled with that from supporting artillery which was firing on call, drove off the German armored vehicles. In the course of the fight for Uberkinger A Company killed twenty of the enemy and captured fifteen without a single American casualty.

115 missing.[51] The 6th Armored Division had lost 94 tanks—of which at least two-thirds could be repaired—but had accounted for 73 German tanks and assault guns, plus an estimated 202 pieces of artillery. Battle casualties suffered by the 6th Armored numbered 162 killed, 725 wounded, and 47 missing.[52]

The 80th Division Attack in the Faulquemont Sector

On 17 November the 80th Division went on the defensive after 102 days of continuous contact with the enemy. The 80th now assumed a blocking role on the left flank of the XII Corps, interdicted the enemy escape routes east of Faulquemont by fire, filled its depleted battalions with replacements, and put its men into dry clothes. It is characteristic of the extreme care now required of commanders who were struggling—under General Patton's critical eye—to reduce the increasing incidence of immersion foot (or trench foot) that most of the messages entered in the 80th Division Journal for these days deal with dry socks, laundry facilities, and the like.

This pause in operations on the north wing of the XII Corps gave the *36th VG Division*, which had taken a very severe beating in the fighting southwest of Faulquemont, an opportunity to reorganize and take some defensive measures before resumption of the battle. On the night of 16–17 November General Wellm, the *36th VG Division* commander, sought permission to withdraw his weakened division across the Nied Allemande River and occupy a new position on the hills north and northeast of Faulquemont, where the Maginot Line works offered the possibility of an organized defense. Generalleutnant der Waffen-SS Max Simon, commanding the *XIII SS Corps*, quickly gave assent since he feared that the American attack would be continued and would shatter his left flank. Wellm's retreat across the Nied Allemande was carried out as scheduled, but the German commander left a reinforced company of the *165th Regiment* in Faulquemont to retain a bridgehead. The French inhabitants of Faulquemont, encouraged by the imminence of "liberation" and the obvious weakness of the German garrison, soon became threatening and on 18 November Wellm removed the small bridgehead force.[53]

[51] 35th Div AAR, Nov 44. The 35th Division had a moderate number of trench foot cases as compared with the 26th Division and 80th Division. The XII Corps Operations Report for November 1944 lists 436 such casualties.

[52] 6th Armd Div AAR, Nov 44.

[53] MS #B–487 (Simon); MS #B–223 (Wellm).

KEEPING WARM AND DRY *was a major problem as cold and rain increased the incidence of trench foot.*

During the brief lull the Third Army commander visited General McBride and casually asked why the 80th Division did not take Faulquemont and the heights beyond. Prompted by this "question" General McBride suggested to the XII Corps commander that the 80th Division be sent up against the Faulquemont position. General Eddy was surprised but gave his consent. Meanwhile, reports from the 80th Division patrols, scouting along the Nied Allemande, indicated that this river line was not strongly held. On 20 November, therefore, after the combined attack by the 35th Division and the 6th Armored had begun moving on the right flank of the 80th, General McBride set in motion a reconnaissance in force to secure bridgeheads north of the river at Faulquemont and Pontpierre.[54] The German rear guard had neglected to destroy the bridge at Faulquemont, and the two leading regiments quickly seized a foothold north of the Nied Allemande. This hold was widened the

[54] Ltr, Maj Gen Horace McBride to Hist Div, 22 Oct 46. The Third Army orders had specified that the 80th Division would contain Faulquemont. See also 80th Div FO No. 15.

following day against slight opposition, for as yet the 80th had not encountered the German main battle position, and a tenuous contact was made with the XX Corps.[55]

The Faulquemont position (*Falkenberg Stellung*), in which the *36th VG Division* had deployed, extended along the north side of a deep draw—marked by the villages of Haute-Vigneulle and Bambiderstroff—about three miles beyond the Nied Allemande; it then angled southeast through Tritteling and Téting, the latter barring the road to St. Avold. Much of the enemy line was based on the Maginot fortifications, but these works were now in a poor state of repair and had a few pieces of usable artillery. In any case the Germans had been given little time to familiarize themselves with the Maginot system and had been unable to strengthen the line with more than a modicum of field entrenchments and wire. The *36th VG Division* was still considerably understrength, although an infantry battalion or two had been borrowed from the *347th Division*, just to the north.

On 25 November, after a five-minute artillery concentration, the 80th Infantry Division attacked with all three regiments, supported by the 702d Tank Battalion, the 610th and 808th Tank Destroyer Battalions, and with the 42d Cavalry Squadron screening its left flank. By 1300 all the main works were in American hands and the fight had dwindled to a progression of mopping-up actions in which the infantry cleared the woods and heights while the tank destroyers methodically blasted the last pillboxes and bunkers at point-blank range.[56] In all, the 80th took about six hundred prisoners. In a subsequent report General Wellm attributed the collapse of the *36th VG Division* on this day to the incessant "drum fire" by the American artillery and the coolness displayed by the American infantry, who advanced calmly through the thickest fire "with their weapons at the ready and cigarettes dangling from their lips." [57]

The broken enemy fell back from the 80th and 5th Divisions, which had made contact, but during 26 November desperate rear guard detachments fought on to cover the retreat. A battalion of the 318th Infantry, on the American north flank, repulsed five counterattacks made by the remnants of the *2d Battalion, 165th Regiment*; then, as if tiring of the matter, nine field artil-

[55] Elements of the 6th Armored reserve had remained in position between the 5th and 80th Divisions.

[56] The 75-mm. tank howitzers only chipped the concrete, but the armor-piercing shells fired by the 90-mm. tank destroyers went straight through six feet of reinforced concrete. Hist Div Combat Interviews.

[57] MS #B-223 (Wellm).

lery battalions laid a TOT on a sixth counterattack—ending both the attack and the enemy battalion. In the center the 319th Infantry in hard fighting drove to within 1,500 yards of St. Avold;[58] the 317th Infantry, coming up from the southwest, reached the high ground overlooking the town. The next day the 318th (Col. Lansing McVickar) and 319th (Col. W. N. Taylor) marched into St. Avold but found none of the enemy: during the night the *XIII SS Corps* had withdrawn to a new line west of the Sarre River.[59]

With the seizure of St. Avold,[60] General McBride turned the 317th (Col. W. M. Lewis) to the northeast on 27 November, in a pursuit calculated to regain contact with the retreating Germans. "Only the infantry could surely get through," reported the regimental commander, and, leaving trucks and half-tracks behind, the 317th moved on foot through the mud. Toward twilight, while marching in column of battalions, the regiment regained touch with the enemy near Seingbouse, about six miles east of St. Avold. Colonel Lewis ordered the 317th to deploy and sent his leading battalion, the 3d, to attack in the direction of Farebersviller while the 1st and 2d Battalions moved forward to go south and north, respectively, of that village.

About 0900 the next morning the 3d Battalion succeeded in getting a foothold in Farebersviller and began a house-to-house fight that went on all through the day. In the village were some two hundred Germans, troops of the *17th SS Panzer Grenadier Division* who had been thrown in piecemeal to hold a section of railway that here formed the new *XIII SS Corps* line. At the far end of Farebersviller a railway embankment ran north and south, providing cover under which a tactical reserve, composed of grenadiers from the *38th SS Panzer Grenadier Regiment* and some light Flak tanks belonging to the *17th SS Reconnaissance Battalion*, was able to mass for sorties into the village or against the American battalions bypassing Farebersviller. During the afternoon, Companies A and C of the 1st Battalion crossed the railroad

[58] During this advance Sgt. Glen M. Stouder, E Company, 319th Infantry in a singlehanded and successful attack cleared the enemy from a house which offered the only cover for his men, who were deployed in the open under intense fire. The DSC was awarded to Sergeant Stouder.

[59] The German withdrawal east of St. Avold allowed CCA, 6th Armored Division, to drive forward on the right of the 80th. As a result General Grow was able for the first time to align both combat commands of the 6th Armored Division facing eastward.

[60] The Germans had planted time bombs in St. Avold. About 1730 on 3 December one of the time bombs exploded in a building occupied by the staff of the 633d Antiaircraft Artillery Battalion. Four officers and eighteen men were killed; some thirty were injured. Within the next hour four other explosions occurred, but all troops had been ordered out into the streets and so escaped injury. Ironically enough, St. Avold had been designated as a "rest area" for the 80th Division.

FAREBERSVILLER

south of Farebersviller and gained the wooded ridge that lay beyond. About 1600 seven German tanks and a company of infantry sliced in between the advance companies and the rest of the battalion. During the night some of the survivors, who had run out of ammunition and medical supplies, found their way back across the railroad. Company B patrols were sent forward into the woods and there surprised a group of enemy guards who were taking thirty walking wounded to the rear. The patrols killed the guards and freed their prisoners.

After the successful foray against the 1st Battalion the German shock troops gathered behind the railroad to drive the 3d Battalion out of the west half of Farebersviller. About 2000, three or four tanks and two or three hundred yelling grenadiers charged the Americans; the latter held on, despite serious casualties, and refused to be driven from the village. On the morning of the 29th friendly tanks and tank destroyers came up and began to shell buildings designated by the infantry. Shortly after noon the 3d Battalion was able to report that it was beginning "to creep forward again," although the largest company had only thirty-five men and one company numbered but sixteen.[61] The Germans, however, had strengthened their force inside the village. When night came the enemy had complete possession of Farebersviller; the remnants of the 3d Battalion were dug in about a thousand yards west of the village. During 29 November the Germans diverted some troops and tanks to deal with the 2d Battalion in the north, launching counterattacks at the beginning and end of the day; they were stopped on both occasions by a curtain of artillery fire.[62] That night General McBride ordered in the 318th Infantry to relieve the 317th Infantry, thus ending the November operations of the 80th Division and an advance—since 25 November—of nearly eighteen miles. During the month the division combat losses had been 513 killed, 2,215 wounded, and 373 missing, a total comparable to the 80th Division casualty list in the heavy fighting of September.[63] But the division had taken 3,943 prisoners.

The November offensive had won very substantial gains for the Third Army in both the XII and XX Corps sectors, but without effecting any penetration of the West Wall or materially hastening the advance on the road to

[61] Hist Div Combat Interviews; 317th Inf Jnl, 28 and 29 Nov 44; 80th Div G–3 Jnl, 29 Nov 44.

[62] Cpl. Thomas W. Pettengill, an aid man with 317th Infantry, was awarded the DSC for his courage in caring for the American casualties under very heavy fire, despite the fact that he was himself suffering from a painful wound.

[63] 80th Div AAR, Nov 44.

the Rhine. Nonetheless the Third Army had taken heavy toll of the enemy. At the close of November the German *First Army* continued to carry eight infantry divisions and four panzer divisions on its troop list, but this was a paper order of battle only. In fact the combat strength of the *First Army* had been reduced to four and a half guns for each mile on the front line and one battalion to each four-mile sector.[64]

[64] *First Army* status report, 28 Nov 1944, in *OB WEST KTB.*

CHAPTER XI

The XX Corps Advance to the Sarre (19 November - 3 December)

The First Attack on the Orscholz Switch Line

No sooner had the 90th and 5th Divisions joined to complete the envelopment of Metz than General Walker began regrouping his armor and cavalry as the first step in a general reorientation of the XX Corps directed northeast toward the Sarre River. Arrangements with General Middleton, commanding the VIII Corps, gave the XX Corps permission to use the Moselle River as an operational boundary on the north, thus placing the Sarre–Moselle triangle in the XX Corps zone and providing space for maneuver on the left flank of that corps. The 3d Cavalry Group (Task Force Polk), which had been probing and pushing its way into the triangle formed by the two rivers while the main body of the XX Corps was fighting farther south, had penetrated about as far into enemy territory as its light-armored squadrons could go. On the afternoon of 19 November the cavalry was brought to a halt by fire from the Orscholz Switch Line (also known to the Americans as the "Siegfried Switch"). (*Map XXXVI*) This line of field works, antitank barriers, and reinforced concrete pillboxes and bunkers had been constructed as an east-west extension at right angles to the main West Wall fortifications which lay beyond the Sarre. In effect the Orscholz position provided a barrier against any advance northward into the triangle whose apex lay at the confluence of the Moselle and Sarre Rivers and denied a turning movement on the north flank of the Saarlautern–Merzig sector of the West Wall.

On 17 November elements of the *416th Division* had begun a withdrawal to the north, folding back fanwise under pressure by the 90th Division and the 10th Armored. This was an orderly movement, and by 19 November the Germans were established in the Orscholz line. At least half of the remaining infantry strength of the *416th* had retreated to the east in company with the *19th VG Division* and there deployed northwest of Merzig on the near bank of the Sarre River. As a result of this split in his division, General Pflieger was left to hold the Orscholz position—a front of some seven and a half miles—with two rifle battalions of the *416th*, two service companies converted to infantry, a fortress machine gun battalion, and a battalion of poorly armed engineers.[1]

Little was known by American intelligence about the exact outline or strength of the Orscholz line. About all that could be definitely established was that the cavalry had been checked by a strong line of field works and fortifications in the sector Nennig–Tettingen–Oberleuken, and that a stronger force would be needed to continue the drive north into the Sarre–Moselle triangle. Late on 19 November, therefore, General Walker ordered the 3d Cavalry Group to hold up its advance and await the heavier armor.

Since the axis of the Third Army offensive lay in a northeasterly direction, aiming at the seizure of the Rhine crossings between Worms and Mainz, General Patton wished to put some troops across the Sarre as far to the north as possible and thus continue the advance to the Rhine with his left flank resting on the Moselle River. Originally the Third Army commander had intended to employ the 83d Infantry Division for this task. But the restrictions which General Bradley had imposed forbade the use of the 83d across the Moselle. Patton, therefore, told the XX Corps commander to send a combat command of the 10th Armored Division into the triangle. General Walker gave orders that CCA of the 10th Armored Division should assemble its dispersed elements and pass through the 3d Cavalry Group in an attack to seize a bridgehead over the Sarre in the vicinity of Saarburg, some twenty miles north of the routes on which the main body of the corps was to move.[2]

On the night of 19 November the body of the 3d Reconnaissance Squadron was deployed in a line running roughly east and west through Besch, Wochern, Borg, and Hellendorf, facing the Orscholz line. To the southeast, patrols from the 43d Reconnaissance Squadron had established observation posts on the hills near Mittel and Unter Tuensdorf, from which the Americans looked down the draws to the Sarre River approximately five thousand yards to the east. The cavalry thus formed a screen covering the left flank of CCB,

[1] MS #B–090 (Pflieger).

[2] General Walker had given orders for an advance to Saarburg before the 3d Cavalry Group encountered the main works of the Orscholz position on the afternoon of 19 November. The first order sent to the 10th Armored Division (at 0920 on 19 November) called for CCB to make the advance to Saarburg. About an hour later the corps commander rescinded this order—possibly because the pincers had closed on Metz—and dispatched the 10th Armored Division (minus CCB) to make the Saarburg attack. 10th Armd Div G–3 Jnl, 19 Nov 44.

10th Armored Division, which was deployed in a series of task forces and teams on a fairly wide front facing the Sarre. Antitank ditches and increasingly stubborn German resistance had prevented any appreciable progress by CCB in the preceding twenty-four hours. At the headquarters of CCA, General Walker's orders arrived just as that combat command was poised to cross the Nied and continue the advance to the east. During the night of 19–20 November, CCA reversed its direction and began a swing back to the west and north in a wide loop designed to bring it onto the positions tenuously secured by Polk's cavalry.

The following night CCA arrived in the sector held by the 3d Reconnaissance Squadron, whose outpost line already was across the German frontier. The cavalry reported that its patrols had worked a way through the dragon's teeth which defined the Orscholz line, and had pushed a short distance north before orders had come down from the XX Corps instructing Colonel Polk to hold in place and await relief by the armor. The cavalry assault guns, in the interim, had laid on a heavy fire in an attempt to maintain the narrow gap opened by the dismounted troopers about a thousand yards north of Borg. General Althaus deployed his combat command along a six-mile front with Task Force Standish on the left and Task Force Chamberlain on the right. His intention was to send the right task force against the sector of the German line north of Borg while the left made a jab at Tettingen and hooked around the German west flank near Besch. On the morning of 21 November CCA moved into the attack in four columns. Behind the armor four reinforcing battalions of field artillery, including one of 8-inch howitzers, were sited to give the combat command additional artillery support when it hit the Orscholz line. The attack on the right gained some initial success, although here as elsewhere in front of CCA the enemy fought desperately. Task Force Chamberlain's eastern column (Team Eisberg) jumped off from the cover of the Forêt de Saarburg in an oblique attack toward the village of Orscholz and drove through the outworks of the Orscholz line. When the attack was about 1,400 yards from the village, very severe artillery and mortar fire from the main German position brought the Americans to a halt. Little was known about these enemy works, and the fight now became an exploratory engagement in which the American artillery ranged in on each pillbox and bunker as its location was spotted by the armored infantry. In the meantime Colonel Chamberlain's western column attacked from Borg along the main road leading toward Kirf and into the gap discovered earlier by the cavalry. Here a line of steel dragon's teeth barred the way. Since there was no antitank ditch in this sector the enemy had blown a large crater in the highway in order to form an antitank barrier between the dragon's teeth flanking the road. Dismounted infantry were able to make a small penetration beyond the crater and the dragon's teeth, but finally were checked by rapid small arms and shellfire from field fortifications backing up the antitank barrier.

Task Force Standish on the left flank was stopped, almost as soon as its advance began, by a long antitank ditch reinforced by pillboxes and dragon's teeth. During the day engineers and armored infantry attempted to throw bridges over the antitank ditch, all the while under intense German fire, but with no success. When the day ended CCA still was held in check by the German line, except at the one point where the small force had worked its way past the crater. Colonel Chamberlain concluded that further preparations must be made before continuing the attack on the right and withdrew his task force to Borg, leaving CCA in approximately the positions it had occupied at the beginning of the day's operations.

CCB had crossed onto German soil on 19 November,[3] but there had received orders from General Morris to hold defensively and contain the Germans west of Merzig while the rest of the division initiated the attack toward Saarburg. The advance of 20 November carried the head of the CCB column forward about two miles and reached Hill 378, some three thousand yards from the Sarre River and Merzig. Because at this point the American troops were well within range of the German guns around Merzig and exposed to continuous shellfire, Brig. Gen. Edwin W. Piburne, the commander of CCB, ordered the men on Hill 378 to fall back to positions on Hill 383, southeast of Wellingen. Actually CCB had driven into a weakly defended portion of the Saar Heights *Stellung*, the line which constituted the last German battle position west of the Sarre River. The enemy interpreted this American advance as a main effort intended to roll up the Saar Heights position and force a crossing near Merzig.[4] Balck therefore threw in the survivors of the tough *25th Panzer Grenadier* Kampfgruppe as shock troops. Late on the afternoon of 21 November this counterattack detachment drove in on the left wing of CCB. A small American outpost force that had been screening east of the Heidwald Woods was driven back along the road toward Launstroff and lost

[3] 10th Armd CCB S–3 Jnl, 19 Nov 44: ". . . head of our column entered Germany at 1032."
[4] MS #B–078 (Mellenthin).

a platoon of tanks. When daylight came the enemy re-formed under cover of the Heidwald to continue the counterattack, but this threat was neutralized by the gunners of the 420th Field Artillery Battalion who poured shells into the woods until the enemy broke. The CCB sector of the front now lapsed into quiet and for the next few days was marked only by desultory frays between patrols.[5]

Back to the north, CCA set about a systematic penetration of the Orscholz line, attacking with dismounted infantry and engineers to reduce the troublesome enemy pillboxes and bridge the antitank ditches and craters. Task Force Standish dispatched a force of tanks and infantry at dawn on 22 November to execute the flank attack against the German right wing which had been outlined in CCA's original plan. These troops succeeded in fighting their way into Nennig, only to find that here the Orscholz line ran in a north-to-south line behind the village, thus covering the enemy flank. The Germans fought fiercely to eject the attackers from Nennig, and in the early afternoon the Americans withdrew under a protective barrage laid down by their supporting artillery. This abortive attack cost fifty-five casualties and five or six tanks. The right wing team of Task Force Standish (Team Eardley) was more successful in a dismounted attack straight along the main road between Wochern and Tettingen. One platoon of infantry, following close behind the advancing fire of its supporting artillery, penetrated the line of dragon's teeth just outside of Tettingen and forced a way into the village, but was quickly driven back to the south. On CCA's right wing Task Force Chamberlain made some headway along the large hogback ridge whose eastern side is marked by the Borg–Kirf road. Chamberlain's armored infantry made a jab north along the ridge road, broke through the dragon's teeth east of the Campholz Woods, and went on to establish a small "bridgehead" about eight hundred yards in depth.[6]

On the night of 22 November CCA held only the one opening through the dragon's teeth. At no point had the field fortifications beyond this antitank barrier been neutralized or reduced. The armored combat command already was deployed on a very extended front, and the experiences of the past two days had demonstrated clearly that additional infantry would be

[5] On 22 November CCB patrols occupied Zeurange, 2½ miles south of Waldwisse. The inhabitants of Zeurange told them that American troops had first entered the village on 22 November 1918.

[6] Details of the CCA attack are given in 10th Armd Div G–3 Jnl; CCA AAR; and Hist Div Combat Interviews.

required if any substantial breach was to be made in the Orscholz line. The precise German strength behind the fortified line was unknown, but the enemy had shown a tenacity which boded ill for hopes of a quick penetration. Actually the scratch force under the *416th* had been reinforced during the day by armored infantry from the *21st Panzer Division*, a unit that still had a German classification as an "attack" division.

Two days before, the XX Corps commander had attached the 358th Infantry, 90th Infantry Division, to the 10th Armored. The CCA commander had been confident that his troops could crack the Orscholz line without help,[7] but at noon on 21 November General Morris finally had ordered the infantry to begin the move northward. Late on the following day the 358th Infantry (Col. C. H. Clarke) was in position to take over the fight. On the morning of 23 November General Morris canceled the scheduled renewal of the CCA attack and ordered the 358th to advance at once, with the mission of capturing the villages of Sinz and Muenzingen three and four thousand yards respectively behind the center of the Orscholz line. The path for the infantry attack lay along the hogback ridge which provided a natural causeway leading north in the direction of Saarburg; therefore once the infantry had made a hole in the Orscholz line and was firmly astride the main section of the ridge the way would be opened for the armor to roll. Lacking precise intelligence data the 358th was none too well briefed as to the specific locations of the works to its front or the number of the enemy opposite, although G–2 estimates did indicate that German reserves had been drawn into this sector to meet the armored attacks of the past forty-eight hours. In addition the 358th had been reduced to about sixty-three percent of its normal strength by the fighting during the envelopment north of Metz.

Colonel Clarke decided to make a co-ordinated attack on Muenzingen with two battalions from the vicinity of Borg, but General Morris directed that one battalion clear the route via Tettingen while another moved on the parallel route from Borg. The 3d (Capt. J. S. Spivey) advanced on the left with Tettingen and Sinz as objectives, and the 2d (Lt. Col. Robert H. Schultz) passed through Task Force Chamberlain on the right. About 1000 the two

[7] A message from the CCA commander on the evening of 21 November reads: "Please note that we have not breached the En Defensive Pos in our immediate front. I have been in contact with both Chamberlain and Standish both of whom assure me that early tomorrow morning they will breach hostile defensive positions and be on their way. I request that CCA be given an opportunity to crack this position tomorrow morning and that the Inf Combat Team be not employed for this purpose." 10th Armd Div G–3 Jnl, 21 Nov 44.

battalions jumped off. The weather was foul and no American planes were aloft, but the armor and its artillery laid down a barrage to aid the advance of the 3d Battalion, 358th, and the 344th Field Artillery Battalion fired in support of the 2d Battalion. By some mischance the tank-supporting fire had not been properly co-ordinated. The 2d Battalion coming up from Borg no sooner reached the line of departure and moved into the attack than it was hit by short-range, high-velocity fire from the tanks of Task Force Chamberlain, which were bogged in the deep mud. Some hours were needed to reorganize the 2d Battalion. It resumed the attack early in the afternoon, but only a few of the troops passed through the dragon's teeth.

The 3d Battalion assembled near Wochern and then swung wide to the right and into the Campholz Woods during a very heavy fog that suddenly enveloped the entire sector and provided concealment over the bare hogback. This flanking movement was designed to avoid a head-on attack along the road to Tettingen. The battalion used ladders to span the ubiquitous antitank ditch, which here extended through the center of the woods, and pushed northward across German trenches and through barbed wire zigzagging under the trees. By dark the 3d Battalion had cleared the woods and captured eight-four prisoners.[8] Its own losses were relatively slight, despite counterattacks by infiltrating Germans who reoccupied pillboxes that had been captured by the 3d Battalion. The latter's strength was too depleted to be able to garrison the pillboxes and continue the attack simultaneously.

At 0630 on 24 November the 2d Battalion again started forward on the right. This time the advance was checked by a storm of machine gun fire sweeping the right flank from a huge bunker at the edge of Oberleuken. An assault team went up against the bunker but was not able to knock it out until nearly noon. Fire from the village itself continued to thin the 2d Battalion ranks, and at 1530 Colonel Clarke sent Colonel Lytle's 1st Battalion (later led by Capt. Thomas Caldecott), which formed his reserve, into Oberleuken, where the fight for the village raged on into the night.

The 3d Battalion also had run into trouble during the morning. The Germans threw in a counterattack using troops armed with flame throwers, in addition to their usual heavy complement of automatic weapons. In beating

[8] During the fight in the woods 2d Lt. Glenn E. Rugh, I Company, 358th Infantry, led a bayonet charge, under withering fire, which cleaned out an enemy trench and netted thirty prisoners. He was awarded the DSC. Pfc. Harold R. McQuay, K Company, mopped up a German machine gun crew in a singlehanded assault. He also was awarded the DSC.

TETTINGEN-BUTZDORF. *Circles indicate pillboxes.*

BUTZDORF
CAMPHOLZ

off the attackers the Americans became somewhat disorganized and did not advance out of the woods until about 1300. Captain Spivey had assigned K Company to take the village of Butzdorf while I Company made for Tettingen, just to the south of Butzdorf. The two assault companies made a left wheel from the woods and started down the slope against the numerous pillboxes dotting the open ground east of the two villages. The attack went slowly during the afternoon. Sixteen pillboxes were taken, but the slow work of buttoning-up each separate pillbox, worming close in through the mud, and knocking it out with demolition charges had consumed the daylight hours. Captain Spivey therefore decided to postpone the final assault until the next morning. Unaware of this decision Capt. Robert B. McHolland and K Company, well known in the 358th as the "Kraut Killers," continued on toward Butzdorf. This company had met less pillbox resistance than its sister company on the left, but just east of Butzdorf it encountered strong machine gun fire sweeping the draw along which the company was moving on the village. Captain McHolland ordered two of his platoons and a section of heavy machine guns to breast the German fire and make a run for Butzdorf. Most of the riflemen and one machine gun crew made it, taking stations in three houses at the edge of the village. Shortly after dark a company of German infantry, reinforced by two tanks, came marching up the road from Tettingen in a column of two's. The lone machine gun, which had jammed during the advance through the mud, could not be made to function and the enemy attacked in a fury of small arms fire and hand grenades. Early in the fight Captain McHolland was killed.[9] The remaining officers soon were casualties. Some thirty-five survivors continued the battle through the night, although their ammunition was dwindling and they had no way of getting word of their plight back to the battalion. One house was literally demolished by German tank and bazooka fire but the men in the two houses remaining were able to hold on until the following day, when relief arrived.[10]

At daylight on 25 November the 3d Battalion began a desperate attack to knock out Tettingen and rescue the survivors in Butzdorf. Company I, lying in the fields east of Tettingen under constant fire from roving self-

[9] Capt. Robert B. McHolland received the DSC for his part in the action of 24 November. He led in breaking up the attack against his command post. When the Germans retreated McHolland and two men pursued them, killing fourteen with hand grenades, wounding seven, and capturing several. The two men were wounded and McHolland was killed while trying to get them back to a building.

[10] See the 358th Infantry After Action Report and battalion journals for this action.

propelled guns and from the German pillboxes still active, watched while the 344th Field Artillery Battalion shelled virtually every house in Tettingen, then charged into the village under cover of smoke put down by the American guns and tanks. Tettingen was cleared in less than thirty minutes, but I Company had suffered many casualties, including all of its officers except one, and L Company had to be committed from reserve to carry the advance on to Butzdorf. In the meantime other American arms had been brought into play. Fighter-bombers interdicted the movement of German reserves[11] by dropping napalm and fragmentation bombs on Sinz and Muenzingen. CCA put a bridge across the antitank ditch south of Tettingen and sent a platoon of tanks into the fight. Two of these tanks joined L Company and the relief of the troops in Butzdorf was executed rapidly. A number of Germans were taken prisoner here, including twenty-one who surrendered to four privates from K Company who had been their prisoners a few minutes before. The relief force, however, was not strong enough to hold this exposed position. Butzdorf was evacuated; then the American artillery blasted the village and the tanks in Tettingen showered it with white phosphorus.

On the right of the regimental zone the 1st Battalion continued a house-to-house battle for the possession of Oberleuken, after beating off a German foray made by a force of tanks and infantry that moved in across the face of the 2d Battalion. The 2d Battalion made some progress, despite a withering fire to its front, and captured the bald top of Hill 388, five hundred yards northwest of Oberleuken. This advance cost the battalion dear; by the end of the day it numbered less than a hundred men in the line.

The three-day battle to penetrate the Orscholz line had drastically reduced the combat strength of the 358th Infantry.[12] Furthermore, exposure in the cold, the mud, and the rain, with only such shelter as could be found in captured pillboxes, had brought on a mounting toll of trench foot casualties. On the evening of 25 November the 10th Armored Division commander and Colonel Clarke agreed that the 358th was in no shape to continue the attack. The corps commander concurred in this decision and on the following day

[11] On 24 November *OB WEST* had given orders that the Orscholz line must be reinforced, because the position "has special importance" as an outwork of the West Wall. The following day *OB WEST* ordered the *404th Volks Artillery Corps*, the *21st Panzer Division*, and a composite regiment to be hurried up to the line (the elements of the *21st Panzer Division* actually had been in and out of the fight). See *Army Group G KTB* of these dates.

[12] The 358th Infantry was at about 40 percent effective strength. Hist Div Combat Interviews.

the infantry were relieved by units of the 10th Armored Division in a highly successful daylight withdrawal.[13] The 358th had captured about five hundred prisoners, forced the deepest penetration of the Orscholz line that would be made during the 1944 campaign, and won high praise from the 10th Armored Division. Now the 358th reverted to the 90th Division and went into division reserve at Veckring Barracks, north of Dalstein. Colonel Clarke was suffering with pneumonia and had to be hospitalized.

The fight at the Orscholz line was not quite ended. About 0130 on 27 November the Germans filtered back into Tettingen and then drove on to attack Borg, well inside the thin American line, with flame throwers and automatic weapons. This last enemy attempt to seal the narrow breach in the line of fortifications was repelled and the armored infantry hunted down the Germans in Tettingen from house to house. American operations against the Orscholz line were halted, however; Oberleuken and Nennig remained in enemy hands, and the attack for a bridgehead at Saarburg was abandoned.

Meanwhile the XX Corps offensive along the main axis toward the Sarre was being carried rapidly northeast by the 90th and 95th Divisions. Since the two-division advance was about to outrun the flank protection offered on the north by CCB of the 10th Armored Division, General Walker decided to turn all of the 10th Armored to the east. On 27 November he issued new operations instructions which assigned the 3d Cavalry Group to relieve CCA of the screening mission on the far north flank of the corps and regrouped the 10th Armored Division preparatory to clearing the remaining German forces from the west bank of the Sarre in the division zone. The armor assembled on 30 November and began the attack toward the river through a low-hanging mist, its armored infantry in the lead and tanks following. CCB, on the right, drove as far as Merzig, where the enemy blew the last two of the Sarre bridges in this sector. Only a few enemy troops remained west of the river to oppose the 10th Armored, and by 0300 on 2 December the last resistance in the Merzig sector west of the Sarre was ended by the capture of Dreisbach, on the north boundary of the division zone. General Walker ordered General Morris to establish an outpost line on the west bank of the Sarre between the 3d Cavalry Group and the 90th Division. Since this defen-

[13] Acting as an artillery forward observer for the 1st Battalion during the withdrawal, 2d Lt. Cecil H. Eller went forward to an exposed position to adjust fire on enemy mortars that had pinned down the infantry. He remained at his hazardous post until he was killed. Lieutenant Eller was awarded the DSC posthumously.

sive mission required only a single combat command, CCB turned back to a rest area from which, on 18 December, it would move to take part in the defense of Bastogne.

The XX Corps Preparations for the Attack Toward the Sarre River

The successful completion of the battle to encircle Metz and neutralize its garrison marked the end of an important phase in the operations of the XX Corps. But the tired and combat-worn divisions had no time to rest on their laurels. At best the greater part of the troops could be given only a few hours of sleep, a bath, and a change to clean, dry clothes, before the XX Corps turned northeast to continue the offensive beside the XII Corps toward the next enemy barriers: the Sarre River and the West Wall.

On 20 November, of General Walker's three infantry divisions, the 90th was east of Metz proper and the 5th and 95th were jammed in and around the city itself. A hasty redrafting of boundary lines inside the city simplified the task of extricating units and regrouping them again under the proper command. The lack of bridges, however, and the difficulties attendant on moving trains and troops through this crowded area—where small groups of the enemy still were fighting—combined to hamper the general reorientation and reorganization required for the drive to the Sarre. Late on 21 November General Walker ordered the 5th Division to relieve the 95th Division, many of whose troops were involved in containing the German forts west of the Moselle. This reshuffling would bring the 95th eastward into the former 5th Division zone and place it on the right of the 90th Division. The 90th had not turned inward toward Metz and at the moment was in the process of wheeling northeast behind an outpost line deployed on the west bank of the Nied which served as a screen for the body of the corps. General Twaddle, whose 95th Division had been chosen to make the main effort to secure crossings at the Sarre, was unwilling to throw his division into what promised to be a hard fight without taking some time for rehabilitation, reorganization—necessitated by the number of casualties among company commanders[14]—and vehicle repair, the last particularly needed by the attached tank battalion (the 778th) after the operations west and north of Metz. The 95th Division commander asked for a four-day delay, time that would be required in any event

[14] 377th Inf AAR, 23 Nov 44.

for regrouping the corps before the resumption of the offensive; so General Walker set 25 November as the date for the new attack toward the Sarre.

The XX Corps Field Order No. 13, issued on the early morning of 22 November, outlined the plan for the three-division operation, placing the 90th Division in the center, the 95th on its right, and the 10th Armored Division on its left. (*Map XXXVII*) General Patton had ordered the XX Corps to destroy the enemy remaining west of the Sarre and to cross that river. Beyond the Sarre River the corps mission would be to penetrate the West Wall, destroy the German formations there, and continue the attack in a northeasterly direction. The burden of this offensive, in mud and rain, across a defended river line, and through the strongly fortified zone of the West Wall, would have to be carried by the infantry. The XX Corps plan gave the 95th Division the task of making the first crossings at the Sarre, in the sector between Saarlautern and Pachten. Once the 95th had a foothold across the river, the scheme of maneuver called upon the division to extend its bridgehead northward in order to facilitate the 90th Division crossing. In addition the 95th was charged with the task of making and keeping contact with the left flank of the XII Corps, whose 80th Division at the moment was held more or less immobile, blocking along the gap between the XII and XX Corps which had opened while the latter was involved at Metz.

The 90th Infantry Division was to begin its attack simultaneously with that of the 95th, clear the enemy out of its zone west of the river, and, when the Sarre was reached, support the 95th Division crossing with all the fire power the division could bring to bear. Once at the Sarre the plan simply called for the 90th Division "to prepare to bridge [the] Saar river within zone in [the] bridgehead established by the 95th Division." During the initial phases of the drive to the Sarre at least one regimental combat team of the 5th Infantry Division was to be left in the Metz sector and there contain the German forts still holding out. General Walker, however, could assume that new troops ultimately would be available to take over the 5th Division containing role, or that the intransigent enemy garrisons would capitulate. Therefore, General Irwin was ordered to prepare plans for an attack with the bulk of the 5th Division anywhere in the corps zone on six hours' notice. The 10th Armored, as noted, was to secure a crossing in the north at Saarburg.

The country between Metz and the Sarre River offered no unusually difficult barriers to foot soldiers and vehicles, although the combination of continuous rains and clay subsoil would slow the speed of any advance. The Nied

River, running obliquely northeast from Bouzonville, near which the bulk of the 90th Division was assembled, could hardly offer the retreating Germans a natural defense line. The Nied, however, did bisect the zone through which the corps would move, making it somewhat difficult for the two infantry divisions to give each other mutual support during the advance to the Sarre line. In general the terrain eastward was moderately rolling and mostly open, with a few patches of dense evergreen forest breaking the monotony of the landscape but providing little continuous cover for any enemy withdrawal. Some minor streams, tributaries of the Nied, cut across the American front and, with their bridges destroyed, were potential sources of delay. A short distance from the Sarre, and just east of the German frontier, the ground rose gradually to a series of heights, which, on the reverse sides, tended to break away sharply to the river. This conformation of high ground was known to the German staff planners as the Saar Heights Position (*Saar-Hoehen Stellung*). Northwest of Merzig the heights lay contiguous to the Orscholz line. West of Pachten, in the 95th Division zone, the heights were particularly rugged and dipped so abruptly at the river as to form a regular escarpment. West of Saarlautern the heights terminated some distance from the Sarre channel, with the result that a natural bridgehead of lower ground extended to the west of the river. The main section of the city of Saarlautern lay in this west bank bridgehead.

In the German scheme of successive defense lines the Saar Heights *Stellung* was the last planned line of resistance in front of the West Wall, which in this sector had been constructed on the east bank of the Sarre generally parallel to the river. The heights constituted a *Vorfeld*, or forward battle position, which could be used either to cover the movement of field forces into the West Wall fortifications or to screen deployment and maneuver for counterattacks launched to deflect any frontal attack against the main works of the West Wall. Although the maps at high German headquarters showed the trace of the Saar Heights *Stellung* as a main line of resistance, it remained in actuality a *geographical* position, strengthened somewhat by temporary field works, but lacking concrete fortifications.[15] It is not surprising, therefore, that the XX Corps G–2 estimates and air photos took little cognizance of the defense possibilities of the Saar Heights.

[15] MS #B–078 (Mellenthin). Both Balck and Rundstedt counted heavily on the natural strength of the Saar Heights *Stellung*. See various orders for withdrawals to this position in *Army Group G KTB* and *OB WEST KTB*.

American intelligence sources predicted that the enemy could throw in the remnants of three infantry divisions (*19th VG*, *347th*, and *462d VG*) to oppose the new XX Corps offensive. It was believed that the German withdrawal to the east, now taking place, would not stop short of the Sarre, and that the enemy forces left behind were incapable of fighting more than minor rear guard and delaying actions. The possibility was recognized that some part of the *21st Panzer Division* and *25th Panzer Grenadier Division*, identified in the fighting at the Orscholz line, might be shifted from the north and used to bolster the enemy forces on the Sarre line.[16] Beyond this, American intelligence and reconnaissance from the air had developed some general knowledge of the outlines and extent of the West Wall; but little detailed information on these fortifications was at hand and more precise acquaintance with their strength and capabilities would have to be developed in actual combat, inasmuch as preliminary ground reconnaissance was denied by the Sarre River barrier.

The German Withdrawal East of Metz

Field Marshal Rundstedt seems to have been far from sanguine as to any hope of long delaying the American advance east of Metz. His fear that the fall of Metz might leave a gap in the lines of the *First Army*, into which General Patton's divisions would wedge their way, found expression as early as 15 November in an unsolicited order that gave the *Army Group G* commander permission to withdraw his right flank to the Saar Heights *Stellung* "if necessary." General Balck was no more willing to accept Rundstedt's conservative and cautious advice than he had been prior to the beginning of the Third Army offensive. Balck apparently believed that the remnants of the *19th VG Division* and *416th Division* which had withdrawn to the Borg–Boulay line on the night of 17–18 November might be able to make a stand. He gave orders that the *347th Division*, just arriving from the *Army Group B* area, should be committed on both sides of Boulay to bolster up the broken and depleted units congregated there.[17] The American maneuver to close the escape routes east of Metz gave the German forces in the Boulay sector a brief respite. But on 19 November the 10th Armored Division attack east of Laun-

[16] XX Corps G–2 Periodic Rpt, 22 Nov 44.

[17] The 347th Division (Trierenberg) had come south from the quiet Eifel sector.

stroff reached the edge of the Saar Heights *Stellung*, and this threat, coupled with that now developing in front of the Orscholz line, caused Balck real concern. *Army Group G* issued a flurry of orders: The *First Army* must hold at the Orscholz line; the Launstroff–Bouzonville sector must be strengthened by "recklessly" stripping forces from the *First Army* center; all penetrations which might be made in the Saar Heights *Stellung* must be wiped out. Finally, Balck ordered Knobelsdorff to rush all the reserves available on the right wing of the *First Army* into the Merzig sector to hold the vital Sarre crossings, a somewhat bootless gesture by the *Army Group G* commander in view of the paucity of reserves along the whole *First Army* front. Subsequently, by considerable juggling of units in the line and with some help from the OKW strategic reserve, Balck was able to form a Kampfgruppe in the Merzig area composed of elements from the *21st Panzer Division* and the *25th Panzer Grenadier Division*. But the deterioration of the situation at the Orscholz line speedily absorbed this last reserve force.[18]

When the XX Corps resumed the eastward attack on 25 November the German *First Army* had in action elements of three weak divisions: the *19th VG Division*, disposed along the German frontier with its right boundary east of Launstroff and its left on the Nied River near Niedaltdorf; *Kampfgruppe Muehlen*, holding a narrow sector behind the Nied River between Niedaltdorf and Bouzonville;[19] and the *347th Division*, whose front extended in a shallow salient along the Nied River south to Boulay and then swung back southeast to an anchor point at the Forêt de St. Avold. Of these units the *347th* was still fairly fresh, but it was only a static division and poorly equipped; the others were hardly more than reinforced regiments. Artillery support was available, although most of the German guns seem to have been already displaced to positions behind the Sarre. The *19th VG Division* had a total of four assault guns for close infantry support, but the others had none. Finally, it should be remarked that even these weak forces could not be employed with the greatest degree of tactical effectiveness, since the Nied River was the boundary between two German corps, the *LXXXII Corps* and the *XIII SS Corps*.

[18] See above, pp. 490–98.

[19] This relict of the *19th* and *559th* had long since been bled white. It had come north from the Morhange sector after relief by the *17th SS*. Weak as the Kampfgruppe was, it continued to have a good reputation, a fact that German writers ascribe to its brave and able officers. MS #B–487 (Simon).

The Advance to the Sarre by the 90th and 95th Divisions

The 5th Infantry Division completed the relief of the 95th at Metz on 23 November and the latter moved east to take up its attack position on the right flank of the 90th Division. The 90th had been holding the Nied River sector with light patrols, as well as part of the line earlier established in the north by the advance of CCB, 10th Armored Division. Now, with the arrival of the 95th, a realignment was carried out along the boundary between the two attack divisions. This boundary line followed the Nied River as far as Bueren and then thrust due east along the main railroad to the Sarre River. The northern boundary for the 90th Division zone of attack ran obliquely northeast through Halstroff and Mondorf, terminating on the Sarre just south of Merzig. The southern boundary of the 95th Division zone at the moment was also the line of demarcation between the XX and XII Corps. This disposition of the XX Corps forces gave the 95th Division a wider front than the 90th. In addition the 90th already was echeloned forward northeast of Bouzonville; which meant that it had only five and a half miles to cover before reaching the Sarre, while the 95th Division, which was making the corps main effort, was sixteen miles from the river.

On the early morning of 25 November the two infantry divisions commenced the drive toward the Sarre, each attacking with two regiments abreast. The enemy had no cohesive line of defense but instead used small detachments of thirty or forty men, holed up in villages along the roads, to fight delaying actions. Blown bridges, swollen streams, and muddy roads caused more delay than did enemy action. The German artillery laid down occasional harassing fire, but fog and haze prevented any effective counterbattery work by the American gunners. The 90th Division progressed about two miles in the course of the day. Its left-wing formation, the 359th Infantry (Col. Raymond E. Bell), which was echeloned in advance of the 357th Infantry (Col. J. H. George), reached the village of Oberesch—only four miles from the Sarre River. The 95th Division, strongly reinforced by artillery from the III Corps and 5th Division, crossed the Nied, advancing with the 377th Infantry (Col. F. E. Gaillard) on the left and the 378th Infantry (Col. S. L. Metcalfe) on the right. By nightfall the division had taken Boulay, Narbéfontaine, Momerstroff, and Hallering, and had begun to move through the Maginot Line. The enemy made no attempt to hold the old fortifications but did engage in occasional sharply contested delaying actions during the course of the day.[20] As the 1st Battalion, 378th, marching in column of companies along the Narbéfontaine–Niedervisse road, came past Hill 384 the Germans opened a surprise fire and inflicted a number of casualties on the battalion, including its commanding officer, Lt. Col. Christian L. Oliver. Company E of the 377th also was hard hit while advancing in the open toward the Bois d'Ottonville. A sudden and withering fire from the woods cut down the company commander and thirty-one men. Pvt. Willie H. Bishop, the company messenger, took charge, withdrew the company from the danger zone, and then directed the removal of the wounded. For this action he was awarded the DSC.

The 10th Armored Division committed CCB to extend the north wing of the attack on 26 November. Its dismounted infantry, supported by fire from field guns, tanks, and chemical mortars, systematically scoured the woods to the front. But most of the Germans in this sector had retired across the Sarre and the combat command met little fire except that from the German guns east of the river. The 90th Division also encountered little resistance on this day, although antitank ditches and mine fields began to appear in its path and slow the advance. In the 95th Division zone the 377th Infantry, making the main effort, advanced about four miles, despite the flooded countryside east of Eblange which forced the regiment to queue in column of battalions and thread its way forward on the one passable road. Toward evening both the 377th and 378th began to meet resistance from small German detachments, which apparently had orders to make a stand. Meanwhile, it had become apparent that the German garrisons holding the forts back at Metz were in no mood for quick capitulation; so General Walker ordered

[20] In October 1941, the Germans had discussed the possibility of using the Maginot Line in the event of an Allied invasion on the Continent. At that time it was concluded that the reconstitution of the fortified works would require too much labor and money. Interestingly enough, some of the German experts also raised the point that their own victories had called into question the value of *any* permanent fortifications. However, recommendations were made that certain parts of the Maginot Line be used to block the road nets leading to the West Wall. (This from a study by the *Kdtr. d.Bef. Eifel und Saarpfalz,* dated 2 Oct 41, in *OKH/General der Pioniere und Festungen.*) In the late summer and early autumn of 1944 some attempts were made to carry out this last recommendation and rearm the line in the Faulquemont and Wittring sectors, but no work was done east of Metz. MS #B–003 (Souchay), MS #B–088 (Claer). So little attention had been paid to the French fortifications since 1940 that on 4 September 1944 the Metz commander had to send a wire to the German Army historians asking for a detailed plan of the Maginot Line. *OKW/Chef der Heeresarchive, Lagebuch,* 4 Sep 44. On 16 November Hitler got around to the question of the Maginot Line and asked his staff how it was armed, to what extent its works had been oriented to face westward, and like questions. However, it was too late to take any action. Office of Naval Intelligence, *Fuehrer Conferences on Matters Dealing with the German Navy,* 1944. The XX Corps G–2 had correctly predicted that the Maginot Line would not be defended. XX Corps G–2 Periodic Rpt, 22 Nov 44.

General Twaddle to extend his reconnaissance to cover the open area on the right flank of the 95th Division which tentatively had been allocated to the 5th Division. The 5th Division commander, however, was able to release the 3d Battalion of the 10th Infantry, and on 27 November it relieved the 2d Battalion, 318th Infantry, which had been holding the Bois de Kerfent at the boundary between the XII and XX Corps.

The 90th Division, pushing forward on a relatively narrow front, was well ahead of the divisions to its flanks by 27 November. General Van Fleet halted his division, except for minor patrolling, and set the engineers to work repairing the roads to the rear so that tanks and tank destroyers could be brought up for the final phase of the advance to the river. The 95th Division, however, was coming forward rapidly and on 27 November made a long drive at the expense of the *347th Division* which put the 377th Infantry within a mile of the German border and brought the 378th up as far as Falck and Dalem. On the following day the 95th Division continued to make progress. The 377th entered Germany. The 378th made slight gains, but then was checked for several hours on its right by intense fire from the large woods east of Falck.[21] At dark the front lines of the 95th were about four and a half miles from the Sarre, roughly abreast of the 90th Division.

General Walker now ordered the two infantry divisions to launch a co-ordinated attack on 29 November. Thus far the Germans had sought to delay the American drive by using small rear guard detachments and extensive demolitions, the main forces withdrawing the while to the Saar Heights *Stellung*. When the 95th began the attack on the morning of 29 November it met more opposition than had been anticipated, for at this point the advance had to be made across the Saar Heights.[22] The 1st Battalion of the 377th fought its way into the village of St. Barbara, located on a narrow spur about two thousand yards from the Sarre. Then tanks and infantry of the *21st Panzer Division* made a counterattack, overran two 57-mm. antitank guns

[21] Here Sgt. Lloyd A. Russell, C Company, 378th Infantry, destroyed a German gun that had knocked out three American tank destroyers. He was awarded the DSC.

[22] Evidence of the stubborn German fight to hold the Saar Heights *Stellung* on 29 November is found in the tremendous rise in ammunition consumption by the XX Corps artillery, which leaped to 21,377 rounds for the 24-hour period. After the breach in the positions of the *347th* on 28 November Balck gave the *First Army* permission to retire to the Saar Heights *Stellung*, but added a peremptory order that this was to be the "last" withdrawal. Knobelsdorff already had reported that *Kampfgruppe Muehlen* and the *347th* were so reduced that in his opinion they could hold no continuous line of resistance. *Army Group G KTB,* 28 Nov 44. On 28 November *OB WEST* ordered the officers responsible for the bad showing of the *347th Division* to be shot without trial. This order was carried out. *Army Group G KTB Anlagen.*

ST. BARBARA. *The area shown in the photograph is indicated on Map XXXVII.*

which had been manhandled into position on the road east of the village, and drove back into St. Barbara, where a bitter fight raged through the night.[23] Other elements of the 377th engaged in a desperate battle with troops from Muehlen's Kampfgruppe who were disposed in and around Kerprich-Hemmersdorf, back to the northwest on the Nied. During the fight Sgt. Andrew Miller of G Company made a one-man assault into the German lines and there met his death. Two platoons rose, one after the other, to follow Miller and took the position. A posthumous award of the Congressional Medal of Honor subsequently cited the intrepid sergeant for "a series of heroic deeds" which had begun in the battles north of Metz and continued until he was killed.

The 378th also found the going tough and received counterattacks all along its front. The 3d Battalion mopped up in Falck, where a detachment from the *347th* had held out during the previous night. When the battalion, supported by some medium tanks, moved east to clear the enemy from the woods and high ground ahead, the Germans lashed back with a succession of counterattacks, six in all, which were dispersed only after hard fighting.[24] In the center the 1st Battalion took Merten and then held the village despite all German efforts to retake it. The 2d Battalion swung out on the left and started an attack toward Berus, but was hit immediately by a counterattack launched by a special "assault group" from *Panzer Lehr.* After a bitter engagement in which the battalion lost heavily and became much disorganized, it fell back toward Merten, reorganizing during the night behind cover offered by a group of farm buildings. The 95th Division had received no less than ten German counterattacks in the course of the day—an earnest of General Balck's intention to defend the Saar Heights *Stellung* in front of Saarlautern. It would appear that all of the available German reserves had been thrown in to stop the 95th; north of the Nied River the 90th met little opposition and by nightfall it had patrols on the west bank of the Sarre.

[23] 377th Inf Jnl, 29 Nov 44. The *21st Panzer Division* troops had been hastily transferred from the Orscholz line on 28 November. Balck had asked for the use of the entire *Panzer Lehr Division* "for two days" to wipe out the American gains made on 27 and 28 November, but Rundstedt denied this request (*Panzer Lehr,* it will be remembered, had been committed in the Sarre-Union sector). *OB WEST KTB,* 28 Nov 44.

[24] Prisoner interrogations indicate that a Kampfgruppe from the *25th Panzer Grenadier Division* had been employed in these counterattacks. Apparently it had assembled in the Warndt Forest, where the *36th VG Division* held a salient at the boundary between the XII and XX Corps. 95th Div G–2 Jnl, 29 Nov 44. At the end of November this detachment of the *25th Panzer Grenadier Division* was pulled out and sent south to aid the rest of the division in the Sarre-Union sector.

On the last day of November the XX Corps began the final battle to destroy the enemy west of the Sarre. The 90th Division, responsible for clearing the triangle formed by the Nied and Sarre Rivers, dispatched the 1st Battalion of the 357th in assault boats across the Nied near Niedaltdorf, thus flanking the hasty field fortifications at the Nied. The battalion then struck east into Bueren, where the enemy continued to contest the possession of the village through the night. In the north the 90th closed up to the Sarre and at dusk occupied Fremersdorf, the largest town on the west bank in the division zone, without a fight. The American thrust in this sector had cut the *19th VG Division* in two, leaving the *74th Regiment* isolated north of Fremersdorf and the *73d Regiment* crowded into the Bueren area.[25]

During the morning of 30 November the 95th Division consolidated its front-line positions and reorganized, after the disorder attendant on the counterattacks of the previous day, to resume the attack. In the meantime the rear echelons of the division worked doggedly to mend the boggy roads and better the supply situation, a necessary preliminary to any crossing attempt. In the afternoon the 377th Infantry hunted down the last Germans in St. Barbara and pushed on its right into Felsberg, where a particularly stubborn knot of the *Panzer Lehr* assault group held the edge of the village and delayed further advance. The 378th moved forward to positions beside the 377th Infantry and took a dominating hill (377) south of Felsberg which the Germans considered the "key" to the Saar Heights. At the end of the day, while not yet at the Sarre, the left wing of the 95th was poised on the slopes which led down to the river in front of the Saarlautern. The two-and-a-half-mile advance to Bueren, by the battalion from the 90th, likewise had moved the American line to the slopes leading down to the Sarre in front of Dillingen, which covered the right flank of the Saarlautern defenses. However, the 378th had not yet fought its way past the high ground on the right flank of the 95th, from which the enemy continued to deny access to the river.

Although the north flank of the two infantry divisions slated to make the river crossing was protected by the 10th Armored Division, which had driven forward to well within light howitzer range of the German defenses at Merzig, the south flank was only weakly outposted and presented some danger. In fact much of the trouble met by the 95th Division had come on its open right flank, where it had attempted to bypass German resistance emanating

[25] MS #B-527 (Britzelmayr).

from the rough, forested salient between the XII and XX Corps. With this potential threat in mind the XX Corps commander attached a task force, commanded by Col. Robert P. Bell, to the 95th Infantry Division. This force, taken from the 5th Infantry Division, consisted of the 10th Infantry (—), 46th Field Artillery Battalion, 5th Reconnaissance Troop, and one company each of engineers, tanks, and tank destroyers. Bell's task force closed in the sector on the right of the 95th Division late in the afternoon of 30 November. General Walker expressly prohibited the use of the task force in the crossing operation, for it was his intention to use the entire 5th Infantry Division to exploit any crossing secured by the 90th and 95th. General Patton, meanwhile, had assigned the 6th Cavalry Group and the 5th Ranger Battalion to the XX Corps, specifying that the Rangers could not be used offensively. These units were organized as a task force under Col. E. M. Fickett, who commanded the 6th Cavalry Group, and on 1 December it assembled near St. Avold with the mission of screening on the XX Corps south flank. The arrival of this force permitted a regrouping on the right of the corps, and the 10th Infantry was released from its protective mission to make an advance on the south flank of the 95th Division.

At the close of November the *First Army* had given ground all along its front. The American XV Corps was driving back the German left and now threatened to break through to Wissembourg and the Palatinate. The XII Corps had made an armored penetration at the German center and was preparing to widen the thrust by a push across the Sarre in the vicinity of Sarreguemines. On the German right the American XX Corps was in sight of the West Wall and in position to carry the attack directly across the Sarre and into the main line of fortifications. (*Map XXXVIII*)

At the moment Hitler considered the XX Corps attack the most serious of all the threats to the West Wall.[26] In the sector between Merzig and Saarlautern the West Wall was more strongly fortified than at any other point—and Hitler had committed himself to the thesis of West Wall impregnability. Furthermore, in this sector the West Wall shielded the great industrial centers of the Saar Basin; on 27 November the *First Army* had been told that its primary mission was the defense of the Saar mines and factories.[27] But al-

[26] *OKH/General der Pioniere und Festungen, Aktennotizen, Band III.* A report of a Hitler staff conference on 28 November 1944 is included in the foregoing.

[27] *Army Group G KTB,* this date. When Knobelsdorff took command of the *First Army* in September he was told to hold the Moselle as long as possible and thus keep the industrial production of the Saar intact. MS #B–222 (Knobelsdorff).

though Hitler may have briefly considered an operation for the recovery of Alsace and Lorraine which would have brought reinforcements to the *Army Group G* front,[28] the project for a great counteroffensive in the Ardennes was never forgotten nor were any but the most meager measures taken to restore the fighting strength of the forces under Balck's command.

The *Army Group G* commander did what he could to wring adequate support from *OB WEST*, and thus indirectly from OKW. He described what he considered to be an alteration in American tactics. Earlier the Americans had attacked in force in a few sectors, giving the Germans opportunity to concentrate at the points of pressure. Now the Americans tended to break up their former large "assault reserves" and launch a whole series of smaller assault detachments in attacks on a wide front. The superior mobility of the American forces allowed a rapid regrouping after the initial penetrations and kept the Germans constantly off balance. These tactics, said Balck, could be met only by building up strong, armored, counterattack reserves behind all parts of the front. But such reserves, as Balck himself admitted, were not available.[29]

The *Army Group G* commander also addressed himself to his troops—in his usual strident manner. On the night of 29 November a general order prescribed "no more withdrawals." The battle now must be fought to weaken the enemy and win time. All traces of the "West Wall psychosis" must be ruthlessly eliminated (apparently the propaganda on the strength of the West Wall had been too successful), and the troops must be told that safety lay not behind concrete but in bitter battle before the German frontier. Finally, wrote Balck, the army group commander will not tolerate "rear-area swine" but will have only soldiers in his command.[30]

Actually there was little Balck or Knobelsdorff could do but issue resounding orders. On 30 November the only reserves on the *First Army* right wing (the *21st Panzer Division* Kampfgruppe) were detailed to make one attack after another in the St. Barbara sector, but without avail. About midnight *Army Group G* ordered Knobelsdorff to pull the right wing of the *LXXXII Corps* back of the Sarre, thus beginning the withdrawal into the West Wall. Subsequently Rundstedt reprimanded Knobelsdorff for this action,

[28] Hitler ordered a special briefing on 26 November for an operation to recover Alsace and Lorraine. A like operation also had been discussed in October. However, nothing came of either of the two staff conferences on the subject. *OKW/WFSt KTB Ausarbeitung, Der Westen.*

[29] *Army Group G KTB,* 28 Nov 44.

[30] *Ibid.,* 29 Nov 44.

but Balck's order had been precise: "He [the *First Army* commander] must not let the *19th VG Division* be destroyed west of the river." [31]

The 95th Division Fight for the Sarre Crossing

Although the enemy continued to evince considerable determination to keep a foothold on the west bank of the Sarre, the 95th Division prepared to buck through this delaying defense and strike immediately across the river. General Twaddle ordered up the 379th Infantry (Col. R. L. Bacon) from reserve, with the intention of sending the fresh regiment through the 377th to force a crossing near Saarlautern. (*Map XXXVII*) This attack was set for 1 December, following a large-scale air assault that was planned to soften up the German defenses along the river. In the days just past, bad flying weather had precluded any extensive co-operation from the air force in the Third Army area. On 1 December the weather broke a little. The IX Bombardment Division had scheduled an assault by eight groups of B–26 bombers, but because of failures in Pathfinder equipment and late arrivals at the initial point only four groups made it to the target zone. The medium bombers struck at Saarlautern, Ensdorf, and Fraulautern; fighter-bombers, sent over from the XIX TAC, worked on interdiction three or four miles east of the river. Visibility was too poor for the kind of pinpoint bombing needed in a river crossing operation and the ground observers reported that the air attack was only moderately successful.[32] At 1235 the last bomber ended its bombing run and General Twaddle gave the word for the 95th Division to advance.

The plan of attack hinged on the effort to be made by the 379th, which was to cross the river near Saarlautern, establish a bridgehead, and then continue the attack by turning sharply north and clearing the east bank in the neighborhood of Rehlingen—thus permitting the 90th Division to cross in that area. On the right the 378th was instructed to sweep the enemy from the west bank and then, on orders from the division commander, force a crossing in its zone and continue the attack to the east. On the left the 377th also had orders to clear out the enemy to its front. During this operation the 379th was to pass through the right wing of the 377th, which would lay down fire to

[31] *Ibid.,* 1 Dec 44.

[32] Ninth AF Summary of Opns, 1 Dec 44. The 322d, 323d, 334th, and 387th Groups took part in this attack.

support the crossing attack by the 379th and then take its place in division reserve.[33]

The G–2 estimate of the number of enemy in front of the 95th Division, on both sides of the river, set the figure at 10,000 with elements of the *559th VG Division*, *347th Division*, and *36th VG Division* represented.[34] The 95th Division had incurred heavier losses than any other division in the XX Corps during the period since 9 November.[35] The inclusion of over thirty-five hundred replacements during November, mostly untried riflemen and officers with no experience in battle, would tend to reduce the combat effectiveness of the division. However, the relatively small number of combat fatigue and sick cases which had been hospitalized by the 95th Division indicated that it was fairly fresh and that its morale was high.[36] Moreover, the 95th approached the fight at the Sarre with an impressive number of guns in support, since the III Corps artillery and the 4th Tank Destroyer Group had been sent forward to aid the division during the crossing operations.

The first hours of the 95th Division attack on the afternoon of 1 December showed that the German troops still west of the river intended to make a fight of it. The 377th Infantry met stiff resistance, but finally completed the job of clearing Felsberg about 1500. Colonel Gaillard then sent his 3d Battalion marching east toward Saarlautern. The 1st Battalion, on the north flank, was pinned down at St. Barbara in an action lasting all afternoon. Enemy tanks and infantry, supported by guns across the river, fought with much determination in the village itself. The 378th, attacking toward the high ground in its front and hampered by an open south flank, also found the going slow and difficult. Slight gains were made on the left, aided by the advance of the 377th, and an important hill near Berus was taken. But the 1st Battalion, advancing on the right where maneuver was restricted by streams and flooded fields, was checked by an enemy detachment holding a hill west of Bisten

[33] 95th Div AAR, 1 Dec 44.

[34] The *87th Regiment* of the *36th VG Division* had been attached to the decimated and disorganized *347th Division*. MS #B–223 (Wellm).

[35] The enlisted casualties in the 95th Division during the month of November totaled 4,246. 95th Div G–1 Jnl, Dec 44.

[36] The XX Corps estimates for November place the number of 95th Division sick at 658. XX Corps AAR, Nov 44. This low figure probably is reasonably accurate. But only the 379th Infantry After Action Report makes a sick return: 177 officers and men during November. An undoubted factor in the high morale of the division was the large number of prisoners it had taken (estimated by the XX Corps at 7,036).

and was forced to fall back on Merten. In spite of these reverses at the flanks of the division, two battalions of the 379th Infantry passed through the 377th and as the day ended swung into the advance down the gentle slope leading to Saarlautern.

The events of 1 December had shattered any German hopes of a systematic and homogeneous defense west of the river. The loss of the high ground near Berus was a matter of special concern to the *First Army* for it meant that the Americans could drive a wedge between the *LXXXII Corps*, forming the army right wing, and the *XIII SS Corps*, which constituted the army center. Knobelsdorff wished to retake the lost hill but found that there was insufficient artillery ammunition at the German guns to support such an attack. Apparently there was a plentiful supply of shells in the dumps at Darmstadt, but these were not reaching the front lines (probably the American air attack was the answer).[37]

Despite the fact that his *First Army* commander had just received a stiff official reprimand from Rundstedt for "continually falling back," Balck issued an order at 2130 for all troops north of an east-west line through Dillingen to retire behind the Sarre. Two hours later he extended the withdrawal zone as far south as Saarlautern and ordered the *XIII SS Corps* to pull its right flank back into the wooded area between Berus and the river.[38] During the night of 1–2 December most of the remaining troops of the *LXXXII Corps* moved across the Rehlingen bridge or were ferried across the Sarre, but rear guard elements of the *21st Panzer Division* remained in the vicinity of St. Barbara and other German detachments congregated to fight a holding action at Saarlautern.

Friendly planes again intervened on the morning of 2 December to help the American infantry. Eight groups of medium bombers, sent over by the IX Bombardment Division, blasted targets in and around Saarlautern. This time the ground observers reported that most of the drops were highly accurate.[39] The bombing must have shaken and scattered the defenders of the city; when the 2d Battalion of the 379th drove into the edge of Saarlautern the enemy reacted slowly and in disorganized fashion. By 1500 the battalion had driven the Germans from the barracks in the western section of the city and started a house-to-house fight deep inside the city itself. Only the 2d

[37] *Army Group G KTB Anlagen*, 3 Dec 44.

[38] *Ibid.*

[39] 95th Div AAR, 2 Dec 44.

Battalion was committed in this engagement, because Colonel Bacon wished to hold his 1st Battalion for use in the crossing and the 3d Battalion had not yet come up.

The 95th Division continued to have trouble on its flanks, and attempts to shake free the regiments at the shoulders of the salient formed by the 379th were countered with desperate resolution. The 1st Battalion of the 377th Infantry finally gave up the effort to clear the resurgent enemy from St. Barbara and withdrew to the west, leaving the division artillery and friendly planes to smash the village.[40] This merciless pounding by shells and bombs ended the fight, and by early afternoon St. Barbara and its key ridge were again in American hands. The 377th began to mop up. By the night of 3 December the regiment had completed its mission of clearing the west bank and was placed in reserve at Wallerfangen.

The 378th Infantry met "extremely bitter resistance" on 2 December. The troops on the left flank fought their way northeast and by nightfall held Pikard, only three thousand yards from the center of Saarlautern. This advance had been made against "some of the most severe resistance the regiment had yet encountered."[41] The regiment now was extended along a very wide front, with the southern wing aligned almost at right angles to the forward line. All attempts to bring the right forward through Falck and Merten were unsuccessful.

The fighting of the past few days had taken heavy toll in the 95th Division, particularly in the ranks of the 377th and 378th. The effective combat strength in four of the infantry battalions was reduced to 55 percent or less. Very few replacements were available. At the close of 2 December the 95th Division G-3 Periodic Report called the division "tired," and for the first time in its

[40] Sgt. Roy E. Holcomb, A Company, 607th Tank Destroyer Battalion, was awarded the DSC for action in the attack against the "enemy-held town" on 1 December. A platoon of tank destroyers had been stopped inside the town by a well-sited German Mark IV. Sergeant Holcomb took a bazooka, crawled to within fifty yards of the tank, partially disabled the tank, and forced it to withdraw. A second enemy tank took over the position. Sergeant Holcomb crawled forward again and fired four rounds, crippling the tank. He was killed by return fire. However, the second German tank withdrew to another position, where it was destroyed by TD fire. Company A of the 377th Infantry made a spirited attack to clear "the newly won town of St. Barbara" at dawn on 1 December when the enemy in "great strength" tried to dislodge the Americans. Twice wounded in this attack, 2d Lt. Frederick K. Baker, A Company, 377th Infantry Regiment, received the DSC.

[41] The hard-fighting Germans were probably from the *87th Regiment, 36th VG Division,* which was nearly destroyed in the battle on the right wing of the *XIII SS Corps.* MS #B-223 (Wellm). Simon, who commanded this corps, says that the *87th* and the remnants of the *347th Division* fought "tooth and nail" in this sector. MS #B-487.

SAARLAUTERN. *The area shown in the photograph is indicated on Map XXXVII. Circles indicate pillboxes.*

record failed to carry the notation of "Excellent" or "Superior" under the Combat Efficiency heading. When more complete reports arrived in the division headquarters the efficiency rating of some battalions was changed to read "very weak." [42] Such was the condition of the division which had yet to force a river crossing in the face of a fortified line. The fortunes of war, however, were about to favor the 95th.

In late afternoon of 2 December an artillery observation plane discovered an intact bridge spanning the Sarre between the center of the city of Saarlautern and the suburb north of the river; this bridge led to the main road connecting Saarlautern and Saarlautern-Roden. The air photo showing this find was sent to the commander of the 379th. After interrogating prisoners on details of the city plan and consulting General Twaddle, Colonel Bacon determined to send his 1st Battalion to seize the bridge. The Sarre makes a loop at the northwestern corner of the city of Saarlautern, and Colonel Bacon decided to take advantage of this configuration by sending the battalion across the near segment of the loop. After this move the attack would dash inland through the northern suburb and take the bridge from the rear or north side. With the bridge in the hands of the 1st Battalion, contact then could be made with the reserve battalion, which was now in position to join the 2d Battalion in the push eastward through the main part of the city.

In the early morning hours of 3 December the 1st Battalion (Lt. Col. Tobias R. Philbin) [43] moved through the barracks area, thus avoiding entanglement in the streets of Saarlautern, and forward to the river. Philbin's troops were fresh, for the battalion had not been engaged since the fighting at Metz. At 0545 the first assault boats shoved off to make the 125-foot crossing. Ten minutes later the whole battalion was on the opposite bank. The noise of the American guns shelling Saarlautern had drowned out all sounds of the crossing and no German outposts were seen as the first troops debarked. Company B and a platoon of Company C, 320th Combat Engineer Battalion, led the surprise attack, double-timing a distance of about two thousand yards through an empty park and down the road to the bridge. Here a light German tank was discovered, sitting beside the bridge exit. In the half-light, shrouded by the fog and rain, the American advance guard moved up to the tank. A German inside the tank suddenly awoke to the danger and started frantically

[42] 95th Div G–3 Jnl, 3 Dec 44.

[43] Colonel Philbin had earlier won distinction in the fighting west of Metz and had been awarded the DSC for bravery in action near Gravelotte.

working his radio, persisting until he was knifed by the commander of D Company. Another made a dash for the switch connected with the demolitions on the bridge and was shot by Colonel Philbin. The engineers, commanded by Lt. Edward Herbert, raced onto the bridge, cut the demolition wires, and surprised and killed four German guards at the opposite end of the bridge. In the meantime L Company, reinforced for this mission, had driven east through the city proper and arrived at the southern end of the bridge. With their backs secure the men of the 1st Battalion faced about and pushed out to the north. The enemy troops on the far side of the river seem to have been widely scattered and were able to gather only small parties of engineers to counterattack, all of which were handily beaten off. But the German artillery, working hard to destroy the bridge structure by shellfire, succeeded in making the bridge so hot that the engineers were unable to remove all the demolition charges until late in the afternoon.[44] At nightfall the bridge still was undamaged and in American hands, the 607th Tank Destroyer Battalion had put tank destroyers across to reinforce the 1st Battalion,[45] and the 2d and 3d Battalions had taken nearly all of the city and tightened the hold on the bridge. After dark the Germans made a daredevil attempt to demolish the bridge by running in tanks loaded with explosives. The leading tank was destroyed when only some two hundred yards from the bridge and this venture was abandoned.[46]

The unexpected American success at the Saarlautern bridge had imperiled the German defense scheme and greatly perturbed the higher German commanders. Field Marshal Rundstedt was informed of what had happened soon after the event and ordered the *First Army* commander to attack at once, destroy the bridge, and hold the east bank of the Sarre "at all costs." *Army Group G* immediately began an investigation, at the behest of *OB WEST*, to assess the blame for the loss of the Saarlautern bridge; it finally reported that the bridge guards had all been killed during the attack and that the

[44] The engineers finally took more than three tons of explosives from the bridge and from chambers built into its stone piers.

[45] The platoon from the 607th was commanded by 1st Lt. Richard A. Reynolds, who led his men through the town and across the bridge to assist the infantry, exposing himself constantly to direct the platoon with no regard for his own safety. Lieutenant Reynolds was killed later in the action. He was awarded the DSC posthumously.

[46] The details of the *coup de main* at the bridge are given in Historical Division Combat Interviews. See also 95th Div AAR, 3 Dec 44.

Americans had engineered a surprise by using a captured German tank.[47] This explanation seems to have been accepted without further question and the matter was dropped. In any event the Americans had a bridge and a foothold across the river, while the enemy on the spot was too weak to prevent the establishment of a real bridgehead—no matter what orders came from Rundstedt's headquarters.

[47] *Army Group G KTB* and *OB WEST KTB* for this date. See also MS #B-078 (Mellenthin). Word of the German failure at the bridge reached Hitler on the following day. Rundstedt's headquarters reported that "the Fuehrer was enraged." *Army Group G KTB Anlagen,* 4 Dec 44.

CHAPTER XII

The XII Corps Attack Toward the West Wall (1-18 December)

At the end of November the Third Army was closing up to the Sarre River. As yet, General Patton's intention to secure at least one bridgehead east of the river in each of the two corps zones had not been realized. It appeared likely, however, that the bulk of the Third Army would soon be across the Sarre. Beyond lay the West Wall, which, insofar as the section facing the Third Army was concerned, remained an unknown quantity. The optimistic prediction by higher headquarters that Patton's troops would reach the Rhine by mid-December had been quietly forgotten. The Third Army commander himself had gradually abandoned the hope of a quick break-through to the Rhine; at this stage he seems to have been concerned simply with driving steadily forward, going as far as his strength and supplies would permit. Meanwhile the First and Ninth Army attack on the Aachen front, begun on 16 November, had run into difficulties. Neither of the two armies had yet reached the Roer River, despite the fact that ten divisions had been put into the attack on a 24-mile front. It seemed possible that a stalemate might result at the Roer River; therefore, at the close of November, the SHAEF and 12th Army Group staffs turned to consider alternative strategy. Progress on the Third Army front and in Alsace, where the 6th Army Group had breached the Belfort Gap position and reached the Rhine, offered some chance of reward. On 27 November Eisenhower ordered General Devers to attack northward with the object of cracking the West Wall west of the Rhine, thus aiding the Third Army in its drive toward the Saar Basin. The SHAEF planning staff, on 28 November, considered the possible results of reinforcing a joint offensive by the Third Army and the 6th Army Group:

More important than the capture of ground would be the destruction of the Germans in the area between the Moselle and the Rhine. It is probable that this offensive will attract considerable German resources from the northern and central sectors, and it is possible that this movement of reserves may resolve the impasse at the Roer. . . . Although the joint Third Army–Seventh Army offensive is not in the most important sector of the front, it offers the best chance of quick returns and of getting the main offensive underway once more.[1]

The Fight for Sarre-Union

By 30 November the XII Corps had come to a halt, except on its projecting right wing where the 4th Armored Division was fighting doggedly to outflank Sarre-Union.[2] The corps front extended some twenty-five miles, with the left wing touching the XX Corps near Béning-lès-St. Avold, on the Rosselle, and the right in contact with the XV Corps near Mackwiller.[3] (*Map XXXIX*) In the north the forward line had not yet crossed the Metz–Sarreguemines railroad. Farther south the XII Corps had closed up to the Maderbach in several places, but the enemy continued to hold a few bridgeheads on its western bank. In the segment formed by the Canal des Houillères de la Sarre and the Sarre River the corps main line of resistance turned somewhat at right angles, since the 25th Reconnaissance Squadron had pushed north to Harskirchen and had cleared the wider portion of the triangle. Beyond the Sarre the 4th Armored Division faced toward Sarre-Union and the hills overlooking the town from the east.

The 4th Armored Division advance had penetrated the southern German defense perimeter around Sarre-Union by 1 December and had attained a point where a direct assault could be made on the town itself. For this operation the 101st Infantry, which had been moved across the Sarre and brought up on the left flank of the 4th Armored Division, would be committed with the armor in a joint attack to bring the infantry straight north into Sarre-Union while the armor made a close-in envelopment on the east.

[1] SHAEF G–3 Notes on Immediate Prospects of Western Front, 28 Nov 44, SHAEF SGS File, Post OVERLORD Planning 381, II.

[2] The tank losses of the 4th Armored Division during November had not been very high: 36 mediums and 10 lights irreparably damaged. The number of killed and wounded also was moderate: 220 and 805, respectively. However, the November battles had taken a heavy toll in the armored infantry battalions; they averaged only half strength at the beginning of December. The nonbattle casualties for the month of November amounted to 1,137 officers and men, mostly from the armored infantry. 4th Armd AAR, Nov 44.

[3] The turn to the north by the XV Corps had extended the battle lines east of the Sarre-Union sector. Here on the *First Army* extreme left wing the *256th VG Division*, the *245th Division*, and the *361st VG Division* faced the XV Corps and fought to bar the road to Bitche and Wissembourg. On 1 December elements of the 44th Infantry Division were echeloned to the right rear of the 4th Armored Division in an attack directed at Tieffenbach.

Sarre-Union was a small manufacturing town, with a prewar population of about three thousand. During the summer and fall of 1944 it had been an important lateral communications center, and now it provided an anchor position for the western wing of the *LXXXIX Corps*. Upon the withdrawal of the main body of the *Panzer Lehr Division* at the end of November, the defense of this area devolved on the *25th Panzer Grenadier Division*, which was equipped with some eighteen tanks of its own and could be reinforced by a Kampfgruppe from *Panzer Lehr*, now in close reserve, or by armor from the *11th Panzer Division*, holding the sector on the right flank of the division. Sarre-Union itself was not strongly held, the main German force being deployed on the hills north and east of the town behind an outpost line running along the road to Mackwiller.

On the morning of 1 December, CCB and the 101st Infantry began a co-ordinated attack. CCB, employing the 8th Tank Battalion and 51st Armored Infantry Battalion, made its push in two columns, the right attacking to take Hill 318, north of Mackwiller, and the left driving in the German outposts east of Rimsdorf.[4] The 101st Infantry launched its attack with the 3d Battalion, formed in a column of companies advancing on Sarre-Union, while the 1st Battalion moved out to clear the Bannholtz woods on the right of the 101st Infantry zone.

CCB found the going slow on the narrow, muddy roads, and became involved in a succession of skirmishes which intensified in violence as the Americans neared Hill 318.[5] Additional tanks and armored infantry from CCA were brought into action in the CCB zone, but the tanks mired down. About noon Company A of the 8th Tank Battalion beat off a detachment of tanks from the *Panzer Lehr* and the armored infantry seized the hill. But the affray had been costly. The attackers suffered eighty-three casualties, including Lt. Col. Arthur L. West, commanding officer of the 10th Infantry Battalion, and Major Van Arnam, commanding officer of the 51st. The 1st Battalion of the 101st Infantry likewise had encountered determined resistance early in the advance. The battalion commander, Lt. Col. L. M. Kirk, was wounded at the outset and his men spent most of the day pinned down by intense fire from the front and flanks. Finally, the progress of the CCB attack forced the Ger-

[4] During December the type of fighting somewhat nullified the task force or combat team organization which had been used by the 4th Armored Division as conventional tactical organization in the earlier battles in Lorraine. Therefore, reference in this chapter generally will be made to the organic units of the division.

[5] In addition to the 4th Armored After Action Reports and Journals, a semiofficial diary kept by Major Spires has been used as a source in reconstructing the 4th Armored operations during early December.

TANKS AND ARMORED INFANTRY *of CCA starting out to aid CCB in the fight for Hill 318 north of Mackwiller.*

man line to give, and with the help of the regimental reserve the 1st Battalion cleared the woods.

The 3d Battalion of the 101st made its approach to Sarre-Union under cover of a ridge line, close to the east bank of the Sarre, which screened the column from the enemy on the hills to the northeast. The two leading companies, I and K, entered Sarre-Union, finding only a handful of Germans. The Americans continued through the north side of the town toward Hill 254, which had been set as the battalion objective, but the enemy on the hill countered with machine gun and mortar fire, inflicting some losses on the attackers.[6] The two rifle companies had had a strength of only about fifty men apiece when the advance began; as night came on they were withdrawn from Sarre-Union, since they were hardly strong enough to hold the town against a determined sortie from the hills.

[6] Sgt. Walter A. Young of I Company here repelled a counterattack with a captured machine gun. He was awarded the DSC.

During the night the Germans reoccupied Sarre-Union and placed combat outposts in the railroad station and the barracks area on the south edge of the town. As a result the 101st Infantry was forced to begin a systematic reduction of the enemy positions on 2 December. A platoon of tank destroyers moved forward and knocked out the enemy antitank guns in the station. In the course of the afternoon, the Americans gained control of the barracks and occupied the town. That night a company of the 104th Infantry which had crossed the Sarre the previous day was sent in to strengthen the defense of the town. East of Sarre-Union the 4th Armored Division cut the Sarre-Union–Domfessel road and seized Hill 332 on the highway to Voellerdingen, leaving only the Oermingen road open for an enemy withdrawal to the north. The Germans fought stubbornly to recover the lost ground, and both of the 4th Armored combat commands had to beat off counterattacks made by a company or two of infantry and supported by single tank platoons hastily thrown in from the *Panzer Lehr*. These counterattacks might have been more serious had not American fighter-bombers swooped down on a concentration of tanks near Domfessel and destroyed several.

Although the net was closing around Sarre-Union, the enemy dealt one last blow at the troops inside the town, this time employing a small Kampfgruppe from the *11th Panzer Division*. At noon on 3 December eight German tanks, supported by the *Begleit (Escort) Company* of the *11th Panzer Division*, charged down the Oermingen road and into Sarre-Union, capturing the command post of I Company and overrunning five 57-mm. antitank guns which had been put in a cemetery overlooking the road but which, as usual, were no match for heavy armor.[7] The American infantry took shelter in the cellars while an artillery forward observer, hidden in a house surrounded by Germans, radioed back for artillery fire. In ten minutes the 105-mm. howitzers of the 101st Field Artillery Battalion and the regimental cannon company fired 380 rounds into the area. This blanket concentration knocked out two German tanks and encouraged the rest to flee the city—leaving the opposing riflemen to fight it out.[8] The following day the 104th Infantry and a company

[7] Capt. Edward R. Radzwich, commanding I Company, was awarded the DSC for bravery shown in this action.

[8] There is considerable disagreement as to the German strength in the counterattack of 3 December, disagreement that points up the difficulty of establishing the exact facts of any confused action such as this. Early reports entered in the XII Corps G–3 Journal say that eleven tanks and three infantry companies were involved. The diary of the commanding officer of the 101st Infantry says that six tanks and about a hundred enemy infantry were encountered. Officers of the 3d Battalion, 101st Infantry, when interviewed in

of the 37th Tank Battalion ended the battle for Sarre-Union by a methodical search of every house, killing or capturing the German infantry who had been unable to escape through the shellfire.[9]

Meanwhile, the 4th Armored Division had been reorganizing under a new commander and waiting in the area around Domfessel for the 26th Division on its left and the 44th Division (of the XV Corps) on its right to come abreast. On 3 December Maj. Gen. Hugh J. Gaffey relinquished his post as the Third Army Chief of Staff to Brig. Gen. Hobart R. Gay and relieved Maj. Gen. John S. Wood, who had commanded the 4th Armored Division in the successful campaign across France and during the heartbreaking actions in the autumn mud.[10] Wood, a brave and energetic commander, had been affected by the strain of battle, like so many of his officers and men. Fatigued as he was, Wood could no longer carry the burden of his command. General Patton and General Eddy reluctantly concluded that he would have to go back to the United States for a rest. The 4th Armored Division itself was badly in need of rest and reorganization. Continuous fighting, under conditions which prewar field manuals had taught were impossible for armor, had seriously reduced its tank complement and induced severe losses among its experienced combat personnel—particularly officers. On the night of 2 December, therefore, when General Patton already had decided to send his chief of staff to relieve General Wood, the XII Corps commander requested that the 4th Armored Division be replaced as quickly as possible by a division from the XV Corps.[11] The 4th Armored, however, had enough of its old élan and drive to make one more substantial push before its relief began on 7 December.

the field recalled the German strength at eight tanks and a company and a half of infantry. Hist Div Combat Interviews. Most of the enemy prisoners were taken from one company, the *Begleit (Escort) Company* of the *11th Panzer Division*. 26th Div G–2 Jnl, 3 Dec 44. In any event it is doubtful whether the rifle strength of the 3d Battalion, 101st Infantry, was more than 150 men at this time.

[9] The German counterattacks on 2 and 3 December had been made by scratch units thrown into action by the *Panzer Lehr* and *11th Panzer Divisions*. Both of these formations were already under orders to go to *Army Group B*. The German reverses on 2 and 3 December were keenly felt in higher commands, and the chief of staff of the *First Army* reports on the night of 3 December that even Wietersheim, "who has nerve," is depressed. *Army Group G KTB* and *Anlagen*.

[10] General Wood was returned to the United States for rest and recuperation; he subsequently took command of the Armored Replacement Training Center. Brig. Gen. H. L. Earnest, who had earlier commanded an independent task force in the dash across northern Brittany, relieved Col. W. P. Withers as commander of CCA, 4th Armored Division.

[11] XII Corps G–3 Jnl, 2 Dec 44: "The 4th Armored Division . . . should be withdrawn as soon as possible. The need for rest and readjustment is acute, because of poor physical condition and some disorganization, due to the loss of key leaders, including the division commander."

The XII Corps Left and Center Advance on Sarreguemines

On 1 December a new Operational Directive alerted the 80th and 35th Infantry Divisions and the 6th Armored Division for an attack on 4 December intended to carry forward the corps left and center in a limited straightening of the line.[12] The 35th Division, theoretically the corps reserve but actually with some elements in the line, relieved CCB, 6th Armored Division, in front of Puttelange on the night of 2–3 December. The 6th Armored Division, in turn, took over a portion of the 80th Division main line of resistance. Here, on the left, XII Corps units already had broken through the main part of the Maginot Line. The general Third Army plan provided for a limited advance by the 80th Division, using one regimental combat team, to gain the commanding ground along the Sarre northeast of Farebersviller. The 6th Armored Division was to drive toward Sarreguemines, meanwhile extending its left flank so as to pinch out the 80th Division, seize the high ground in the Cadenbronn area, and clear the west bank of the Sarre. The 35th Division, on the right of the 6th Armored, was earmarked to continue the drive alongside the 26th Division and 4th Armored Division once the left and center of the corps had been brought up to or across the Sarre River.

The German troops facing the XII Corps were in poor condition to sustain any determined attack and were greatly outweighed in numbers and materiel.[13] On the right wing of the *XIII SS Corps* the *36th VG Division*—badly mauled but still reckoned a good division—had pulled back to the northeast. It was now stationed in the Warndt Forest area facing the 5th Infantry Division and the American cavalry detachments screening the gap between the XX and XII Corps. Opposite the 80th Division and the 6th Armored, along a front extending from the Rosselle River to a point just south of Puttelange, the *17th SS Panzer Grenadier Division* was deployed. This division had been in almost continuous action since early June 1944, and was about worn out. Numerous changes in command at all echelons and the constant admixture of untrained troops and unwilling *Volksdeutsche* from Eastern Europe had robbed the division of its character as an elite formation. The *17th SS* artillery, however, still retained a high reputation. On 4 December the division had a ration strength of 4,000, of which number only 1,700 were classed as infantry

[12] XII Corps Operational Directive No. 46.

[13] The German strength figures given in this paragraph are taken from a strength report forwarded by *Army Group G* to *OB WEST* as of 4 December 1944. See also estimates in MS #B–078 (Mellenthin).

effectives. South of Puttelange the *11th Panzer Division* was still in the line, although numerous and peremptory orders had come down from OKW to send the division north to the Aachen area. Very heavy fighting had reduced the division to some twenty tanks and assault guns; its total complement numbered 3,500 officers and men, but only 800 of these were armored infantry. Despite this weakness the *11th Panzer Division* remained on the Wehrmacht list of "attack" divisions.

Just before daylight on 4 December the 35th Division led off in the three-division attack. An artillery preparation had been denied in order to gain tactical surprise, and this decision paid dividends. On the left the 134th Infantry crossed the Maderbach in assault boats, encircled Puttelange, and were in possession of the city before the *17th SS* outposts could offer any resistance. The German infantry were found sleeping in their foxholes and billets; the whole business was concluded so quickly and quietly that the regiment lost only one man. On the right the 320th Infantry had a stroke of bad luck when the advance guard ran into a column of German infantry moving up to relieve their outposts on the east bank of the Maderbach. Meanwhile the 2d Battalion had crossed near Rémering-lès-Puttelange and started east along the main road. At the first crossroads the battalion encountered a large patch of barbed wire entanglements. While the column was halted the enemy brought down a terrific shelling, immobilizing the battalion for several hours.[14] While the right-wing advance was checked, the 35th Division left succeeded in driving a deep salient in the German lines east of Puttelange and General Eddy ordered General Baade to continue the attack toward the Sarre, supporting the 26th Division or taking over its mission if so required.

The 6th Armored Division and 80th Division began their attack well after daylight on 4 December. It was preceded by an intense fire from the corps artillery which lasted for an hour and eight minutes and blasted the Germans out of their forward positions.[15] On the extreme left of the corps the 80th Division put the 318th Infantry (reinforced by a company from the 702d Tank Battalion and a company from the 610th Tank Destroyer Battalion) into a limited-objective attack and took Farebersviller, which had been so

[14] During the fight near Rémering Sgt. Joseph J. Lazarski, E Company, 320th Infantry, led his platoon in an attack to wipe out a concentration of enemy machine guns. When all but two had been accounted for Sergeant Lazarski went on alone, was severely wounded, but silenced these last machine guns. He was awarded the DSC.

[15] In the first days of December the XII Corps artillery had fired an average of 9,000 rounds per day. But on 4 December the ammunition expended rose to 27,575 rounds. XII Corps Opns Rpt, 4 Dec 44.

tough an obstacle for the division a few days earlier. Then the regiment drove the Germans off the hills to the northeast, rounding up 327 prisoners during the day. South of the 318th Infantry, CCA of the 6th Armored Division inaugurated an attack with dismounted infantry and supporting tank platoons to take the high ground in the vicinity of Mont de Cadenbronn. The combat command made its advance along two east-west ridge lines, easily reducing the villages in the valley with artillery and tank guns firing from the heights. Since the 318th Infantry had halted after reaching its objective, CCA was forced to attack with its north flank in the air. Toward the end of the day one of its tank columns, which was moving to encircle Cadenbronn from the north, came under flanking fire from German 88's located beyond the range of the American tank guns and lost eight tanks.

The second day of the XII Corps attack toward the Sarre was carried by the 6th Armored Division and the 35th Division against little resistance. The remaining enemy infantry hurriedly crossed behind the Sarre, and the German batteries displaced to safer positions. By midafternoon CCA patrols were on the bluffs overlooking the river north of Sarreguemines and the command had its guns ranging in on Grosbliederstroff. In the meantime the 2d Cavalry Group had moved forward along the north bank of the Rosselle River, where it had been scouting on the left flank of the corps. During the day a cavalry patrol passed the German frontier near St. Nicolas, one of the first—if not the first—incursions by the XII Corps on the soil of the Third Reich. Subsequently the cavalry crossed the Rosselle near the village of Rosbruck and started east to cover CCA's open flank.

In the 35th Division zone all battalions of the 134th and 320th Infantry Regiments put patrols along the west bank of the Sarre before dark. The 2d Battalion of the 134th Infantry reached the southeastern outskirts of Sarreguemines and there began a five-day battle for control of the city. Sarreguemines, an industrial center with a prewar population of around 15,000, occupied a commanding site at the confluence of the Sarre and Blies Rivers—both of which had to be crossed during the northeastwardly advance by the XII Corps. The British and American air forces had used the city as a target for some months past because of its importance as a rail center, and as a result the German garrison had sought to protect itself by building numerous concrete bomb shelters. These shelters and the many substantial factory buildings made the city a demifortress for the troops of the *17th SS* now acting as defenders.[16] The Americans' task was made even more difficult by the fact that Sarreguemines is built on both sides of the Sarre; once the enemy relinquished his hold west of the river he could continue the fight from buildings in the eastern part of the city—which is what he did.

CCA put a one-tank task force into Sarreguemines on 6 December, although as the result of erroneous information. Colonel Hines, the CCA commander, had been told that troops of the 35th Division were in possession of the town and set off with his S–3, Lt. Col. A. N. Ward, on a liaison trip. Inside the town the single American tank received an ovation from the French members of the population—but found no other Americans. Hines decided to wait until the infantry came in from the south. Eventually he made contact with the 2d Battalion of the 134th Infantry, which had arrived in the outskirts of Sarreguemines the previous evening. Light tanks then were brought in from CCA to support the infantry in the fight to clear the western sector of the city. By midafternoon of 6 December the 6th Armored had completed the mission assigned by the XII Corps. The division would now assume a defensive role, extending its zone to the north and covering the north flank of the XII Corps between the 35th Division on the right and the XX Corps on the left. The slow advance in the autumn mud had cost the 6th Armored heavily in tanks and men; the armored infantry in particular had been reduced by battle and by combat fatigue. The Lorraine Campaign had given little opportunity for the dashing tactics and rapid movement that had characterized the 6th Armored drive across Brittany. But the division had punched and probed its way to the Sarre under conditions of terrain and weather as difficult as those any American armored division in the European Theater of Operations would be called upon to endure.

At the end of 6 December the 6th Armored and 35th Divisions held the western bank of the Sarre in force from Grosbliederstroff to Wittring, a distance of about ten miles. Late in the evening General Eddy canceled the orders for the 35th Division to cross the Sarre, pushing the date ahead until 8 December when the 26th Division could be in position to attack alongside the 35th. South and east of Wittring the French had built one of the strongest

[16]The *17th SS Panzer Grenadier Division* was only the wreck of a division and Balck believed it incapable of putting up much of a fight. Since the *17th* belonged to the *Waffen-SS* it could be reconstituted and re-equipped only by Himmler, who showed little interest in the fate of this division. On 5 December, therefore, Balck asked *OB WEST* for another division to replace the *17th SS*, but without effect. *Army Group G KTB*

sectors of the Maginot Line. The 26th Division was now in process of closing up to this section of the Maginot Line, and the XII Corps commander envisaged a co-ordinated attack in which the 35th and 26th Divisions would crack the two wings of the German position, the one breaching the line on the Sarre while the other drove through the Maginot Line.

The 4th Armored Division Drive from Domfessel to Singling

The American seizure of the hills east of Sarre-Union had compressed the opposing German forces into the narrow, wooded area between the Sarre River and Eichel Creek. On the night of 3 December the *25th Panzer Grenadier Division* and the tank detachment from the *11th Panzer Division* started a retreat northeast across the Eichel. General Gaffey began the pursuit the next day, with both combat commands moving to establish a bridgehead across that stream. CCB, on the left, overran a few small rear guard detachments, and shortly after noon the 8th Tank Battalion took on ten enemy tanks near Voellerdingen, destroying two and driving off the rest. A small task force (Maj. A. F. Irzyk) fought its way into Voellerdingen and there captured a bridge intact; by nightfall CCB had an advance guard across on the enemy bank of the Eichel. During the night enemy patrols tried to destroy the bridge but were beaten off.

CCA, which had been reinforced by the 37th Tank Battalion, in reserve since 19 November and now in good condition by comparison with the other battle-worn battalions, sent a task force (Maj. Harold Cohen) to take Domfessel. The village was only lightly held by a small force from the *Panzer Lehr*, but the Germans had torn up the road which ran through it.[17] As a result the command was halted while the advance detachment filled in craters, cleared a way around a blown overpass, and bridged a creek in the center of the village. While the Americans were stopped here, the German artillery opened up with heavy guns and knocked out five tanks. This was only the beginning of the losses which the 4th Armored would suffer under heavy and accurate artillery fire from German batteries and self-propelled single guns now emplaced northeast generally out of American artillery range.[18]

[17] Sgt. Paul Porter, B Company, 53d Armored Infantry Battalion, was awarded the DSC for "repeated acts of heroism" at Domfessel, engaging the enemy in hand-to-hand combat "wherever he encountered them." Sergeant Porter was wounded while attempting to rescue a wounded medical aid man.

[18] The organic German artillery was reinforced by the *401st Volks Artillery Corps*.

During the morning of 5 December the 35th Tank Battalion and the 53d Armored Infantry Battalion gained a bridgehead across the Eichel for CCA. About noon the fresh 37th Tank Battalion passed through the bridgehead to begin a dash in the direction of Bining under orders from General Gaffey to go as far as possible, but with a limiting objective set at Rimling. Although Bining itself was not important, the little village controlled the entrance to Rohrbach-lès-Bitche, an important communications center and barracks area. At this moment, when the XII Corps was trying to take Sarreguemines, the possession of Rohrbach was an essential preliminary to cutting one of the main road and rail routes for German escape to the east. In addition Rohrbach lay athwart the line of retreat for the Germans being driven out of the Forêt de Montbronn by the northward advance of the XV Corps.

Since the ground was too soft to allow movement across country, Colonel Abrams' tanks started out along the main highway leading to Bining. The enemy had prepared for such an attack and had massed the artillery of the *11th Panzer Division* and *25th Panzer Grenadier Division* to cover the road. Colonel Abrams, therefore, turned to a secondary road with the intention of wheeling near the little hamlet of Singling[19] and outflanking Bining from the west. Actually the Singling area was as dangerous to tanks as the Bining approach, for the former lay among the works of the Maginot Line and was under the guns of German batteries emplaced on the hills to the north. About a mile south of Singling the leading tank company lost five tanks simultaneously to direct hits. Daylight was ending, the 37th Tank Battalion had lost fourteen tanks to enemy guns and mud during the move north, and artillery and infantry were needed; therefore Colonel Abrams withdrew out of range.

During the day CCB had put its armored infantry on tanks and had driven as far north as Schmittviller. Since this move placed CCB in a position to thrust toward Singling, General Gaffey outlined orders that would assign the village to CCB with the intention of turning Colonel Abrams back toward Bining and Rohrbach. Abrams, closer to the action than the division commander and impressed with the danger involved in making a wheel toward Bining while the enemy still held Singling, requested permission to attack Singling and at least neutralize that village before continuing the advance on Bining. CCB was still some distance from the battlefield and the 4th Armored commander gave Colonel Abrams a free hand. Reinforced on

[19] The Singling action is described by Gordon A. Harrison in *Small Unit Actions*, a volume in the AMERICAN FORCES IN ACTION series prepared by the Historical Division, War Department.

the morning of 6 December by the 51st Armored Infantry Battalion, a field artillery battalion, and some tank destroyers, the two remaining medium tank companies of the 37th moved in to bring Singling under fire.

The village was defended by the *1st Battalion* of the *111th Panzer Grenadier Regiment*, which even at reduced strength totaled more rifles than the 51st Armored Infantry Battalion could muster. In addition, enemy tanks and assault guns were at hand to intervene in Singling and a large number of German guns were located on the high ground to the north. Finally, the town of Singling was an organic part of the Maginot Line; its periphery was dotted with bunkers, pillboxes, and gun emplacements. It soon became apparent that Singling and the covering guns on the hills could not be neutralized by fire alone. Colonel Abrams ordered up the armored infantry—which had been earmarked to take Bining—and a fight ensued for the possession of the village. When night fell a company of armored infantry and a company of tanks had a foothold in Singling, but it could not be retained under the very muzzles of the guns on the hills, and the task force withdrew. However, the fight for Singling had enabled a company of light tanks, some cavalry, and an attached battalion of the 328th Infantry to take Bining during the day. At 1815 word reached General Gaffey that the 12th Armored Division of the XV Corps would begin the relief of his tired and weakened division the next morning. The 4th Armored held in place. By 8 December most of its troops were out of the line and en route across the Sarre to rest areas near Cutting and Loudrefing.

The fighting strength of the 4th Armored Division had drained away perceptibly as its tanks were destroyed and its veteran infantry and tank crews were reduced in action after action.[20] But in spite of the fact that it

[20] Losses in experienced officer personnel had been very high since 8 November: a number of companies had had a 100 percent turnover in officers, and the battalion staffs had been decimated. The armored infantry, of course, suffered high casualties. On 2 December the 51st Armored Infantry Battalion had a rifle strength of 160 and the 53d had only 126. Company B, 51st Armored Infantry Battalion, received 128 replacements for losses between 9 November and 6 December. Tank losses also were severe. The 8th Tank Battalion, already crippled by the loss of nearly a whole medium tank company at Baerendorf, lost 14 tanks in operations between 3 and 6 December. XII Corps G–3 Jnl, 2 Dec 44. The casualties inflicted on the tank crews were particularly damaging to the division since the replacements coming in at the end of the Lorraine Campaign usually were converted riflemen or headquarters personnel who knew nothing about tanks. In one batch of replacements sent to the 37th Tank Battalion only two men had ever seen the inside of a tank—one of these as the result of having once been given a ride by a cousin in the Armored Force while training in the United States. During the latter part of 1944, training at the Armored Replacement Training Center had deteriorated and few replacements were being turned out. See The Armored Force Command and Center, AGF Study No. 27 (Historical Division, War Department).

had been fighting under conditions ill suited for armored action, the division had succeeded in fulfilling the mission of armor and had rolled up the German defense line on the Sarre for a distance of twenty miles across the front of the XII Corps zone of advance.

The Last Phase of the Advance Toward the West Wall

On 7 December the XII Corps regrouped for the next phase of the advance to the northeast. The main effort would be made by the 35th and 26th Divisions attacking abreast. The object was to bring the XII Corps into positions from which a final assault would be launched to penetrate the section of the German West Wall extending from Saarbruecken to Zweibruecken. The 6th Armored Division and the 2d Cavalry Group relieved the 80th Division, which moved back to rest areas around St. Avold. Its departure left the armor and cavalry to guard the left flank of the corps and contain Saarbruecken—which was being subjected to a daily pounding by 240-mm. howitzers and 4.5-inch guns. The 35th Division, at the moment involved in a fight for the west half of Sarreguemines, was nevertheless ready with engineer equipment and smoke generators to cross the Sarre River south of the city. The 26th Division had been following hard on the heels of the 4th Armored Division and on 5 December made the greatest gains it had won since the opening of the Lorraine Campaign. Two days later the forward elements of the division were within sight of the Maginot Line forts at Wittring and Achen.[21] The 4th Armored Division was moving out to rear areas with the pleasant prospect of warm billets and three hot meals a day, as well as with the task of recovering the scores of disabled tanks and vehicles from mud and mine fields now far behind the battle line. The 12th Armored Division (Maj. Gen. R. R. Allen),[22] fresh to the European Theater of Operations and untried, was in process of relieving the 4th Armored Division.[23]

[21] Pvt. Gordon E. Huggins, K Company, 104th Infantry, received the DSC as a result of action on 7 December. Picking up a defective grenade he smothered it against his body to save his comrades standing near. Private Huggins lost a hand and received severe fragment wounds.

[22] General Allen, a graduate of Texas A. and M. College, had joined the Army as a cavalry officer. He served in France from 1917 to 1919 with the 3d Cavalry. In 1940 he joined the 1st Armored Regiment at Fort Knox, and thereafter served with various armored units. General Allen was commanding the 20th Armored Division when, in September 1944, he was dispatched by plane to England, there taking command of the 12th Armored Division.

[23] The decision to relieve the 4th Armored Division followed General Eddy's letter of 2 December to General Patton in which he suggested that the XV Corps had a narrower front than the XII Corps and

The German *First Army* was ill disposed to meet a further attack by the XII Corps. Artillery ammunition was running short; on a number of days past the entire *First Army* had been able to fire no more than 7,000 rounds.[24] Armor was available only in small allotments of ten or twelve tanks. The infantry divisions were burned out, and the 5,700 replacements that had arrived during the first week of December were, to use one German general's expression, only drops of water on a hot stone.

To make matters worse, *OB WEST* was insistent on compliance with the orders which it had received from OKW at the beginning of December for the relief of *Panzer Lehr*, the *11th Panzer Division*, and the *401st* and *404th Volks Artillery Corps*. Knobelsdorff, the *First Army* commander, had made an issue of the matter by publicly stating that he could not take responsibility for defense of the West Wall if he lost these troops. But Knobelsdorff, for this and other reasons, had been replaced by General der Infanterie Hans von Obstfelder. Balck, the *Army Group G* head, continued to negotiate with *OB WEST* for the retention of the armor and artillery and succeeded in holding on to these formations after the deadline set for their relief. Rundstedt, however, attempted to coerce Balck into acquiescence with word that the order stripping the *First Army* had come "from the highest source." Rundstedt himself was determined that *Army Group B* should receive these reinforcements, even at the expense of Balck's weakened lines, since he feared that the Allies would make a break-through east of Aachen and drive out onto the Cologne Plain. Either Balck's argument that he had gasoline sufficient to move only one division or the steadily deteriorating situation on the *First Army* front led to a compromise on 5 December, whereby the *Panzer Lehr*

had divisions in reserve, one of which could replace the 4th Armored Division. After General Patton and General Patch agreed to this exchange the commanding generals of the XII and XV Corps met at Fénétrange on 6 December and arranged the details of the relief. The 12th Armored Division was in effect "loaned" to the XII Corps, but the corps' boundaries remained unchanged; as a result the division operated in the XII Corps zone under XV Corps command. See Seventh Army Opns Instructions No. 30, 6 Dec 1944. On 10 December Generals Haislip and Eddy made the following arrangements: the 12th Armored Division will attack with the 26th Division "if going looks easy"; if the 44th Division "gets up," the 26th Division, the 12th Armored Division, and the 44th Division will make a co-ordinated attack to penetrate the Maginot Line. See XII Corps G–3 Jnl. General Haislip did not want to commit the 12th Armored in an all-out attack until it had some battle experience.

[24] Not only was artillery ammunition in short supply, but the number of guns available to the Germans was far less than the number the Allies could bring to bear in the support of any operation. On 12 December *OB WEST* had on the Western Front 5,422 pieces of artillery, including coastal guns and antiaircraft guns of all calibers. The Eastern and Southeastern Fronts combined had 10,078 guns. *OKH/Stab Gen. Art. Beim Gen. St. d. H. KTB Anlagen #830*. This number of guns gave three guns to each kilometer on the Eastern and Western Fronts. *OKH/Stab Gen. Art. beim Gen. St. d. H. KTB Anlagen #860*.

Division and the *401st Volks Artillery Corps* started the move to the north while the *11th Panzer Division* and the *404th Volks Artillery Corps* remained in *Army Group G.*

This arrangement gave Balck only half a loaf. The *First Army* north wing was heavily engaged and the American XX Corps had driven into the first line of West Wall defenses in the Saarlautern sector. Since a breakthrough appeared imminent Balck had moved a part of the *11th Panzer Division* to the Saarlautern front on 3 December and diverted the *719th Division*, which originally had been designated as reinforcement for the hard-pressed *XIII SS Corps*, to the north. This fragmentization of the *11th Panzer Division*, the loss of the expected *719th Division*, and the relief of the *401st Volks Artillery Corps* left the *XIII SS Corps* in a poor way to meet the renewal of the American XII Corps attack.

The *Army Group G* commander was not unaware of this threat at the center of the *First Army* line; on 7 December he sent out an urgent request for "immediate" reinforcement on the grounds that the Americans were in position to achieve a "strategic penetration" along the Saarbruecken–Kaiserslautern axis which might reach Frankfurt and the Rhine. But Balck was not only fearful that his right and center might collapse; he was also concerned lest his left wing—touching on the Rhine—be broken by the American XV Corps and the road to the Palatinate thus be opened. On 8 December the three weak divisions in the line facing the XV Corps were reorganized as a special command, *Group Hoehne*, under a well-known veteran of the Eastern Front. Now *Army Group G* consisted only of the *First Army*, aligned roughly on the Sarre River, and *Group Hoehne*, deployed diagonally east of Bitche on a front extending through Hagenau to the west bank of the Rhine. Since the *Nineteenth Army* no longer had contact with the *First*, having withdrawn its right wing behind the Rhine, the *Nineteenth* would operate as a separate command under Reichsfuehrer-SS Heinrich Himmler, now *Oberbefelshaber Oberrhein* (C-in-C Upper Rhine). Needless to say, all of Balck's attempts failed to persuade OKW that a further withdrawal of the *Nineteenth Army* would have less far reaching consequences than a collapse of some portion of the *First Army* front. Not only was Balck unable to wrest any troops from Himmler but he was hard pressed to save the replacement battalions marked for his own front from reaching Himmler.

On 8 December Rundstedt appealed to OKW in an effort to call Hitler's attention to the dire conditions on the Western Front. Rundstedt permitted himself the liberty of a protest. There were, he said, too many German troops on the Eastern Front, which at the moment was generally quiet. Some of these troops should be brought back to bolster up the Western Front. Rundstedt's second complaint concerned Reich Minister Albert Speer, who, he noted, had been releasing very high figures for the production of artillery ammunition, but without getting the ammunition to the guns.

Since Rundstedt's plea fell on deaf ears, the following day he agreed to let Balck make a direct appeal to OKW with his own special problems. Balck talked to Generalleutnant August Winter, Jodl's deputy, told him how bad the situation was, and asked for moderate reinforcement: 40 to 50 assault guns, 30 to 40 tanks and an equal number of light guns, 6 new replacement battalions, and the *103d Panzer Brigade*. Winter gave what had now become the stock answer at OKW: Jodl was fully aware of the situation but could make no promises. *Army Group G*, therefore, would have to meet the onslaughts of three full-strength American corps with fourteen "paper divisions" whose actual strength (as reckoned by *OB WEST*) was equivalent to that of four or five infantry divisions and one reinforced armored division.[25]

Before sunrise on 8 December the 35th and 26th Divisions attacked to cross their respective barriers, the Sarre River and the Maginot Line. The bend in the Sarre between Sarralbe and Wittring formed the boundary between the two divisions. In the 35th Division zone General Baade began his attack at 0500 with the 134th and 320th Infantry. On the right the two leading battalions of the 320th Infantry crossed the river in assault boats and completely surprised the enemy infantry, many of whom had deserted the cold, water-filled foxholes at the river's edge and were found asleep in the houses bordering the east bank.[26] The 3d Battalion, which had intended to cross at Zetting, was pinned down on the west bank by artillery and machine gun fire from positions built into the cliffs across the river. The battalion was unable to cross until the night of 8 December when the engineers put in an infantry footbridge near Wittring. During the day the enemy formed a coun-

[25] German information on these first days of December has been taken from the *Army Group G KTB* and *Anlagen; OB WEST KTB;* MS #T–122 (Zimmermann *et al.*); and MS #B–078 (Mellenthin). It is interesting to notice that, hard pressed as Rundstedt was, he protested against the OKW plan to use the *Hitlerjugend* born in 1928 as replacements in the field forces of the Wehrmacht. *OB WEST KTB,* 7 Dec 44.

[26] Some of the enemy did put up a fight in entrenchments near the bank. Sgt. Raymond M. Kirkland, F Company, 320th Infantry, made a singlehanded attack against one position and destroyed two machine guns. He received the DSC.

terattack to hit the 320th Infantry, but this threat was literally blown to pieces by a TOT, followed by a strike with fighter-bombers and still another TOT —the whole effort reinforced by fire from a phalanx of tank destroyers lined up on the west bank.[27]

The 134th Infantry crossed with little trouble and virtually no losses, using a demolished railroad bridge south of Sarreguemines. By 0830 all three battalions were on the enemy bank. The 3d Battalion pushed out on the right to mop up Sarreinsming, a favorable site for bridging operations, and the 1st and 2d Battalions marched northeast astride the railroad line. The 2d Battalion, on the open left flank of the 35th Division, came under a rain of mortar and artillery shells from Sarreguemines and the enemy-held heights north of the city. About 1315 some thirteen to fifteen German tanks, bearing infantrymen on their decks, came out of Neunkirch and bore down on the 2d Battalion, intent on the kill. Fortunately, ground and air observation posts sighted the enemy counterattack as it was forming. The American artillery across the river was still close enough to give support to the attacking infantry and after fifteen minutes of hot work by nine field artillery battalions the enemy broke and fled.[28] Nonetheless, the first day of the advance was made at heavy cost to the 2d Battalion; by dark its companies were reduced to a rifle strength averaging thirty men apiece. The 35th Division, however, had exacted such heavy toll from the *11th Panzer Division* armored infantry that the day after the attack German records listed the *110th Panzer Grenadier Regiment* as "nearly destroyed."

While the 35th Division was pushing east out of the Sarre bridgehead on the morning of 8 December, the 26th Division drove forward to crack the Maginot Line. A thirty-minute preparation by corps and division artillery, followed by a bombing and strafing mission in which five squadrons of the XIX TAC took part, inflicted very severe losses on the German troops in le

[27] The 320th Infantry After Action Report for December 1944 points with pride to the 8 December attack as an example of a well-conducted river crossing.

[28] 134th Inf Jnl, 8 Dec 44; Hist Div Combat Interviews. A battalion of infantry was employed in this abortive counterattack, combining with the tanks to form what was a sizable task force for the *First Army* front in December. Apparently this failure in the *XIII SS Corps* sector was the capsheaf to a number of such untoward experiences. Late on 8 December Balck issued a general directive: "The experiences of the last days have taught that the enemy artillery, employing air or ground observation, easily destroys our own counterattacks before they are actually formed." Therefore, said Balck, counterattacks in the future are to be launched only at twilight, during the night, or in fog—unless enemy observation is denied by woods or by bad weather. Since the Americans have a distaste for hand-to-hand fighting the counterattack must be made so as to close with them as quickly as possible. *Army Group G KTB*, 8 Dec 44.

Grand Bois and in the trenches around the Maginot forts. The 328th and 104th jumped off about 1000. On the right the 104th faced four mutually supporting forts in and around the village of Achen—about 3,000 yards west of the Singling positions which the 4th Armored Division had engaged two days earlier. In the 328th zone two works, Fort Wittring and Fort Grand Bois, lay on the edge of le Grand Bois in such a position as to threaten the interior flanks of both the 26th and 35th Divisions. Actually these Maginot Line forts no longer presented any great tactical problem, though they appeared forbidding enough to the assault teams sent against them. Most of the German troops in the area already had withdrawn into the Bois de Blies-Brucken, leaving skeleton garrisons to man the machine guns in the forts.

The Achen forts quickly capitulated in the face of regular assault tactics, containing fire, and white phosphorus grenades,[29] but the assault companies of the 328th Infantry had more trouble. Company K reached Fort Wittring in the middle of the afternoon, after clearing the pillboxes surrounding the main work, and found it to be sited on a large mound, closely hemmed in on three sides by the buildings of an extensive factory—reputed to be a source of fuel for jet-propelled planes. The fort was a conventional reinforced concrete type with revolving cupolas and steel-covered firing slits. Napalm bombs, used during the air strike in the morning, had missed the fort by a considerable distance. Shells from a tank destroyer that was run forward only chipped the concrete walls; however, the tank destroyer crew was able to engage and neutralize a 20-mm. gun firing from the cupola. Next, the 155-mm. guns were brought into action against the fort—without success. Just before dark a sergeant made a rush up the mound and threw a grenade against the main steel door while his mates peppered the firing slits from the neighboring factory buildings; a machine gun cut him down. Later some German dynamite was found at a bridge near by. Armed with this, engineers and infantry set out for another try, but the dynamite failed to burst the door. Finally, as dawn approached, an assault team put a couple of hundred pounds of plastic charges against the door. This time the explosion cracked the steel door, detonated the ammunition inside, and smeared the garrison—some thirty men—against

[29] Maj. Leon D. Gladding, commanding the 1st Battalion, 104th Infantry, received the DSC for gallantry in the fight around Achen. When one fort checked the left flank of the battalion Major Gladding led four men through the enemy wire around the fort. While his men covered him Gladding went on alone, cleared one bunker with a white phosphorous grenade, and charged the other, firing his submachine gun. One German officer and nineteen men surrendered to Gladding.

the wall like the bodies of so many flies. Company L, making the assault against Fort Grand Bois, meanwhile had encountered ten complete rows of double-apron barbed wire, and since there were no bangalore torpedoes to blow the wire the company had to wait until dark to begin the task of cutting through. Daylight came before a path could be cleared, and L Company withdrew to the surrounding woods; then the German garrison evacuated the fort.[30]

With the main positions of the Maginot Line now behind it the 26th Division marched northeast toward Gros-Réderching. The 104th Infantry took the town on 10 December, thus bringing the division within ten miles of the West Wall. General Paul had been told the day before that his division was about to be relieved by the 87th Division, which had just arrived in the Metz area, but he and his officers and men were eager to reach Germany before the relief took place. Although elements of the 26th Division began to shuttle to Metz on 10 December, the 328th Infantry drove on, finally getting a company across the German frontier just before it was relieved by the 347th Infantry on the night of 12–13 December.

While the 26th Division drove through the Maginot Line the 12th Armored Division, on its right, received its first battle indoctrination. Early on the morning of 9 December Task Force Wells (Lt. Col. C. W. Wells) took Singling, thus advancing to cover the right flank of the 26th Division attack. The next day Rohrbach-lès-Bitche fell and CCA, 12th Armored Division, moved its tanks forward to drive through the remaining Maginot Line positions to the north. In the initial attempt the 23d Tank Battalion (Lt. Col. M. C. Meigs) was hit by accurate antitank fire and lost six medium tanks. A second attempt on 11 December also was repulsed and the battalion commander was killed. In an attack the following day CCA reached Bettviller, which had been assigned as the division objective, and here it held in place.[31]

The 26th Division successes at Wittring and Achen provided some security for the right flank of the 35th Division. But although the right wing of the 35th was able to forge ahead with little opposition the 134th Infantry on the left continued to receive heavy fire, and its supply people and litter bearers were being picked off by snipers in Sarreguemines. To remove this thorn from the side, General Baade sent the 1st Battalion of the 137th Infantry

[30] Hist Div Combat Interviews; 328th Inf AAR, Dec 44.

[31] 12th Armd Div AAR, Dec 44. Ltr, Maj Charles P. Chapman to Hist Div, 17 Jan 47

from reserve to finish mopping up the last resistance in the portion of the city west of the river; before dawn on 10 December he dispatched the rest of the regiment across the Sarre to clear eastern Sarreguemines.

During the first two days of the bridgehead operation the 35th Division had been stranded on the enemy bank without tanks or supply vehicles and with only a few light 57-mm. antitank guns and a single tank destroyer. Although the German infantry forces had failed to defend the river line with their usual vigor the German artillery was extremely active, pouring a continuous fire in on the American bridging sites. On 9 December the 81st Chemical (SG) Company brought smoke generators down to the river and laid a smoke screen to cover the activity at the crossings. The German gunners increased their tempo, but the men at the generators—fighting their first battle—stayed with their equipment. Eventually the smoke screen attracted such a heavy shelling that all efforts on the bridges had to be abandoned. Nightfall provided better cover and the 1135th Engineer Combat Group, reinforced by the 60th Engineer Combat Battalion, rushed construction at the bridge sites. By midnight two Class 40 bridges were in place and on the morning of 10 December the XII Corps had ten vehicular bridges over the Sarre.

For the next two days the lead regiments of the 35th fought their way toward the Blies River in the midst of snow and bitter wind, while the 137th Infantry conducted a battle all its own in and around Sarreguemines. Here the fight went on from floor to floor, in the larger buildings, and from one air raid shelter to the next. Buildings were honeycombed with connecting passages running the length of entire blocks. Cellars were "mouseholed" in such a fashion that a BAR burst or a grenade through a window would not suffice and the enemy sniper or machine gunner had to be pried out. On 10 December F Company (Capt. J. S. Giacobello) cornered a company of German infantry in a pottery factory near the south edge of the city and killed or captured the lot in a hand-to-hand fight that raged for three hours from one kiln to the next.[32] By 11 December the city of Sarreguemines was clear, except for a handful of die-hard snipers.

The 137th Infantry meanwhile moved northeast to Frauenberg, where it could block any enemy threat to the 35th Division left flank, but the regiment came under bitter and continuous harassing fire from the German guns

[32] Captain Giacobello received the DSC for bravery in this action. Company F was awarded a Distinguished Unit Citation.

covering the *17th SS* withdrawal across the Blies.[33] With the 137th far enough forward to protect his exposed left flank, General Baade ordered an attack to be made on the morning of 12 December which would put the 35th Division across the Blies River. In contrast with the weak resistance shown at the Sarre River line the enemy was prepared to make a real fight for the Blies River positions. The *17th SS Panzer Grenadier Division* faced the left wing of the 35th Division with the *38th SS Panzer Grenadier Regiment* in the line. The *11th Panzer Division*, drastically reduced in rifle strength but still a hard-fighting outfit, was entrenched along the southern loop of the Blies with its left flank resting on the ridge line west of Obergailbach.[34]

At the Blies the enemy possessed superior observation, which had been lacking at the Sarre, and from hills in the narrow salient formed by the river near Bliesgersviller German observers could look down the American left flank and front for nearly 6,000 yards. Opposite the American right the enemy positions on the high ground around Obergailbach, which rose above the positions held by the 35th Division, estopped any flanking movement to turn the Blies River line from the south. Prevailing winds and the extended area involved ruled out the use of smoke to mask the American assault.[35] In short, General Baade had to send his division across the river the hard way—in a frontal attack.

On the night of 11 December the 35th Division took up positions for the assault on the following morning. In the center the 134th Infantry was given the mission of crossing the Blies at Habkirchen and continuing the attack toward Wolfersheim, the regimental objective. On the left the 137th Infantry was assigned Bliesransbach as an objective; its seizure would place the regi-

[33] The enemy too had a rough time at the hands of the artillery. The 945th Field Artillery Battalion (155-mm. howitzer) and the 731st Field Artillery Battalion (155-mm. gun) picked up a German tank park near Bebelsheim, some 5,000 yards northeast of Frauenberg, and crippled or destroyed several of the enemy tanks.

[34] The *11th Panzer Division* and *25th Panzer Grenadier Division* were now under a new command, the *XC Corps* (General der Infanterie Erich Petersen). The *XC Corps* was a scratch command which had been brought in to free the *XIII SS Corps* staff for the Saarlautern fight. It had almost no corps troops. The corps artillery consisted of one battalion of light howitzers and one battalion of mixed Flak. MS #B–071 (Petersen). On 11 December the *11th Panzer Division* was reported as at the end of its armored infantry strength and Balck ordered that it use its tanks in defensive tactics. The *11th* had just received twenty new Panthers.

[35] The 35th would have had to rely on generators and smoke pots. At this time the XII Corps had no 4.2 chemical mortars, which might have been more effective under the circumstances. Throughout the Lorraine Campaign the bulk of the Third Army chemical units went to the XX Corps.

ment again in a blocking position on the exposed left flank of the division. The 320th Infantry, on the right, was ordered to take Nieder-Gailbach by an advance astride the Blies. Attainment of these objectives would put the 35th Division close to the West Wall and in position for a break-through in company with the new 87th Infantry Division and such other forces as General Patton might have at hand.

The main effort in the crossing attack on 12 December fell to the 1st Battalion of the 134th Infantry, whose regimental objective lay some distance beyond the objectives given the two flanking regiments. In the early morning hours the 1st Battalion moved through rain and darkness down to the river, clearing the tree trunks and branches that the enemy had felled to barricade the one usable road. About 0500 B and C Companies, reinforced by a platoon of D Company, arrived at a point on the west bank of the Blies directly across from the little village of Habkirchen. Here the flooded stream was some sixty feet wide. Patrols were unable to locate a ford and the two companies crossed in plywood boats, one following another. As usual in these crossings some boats capsized in the swift current and seven or eight men were drowned. Thus far the only indication of the enemy was an occasional shell. On the east bank the Americans silently put the German guards out of the way and moved into the section of Habkirchen which lay north of a small creek known as the Mandelbach. Surprise continued to work for the attackers. In a large building close to the bank the Americans captured a German company at breakfast. The prisoners were incarcerated in the cellar and the building became the center for further expansion into the north half of the village. Plans had been laid for a co-ordinated assault on Habkirchen in which both the 1st and 3d Battalions would take part, but a series of misadventures delayed the reinforcing elements.[36] The two small rifle companies and the machine gun platoon were left on the enemy bank to fight alone. Company B led the penetration inside the village but lost all its officers, became disorganized, and

[36] The boats used by the assault wave of the 1st Battalion were shot up or lost in the swift current and Company A was held up on the west bank until the engineers, working under fire, could put in a footbridge. The 3d Battalion had planned to ford the Blies, but on the night of 11 December a patrol found that the water at the chosen site had risen above fording depth. Next, the trucks carrying the eight boats available to the battalion found the road to the river's edge blocked by a disabled tank destroyer and were forced to make a wide detour. Finally, when the boats reached the river they were lost in the rapid current, and as daylight came the 3d Battalion had to withdraw from the bank under fire. Hist Div Combat Interviews.

fell prey to the enemy. During the day and the ensuing night some thirty men filtered back to join C Company.[37] Casualties in the latter company also were heavy, and as the day ended Capt. Williams M. Denny withdrew the survivors to a handful of houses grouped about the large building captured in the morning. Successive attempts by troops of the *38th SS Panzer Grenadier Regiment* to wipe out Denny's small force came under American fire from both sides of the river. Mortar crews and heavy machine gun sections located in buildings on the west bank maintained a constant fire, at distances of three and four hundred yards, to cover their comrades. The 161st Field Artillery Battalion directed the American guns and tank destroyers, laying TOT's on the neighboring sectors from which German reinforcements might gather, smoking enemy observation posts, firing "road runners" on the entrances to Habkirchen, and maintaining a defensive barrage which, as enemy prisoners later attested, effectively isolated the battle being fought in the village.[38] At 0015 on 13 December the Germans moved in on Denny's command with tanks and infantry, apparently intent on ending the fight. Slowly the Americans were pushed back toward the river, but their defense never broke; about 0400, reinforcements in the form of two companies of the 3d Battalion, 134th Infantry, debouched from assault boats into the middle of the fight.

Other friendly troops also were crossing in the early morning darkness and the 35th Division began to get a secure grip east of the Blies. To the south the 320th Infantry took a hand in the battle for a bridgehead. The regiment had been checked in earlier attempts to close up to the Blies by the enemy possession of the valley town of Bliesbruck, situated on the American side of the river. On 12 December the 1st and 3d Battalions of the 320th Infantry, reinforced by a company of tanks, returned to the attack at Bliesbruck. In the face of withering machine gun fire, thickened by shells from German tanks on the opposite bank, the Americans drove the enemy from the town and reached the river bank, thus clearing the way for a crossing. At 0300 the next morning the 320th sent one battalion over the Blies and by the night of 13 December held Hill 312, which overlooked Habkirchen and spiked down the right flank of the American bridgehead. North of Habkirchen a small party from the 137th Infantry made a crossing on the early morning of 13

[37] The enemy captured about sixty Americans on 12 December. *Army Group G KTB Anlagen* of this date.

[38] The XII Corps expenditure of artillery ammunition jumped to 18,809 rounds on 12 December.

December, but it was pinned down by the German batteries farther north and did not affect the course of the fight for Habkirchen. Inside Habkirchen Denny's reinforced command continued the struggle for the houses on the east bank. The enemy stubbornly persisted in his efforts to drive the Americans back into the river. Casualties on both sides mounted rapidly, and late on the afternoon of 13 December the combatants agreed to a brief truce in order to care for the wounded lying in the no man's land between the houses.

When night fell more troops moved across the Blies to expand and consolidate the bridgehead. The 2d Battalion of the 134th, reinforced by Company K, made a predawn crossing on 14 December and marched to encircle Habkirchen from the south. This maneuver surprised the Germans on the opposite bank, so much so that one of their platoons fell in behind Company K as it marched north along the river and accompanied the American column until Company K noted these "reinforcements" and captured them. When daylight came the 2d Battalion was on a hill east of Habkirchen, but here the German gunners discovered the Americans and poured in a murderous fire, an estimated 600 rounds in thirty minutes. By the close of the day the battalion was reduced to a combat strength of eighty men and four officers.

Nevertheless the battle for Habkirchen was turning against the enemy.[39] The battered troops of the 134th Infantry drove the Germans back to the creek, while tank destroyers across the river fired directly into the houses and bunkers held by German detachments. During the night of 14–15 December the American engineers laid a Bailey bridge across to Habkirchen. At daylight tanks and tank destroyers intervened in the fray, carrying the battle to the enemy and finally clearing the village shortly after noon.[40]

The fight for Habkirchen had more than halved the combat strength of the 134th Infantry, and the rifle strength throughout the rest of the division also had been whittled away in the past days of intense action; the 35th Division swung into line for the last drive toward the West Wall with its ranks seriously depleted. The enemy, for his part, now was defending what his leaders had called "the sacred soil of the Reich" and contested the possession of every wood lot and hill until he was killed. The 35th Division and the adjacent 87th took very few prisoners in these next days of bloody fighting.

[39] The enemy reinforced his troops around Habkirchen on 14 December with some two hundred men from the *165th Regiment* of the *36th VG Division*. *Army Group G KTB* of this date.

[40] Details of the fight for Habkirchen are taken from the 134th Inf Jnl; Hist Div Combat Interviews; Interv with Lt Col Dan E. Craig, Washington, 24 Jul 47. Both C Company and the 2d Platoon of D Company were awarded the Distinguished Unit Citation.

TOUGH FIGHT IN HABKIRCHEN *was brought to an end on 15 December by tanks and tank destroyers after a three-day struggle by infantry.*

In the north the 137th Infantry got a taste of what the German grenadier would do on his own ground when, after driving deep into the Breiterwald wood on 15 December, the 3d Battalion was counterattacked and driven out, suffering heavier casualties than in any other action during the Sarre campaign.[41] On the right also the Germans fought bitterly, but the 347th Infantry (Col. S. R. Tupper) swung over to the left in the 87th Division zone, cut off part of the *110th Panzer Grenadier Regiment*, and took Obergailbach and the high ground overlooking the Blies.[42] This maneuver reduced the resistance which the 320th Infantry was meeting in its advance astride the Blies; however, Nieder-Gailbach remained in enemy hands until 18 December when the 2d Battalion took the village after a hard fight.

[41] The strength of the 3d Battalion rifle companies on the night of 15 December follows: I—30 men and 2 officers; K—60 and 3; L—11 and 2.

[42] During the fight for Obergailbach Pfc. Harry Ellis, G Company, 347th Infantry, made a lone advance across a hundred yards of open, fire-swept ground, passed through a hedgerow, and mopped up two machine gun positions with his BAR. He received the DSC.

The 87th Infantry Division (Brig. Gen. Frank L. Culin)[43] was a new arrival in the European Theater of Operations. After a short staging period in England the division began to ship out from Southampton on 23 November, but storms in the English Channel delayed debarkment and the entire division was not on the Continent until 6 December. Originally, General Patton planned to give the 87th Division some combat training under the new III Corps in the Metz area. There, on 8 December, the 345th Infantry (Col. Douglas Sugg) began the relief of the 2d Infantry, 5th Division, just failing to receive the surrender of Fort Driant which took place fifteen minutes before command in the area passed to the 87th Division. The next day the 87th Division was assigned to the XII Corps to replace the battle-weary and understrength 26th Division in a reciprocal change of positions, and the 346th Infantry (Col. N. A. Costello) moved by truck to Gros-Réderching, relieving the 104th Infantry on 10 December. Thereafter the trucks shuttled back and forth between Metz and the XII Corps front while units of the two divisions, side by side in the line, continued to move slowly toward Rimling. By 14 December General Culin had his division together, supported by a 4th Armored formation—the 25th Reconnaissance Squadron—which had taken over this mission from the 12th Armored Division. At noon of that day the 87th Division won its first important objective by taking Rimling. As the division approached the German frontier, however, resistance stiffened and the enemy troops (probably the *37th SS Panzer Grenadier Regiment* and elements of *Kampfgruppe Lehmann*) began to counterattack, while the American front-line battalions were submitted to increasingly heavy shelling.

Two days later the 35th Division and the 87th Division started a series of grim battles, generally fought in not more than battalion strength, to clear the small forests and wood lots held by the German infantry as outworks to the West Wall. Here again the German grenadier proved himself an able woods fighter, and the German artillery, firing accurately at long ranges, very often drove the Americans off such ground as they had taken. The 35th Division suffered most in this fighting; its rifle strength was insufficient to drive home successful attacks on any but narrow frontages, and its open left flank forced the division to fight with head over shoulder. The German troops

[43] General Culin had joined the Regular Army in 1916 as an infantry officer, after graduation from the University of Arizona. During World War I he served with the 30th Infantry in the Aisne defensive, the Aisne–Marne and the Meuse–Argonne offensives. General Culin assumed command of the 87th Division in October 1944.

facing the 35th and 87th were in much worse condition than the Americans, however, and on the night of 16 December the *XC Corps* commander was forced to warn his superiors that the German infantry line was so thin that no serious attempt at a break-through could be checked.[44]

General Patton ordered the 6th Armored Division to make an attack in the Forbach sector on 17 December and so relieve pressure on the left wing of the 35th Division, but word of the great German counteroffensive in the Ardennes led the Third Army commander to cancel this move. On 18 December, one day before the target chosen by General Patton for an all-out offensive by the XII Corps against the West Wall, the 87th Division was ordered to halt its attack.[45] Next day the 35th Division stopped in its tracks with orders to hold and consolidate before withdrawal from the battle line. When its relief was completed, two days later, the 35th had been in the line for a period of 162 consecutive days.

At midnight on 20 December the XV Corps took over the XII Corps zone and the following night General Eddy opened his forward command post in Luxembourg, preparatory to the Third Army counterattack against the southern wing of the German offensive. The Ardennes counteroffensive had in effect served the enemy as a spoiling attack, even in those sectors of the battle line far from the center of impact.

[44] *Army Group G KTB Anlagen.* On 16 December the *257th VG Division* began a piecemeal replacement of the *11th Panzer Division,* which was earmarked for OKW reserve. But the *XC Corps* still was hard pressed and greatly outnumbered.

[45] On 13 December General Patton, General Vandenberg (Ninth Air Force commander), and their staffs had begun planning for a joint air-ground attack against the West Wall with a readiness date set at 19 December. It was intended that, after three or four days of intensive bombing by the Ninth Air Force and the Royal Air Force, the XII Corps would launch the ground attack to penetrate the West Wall. Elements of the Seventh Army also were expected to join in the offensive shortly after the XII Corps attack began.

CHAPTER XIII

The XX Corps Battle at the West Wall (4-18 December)

After weeks of severe fighting, troops of the Third Army finally had come up against the fortifications of the German West Wall. On 3 December, following the seizure of the Saarlautern bridge, the 1st Battalion of the 379th Infantry, 95th Division, captured two bunkers that commanded the exit from the span.[1] Although somewhat isolated, the twin bunkers were part of the West Wall system; their seizure marked the beginning of a slow, bloody attempt to chip and pry an opening that would lead to the Rhine.

The XX Corps entrance into this formidable fortified zone was not the first made by the Allied arms. As early as 11 September advance guards of the 5th Armored Division operating on the right wing of the First Army had captured the first bunkers in the West Wall position. (*Map IV*) This initial penetration was made in a sector some eighteen miles northeast of Trier, near Wallendorf, which, like many parts of the West Wall at the beginning of September, had not yet been fully manned. Subsequent German reports indicate that CCR (reinforced) of the 5th Armored Division went clear through the West Wall before being driven back by a hastily organized counterattack.[2] It is not clear whether the Americans on the spot realized at the time what they had done.[3] Aerial reconnaissance failed to show many of the overgrown positions in the West Wall, and most of the intelligence reports on the subject dated back to 1940.[4] As a result the Allied maps of September 1944 possessed only very general tracings of the West Wall and often were

[1] 1st Bn, 379th Inf, Jnl, 3 Dec 44.

[2] MS #B–006a (Beyer) and MS #B–081 (Beyer); *Army Group B KTB Anlagen* for this period; *OKW/WFSt KTB Ausarbeitung, Der Westen*. General Wissmath, commanding in this sector, was relieved. *Personalakten*. To the north of this abortive operation, the 4th Infantry Division in mid-September effected a penetration of the West Wall along the Schnee Eifel.

[3] FUSA Rpt of Opns, I, pp. 50ff. See also a series of eight Historical Division Combat Interviews on the Wallendorf operation which was obtained in November 1944.

[4] See TUSA Target Area Analysis Nos. 9, 10, 11.

in disagreement with one another. Then, too, the Germans had built fortifications in various positions forward of the West Wall proper. The resulting complex puzzled even the German staffs: on 21 September, for example, *OB WEST* was forced to give *Army Group G* a ruling as to what really constituted the West Wall.[5] However, when the First Army hit the West Wall defenses at Aachen in mid-September there was no question that the hard-fought advance was being made against the main German fortifications. The Aachen sector was the second most heavily fortified portion of the entire West Wall—the Saarlautern sector ranked first—but although the First Army had effected a breach in the Aachen area the subsequent stalemate at the Roer had prevented a thoroughgoing exploitation of this Allied penetration.

Hitler had set the Third Reich to building an "impregnable" wall in the West in 1936. At that time only the fortifications reaching from the Moselle south and east to the Rhine were called the "West Wall," but in 1938 Hitler extended the name to the entire system—a fact probably unknown to the composers of the popular marching song of 1940 when they immortalized the "Siegfried Line." A series of extensions had been planned at either end of the West Wall in 1940, but the quick German victory in France and the necessity of moving the defenses of the Third Reich forward to the Channel and the Atlantic forced these plans into the discard.[6] A little work on the original West Wall between the Moselle and the Rhine was done during the succeeding years; however, no real effort was made to strengthen the entire line prior to 20 August 1944, when Hitler issued a decree for a levy of "people's" labor to put these fortifications in repair. Concrete, steel, machinery, and manpower—not to mention the heavy arms required for antitank defense—all were in very short supply in the autumn of 1944, but by December the West Wall had been somewhat strengthened in those areas where the Allied forces had not won an early foothold.

The West Wall, as it existed in 1944, had its northern terminus at Roermond, near the southeastern corner of the Netherlands. The fortified zone extended south through the Aachen sector, where a second zone backed up the first as a double barrier to any advance into the Cologne Plain; continued along the eastern border of Luxembourg; looped to the east bank of the Sarre, which it followed to a point northeast of Forbach; then turned gradually east until it reached the Rhine in the vicinity of Karlsruhe. Here the West Wall

[5] *Army Group G KTB,* 18 and 21 Sep 44.

[6] MS #T–121 (Zimmermann *et al.*). See also German planning maps of 1940.

followed the German bank of the Rhine, coming to an end at Basel and the Swiss frontier.

Throughout its length the West Wall zone had been planned with an admirable eye for ground. Where the terrain denied cross-country movement by large mechanized forces the German fortifications were relatively weak and scattered. Where the ground offered a corridor to the attacker the fortifications were the strongest and provided mutual support by works in great density. It is true that the West Wall was of 1940 vintage and that warfare had made considerable advances by the fall of 1944. German staff officers recognized several weaknesses in the four-year-old system. First, it lacked the antitank defenses necessitated by the newer, heavier tanks. Second, many of the smaller works were not adequately protected against aerial bombardment, and the whole line had insufficient antiaircraft artillery. Next, the bunkers seldom were built to mount guns of calibers larger than 75-mm., and the smaller pillboxes could not use the 1942 model machine gun in embrasures constructed for the MG 34. Furthermore, the entire system was so complex as to require a considerable familiarity with the individual works by those who manned them. Germany's lack of manpower in 1944 forbade the necessary training period in the West Wall; as a result most formations entered the fortifications with the Allies hot on their heels and with no time to co-ordinate the defense of their own particular sector. In addition, co-ordination of fire plans and tactical dispositions was made difficult by the lack of communications equipment—switchboards, wire cables, radios, and the like—in the fortified zone. Finally, the original German plans had been predicated on one division in each four miles of the line, plus large field forces in reserve.[7] In early December 1944, however, the *First Army* would defend the West Wall with an average force of one division—much under the 1940 strength—per ten miles of front. Elsewhere single German divisions held as much as twenty-mile sectors in the West Wall.[8] All these factors contributed to a reasonable skepticism by many German field commanders as regards the "impregnable" nature of the West Wall. Rundstedt, for example, freely characterized the West Wall fortifications as "mouse traps." But many of their points

[7] *Ibid.;* MS #B–308 (Zimmermann).

[8] These estimates are based on various German situation maps, plus the *First Army* estimate of 2 December 1944. See *Army Group G KTB Anlagen.* On 11 December *Army Group G* was defending with one-half the strength it was supposed to have in the West Wall.

of weakness would be negated by the bad weather of the late fall and winter months, which drastically limited close tactical support by the Allied air forces, curtailed the use of heavy armor in cross-country maneuver, and shifted the burden of attack almost entirely to the infantry. Even the tremendous superiority enjoyed by the Allies in the artillery arm (with better guns and projectiles than those of 1940) would be partially erased when the ground fogs and lowering clouds of the late months cut down observation, thus somewhat restoring an equilibrium between the 1944 gun or howitzer and the 1940 bunker.

The section of the West Wall which the XX Corps proposed to attack was now regarded by the Germans as the strongest in the entire West Wall system. Two factors had worked to make it so. In January 1939 Generaloberst Walther von Brauchitsch, then Commander in Chief of the German Army, had prepared an estimate of the French plan of attack in the event of war. Brauchitsch and the General Staff concluded that the French would make a strong attack between Merzig and Saarlautern, aimed at reaching the Rhine Valley. (*Map XXXVII*) As a result of his recommendations this particular part of the West Wall was strengthened;[9] subsequently more works were added in the last part of 1943 and the early months of 1944. As for the second factor: the Allies had reached the West Wall in the strong Aachen area before much of anything was done to rearm the fortifications or build auxiliary field works;[10] in the Merzig–Saarlautern sector, however, the Germans had been given time to arm the line and strengthen the original works with trenches, wire and some additional reinforced concrete.

In the area between Beckingen and Ensdorf, where the XX Corps would launch its attack, the forward part of the West Wall zone bordered the east bank of the Sarre River. At some points the bunkers and wire reached to the river; at others they lay as much as half or three-quarters of a mile inland. This forward zone was thickest in and around the cities of Fraulautern, Saarlautern-Roden, and Dillingen, here averaging nearly a mile in depth. Farther to the east the German works continued, although in much less strength, to a second main zone which began on the higher ground some five or six miles

[9] *OKH/General der Luftwaffe beim Oberbefehlshaber des Heeres KTB Anlagen*, 18 Jan 39. The French had in fact considered an offensive in this area. See Gen. Maurice Gustave Gamelin, "Directive pour l'Offensive entre Rhin et Luxembourg," dated 8 June 1938, in *Servir* (Paris, 1946–47), III, 26–32.

[10] MS #T–121 (Zimmermann *et al.*).

east of the Sarre.[11] This second zone was deeper than the first, but the state of its defenses in 1944 is unknown. Actually it was a part of a semicircular fortified zone known as the Hilgenbach *Stellung*, which extended from Beckingen to the Blies River west of Zweibruecken and was intended as a kind of tampon in the event of a penetration in the forward zone. Still another barrier, the Westmark *Stellung*, existed farther east in the Trier–Zweibruecken area. The fortifications in this zone, however, had never been completed.[12]

Hoernlein's *LXXXII Corps*, deployed in the West Wall positions in front of the American XX Corps, had been badly shattered during the battles west of the Sarre, but had withdrawn across the river in good order. In the north the *416th Division* had regrouped and now held the Orscholz line and the Sarre–Moselle triangle as an anchor for the main West Wall defenses. East of the Sarre the *19th VG. Division* was deployed with its right flank touching the Orscholz line and its left resting on the village of Beckingen. The *73d Regiment* held the north wing, the *74th Regiment* held the south, and the *59th Regiment* was assembling in the rear at Dueppenweiler. The *19th VG Division* had been reduced to one-third its normal strength by the time it reached the West Wall and was reported as "completely fought out," with only 630 infantrymen left.[13] Officer losses had been extraordinarily high throughout the division and much of its heavy equipment had been lost west of the river. The replacements handed the *19th* when it crossed the Sarre were uniformly rated as poor. They included a Luftwaffe security battalion of some six hundred untrained men, a fortress battalion, and a *Volkssturm* battalion. The latter was relegated to the Hilgenbach *Stellung* in the rear. This was the standard disposition of the *Volkssturm* during the first days of the December fighting, although occasionally a company would be caught in the forward line before it could be relieved and the American intelligence officers would have a field day predicting that these old men and beardless youths were harbingers of the imminent dissolution of the German Army.[14]

[11] The above analysis is based on German 1:25,000 and 1:5,000 maps made in 1939 and 1940. The Allied defense overprints made on these same maps in 1944 show the various alterations in the German defenses. Actually, few bunkers had been added since 1940, but a number appear to have been strengthened.

[12] The entire West Wall system in the sector south of the Moselle is shown on a *Baustandskarte: Saarphalz, Oberrhein*, dated 25 January 1945, in *OKH/General der Pioniere und Festungen*.

[13] MS #B–527 (Britzelmayr). Strength figures for this and other divisions of the *LXXXII Corps* are taken from a report to *OB WEST* made as of 4 December. *Army Group G KTB*, 4 Dec 44.

[14] Hitler had called up the *Deutsche Volkssturm* on 8 October 1944. The levy extended to all German males between the ages of 16 and 60. In December 1944, there were still a great many restrictions on the use of the *Volkssturm* as combat troops.

The *21st Panzer Division* and *Kampfgruppe Muehlen* (the latter reinforced by an "assault" detachment from *Panzer Lehr*) held the Sarre line from Beckingen to the boundary between the *LXXXII* and *XIII SS Corps* south of Ensdorf. In theory the *21st Panzer Division* was a counterattack reserve, although the *First Army* continued to warn higher commands that this division could not be considered an "attack unit." On 4 December the *21st* had only two hundred effectives all told among its armored infantry. However, replacement quickly were brought in and the tank strength of the division was raised to seventeen Mark IV's and V's.[15] In the past the *21st Panzer Division* had been reputed to have good morale, but now its fighting spirit had declined, partially, at least, because of Allied bombing raids over Wehrkreis VI where most of the troops in the panzer division lived.[16] *Kampfgruppe Muehlen* had reached a new low—even for that battered outfit—and the division staff was serving in the line. The *total* strength of the Kampfgruppe on 4 December was 360 officers and men, but replacements were added to bring the formation up to the strength of a weak regiment. The *LXXXII Corps* was reinforced by five battalions of field artillery under the *404th Volks Artillery Corps*, totaling about a hundred pieces of various makes and calibers. The *404th* was hard pressed for shells, however, and its officers were mostly superannuated infantrymen with little experience in artillery.[17] The battalions were grouped on the high ground northeast of Saarlautern-Roden.

An additional division had been promised the *First Army*. This was the *719th Division* (Generalleutnant Felix Schwalbe), which on 4 December began to detrain at Saarbruecken after a move south from Holland. The *719th* had been employed in the Netherlands as an over-age garrison unit, but had been caught up in the fighting there just before the switch to the *First Army*. The infantry were considered poor, although they proved better than anticipated, and the division artillery train was characterized as the "Artillery Museum of Europe."[18] So hard beset was the whole *First Army* front that for some days the higher German commands could not decide where the various trainloads of the *719th* should be committed. The division was shuttled forward and back in answer to orders and counterorders until the *Army*

[15] *Army Group G KTB*, 6 Dec 44. MS #B–078 (Mellenthin).

[16] *Army Group G KTB*, 6 Dec 44. Wehrkreis VI included the Westphalian area which had taken such a beating from the RAF.

[17] *Army Group G KTB*, 6 Dec 44.

[18] *Ibid.*

Group G staff named it "our gypsy division." The *719th* finally came to rest in the Saarlautern sector of the West Wall.

The forces listed above were obviously not strong enough to garrison the West Wall defenses properly. On 4 December the *First Army* reported that it could not man all of the works in the forward zone and would have to place the available troops in the first line of bunkers. Defense in depth, therefore, the tactic on which the West Wall was based, would really mean retirement from one layer of fortifications to another in what amounted to linear tactics. Hitler himself had intervened to order that there be at least one man in each and every pillbox or bunker, but this order—though several times repeated—had little practical effect when the single occupant was an old man or a boy from the *Volkssturm*. Psychologically, however, the defenders of the West Wall were in a position to make a stubborn fight. This was the "last line," here the German soldier fought to defend German soil, and here he had the greatest amount of artificial protection that he could hope to find.[19]

The 95th Infantry Division Expansion of the Saarlautern Bridgehead

The capture of the Saarlautern bridge was followed on 4 December by a rapid regrouping in the 95th Division sector intended to exploit this new and unforeseen situation. The 3d Battalion of the 379th Infantry crossed the bridge, which the German gunners still were trying to destroy, and attacked obliquely to the right toward the suburb of Fraulautern. This fortified area lay in the West Wall and formed a barrier to future American deployment and maneuver east of the river. (*Map XL*) The *21st Panzer Division* had finally gathered a small force to counterattack, and about 1000 the American 1st and 3d Battalions were hit by two companies of infantry, reinforced by five tanks.[20] The American tank destroyers, which had been rushed across the bridge the day before, here proved their worth, knocking out two of the German tanks and so discouraging the rest that they turned and fled;[21] the enemy infantry were driven off by the American riflemen and machine gunners. After this

[19] See *Army Group G KTB*, 5 Dec 44, for a discussion of the German tactical plans for the defense of the West Wall.

[20] The Americans estimated that the counterattack detachment was made up of one or two companies. 95th Div AAR, 4 Dec 44. Actually it consisted of two grenadier battalions—a commentary on the effective strength of the German units at this time. *Army Group G KTB Anlagen*.

[21] Cpl. Eugene L. Lafountain of B Company commanded the tank destroyer that made the two kills. His vehicle was hit and set ablaze, but although he was wounded he continued to fire until his comrades had found cover. Corporal Lafountain received the DSC.

EN RAILWAY YARDS FRAULAUTERN

FRAULAUTERN. *Circles indicate pillboxes.*

SAARLAUTERN
TO SAARLAUTERN BRIDGE
BRICKYARD

brief interruption the 1st Battalion pushed slowly north toward Saarlautern-Roden, while the 3d Battalion continued the attack into the Fraulautern outworks, beginning an inconclusive and hard-fought battle for possession of the suburb which did not end for the 95th Division until the 5th Division took over the fight on 17 December. The two battalions of the 379th made little progress on 4 December. German pillboxes and bunkers were less thickly clustered in the open space between the bridge and Saarlautern-Roden and Fraulautern than in the two towns themselves, but the enemy had assembled much of his artillery behind Saarlautern-Roden and maintained a constant barrage on the open approaches.[22] All of the XX Corps artillery that could be brought to bear concentrated on shelling Saarlautern-Roden and the hills beyond, but with only limited success. As later events showed, the supremacy of the American artillery arm, which had marked nearly every step of the fight across France, would be reduced considerably during the whole period of battle in the Saarlautern bridgehead. Continuous bad weather curtailed aerial observation. The common German use of flash-hider salt, which here proved to be a very effective means of reducing muzzle flash and thwarting American flash-ranging techniques, further limited the effectiveness of counterbattery fire by the American artillery. Moreover, the enemy was able through this and subsequent days to pound the bridgehead with his heavy guns, while his own battery positions were out of range of the American medium and heavy field artillery battalions emplaced west of the Sarre. But as usual the number of American batteries engaged was vastly superior to the number of opposing German batteries. The American artillery would average approximately 15,000 rounds expended in each day of action, as compared with what the "shell-rep" teams estimated to be a maximum German expenditure of 6,000 rounds on the days of the most intense enemy fire.

It must be noted here that American air power was of relatively little use in complementing the efforts of the artillery arm during the fighting in the bridgehead. Almost continuous bad weather during the first weeks of December permitted the heavy and medium bombers to intervene only on occasion; when they did come into the area they were forced to bomb through the overcast, with generally unsatisfactory results.[23] The fighter-bombers, working

[22] The Germans used 78 guns to support the *21st Panzer Division* counterattack. *Army Group G KTB Anlagen*.

[23] Other factors also contributed to the lack of bomber support. The American First Army was engaged in the battles east of Aachen and had air priority. Pathfinder equipment sometimes failed and wiped out scheduled missions. See Ninth AF Monthly Summary, Dec 44.

closer over their targets but carrying small bomb loads, were called upon to render most of the air support given the XX Corps. Yet even the XIX TAC, well known in the Third Army for flying in all kinds of weather, could give but little support to the effort on the ground. Photo-reconnaissance flights showed mostly cloud and mist patches on the pictures taken during these weeks, adding to the difficulties inherent in attacking a deep zone of strong fortifications.

While the 379th Infantry (—) pushed out from the Saarlautern bridge, the 378th Infantry advanced to the near bank of the river on the southeastern edge of Saarlautern. Although the regiment had been engaged against the enemy in the southern suburbs as early as 3 December, its right flank was held in check for some hours. Lisdorf, the town south of Saarlautern from which the 378th was to launch a crossing attack, was not taken until 4 December. General Twaddle then ordered the 377th up from reserve, with instructions to relieve the rear elements of the 379th inside Saarlautern, as well as the troops of the 378th at the edge of the city. When the reserve regiment came up, the 378th assembled in Lisdorf, on the west bank of the Sarre, preparatory to an assault crossing set for the morning of 5 December.

The 378th Infantry, using two battalions in the assault, made a successful predawn crossing as planned, receiving only a small amount of small arms fire. The German West Wall fortifications at this point did not extend as far as the river bank, but when the 3d Battalion, moving on the left, came up against the first belt of pillboxes outside the village of Ensdorf the enemy fire increased sharply. Nevertheless this first phase of the attack inland moved slowly ahead; by noon the 3d Battalion had penetrated the forward line of pillboxes and was at the edge of Ensdorf. The 1st Battalion, on the right, crossed the railroad line south of the village but here was halted by direct fire from concrete works whose weapons covered the open ground beyond. All told, the two battalions captured fourteen or fifteen pillboxes during the first day's operations—but the toughest sections in the West Wall yet were to be engaged.

North of Saarlautern, the 2d Battalion of the 379th crossed the bridge on the early morning of 5 December, passed through the lines of the 1st Battalion, and attacked toward Saarlautern-Roden. The 2d Battalion reached the edge of the city before receiving the usual German counterattack, and this was repulsed. Four pillboxes, built to cover the southern entrance to Saarlautern-Roden, checked further advance. The remainder of the daylight hours were needed to reduce three of the four. Over on the right flank the 3d Battalion, in a day marked by hard fighting, won a foothold at the south edge of Fraulautern and cleared most of four blocks. Again pillboxes, manned by machine gun crews and a few covering riflemen, were the chief obstacle; built into the streets and between houses each required discovery and the slow process of "buttoning up," approach, and demolition before the advance could proceed.

The fighting on 6 December gave the troops of the 95th Division a real taste of the difficulties attendant on forcing a way through the West Wall. In Saarlautern-Roden, Fraulautern, and Ensdorf, the enemy contested every yard of ground, every house, and every street, filtering behind the American lines in small groups each time a pillbox or a block of houses was taken, and forcing the American infantry to turn back and fight for each strong point two or three times. In the northern sector the 2d Battalion of the 379th was hit during the early morning by an intense shelling estimated to be about fifteen hundred rounds in a matter of three hours.[24] It refused to be disorganized or demoralized and fought its way slowly, house by house and room by room, into Saarlautern-Roden. The 1st Battalion, which had come forward on the right of the 2d, paralleled its dogged advance, but at the end of the day was stopped short by "a warehouse full of Germans." The 3d Battalion was able to report a net gain of only one city block in Fraulautern.

The two battalions of the 378th Infantry in the Ensdorf sector also found the going slow and the enemy determined. While the 3d Battalion hammered away at strong points within the town the 1st Battalion reduced fourteen pillboxes in the zone south of Ensdorf. Here the flat, open terrain was barren of cover and the 1st Battalion found that all movement in daylight was answered by sharp fire and led to high losses. As a result, the gains made by this battalion were confined to the hours of darkness, when the German pillboxes could be engaged without incurring needlessly heavy losses. The 2d Battalion of the 378th had not yet been able to cross the river, because the enemy gunners had brought the Lisdorf crossing site under extremely heavy fire. Never-

[24] This barrage was laid down preparatory to a counterattack by a hodgepodge Kampfgruppe which had been thrown together at Dillingen in an attempt to recapture the Saarlautern bridge. Although some six hundred Germans were employed the counterattack never really got under way, and the fight developed into a holding action against both the 95th and 90th. *Kampfgruppe Lier,* the counterattack group, consisted of a battalion from the *21st Panzer Division,* a company of engineers, "untrained flyers" from Wehrkreis XII, and about three hundred men from the *Lehr Battalion* of the *First Army Weapons School. Army Group G KTB Anlagen,* 5–6 Dec 44.

theless General Twaddle now had five infantry battalions across the Sarre in position to continue the attack against the West Wall and expand the Saarlautern bridgehead. The 95th Division, however, was no longer alone on the enemy bank of the Sarre. On 6 December the 90th Division seized a bridgehead in the Dillingen area about two miles north of Saarlautern, and the XX Corps attack against the West Wall began to assume new proportions.

The 90th Infantry Division Crosses the Sarre

Even before the 95th Division began the fight to make a crossing at the Sarre it had become apparent that the strength of the German forces deployed in front of the XX Corps might make it impossible for the 95th Division to roll up the enemy defense line facing the 90th Division at the river. Therefore, on 2 December, General Van Fleet and his staff began to make new plans and troop dispositions with an eye to an attack in which the 90th Division would secure its own bridgehead. Across the river in front of the 90th Division was a high, steep hill mass, extending from a point opposite Rehlingen northwest to Merzig. (*Map XXXVII*) Observers on the west bank of the Sarre could tell that this high ground was covered with pillbox positions and laced with trenches, but the detailed and pinpoint information essential to an assault against such well-fortified terrain was lacking. The absence of this vital information, coupled with the obvious tactical advantage possessed by the defender on the hill mass, led General Van Fleet to conclude that the cost of an attack at this point would be far too great. Southeast of Rehlingen the far bank of the Sarre led back into more moderate high ground. Since this sector appeared to offer fewer obstacles to the attacker, the 90th Division commander asked General Walker to shift the right boundary of the division to the south, forming a new line extending from Wallerfangen on the west bank, along the Prims River, an eastern tributary of the Sarre. This change placed the heavily defended German city of Dillingen in the 90th Division zone of attack east of the Sarre and would not completely remove the threat posed by the enemy artillery, but it would permit General Van Fleet to maneuver his assault forces beyond the range of small arms and light artillery fire coming from the hill mass north of Rehlingen.[25]

[25] 90th Div AAR, 2 Dec 44. See also Ltr, Lt Gen J. A. Van Fleet to Hist Div, 18 May 49.

At dark on the night of 2 December the 90th Division began a shift to strengthen and extend the right wing in preparation for the attack to secure a crossing. The 359th Infantry took over the task of manning what had been the division front north of the Nied River, outposting the river with small pickets and grouping its battalions in defilade to give protection from the constant enemy shelling. The 357th Infantry assembled around Bueren and sent a combat patrol into Rehlingen, which was found empty of hostile troops. The 358th Infantry (now commanded by Lt. Col. F. H. Loomis), having completed some degree of rehabilitation after the bitter fight at the Orscholz line, was ordered to hold in readiness for a move from the Veckring training ground directly into a forward assembly area on the right wing of the division. During the night the engineers cleared mines from the approaches to the river and marked the routes to be taken. Two battalions of field guns were shifted to positions on the right, while tank destroyers, self-propelled guns, and heavy machine guns were moved down toward the river under cover of harassing fire laid on enemy positions opposite the 359th. Since the Saarlautern bridgehead secured by the 95th Division early on 3 December was very confined and permitted little room for maneuver, it appeared likely that the Germans would be able to contain the 95th for some time. General Walker therefore dispatched orders for the 90th Division to cross within its new zone at the earliest practicable hour. The 358th arrived in assembly areas near St. Barbara late in the afternoon of the following day and, with his division now in hand, General Van Fleet set the attack for the early morning of 6 December.

The high ground on which the 90th Division stood permitted excellent observation across the Sarre but was so rugged as to restrict riverward traffic to the roads at Itzbach and Wallerfangen, in effect forcing the 90th to make any crossing attempt near these two sites. The Sarre, normally some two hundred feet wide, has flooded its banks, increasing the difficulties of an attack crossing. Beyond the river the West Wall defenses began at the very bank and continued eastward, with great pillbox density, to an unknown depth. Between the Sarre and the Merzig–Saarlautern rail line, which here paralleled the river, extended a flat, open space about fifteen hundred yards across, defended by trenches and pillboxes. Opposite the 358th lay the cities of Dillingen and Pachten, known to be strongly fortified and defended. Just north of the twin cities, in the 357th zone, the ground rose from the rail line to a moderately high, wooded ridge, which ran back to the northeast and was bordered on the south by the Prims River. This ridge was chosen as the main axis for the 90th Division attack east of the Sarre. But once beyond the river the left flank of the division would lie open and exposed to long-range fire and possible counterattack from the hill mass north of Rehlingen.

On 5 December the 90 Division commander met with his staff and line officers and mapped out the plan for the attack. The 357th and 358th, left and right respectively, would attack abreast, each using two battalions. The 359th, after making a demonstration by intense fire to attract the enemy's attention farther north, was to pass through a bridgehead won by either of the assault regiments, or attack straight across the Sarre if circumstances seemed to warrant such a maneuver. The initial objective for the division would be the high ground between Dueppenweiler and Piesbach, that is, the highest section of the ridge line north of the Prims River. This objective lay a little over four miles beyond the Sarre. According to the plan of maneuver the 358th Infantry would first have to capture Pachten and Dillingen, then block any enemy approach along the narrow corridor formed by the valley of the Prims, and finally drive down the ridge to Piesbach.[26] The 357th was given the task of striking rapidly eastward to seize a hold on the segment of the ridge defined by two little streams, the Haien Bach and the Kondler Bach. Once in position on the ridge, the 357th was ordered to block hostile efforts from the north and hold until the 358th had cleared the twin cities, whereupon the two regiments would attack abreast along the ridge to the initial division objective. No detailed planning was possible, or attempted, for operations beyond the Dueppenweiler–Piesbach line. Each of the assault regiments was given an engineer battalion as reinforcement for the crossing attack. Five battalions of field artillery were available to reinforce the organic artillery of the 90th, and an additional six battalions were grouped so as to support either the 90th or 95th. Behind these battalions was emplaced still more corps and army artillery. Finally, the greater part of six tank destroyer battalions was disposed along the west bank so as to give close fire support in the corps zone during and after the crossing attack.

In the days just prior to 6 December, American intelligence estimates had been rather optimistic, which explains in part the ambitious nature of the

[26] The day before the 90th Division crossing, the 322d Group of the IX Bombardment Division hit Dueppenweiler with B–26's in an attempt to soften it up for the infantry. This was the last effort over the Saarlautern sector by the IX Bombardment Division.

90th Division scheme of maneuver.[27] Little was known of the precise location of hostile units east of the river. The G–2's at the various American headquarters believed that the German troops holding the Dillingen sector were poor, their morale shattered by the bloody and costly retreat from the Moselle. The West Wall fortifications were considered to be intrinsically strong, but only weakly held. On the other hand, the enemy concentration of artillery east of the Sarre was estimated to be stronger than that which had opposed any previous river crossing; all intelligence estimates agreed in pointing up this feature of the German defense.

While the 90th Division made preparations for the attack, the combat command of the 10th Armored Division, holding the river line farther north, engaged in a demonstration, firing around the clock in an attempt to pin the attention of the enemy to that sector. General Walker ordered that the shelling be continued until the afternoon of 5 December. By that time the hostile artillery was reacting with intense counterbattery fire, although this may have been an attempt to screen troop movements which American observers had noticed as early as 4 December to be taking place behind the German lines.

About 0100 on the morning of 6 December the troops selected to make the crossing moved silently through the darkness down to the water's edge. The 1st Battalion (Maj. W. E. DePuy) of the 357th was in position on the left and moved to a crossing site just southeast of Rehlingen. (*Map XLI*) The 2d Battalion (Maj. B. O. Rossow) assembled at a site slightly south of a demolished railroad bridge that lay below Bueren. In the zone of the 358th, the 1st Battalion (Maj. A. L. Nichols) gathered at the river north of Wallerfangen; the 3d Battalion (Maj. J. S. Spivey), on its left, climbed down the vertical cliffs at Oberlimberg to reach a position for the crossing. About 0415 the leading waves shoved off in assault boats.[28] Surprise was complete, except for an incident on the left where the accidental firing of some .50-caliber machine guns in Rehlingen brought hostile fire down on the 1st Battalion of the 357th. At 0430, as the leading American infantry hit the enemy bank, the XX Corps artillery opened fire, laying counterbattery and neutralizing fire on thirty-nine German battery positions which had been plotted earlier. A total of over six hundred guns (field artillery, tank destroyers, and regimental

[27] 358th Inf S–2 Jnl and 90th Div G–2 Jnl, both for the period 2–5 Dec 44.

[28] The 179th Engineer Combat Battalion and the 206th Engineer Combat Battalion were attached to the 357th Infantry and 358th Infantry respectively.

VEHICULAR FERRY SITE RAILWAY YARDS

PACHTEN. *Circles indicate pillboxes.*

cannon) expended 8,000 rounds in forty-five minutes.[29] As daylight broke, the 359th Infantry and the 10th Armored Division opened fire on the fortifications visible across the river, and the 161st Smoke Generator Company added a demonstration with fog oil as if covering preparations for additional crossings north of the 90th Division zone.

The American advance across the flats east of the river moved forward in uneven cadence. Machine gun fire searched the open ground. Hostile guns and mortars lobbed shells on the infantry, despite the intense concentration of American counterbattery fire. Pillboxes barred every forward movement, yet there was a marked lack of German co-ordination. In the 357th zone the 1st Battalion advanced about a mile and a quarter on the left. During most of the day, however, the infantry on the right were pinned down in such shallow foxholes as they could scoop out of the clay, widely dispersed with little chance of reorganization, and harassed by sorties from pillboxes that they could not approach.[30] The gist of the reports filtering back across the river to the 357th Infantry command post was that the situation was "fluid"; beyond this little could be said.

The 358th Infantry attack toward Pachten and Dillingen initially promised success. The 1st Battalion moved forward on the road north of the Prims River. Here the enemy offered little opposition until the battalion reached its first phase line, the railroad tracks at the edge of Dillingen, where the battalion halted to reorganize before the assault into the city. Losses had been slight, although the right flank of the battalion, resting on the Prims River, was under enfilade by Germans on the south bank. The 3d Battalion, heading toward Pachten, came under fire as it crossed the open ground south of the city; but it hurried forward, bypassing the pillboxes studding the approaches, and succeeded in fighting its way into the first rows of houses just short of the tracks.[31]

[29] A heavy overcast precluded aid by the XIX TAC. Later in the day, however, the fighter-bombers struck at the roads in the enemy rear.

[30] 357th Inf AAR, 6 Dec 44.

[31] 358th Inf AAR, 6 Dec 44. Sgt. Joseph E. Williams, B Company, 315th Engineer Combat Battalion, received the DSC for gallantry in action at Pachten on 6 December. He volunteered to breach an enemy pillbox, and although wounded before he could reach the pillbox Sergeant Williams continued on and fired his charge. He refused to be evacuated, advanced on another pillbox, was again wounded, but finished by taking sixteen prisoners. During the night of 6 December Pvt. Ernest O. Johnson, I Company, 358th Infantry, was with a patrol that was stopped by fire from a bunker. Johnson got a plank, laid it from the top of a neighboring house over to the bunker, crawled across, dropped a couple of grenades down the ventilator, and forced the occupants of the bunker to surrender. Private Johnson received the DSC.

DILLINGEN. *Circles indicate pillboxes.*

The Germans opposite the 90th Division recovered only slowly from their initial surprise; most of their reserves were assembled on 6 December in the Saarlautern sector opposite the 95th Division. No attempt at a counterattack was made until 1730, when hostile tanks and infantry struck at the lines of the 357th and 358th. This onslaught was readily repelled by the American field guns west of the Sarre. Meanwhile the rifle companies of the 2d Battalion (Maj. William Wallace) crossed on a temporary footbridge to join the rest of the 358th, deploying in the rear of the 3d Battalion where the hostile pillboxes were still very much alive. The reserve battalion of the 357th Infantry (the 3d) was not able to cross the river until nearly midnight, for enemy machine guns had swept the crossing site with bullets during the daylight hours. Attempts to put in a heavy bridge or ferry, made during the night of 6–7 December, failed. Cables broke and anchors would not hold in the mud. The trucks moving treadway ferry equipment down to the river were destroyed by high velocity field guns. A few "alligators" were brought forward, but proved incapable of negotiating the mud at the river's edge.

The events of the last days in the Saarlautern sector had caused much concern at all of the higher German headquarters. Hitler reacted in characteristic fashion by ordering that immediate punitive measures be taken against all persons involved in the loss of any West Wall position, since, as he expressed it, the West Wall was "the strongest defense of the Reich." The *Army Group G* commander and the C-in-C West warned that the Americans might break through the Saarlautern zone and roll up the inner flanks of both *Army Group G* and *Army Group B* in an eccentric attack. They varied such reports with warnings that the *First Army* might be enveloped by a concentric attack via Saarlautern and Sarreguemines. Balck asked for reinforcements but had little success. Rundstedt finally allowed the *First Army* to retain the *11th Panzer Division* and the *404th Volks Artillery Corps*, both of which had earlier been ordered north to the Aachen front. He dispatched some *11th Panzer* tanks from the Sarreguemines sector to reinforce the troops at Saarlautern. Throughout the *LXXXII Corps* area officers were combed out of the staffs and headquarters in order to provide one officer for each bunker.[32]

Meanwhile some changes were in process within the *Army Group G* command. Balck himself continued to weather the storms, such as those unleashed

[32] *Army Group G KTB* and *OB WEST KTB*, 1–6 Dec 44.

by the loss of the Saarlautern bridge, but General Knobelsdorff was less fortunate as commander of the *First Army*. At the very beginning of December Rundstedt had started to send down caustic comparisons of the *First* and *Nineteenth Armies*—all to the advantage of the latter. Knobelsdorff tried to defend himself, but on 4 December a successor arrived in the person of General Obstfelder. Knobelsdorff was given a fortress command in Germany, probably because Rundstedt was kind enough to ascribe his relief officially to "sickness" brought on by Knobelsdorff's hard experiences on the Eastern Front. His successor had been recommended for an army command by Field Marshal Model, after having led the *LXXXVI Corps* on the Western Front. Obstfelder, however, had no particularly outstanding reputation and was known as a cautious man, prone to details.[33]

Mellenthin, who had arrived in *Army Group G* in September as Balck's chief of staff, also was relieved, on 5 December, by Generalmajor Helmut Staedke, a veteran of the Eastern Front. Mellenthin, however, had lived up to his earlier reputation as an able staff officer and apparently was relieved for reasons of army politics. He had at various times criticized Generaloberst Heinz Guderian, chief of staff at OKH, and the latter finally was able to secure Mellenthin's dismissal from the General Staff Corps. Eventually, as things grew worse in February of 1945, Mellenthin was brought back in favor and made chief of staff in the *Fifth Panzer Army*.[34] General Feuchtinger, the *21st Panzer Division* commander, also had won black marks because of the failures of the *21st*'s counter measures on 5 and 6 December. Word was given out that he had lost his drive and should be relegated to an administrative post, but somehow Feuchtinger held on to his division.

As a result of the steady worsening of the situation in the Saarlautern sector Hitler had sent a personal order that the peregrinating *719th Division* should be committed there. Ten tanks also had arrived from the *11th Panzer Division*, plus a few tank destroyers and some motorized engineers. The bulk of these reinforcements was thrown into action against the 90th Division on 7 December with orders to destroy the Dillingen–Pachten bridgehead. The first German effort was made shortly after dawn when two companies of engineers and four Mark IV tanks drove into the positions held by the 3d Battalion of the 358th at the edge of Pachten. American guns and infantry broke up this

[33] *Personalakten*.

[34] MS #A–999 (Mellenthin).

attack before it could make much headway; the 3d Battalion then spent the rest of the day organizing a firm front on the west side of the railroad tracks. The 2d Battalion, now in the center, was forced to clear a number of pillboxes that separated it from the 1st Battalion. Pillboxes left intact in the rear of the infantry advance continued to be a problem throughout the operation. Even after they were cleared and the troops within killed or captured, other Germans would slip through the American lines at night and man them once more, forcing the infantry-engineer assault teams to repeat the costly process of attack and capture.

In the sector held by the 357th the 2d Battalion made an attack that brought it up on the right of the 1st Battalion; the two thus formed a salient reaching out about eight hundred yards to the northeast of the Pachtner Koepfe. The supply routes back to the river, however, were very precarious and the Americans delayed a further advance until the ground which had been won could be consolidated.[35] The 357th was just in process of reorganizing when the enemy launched a counterattack south from Beckingen, apparently trying to roll up the exposed left flank of the division. This assault was the German main effort, made by some 1,100 infantry who stubbornly pressed forward until artillery and small arms fire had stricken at least one hundred and fifty dead before the American positions. The Germans finally withdrew in disorder, but a few had filtered through to the rear of the regiment.[36] Behind the thin perimeter formed by the 1st and 2d Battalions, the reserve battalion fought to reduce the pillboxes still active and to destroy the snipers and little knots of determined German infantry who were hindering movement on the roads leading back to the river. Meanwhile assault teams made determined efforts to clear a corridor through the thick concentration of pillboxes north of Pachten which thus far had barred contact between the two American regiments, but with little success.

At the close of 7 December the 90th Division still lacked a vehicular bridge across the Sarre, although an improvised footbridge was in use. German observation posts on the heights north of Rehlingen had a complete view of

[35] 357th Inf AAR, 7 Dec 44.

[36] The German counterattack must have suffered somewhat from lack of co-ordination for it was made by the *59th Regiment* of the *19th VG Division,* one battalion of the *87th Regiment* of the *36th VG Division,* two battalions of the newly arrived *723d Regiment, 719th Division,* elements of the *668th Engineer Battalion (mtzd),* six tanks from the *11th Panzer Division,* and two tank destroyers from the *654th Tank Destroyer Battalion.* Most of these units had just come into the sector. *Army Group G KTB Anlagen,* 7 Dec 44.

the river and all movement in daylight brought down a rain of shells. Smoke shells had been lobbed onto the heights by 4.2 chemical mortars, as many as 1,600 rounds in the one day, but without appreciably lessening the accuracy or intensity of the German fire.[37] Smoke generators working on the west bank were of little value: the smoke dissipated in the veering air currents above the river. Drums of oil could not be moved to the east bank to supply smoke there. As a result, all engineer work along the river had to be confined to hours of darkness and all bridging equipment was moved down to the banks through the pitch black, along steep roads made slippery and treacherous by constant rain. On the night of 7–8 December the troops across the Sarre were resupplied by boat, but the river had risen over two feet during the day and navigation was increasingly difficult.[38]

During 8 December the enemy held the initiative. The 2d and 3d Battalions of the 358th Infantry in Pachten were harassed by continuous local attacks made by the *21st Panzer Division* infantry, as well as by extremely severe shelling; however, the Americans were able to inflict substantial losses on the enemy whenever the latter sallied out of his fortified positions. The 1st Battalion attempted to continue the attack eastward, but when the battalion crossed the railroad tracks it was hit by fire from the warehouses along the open siding area and driven back. A part of C Company later managed to cross the tracks and seize a hold on the Dillingen railroad station. Farther south some of the 1st Battalion troops fought their way into the municipal slaughterhouse, west of the railroad, which had assumed considerable tactical importance because of its position in enfilade on the right flank of the 358th. These successes represented all the American gains in the bridgehead.[39]

At the first light of dawn on 8 December troops of the *719th Division* launched a vicious assault from the northeast and east against the 357th Infantry, apparently intending to erase the 90th Division lodgment area on the east bank of the Sarre.[40] About six hundred German infantry and at least a

[37] The Germans in this area did find artillery observation much hampered by the American smoke. MS #A–972 (Muehlen).

[38] 357th Inf Jnl, 7 Dec 44; 90th Div AAR, 7 Dec 44.

[39] About noon the 513th Squadron of the XIX TAC hit a concentration of German tanks at the southeastern edge of Dillingen. The American rockets and 500-lb bombs did much damage, giving the *First Army* an alibi for its failures on this date. *Army Group G KTB Anlagen,* 8 Dec 44.

[40] Hitler had given orders that the rest of the *Army Group G* front was to go over to the defensive while the *719th Division* concentrated to wipe out the American bridgehead north of Saarlautern "at once." On 8 December, however, the *719th* was still being committed piecemeal. *Army Group G KTB Anlagen,* 8 Dec 44.

dozen tanks took part in the initial counterattack, which succeeded in making some penetration in the lines of the 357th. Although this major counterattack finally was repulsed, smaller groups of the enemy, reinforced by a few roving tanks and assault guns, continued to press hard against the American lines all through the day.[41] A platoon from C Company, manning a road block on the Beckingen highway, was overrun momentarily by an attack which brought the German grenadiers right into the American foxholes and trenches. In the ensuing hand-to-hand fight the American infantrymen killed or captured several of the attackers and restored the position. Elsewhere along the perimeter defended by the 1st and 2d Battalions the Germans advanced to the assault in closed ranks, suffering "extravagant losses" from small arms fire but continuing forward. These frontal assaults in daylight offered perfect targets for the American gunners and it remained for the artillery to give the quietus to each attack formation.

This kind of close combat took its toll in the American ranks as well as in the German. The rifle strength of the 357th Infantry already was perilously small as the result of the ravages of trench foot. Unlike the zone held by the 358th Infantry, the northern sector had very few buildings in which the infantry might take cover. A large part of the 357th Infantry had stood or lain for hours in water-filled foxholes and trenches. Each casualty, whether caused by a bullet or crippled feet, further weakened the overextended American front. The reserve battalion could not be used to fill the gaps in the main line of resistance: it had been dissipated, a squad at a time, to garrison the captured pillboxes in the American rear. At the close of the day the ranking battalion commander, Lt. Col. J. H. Mason, sent word back across the river that the situation was "critical," and the regimental commander gave orders to withdraw the overextended and weakened battalions to a shortened line.[42]

Operations on the South Flank of the XX Corps

At the beginning of December the right wing of the *XIII SS Corps* held a salient northeast of St. Avold athwart the boundary between the XII and XX Corps. The XII Corps drive in the Sarreguemines sector and the XX

[41] The *686th Antitank Battalion (heavy)* had arrived in the woods behind Dillingen with 27 guns. The original plan had been to use the battalion in close support of the *719th*, but this idea had to be abandoned because the heavy carriages of the 88-mm. pieces could not be used in the close confines of the pillbox area. *Army Group G KTB Anlagen*, 8 Dec 44.

[42] 357th Inf Jnl and 90th Div AAR, both of this date.

Corps attack at Saarlautern had increased the angle between the axes of advance for the two corps and widened the gap between their main forces. This divergence may be explained in part by the direction in which lay the strategic objectives assigned the XII and XX Corps and the bend, at this point, in both the West Wall and the German frontier. The terrain northeast of St. Avold in any case was most unpromising. This area generally is known as the Warndt Forest, although in reality the Warndt is surrounded by a series of smaller forests such as those of St. Avold and Houve. Not only is this country heavily wooded, but it is extremely rugged, marked by mining towns and shafts. What few roads cross the Warndt are poor. In the years before World War II the French Genéral Staff had written off this sector as being generally too difficult for offensive operations and had planned to bypass the Warndt in any advance to the Sarre River. The Third Army had adopted a like scheme of maneuver, with the result, as already noted, that the advance of the 95th Division on the XX Corps right ran into considerable trouble at the hands of the *XIII SS Corps* troops (elements of the *36th VG* and *347th Divisions*) who were gathered in the rugged salient.

The XII Corps left was deployed in echelon and thus somewhat protected against the enemy in the Warndt, although the commitment of the 10th Infantry on the extreme right of the XX Corps initially had been ordered to give cover for the 80th Division. The subsequent Sarre crossing in the Sarreguemines sector had swung the XII Corps wide of the Warndt, leaving the corps cavalry and 6th Armored Division patrols to screen along the Rosselle River on the shoulder of the German salient. The main part of this difficult, enemy-held terrain lay in the zone of the XX Corps, uncomfortably close to the Saarlautern bridgehead.

The XX Corps plan to place General Irwin's 5th Division on the corps right, as soon as a part of the 5th could be relieved at the Metz forts, was put in motion on 1 December. Irwin's command was assigned a narrow zone on the right of the 95th Division. The 5th Division right in turn was covered by the 6th Cavalry Task Force, which had been employed earlier as a screening force in the Forêt de St. Avold. General Walker intended that the 5th Division should advance to the Sarre, clearing the Warndt salient as it progressed, and arriving on the river between Buss and Voelklingen. As yet General Patton had not definitely decided to release Irwin's division for use across the Sarre.

On 2 December the 3d Battalion of the 11th Infantry moved east from Metz to join the 1st and 2d Battalions of Colonel Bell's 10th Infantry, which were attacking through the southwest corner of the Forêt de la Houve. Meanwhile progress was slow. The Germans had strengthened the natural defensive features of this broken, heavily wooded ground by ingenious field works and obstacles; in the mining villages they fought stubbornly from shafts and pits. At Creutzwald, on 3 December, troops of the 10th Infantry fought a day-long battle to dislodge the Germans from mine shafts and houses. On the same day the 6th Cavalry Group and the 5th Ranger Battalion were hit by two counterattacks west of Lauterbach, but beat off the enemy and continued the advance.[43] The Germans returned to counterattack on 4 December, this time striking K Company of the 10th Infantry. The American infantry held their ground, despite rising losses, until tank destroyers from the 818th Tank Destroyer Battalion swung into firing positions and put an end to the enemy assault.[44] The 3d Battalion of the 11th Infantry came in on the right of the 10th during 4 December, beginning an advance to cross the Rosselle and clear the enemy between that river and the Sarre. Lauterbach, a key crossroads village, was taken without a fight on 5 December. The enemy was beginning to weaken, although artillery and mortar fire increased to cover the withdrawal toward the Sarre. By 7 December the 10th had reached its objectives on the near bank of the river and tied in with the 95th Division. Two days later the regiment was relieved by the 6th Cavalry Group—the cavalry had taken over the southern sector earlier—and the entire 5th Division assembled to begin training in preparation for a future attack against the West Wall fortifications.

[43] Pvt. J. R. Holland, F Company, 6th Cavalry Reconnaissance Squadron, was awarded the DSC for gallantry during the advance on 3 December. The tank ahead of Holland was hit by shellfire and the crew of Holland's tank were forced to take shelter in a pillbox. Holland dismounted a .30-caliber machine gun and went forward alone, firing from the hip. When he reached the lead tank he found that the platoon leader and his crew were dead.

[44] Capt. F. L. Bradley of the 10th Infantry made a dash under intense artillery fire to reach the friendly tank destroyers. Although he was wounded, he led the tank destroyers into position to repel the German counterattack. Captain Bradley was awarded the DSC. Other deeds of gallantry during 4 December were recognized on the 10th Infantry front. Pfc. D. C. Wideman of L Company made a singlehanded assault and killed the crew of a hostile machine gun. He died of wounds received in this fight and was awarded the DSC posthumously. Pfc. W. D. Haag, also of the 10th Infantry, was checking a wire break close to a battalion command post when he saw a German patrol moving in. He shouted a warning and then, although he was unarmed, rushed the enemy. Haag was killed, but his comrades shot six of the Germans and took the rest prisoner. He was awarded the DSC posthumously.

The 95th Division Fight at the West Wall, 7–18 December

The fortified area in which the 95th Division had begun a penetration was one of the strongest sectors of the entire West Wall. The city of Saarlautern itself had been cleared without much difficulty, since it lay on the west bank of the Sarre River and did not constitute a part of the West Wall proper. But the suburbs on the east bank, Saarlautern-Roden, Fraulautern, and Ensdorf, were most heavily fortified and their defenses well integrated. (*Map XL*) Pillboxes and bunkers constituted the main obstacles to an advance through this sector. Spread in great density, these works were found everywhere: they guarded the approaches to the fortified towns, they were built to command cross streets, and they nested inconspicuously between ordinary dwellings. Some pillboxes were small, with only one or two firing apertures for small arms and machine guns. Other pillboxes and bunkers had as many as sixteen rooms, extending for two or three levels below the ground. These works were built of reinforced concrete, some having roofs and walls that were ten feet thick; most were impervious to anything but a direct hit by heavy artillery or an aerial bomb. The high-velocity projectiles fired by the 90-mm. gun generally were unable to cope with these works, as shown by the experience of one crew, serving a self-propelled 90-mm. gun, which fired seventy-five rounds at a range of less than one hundred yards without breaching or neutralizing the pillbox target. Many of the reinforced concrete works were skillfully camouflaged, giving the harmless appearance of manure piles, mounds of earth, and ordinary buildings. In one case a bunker simulated the appearance of a suburban railroad station with ticket windows appropriately marked. It was discernible as a fraud only when the attackers were within rifle range. Some of the pillboxes and bunkers inside the towns could not be precisely located until all of the surrounding buildings were razed by shelling and bombing. Besides having formal field works of the pillbox or bunker type, the enemy had turned ordinary dwellings, shops, and factory buildings into miniature forts by the use of sandbags, wire, and concrete reinforcement.[45] Most of these defensive works were occupied initially by third-rate troops from the *Volkssturm* companies, but as the tide of battle moved into the city sectors these troops were replaced by first-line units. In addition, roving assault guns, dual-purpose 88's, and tanks reinforced the city defenses,

[45] See various detailed descriptions in the 95th Div AAR, Dec 44.

TO SCHWALBACH

ENSDORF. *Circles indicate pillboxes.*

SAAR RIVER
TO LISDORF

fighting in the narrow streets where they could be protected by their own infantry and where the American tanks or tank destroyers could not readily bring them within range. German artillery and heavy-caliber mortar fire continued to be intense and accurate through all of this fighting and reached a volume in both the 90th and 95th Division zones never before experienced by these divisions.

The American attack, both here and in the zone of the 90th Division, was hampered by the fact that the main German defenses crowded so close to the east bank of the Sarre as to prevent proper tactical deployment for assault in front of the fortified line and seriously hamper the amassing of supplies within close supporting distance of the assault forces. Poor weather denied the troops on the ground the kind of tactical co-operation by the air force which had made the going easier for the infantry in the early battles across France. Limited observation and the difficulty of moving medium and heavy field artillery across the river and into a bridgehead still under small arms fire at many points further curtailed the conventional use of the combined arms in assault against the West Wall.

Nearly every pillbox or bunker captured by the Americans entailed some reduction in the actual rifle strength on the firing line. At no time were sufficient explosives available to demolish any large number of these enemy works. The engineers welded shut the steel doors and casemates on some pillboxes, but there was never sufficient welding apparatus to make this a general practice. Bitter experience soon taught the Americans that each captured pillbox or bunker must be occupied to prevent German infiltration and the reoccupation of a presumably "dead" work. The type of close combat which continued for so long in the Saarlautern bridgehead, and in the Dillingen area as well, not only resulted in numerous combat casualties, but also was distinguished by a high rate of sick and combat-fatigue cases. This kind of fighting was disheartening enough for veterans; it was worse for the inexperienced soldier. In the case of the 95th Infantry Division, for example, the body of the division —as it stood in November—had had two years of training in the United States. Now, like the rest of the American divisions actively engaged on the Western Front, the 95th Division had to rely more and more on green replacements who were being thrown into battle with generally no more than basic or refresher training. These replacements did not suffice to fill the gaps in the ranks, for an alarming shortage was already making itself felt as the replacement depots and battalions ran dry.

In the face of such difficulties the rate of progress made by the 95th Division attack was very slow, measurable in terms of a block of houses cleared or a few pillboxes captured. On 7 December the 379th Infantry edged ahead in Saarlautern-Roden. The 2d Battalion, on the left, repelled sorties by small batches of infantry and roving tanks, cleared one city block, and late in the afternoon crossed the railroad tracks, after the 1st Battalion had taken a factory in which a hidden tank was holding up the advance on the right. The 3d Battalion, which had been engaged at Fraulautern, was relieved by the 2d Battalion of the 377th Infantry and returned to join the rest of the regiment, while the 377th took over the attack in Fraulautern and the protection of the all-important bridge at Saarlautern. The 378th Infantry was held almost to a standstill in the Ensdorf sector under exceedingly severe shelling that knocked out all support bridges as fast as they were put in and made it impossible to cross the 2d Battalion, still west of the Sarre River. Finally, on 8 December, the 2d Battalion was brought across and added its weight to the attack on Ensdorf. Throughout this and the following days, the 378th was handicapped by the necessity of using its riflemen in carrying parties (since no vehicles could be brought across), by the lack of any tank destroyer or tank support, and, in addition, by the fact that the right wing of the regiment was in the air.

During 8 and 9 December the 95th Division fought on, house to house and pillbox to pillbox, but with little to show for its efforts.[46] Behind the battalions the Sarre River was rising rapidly; by 9 December it had swollen to a width of between four hundred and five hundred feet in the 378th area, which as yet had no bridge and could be supplied only by strenuous efforts on the part of the assault boat crews. The Saarlautern bridge served to supply the other two regiments across the river and made it possible for the whole of the 607th Tank Destroyer Battalion and 778th Tank Battalion to reinforce the attack, with considerable impetus to the morale of the infantry.

[46] The 377th Infantry Journal for this period is typical, with the laconic entry, "took another pillbox," repeated after long intervals. The American engineers distinguished themselves in both the 90th and 95th Division zones during this bunker fighting. On 7 December the 95th Division After Action Report pays special tribute to the work of the 320th Engineer Combat Battalion. Enemy participants in these engagements agree in recognizing the "bunker knack" of what they call the American "special troops." The bazooka was particularly valuable in this kind of fighting, despite its high percentage of misfires. Bazooka training had been neglected in the United States (see AGF Study No. 12), and the 95th Division was forced to give such training immediately in the rear of the forward lines.

Finally, on 10 December, resistance in Fraulautern began to crack a little.[47] The 377th, still fairly fresh, wedged through the fourth and fifth city blocks, after capturing a large hotel whose defenders had beaten off several assaults. Characteristic of this close-quarter fighting, the battle for the hotel progressed from room to room and ended in a hand-to-hand struggle in the ballroom. Said a squad leader, "There was plenty of dancing in that ballroom today, but it sure wasn't a slow fox trot." [48] German counterattacks checked the 378th and 379th on 10 December, but the next day brought gains, dearly won as usual, along most of the 95th Division front. In Fraulautern the 377th Infantry drove the Germans back across the railroad line in the center of the city. The enemy fought as stubbornly as ever, but there were a few indications that the will to resist was weakening; the regiment was encouraged greatly when Lt. Peter H. Skala, an IPW (Interrogation Prisoner of War) officer, was able to talk the defenders of four pillboxes into surrendering without a fight.[49] At Ensdorf the 378th cleared most of five city blocks. But in Saarlautern-Roden the 379th Infantry made little progress, becoming involved in a stiff fight to take a large brickyard that blocked the advance on the left flank.

This brief spurt forward came to an end on 12 December, although the 377th took several more blocks in Fraulautern. At the close of this day the 378th Infantry was able to report that after four days of fighting it had taken a cluster of four interlocking pillboxes. Such was the measure of advance in this battle. During the next few days the 95th Infantry Division made a little progress through Ensdorf and Fraulautern.[50] The Germans were fighting with what seemed to be little cohesion or direction, although the individual soldier showed stubborness and determination.[51] But if the enemy was weakening, so was the 95th Division. As early as 12 December the combat efficiency of

[47] The 512th Squadron of the XIX TAC made two raids in front of the 95th Division on 10 December, which may have contributed to the infantry rate of progress.

[48] 377th Inf AAR, 10 Dec 44.

[49] The German commanders were concerned over the large number of "missing" in this period, since the ratio between the "missing" and actual casualties was out of balance. The *First Army* reported as "missing" 19 officers, 215 noncoms and 2,128 men during the period 29 November–10 December. Balck at once began an investigation. *Army Group G KTB,* 11 Dec 44.

[50] On 15 December Balck told *OB WEST* that the American attack had penetrated the "bunker line" in three places "on both sides of Saarlautern." *Army Group G KTB.*

[51] On 11 December the German line needed reinforcement so urgently that a battalion of *Volkssturm* was put in the forward line at Ensdorf. The battalion was so poorly trained that Balck yanked it out of the fight almost as soon as it was committed. *Army Group G KTB,* 11 Dec 44. On 15 December the main body of the *21st Panzer Division* was relieved and sent to the endangered left flank of *Army Group G.*

the division[52] (an index largely based on actual rifle strength) had been rated at 61 percent; 2,000 replacements were needed but were lacking. On 13 December, therefore, the XX Corps commander attached a battalion of the 2d Infantry to the 377th Infantry as bridge guards, the first step in bringing the 5th Infantry Division across to relieve the weary troops in the Saarlautern bridgehead. On 16 December, first word of the German counteroffensive in the Ardennes reached the Third Army. But no change was made in the plans to relieve the battle-worn 95th Division. By 0400 on 17 December the 11th Infantry had taken over the 379th Infantry battle at Saarlautern-Roden, and at midnight the 2d Infantry had completed the relief of the 377th Infantry in Fraulautern, where the 377th was able to turn over a greater part of the city. General Irwin took command of the Saarlautern bridgehead the next morning and the 95th Infantry Division, minus the 378th Infantry, moved out of the line after fifty-eight consecutive days of combat. Its respite would be very brief. The Third Army was about to intervene in the Ardennes battle and elements of the 95th Division would be returned to the bridgehead to free the 5th Division for use in the new American offensive. Nonetheless the 5th Division had time to make very considerable progress forward, as it did on 18 and 19 December. General Irwin's troops were generally fresh, the companies were mostly at full strength, and the 95th Division already had driven through the main bunker lines of the forward West Wall zone.[53] Time was lacking, however, for the 5th Division to capitalize on its gains.

The 378th Infantry was not included in the relief on 17 December because General Patton had ordered the regiment to continue the fight for a bridgehead in the Ensdorf area. Here the river was returning to its normal channel,

[52] Although the combat strength of the 95th Division declined, its fighting spirit continued strong. Numerous deeds of heroism marked this period of the battle, of which only a few could be officially recognized. Sgt. Lemuel G. Tilson, F Company, 377th Infantry, received the DSC for his feats on 12 December at Fraulautern. A platoon from F Company was isolated, with many casualties. Tilson organized a squad to rescue them. Attacking the building in which the wounded were held prisoners, Tilson fought his way inside, from room to room, with grenades. Twenty Germans surrendered and the American casualties were evacuated. Sgt. Earl F. Thurston, I Company, 377th Infantry, also received the DSC. At Fraulautern on 15 December when his squad was held up by rifle and machine gun fire, the sergeant crawled around to the rear of the position, killed one man with his pistol, another with his knife, then routed the machine gun crew with pistol fire and turned the gun on the enemy in surrounding trenches. Capt. Herbert H. Hardy, commanding G Company, 377th Infantry, also was awarded the DSC for the fearless leadership he demonstrated in this fighting.

[53] The existence of a second fortified zone behind Fraulautern and Saarlautern-Roden permitted the German high commands to view the American penetration as only a "technical break-through." *Army Group G KTB Anlagen,* 16 Dec 44.

and on the night of 15–16 December six antitank guns were ferried across. By 17 December the engineers had a bridge in. Guns and supplies began to roll, but the 378th Infantry was not to be allowed to carry out its mission of expanding the bridgehead. On 20 December the last covering troops evacuated Ensdorf and withdrew across the Sarre as part of General Patton's plan to fight a containing battle at the Sarre while turning the bulk of his forces north to meet the German offensive.

The progress of the 95th Infantry Division in the attack east of the Sarre River had been marked on the Third Army situation maps in terms of yards won or lost. But to the staff and line of the 95th the story of this bitter fight was best expressed by the number of buildings and fortifications wrested from a determined enemy. During the period 1 December to 18 December the 95th Division had captured 146 pillboxes and 1,242 defended houses or other buildings. In addition the division had taken over three thousand prisoners and inflicted very heavy casualties on the enemy (estimated by the Americans, albeit superficially, at over five thousand dead and wounded). In the same period the 95th Division had lost close to two thousand officers and men in battle, plus at least six hundred hospitalized as nonbattle casualties, these losses totaling one third of the combat strength with which the 95th Division had started the December operation.[54]

The 90th Division Fight at the West Wall Continues, 8–19 December

On 7 December General Van Fleet had decided to commit his reserve, the 359th Infantry, in the Dillingen bridgehead battle (*Map XLI*) This decision to reinforce the flagging efforts of the attacking force east of the Sarre was strengthened on the following day by reports coming in from the 357th which indicated that the situation on the exposed left flank was growing steadily worse. At noon on 8 December the reserve regiment began to assemble around Bueren and Itzbach in preparation for a crossing that night, leaving its supporting weapons and a small detachment from the cannon

[54] Accurate figures on the 95th Division losses for the period 1–18 December are difficult to determine since the reports by the XX Corps, the 95th Division, and the regimental headquarters are considerably at variance. The *final* casualty report made by the 95th Division G–1 has been used here: 20 officers and 413 men killed; 51 officers and 1,365 men wounded; 4 officers and 93 men missing; 35 officers and 576 men hospitalized as nonbattle casualties. Temporary losses from battle fatigue and exposure were much higher than those listed here, since many more officers and men were taken out of the line for these causes than ever were hospitalized.

companies and antitank platoons of the three regiments to hold the old outpost line on the west bank of the river. The 90th Division commander planned for the reserve regiment to cross the river in the zone of the 357th Infantry and then attack between the two regiments already east of the Sarre. He hoped that the fresh formation would crack the stalemate at Dillingen, but to do so the reserve regiment would have to capture the high ground northeast of Dillingen and, in addition, destroy the enemy salient separating the 358th from the 357th. The initial objective assigned the 359th was the southwest edge of the Huettenwald heights, just north of Dillingen and about one thousand yards east of the railroad line at which the 358th had been checked.[55]

During the night of 8–9 December the 359th moved down to the river. The crossings were made as planned, one battalion following the other as the assault craft were released, and at 0700 the 3d Battalion, bringing up the rear, finished debarking on the east bank. The two battalions in the lead had marched inland immediately, passing through the right wing of the 357th and crossing the railroad tracks. At dawn the battalions began the attack up the pillbox-infested slopes to the east, with the 1st Battalion on the right (and about a thousand yards north of Dillingen) and the 2d Battalion on the left. These fresh troops attacked with vigor and determination, but no speedy advance was possible so long as the enemy, behind reinforced concrete, held the ground above.[56] By dark, however, the leading infantry were within two hundred yards of the Haien Bach, a small stream that here ran north and south along the edge of the Huettenwald. The 3d Battalion, under orders to gain contact with the 358th Infantry, made its attack due south toward Pachten. Immediately, it came under fire from the pillboxes in the long, slender enemy salient which, reaching nearly to the Sarre, had frustrated earlier attempts to link up the American forces in the 90th Division zone. This fortified area was strongly manned and hard to penetrate. The pillboxes were grouped so as to give mutual support and the whole position was reinforced by two forts, or large bunkers, so strongly constructed that they had successfully withstood direct hits by shells from the American 240-mm. howitzers. The approach taken by the 3d Battalion lay across flat ground completely barren of cover and swept by fire. At the end of this first day the battalion could report no

[55] 359th Inf AAR, 8 Dec 44.

[56] Sgt. Vernie A. Lindsay, C Company, 359th Infantry, received the DSC for his outstanding work during this attack. While engaged against a strong bunker position Lindsay's platoon was checked by heavy fire. Lindsay made a one-man attack armed with as many grenades as he could carry, killed several of the enemy, captured the rest, and took the bunker.

progress; in fact it had been forced to take shelter, under the searching German fire, in the few houses along the railroad track. The two companies of the 3d Battalion, 357th Infantry, already engaged in a fight to drive through this enemy salient farther to the west, cleared a few pillboxes during the day, but later lost most of them to German infiltration.

Although the advance by the 359th Infantry lessened the German pressure on the right flank of the 357th during 9 December, the situation on the left and center of the latter's thin line grew more desperate by the hour as assault after assault hit at the American positions and bounced back, each claiming casualties among the defenders. The 1st Battalion, aligned east of the Beckingen–Pachten road, was in a particularly precarious state. Its ranks were so reduced that some men whose feet were too swollen by trench foot to permit walking were carried by their comrades to the forward foxholes. The platoon from C Company which had been stationed at the road block positions astride the Beckingen–Pachten road was the target of persistent German attacks. At dawn each morning the enemy maneuvered in on the platoon and attacked to wipe out the detachment. But each assault was repelled and this anchor for the left wing of the 357th Infantry held fast.[57]

The 358th Infantry continued to battle along the railroad tracks in Dillingen. The 3d Battalion resumed its efforts to clear the buildings west of the tracks, using a captured 75-mm. gun and twenty-two rounds that fitted the piece to blast the houses in which the enemy fought most stubbornly. This enemy gun was the only field piece that the 90th Division possessed east of the river, and the sole item of antitank artillery. In the center the 2d Battalion initiated a futile assault to cross the railroad. Company F discovered a tunnel under the tracks, but the men who got through were cut off and captured by the Germans on the other side. The 1st Battalion, on the right, was subjected to heavy attacks by superior forces in the slaughterhouse area, the fight surging back and forth in the buildings at this strong point without any decisive result.[58]

Behind the 90th Division the Sarre was still at flood stage. Late in the afternoon of 9 December the engineers began rafting operations in the 358th Infantry zone, ferrying across a few jeeps and light antitank guns. In the

[57] 357th Inf AAR, 9 Dec 44.

[58] 358th Inf AAR, 9 Dec 44. The 358th Infantry had not sustained anything like the number of casualties suffered by the 357th. On this date the 358th lost 53 officers and men, reporting the losses as "heavy casualties."

SLAUGHTERHOUSE AREA IN DILLINGEN. *Circles indicate pillboxes.*

TO SAARLAUTERN-RODEN

early evening the first tank debarked from the treadway ferry, but this and the tanks following could not be used on the left flank of the division, where armor was most needed, so long as the hostile fortified salient separated the 358th from the rest of the division. Assault boats and carrying parties remained the only means of supplying the 357th and 359th, although four P-47's, flown by pilots of the XIX TAC, swept over the 357th at treetop level and dropped urgently needed medical supplies squarely in the drop zone that had been marked by the infantry. The hard-pressed 357th received additional help in the form of two hundred replacements who were crossed in assault boats and sent immediately into line.[59]

December 10 was a day of snow and rain, chilling and soaking the men in the foxholes. It was also the day on which the entire force of the *719th Division* finally was brought to bear against the 90th Division bridgehead defenses. Balck's threats and fulminations had accomplished little as to rerouting the wandering *719th* or remedying the disorder that had resulted from the conflicting missions assigned the division. On 9 December the bulk of the *719th* had been rounded up and was in process of assembling in the woods east of Saarwellingen. But when the division began the march west to its attack positions a traffic jam resulted; the division artillery, nineteen light and eleven heavy guns, could not be moved forward to support the scheduled attack. The *Army Group G* commander was furious, started court martial proceedings, and issued the strictest kind of injunctions for the *719th* to make a full-scale attack on the morning of 10 December.[60]

Just before dawn the *719th* and the *19th VG Division* began piecemeal attacks all along the American line, while the German artillery, numbering some 110 guns, increased its shelling to a tempo the 90th Division had not heretofore encountered in the bridgehead. The 90th Division, with all its rifle battalions committed, was not able to take the initiative and during most of the day could only hold grimly to its positions. The 357th Infantry was hard hit, since the main effort by the *719th* was thrown against it, but continued to beat off each assault.[61] The 359th Infantry fought a seesaw battle in

[59] 90th Div AAR, 9 Dec 44.

[60] *Army Group G KTB Anlagen,* 9 and 10 Dec 44. Balck told his staff that "everything" depended on this attack.

[61] An enemy counterattack on 10 December forced two infantry platoons to retreat. Sgt. James L. McDonald, A Company, 357th Infantry, led a bold attack to retake the position, killed several of the enemy, and drove the rest out of the entrenchments which had been lost. Sgt. McDonald was awarded the DSC.

the pillboxes west of the Haien Bach against enemy sallies coming down the slopes. The 3d Battalion fought its way into the fortified salient, making a desperate attempt to join hands with the 358th Infantry to the south, but by nightfall had lost nearly all organization as its squads and platoons were cut off in captured pillboxes or isolated and pinned to the earth by raking machine gun fire. The 358th received a terrific pounding by the German guns and several counterattacks.[62] Company F, which had won a precarious footing east of the track, was forced to withdraw. Elsewhere the regiment held its ground[63] and L Company succeeded in destroying five German tanks. Company A was hit and surrounded by a very strong enemy force intent on retaking the slaughterhouse area. For several hours telephone connections with the company were severed and the company was reported lost, but at the end of the day this strong point was still in American hands. Late in the afternoon the 1st Battalion saw the Germans forming east of the tracks for a final assault. Hastily organizing a counterattack, elements of A and B Companies dashed across the tracks, wheeled left through a cemetery and into a fortified church on the enemy flank. This unexpected assault broke up the German formation. The exposed position was untenable, however, and the American troops withdrew from their temporary shelter as soon as darkness gave them the opportunity.[64]

Supply for the 90th Division continued to be handled by assault boats, for the river dropped abruptly and stranded the heavy ferry, which German guns then damaged when veering winds blew away the smoke screen at the crossing site. The shoestring nature of the supply lines on the left flank and their continued interruption by German raiding parties made General Van Fleet decide to regroup the 357th. To do this he ordered the 1st and 2d Battalions to redress their lines on a shortened front, and withdrew the 3d Battalion from the attack on the fortified salient, setting it to secure the supply roads close behind the battalions in the line. He further ordered the 359th to continue the attack to the east, but to use its 3d Battalion to force a way to the 358th in the sector north of Pachten.[65]

[62] Col. Jacob W. Bealke, Jr., took command of the 358th Infantry on 10 December, relieving Lt. Col. Frederick H. Loomis, who returned to his old position as regimental executive officer.

[63] Some credit for the stand by the 358th must go to the 513th Squadron of the XIX TAC which intervened in the fighting during the afternoon with napalm and 5-inch rockets. This was the last major direct-support mission flown by the XIX TAC during the December battle at the XX Corps bridgehead.

[64] 1st Bn, 358th Inf, Jnl, 10 Dec 44.

[65] 90th Div G–3 Jnl, 10 Dec 44.

On 11 December the 357th withdrew its lines in the north and northeast as the division commander had directed.[66] The 358th and 359th confined their activities to probing for a corridor through the fortified salient still separating the two, after the 359th was hit by a German night attack that drove in between the 1st and 3d Battalions and recaptured three pillboxes and their occupants. All efforts to reduce the pillboxes in the salient by direct assault were fruitless, as was precision shelling by heavy artillery west of the Sarre. During the day General Van Fleet brought the scratch covering force from the west bank to fill the gaps in the firing line, leaving the 90th Reconnaissance Troop to patrol west of the Sarre. This movement brought on so much enemy shelling as to indicate the possibility that the Germans might attempt to flank the 90th Division by a counterattack across the Sarre, and General Walker alerted the 10th Armored Division to meet such a riposte if it should come.[67]

The following day brought the successful completion of the scheme of maneuver outlined on 10 December by the division commander. The 3d Battalion of the 357th finished mopping up the pillboxes and knots of enemy riflemen which had harassed the rear of the regiment all through the operation. For the first time the left flank of the 90th Division was stabilized. The 358th and 359th finally made contact and established a lateral corridor through the German fortified salient. This feat was accomplished by a combination of accurate artillery fire, daring infantry assault tactics, and a kind of "homegrown" psychological warfare. The 8-inch and 240-mm. howitzers that had been brought to bear on the German pillboxes produced real results on 12 December, smashing some by direct hits and badly shaking the nerves of the defenders in the rest. A combat patrol sent out from the 359th on the previous day, and written off for lost when it failed to report, turned up in possession of one of the key pillboxes, making the task of the following assault teams much easier.[68] The 358th pressed into service a Luxemburger known as "the

[66] Sgt. Aubrey G. Edwards, K Company, 357th Infantry, and his squad were surrounded while holding a pillbox that protected the 3d Battalion flank. Sergeant Edwards rushed out of the pillbox in the face of intense fire and although he was wounded killed seven and wounded three of the Germans with his rifle. This diversion allowed the rest of the squad to emerge and the surviving enemy surrendered. Sergeant Edwards was given the DSC.

[67] XX Corps G–3 Jnl, 11 Dec 44.

[68] An incident in the 357th Infantry zone illustrates the tactics of this pillbox combat. A platoon from I Company captured a large pillbox by conventional assault tactics, buttoning up the defenders by fire and then blasting in the steel doors with demolition charges. The platoon neglected to post riflemen outside the captured pillbox; so a German combat patrol quickly closed in, sealed the Americans inside the pillbox with small arms fire, and captured all thirty-one men. The following day the Americans buttoned up the pillbox in exactly the same way, laid satchel charges that killed sixteen of the enemy, and took

VEHICULAR TREADWAY FERRY *in the 358th Infantry zone was left stranded by the receding river on 9 December, but became operational again three days later.*

old Kraut." He succeeded in convincing the occupants of five strong pillboxes that wisdom was the better part of valor, after condign threats that they would all "be blown to hell." The first contact between the 358th and the two regiments in the north was made about 1530. Fortunately the winds now favored the Americans, the smoke screen held, the vehicular ferry was again put into operation, and by late afternoon one company each of tanks and tank destroyers had been put across. Two tank platoons were sent at once through the corridor to the 357th. Although all but four of the tanks mired down before they reached the regiment, their presence brought a considerable lift to the flagging spirits of the men in the foxholes.[69] Meanwhile the 358th turned its attention toward Dillingen and began preparations to resume the

the twenty-five dazed survivors as prisoners. In one such episode on 16 December Pfc. James R. Pfleger, I Company, 357th Infantry, voluntarily made a dash out of a surrounded pillbox in broad daylight to get help for his trapped comrades. He succeeded in bringing aid before the sixteen men in the pillbox were wiped out. Private Pfleger was awarded the DSC.

[69] Another bright spot came in the 358th Infantry area where the fight for the slaughterhouse paid off and the "doughs" now were eating steaks and French-fried potatoes.

attack. Corps artillery blasted the city, the 4.2 chemical mortar companies of the 81st Battalion laid in 2,500 rounds of white phosphorus, and by nightfall Dillingen was burning brightly.

In reports on the morning of 12 December, the "combat efficiency" of the 90th Division was rated at 43 percent, the result of the exhausted condition of the troops and the acute shortage of replacements. It is true that the arrival of the armor and antitank support plus the final tie-up of all three regiments raised morale appreciably during the day. But the chief difficulties facing the division still obtained: gravely reduced rifle strength in the battalions and the necessity of holding on to the innumerable pillboxes after their seizure, for here, as in the 95th Division bridgehead, demolition supplies were insufficient to destroy more than a very few of the captured enemy works.

General Van Fleet decided to concentrate the limited strength of the 90th Division in a determined effort to complete the capture of the city of Dillingen. Devastated though the city was, it would offer some cover from the winter cold and rain and provide a defensive position more easily held than the open terrain on which the American main line of resistance now was drawn. Once Dillingen was secured the 357th Infantry could be withdrawn from its exposed sector and aligned as flank protection in the Pachten–Dillingen area. Furthermore, the capture of Dillingen would put the 90th Division in possession of the Prims River crossing at the south edge of the city from which a main highway, skirting the swamp land to the west, led to Saarlautern-Roden and possible contact with the 95th Division.[70]

General Van Fleet set 15 December as the date for the renewal of the attack, giving time for the 90th to regroup and build up its stock of supplies and ammunition east of the Sarre. The last was no easy task, for the bottom had gone out of the muddy road between the river and Pachten; to make matters worse, at noon on 14 December the German guns again knocked out the vehicular ferry. Nevertheless, by the night preceding the attack ample supplies were at hand and enough vehicles had been crossed to relieve the infantry engaged as carrying parties.

The Saarlautern–Dillingen bridgehead meanwhile had lost its paramount place as the greatest threat to the German forces under *Army Group G.* The offensive by the American Seventh Army along the west bank of the Rhine had gained momentum on 11 December and promised to drive straight

[70] 90th Div AAR, 13 Dec 44.

through the weak forces under *Group Hoehne* who were fighting with their backs to the West Wall. Here in the Wissembourg sector, on the edge of the Rhine Valley, the West Wall was none too strong, consisting as it did of only a single fortified line. Furthermore, *OB WEST* reckoned the ratio between the opposing forces as 10 to 1 in favor of the Americans. By 14 December the German situation had deteriorated so markedly that Rundstedt's headquarters expected "hourly" to receive news that the Americans had broken through into the Palatinate. The battle now could only be one to win time and to hold until the great Ardennes counteroffensive was unleashed.[71]

Needless to say Balck could expect no help from the armies in the OKW strategic reserve. Requests for help from the *Nineteenth Army* only resulted in the brusque statement by Jodl that no troops could be taken away from Himmler. Balck did the only thing he could do and commenced to strip the rest of the *Army Group G* front in order to reinforce General Hoehne. With his eye on the double zone of fortifications in the Saarlautern sector Balck gave orders that the remainder of the *21st Panzer Division* and all of the *404th Volks Artillery Corps* were to be relieved from the bridgehead battle and sent to the south. The *First Army* commander, General Obstfelder, pleaded and even argued, then fell back on the conventional alibi that he lacked the gasoline necessary to move these troops out of his area. By various dodges Obstfelder managed to delay the departure of the *21st* and the *404th*, but by 15 December only the rear elements of these units were left in the Saarlautern–Dillingen area. In the meantime *OB WEST* had secured the *526th Replacement Division* to take the place of the *21st Panzer Division*, but the movement of the former was long delayed and on 15 December only a few of its troops had arrived in front of the XX Corps bridgehead.[72]

Early on the morning of 15 December the 90th Division attack to mop up Dillingen jumped off as planned under a dense smoke screen put down by the 4.2 mortars. Two battalions of the 358th Infantry led off in an assault across the railroad tracks and fought their way under terrific enemy fire into the streets and houses of Dillingen, followed closely by tanks and tank destroyers. Within a few hours the Germans began to break and when night

[71] Balck knew that some large project was in the offing but probably had not been briefed on the exact details. Rundstedt, of course, was involved in the planning and had constantly told Balck "to fight for time."

[72] See the *Army Group G* and *OB WEST KTB*'s for this period.

came the 358th had cleared the buildings for some three hundred yards east of the tracks. The 359th Infantry gained about five hundred yards, against moderate resistance.[73] In the late afternoon elements of the two regiments met on the north side of the city. The Americans had penetrated the main line of defenses in the Dillingen sector and mopped up numerous bunkers. The Germans could no longer defend along a co-ordinated line, but instead would have to hold at individual strong points and in islands of resistance. The success of this attack allowed General Van Fleet to risk weakening his left flank. On 16 December he took the battered and depleted 1st Battalion from the 357th and sent it back across the river for a few hours' rest. The remaining battalions of the 357th were in little better state than the 1st, although refleshed somewhat by the arrival of the scratch force from the west bank.[74] Indeed, the rifle strength of the entire division was so low that the division commander was forced to eliminate all antitank platoons and reduce the cannon companies and mortar platoons in order to provide more infantry for the continuation of the attack.

After the drive into Dillingen the German forces, now stripped of the *21st* and *404th*, failed to react with their usual counterattack tactics and a lull developed along the front.[75] General Van Fleet purposely postponed any continuation of the attack at Dillingen since he wished to give the 5th Division time to relieve the 95th Division in the Saarlautern bridgehead and initiate a drive that would bring its lines forward alongside the 90th. On 18 December the 3d Battalion, 359th Infantry, and the 2d Battalion, 358th, made a co-ordinated drive in Dillingen. The division commander strictly enjoined a "cautious attack," for he was most anxious to avoid excessive casualties and did not want to attract any strong German reaction until the 5th Division was abreast of the 90th.[76] In spite of these limitations the advance moved forward very swiftly; resistance was astonishingly light and only twenty-two prisoners were

[73] Sgt. John W. Muza, G Company, 359th Infantry, charged inside a large enemy bunker, peppered the interior with hand grenades, and forced the surrender of about 125 Germans. Sergeant Muza was awarded the DSC.

[74] On 16 December the company strengths in the 357th Infantry, listed in numbers of officers and men, were as follows: A—4 and 54; B—2 and 18; C—1 and 54; D—4 and 35; E—4 and 55; F—6 and 65; G—4 and 62; H—5 and 53; I—3 and 55; K—4 and 83; L—5 and 96; M—6 and 83. 357th Inf S-1 Jnl, 16 Dec 44.

[75] At 0600 on 16 December the *Army Group G* commander was informed by *OB WEST* that the Ardennes counteroffensive had begun. His orders now were to fight a containing action and concentrate on patrolling that would identify American withdrawals from his front.

[76] 358th Inf AAR, 17 Dec 44.

taken. Within three hours the assault battalions had cleared eleven blocks and most of Dillingen was in American hands. But the 90th Infantry Division was soon to lose its hard-won ground. On the afternoon of 19 December General Patton ordered the division commander to begin the evacuation of the 90th Division bridgehead. The Third Army was in the process of shifting its divisions toward the Ardennes.[77] There were some indications that the enemy was assembling a force in the Sarre–Moselle triangle, from which base a German attack could be mounted against the new American line of communications.[78] General Patton needed every division that could be freed. For the time being the Saarlautern bridgehead would suffice to ensure a foothold east of the Sarre, in the event that the Third Army should return to the offensive in this area.[79]

Lacking a bridge, the withdrawal of nine infantry battalions and about a hundred vehicles was a delicate operation. Through three successive nights the 90th Division moved men, weapons, tanks, trucks, and tank destroyers back over the Sarre.[80] At 1040 on 22 December the rear guard arrived on the west bank, while the American guns smashed Pachten and Dillingen with salvo after salvo.[81] An unknown battalion clerk wrote *finis* to the operation: "This was the first time this Battalion ever gave ground and even though it was a strategic retreat rather than tactical, it still hurt." [82] During the December battle on the Sarre the 90th Division had captured 1,298 prisoners and inflicted heavy losses on the enemy. But the 90th Division also had suffered severely, particularly among its veteran officers and men, and had lost 239 killed, 924 wounded, approximately 440 missing, as well as over a thousand officers and men evacuated as sick, battle-exhaustion, or battle-injury cases, the whole totaling more than one-third of its strength on 1 December.[83]

[77] The subsequent operations of the Third Army will be described in H. M. Cole, The Ardennes, a volume now under preparation in this series.

[78] 90th Div AAR, 19 Dec 44. This German concentration in the triangle actually did not exist; there were less than six battalions all told in the area.

[79] General Patton and General Walker were anxious to hold on to the Saarlautern bridgehead because they expected to continue the XX Corps offensive as soon as the Ardennes counteroffensive was halted.

[80] The German observers were aware of each stage in the withdrawal. MS #A–972 (Muehlen).

[81] Among the last troops to leave the bridgehead were elements of the 84th and 161st Smoke Generating Companies. Smoke generator units had taken an important part in the Sarre operation, although the prevailing winds (before 11 December) had played havoc with the smoke screen laid over the river. During the crossing and recrossing of the Sarre the XX Corps used 167,050 gallons of fog oil, plus 8,500 smoke pots.

[82] 3d Bn, 358th Inf, Jnl, 20 Dec 44.

[83] 90th Div G–1 and G–4 Jnls.

CHAPTER XIV
Conclusion

Estimates by the Enemy

At the end of 1944 the German training staffs published a series of "Battle Experiences,"[1] containing the official enemy estimate of the American soldier, his tactics, and his weapons. For the most part this German's-eye view is presented in the form of a "catch-all" characterization of the American troops fighting on the Western Front; in numerous instances, however, generalizations are supported by examples chosen from the Lorraine sector. Since the "Battle Experiences" were prepared for and issued to the troops, they contain much that stems from the politico-military dogmas of the Nazi party or that obviously is intended to raise the morale of the individual German soldier.

Despite recognition that the individual American was a more skilled and tenacious fighter in the fall of 1944 than in the early weeks after the Normandy landings, the *doctrine* of the superiority of the German infantryman did not alter. Stripped of the numerous propaganda reasons put forth to support this allegation, the core of the argument is as follows: the American soldier depends upon tremendous materiel support to bring the battle to a successful conclusion; when he is denied heavy support by the combined arms the "drive" in the attack dwindles; he avoids close combat, dislikes night fighting, and surrenders readily—all symptoms of his poor quality as a soldier.

The German soldier was alerted to capitalize on several peculiarities shown by American troops. The Americans were depicted as being careless with radio conversations, although the radio silence of the Third Army armored divisions before the 8 November offensive was admitted to have been notably successful in misleading German intelligence. The Americans tended to start their attacks late in the forenoon and to "call off the war" at midnight. American security during hours of darkness was careless, particularly on rainy nights. The individual American soldier was "more tenacious" on the defensive than in the attack. American infantry and tanks tended to stick to streets and roads; tanks avoided woods and heavy underbrush.

[1] *OKH Gen. St. d. H., Abt. Fremde Heere West: Einzelnachrichten des Ic Dienstes West.*

Besides including such derogatory comments, the German "Battle Experiences" described in detail those aspects of American tactics and techniques believed to be worthy of emulation. High on all lists was the effective co-operation between infantry and tanks, tanks and planes. American artillery was an object of praise. It was distinguished, said German observers, by a speedy system of communication, accurate fire, a plentiful supply of ammunition, greater range than that of comparable German types, skilled employment of artillery planes as aerial OP's, and extensive use of white phosphorus. The American replacement system was regarded as very effective, although the German writers agreed that the national wealth of manpower was a basic factor in helping make it so. American tactical leadership was rated highly, learning with surprising rapidity, as it seemed to do, from its own failures and from the enemy.

Planning and preparation appeared to err, from the German point of view, on the side of caution. The Germans found what they considered evidence of hypermethodical thinking, and of a tendency to make success absolutely certain, in the practice of combining one armored division with two infantry divisions. They agreed, however, that the motorization of American infantry formations prevented the infantry from acting as a drag on the armor. This cautious approach to tactical problems was seen also in the practice of using battalion attacks, heavily supported by all arms, to open a hole on a narrow front. The later "Battle Experiences" noted that the Americans were trying to break away from "sterile" limited-objective attacks on a narrow front, but that when improvisation failed the American leadership quickly reverted to cautious tactics. The XII Corps attack on a broad front on 8 November was singled out particularly as evidence of an attempt to break away from small-scale and "riskless" solutions. In connection with this attack, it was observed that artillery fires massed all along the front made it impossible to determine what the points of penetration might be. On the other hand, the German observers pointed to the XX Corps attack across the Moselle north of Metz as a good example of the satisfactory results to be attained by a very limited use of artillery fire prior to the assault. The final drive toward Sarreguemines was regarded as a reversion to the tactics of improvisation and quick exploitation which, in the German view, had characterized Patton's use of armor in the break-out at Avranches. But the "Battle Experiences" expressed surprise that the American armor tended, at the close of the autumn campaign, to be parceled out in small detachments intermixed with the infantry divisions.

To what extent the above observations are valid and valuable can best be determined by the trained soldier who has made an unbiased and critical study of the operations in Lorraine and in other areas of the Western Front during the autumn and early winter of 1944. It would be a mistake, albeit human, to take satisfaction in those points chalked up to the credit of the American arms while giving arbitrary dismissal to each unfavorable item in these enemy appraisals.

Losses Suffered by the Combatants

Losses inflicted on the German forces in Lorraine were high. Although the number of Germans killed and wounded cannot be determined with any degree of exactness, it is known that at least 75,000 prisoners passed through the Third Army cages during the Lorraine operation. It is impossible to give any reasonably accurate statement of German losses in tanks, guns, and vehicles. During September the enemy had amassed the greatest number of armored fighting vehicles that he was to employ against the Third Army at any time in the Lorraine Campaign. The tank losses sustained by the German armored brigades and divisions in the September battles had been much higher than those inflicted on the American armored formations. In November and December, however, American tank losses incurred in the course of the slow advance through the Lorraine mud probably were considerably higher than those of the enemy. The damage and destruction inflicted on German transport and artillery by the Third Army and the XIX Tactical Air Command were very much greater than that visited by enemy action on the Third Army. Materiel losses sustained by General Patton's command in the period 1 September to 18 December are cited below:[2]

Light tanks	105
Medium tanks	298
Vehicles	1,080
Artillery (75-mm. and larger)	34

It must be added that the German ability to replace materiel losses in any category of equipment was markedly inferior to that of the Allies. If the campaign be considered as a battle of attrition, which indeed it was during

[2] TUSA AAR, I.

the last weeks, the Third Army had done much on this secondary front to weaken the Wehrmacht.

The Third Army had suffered 55,182 killed, wounded, and missing in Lorraine (a total casualty list substantially less than the number of Germans captured, not to speak of the enemy roster of dead and wounded).[3]

Killed in action	6,657
Wounded in action	36,406
Missing in action	12,119

This list of combat casualties does not represent the sum total of the American losses suffered in the Lorraine Campaign. The number of so-called "nonbattle" casualties—those evacuated because of fatigue, exposure, and disease—is officially reported as 42,088 officers and men. Statistics compiled on these cases during and after the campaign generally are unreliable and tend to minimize this type of casualty. In November, however, when the system of reporting nonbattle casualties was more or less regularized, Third Army records show a total of 15,737 nonbattle casualties as against 22,773 battle casualties; and it is probable that the same ratio continued through the first three weeks of December, if indeed the proportion of nonbattle casualties did not increase.

During November and December the front-line troops of the Third Army were hard hit by trench foot, a disease in which the feet, through continued exposure to dampness and cold, became painfully swollen, discolored, and sometimes gangrenous.[4] Trench foot first attained epidemic proportions among the American armies on the Western Front about 10 November. The Third Army, which had begun the November offensive, showed a higher incidence of the disease during this initial stage than any of the other American armies. From 16 November until the middle of December the incidence of trench foot began a slow but progressive decline, this decline being most apparent in the Third Army divisions. New provision for the laundering and issue of clean socks, extensive educational campaigns, and tightened disciplinary measures helped to reduce the number of trench foot cases. But the occurrence of the disease bore a direct and demonstrable relation to the tactical situation in any given area: so long as troops had to continue in sections

[3] TUSA G–1 Periodic Rpt, Nos. 5 through 43. These figures cover the period 1 September–18 December 1944.

[4] Medical aspects of the operations in 1944 will be treated in the official history now being compiled by the Historical Division, Office of the Surgeon General.

of the line where there was no cover and where rotation in the fox holes could not be effected, just so long the disease continued to reduce the rifle strength.

Records of the German units opposing the Third Army make no reference whatever to trench foot and it is clear that this disease was not regarded as a problem in the enemy camp. The enemy freedom from trench foot, at a time when the Third Army was being hit severely by the malady, is difficult to explain. Contemporary interrogation of German medical personnel revealed little save the fact that at this stage of the war the Wehrmacht did not regard trench foot as a problem. The German boot, the cloth wrappings with which the German soldier bound his feet, the foot salve issued by the German medical aid men, all were analyzed without result. But it would seem that the enemy success in avoiding trench foot may be ascribed primarily to two factors. First, many of the troops facing the Third Army were seasoned veterans of campaigns on the Eastern Front. During the winter of 1941-42 the German armies in Russia, ill-prepared as they were to face the rigors of the Russian cold, had suffered severely from exposure and frostbite. The lessons of this first winter campaign were quickly assimilated by the Wehrmacht. Second, the German soldier in late 1944 lacked the mechanized transport (and the freedom to use such transport) which characterized the Allied armies. Inured to long marches on foot, the individual soldier was physically prepared to withstand foot disease and practiced in its prevention.

Combat fatigue also contributed heavily to the losses sustained by combat elements of the Third Army during the Lorraine Campaign. The practice of leaving divisions in the line for very long periods and filling gaps in the ranks with individual replacements quite naturally increased the rate of combat fatigue as the campaign wore on. Before the November drive, however, the American replacement system in the ETO was able to make good the total losses (both from battle and nonbattle casualties) of the Third Army. The bitterly contested advance in November, made under difficult conditions of weather and terrain, resulted in a high casualty rate which could not be equaled by the number of replacements available. In this month the Third Army received only 26,981 replacements, although its casualty list numbered 38,510. By 30 November there was a shortage of 10,184 officers and men—mostly infantry, tankers, and medical aid men—in the divisions. On 1 December the Third Army was 8,213 understrength in infantry alone.[5] By 6 De-

[5] TUSA Diary, 1 Dec 44.

cember the Army Ground Force replacement system had broken down entirely, so far as the Third Army was concerned, and no troops were available in the army replacement depots. General Patton wished to maintain one infantry division in each corps at full strength, selecting the 5th Division for the XX Corps and the 87th Division for the XII Corps. In order to secure the necessary replacements the Third Army Commander ordered that 5 percent of all nondivisional units should be converted to riflemen, dispatching the new "infantry" to be retrained by the 87th Division which was still in the Metz area under the III Corps. On 15 December another 5 percent was cut from the army and corps troops, making a total of approximately 6,500 trainees that were added to the rifle strength of the Third Army under this plan. In the opinion of the line commanders, however, the cursoriness of the training given these replacements was a distinct liability that imposed great burdens and led to heavy casualties among the veteran noncoms and company officers.

Supply

When the Third Army started operations to force the Moselle line in early September, it was almost entirely dependent on truck-borne supply. The famous Red Ball Express was moving supplies from Cherbourg and the Normandy beaches to dumps at Sommesous, south of Reims, a round trip of 670 miles. Army truck companies carried this tonnage to army supply points, or themselves made the long journey to Normandy. Fortunately, the railroad system east of Paris was relatively intact and soon was in operation behind the advancing armies. The Third Army opened its first railhead on 15 September at Verdun. By 26 September the Red Ball Express ended the run east of Paris, limiting itself to hauling supplies from Normandy to the new rail terminals in the vicinity of Paris. Truck transport continued to move much of the tonnage coming into the Third Army dumps, but the creation of great railheads in the Reims and Toul areas made possible a considerable expansion of the army supply system. The October lull allowed the Third Army a greater degree of logistical stability than it had previously known. Reserves were created; army dumps, truckheads, and railheads moved up close to the corps rear boundaries. During October the Third Army received 97,955 long tons of supplies, most of the quartermaster items and artillery ammunition arriving by rail. By the beginning of the November offensive the supply situation on the Continent was so much improved that the Third Army was able to make requests for specific items of supply instead of relying upon the delivery of gross tonnages. Gasoline was no longer a supply problem; during November the army received more POL than it had requested.

The battles east of the Moselle, during November and December, required a displacement to bring the army supply installations across the river. The first army supply point east of the Moselle opened about 14 November, dispensing POL. By the end of November a small quartermaster railhead was in operation at Château-Salins, using a spur from the railroad bridge that had been rebuilt north of Nancy. However, the supply shift east of the Moselle had not yet been completed when the Third Army turned north toward the Ardennes. Until the end of the Lorraine Campaign the bulk of supplies destined for the Third Army entered the Continent by way of Normandy ports and beaches, although in October the port of Le Havre began shipments to Reims, and some supplies later reached the Third Army by way of Marseille.

The rations issued to Third Army troops varied little during the campaign. As a rule 65 to 70 percent of the food supplied came in the form of the B ration, a modified garrison ration with some fresh meat, white bread, and newly roasted coffee, but with no fresh fruit (except oranges) or fresh vegetables. The man actually in the line usually lived on the C ration, its canned meat and hash hard to digest even when heated, or the K ration, with its unchanging sequence of processed meat and egg, processed cheese, and "meat component." In November a new and more palatable C ration arrived in the form of spaghetti and meat balls; the popularity of this meal was attested to immediately by numerous entries in unit journals, sandwiched in among reports on patrol activities or strength returns. The Thanksgiving dinner, for decades a high point in Army quartermaster efforts, also was a subject for enthusiastic report by troops in combat. On 23 November all the men who could be reached were given a pound of turkey, a half-pound of chicken, and as many of the conventional trimmings as the company cook could provide. Those troops in forward positions were rotated in the next several days in order that every combat soldier could have his Thanksgiving dinner.[6]

[6] For a detailed history of supply see Ruppenthal, Logistical Support.

Morale Factors; Civilian Problems

Periodic rest and rehabilitation for troops in the line, which had been taught as a matter of doctrine in service schools between the two world wars, were limited by the practice of keeping divisions in action for long periods and maintaining their combat strength through the replacement system. In December the XII Corps set up a Rest Center at Nancy staffed by the American Red Cross, but the tactical situation on the XX Corps front precluded such an establishment in the Metz area. Rest for most troops meant a few hours in some demolished village behind the lines, a hot shower, coffee and doughnuts served by a Red Cross "Clubmobile," and the chance to see a movie or a traveling USO show. Marlene Dietrich played to Third Army audiences for nine weeks, by far the longest tour of the "name" shows, during which time over 37,000 troops saw her performance. In general, however, entertainment was provided by the lesser known USO performers, who stayed with the army throughout the campaign, and by the traveling "jeep shows," manned by two or three soldier-performers. Radio receivers for combat units arrived early in the campaign. As troops moved into billets they had a chance to hear the special programs broadcast by the Armed Forces Network, or the jazz recordings played on a popular Berlin program which began with "Over There" and signed off nostalgically with "Home Sweet Home." Much reading matter reached the troops, even those in forward positions. The daily newspaper, *Stars and Stripes*, which on occasion was enlivened for General Patton's troops by Mauldin's sardonic cartoons on Third Army discipline, went up to the lines with mail and rations. *Yank*, famous for its ultramammary and undraped "pin-up girls," came along once a week. But it is probable that of all the so-called "morale services" none were as important as mail from home and the supply of cigarettes. Early in October, when the Third Army front began to stabilize, a special daily train loaded with 400 tons of mail was run to the army area with the letters and packages that had accumulated at the beaches during the period of mobility. The "cigarette crisis" of October and early November, in its turn, was a matter of concern from the army headquarters up through the chain of higher command.

Military operations in Lorraine were little affected by the civilian life of this populous region. On the French side of the border the retreating Germans evacuated few inhabitants besides their own party and customs officials.

In Germany some large-scale movements of the civilian population took place, particularly in the Saar Basin, but even the German civilians tended to stick doggedly to their homes. Usually the civilian population, both French and German, took to their cellars while the battle, literally, passed over their heads. At Sarreguemines, for example, it was estimated that two-thirds of the inhabitants remained in the city while the American and German troops fought for its possession. Of course there was a considerable number of refugees—13,274 in the Third Army zone at the end of September and 32,735 at the close of November. Many of them were Russians, Poles, and Yugoslavs who had furnished slave labor in the mills and mines. The detachments of the 2d European Civil Affairs Regiment, the French officials, and the Third Army military police who handled the civilian population acted on "stand fast" orders designed to prevent mass movement on the main supply roads or the free circulation of potential spies. The Moselle River was marked as a "no passage" line for all civilians, partly to keep the roads free and to maintain security, but also because of the continuing fear that typhus might break out and strike the American troops.

Air-Ground Co-operation

One outstanding feature of the Lorraine Campaign was the co-operation between the XIX Tactical Air Command and the Third Army. To a considerable degree this must be attributed to the excellent relations between General Weyland, General Patton, and their respective staffs. The Third Army commander, conscious of the problems, limitations, and capabilities of air support, allowed himself to be guided by General Weyland, by Col. James Ferguson, the A–3 of the XIX TAC, and by Lt. Col. I. P. Murray, his own G–3 Air. General Weyland, in turn, extended himself and his command to meet the requests of the Third Army whenever the weather and the priorities imposed by higher headquarters permitted.

It must be said that the role played by the weather became increasingly important in the course of the campaign as a factor limiting air-ground cooperation. The fighter-bombers, from the Moselle eastward, were never capable of the continuous and spectacular support which had stamped the pursuit operations in August. The decline in the number of sorties flown by the XIX TAC, indicated in the following table, clearly shows the impact of unfavorable seasonal weather (although it should be added that the strength of Weyland's command was reduced somewhat in the late fall).[7]

August	12,292 sorties
September	7,791 sorties
October	4,790 sorties
November	3,509 sorties
1–22 December	2,563 sorties

During September the XIX TAC moved its bases eastward, as operations against Brest came to a close, setting up on airfields overrun by the Third Army in the area north and east of Chalôns-sur-Marne. By the end of the month all bases were sited within fifty miles of the army front. About 22 September General Weyland moved his advance headquarters to Etain, where General Patton was located; the two commanders lived as neighbors throughout the remainder of the campaign.

During September the XIX TAC combined efforts to interdict enemy movement into the battle area with close tactical support against objectives on the immediate army front. During the pursuit across France the ground forces had frequently been hampered by the all too effective air attacks against bridges lying in the path of the advance; as early as 1 August Patton had requested Weyland to leave intact the bridges along the Third Army axis. On 2 September the Allied Expeditionary Air Force ordered a stop to indiscriminate attacks on bridges and rail yards, adding an injunction against rail cutting, except for immediate tactical purposes. Air support in the days following tended to concentrate on strafing enemy troop movement, flying cover over the attacking ground troops, and bombing suspected German concentrations in such places as Metz, the Forêt de Haye and the Forêt de Parroy. The XIX TAC raids over the latter points were abetted by bombers from the IX Bombardment Division. As the Third Army advance came to a halt in late September, the XIX TAC reverted to its rail-cutting tactics in an attempt to prevent German reinforcement on the Lorraine front, but a stretch of bad weather intervened to cripple this effort.

The stalemate in October resulted in some changes in the air program. The Third Army artillery was emplaced in positions from which most targets to the immediate front could be handled. As a result XIX TAC, rein-

[7] TUSA AAR, I.

forced on occasion by the IX Bombardment Division, set about strafing and smashing German supply dumps, barrack centers, and troop columns in the area between the Sarre and Rhine Rivers. Trier, Saarbruecken, Forbach, Zweibruecken, Sarreguemines, Bad Kreuznach, and Homburg appeared again and again on the target lists during these days. Uncertain weather precluded any extensive policing of cuts made in the German rail lines; therefore, on 2 October the prohibition against attacking railroad bridges and yards was lifted. The enemy, who was making considerable movement during this lull, was forced to travel on poor flying days, make his marches at night, or take his chances in the daylight. Weyland received a squadron of P–61 night fighters (the 425th) early in October, but the number of these planes was too small to have much effect.

Despite the poor weather and the short days in November the XIX TAC was able to give considerable support in the initial phases of the Third Army offensive, flying 2,114 sorties between the 8th and 19th. A concentrated effort was made, as in early October, against the Metz–Thionville position, but in general the fighter-bombers joined in the ground attack from village to village. In this fighting the XIX TAC used an extremely effective procedure: the lead planes dropped 500-lb. general purpose bombs to split the stone houses open; then fragmentation bombs were used to catch the enemy troops; finally napalm bombs set the village ablaze. The German ground forces, however, were better able to retaliate in November, since the number of Flak batteries opposite the Third Army had been greatly increased, and the low-flying American squadrons suffered considerable loss. The army met this new development with an anti-Flak program, in which the ground batteries massed their fire on all known locations of German Flak while the fighter-bombers were overhead. Reports by the American pilots indicate that this inverted type of air-ground co-operation was fairly successful.

Poor flying weather in December further curtailed the air support available to the Third Army, now battling where pinpoint bombing was needed. From 1 December until the Lorraine Campaign ended, the XIX TAC had only six days suitable for full-scale operations. Tactical reconnaissance, always an important feature of the support furnished by Weyland's command, was severely hampered by the December weather. The Third Army's own light craft, the ubiquitous and valuable artillery liaison planes, flew when they could; but they too had only limited usefulness. As a result the army fought its way forward over difficult ground and through layers of fortifications with a patch over one eye. Nonetheless the XIX TAC and the IX Bombardment Division were able to intervene with some effect in the XX Corps battle for the Sarre bridgehead—a last contribution to the Lorraine Campaign.

Little has been said of the strategic efforts by the Allied Air Forces as these affected operations by the Third Army. Any chain of cause and effect between the thousand-bomber raids over Mannheim, as an example, and tactical events on the Lorraine front would be difficult to link together. Yet in one respect the entire course of the Lorraine Campaign was affected in demonstrable fashion by the strategic air war. Few of Patton's troops ever saw more than a single German plane at a time, although they may have been subjected to a short night bombing or may have heard a few enemy reconnaissance planes chugging overhead in the darkness, making their rounds as "bed check Charlies." The supremacy in the air achieved by the Allied Air Forces before the invasion of Normandy, and retained after D Day, allowed the Third Army a degree of tactical mobility and logistical freedom that was nearly absolute insofar as any threat from the Luftwaffe was concerned. During the first week of September, it is true, the *II Fighter Corps (Jagdkorps)* succeeded in breaking through in some force, striking at the 4th Armored Division and the bridges over the Meuse, but without much effect. On 6 September the *II Fighter Corps* recorded 110 sorties aimed at the troops and bridges west of Metz, but apparently much of this effort was deflected far short of the target area by American planes. In the meantime the *IX Air Corps (Fliegerkorps)* had essayed a series of night raids against the Marne and Meuse bridges held by the Third Army. Here the concentration of antiaircraft artillery made things so hot for the German bombers that they consistently missed their targets. On 7 September the Luftwaffe reported 337 planes ready for a major effort, presumably aimed at the Third Army, but poor flying weather and lack of aviation fuel kept most of the planes on the ground. In the weeks that followed, the *Third Air Force*, the German tactical air command on the Western Front, turned its attention to the Allied armies in the north. On the 19th of September and again on the 24th German attack planes were diverted from the northern front to fly cover over the *Fifth Panzer Army*, then fighting to break into the right flank of the Third Army. Either the Luftwaffe lacked the planes and gasoline to make a major effort, or the American fighters cut down the enemy short of their goal; in any case the Third Army antiaircraft batteries reported this period as a "quiet week." By the end of September the threat of German planes over the Third Army area had dwindled to the point that

American vehicles were driving as far as the corps rear boundaries with their headlights full on. Until the close of the campaign Patton's antiaircraft gunners continued to knock down German planes, but these were few in number and usually engaged in reconnaissance missions.

The impact of the great Allied air offensive against the war production of the Third Reich was undoubtedly felt by the German ground forces facing the Third Army, although this is less susceptible to documentation than the far-reaching effects of the Allied control of the air. But if the effects of fluctuations in the production of armored vehicles induced by the great bombing raids over Mannheim and Kassel did not reach as far as the German armored formations in Lorraine, it is certain that the vicissitudes encountered by the enemy supply columns and trains moving ammunition, gasoline, and heavy equipment to the Western Front must be attributed in large part to the strategic air offensive mounted by the American Air Forces and the RAF.

Materiel

Throughout the Lorraine Campaign the Third Army enjoyed a marked superiority over the enemy in materiel, at least by any quantitative comparison. The employment of the artillery arm offers an excellent example of this superiority. Just before the November offensive Hitler increased the allocation of guns and ammunition on the *Army Group G* front; the new allocation was continued until the eve of the Ardennes offensive. During the period 11 to 20 November *Army Group G* used 143 batteries (approximately 600 pieces) and fired 205,660 rounds against the Third Army and the 6th Army Group. Across the lines the Third Army alone employed nearly 1,000 pieces, including tank destroyers firing in an artillery role. As contrasted with an average daily expenditure by the entire *Army Group G* artillery amounting to a little more than 22,000 rounds during this period, the XII Corps alone fired 17,677 rounds on 11 November and subsequently increased its fire on 25 November to 24,346 rounds. During the fight for the Saarlautern–Dillingen bridgehead the XX Corps artillery fired an average of somewhat over 15,000 rounds per day. The enemy artillery in this sector, reinforced by Hitler's orders, fired about 6,000 rounds per day.

The Lorraine Campaign was too limited in duration to see much change in armament and equipment. The towed 3-inch gun in the separate tank destroyer battalions was gradually replaced by the self-propelled, high-velocity

90-mm. gun. In general the tank destroyer functioned as an assault gun accompanying the infantry or as a field piece thickening fires by the corps or division artillery. Although often employed successfully against hostile tanks the tank destroyer usually made its kills at long ranges. Toward the end of the campaign the 540 tank destroyers then in the Third Army reverted to type as weapons for direct fire, working in close support of the infantry and armor against pillboxes, antitank guns, machine gun emplacements, and the like. In December the tank destroyers with the XX Corps fired 27,289 rounds in direct fire and only 900 rounds indirect, as compared with 24,741 rounds indirect and 2,422 rounds direct during November. The 57-mm. antitank gun remained in general use throughout the campaign, although the 6th Armored Division officially scrapped this weapon and a few other units simply abandoned the gun along the way. It had little value when employed against hostile armor, and its use against infantry was restricted by the limited issue of canister. The bazooka began to appear as a popular weapon toward the close of the campaign. There are relatively few recorded instances in which the bazooka was successfully employed against German armor, but the engineers and infantry found it useful in reducing machine gun emplacements and pillboxes. The BAR, one of the oldest weapons in the American Army, had a considerable vogue in both infantry and armored divisions. Nearly every unit carried more BAR's than called for in the Tables of Equipment—one explanation of the constant shortage of this item in the depots.

Lorraine was a good testing ground for the American medium tank, the M–4. The army commander was a student of tank warfare; moreover, he was willing to give his armored formations a free hand. The two armored divisions that continued with the Third Army throughout the campaign had won recognition even before they reached the Moselle. Patton employed his tanks under favorable and unfavorable conditions alike. They fought in large-scale armored battles, tank against tank, and supported the infantry in an assault gun role. So varied was the armored experience in Lorraine that at first glance it would seem possible to give an accurate and final evaluation of the combat characteristics of the M–4 tank as opposed to the German Mark IV and the Panther. But the battles in Lorraine were not fought under conditions conducive to a clean-cut decision on the relative merits of the opposing armor, even when, as in September, tank was pitted against tank. In the first place, the American tanks always outnumbered those thrown against them. Second, in the largest armored battles the enemy was forced to employ untrained tank crews against the veteran Americans and French. Finally, the German tanks had to operate with no air cover and with very limited artillery support. The competing claims for German tank kills made by the Allied armor, fighter-bombers, and artillery give some clue to the crushing weight of this combination of arms when hurled against tanks fighting almost unaided.

During the Lorraine Campaign General Patton and a few of his armored commanders were called upon to furnish "testimonials" as to the efficacy in action of the M–4 tank. These "testimonials" may have had some value in building public confidence in American armored equipment, but they should not be taken as a critical evaluation of the American medium tank. The M–4, mounting the short-barreled 75, was outgunned by the Panther (Mark V). The M–4 was less adequately protected by armor than was the Panther. The American medium tank, however, had some important points of superiority. It was more mobile than either the Mark IV or the Panther, although less maneuverable than the latter. Its gyrostabilizer and power traverse permitted a greater flexibility and rapidity of fire than the enemy tanks could attain. It may therefore be said that, while the American tank at this period of the war had been outdistanced in the race to pile more armor and heavier guns on the tank chassis, certain features of mechanical superiority and weight of numbers kept the M–4 in the running. During 1944 higher American headquarters made various attempts to redress the balance in armament and weaponing. Experiments were conducted with an eye to improving the American armor-piercing projectile. A number of modified M–4's with heavier armor were sent to the European Theater of Operations, but only a few specimens of the new model reached the Third Army. The 76-mm. tank gun began to replace the short-barreled 75 as the Lorraine operations progressed and the new 105-mm. howitzer mounted in headquarters tanks proved to be very useful (particularly when fired in battery). Nonetheless the Americans fought the Lorraine tank battles with a relatively obsolescent weapon.

Characteristics of Operations

In the course of the Lorraine Campaign, the tactics of the Third Army were modified considerably by reason of the terrain, the weather, and the nature of enemy resistance. The earlier drive across western France had seen the fortunate combination of a dashing armored commander, ground suited for tank action, and an almost complete demoralization and disorganization in the forces of the enemy. The subsequent German stand at the Moselle line benefited, it is true, from the logistical lag in Allied operations, but in its more important implication the re-establishment of an organized front typified the amazing powers of recuperation still possessed by the Wehrmacht throughout 1944. This revival of the will to resist is shown by the fact that the Third Army took only 10,000 more prisoners in the period 1 September to 20 December than it captured during the single month of August.

In contrast to the pursuit period, operations in Lorraine were characterized by prepared assaults to gain river crossings, battles to break out of shallow bridgeheads, and limited-objective attacks against well-organized positions. Occasionally the weather, the ground, and the tactical situation permitted a wide sweep and a fairly deep penetration, in the manner so common during the August drive. Occasionally, too, the Third Army made a co-ordinated attack on a broad front, reminiscent of attacks on a much larger scale in World War I. In general, and this was particularly true of the last weeks in Lorraine, separate attacks were made on relatively narrow fronts, aiming at the seizure of one or two points and concentrating every available weapon in support. This procedure cut losses but also took much time; in addition it permitted the weaker German artillery some measure of concentrated fire. In November and December, swampy ground, a limited road net, fogs rising from the river basins, and fewer hours of daylight all combined to slow the American advance. (*Map XLII*) The more the attack slowed down, the more obstacles the enemy could place in the path of the advance. Patton's dictum that "the flanks can take care of themselves" required considerable revision in the last weeks of the campaign. Bypassing the enemy and operating with open flanks had proved successful in periods of rapid advance, but as the Third Army neared the Sarre and the offensive slowed to an "infantry pace" any cavalier disregard for the flanks became the exception rather than the rule. In this connection, however, it must be remembered that the strength of the German forces opposing the Third Army did not, after September, allow counterattacks on any large scale. Therefore some "calculated risk" was possible up to the close of the campaign.

The fight for observation and ground was a conspicuous feature in the early days of the battle for Lorraine. In part this resulted from the sharply etched character of the Moselle Plateau, in part from the flair for choosing and defending terrain which seemed to mark most German formations and commanders. The resumption of the offensive after the October pause introduced a general change in which the fight was waged from village to village, rather than from hill to hill. Unusually heavy rains and bitter cold forced both sides to leave the wooded areas, which had earlier served as bivouac and assembly positions, and seek shelter in towns, villages, and farmsteads. Some advantages accrued to the American forces in this type of warfare. Villages could be readily encircled and the garrisons could be prevented from withdrawing to fight another day. The advance from village to village made it easier to keep supply routes open. Enemy troops assembled in buildings offered a better target from the air than when hidden in wood lots and forests—despite the protection offered by the stone walls and cellars that characterized the Lorraine communities. On the other hand, the task of mopping up such centers of resistance was of necessity a slow business in a populous region like the Lorraine plain.[8] If the Americans occupied a village late in the limited hours of daylight they might reasonably expect to be the object of a counterattack. Furthermore, throughout this campaign the German on the defensive proved his ability to accomplish much with little; given the protection provided in one of the Lorraine villages the German was capable of a delaying action out of all proportion to his numbers.[9]

The relation of armor to infantry altered perceptibly as the Lorraine Campaign progressed and tank going deteriorated. This change was indicated by attempts to convert antitank gunners and other armored division personnel to armored infantry, by numerous complaints that the armored division lacked an adequate complement of armored infantry in the Tables of Organization, by the rising proportion of casualties in the infantry organic to the armored division, and by the continuing demand from armored commanders for close support by the "doughs." Patton's tanks continued to prove their worth throughout the campaign in exploitation and as weapons giving mobility and shock effect. However, the mass and depth in which tanks could be employed constricted severely as the road nets dwindled near the German frontier and cross-country movement ended in the mud. Nor did the operations in Lorraine conclusively prove Patton's contention that armor could breach fortified positions constructed in depth. Although the Germans were seldom able to

[8] In November, for example, the XII Corps advance captured 279 towns and villages.

[9] A number of the German commanders who were interrogated at the close of the war reaffirmed the World War I axiom that the attacker requires a three-to-one superiority over the defender so long as the latter is holding an organized position. A few German officers have set the ratio at six to one.

collect any sizable armored formation for employment as a unit against the Third Army, the history of operations in Lorraine indicates the attraction of armor to armor. While the self-propelled tank destroyer was often able to seek out and destroy tanks, a role also common to the German self-propelled long-barreled 75-mm. and 88-mm. gun, the most successful weapon employed in Lorraine against German tanks was the American tank.

From beginning to end of the Lorraine Campaign the Third Army had liberated or conquered approximately 5,000 square miles of enemy-held territory. Tactically, the Lorraine operations of the Third Army had resulted in the loss to the enemy of three highly important defensive positions, those of the Moselle, the Nied, and the Sarre Rivers. The West Wall still stood in the path of a drive to the Rhine, but the Third Army had drastically reduced the German space for maneuver west of that river. Strategically, the Third Army campaign had resulted in the loss to the German war economy of the military production based on the mines of Lorraine and the Saar Basin, although in the latter case some work continued even after the factories and rolling mills were in range of heavy artillery. Besides, the battle for Lorraine had forced the German high command to divert substantial forces from the defense of the Ruhr. This dispersion of enemy resources, especially armor, had been particularly telling in the early phases of the battle for the Aachen gateway. General Patton's persistent offensive during November and early December also had delayed the movement of key German divisions from the Third Army front to the strategic reserve that was being assembled, trained, and re-equipped for employment in the December counteroffensive. It is true that this enemy counteroffensive worked to deflect General Patton's divisions short of the Rhine and brought the Lorraine Campaign to an abrupt conclusion. (*Map XLIII*) But the German forces had been so badly shattered in Lorraine that the Third Army was able to disengage on this front with relative ease as it turned to intervene in the battle of the Ardennes.[10]

[10] For the story of this operation, see Cole, The Ardennes, now in preparation.

Third Army Staff Roster as of 1 September 1944

Commanding General
Lt. Gen. George S. Patton, Jr.

Chief of Staff
Maj. Gen. Hugh J. Gaffey

Deputy Chief of Staff
Brig. Gen. Hobart R. Gay

Deputy Chief of Staff (Operations)
Col. Paul D. Harkins

Assistant Chief of Staff G–1
Col. Frederick S. Matthews

Assistant Chief of Staff G–2
Col. Oscar W. Koch

Assistant Chief of Staff G–3
Col. Halley G. Maddox

Assistant Chief of Staff G–4
Col. Walter J. Muller

Assistant Chief of Staff G–5
Col. Nicholas W. Campanole

Adjutant General
Col. Robert E. Cummings

Antiaircraft Artillery
Col. Frederick R. Chamberlain

Artillery
Col. Edward T. Williams

Chaplain
Col. James H. O'Neill

Chemical Warfare
Col. Edward C. Wallington

Engineer
Col. John F. Conklin

Finance
Lt. Col. Charles B. Milliken

Inspector General
Col. Clarence C. Park

Judge Advocate
Col. Charles E. Cheever

Medical
Col. Thomas D. Hurley

Ordnance
Col. Thomas H. Nixon

Provost Marshal
Col. John C. MacDonald

Quartermaster
Col. Everett Busch

Signal
Col. Elton F. Hammond

Special Service
Lt. Col. Kenneth E. Van Buskirk

Secretary of the General Staff
Maj. George R. Pfann

Glossary

A Gp	Army Group
AAF	Army Air Forces
AAR	After Action Report
AEAF	Allied Expeditionary Air Force
AEF	American Expeditionary Force (World War I)
AGO	The Adjutant General's Office
AI	Armored infantry
Alligator	Amphibian tracked vehicle
Anlage	Appendix or annex
AUS	Army of the United States
Bailey bridge	Portable steel bridge of the "through" type. The roadway is supported by two main trusses composed of 10-foot sections called "panels" pinned together to form a continuous truss. Capacity may be increased by adding extra trusses alongside the first, by adding an extra truss on top of the first to make a second story, or by both means.
Bangalore torpedo	Metal tube packed with high explosive
BAR	Browning automatic rifle
Baustandskarte	German engineer map, showing status of construction
Bazooka	Rocket launcher, hand-carried
Bazooka pants	Additional armor to protect tank tracks from antitank fire
BBC	British Broadcasting Corporation
Bouncing Betty	Bounding type of German antipersonnel mine that explodes three to five feet in the air
Burp gun	German submachine gun
CCA	Combat Command A, one of the major, flexible, combat formations in armored division
CCB	Combat Command B, in armored division
CCD	Combat Command D, in French armored division
CCL	Combat Command L, in French armored division
CCR	Reserve Combat Command, in armored division
CCS	Combined Chiefs of Staff
CCV	Combat Command V, in French armored division
C-in-C	Commander in Chief
CofS	Chief of Staff
Dragon's teeth	Concrete pillars or iron posts erected as tank barriers
DSC	Distinguished Service Cross
DUKW	2½-ton, 6 × 6 amphibian truck, used for short runs from ship to shore

Ersatzheer	German Replacement Army
ETO	European Theater of Operations
ETOUSA	European Theater of Operations, U.S. Army
Ex O	Executive officer
FA	Field artillery
Fahnenjunkerschule	German officer candidate school
Feldgendarmerie	German military police
Feldgericht	Military tribunal of summary nature
Feldheer	Field army
Festung	Fortress
FFI	French Forces of the Interior
Flash-hider salt	Chemicals mixed with explosive to reduce muzzle flash
Fliegerkorps	Corps-type operational command of the Luftwaffe
Fuesilier battalion	Separate infantry battalion performing both reconnaissance and support in German division
FUSA	First U.S. Army
FWD	Forward headquarters
G–1	Personnel section of divisional or higher staff
G–2	Intelligence section
G–3	Operations section
G–4	Supply section
General der Luftwaffe beim Oberbefehlshaber des Heeres	Air Force general acting as liaison officer with Commander in Chief of the Army
Gen. Qu.	*General Quartiermeister* (Chief of supply and administration for the German Army)
Gen. St. d. H.	*Generalstab des Heeres* (General Staff of the Army)
Gkdo.	*Generalkommando* (Corps-type headquarters)
GMDS	German Military Documents Section, AGO
Grouser	Steel piece welded to tank track to increase traction in mud
Halb-soldaten	"Half-soldiers": over-age or inferior German soldiers
Half-track	Combination wheeled and tracked armored personnel carrier
Heeresarchiv	German Army Archives
Heeresarzt	Surgeon General of the German Army
Hilfswillige	Volunteer auxiliaries (non-German)
Hitlerjugend	Hitler Youth
Jabo	German nickname for fighter-bomber
Jagdkorps	German fighter-plane command, corps type
Jeep	¼-ton vehicle, personnel carrier
Kampfgruppe	German combat group of variable size
Kdtr. d. Bef.	*Kommandantur der Befestigungen* (Fortification Command)
KIA	Killed in action
KTB	*Kriegstagebuch* (war diary)

Lagebuch	Collection of reports, usually on the military situation
Landesschuetzen	Home Guard, sometimes employed outside Germany
Luftflotte	An air force of the Luftwaffe
Luftwaffe	German Air Force
M–4 (Sherman)	American medium tank
Marching fire	Firing by troops while erect and advancing
Mark IV	German medium tank
Mark V (Panther)	German medium tank with heavy armor and high velocity gun
MG 34	German machine gun, model 1934
MIA	Missing in action
MII	Military Intelligence Interrogation
MLR	Main line of resistance
MP	Military police
Mtzd	Motorized
Nachrichtenschule	Signal school
Napalm	Incendiary bomb containing butane and petroleum jelly
NCO	Noncommissioned officer
OB WEST	*Oberbefehlshaber West* (Highest German ground headquarters of the Western Front)
Obkdo.	*Oberkommando* (Headquarters of an army or higher military organization)
OKH	*Oberkommando des Heeres* (High Command of the Army)
OKW	*Oberkommando der Wehrmacht* (High Command of the Armed Forces)
ONI	Office of Naval Intelligence
OP	Observation post
Org. Abt.	*Organizations Abteilung* (Staff subdivision in charge of organization)
Ostheer	German Army on the Eastern Front
Panther (Mark V)	German medium tank with heavy armor and high velocity gun
Panzerfaust	Recoilless antitank grenade launcher, hand-carried
Pathfinders	Aircraft that lead a formation to the drop zone, release point, or target
Personalakten	Individual personnel files of German officers
POL	Petrol, oil, and lubricants
Road runner	Artillery fire which is "walked" along a road to cover successive segments
S–1	Personnel section of regimental or lower staff
S–2	Intelligence section
S–3	Operations section
S–4	Supply section
SG	Smoke generator
SGS	Secretary of the General Staff

SHAEF	Supreme Headquarters, Allied Expeditionary Force
Shell-rep team	Team for reporting rate and type of enemy artillery fire
S-mine	German antipersonnel mine
SS	*Schutzstaffel* (Elite Guard)
Stab Gen. Art. beim . . .	Chief Artillery Officer at . . .
Stellung	Selected position, sometimes organized
TAC	Tactical Air Command
TD	Tank destroyer
TF	Task force
Tiger	German heavy tank
T/O	Table of Organization
Todt workers	Laborers on fortifications, the name being derived from the name of a German official
Tommy gun	Thompson submachine gun
TOT	Time on target, a method of timing artillery fire from various points to fall on a given target simultaneously
Tree burst	Explosion of shells against trees, designed to destroy troops underneath
TUSA	Third U.S. Army
Unterfuehrerschule	Noncommissioned officers' school
USFET	U.S. Forces, European Theater
USO	United Service Organizations
VG	Volksgrenadier
Volksdeutsche	Citizens of a country other than Germany who were considered Germans racially
Volkssturm	A people's militia, partially organized in one of the last steps of German mobilization for total war
Waffen-SS	SS as a military organization
WDGO	War Department General Orders
Wehrkreis	German Army administrative area, for the most part inside Greater Germany
WFSt	*Wehrmachtfuehrungsstab* (Armed Forces Operations Staff)
WIA	Wounded in action

Table of Equivalent Ranks

U.S. Army	*German Army and Air Force*	*German Waffen-SS*
None	Reichsmarschall	None
General of the Army	Generalfeldmarschall	Reichsfuehrer-SS
General	Generaloberst	Oberstgruppenfuehrer
Lieutenant General	General der Infanterie	Obergruppenfuehrer
	Artillerie	
	Gebirgstruppen	
	Kavallerie	
	Nachrichtentruppen	
	Panzertruppen	
	Pioniere	
	Luftwaffe	
	Flieger	
	Fallschirmtruppen	
	Flakartillerie	
	Luftnachrichtentruppen	
Major General	Generalleutnant	Gruppenfuehrer
Brigadier General	Generalmajor	Brigadefuehrer
None	None	Oberfuehrer
Colonel	Oberst	Standartenfuehrer
Lieutenant Colonel	Oberstleutnant	Obersturmbannfuehrer
Major	Major	Sturmbannfuehrer
Captain	Hauptmann	Hauptsturmfuehrer
Captain (Cavalry)	Rittmeister	
First Lieutenant	Oberleutnant	Obersturmfuehrer
Second Lieutenant	Leutnant	Untersturmfuehrer

Basic Military Map Symbols*

Symbols within a rectangle indicate a military unit, within a triangle an observation post, and within a circle a supply point.

Military Units—Identification

Antiaircraft Artillery . . . .

Armored Command . . . .

Army Air Forces . . . .

Artillery, except Antiaircraft and Coast Artillery . . . .

Cavalry, Horse . . . .

Cavalry, Mechanized . . . .

Chemical Warfare Service . . . . G

Coast Artillery . . . .

Engineers . . . . E

Infantry . . . .

Medical Corps . . . .

Ordnance Department . . . .

Quartermaster Corps . . . . Q

Signal Corps . . . . S

Tank Destroyer . . . . TD

Transportation Corps . . . .

Veterinary Corps . . . .

Airborne units are designated by combining a gull wing symbol with the arm or service symbol:

Airborne Artillery . . . .

Airborne Infantry . . . .

*For complete listing of symbols see FM 21–30, from which these are taken.

Size Symbols

The following symbols placed either in boundary lines or above the rectangle, triangle, or circle inclosing the identifying arm or service symbol indicate the size of military organization:

Squad . . . . ●

Section . . . . ●●

Platoon . . . . ●●●

Company, troop, battery, Air Force flight I

Battalion, cavalry squadron, or Air Force squadron II

Regiment or group; combat team (with abbreviation CT following identifying numeral) III

Brigade, Combat Command of Armored Division, or Air Force Wing . X

Division or Command of an Air Force XX

Corps or Air Force XXX

Army XXXX

Group of Armies XXXXX

EXAMPLES

The letter or number to the left of the symbol indicates the unit designation; that to the right, the designation of the parent unit to which it belongs. Letters or numbers above or below boundary lines designate the units separated by the lines:

Company A, 137th Infantry . . . . A 137

8th Field Artillery Battalion 8

Combat Command A, 1st Armored Division . . . . A 1

Observation Post, 23d Infantry 23

Command Post, 5th Infantry Division 5

Boundary between 137th and 138th Infantry . . . . 137 —III— 138

Weapons

Machine gun . . . .

Gun . . . .

Gun battery . . . .

Howitzer or Mortar . . . .

Tank . . . .

Self-propelled gun . . . .

Bibliographical Note

The military historian who attempts to record the history of the European Theater of Operations is faced with an astounding amount of documentary materials. The After Action Reports and journals of the sixty-one American divisions in the ETO alone form a collection weighing some thirty-seven tons. The main problem for the historian, therefore, is not that of finding information, but of cutting down and compressing the materials at hand. Gaps in the records do occur, but as a rule these are the occasion for minor irritation rather than major concern. The records of all the higher headquarters, including SHAEF and the War Department, have been collected and opened to the historian. Here the practice of making multiple copies of even the most secret dispatches or orders insures against the possible disappearance of a significant original.

What the historian has gained by the widespread use of such mechanical aids as the typewriter, the teleprinter, and the mimeograph is partially offset by the ease with which commanders, traveling by jeep and liaison plane, now meet face to face for informal, unrecorded, but nonetheless decisive, discussion. The commands and decisions stemming from such meetings find their way into the written record, but the personal exchanges and the reasoning that culminates in the decision often are irretrievably lost to the historian, despite attempts through oral and written interrogation to plumb the memories of the commanders involved. It is doubtful whether the spate of memoir literature which we may expect at some later date will fill the lacunae acceptably.

Information on tactical units comes from three general sources: the unit journals, the After Action Reports required by Army Regulations, and interviews conducted by historical officers during and after battle. The unit journals, containing messages and orders, are an absolutely reliable guide to what was known at the time. Overlays showing troop dispositions, reports on patrols, intelligence estimates, and similar material are appended to these journals. The After Action Reports, compiled at the close of each month of operations, are based to a considerable extent on the unit journals but also contain information not normally recorded in the form of messages or orders. Errors will be found in the After Action Reports. The percentage of error increases in progression up the echelon of command, since the army corps After Action Report tends to rely on that coming from the division, and the division normally uses the After Action Report prepared by its regiments. The After Action Report, however, is the most convenient guide through the maze of combat information and the historian can soon determine the quotient of reliability for the individual unit preparing it. Unit journals and After Action Reports prepared in the ETO are now in the possession of the Historical Records Section, Office of the Adjutant General.

During operations in Europe historical officers attached to the various armies interviewed officers and men who took part in or directed the fighting. More than two thousand of these Combat Interviews are on file in the Historical Division. Their coverage varies from the interrogation of one officer to that of an entire combat formation. Some interviews were obtained while the unit was in action; others were secured weeks after the action occurred. The hours and dates reported in the Combat Interviews are often in error, for these are things which the soldier, living in twelve-hour periods, quickly forgets. The Combat Interviews also reflect the extreme localization of knowledge that occurs on the battlefield and cannot be accepted as final evidence when reference is made to units supporting or adjacent to the formation from which the interview comes. This corpus of Combat Interviews, however, is one of the most valuable sources of information available to the historian. It fleshes out the framework of events chronicled in the unit journals and provides additional testimony to help resolve disputed questions of fact.

Information on the enemy comes from two general sources: War Diaries (*KTB*'s) and other German Army documents now in our possession; manuscript histories prepared after the war by German officers who played a part in the events they describe. The collection of German Army records (held by the German Military Documents Section, Office of the Adjutant General, for the United Kingdom and the United States) is by no means complete. Tons of such documents were destroyed by the Germans or by looters and vandals. Large collections of War Diaries, particularly in the Potsdam archives, went to the USSR and are not available to the Western historian. Nonetheless the enemy records extant and available suffice for the compilation of a reasonably complete and accurate account of the German armies that faced the Allies on the Western Front during the campaigns of 1944 and 1945. Enemy information derived from contemporary documents has been augmented by approximately one thousand manuscript histories written after the war by German officers in Germany under the direction of Col. H. E. Potter, USA. This collection, to which additions on the later phases of the war in Europe are still being made, is in the possession of the Historical Division. Although these manuscript histories depend almost entirely on the unaided memories of their writers they add immeasurably to our knowledge of the enemy operations. When checked against German Army documents and Allied sources the manuscripts show an amazing degree of accuracy and objectivity (probably explained by the professionalism of the German officer corps, the academic traditions of the German General Staff, and the destruction of those German military institutions to which personal reputations have been attached).

The amount of information on operations in the ETO which has found its way into print since the end of the war is rather limited. A number of semiofficial histories prepared by corps, divisional, and regimental associations have been published in Germany and the United States. Such works vary greatly in value, but all those pertinent to the present volume have been examined. Thus far the only memoirs that refer in any detail to the Lorraine Campaign are those of General Eisenhower and General Patton. These two works have been used, but as a rule reference in the present volume is made to the original documents from which the memoirs derived their information.

Index